6,000 WORDS

6,000 WORDS

A Supplement to Webster's Third New International Dictionary

A Merriam-Webster®

G. & C. MERRIAM CO. *Publishers*
Springfield, Massachusetts, U.S.A.

CONTENTS

Library of Congress Cataloging in Publication Data
Main Entry under title:

6,000 words

1. English language — Dictionaries. 2. Words, New — English — Dictionaries. I. Webster's third new international dictionary of the English language, unabridged.
PE1630.S5 423 75-45056

ISBN 0-87779-007-8

MADE IN THE UNITED STATES OF AMERICA

34567 RRD 79

Preface

A dictionary begins to go out-of-date the moment it is published, for the English language does not freeze upon the date of publication, but continues to grow and change. When Webster's Third New International Dictionary appeared in 1961, it provided as complete coverage of contemporary American English as was then available. But the editing of the Third had begun more than a decade earlier; the language did not stand still during the editing, nor has it since. To try to keep abreast of the living language, Merriam editors added an eight-page Addenda section to Webster's Third in 1966 and increased it to sixteen pages in 1971.

6,000 Words is essentially the most recent Addenda section of Webster's Third New International Dictionary. The Addenda section serves two purposes: to record as many as space will permit of the new words and meanings that have become established since Webster's Third was edited and to enter those older words that for various reasons had been passed over in the earlier editing. This book differs from the Addenda proper in that it has replaced a number of the words in the second category with newer terms for which the Addenda section is physically too small. In addition the somewhat larger compass of a separate book has permitted the inclusion of a more generous selection of quoted illustrations than is possible in the Addenda proper. Still, 6,000 Words has one disadvantage of an Addenda section. It cannot be self-contained; the reader will find it necessary to consult another dictionary for terms—especially technical terms—which are unfamiliar. Every word used in 6,000 Words can be found in Webster's Third or in 6,000 Words; most can be found in a good desk dictionary like Webster's New Collegiate Dictionary.

In order to get such satisfaction and pleasure as a dictionary affords, one must learn how to use it—that is, how to interpret the information contained in each entry. This knowledge involves mainly an ability to recognize different typefaces, a number of abbreviations that occur over and over, and a few traditional dictionary devices. Every reader is therefore urged to read the Explanatory Notes after this preface carefully. Following these the reader will find an informative section on the recent growth of English vocabulary, the fields which yield new words, the processes of word-formation, and the means by which Merriam editors record and define new words and meanings, then a list of pronunciation symbols and a list of abbreviations.

Editorial Staff

Editorial Directors
Mairé Weir Kay
Frederick C. Mish
Henry Bosley Woolf (retired)

Senior Editors
E. Ward Gilman • Roger W. Pease, Jr.

Associate Editors
Gretchen Brunk • Robert D. Copeland • Grace A. Kellogg • James G. Lowe

Assistant Editors
Michael G. Belanger
John K. Bollard • Julie A. Collier • Kathleen M. Doherty
James E. Shea, Jr. • Anne H. Soukhanov • Raymond R. Wilson

Editorial Assistant
Francine A. Socha

Department Secretary
Hazel O. Lord

Head of Typing Room
Evelyn G. Summers

Clerks and Typists
Maude L. Barnes • Gwendolyn L. Belton • Florence Cressotti
Ruth W. Gaines • Helene Gingold
Patricia Jensen • Mildred M. McWha • Catherine T. Meaney
Frances W. Muldrew • Mildred C. Paquette • Genevieve M. Sherry

6a • Explanatory Notes

ENTRIES

A boldface letter or a combination of such letters set flush with the left-hand margin of each page is a main entry. The main entry may consist of letters set solid (as **firmware**), of letters joined by a hyphen (as **de-escalate**), or of letters separated by one or more spaces (as **living will**).

The main entries follow one another in alphabetical order letter by letter. Those containing an Arabic numeral are alphabetized as if the numeral were spelled out.

A main entry marked with an asterisk (as **face-off***) is not a new word, but a new sense of a word already entered in Webster's Third New International Dictionary.

When one new main entry has exactly the same written form as another, the two are distinguished by superscript numerals preceding each word (as ^{1}**photochromic** *adj* and ^{2}**photochromic** *n*). Main entries marked with asterisks are not given such superscript numerals.

The centered periods within entry words indicate points at which a hyphen may be put at the end of a line of print or writing. They are not shown at the second and succeeding homographs of a word or for asterisked entries. There are acceptable alternative end-of-line divisions just as there are acceptable variant spellings and pronunciations, but for reasons of space no more than one division is shown for any entry in this dictionary. Without being dogmatic, we simply offer these divisions as a guide for writers, typists, and printers aiming at a consistency of end-of-line division in their work.

A double hyphen ⸗ at the end of a line in this dictionary stands for a hyphen that belongs at that point in a hyphened word and that is retained when the word is written as a unit on one line.

When a main entry is followed by the word *or* and another form (as *or* **Chomskyan** at **Chomskian**), the two forms are equal variants. Both are standard, and either one may be used according to personal inclination. When another form is joined to the main entry by the word *also*, the form after *also* is a secondary variant and occurs less frequently than the first. Secondary variants belong to standard usage and may be used according to personal inclination. If there are two secondary variants, the second is joined to the first by *or*.

Variants whose spelling puts them alphabetically more than a page away from the main entry are entered at their own alphabetical places.

A main entry may be followed by one or more derivatives (as **cablecaster** *n* at **cablecast** *vt*) or by a homograph with a different functional label (as **cablecast** *n* at **cablecast** *vt*). These are run-on entries. Each is introduced by a lightface dash and each has a functional label. They are not defined, however, since their meanings are readily derivable from the meaning of the root word.

A few main entries may be followed by one or more phrases (as **hang five** and **hang loose** at **hang***) containing the entry word or an inflected form of it. These are also run-on entries. Each is introduced by a lightface dash but there is no functional label. They are, however, defined since their meanings are more than the sum of the meanings of their elements.

Boldface words that appear within parentheses (as **angiotensin II** at **angiotensin**) are run-in entries. They are related to the entry word in an obvious way and their meaning should be clear from the context in which they occur.

A guide word is printed at the top of each page. On a left-hand page the guide word is usually the alphabetically first entry on the page; on a right-hand page it is usually the alphabetically last entry on the page. Thus the two guide words on a two-page spread indicate that the entries falling alphabetically between them may be found on those pages. Any boldface word—a main entry with definition, a variant, an inflected form, a defined or undefined run-on—may be used as a guide word.

PRONUNCIATION

The matter between a pair of reverse slant lines \ \ following the entry word indicates the pronunciation. The symbols used are explained in the chart printed on pages 18a and 19a.

Pronunciation is shown for most entries in this book. Some entries, however, are common words for which new senses have developed in recent years. No pronunciation is shown for words which have been found to occur commonly in their earlier senses in textbooks and supplementary reading in the elementary school curriculum and which therefore may be considered as belonging to the current general vocabulary, e.g. **country, estimate, into.** Similarly, no pronunciation is normally shown for common elements of open compounds, e.g. **American dream, beef Wellington** \-ˈweliŋtən\, **blue stellar object** \-ˌstelər-\, **command module** \-ˌmäj(ˌ)ü(ə)l\, **line judge.**

All the pronunciation variants shown for entries or parts of entries may be considered acceptable in educated English speech. Variation in pronunciation falls into two main categories, predictable and unpredictable. Predictable variants are those for which one speaker's pronunciation differs from another's because their dialects or speech patterns are different. This type of variation may be predicted from the speaker's pronunciation of other words. One type of predictable variation often recorded in this book is the so-called "loss" of \r\ before a consonant or pause in the speech of many Americans from New England, New York City, and much of the South and that of most southern British speakers. Unpredictable variation, on the other hand, may occur in any dialect, and there is no certain way of telling from a speaker's treatment of other words which variant he might use for a particular utterance of a word with unpredictable variants. For instance, some speakers put more stress on the first syllable of **acadamese** than on the second; others stress the second syllable more than the first. The order of pronunciation variants in this book does not mean that the first is to be preferred over the second or even that it is more frequent; with two equally acceptable variants one of them must be printed before the other. Variants preceded by *also* are appreciably less frequent than unlabeled variants, and those preceded by *sometimes* are infrequent; however, no variant with either of these labels should be considered unacceptable simply on the basis of relative infrequency.

Entries labeled *abbr* are not normally given a pronunciation respelling in this work; the pronunciation may be assumed to be that of the individual constituent letters: **FOBS** *abbr,* **ISBN** *abbr.* However, abbreviations are given a pronunciation respelling if evidence of a pronunciation other than that of the constituent letters appears in the Merriam-Webster pronunciation files: **gox** \ˈgäks\ *abbr,* **TEFL** \ˈtefəl\ *abbr.* For these it can be assumed that some people may pronounce the constituent letters, even though such a pronunciation is not shown. Some abbreviations are not initialisms but are shortened forms of words or parts of words. Many of these are automatically expanded in speech; for instance, **kbar** is probably most often pronounced like **kilobar**, though it may possibly also be pronounced in a way analogous to the pronunciation of the noun **krad** \ˈkāˌrad\. In entries of this class no pronunciation is shown unless evidence appears in our pronunciation files: **nsec** *abbr,* **oceanog** *abbr,* **obstet** *abbr.*

The following devices are used in the pronunciation transcriptions in addition to the character symbols:

\, ;\ A comma separates pronunciation variants, e.g. **fentanyl** \fenˈtanᵊl, ˈfentᵊnˌil\. A semicolon separates groups of variants, as at **medullin** \məˈdələ̇n, me-; ˈmedᵊlə̇n, ˈmejəl-\ where the variants transcribed in full would be \məˈdələ̇n, meˈdələ̇n, ˈmedᵊlə̇n, ˈmejələ̇n\.

\( ), (\ Parentheses indicate that the enclosed symbols are present in some utterances and not in others; for example, \ˈeb(y)əˌlizəm\ indicates two pronunciation variants for **ebullism**, \ˈebyəˌlizəm\ and \ˈebəˌlizəm\. In entries such as **lekvar** \ˈlekˌvär, -ˌvȧ(r\ where the pronunciation of so-called "*r*-droppers" is distinguished from that of "*r*-keepers," \(r\ with no closing parenthesis indicates that the *r*-dropper may pronounce the \r\ when a vowel initial word or suffix follows without pause but not otherwise.

\-\ A hyphen is used at the beginning or end of a pronunciation respelling to show that not all of the boldface entry is transcribed. The missing part may be supplied from another entry, from a preceding variant within the same pair of reversed slants, or in the case of open compounds, from the pronunciation of a common word which is not entered separately in this dictionary.

\ˈ ˌ ˈˌ\ Three levels of stress are indicated in this dictionary: primary stress \ˈ\ as in **granola** \grəˈnōlə\, secondary stress \ˌ\ as in the first syllable of **kung fu** \ˌkəŋˈfü\, and no stress at all, as in the second syllable of **lexis** \ˈleksə̇s\. The stress marks stacked together \ˈˌ\ mean "either \ˈ\ or \ˌ\." Items with a stress pattern like that of **laid–back** \ˈˌlādˈˌbak\ should be interpreted as indicating that when one of the stressed syllables has primary stress the other has secondary, or that both may have secondary stress, as is common in running speech for adjectives and even nouns in attributive position where the primary stress may fall on the word being modified. Thus the transcription for **laid–back** represents \ˈlādˌbak, ˌlādˈbak, ˌlādˌbak\. Stress is especially variable in compounds, depending on context, emphasis, and personal preference. Fully French pronunciations are shown without any stress marks, as in the usual practice of transcribers of French. Heaviest stress generally falls on the last syllable of French words pronounced in isolation, though no such precise rule can be given for French pronunciation in running speech. The placement of stress marks in this book is not intended to indicate syllable division; see the section on \·\ following.

\·\ Syllable division is not regularly indicated in the pronunciation transcriptions. However, we have found it desirable to indicate what we will here call syllable division in some cases where confusion might arise otherwise. This is shown by the use of a centered dot \·\. It occurs, for instance, between the third and fourth syllables of the plural of **corpus allatum, corpora allata** \ˌkȯrpərə·əˈlād·ə, . . .\, to indicate that the two adjacent vowels are in separate syllables. In the entry **FORTRAN** \ˈfȯr·ˌtran\ the centered dot indicates that the variety of \t\ used in this word is that heard at the beginning of a word or syllable as in *tan* or *train*, and not that heard at the end of a word or syllable as in *foot* or *fort*. That is to say, the centered dot shows that the *tr* in **FORTRAN** is pronounced as in *four transoms*, not as in in *Fort Ransom*. The centered dot following the character in the symbol \d·\ is not meant to represent syllable division. The use of this symbol is explained in some detail in the Pronunciation Guide to Webster's Third. \d·\ should be thought of as a single character representing a sound heard in the speech of most Americans in both *madder* and *matter*.

\÷\ The symbol \÷\ preceding a variant indicates that although the variant occurs in educated speech many people consider it unacceptable. For example, at the entry for **escalate** the variant \÷-kyə-\ is included because it has been heard from a number of educated speakers including highly placed government officials, members of Congress, and journalists or news commentators with nationwide radio and television exposure. The absence of a representative in the spelling for the \y\ in this pronunciation variant may have given rise to the objections to its acceptability, but spelling should not overly influence the transcription of the spoken language.

FUNCTIONAL LABELS

An italic label indicating a part of speech or some other functional classification follows the pronunciation or, if no pronunciation is given, the main entry. The eight traditional parts of speech are abbreviated thus: *adj* (adjective), *adv* (adverb), *conj* (conjunction), *interj* (interjection), *n* (noun), *prep* (preposition), *pron* (pronoun), *vb* (verb).

Other italicized labels used to indicate functional classifications that are not traditional parts of speech include these: *vi* (verb intransitive), *vt* (verb transitive), *abbr* (abbreviation), *comb form* (combining form), *prefix, service mark, suffix, symbol, trademark*. Functional labels are sometimes combined.

INFLECTED FORMS

NOUNS

The plurals of nouns are shown in this dictionary when suffixation brings about a change of final *-y* to *-i-*, when the noun ends in a consonant plus *-o* or in *-ey*, when the noun has an irregular plural or a zero plural or a foreign plural, when the noun is a compound that pluralizes any element but the last, when the noun has variant plurals, and when it is believed that the dictionary user might have reasonable doubts about the spelling of the plural.

heavy* *n, pl* **heavies**
[2]**hetero** . . . *n, pl* **-eros**
bogey* . . . *n, pl* **bogeys**
dong . . . *n, pl* **dong**
granum . . . *n, pl* **grana**
halala . . . *n, pl* **halala** *or* **halalas**
bialy *n, pl* **bialys**
goofy-foot . . . *n, pl* **goofy-foots**

Cutback inflected forms are frequently used when the noun has three or more syllables:

helicity . . . *n, pl* **-ties**

The plurals of nouns are usually not shown when the base word is unchanged by suffixation, when the noun is a compound whose second element is readily recognizable as a regular free form, or when the noun is unlikely to occur in the plural.

Nouns that are plural in form and that regularly occur in plural construction are labeled *n pl:*

granny glasses *n pl*

Nouns that are plural in form but that do not always take a plural verb are appropriately labeled:

gyrodynamics . . . *n pl but sing in constr*

VERBS

The principal parts of verbs are shown in this dictionary when suffixation brings about a doubling of a final consonant or an elision of a final *-e* or a change of final *-y* to *-i-*, when the verb ends in *-ey*, when the inflection is irregular, when there are variant inflected forms, and when it is believed that the dictionary user might have reasonable doubts about the spelling of an inflected form.

grab* *vt* **grabbed; grabbing**
goose* *vt* **goosed; goosing**
gussy up *vt* **gussied up; gussying up**
hang* *vb* **hung; hanging**
input . . . *vt* **inputted** *or* **input; inputting**

Cutback inflected forms are usually used when the verb has three or more syllables and when it is a compound whose second element is readily recognized as an irregular verb:

habituate* . . . *vi* **-ated; -ating**

The principal parts of verbs are usually not shown when the base word is unchanged by suffixation or when the verb is a compound whose second element is readily recognizable as a regular free form.

ADJECTIVES & ADVERBS

The comparative and superlative forms of adjectives and adverbs are shown in this dictionary when suffixation brings about a doubling of a final consonant or an elision of a final *-e* or a change of final *-y* to *-i-*, when the word ends in *-ey*, when the inflection is irregular, and when there are variant inflected forms. The superlative forms of adjectives and adverbs of two or more syllables are usually cut back:

grungy . . . *adj* **grun·gi·er; -est**

The inclusion of inflected forms in *-er* and *-est* at adjective and adverb entries means nothing more about the use of *more* and *most* with these adjectives and adverbs than that their comparative and superlative degrees may be expressed in either way.

The comparative and superlative forms of adjectives and adverbs are usually not shown when the base word is unchanged by suffixation or when the word is a compound whose second element is readily recognizable as a regular free form.

Inflected forms are not shown at undefined run-ons.

CAPITALIZATION

Most entries in this dictionary begin with a lowercase letter. A few of these have an italicized label *often cap,* which indicates that the word is as likely to be capitalized as not, that it is as acceptable with an uppercase initial as it is with one in lowercase. Some entries begin with an uppercase letter, which indicates that the word is usually capitalized. The absence of an initial capital or of an *often cap* label indicates that the word is not ordinarily capitalized:

icekhana . . . *n*
joual . . . *n, often cap*
Sasquatch . . . *n*

The capitalization of entries that are open or hyphened compounds is similarly indicated by the form of the entry or by an italicized label:

cabana set *n*
spaghetti western . . . *n, often cap W*
Fabry's disease *n*
cable TV *n*
Hardy–Weinberg *adj*

A word that is capitalized in some senses and lowercase in others shows variations from the form of the main entry by the use of italicized labels at the appropriate sense.

Lacombe . . . *n*. . . **2** *often not cap*

ETYMOLOGY

The matter in boldface square brackets preceding the definition is the etymology. Meanings given in roman type within these brackets are not definitions of the entry, but are meanings of the italicized words within the brackets.

The etymology gives the language from which a word borrowed into English has come. It also gives the form or a transliteration of the word in that language, if the form in that language differs from that in English.

Whenever a language name appears in an etymology without an expressed form or without an expressed meaning, the form or meaning of the etymon in that language is the same as that of the word immediately preceding. If a language name which begins an etymology has no expressed form or meaning, the form of the word in that language is the same as the form of the entry word, or the meaning is the same as that of the first definition of the entry.

When an italicized word appears in an etymology with no language label, that word belongs to the same language as the word immediately preceding.

In some cases the expression "deriv. of" replaces the more usual "fr." This indicates that one or more intermediate steps have been omitted in tracing the derivation.

Small superscript numerals following words or syllables in an etymology refer to the tone of the word or syllable which they follow. They are, therefore, used only with forms cited from tone languages.

An etymology is usually not given for a word formed in English by compounding, affixation, or functional shift. Such an absence indicates that the etymology is expected to be self-evident. When several words formed from the same English prefix are entered, only the first is etymologized.

USAGE

Two types of status labels are used in this dictionary—regional and stylistic—to signal that a word or a sense of a word is not part of the standard vocabulary of English.

A word or sense limited in use to one of the other countries of the English-speaking world has an appropriate regional label:

clanger . . . *n, Brit*

The stylistic label *slang* is used with words or senses that are especially appropriate in contexts of extreme informality:

scag . . . *n, slang*

There is no satisfactory objective test for slang, especially with reference to a word out of context. No word, in fact, is invariably slang, and many standard words can be given slang applications.

When the application of a word or sense is very limited, the definition may be preceded by an italic guide phrase that points out the limitation:

scramble* *vi* . . . *of a football quarterback*

Definitions are sometimes followed by usage notes that give supplementary information about such matters as idiom, syntax, and semantic relationship. A usage note is introduced by a lightface dash:

schmear . . . — usu. used in the phrase *the whole schmear*
plastic . . . — often used as a generalized term of disapproval
performance* . . . — contrasted with *competence*

Definitions are frequently followed by illustrative quotations and verbal illustrations that show a typical use of the word in context. These illustrations are enclosed in angle brackets, and the word being illustrated is set in italic.

SENSE DIVISION

A boldface colon is used in this dictionary to introduce a definition; it is also used to separate two or more definitions of a single sense.

Boldface Arabic numerals separate the senses of a word that has more than one sense and boldface letters separate subsenses.

A particular semantic relationship between senses is sometimes suggested by the use of one of the italic sense dividers *esp, specif, also,* or *broadly.*

The sense divider *esp* (for *especially*) is used to introduce the most common meaning included in the more general preceding definition. The sense divider *specif* (for *specifically*) is used to introduce a common but highly restricted meaning subsumed in the more general preceding sense.

The sense divider *also* is used to introduce a meaning that is closely related to the preceding sense but that may be considered less important. The sense divider *broadly* is used to introduce an extended or wider meaning of the preceding definition.

The order of senses is historical: the sense our evidence shows to have been first used in English is entered first.

When an italicized label follows a boldface numeral, the label applies only to that specific numbered sense. It does not apply to any other boldface numbered senses.

CROSS-REFERENCES

Three different kinds of cross-references are used in this dictionary: directional, synonymous, and cognate. In each instance the cross-reference is readily recognized by the lightface small capitals in which it is printed. Every occurrence of small capitals refers the reader to another entry in 6,000 Words.

A cross-reference following a lightface dash and beginning with *compare* is a directional cross-reference. It directs the dictionary user to look elsewhere for further information:

plateglass . . . *adj* . . . — compare OXBRIDGE, REDBRICK

A cross-reference following a boldface colon is a synonymous cross-reference.

apocynthion . . . *n*. . . **:** APOLUNE

A synonymous cross-reference indicates that a definition at the entry in this dictionary cross-referred to can be substituted as a definition for the entry or the sense in which the cross-reference appears. A lightface numeral following a synonymous cross-reference refers to a sense number at the entry cross-referred to.

magnetoplasmadynamic . . . *adj* **:** HYDROMAGNETIC 1

A cross-reference following an italic *var of* ("variant of") is a cognate cross-reference:

schtick *var of* SHTICK

ABBREVIATIONS & SYMBOLS

Abbreviations and symbols are included as main entries in the vocabulary:

ICU *abbr* intensive care unit
p* *symbol*. . .

Abbreviations have been normalized to one form. In practice, however, there is considerable variation in the use of periods and in capitalization (as *bpi, b.p.i., BPI, B.P.I.*), and stylings other than those given in this dictionary are often acceptable.

The Recent Growth of English Vocabulary • 13a

The vocabulary of English, like that of every other living language, is constantly growing. This growth is certainly not new. Always, as men have met with new objects and new experiences and have developed new ideas, they have needed new words to describe them. New words and new meanings for old words are the reason for this book. In the sections that follow, we will indicate some of the areas that produce new words, the ways in which new words are formed, and how new words get into the dictionary.

Where Do They All Come From?

Science and technology are probably the most prolific providers of new words today. Most spectacularly, perhaps, they have combined to take men to the moon and bring them back, and they have sent unmanned craft even farther into space. The exploration of the moon has given us words for novel experiences: *moonwalk, earthrise.*

The closer exploration of the moon has also brought changes in our conception of more familiar experiences. We have long been familiar with the moon's maria, those large dark areas which appear to the naked eye of the earthbound observer to be the features of the man in the moon. We long ago borrowed the Latin word *mare* "sea" to refer to these dark patches. We now know that the moon has highlands, too, contrasting with the low-lying maria. These we call *terrae,* contrasting Latin *terra* "land" with *mare* "sea." And we have long been aware that the earth and the other planets orbit the sun. We have referred to a planet's greatest distance from the sun as its *aphelion,* the least distance as its *perihelion.* Now that we are able to orbit the moon we speak analogously of a moon satellite's *apolune* and *perilune.* But we have not yet settled down with these words; we have created variants, borrowing from both Greek and Latin, even from mythology. We base *apolune* and *perilune* on the Latin word for the moon, *luna; aposelene, aposelenium, periselene,* and *periselenium* on the Greek *selēnē.* And we use the name of *Cynthia,* goddess of the moon, in *apocynthion* and *pericynthion.*

It is not only our exploration of *deep space* which adds to our extraterrestrial vocabulary. Earthbound astronomers continue to make new discoveries and formulate new theories. We hear about *quasars, pulsars, neutron stars,* and the mysterious *black hole.* The *big bang theory* and the *steady state theory* offer us alternative explanations of the origin of the universe. We learn that the earth moves in a mysterious way, *Chandler's wobble,* not yet explained; and we can be sure that efforts to explain the wobble will add further to our scientific vocabulary.

Other fields of scientific study are also adding to the English vocabulary. For all the years men have lived on the earth, they have not exhausted the study of the earth's natural history. It is true that discoveries of undescribed and uncataloged animals and plants are not as frequent as they were in earlier ages, when whole continents were being opened up for scientific exploration. Nor have we yet discovered living things in our exploration of outer space. But we shall probably never feel confident that we know all the forms of life. Few new discoveries are as striking or as controversial as that, as yet unconfirmed, of a large nonhuman primate in the Pacific Northwest. Whether or not he exists, the animal's names, *Sasquatch* and *bigfoot,* are now a part of our language. Other animals, although not new to science, are new to America. For example, two immigrants from abroad, the *walking catfish* and the *imported fire ant,* are making their presence felt in the southeastern United States, and their names have become established in American English.

The discovery of the mechanism of protein synthesis has made genetics a fertile provider of new terms, giving us the *Watson-Crick model* of DNA, the *genetic code, messenger RNA,* and a new meaning for *template* among many others. And as physicists pry deeper and deeper into the atomic nucleus they have discovered more subatomic particles: *kaon, lambda,* and *muon,* for example. They have discovered *antimatter,* studied *isospin,* and used *spark chambers.* Medicine too is a major contributor of new terms such as *busulfan, open-heart* surgery, the *sudden infant death syndrome,* and the famous *pill.* Mathematics has become more noticeable especially since the revising of the subject as taught in school. *Fourier transform, open sentence, onto,* and *truth set* are among the mathematical terms that will be found herein.

Technological sophistication always seems to make things faster or smaller, as such terms as *SST, computerization,* and *microminiaturization* attest. Programmers communicate with computers in *FORTRAN, COBOL,* or *BASIC* and computers talk to each other in *ASCII* or *EBCDIC.* Technical improvement in *microforms* has made possible the business of *micropublishing.* Tiny *integrated circuits* make the pocket calculator possible. And in even more familiar applications technology has supplied the *flashcube,* the *microwave oven,* and the *Wankel engine.*

Some technological advances are less benevolent than these, however. Our capacity for military destructiveness is constantly increasing, and with it our military vocabulary. We have *ABMs, SAMs,* and *MIRVs.* We have *overkill.* We can talk almost casually about the possibility of nuclear war, and we have a new unit of measurement to use in such discussions, the *megadeath.* Our long military involvement in Vietnam also increased our vocabulary. We sought to justify our actions by the *domino theory.* We disparaged the *Cong* by calling them *dinks* or *slopes.* The *Green Berets* became a household word, and the common foot soldier became a *grunt.* The division of American opinion on our undeclared war gave us *doves* and *hawks.* And the words we brought out of the war were not only military: the appearance in American English of such words as *ao dai* and *hootch* was a by-product of our military involvement in Southeast Asia.

But science and technology are not the only sources of new words. The decade and a half since the publication of Webster's Third has seen considerable political and social ferment and this ferment has left its mark on the language. The young people of the English-speaking world have become more numerous as well as more visible and more vocal. Many of them have spurned the *establishment* to join the *counter-culture* as *hippies* or *flower people.* The music of the young has given us *acid rock, hard rock,* and *folk rock,* which are all cheered loudly by *teenyboppers* and *groupies.*

So many young people have become involved with the drug subculture that the jargon of drugs has won a prominent place in the consciousness of contemporary America. We talk of *uppers* and *downers, acid, pot, dexies,* and *smack,* of people who have *OD'd,* and of people *busted* for trying to smuggle in a couple of *keys.*

Minorities as well as the young have made themselves heard. The civil rights movement that began with *freedom rides* and *sit-ins* has made us all more aware of black culture. Black culture itself has given us many new words. A new academic subject, *black studies,* has been added to the curriculum of many schools. And *Afro, dashiki,* the *Black Panthers,* the *Black Muslims,* and *soul* are familiar to most of us. Other minorities have also become more politically active and more visible: we are now familiar with both *Chicanos* and *Native Americans.* From the women's movement we get such terms as the now widely used *Ms., sexism, chairperson,* and *chairone.* Rounding out the group are politically active *golden-agers* who call themselves *Gray Panthers* and fight *ageism.*

The changing attitude of Americans toward sexual matters and materials has also contributed to the language. Movies are now rated *G, PG, R,* or *X,* and people may be *A.C./D.C.* The homosexual subculture has become more open, bringing into general use such terms as *homophile, gay, butch,* and *camp.*

Education is another source of new vocabulary, giving us *underachiever, open classroom, TA, grade-point average, CAI,* and *pass-fail* grading. Increasing interest in the consumer has given us *consumerism, callback, unit pricing,* and *generic.*

Entertainment has always been a source of new words. We have *sitcoms* and *shoot-'em-ups* on television and *call-in* programs on radio; at the neighborhood movie theater we might watch a *spaghetti western.* We might see *guerrilla theater* or a *happening.* Sports continues its steady production of vocabulary with new sports such as *roller hockey* and new ways of playing old ones, such as baseball's *designated hitter.* Television coverage of football fills weekends with *blitzes, split ends, square outs,* and *squib kicks.* Those who care *zilch* about football may go to the track and play the *perfecta, superfecta,* or *trifecta.* The *martial arts* of the Far East have given us *aikido* and *kung fu* along with *dan, dojo,* and *black belt.* Surfing has created a whole new vocabulary, including *head-dip, hang five, goofy-foot, hotdog,* and the less sporting *hodad* and *beach bunny.*

Cooking too has added to the English vocabulary. From *aioli* to *zuppa Inglese* English has borrowed a host of terms from foreign cuisines, including *coq au vin, marinara* sauce, and *wok.* The vocabulary of food has also been increased by such domestic contributors as the *corn chip* and *green goddess dressing.*

How Are They Formed?

English gets its new vocabulary from many fields, some very new. But these new words are, for the most part, created or derived in a number of time-honored ways. Not all new words, in fact, are really new. Old words are frequently given new meanings to fit new situations. *Angel,* for example, is the name of a spiritual being believed by many to be able to exert an influence on men without their being aware of his presence. Now the word *angel* is used also for a radar echo whose cause is not visually discernible. Because the dove is a traditional symbol of peace and the hawk is a predatory bird, *dove* has come to be used for a conciliatory person, *hawk* for one who is militant. We have long been familiar with the *Mafia* as a secret criminal society; now the use of the word has been extended so that any clique may be called a *Mafia.*

Some new words are new not in form but in function. By functional shift an old noun, for example, may come to be used as a new verb. The noun *clone* means "an aggregate of the progency of an individual, reproduced asexually." *Clone* has now been made into a verb, meaning "to grow as a clone or to culture into a clone." The noun *update,* meaning "an updating", comes by functional shift from the verb *update.* Similarly, the adjective *soul* comes from the noun, the noun *commute* from the verb, the verb *format* from the noun.

Of course the words most obviously new are those whose forms have not been used before, whether in earlier senses or in other functions. One common method of forming new words is compounding, combining two (or more) old words to form a new one. Typical compounds are such words as *fake book, far-out, pantsuit, uptight, goof-off, acidhead, strawberry jar, end-of-day glass, floating decimal, water bed, litterbag, splashdown.* Some of these words occur in more than one styling—closed (*acidhead*), hyphenated (*acid-head*), or open (*acid head*)—but only the most common will appear in the dictionary. Some new words are compounds of parts of older words. *Gravisphere,* for example, adds *sphere* to the *gravi-* of *gravity. Underwhelm* is formed from *under* and the *-whelm* of *overwhelm.*

Sometimes words which are combined seem to overlap. Two words which have letters or sounds in common may be blended. Typical blends are such new words as *cremains,* from *cremated* and *remains, boatel,* from *boat* and *hotel,* and *Franglais,* blended in French of *français* (French) and *anglais* (English).

Many word elements occur only in combinations, never alone. These are affixes (prefixes and suffixes) and combining forms. Many old affixes and combining forms are very prolific. The prefix *anti-,* for example, has given us *antihero, antiheroine, antiparticle, antipollution, antismog,* and a host of other new words. From *non-* we derive such words as *nonbook, nondiscrimination, nonnegative,* and *nonperson.* The suffix *-ese,* which denotes a jargon, has formed *academese, computerese, educationese.* The combining form *-logy* has been especially prolific in recent years, yielding terms for such studies as *erotology, futurology, Pekingology,* and *planetology.* Nor is the English language content with its already large hoard of affixes and combining forms; it creates or borrows new ones like the suffix *-manship,* taken from *sportsmanship* and used to form such words as *gamesmanship* and *grantsmanship;* like the suffix *-nik,* borrowed from Yiddish and used in *peacenik, neatnik,* and their relatives; like the combining form *-in,* which we find not only in the original *sit-in,* but very widespread, as in *love-in* and *teach-in,* and like the very frequently used new combining form *mini-,* in *minibus, minicomputer,* and *ministate.*

Many new words are simply shortened forms, or clippings, of older words. By shortening we derive *deli* from *delicatessen, mayo* from *mayonnaise, mod* from *modern, narc* from *narcotics agent.* Some words are formed as acronyms from the initial letters of the parts of a compound term. In this way we have created *COBOL* from *common business oriented language, LSD* from *lysergic acid diethylamide,* and *WASP* from *white Anglo-Saxon Protestant.*

A process somewhat similar to clipping is known as back-formation. A back-formation is formed from an already existing word by subtracting a real or supposed affix. *Gangling,* for example, looks as if it ought to be the present participle of a verb, so we create a new verb *gangle,* removing the supposed derivative suffix *-ing. Laser,* although it is an acronymic formation from *light amplification by simulated emission of radiation*, looks like an agent noun formed from a verb. So we remove the apparent agent suffix and form the verb *lase*. In like manner, we have created the back-formations *free-associate* from *free association* and *one-up* from *one-upmanship*.

Many new English words are not products of English word formation at all. They are borrowed from other languages. For much of its history English has been a great borrower, building its vocabulary by culling languages all over the world for new and useful terms. From the French, English has taken such words as *après-ski*, *extraordinaire*, *bidonville*, and *yé-yé* (the last borrowed earlier by French from English *yeah-yeah*). We have borrowed Italian *autostrada* and *ciao*, Portuguese *favela*, German *gemütlich* and *gemütlichkeit*, Swedish *ombudsman*, Mexican Spanish *macho* and *machismo*, Hindi *tabla*, Sanskrit *tala*, Chinese *wok*, Japanese *ikebana*, Tahitian *mai tai*.

We have borrowed such words as *flokati* from modern Greek and gone back to classical Greek for *lexis*. One language from which English has borrowed extensively is in a unique position. Yiddish is a language foreign to English, but it is spoken by many English-speaking American Jews, who often lard their English with Yiddish words. And many Yiddish words have passed into the speech of non-Yiddish-speaking Americans. Especially prominent among these borrowings are derogatory terms like *klutz*, *nebbish*, *schlepp*, and *schlock*. But also from Yiddish come *chutzpah* (perhaps derogatory), *bialy*, and *maven*.

Sometimes English compounds are borrowed from other languages, but their components are translated into English. These are called loan translations. *Black humor* is a loan translation from French *humour noir*. French *objet trouvé* has entered English both as a straight borrowing and as a loan translation (*found object*). Occasionally we translate only part of a compound we are borrowing. *Auteur theory*, for example, is a part translation of French *politique des auteurs*.

Some new words come from the names of people or places. The *Alfvén wave*, for instance, was named for Swedish astrophysicist Hannes Alfvén, *Chandler's wobble* for American astronomer Seth Carlo Chandler. A jacket of eastern appearance is called either *Mao*, after Mao Tse-tung, or *Nehru*, after Jawaharlal Nehru. *A-go-go* comes from a café and discotheque in Paris, the Whisky à Gogo.

Trademarks are another source of new words. Although a trademark is owned by a particular company and used for a specific class of products, some trademarks become so familiar that they are used by many people for similar products. Of course a company that owns a trademark will try to protect its property and maintain the association of the trademarked name with its product alone. But occasionally a trademark does become generic. *Granola*, formerly a trademark, is now a generic name for a cereal mixture whose basic component is rolled oats. Sometimes a trademark for one product is borrowed and used as a general word for something else. *STP* is a trademark for a motor fuel additive, but it is commonly applied to a psychedelic drug. Other trademarks, although they do not become generic, do produce derivatives by functional shift. The trademark *Mace*, for example, has given us the verb *mace*. Some trademarks which have not become generic occur so often in speech and writing that they deserve a place in a dictionary, even though they cannot really be considered a part of the general vocabulary of English. Those entries known to be trademarks or service marks are so labeled and are treated in accordance with a formula approved by the United States Trademark Association. No entry in this dictionary, however, should be regarded as affecting the validity of any trademark or service mark.

Many new words are onomatopoeic, imitative of nonspeech sounds. *Chugalug* imitates the sound of swallowing liquid, *bleep* a high-pitched sound of electronic equipment, *zap* the sound of a gun. Some words are simply coined ex nihilo, but these are relatively rare. One such is *quark*, which was coined by the physicist Murray Gell-Mann in 1964 during a discussion of a new theory apparently by his garbling another term he had meant to propose for the particle.

How Do They Get Into Merriam-Webster Dictionaries?

It is one thing for a word to get into the language and quite another for it to get into a dictionary. The definitions in this book, as in all Merriam-Webster dictionaries, are based upon our voluminous files of citations. The editorial staff regularly reads a variety of periodicals, as well as fiction and nonfiction books in many fields. Every editor spends a part of each working day reading and marking. When he comes across a word that is not in our dictionaries or that is used in a new or striking way, he underlines the word and brackets enough of its context to make the word's meaning clear. (Sometimes, it is true, a word's meaning will not be clear no matter how much context surrounds it. When this happens, the only thing an editor can do is mark it anyway, simply for its occurrence, and hope that the word will turn up elsewhere, more intelligibly used.) The passages marked in this manner are put on 3x5 slips of paper, called citation slips, and filed alphabetically. When a new dictionary is being written, a definer will take all the citations for a particular word, sort them according to grammatical function (such as noun or verb) and possible separable segments of meaning, read them carefully to determine the meaning of the word as it is used, and write a definition. The definitions, then, are based not on an editor's idea of what words ought to mean but rather on the meanings actually given to words by the speakers and writers of English who use them.

Not every word that is represented in the citation files will be entered in a dictionary. A single citation or two is not normally considered evidence of a word's establishment as part of the general vocabulary. We look for the use of a word in a variety of sources, and for its occurrence over several years. Some words enjoy a brief vogue, when they are on practically every tongue, then disappear. The division of British youth a few years ago into *Mods* and *Rockers* seemed destined to add these terms to the general vocabulary. But after a couple of years the division faded away and with it the words. A more recent example was the highly publicized phenomenon of *streaking.* It went out of fashion after about six months, and the word has been rarely seen since. Such words as *Mod, Rocker,* and *streaking* are items of interest for a historical dictionary, but are unlikely to enter a general dictionary.

Some of our 6,000 Words are older than the 1960s. They appear here because, for one reason or another, they were not entered in Webster's Third New International Dictionary. Some words, although they had been in the spoken language for years, did not appear in print until recently or appeared so rarely as to be caught only once or twice, or not at all, by our reading and marking program. *Mayo* has probably been heard at lunch counters for forty years or more, but it was only in the early 1960s that we began to see it in print. Another word, *frog* "a spiked or perforated holder used to keep flowers in position in a vase", is quite old. Even now it has been cited only very rarely by our readers and markers. But after the appearance of Webster's Third, a number of correspondents questioned its absence from that book, so it was entered among the addenda.

In some fields, our reading and marking program was fairly weak in the past. In mathematics, for example, such words as *counterexample* and *Fibonacci number,* although they are not new, have only recently caught the attention of the markers and definers. Some older words did not appear in Webster's Third because they were rejected by outside consultants. One such is *sprechstimme,* which was rejected by the music consultant with the note "The time will come . . . when this word will or must, be entered". His note is dated 1957 and the citational evidence, now more than three times what it was in 1957, shows that *sprechstimme* deserves entry.

Some words have an air of antiquity not because they themselves are old but because the objects with which they are associated are old. The controversial *homo habilis,* for example, although he is a fossil about two million years old, was not discovered until 1964. And though typists have been taught for years with the aid of such sentences as "The quick brown fox jumps over the lazy dog", we knew of no word for such sentences until 1964, when we first met *pangram* in print.

18a • Pronunciation Symbols

ə .... in unstressed syllables as in banana, collide, abut, maker; in stressed syllables as in humdrum, abut, and by *r*-keepers in bird

ə̇ .... two-value symbol meaning \ə\ or \i\ in unstressed syllables only

^{ə} ..... immediately preceding \l\, \n\, \m\ as in battle, cotton, and one pronunciation of **open** \'ōp^{ə}m\; immediately following \l\, \m\, \r\ as often in French table, prisme, titre

ə̄, əi .. alternative pronunciations used by *r*-droppers in stressed positions where *r*-keepers have \ər\ as in bird

a .... mat, map, mad, man, pass, stamp

ā .... day, fade, aorta, drape, cape, date

ä .... bother, cot, and with most Americans father, cart

ȧ .... father as pronounced by speakers who do not rhyme it with *bother;* aunt as pronounced by speakers who do not rhyme it with *pant* or *font;* farther, cart as pronounced by *r*-droppers; French patte

au̇ .. now, loud, out, some pronunciations of talcum (see \u̇\)

b .... baby, rib

ch ... chin, nature \'nāchə(r)\ (actually, this sound is \t\ + \sh\)

d .... elder, undone, glad

d· .... as in the usual American pronunciation of duty, latter; \t\ is always to be understood as an alternative

e .... bed, pet

ē .... in stressed syllables as in beat, nosebleed, evenly, sleepy; in unstressed syllables as in one pronunciation of evenly, sleepy, envious, igneous (alternative \i\)

f .... fifty, cuff

g .... go, big

h .... hat, ahead

hw .. whale as pronounced by those who do not have the same pronunciation for both *whale* and *wail*

i ..... bid, tip, one pronunciation of active, evenly (alternative unstressed \ē\)

ī .... site, side, buy (actually, this sound is \ä\ + \i\ or \ȧ\ + \i\)

j ..... job, gem, judge (actually, this sound is \d\ + \zh\)

k .... kin, cook, ache

k̲ .... as in one pronunciation of loch (alternative \k\); German ich, buch

l ..... lily, pool, cold

m ... murmur, dim, nymph

n .... no, own

^{n} .... indicates that a preceding vowel or diphthong is pronounced with open nasal passages as in French *un bon vin blanc* \œ^{n}bō^{n}va^{n}blä^{n}\

ŋ .... sing \'siŋ\, singer \'siŋə(r)\, finger \'fiŋgə(r)\, ink \'iŋk\

ō .... **bo**ne, kn**ow**, b**eau**

ȯ .... s**aw**, **a**ll, gn**aw**

œ ... French b**œ**uf, German H**ö**lle

œ̄ the vowel \œ\ but with longer duration as in French b**eu**rre

œ̄ ... French f**eu**, German H**öh**le

ȯi ... c**oi**n, destr**oy**, s**awi**ng

p .... **p**e**pp**er, li**p**

r .... **r**a**r**ity, **r**ead; ca**r** and ca**r**d as pronounced by *r*-keepers

s .... **s**our**c**e, le**ss**

sh ... with nothing between, as in **sh**y, mi**ss**ion, ma**ch**ine, spe**c**ial (actually this is a single sound, not two)

t .... **t**ie, a**tt**ack; one pronunciation of la**tt**er (alternative \d•\)

th ....with nothing between, as in **th**in, e**th**er (actually this is a single sound, not two)

th̲ ....**th**en, ei**th**er, **th**is (actually this is a single sound, not two)

ü .... r**u**le, y**ou**th, union \'yünyən\, few \'fyü\

u̇ .... p**u**ll, w**oo**d, t**oo**k, curable \'kyu̇rəbəl\, some pronunciations of mil**k** \'miu̇k\, talcum \'tau̇kəm\

ue ....German f**ü**llen, h**ü**bsch

ue̅ ....French r**ue**, German f**üh**len

v .....**v**i**v**id, gi**v**e

w ... **w**e, a**w**ay; in some words having final \(ˌ)ō\ or \(ˌ) yü\ variant \əw\ occurs before vowels as in foll**ow**ing \'faləwiŋ\, covered by a variant \ə(w)\ at the entry word

y ....**y**ard, **y**oung, cue \'kyü\, union \'yünyən\

z.....**z**one, rai**s**e

zh....with nothing between, as in vi**si**on, azure \'azhə(r)\ (actually this is a single sound, not two)

\ ....slant line used to mark the beginning and end of a transcription

, ; ....a comma separates pronunciation variants; a semicolon separates groups of variants

(), (..indicate that what is symbolized between or after is present in some utterances but not in others

ˈ, ˌ, ˈˌ ...\ˈ\ precedes a syllable with primary (strongest) stress; \ˌ\ precedes a syllable with secondary (next-strongest) stress; combined marks \ˈˌ\ precede a syllable whose stress may be either primary or secondary

• .... used to indicate syllable division where confusion might otherwise arise (see also \d•\)

÷ ... indicates that many regard as unacceptable the one pronunciation immediately following, as in *escalate* \'eskəˌlāt, ÷-kyə-\

20a • Abbreviations in This Work

AAUP	American Association of University Professors
ab	about
abbr	abbreviation
adj	adjective
adv	adverb
advt	advertisement
alter	alteration
Am, Amer	American
AmerSp	American Spanish
Ar	Arabic
b	born
B.C.	before Christ
Biog	Biography
Biol	Biological
Brit	British
Bull	Bulletin
C	centigrade
cal	caliber
Canad	Canadian
CanF	Canadian French
Cant	Cantonese
cent	century
Chem	Chemical
Chin	Chinese
Co	Company
comb	combining
conj	conjunction
constr	construction
contr	contraction
Dan	Danish
D.C.	District of Columbia
deriv	derivative
dial	dialect
dim	diminutive
Du	Dutch
E, Eng	English
Esk	Eskimo
esp	especially
Eve	Evening
F	French
fem	feminine
fl	flourished
Fla	Florida
fr	from
Fr	French
freq	frequentative
G, Ger	German
Gk	Greek
Heb	Hebrew
Hung	Hungarian
Icel	Icelandic
Ill	Illinois
imit	imitative
interj	interjection
Introd	Introduction
irreg	irregular
ISV	International Scientific Vocabulary
It, Ital	Italian
Jap	Japanese
Jour	Journal
Jr.	Junior
L	Latin
LHeb	Late Hebrew
lit	literally
Lit	Literary
LL	Late Latin
Mag	Magazine
Mass	Massachusetts
MD	Middle Dutch
MexSp	Mexican Spanish
MF	Middle French
MHG	Middle High German
MLG	Middle Low German
modif	modification
n	noun
NE	northeast
neut	neuter
Nev	Nevada
NGk	New Greek
NHeb	New Hebrew
NL	New Latin
Norw	Norwegian
obs	obsolete
OE	Old English
OF	Old French
OHG	Old High German
OIt	Old Italian
ON	Old Norse
orig	originally
part	participle
Pek	Pekingese
perh	perhaps
Pg	Portuguese
pl	plural
Pol	Polish
prep	preposition
prob	probably
pron	pronoun
Prov	Provençal
Russ	Russian
Sat	Saturday
Sc	Scots
Scand	Scandinavian
Scot	Scottish
sing	singular
Skt	Sanskrit
Slav	Slavic
So	South
Sp	Spanish
specif	specifically
Supp	Supplement
Sw, Swed	Swedish
trans	translation
U.S.	United States
U.S.S.R.	Union of Soviet Socialist Republics
usu	usually
v, vb	verb
var	variant
vi	verb intransitive
VL	Vulgar Latin
vt	verb transitive
Vt	Vermont

A Supplement to Webster's Third New International Dictionary

A

a* *abbr* atto-

A and R *abbr* artists and repertory

ABD \ˌā(ˌ)bēˈdē\ *n* [*a*ll *b*ut *d*issertation] : a doctoral candidate who has completed the required course work and examinations but not the dissertation

Abe·lian \əˈbēlyən, -lēən\ *adj* [Niels *Abel* †1829 Norw. mathematician] : combining elements or having elements that combine in such a manner that the result is independent of the order in which elements are taken : commutative <*Abelian* ring> <the real numbers under addition comprise an *Abelian* group>

ab·la·tor \aˈblād·ə(r)\ *n* [LL, one that removes, fr. *ablatus*, suppletive past part. of *auferre* to remove] : a material that provides thermal protection (as to the outside of a spacecraft on reentry) by ablating

ABM \ˌā(ˌ)bēˈem\ *n* : ANTIBALLISTIC MISSILE

abort* \əˈbȯ(ə)rt, -ȯət\ *n* : the premature termination of an action, procedure, or mission relating to a rocket or spacecraft <a launch *abort*>

ab·scis·ic acid \(ˌ)abˌsizik-, -ˌsis-\ *n* [*abscis*ion (var. of *abscission*) + *-ic* relating to] : a growth-inhibiting plant hormone widespread in nature and made synthetically that promotes leaf abscission and dormancy and has an inhibitory effect on cell elongation — called also *abscisin II, dormin*

ab·scis·in *also* **ab·scis·sin** \ˈabsəsən, abˈsisᵊn\ *n* [*abscis*ion, *absciss*ion + *-in* chemical compound] : any of a group of plant hormones (as abscisic acid) that tend to promote leaf abscission and inhibit various growth processes

absurd* *adj* **1** : having no rational or orderly relationship to man's life : meaningless; *also* : lacking order or values <adults have condemned them to live in what must seem like an *absurd* universe —Joseph Featherstone> **2** : dealing with the absurd or with absurdism

absurd *n* : the state or condition in which man exists in an irrational and meaningless universe and in which man's life has no meaning outside his own existence <no . . . existential *Absurd* to perplex us —Dwight Macdonald> <the black humor of the *absurd* —Mark Phillips>

ab·surd·ism \əbˈsərdˌizəm, ab-, -ˈz-, -əd-, -əid-\ *n* : a philosophy based on the belief that man exists in an irrational and meaningless universe and that his search for order brings him into conflict with his universe

[1]ab·surd·ist \-dəst\ *n* : a proponent or adherent of absurdism; *esp* : a writer who deals with absurdist themes

[2]absurdist *adj* : of, relating to, or dealing with absurdism

aca·de·mese \ə¦kadə¦mēz, ¦akəd-, -ēs\ *n* [*academ*ic + *-ese* jargon] : a style of writing held to be characteristic of those in academic life <the usual scholarly biography, written in barbarous *academese* —Dwight Macdonald>

acceptable* *adj* : capable of being endured : supportable, tolerable <maximum *acceptable* damage from nuclear attack> <concluded that environmental damage caused by the line could be held to an "*acceptable* minimum" —Robert Gillette>

access *vt* : to get at : gain access to <accumulator and index registers can be *accessed* by the programmer —*Datamation*>

access time *n* : the time lag between the time stored information (as in a computer) is requested and the time it is delivered

AC/DC \¦ā(ˌ)sē¦dē(ˌ)sē\ *adj* [fr. the likening of a bisexual person to an electrical appliance which can operate on either alternating or direct current] : sexually oriented to both sexes : bisexual <help the *A.C./D.C.* youngster to shape his actions in a heterosexual direction —R.H. Kuh>

ace* *vt* **aced; ac·ing** : to earn the grade of A on (an examination)

ac·et·amin·o·phen \ˌasəd·ə'minəfən, əˌsēd-·\ *n* [*acet*ic + *amino-* containing an amino group + *phen*ol] : a crystalline compound $C_8H_9NO_2$ that is a hydroxy derivative of acetanilide and is used in chemical synthesis and in medicine to relieve pain and fever

ac·e·to·hex·amide \¦asəd·ō¦heksəməd, ə¦sē-, -ˌheks¦aməd, -ˌmīd\ *n* [N-(p-*acet*ylphenylsulfonyl)-N′-cyclo*hex*ylurea + *amide*, chemical family name for ureas] : a sulfonylurea drug $C_{15}H_{20}N_2O_4S$ used in the oral treatment of mild diabetes to lower the level of glucose in the blood

ace·tyl–coA \ə'sēd·əl'kō'ā; 'asəd·əl-, -əˌtēl-\ *n* [*acetyl co*enzyme *A*] : a compound $C_{25}H_{38}N_7O_{17}P_3S$ formed as an intermediate in metabolism and active as a coenzyme in biological acetylation

acid* *n* : a hallucinogenic drug lysergic acid diethylamide : LSD

acid·head \'asədˌhed\ *n* : a person who frequently uses LSD

acid rock *n* : rock music with lyrics and sound relating to or suggestive of drug-induced experiences

acoustic* *also* **acoustical*** *adj* : of, relating to, or being a musical instrument whose sound is not electronically modified <an *acoustic* guitar>

acous·to·electric \ə¦küstō·ə¦lektrik\ *adj* : of or relating to electroacoustics : electroacoustic

acquire* *vt* **ac·quired; ac·quir·ing** : to locate and hold (a desired object) in a detector <*acquire* a target by radar>

ac·ra·sin \'akrəsən\ *n* [*Acrasia*, a genus of fungi related to the slime molds + *-in* chemical compound] : a substance and esp. cyclic AMP that is secreted by the individual cells of a slime mold and that causes them to aggregate into a multicellular mass

ac·ro·lect \'akrəˌlekt, -rō-\ *n* [*acro-* top (fr. Gk *akro-*, fr. *akros* topmost, extreme) + *-lect* (as in *dialect*)] : the most prestigious dialect of a community — compare BASILECT

ac·ti·no·spec·ta·cin \ˌaktənō'spektəsən\ *n* [*actino*mycete + NL *specta*bilis (specific epithet of *Streptomyces spectabilis*, species of actinomycete) + E -my*cin* substance obtained from a fungus, fr. *streptomycin*] : a broad-spectrum antibiotic from a soil actinomycete (*Streptomyces spectabilis*) that is esp. effective against penicillin-resistant venereal infections

action* *n* : the most vigorous, productive, or exciting activity in a particular field, area, or group <go where the *action* is> <obvious to women in the office ghetto that they are not getting the *action*, but only the crumbs —Margaret Dawson>

action painting *n* : nonrepresentational painting marked esp. by thickly textured surfaces and by the use of improvised techniques (as dribbling, splattering, or smearing) to create apparently accidental pictorial effects — **action painter** *n*

action potential *n* : a recorded change in potential (as between the inside of a nerve cell and the extracellular medium) during activity of a cell or tissue

ac·ti·va·tion analysis \ˌaktə'vāshən-\ *n* : a method of analyzing a material for chemical elements by bombarding it with nuclear particles or gamma rays to produce radioactive atoms whose radiations indicate the identity and quantity of the parent elements

active transport *n* : a movement of a chemical substance by the expenditure of energy through a gradient (as across a cell membrane) in concentration or electrical potential and opposite to the direction of normal diffusion

ACV *abbr* **1** actual cash value **2** air-cushion vehicle

add* *n* : an instance of addition < the computer does an *add* in 7 microseconds >

additive identity *n* : an identity element (as 0 in the group of whole numbers under the operation of addition) that in a given mathematical system leaves unchanged any element to which it is added

additive inverse *n* : a number of opposite sign with respect to a given number so that addition of the two numbers gives zero < the *additive inverse* of 4 is –4 >

ad·dress·able \ə¦dresəbəl\ *adj* : accessible through an address (as in the memory of a computer) < *addressable* registers in a computer >

aden·o·sine mo·no·phos·phate \ə¦denə,sēn,mänə'fäs,fāt, -əsən-, -mōn-\ *n* **1** : AMP **1** **2** : CYCLIC AMP

ad·e·no·vi·rus \¦adᵊnō¦vīrəs\ *n* [adenoid + connective -o- + virus] : any of a group of DNA-containing icosahedral animal viruses orig. identified in human adenoid tissue, causing respiratory diseases (as catarrh), and including some capable of inducing malignant tumors in experimental animals — **ad·e·no·vi·ral** \-rəl\ *adj*

ad·e·nyl·ate cy·clase \¦adᵊn¦ilət'sī,klās, -l,āt-, -āz\ *n* [adenylate fr. adenyl + -ate derivative compound; cyclase fr. cyclic AMP + -ase enzyme] : ADENYL CYCLASE

ad·e·nyl cyclase \¦adᵊn,il-\ *n* : an enzyme that catalyzes the formation of cyclic AMP from ATP

¹ad·mass \'ad,mas\ *n* [advertising + mass] : a system of commercial marketing that attempts to influence great masses of consumers by mass-media advertising; *also* : a society thus influenced

²admass *adj* : of, characterized by, or influenced by admass

ADP* *abbr* automatic data processing

ad·re·no·cor·ti·co·ste·roid \ə¦drēnō,kȯrd·əkō'sti(ə),rȯid, -ren-, -,ste(ə),-\ *n* [adrenocortical + connective -o- + steroid] : a steroid (as cortisone or hydrocortisone) obtained from, resembling, or having physiological effects like those of the adrenal cortex

ad·re·no·cor·ti·co·tro·phin \-'trōfən, -äf-\ *or* **ad·re·no·cor·ti·co·tro·pin** \-'trōpən, -äp-\ *n* [adrenocorticotrophic or adrenocorticotropic + -in chemical compound] : a protein hormone of the anterior lobe of the pituitary gland that stimulates the adrenal cortex : ACTH

advance man* *n* : an aide (as of a political candidate) who makes a security check or handles publicity in advance of personal appearances by his employer

ad·vect \(')ad¦vekt\ *vt* [back-formation fr. advection] **1** : to convey (as water) horizontally by advection **2** : to transport (as moisture) by advection

aeon* *n* : a unit of geologic time equal to one billion years

ae·quo·rin \ē'kwȯrən, -ōr-\ *n* [Aequorea + -in chemical compound] : a bioluminescent protein of jellyfish (genus *Aequorea*) that emits light in response to the addition of calcium or strontium

aer·o·bics \¦a(ə)¦rōbiks, ¦e(ə)-, ¦āə-\ *n pl but sing or pl in constr* [fr. aerobic, after such pairs as *calisthenic: calisthenics*] : a system of physical conditioning that stresses exercises (as running, walking, or swimming) designed to increase oxygen consumption for the purpose of improving circulatory function esp. of the heart and lungs

aer·on·o·my \a(ə)'ränəmē, e(ə)'-, ,āə'-\ *n* [aero- air (deriv. of Gk aēr air) + -nomy sum of knowledge regarding a field, deriv. of Gk nemein to distribute] : a science that deals with the physics and chemistry of the upper atmosphere — **aer·on·o·mer** \-mə(r)\ *n* — **aer·o·nom·ic** \,a(ə)rə'nämik, ,e(ə)r-, ,āər-\ *adj*

aero·plank·ton \¦a(ə)rə¦plaŋ(k)tən, ¦e(ə)rə-, ¦āərə-, -rō-, -,tän\ *n* : small airborne organisms (as flying insects)

¹aero·space \'a(ə)rə,spās, 'e(ə)r-, 'āər-\ *n* **1** : space comprising the earth's atmosphere and the space beyond **2** : a branch of physical science that deals with aerospace **3** : the industry involved in the manufacture of aerospace vehicles

²aerospace *adj* : of or relating to aerospace, to vehicles used in aerospace or the manufacture of such vehicles, or to travel in aerospace < *aerospace* research > < *aerospace* medicine >

aero·train \-rə-,trān\ *n* : a propeller-driven vehicle that rides on a cushion of air astride a single rail

affirmative action plan *or* **affirmative action program** *n* : a plan that encourages the employment of members of minority groups and women

Af·ghan·i·stan·ism \af'ganə,sta,nizəm, -stə,-\ *n* [fr. the remoteness of Afghanistan from America] : the practice (as by a journalist) of concentrating on problems in distant parts of the world while ignoring controversial local issues

af·la·tox·in \,aflə'täksən\ *n* [NL *Aspergillus flavus*, species of mold + E *toxin*] : any of several mycotoxins that are produced esp. in corn or oilseed meals by molds (as *Aspergillus flavus*), are implicated in the death of livestock, and are suspected of being carcinogenic

A–frame* \'ā,frām\ *n* [fr. the resemblance of the shape of the facade to a capital A] : a building (as a house) that typically has a triangular front and rear wall and a roof reaching to or nearly to the level of the ground floor

[1]Af·ro \'a(,)frō\ *adj* [*Afro-* African] : having the hair shaped into a round bushy mass < bouffant *Afro* hairstyles —*N.Y. Times* >

[2]Afro *n, pl* **Afros** : an Afro hairstyle < his hair stood out about four inches all over his head in one of the best *Afros* I had ever seen —Frank Leonard > — **Af·roed** \'a(,)frōd\ *adj*

af·ter·burn·er* \'aftə(r),bərnə(r), -,bən-, -,bəin-\ *n* : a device for burning or catalytically destroying unburned or partially burned carbon compounds in exhaust (as from an automobile)

af·ter·tax \'aftə(r)'taks\ *adj* : remaining after payment of taxes and esp. of income tax < *aftertax* earnings >

age·ism *also* **agism** \'ā(,)jizəm\ *n* [*age* + *-ism* (as in *racism*)] : prejudice or discrimination against a particular age-group and esp. against the elderly < fighting *ageism* through . . . a group of elderly activists —Mary Ann Meyers > — **age·ist** *also* **agist** \-əst\ *adj*

Age of Aquar·i·us \-ə'kwarēəs, -wer-, -wār-\ : an astrological age of freedom and brotherhood

ag·gior·na·men·to \ə,jȯ(r)nə'men(,)tō\ *n* [It, fr. *aggiornare* to bring up to date, fr. *a* to (fr. L *ad*) + *giorno* day, fr. LL *diurnum*, fr. L, neut. of *diurnus* of the day, fr. *dies* day] : a bringing up to date < the enthusiasts of *aggiornamento* and the defenders of older, stricter ways —*Time* >

[1]a–go–go \ä'gō(,)gō, ə'g-\ *n, pl* **a–go–gos** [*Whisky à Gogo*, café and discotheque in Paris, France, fr. F *whisky* whiskey + *à gogo* galore, fr. MF] **1** : DISCOTHEQUE **2** : a usu. small intimate nightclub for dancing to live music and esp. rock 'n' roll

[2]a–go–go *adj* **1** : of, relating to, or being an a-go-go or the music or dances performed there < *a-go-go* dancers > **2** : characterized by rapid frenetic movement or tempo < the *a-go-go* rhythm of change in our century —Ted Palmer > **3** : being in the latest style < psychiatry *a-go-go* —Charles Schulz >

ag·o·nis·tic* \,agə'nistik\ *adj* : of, relating to, or being aggressive or defensive social interaction (as fighting, fleeing, or submitting) between individuals usu. of the same species < *agonistic* behavior > < *agonistic* encounters between warblers >

ago·ra \,ägə'rä\ *n, pl* **ago·rot** \-'rō\ [NHeb *ăgōrāh*, fr. Heb, a small coin] **1** : a monetary unit of Israel representing $^{1}/_{100}$ of a pound **2** : a coin representing one agora

agrav·ic \(')ā'gravik\ *adj* [*a-* not (fr. Gk) + *gravity* + *-ic* relating to] : of or relating to a theoretical condition of no gravitation

ag·ro–in·dus·tri·al \'a(,)grō-ən'dəstrēəl\ *adj* [*agriculture* + connective *-o-* + *industrial*] : of or relating to production (as of power for industry and water for irrigation) for both industrial and agricultural purposes

ai·ki·do \,īkē'dō, -kə-\ *n* [Jap *aikidō*, fr. *ai-* together, mutual + *ki* spirit + *dō* district, province, art] : a Japanese art of self-defense employing locks and holds and utilizing the principle of nonresistance to cause an opponent's own momentum to work against him

ai·o·li \(ˈ)īˌōlē, (ˈ)āˌ-, -li, *F* àyòlē\ *n* [Prov, fr. *ai* garlic (fr. L *allium*) + *oli* oil, fr. L *oleum*] : a sauce made of crushed garlic, egg yolks, olive oil, and lemon juice and usu. served with fish, cold meat, or vegetables : garlic mayonnaise

air bag *n* : a bag designed to inflate automatically in front of riders in an automotive vehicle in case of accident to protect them from pitching forward into solid parts (as the dashboard or windshield)

air battery *n* [fr. the oxidation's being produced by exposure to pressurized air] : a rechargeable battery in which current is generated as a result of oxidation of a metal

air·bus \ˈa(ə)rˌbəs, ˈe(ə)rˌ-, ˈaəˌ-, ˈeəˌ-\ *n* : a short-range or medium-range subsonic jet passenger airplane

air cavalry *or* **air cav** \-ˈkav\ *n* **1** : an army unit that is transported in air vehicles and carries out the traditional cavalry missions of reconnaissance and security **2** : an army unit that is esp. equipped and adapted for transportation in air vehicles but is organized for sustained ground combat

air–cush·ion \-ˌkůshən, *sometimes* -shin\ *also* **air–cushioned** *adj* : of, relating to, or being a vehicle that is used for transporting material or traveling over land or water and that is supported a short distance above the surface on a cushion of air produced by downwardly directing fans

air door *n* : a temperature-controlled strong usu. upward current of air used instead of a door (as at a store)

air·er \ˈe(ə)rə(r), ˈa(ə)-\ *n, Brit* : a frame on which clothes are aired or dried

air·mo·bile \ˌa(ə)rˌmōbəl, ˌa(ə)rˈmōˌbēl, ˌe(ə)rˌ-, ˌaəˌ-, ˌeəˌ-, -ˌbīl\ *adj* : of, relating to, or being a military unit whose members are transported to combat areas usu. by helicopter

air piracy *n* : the hijacking of an airplane : SKYJACKING <held . . . on a charge of *air piracy* in the plot to hijack the plane for $ 502,000 ransom —*Springfield (Mass.) Union*> — **air pirate** *n*

air·play \ˈa(ə)rˌplā, ˈe(ə)rˌ-, ˈaəˌ-, ˈeəˌ-\ *n* : the playing of a phonograph record on the air by a radio station

air·shed \-ˌshed\ *n* [*air* + *-shed* (as in *watershed*)] : the air supply of a given region; *also* : the geographical area covered by such an air supply

air taxi *n* : a small commercial airplane that makes short trips to localities not served by regular airlines

air·tel \ˈa(ə)rˌtel, ˈe(ə)rˌ-, ˈaəˌ-, ˈeəˌ-\ *n* [*air* + ho*tel*] : a hotel situated at or close to an airport

air·time \-ˌtīm\ *n* : the time or any part thereof that a radio or television station is on the air

aka *abbr* also known as

albatross* *n* [fr. the albatross killed by the ancient mariner and subsequently hung about his neck in the poem *The Rime of the Ancient Mariner* (1798) by S. T. Coleridge † 1834 Eng. poet] **1** : something that causes persistent deep concern or anxiety **2** : something that makes accomplishment particularly difficult : an encumbrance <this regulatory *albatross* inhibits any marketing scheme that might lure commuters —Charles Luna>

al den·te \(ˌ)älˈden·(ˌ)tā, -àl-, -al-\ *adj* [It, lit., to the tooth] *of food* : cooked no more than enough to retain a somewhat firm texture <the pasta arrived piping hot . . . and properly *al dente* —Milton Glaser & Jerome Snyder>

al·do·ste·ron·ism \alˈdästəˌrōˌnizəm, ˌal(ˌ)dōstəˈr-\ *n* : a condition that is characterized by excessive production and excretion of aldosterone and typically by loss of body potassium, muscular weakness, and elevated blood pressure

ale·a·tor·ic \ˌālēəˌtȯrik, -tär-\ *adj* [L *aleator* dice player, gambler (fr. *alea* dice game)] *of music* : characterized by chance or random elements

ale·a·to·ry* \ˈālēəˌtōrē, -ˌtȯr-, -ri\ *adj* : ALEATORIC

Alf·vén wave \ˌal(f)ˌvān-, -ˌven-\ *n* [Hannes *Alfvén* *b* 1908 Swed. astrophysicist] : a transverse electromagnetic wave that propagates along the lines of force in a magnetized plasma

ALG *abbr* antilymphocyte globulin; antilymphocytic globulin

al·ge·bra* \ˈaljəbrə\ *n* : LINEAR ALGEBRA 2

AL·GOL \ˈal͵gäl, -gȯl\ *n* [*algo*rithmic *l*anguage] : an algebraic and logical language for programming a computer

al·go·rithm* \ˈalgə͵rit͟həm, -th-\ *n* : a procedure for solving a mathematical problem (as finding the greatest common divisor) in a finite number of steps that frequently involves repetition of an operation; *broadly* : a step-by-step procedure for solving a problem or accomplishing an end <the *algorithm* used by the computer in comparing footprints —*Technical News Bull.*> — **al·go·rith·mic*** \¦algə¦rit͟hmik, -th-\ *adj* — **al·go·rith·mi·cal·ly** \-mək(ə)lē, -mēk-, -li\ *adv*

ali·es·ter·ase \¦alē¦estə͵rās, -āz\ *n* [*ali*phatic + *esterase*] : an esterase that promotes the hydrolysis of ester links esp. in aliphatic esters of low molecular weight

A–line \ˈā¦līn\ *adj* [fr. the resemblance of such a garment's outline to that of a capital A] : having a flared bottom and a close-fitting top — used of a garment <an *A-line* skirt>

all–night·er \(͵)ȯlˈnīd·ə(r)\ *n* : something that lasts throughout the night <classes, meetings, eye-straining hours in the library, and *all-nighters* over last-minute papers —Nora Peck>

al·lo·ge·ne·ic \¦aləjə¦nēik, -lō-\ *also* **al·lo·gen·ic** \-¦jenik\ *adj* [*allogeneic* fr. *allo-* other, different (fr. Gk, fr. *allos* other) + *-geneic* (as in *syngeneic*); *allogenic* fr. *allo-* + *genic*] : sufficiently unlike genetically to interact antigenically but of the same species <*allogeneic* skin grafts> — compare SYNGENEIC

al·lo·graft \ˈalō͵graft, ˈalə-\ *n* [*allo-* + *graft;* fr. its being a graft from another individual] : a homograft between genetically dissimilar individuals — **allograft** *vt*

al·lo·pu·ri·nol \͵alōˈpyu̇rə͵nȯl, -͵nōl\ *n* [*allo-* + *purine* + *-ol* compound containing hydroxyl] : a drug $C_5H_4N_4O$ used to promote excretion of uric acid esp. in the treatment of gout

al·lo·ste·ric \¦alə¦sterik, -ti(ə)r-\ *adj* [*allo-* + *steric* relating to the arrangement of atoms in space] : of, relating to, or being alteration of the activity of a protein (as an enzyme) by combination with another substance at a point other than the chemically active site — **al·lo·ste·ri·cal·ly** \-rək(ə)lē, -rēk-, -li\ *adv*

al·lo·transplant \͵alōˈtran(t)s͵plant, ͵aləˈ-, -nz͵-\ *vt* : to transplant between genetically different individuals of the same species — **al·lo·trans·plant** \¦alō¦-, ¦alə¦-\ *n* — **al·lo·trans·plan·ta·tion** \¦alō͵tran(t)s͵plan·¦tāshən, -nz-, -splən-\ *n*

al·lo·type* \ˈalə͵tīp\ *n* : an isoantigenic immunoglobulin — **al·lo·typy** \-pē, -pi\ *n*

al·pha \ˈalfə, ˈau̇fə\ *adj* [short for *alphabetic*] : being or done in the order of the alphabet : alphabetic <an *alpha* sort done by computer>

al·pha–ad·ren·er·gic \¦alfə͵adrə¦nərjik\ *adj* : of, relating to, or being an alpha-receptor <*alpha-adrenergic* blocking action>

alpha–adrenergic receptor *n* : ALPHA-RECEPTOR

alpha decay *n* : the radioactive decay of an atomic nucleus by emission of an alpha particle

alpha he·lix \-¦hēliks\ *n* : the coiled structural arrangement of many proteins consisting of a single amino-acid chain that is stabilized by hydrogen bonds — **al·pha–he·li·cal** \͵alfəˈheləkəl, -hēl-\ *adj*

al·pha·met·ic \¦alfə¦med·ik\ *n* [*alpha*betic + arith*metic*] : a mathematical puzzle consisting of a numerical computation with letters substituted for numbers which are to be restored through mathematical reasoning

al·pha–re·cep·tor \ˈalfə·rə͵septə(r), -rē͵-\ *n* : a receptor that responds to or is activated by epinephrine and levarterenol but not isoproterenol and that is associated with vasoconstriction, relaxation of intestinal muscle, and contraction of the myometrium, nictitating membrane, iris dilator muscle, and splenic smooth muscle —compare BETA-RECEPTOR

alpha rhythm *or* **alpha wave** *n* : an electrical rhythm of the brain that can be recorded by an electroencephalograph, occurs 8 to 13 cycles per second, and is often associated with a state of wakeful relaxation

Al·pine* \ˈal͵pīn, *also* ˈalpən\ *adj* : of or relating to competitive ski events consisting of slalom and downhill racing — compare NORDIC

Alpine hat *n* : an often green felt hat with a narrow brim, pointed crown, and an ornamental feather or brush

aman·ta·dine \ə'mantə,dēn\ *n* [*amantad-* (fr. anagram of *adamantane*) + am*ine*] : an antiviral drug used esp. to prevent infection (as by an influenza virus) by interfering with virus penetration into host cells

am·bi·plas·ma \¦ambə̇¦plazmə, -bē-\ *n* [*ambi-* both (fr. L) + *plasma*] : a hypothetical plasma that is held to consist of matter and antimatter

am·bi·po·lar \-¦pōlə(r)\ *adj* : relating to or consisting of both electrons and positive ions moving in opposite directions <an *ambipolar* diffusion>

am·bi·sex·trous \-¦sekstrəs\ *adj* [*ambi-* + *sex* + *-trous* (as in *ambidextrous*)] : UNISEX

Am·er·asian \¦amər¦āzhən, -¦āshən\ *n* : a person of mixed American and Asian descent

American dream *n* : an American social ideal that stresses egalitarianism and esp. material prosperity <much pride, some anger, more self-respect and self-reliance, but most of all love and the recognition of the dignity and integrity of all human beings are what is most needed if the *American dream* is to become a reality —K.S. Tollett>

am·e·thop·ter·in \,amə'thäpt(ə)rən\ *n* [*a*mino- containing an amino group + *meth*yl + *pter*oyl the radical $(C_{13}H_{11}N_6O)CO$ + *-in* pharmaceutical product] : METHOTREXATE

ami·no·ac·id·uria \ə¦mēnō,asə̇¦dyu̇rēə, -ür-\ *n* [NL, fr. *amino acid* + *-uria* presence in urine] : a condition in which one or more amino acids are excreted in excessive amounts

ami·no·trans·fer·ase \-¦tran(t)s(,)fər,ās, -nz,f-, -,āz\ *n* : an enzyme promoting transamination

ami·no·tri·a·zole \-¦trīə,zōl, -(,)trī¦a,zōl\ *n* : AMITROLE

am·i·trip·ty·line \,amə·'triptə,lēn, -ələ̇n\ *n* [*ami*no- + *tript-* (alter. of *trypt-* — as in *tryptophan*, an amino acid) + *-yl* chemical radical + *-ine* chemical substance] : an antidepressant drug $C_{20}H_{23}N$

am·i·trole \'amə·,trōl\ *n* [*ami*no- + *tri*az*ole* $C_2H_3N_3$] : a systemic herbicide $C_2H_4N_4$ used in areas other than food croplands

am·nio·cen·te·sis \,amnēō(,)sen·'tēsə̇s\ *n, pl* **-te·ses** \-'tēsēz\ : the surgical insertion of a hollow needle through the abdominal wall and uterus of a pregnant female and into the amnion esp. to obtain amniotic fluid for the determination of sex or chromosomal abnormality in the fetus

am·ni·og·ra·phy \,amnē'ägrəfē\ *n, pl* **-phies** [*amnion* + radio*graphy*] : radiographic visualization of the outlines of the uterine cavity, placenta, and fetus after injection of a radiopaque substance into the amniotic sac

am·ni·os·co·py \-'äskəpē\ *n, pl* **-pies** [*amnion* + *-scopy* observation, fr. Gk *-skopia*, fr. *skeptesthai* to watch, look at] : visual examination of the amniotic cavity and its contents by means of an optical instrument surgically inserted through the abdominal wall

AMP \,ā,em'pē\ *n* [*a*denosine *mono*phosphate] **1** : a mononucleotide of adenine $C_{10}H_{12}N_5O_3H_2PO_4$ that was orig. isolated from mammalian muscle and is reversibly convertible to ADP and ATP in metabolic reactions — called also *adenosine monophosphate* **2** : CYCLIC AMP

am·pho·ter·i·cin \,amfə'terəsən\ *n* [*amphoteric* capable of reacting chemically either as an acid or as a base (fr. Gk *amphoteros* each of two, fr. *amphō* both) + *-in* chemical compound] : either of two antibiotic drugs obtained from a soil actinomycete (*Streptomyces nodosus*); *esp* : the one (**amphotericin B**) useful against deep-seated and systemic fungal infections

am·pi·cil·lin \¦ampə̇¦silən\ *n* [*ami*no- + *pen icillin*] : an antibiotic of the penicillin group that is effective against gram-negative bacteria and is used to treat various infections of the urinary, respiratory, and intestinal tracts

an·a·dama bread \¦anə¦damə-, -dȧm-\ *n* [origin unknown] : a leavened bread made with flour, cornmeal, and molasses

ana·gen·e·sis* \,anə'jenəsə̇s\ *n* : linear evolutionary change in which one group replaces another without branching into distinct forms — **ana·ge·net·i·cal·ly** \¦anəjə̇¦ned·ək(ə)lē\ *adv*

an·a·log *also* **an·a·logue** \ˈanᵊlˌȯg, -äg\ *adj* **1** : of, relating to, or being an analogue **2 a** : of or relating to the representation of data by continuously variable physical quantities **b** : of or relating to an analog computer

analyst* *n* : SYSTEMS ANALYST

an·am·nes·tic* \ˌanəmˈnestik, -nˌam-\ *adj* : of or relating to a second rapid increased production of antibodies in response to an immunogenic substance after serum antibodies from a first response can no longer be detected in the blood

an·a·tom·i·co- \ˌanəˌtämə(ˌ)kō\ *or* **anat·o·mo-** \əˈnad·ə(ˌ)mō\ *comb form* : anatomical and : anatomical < *anatomico*pathological > < *anatomo*clinical >

an·au·tog·e·nous \ˌan(ˌ)ȯˌtäjənəs, ˌanəˌt-\ *adj* [*an-* not (fr. Gk) + *autogenous*] : requiring a meal of blood to produce eggs < *anautogenous* mosquitoes >

an·chor·man \ˈaŋkə(r)ˌman, -kə(r)mən\ *n* **1** : a newscaster who coordinates the related activities of other usu. remotely located broadcasters (as at a political convention) so as to produce a coherent program **2** : the moderator of a discussion group (as on radio or television)

an·chors \ˈaŋkə(r)z\ *n pl, slang* : the brakes of a motor vehicle

AND \ˈand\ *n* : a logical operator equivalent to the sentential connective *and* < *AND* gate in a computer >

an·dro·stene·di·one \ˌandrəˌstēnˌdīˌōn, -ˈstēndēˌ-\ *n* [*andros*terone, a male sex hormone + *-ene* unsaturated carbon compound + *-dione* chemical compound with two carbonyl groups] : a steroid sex hormone that is secreted by the testis, ovary, and adrenal cortex and acts more strongly in the production of male characteristics than testosterone

angel* *n* : a radar echo caused by something not visually discernible

an·gio·ten·sin \ˌanjēōˈten(t)sən, -jōˈ-\ *n* [blend of *angiotonin* and *hypertensin*] : either of two forms of a kinin of which one (**angiotensin II**) is an octapeptide with vasoconstrictive activity; *also* : a synthetic amide of the physiologically active form used to treat some forms of hypotension

an·gio·ten·sin·ase \-səˌnās, -āz\ *n* : any of several enzymes in the blood that hydrolyze angiotensin

¹An·glo·phone \ˈaŋ(ˌ)glōˌfōn, -glə-\ *or* **An·glo·phon·ic** \ˌaŋglōˈfänik, -glə-, -ēk\ *adj* [*Anglophone* fr. F, fr. *anglo-* English + *-phone* (as in *francophone* French-speaking); *Anglophonic* fr. *Anglophone* + *-ic* relating to] : having or belonging to an English-speaking population esp. in a country where two or more languages are spoken

²Anglophone *n* : an English-speaking person esp. in a country where two or more languages are spoken

angry young man *n* [*Angry Young Man*, autobiography (1951) of Leslie A. Paul *b*1905 Eng. journalist] : one of a group of mid-20th century British writers whose works express the bitterness of the lower classes toward the established sociopolitical system and toward the mediocrity and hypocrisy of the middle and upper classes

angular perspective *n* : linear perspective in which parallel lines along the width and depth of an object are represented as meeting on two separate points on the horizon that are 90 degrees apart as measured from the common intersection of the lines of projection : two-point perspective

annihilate* *vi* **-lat·ed; -lat·ing** : to undergo annihilation <an elementary particle and its antiparticle *annihilate* when they meet>

annual percentage rate *n* : a measure of the annual percentage cost of consumer credit (as in installment buying or a charge account) that is required by law to appear on statements of credit accounts and is variously computed but always takes into consideration the amount financed, the amount of the finance charges, and the schedule of repayment

an·ovu·lant \aˈnävyələnt, -ōv-\ *n* : an anovulatory drug — **anovulant** *adj*

an·ovu·la·tion \(ˌ)anˌävyəˈlāshən, -ˌōv-\ *n* [*an-* not (fr. Gk) + *ovulation*] : temporary or permanent cessation of ovulation

an·ovu·la·to·ry* \(ˈ)anˈävyələˌtōrē, -ˈōv-, -ˌtȯr-, -ri\ *adj* : suppressing ovulation < *anovulatory* drugs >

answering service *n* : a commercial service that answers telephone calls for its clients

an·thro·po·sere \an'thräpə,si(ə)r, 'an(t)thrəpə-, -,siə\ *n* [*anthropo-* human (deriv. of Gk *anthrōpos* human being) + *sere* series of ecological communities, fr. L *series* series] : NOOSPHERE 1

an·thro·sphere \'an(t)thrə,sfi(ə)r, -,sfiə\ *n* [*anthro*po- + *sphere*] : NOOSPHERE 1

an·ti·abor·tion \¦an,tīə¦bórshən, ¦antē-, ¦antə̇-, -¦bó(ə)sh-\ *adj* [*anti-* against (deriv. of Gk *anti* against) + *abortion*] : opposed to abortion < *antiabortion* lobbyists > — **an·ti·abor·tion·ist** \-ə̇st\ *n*

an·ti·al·ler·gic \-ə¦lərjik, -¦lə̄j-, -¦ləij-, -ēk\ *also* **an·ti·al·ler·gen·ic** \-,alə(r)¦jenik\ *adj*: tending to relieve or control allergic symptoms — **antiallergic** *also* **antiallergenic** *n*

an·ti·anx·i·ety \-aŋ¦zīəd·ē, -ət-, -i\ *adj* : tending to prevent or relieve anxiety < *antianxiety* drugs >

an·ti·ar·rhyth·mic \-(,)ā¦rithmik, -mēk\ *adj* : tending to prevent or relieve arrhythmia < an *antiarrhythmic* agent >

an·ti–art \'an,tī,ärt, 'antē-, 'antə̇-, -,ȧt\ *n* : art (as dada) based on premises antithetical to traditional or popular art forms

an·ti·at·om \-,ad·əm, -,atəm\ *n* : an atom comprised of antiparticles

an·ti·au·thor·i·tar·i·an \¦an,tīó,thärə¦terēən, ¦antē-, ¦antə̇-, -ə,th-, -thór-\ *adj* : opposed or hostile to authoritarians or authoritarianism — **an·ti·au·thor·i·tar·i·an·ism** \-ēə,nizəm\ *n*

an·ti·aux·in \-¦óksə̇n\ *n*: a plant substance that opposes or suppresses the natural effect of an auxin

an·ti·bal·lis·tic missile \-bə¦listik-, -ēk-\ *n* : a missile for intercepting and destroying a ballistic missile — called also *ABM*

an·ti·bary·on \-¦barē,än\ *n* : an antiparticle of a baryon (as an antiproton or antineutron)

an·ti·black \-¦blak\ *adj* : opposed or hostile to people belonging to the Negro race — **an·ti·black·ism** \-,izəm\ *n*

an·ti·bus·ing \-¦bəsiŋ\ *adj*: opposed to the busing of schoolchildren < *antibusing* demonstrators >

an·ti·can·cer \-¦kan(t)sə(r)\ *also* **an·ti·can·cer·ous** \-sərəs\ *adj* : used or effective against cancer < *anticancer* drugs >

an·ti·co·ag·u·late \¦an,tī(,)kō¦agyə,lāt, ¦antē-, ¦antə̇-\ *vt* : to hinder the clotting of the blood of esp. by treatment with an anticoagulant — **an·ti·co·ag·u·la·tion** \-,agyə¦lāshən\ *n* — **an·ti·co·ag·u·la·tive** \-¦agyələd·iv, -ətiv\ *adj*

an·ti·co·don \-¦kō,dän\ *n*: a triplet of nucleotide bases in transfer RNA that identifies the amino acid carried and binds to a complementary codon in messenger RNA during protein synthesis at a ribosome

an·ti·con·vul·sant \-kən¦vəlsənt\ *or* **an·ti·con·vul·sive** \-¦vəlsə̇v, -sēv\ *adj* : used or tending to control or ward off convulsions (as in epilepsy) — **anticonvulsant** *or* **anticonvulsive** *n*

an·ti·crop \-¦kräp\ *adj* : destructive to or directed against crops < *anticrop* chemical weapons >

an·ti·de·pres·sant \-də̇¦presᵊnt, -dē-\ *or* **an·ti·de·pres·sive** \-¦presə̇v, -sēv\ *adj* : used or tending to relieve psychic depression — **antidepressant** *n*

an·ti·deu·ter·on \-¦d(y)üdə,rän\ *n* : the antimatter counterpart of deuteron

an·ti·di·ure·tic hor·mone \-,dī(y)ə¦red·ik¦hór,mōn, -¦hó(ə),-\ *n* : a polypeptide hormone secreted by the posterior lobe of the pituitary that increases blood pressure and decreases urine flow : vasopressin

an·ti·dump·ing \¦an,tī¦dəmpiŋ, ¦antē-, ¦antə̇-\ *adj* : designed to discourage the importation and sale of foreign goods at prices substantially lower than domestic prices < *antidumping* tariffs > < rash of U.S. *antidumping* actions against Japanese television sets and other goods —*Chem. & Engineering News* >

an·ti·elec·tron \-ə̇¦lek·¦trän\ *n* : the antiparticle of the electron : positron

an·ti·emet·ic \-ə̇¦med·ik, -ēk\ *adj*: used or tending to prevent or check vomiting < *antiemetic* drugs > — **antiemetic** *n*

an·ti·en·vi·ron·ment \-ən¦vīrənmənt, -¦vī(ə)r(n)-\ *n*: something (as a work of art) that points up aspects of the actual environment by contrast — **an·ti·en·vi·ron·men·tal** \-ən,vīrən¦mentᵊl, -,vī(ə)r(n)-\ *adj*

an·ti·es·tab·lish·ment \-ə¦stablishmənt\ *adj* : opposed or hostile to the social, economic, and political principles of a ruling class (as of a nation) < *antiestablishment* candidates with long records of opposition to various national policies —N.C. Miller >

an·ti·fem·i·nist \-¦femənəst\ *adj* : opposed to feminism < the *antifeminist* view that intensity of purpose in a woman is unnatural and therefore unladylike —Elizabeth L. Cless > — **an·ti·fem·i·nism** \-,nizəm\ *n* — **antifeminist** *n*

an·ti·fer·til·i·ty \-fə(r)¦tiləd·ē, -ətē, -i\ *adj* : having the capacity or tending to reduce or destroy fertility : contraceptive < *antifertility* agents > < *antifertility* properties of a new drug >

an·ti·flu·o·ri·da·tion·ist \¦an,tī,flu̇rə¦dāsh(ə)nəst, ¦antē-, ¦antə-, -ōr-, -ȯr-\ *n* : a person opposed to the fluoridation of public water supplies

an·ti·foul·ant \-'fau̇lənt\ *n*: a substance (as paint for use on the bottom of a boat) designed to prevent, reduce, or eliminate fouling

an·ti·fun·gal \-¦fəŋgəl\ *adj* : used or effective against fungi : fungicidal < *antifungal* drugs > < *antifungal* activity > < *antifungal* properties >

an·ti·gal·axy \-¦galəksē, -si\ *n* : a hypothetical galaxy comprised of antimatter

an·ti·glob·u·lin \-¦gläbyələn\ *n* : an antibody that combines with and precipitates globulin

¹an·ti·grav·i·ty \-¦gravəd·ē, -i\ *adj* : reducing or canceling the effect of gravity or protecting against it < an *antigravity* suit > < tracheophytes developed an *antigravity* and a water-conducting mechanism —P.B. Weisz >

²antigravity *n* : a hypothetical effect resulting from cancellation or reduction of a gravitational field

an·ti·he·li·um \¦an,tī¦hēlēəm, ¦antē-, ¦antə-\ *n*: the antimatter counterpart of helium

an·ti·he·mo·phil·ic \-,hēmə¦filik\ *adj* : counteracting the bleeding tendency in hemophilia

an·ti·he·ro \-¦hē(,)rō, -¦hi(ə)r(,)ō\ *n* : a protagonist who is notably lacking in heroic qualities (as resoluteness or effectiveness) < the quintessential *antihero* of the Age of Anxiety, a textbook case of contemporary alienation with whom intellectuals could easily identify —J.W. Aldridge > < an *antihero* who scorned law and morality in his lust for money —*Current Biog.* > — **an·ti·he·ro·ic** \-hə¦rōik, -he-, hē-\ *adj*

an·ti·her·o·ine \-¦herəwən, -¦hir-\ *n* : a female antihero < his *antiheroine,* Christy, is fearful and compliant to the point of lacking personal dignity —Phil Frankfeld >

an·ti·hu·man \-¦(h)yümən\ *adj* : acting or being against man; *esp* : reacting strongly with human antigens

an·ti·hy·dro·gen \-¦hīdrəjən, -rēj-\ *n* : the antimatter counterpart of hydrogen

an·ti·hy·per·tens·ive \-¦hīpə(r)¦ten(t)səv\ *adj* [*anti-* + *hypertens*ion high blood pressure + *-ive* tending toward] : used or effective against high blood pressure < *antihypertensive* drugs > — **antihypertensive** *n*

an·ti–in·flam·ma·to·ry \¦an,tīən¦flamə,tōrē, ¦antē-, ¦antə-, -tȯr-, -ri\ *adj* : counteracting inflammation < *anti-inflammatory* drugs > < *anti-inflammatory* effects >

an·ti·lep·ton \-¦lep,tän\ *n* : an antiparticle (as a positron or an antineutrino) of a lepton

an·ti·leu·ke·mic \-lü¦kēmik, -ēk\ *also* **an·ti·leu·ke·mia** \-¦kēmēə\ *adj* : counteracting the effects of leukemia < *antileukemic* effect of a drug >

an·ti·lit·ter \-¦lid·ə(r), -itə-\ *adj* : serving to prevent or discourage the littering of public areas < *antilitter* laws >

an·ti·lym·pho·cyte glob·u·lin \-¦lim(p)fə,sīt'gläbyələn\ *n* : serum globulin containing antibodies against lymphocytes that is used similarly to antilymphocyte serum

antilymphocyte serum *n* : a serum containing antibodies against lymphocytes that is used for suppressing graft rejection caused by lymphocyte-controlled immune responses in organ or tissue transplant recipients

an·ti·lym·pho·cyt·ic globulin \-,lim(p)fə¦sid·ik-\ *n* : ANTILYMPHOCYTE GLOBULIN

antilymphocytic serum *n* : ANTILYMPHOCYTE SERUM

[1]**an·ti·mis·sile** \¦an,tī¦misəl, ¦antē-, ¦antə̇-, *chiefly Brit* -¦mis,īl\ *adj* : designed as a defense against missiles <an *antimissile* system>

[2]**antimissile** *n* : ANTIMISSILE MISSILE

antimissile missile *n* : a missile for intercepting another missile in flight; *esp* : ANTIBALLISTIC MISSILE

an·ti·mi·tot·ic \-,mī¦täd·ik, -ēk\ *adj* : inhibiting or disrupting mitosis <*antimitotic* drugs> <*antimitotic* activity> — **antimitotic** *n*

an·ti·mu·ta·gen·ic \-,myüd·ə¦jenik, -ēk\ *adj* : decreasing the frequency of mutation either by inhibiting the action of mutagens or by reducing spontaneous mutation

an·ti·neo·plas·tic \-,nēə¦plastik\ *adj* : inhibiting or preventing the growth and spread of neoplasms or malignant cells

an·ti·noise \-¦nȯiz\ *adj* : designed or acting to reduce noise level <an *antinoise* ordinance>

an·ti·nov·el \¦an,tī¦nävəl, ¦antē-, ¦antə̇-\ *n* : a work of fiction that lacks most or all of the traditional features (as coherent structure or character development) of the novel — **an·ti·nov·el·ist** \-lə̇st\ *n*

an·ti·nu·cle·ar \-¦n(y)üklēə(r), ÷ -kyələ(r)\ *adj* : tending to react with cell nuclei or their components (as DNA) <*antinuclear* antibodies>

an·ti·ob·scen·i·ty \-,äb¦senə̇d·ē, -əb-, *also* -sēn-\ *adj* : designed to prevent or restrict the dissemination of obscene materials <*antiobscenity* laws>

an·ti·par·a·sit·ic \-,parə¦sid·ik, -ēk\ *adj* : acting against parasites <*antiparasitic* drugs>

an·ti·par·ti·cle \ˈan,tī,pärtə̇kəl, ˈantē-, ˈantə̇-, -,pȧd·-\ *n* : an elementary particle identical to another elementary particle in mass but opposite to it in electric and magnetic properties that when brought together with its counterpart produces mutual annihilation

an·ti·pol·lu·tion \¦an,tīpə¦lüshən, ¦antē-, ¦antə̇-\ *adj* : intended to prevent, reduce, or eliminate pollution <*antipollution* devices on automobiles> <*antipollution* regulations> — **an·ti·pol·lu·tion·ist** \-ə̇st\ *n*

an·ti·pov·er·ty \-¦pävə(r)d·ē, -i\ *adj* : of or relating to action designed to relieve poverty <*antipoverty* programs>

an·ti·psy·chot·ic \-(,)sī¦käd·ik, -ēk\ *adj* : tending to alleviate psychosis or psychotic states <an *antipsychotic* drug> — **antipsychotic** *n*

an·ti·quark \ˈan,tī¦kwärk, ˈantē-, ˈantə̇-, -¦kwȯrk\ *n* : the antiparticle of the quark

antique* *vb* **an·tiqued; an·tiqu·ing** : to shop around for antiques <an afternoon of *antiquing* and browsing in the dozen or so shops and restaurants that make up this quaint . . . community —Jane L. Gregory>

an·ti·rac·ism \¦an,tī¦rā,sizəm, ¦antē-, ¦antə̇-, *also* -,shizəm\ *n* : adherence to the view that racism is a social evil — **an·ti·rac·ist** \-¦rāsə̇st, *also* -shə̇st\ *n or adj*

an·ti·rad·i·cal \-radə̇kəl, -dēk-\ *adj* : opposed to radicals or radicalism <the thoroughly *antiradical* sheriff —H.F. May>

an·ti·rheu·mat·ic \-(,)rü¦mad·ik, -rə-, -ēk\ *adj* : alleviating or preventing rheumatism — **antirheumatic** *n*

an·ti·sci·ence \-¦sīən(t)s\ *n* : a system or attitude or cult that rejects scientific methods or the value of science to man; *also* : one that denies the value of basic scientific research — **an·ti·sci·en·tif·ic** \-,sīən¦tifik, -ēk\ *adj*

an·ti·sci·en·tism \-¦sīən,tizəm\ *n* : ANTISCIENCE

an·ti·sex \-¦seks\ *or* **an·ti·sex·u·al** \-¦seksh(ə)wəl, -shəl\ *adj* : antagonistic toward sex; *esp* : tending to reduce or eliminate the sex drive or sexual activity

an·ti·sex·ist \-¦seksə̇st\ *adj* : opposed to sexism

an·ti·skid \¦an,tī¦skid, ¦antē-, ¦antə̇-\ *adj* : designed to prevent skidding <*antiskid* braking systems>

an·ti·smog \-¦smäg, *also* -¦smȯg\ *adj* : designed to reduce pollutants that contribute to the formation of smog <*antismog* devices on automobiles>

an·ti·stat \¦an,tī¦stat, ¦antē-, ¦antə̇-\ *or* **an·ti·stat·ic** \-¦stad·ik, -ēk\ *adj* [*antistat* short for *antistatic*] : reducing, removing, or preventing the buildup of static electricity

<the can't-be-copied *antistat* nylon crepe the women's wear industry is mad for —*advt*> <an *antistatic* coating>— **antistatic** *n*

an·ti·tu·ber·cu·lous \-t(y)u̇ˈbərkyələs, -təˈ-\ *or* **an·ti·tu·ber·cu·lo·sis** \-ˌbərkyəˈlōsə̇s\ *or* **an·ti·tu·ber·cu·lar** \-ˈbərkyələr\ *adj* : used or effective against tuberculosis < *antituberculous* drugs > < *antituberculous* activity >

an·ti·tu·mor \-ˈt(y)ümə(r)\ *also* **an·ti·tu·mor·al** \-mərəl\ *adj* : ANTICANCER < *antitumor* agents > < *antitumor* activity >

an·ti·uto·pia \-yu̇ˈtōpēə\ *n* **1** : DYSTOPIA **2** : a work describing an antiutopia — **an·ti·uto·pi·an** \-pēən\ *adj*

an·ti·war \-ˈwȯ(ə)r, -ˈwȯ(ə)\ *adj* : opposed to war < *antiwar* protests >

an·ti·white \-ˈ(h)wīt\ *adj* : opposed or hostile to people belonging to a light-skinned race — **an·ti·whit·ism** \-ˈ(h)wīd·ˌizəm\ *n*

an·ti·world \ˈanˌtīˌwər(ə)ld, ˈantē-, ˈantə̇-, -ˌwəld, -ˌwəild\ *n* : the hypothetical antimatter counterpart of a world

ao dai \ˌäōˈdī, ˈa-\ *n, pl* **ao dais** [Vietnamese *áo dài*, fr. *áo* jacket, tunic (of Chinese origin — akin to Chin (Pek) ao^3 jacket) + *dai* long] : the traditional dress of Vietnamese women that consists of a long tunic with slits on either side and wide trousers

A-OK \ˌā(ˌ)ōˈkā\ *adj* : being entirely without fault or defect : perfect <the fuses were all *A-OK* —John Gould>

ape \ˈāp\ *adj* : being beyond restraint : crazy, wild — usu. used in the phrase *go ape* <went *ape* over another girl —*Boston Sunday Globe Mag.*>

aperture card *n* : a punch card for data processing in which one or more frames of a microfilmed document are mounted

aph·o·late \ˈafəˌlāt\ *n* [prob. fr. *a*ziridinyl, a chemical radical + *pho*sphorine, a chemical compound + *-ate* derivative compound] : a chemosterilant $C_{12}H_{24}N_9P_3$ esp. effective in controlling houseflies

aph·ox·ide \(ˈ)aˈfäkˌsīd, *also* -ksə̇d\ *n* [prob. fr. *a*ziridinyl + *ph*ospine, a chemical compound + *oxide*] : TEPA

apo·ap·sis \ˌapōˈapsə̇s\ *n, pl* **-ap·si·des** \-ˈapsə̇ˌdēz \ [NL, fr. *apo-* away from (deriv. of Gk *apo* away from) + *apsis*] : the apsis that is the greatest distance from the center of attraction

apo·cyn·thi·on \ˌapəˈsin(t)thēən\ *n* [NL, fr. *apo-* + *Cynthia*, goddess of the moon (fr. Gk *Kynthia*) + *-on* (as in *aphelion*)] : APOLUNE

apo·lune \ˈapəˌlün\ *n* [*apo-* + *-lune*, fr. L *luna* moon] : the point in the path of a body orbiting the moon that is farthest from the center of the moon

apo·se·lene \ˈapəsə̇ˌlēn\ *n* [ISV *apo-* + *-selene*, fr. Gk *selēnē* moon] : APOLUNE

apo·se·le·ni·um \ˌapəsə̇ˈlēnēəm\ *n* [NL, fr. *apo-* + Gk *selēnē* moon + NL *-ium*, alter. of *-ion* (as in *aphelion*)] : APOLUNE

Ap·pa·la·chian \ˌapəˈlāchən, -ˈlach-, -ˈlāsh-, -chēən\ *n* : a white native or resident of the Appalachian mountain area <blacks and *Appalachians* competing for the same scarce jobs, housing, and recreational facilities —James Adams>

ap·ple-pie* \ˌapəlˈpī\ *adj* [fr. the tradition that apple pie is a quintessentially American dish] : of, relating to, or characterized by traditionally American values <concerned with the recovery of a lot of *apple-pie* virtues after an era of turmoil and flux —E. B. Fiske>

¹après-ski \ˌäˌprāˈskē\ *n* [F, fr. *après* after + *ski* ski, skiing] : social activity (as at a ski lodge) after a day's skiing

²après-ski *adj* : of, relating to, or suitable for après-ski <appear on slopes and around crackling fires in their newest ski and *après-ski* clothes —*Women's Wear Daily*> <offers its typically cosmopolitan clientele . . . unsurpassed accommodations, diverse *après-ski* pastimes and calculated Alpine charm —*Playboy*>

aqua·naut \ˈakwəˌnȯt, ˈäk-, -nät\ *n* [*aqua* water (fr. L) + *-naut* (as in *astronaut*)] : a scuba diver who lives beneath the surface of water for an extended period and carries on activities both inside and outside his underwater shelter

aquaplane* *vi* : HYDROPLANE

ar·a·besque* \ˌarəˈbesk, ˈer-\ *n* : a contrived intricate pattern of verbal expression < *arabesques* of alliteration —C.E. Montague>

ar·bo·vi·rus \ˌärbəˈvīrəs\ *n* [*ar*thropod-*bo*rne *virus*] : any of various viruses transmitted by arthropods and including the causative agents of encephalitis, yellow fever, and dengue
ar·cho·saur \ˈärkəˌsȯ(ə)r\ *n* : a member of the reptilian subclass Archosauria
arc·jet \ˈärkˌjet, ˈåk-\ *n* : ARC-JET ENGINE
arc–jet engine *n* : a rocket engine in which the propellant gas is heated by an electric arc
area code *n* [fr. its designation of major subdivisions of the territory of the United States] : a 3-digit code used in dialing long-distance telephone calls
area rug *n* : a rug designed to cover a limited area within a room
ar·eo·cen·tric \ˌarēōˈsen·trik, -ēəˈ-\ *adj* [*areo-* (fr. Gk *Areios* of Ares, the Greek god of war, fr. *Arēs* Ares) + *-centric* having as a center] : having or relating to the planet Mars as a center
Ar·gy·rol \ˈärjəˌrȯl, -ˌrōl\ *trademark* — used for a silver-protein compound whose aqueous solution is used as a local antiseptic esp. for mucous membranes
arm–twist·ing \ˈärmˌtwistiŋ, ˈåm-\ *n* : the use of direct personal pressure in order to achieve a desired end <for all the *arm-twisting*, the . . . vote on the measure was unexpectedly tight —*Newsweek*>
arm wrestling *n* : a form of wrestling in which two opponents sit face to face gripping usu. their right hands and setting corresponding elbows firmly on a surface (as a tabletop) in an attempt to force each other's arm down : Indian wrestling
array* *n* : an arrangement of computer memory elements (as magnetic cores) in a single plane
ar·res·tant \əˈrestənt\ *n* : a substance that causes an insect to stop locomotion
art de·co \ˌär(t)dāˈkō; (ˈ)är(t)ˈdā(ˌ)kō, -de-; -å(t)-\ *n, often cap A&D* [F *Art Déco,* fr. *Exposition Internationale des Arts Décoratifs et Industriels Modernes,* an exposition of modern decorative and industrial arts held in Paris, France, in 1925] : a popular decorative style of the 1920s and 1930s characterized esp. by bold outlines and colors and by streamlined and geometric forms
artificial intelligence *n* : the capability of a machine to imitate intelligent human behavior (as reasoning, learning, or the understanding of speech)
art·mo·bile \ˈärtmōˌbēl, ˈåt-\ *n* : a trailer that houses an art collection designed for exhibition on road tours
ASCII \ˈas(ˌ)kē\ *n* [*A*merican *S*tandard *C*ode for *I*nformation *I*nterchange] : a code for representing alphanumeric information (as in a data processing system)
ash* *n* [OE *æsc,* lit., ash tree, name of the corresponding runic letter] : the ligature *æ* used in Old English to represent a low front vowel
as·par·to·kinase \əˌspärd·ōˈkīˌnāz, -ās\ *n* [*aspart*ic acid + connective *-o-* + *kinase,* an enzyme] : an enzyme that catalyzes the phosphorylation of aspartic acid by ATP
asphalt jungle *n* : a big city or a specified part of a big city <the *asphalt jungle* around Times Square —E.R. Bentley>
¹-ass \ˌas, *also* ˌås\ *adj or adv comb form* [*ass* buttocks] — used as a derogatory intensive <a fancy-*ass* limited edition at ten bucks a throw —*East Village Other*> <a story that's dead-*ass* wrong —J.D. Ehrlichman>; often considered vulgar
²-ass *n comb form* : a contemptible person <smart*ass*> <my son is a wise*ass.* He answers the telephone with cracks —Richard Reeves> — often considered vulgar
as·sem·blage* \əˈsemblij, -lēj; ˌaˌsä(^{n})mˈbläzh, ˌåˌs-, -sä^{n}ˈb-, -låzh\ *n* **1** : an artistic composition made from scraps, junk, and odds and ends (as of paper, cloth, wood, stone, or metal) **2** : the art of making assemblages — **as·sem·blag·ist** \-jəst, -zhəst\ *n*
assembler* *n* : a computer program that automatically converts instructions written in a mnemonic code into the equivalent machine code
assembly* *n* : the translation of mnemonic code to machine code by an assembler
assembly language *n* : a mnemonic language for programming a computer that is a close approximation of machine language
assist* *n* : a mechanical device that provides assistance
As·ti spu·man·te \ˌästē(ˌ)spüˈmän(ˌ)tā, ˌas-, ˌås-, -sti-, -spəˈ-, -tē\ *n* [It, lit., sparkling Asti] : a white sparkling wine made in the Asti province of Piedmont

as·tri·on·ics \ˌastrēˈäniks\ *n pl but sing or pl in constr* [*astr*onautics + *-ionics* (as in *avionics*)] : electronics applied to astronautics

as·tro·bi·ol·o·gy \ˈas(ˌ)trōˌbīˈäləjē, -ji\ *n* [*astro-* star, outer space (deriv. of Gk *astron* star) + *biology*] : EXOBIOLOGY — **as·tro·bi·o·log·i·cal** \-ˌbīəˈläjəkəl, -jēk-\ *adj* — **as·tro·bi·ol·o·gist** \-ˌbīˈäləjəst\ *n*

as·tro·bleme \ˈastrəˌblēm\ *n* [*astro-* + Gk *blēma* throw, missile, wound from a missile, fr. *ballein* to throw] : a scar on the earth's crust made by the impact of a meteorite

as·tro·chem·is·try \ˈastrōˈkeməstrē, -tri\ *n* : the chemistry of the stars and interstellar space — **as·tro·chem·ist** \-ˈkeməst\ *n*

as·tro·dy·nam·ics \ˈas(ˌ)trōˌdīˈnamiks, *sometimes* -də-\ *n pl but sing or pl in constr* : dynamics that deals with objects in outer space — **as·tro·dy·nam·ic** \-ˈnamik\ *adj* — **as·tro·dy·nam·i·cist** \-ˈnaməsəst\ *n*

as·tro·ge·ol·o·gy \ˈas(ˌ)trō(ˌ)jēˈäləjē, -ji\ *n* : a branch of geology that deals with celestial bodies — **as·tro·geo·log·ic** \-ˌjēəˈläjik, -jēk\ *adj* — **as·tro·ge·ol·o·gist** \-(ˌ)jēˈäləjəst\ *n*

ath·ero·gen·e·sis \ˈathərōˈjenəsəs\ *n* : the production of atheroma

ath·ero·gen·ic \ˈathərōˈjenik\ *adj* : relating to or tending to produce degenerative changes in arterial walls

At·lan·ti·cism \ətˈlantəˌsizəm, at-\ *n* : a policy of military, political, and economic cooperation between European and North American powers — **At·lan·ti·cist** \-ntəsəst\ *n*

at·mo·sphe·ri·um \ˌatməˈsfirēəm\ *n* [*atmosphere* + *-ium* (as in *planetarium*)] **1** : an optical device for projecting images of meteorological phenomena (as clouds) on the inside of a dome **2** : a room housing an atmospherium

ATPase \ˌāˌtēˈpēˌās, -ˌāz\ *n* : an enzyme that hydrolyzes ATP; *esp* : one that hydrolyzes ATP to ADP and inorganic phosphate

at·ra·zine \ˈa·trəˌzēn\ *n* [ISV *atr-* (perh. fr. L *atr-*, *ater* black, dark) + tri*azine*] : a photosynthesis-inhibiting persistent herbicide $C_8H_{14}ClN_5$ used esp. to kill annual weeds and quack grass

at·tack·man \əˈtakˌman, -kmən\ *n* : a player (as in lacrosse) assigned to an offensive zone or position

at·to- \ˈad·(ˌ)ō, -d·ə\ *comb form* [ISV, fr. Dan or Norw *atten* eighteen, fr. ON *āttjān*] : one quintillionth (10^{-18}) part of

at·trit \ə·ˈtrit, a·ˈ-\ *vt* [back-formation fr. *attrition*] : to weaken or reduce by attrition <had little success in *attriting* the enemy>

attrition* *n* : a usu. gradual loss of personnel from causes normal or peculiar to a given situation (as death, retirement, and resignation in a labor force or failure and dropout among students) often without filling the vacancies <the total number of employees was reduced . . . through normal *attrition* and adjustments based on business considerations —*Annual Report E.I. DuPont De Nemours & Co.*> <student *attrition* rate is very high —J.M. Ziegler>

au bleu \(ˌ)ōˈblœ̄, -ˈblə̄, -ˈblü\ *adj (or adv)* [F, lit., to the blue; fr. the fact that the skin of fish cooked in this manner turns blue] : cooked by boiling in acidulated water immediately after being killed and cleaned but without being washed or scaled — used esp. of trout

audible *n* [*audible*, adj.] : a substitute offensive play or defensive formation called at the line of scrimmage in football

au·dio–lin·gual \ˈȯdē(ˌ)ōˈliŋg(yə)wəl\ *adj* [*audio-* hearing (fr. L. *audire* to hear) + *lingual*] : involving the use of listening and speaking drills in language learning

au·dio·phile \ˈȯdēōˌfīl\ *n* [*audio* relating to high fidelity + *-phile* lover, deriv. of Gk *philos* beloved, loving] : one whose hobby is high-fidelity audio systems

au·dio·tape \ˈȯdēōˌtāp\ *n* : a tape recording of sound

au·dio·typ·ist \ˈȯdē(ˌ)ōˈtīpəst\ *n* : one who types directly from a tape recording — **au·dio·typ·ing** \-piŋ\ *n*

au·dio·vi·su·als \ˌȯdēōˈvizh(ə)wəlz, -zhəlz\ *n pl* : instructional materials (as filmstrips accompanied by recordings) that make use of both hearing and sight

au pair girl \(ˈ)ōˈpa(ə)r-, -ˈpe(ə)r-\ *or* **au pair** *n* [F *au pair* on equal terms] : a foreign girl who does domestic work for a family in return for room and board and the opportunity to learn the English language

aus·form \ˈȯsˌfȯ(ə)rm, -ȯ(ə)m\ *vt* [*aus*tenitic + de*form;* fr. the deformation's taking place while the steel is still in the austenitic form] : to subject (steel) to deformation and then to quenching and tempering in order to increase the strength, ductility, and resistance to fatigue failure

au·teur \ōˈtər, -tœœr\ *n* : a film director whose practice accords with the auteur theory

au·teur·ism \-ˌizəm\ *n* : AUTEUR THEORY — **au·teur·ist** \-əst\ *n or adj*

auteur theory *n* [part trans. of F *politique des auteurs,* fr. *auteur* author; fr. the view that the director is the true author of a film] : a theory in film criticism that considers the director to be the primary creative force in a motion picture

au·to·clav·able \ˌȯd·əˌklāvəbəl, -d·ōˌ-\ *adj* : able to withstand the action of an autoclave < *autoclavable* laboratory equipment >

au·to·cross \ˈȯd·əˌkrȯs, -d·ō-, ˈäd·-, *also* -ˌkräs\ *n* [*auto* + *cross*-country, n.] : an automobile gymkhana

au·to·drome \-ˌdrōm\ *n* [*auto* + *-drome* racecourse, deriv. of Gk *dromos;* akin to Gk *dramein* to run] : an automobile racetrack

au·tog·e·nous* \(ˈ)ȯˌtäjənəs, əˌ-\ *or* **au·to·gen·ic*** \ˌȯd·ōˌjenik\ *adj* : not requiring a meal of blood to produce eggs < *autogenous* mosquitoes >

au·to·im·mune \ˌȯd·ōəˌmyün\ *adj* [back-formation fr. *autoimmunization*] : of, relating to, or caused by autoantibodies < *autoimmune* diseases > — **au·to·im·mu·ni·ty** \-əˌmyünəd·ē, -i\ *n* — **au·to·im·mu·ni·za·tion** \-ˌimyənəˈzāshən, -əmˌyünə-\ *n* — **au·to·im·mu·nize** \-ˌimyəˌnīz\ *vt*

au·to·ma·nip·u·la·tion \-məˌnipyəˌlāshən\ *n* [*auto-* self, same (fr. Gk, fr. *autos* same, self) + *manipulation*] : physical stimulation of the genital organs by oneself — **au·to·ma·nip·u·la·tive** \-məˌnipyələd·iv\ *adj*

automatic* *n* : AUDIBLE

au·to·net·ics \ˌȯd·ōˈned·iks, -d·əˈ-\ *n pl but usu sing in constr* [*auto-* self, automatic + *-netics* (as in *cybernetics*)] : a branch of knowledge dealing with automatic guidance and control systems

au·toph·a·gy \ȯˈtäfəjē\ *n* [*auto-* self, same + *-phagy* eating, fr. Gk *-phagia,* fr. *phagein* to eat] : digestion of cellular constituents by enzymes of the same cell — **au·toph·a·gic** \-jik, -jēk\ *adj*

au·to·reg·u·la·tion \ˌȯd·ōˌregyəˌlāshən\ *n* [*auto-* self + *regulation*] : the maintenance of relative constancy of a physiological process under varying conditions by factors inherent in an organ or tissue — **au·to·reg·u·la·tive** \-ˌregyəˌlād·iv, -yələd·-, -ēv\ *adj* — **au·to·reg·u·la·to·ry** \-ˌregyələˌtōrē, -ˌtȯr, -i\ *adj*

au·to·route \ˈȯd·əˌrüt, -d·ō-, ˈäd·-; *F* ȯtȯrüt, ō-\ *n* [F, fr. *auto* automobile (fr. *automobile*) + *route* road] : a high-speed multilane motor road in France

au·to·stra·da \ˌau̇d·ōˈsträdə, ˌȯd·-\ *n, pl* **autostradas** *or* **au·to·stra·de** \-äd(ˌ)ā\ [It, fr. *auto*mobile automobile (fr. F) + *strada* street, fr. LL *strata* paved road] : a high-speed multilane motor road first developed in Italy

auxo·troph \ˈȯksəˌtrōf, -äf\ *n* : an auxotrophic strain or individual

auxo·tro·phic \ˌȯksəˈtrōfik, -äf-\ *adj* [*auxo-* growth (fr. Gk, fr. *auxein* to increase) + *-trophic* relating to nutrition, deriv. of Gk *trephein* to nourish] : requiring a specific growth substance beyond the minimum required for normal metabolism and reproduction < *auxotrophic* mutants of bacteria > — **aux·ot·ro·phy** \ȯkˈsätrəfē\ *n*

avale·ment \ȧvȧl(ə)mä^{n}\ *n* [F, lit., swallowing, fr. *avaler* to lower, swallow, fr. MF] : the technique of allowing the knees to flex and thus absorb bumps when skiing and turning at high speed so that the skis will remain in constant contact with the snow

aversion* *n* : a tendency to extinguish a behavior or to avoid a thing or situation and esp. a usu. pleasurable one because it is or has been associated with a noxious stimulus < conditioning of food *aversions* by drug injection >

aversion therapy *n* : therapy intended to change habits or antisocial behavior by inducing a dislike for them through association with a noxious stimulus

aver·sive* \ə'vərsiv, -'vəs-, -'vəis-, -ziv\ *adj* : tending to avoid or causing avoidance of a noxious or punishing stimulus <behavior modification by *aversive* stimulation> — **aver·sive·ly** \-lē, -li\ *adv*

av·go·lem·o·no \ˌävgō'leməˌnō\ *n* [NGk *augolemono*, fr. *augon* egg + *lemonion* lemon] : a soup made of chicken stock, rice, egg yolks, and lemon juice

aviator glasses *n pl* : eyeglasses having a lightweight metal frame and usu. tinted lenses

avoidance* *n* : an anticipatory response undertaken to avoid a noxious stimulus <conditioned *avoidance* in mice>

avoid·ant \ə'vȯidᵊnt\ *adj* : characterized by turning away or by withdrawal or defensive behavior <the *avoidant* detached schizophrenic patient —Norman Cameron>

ax* *or* **axe*** *n* : any of several musical instruments (as a guitar or a saxophone) <these cats were blowing their horns, their *axes*, whatever they had —Claude Brown>

aza·se·rine \ˌazə'seˌrēn, -siˌ-, -rən\ *n* [di*az-* containing the group N_2 + *acetyl* + *serine*, a crystalline amino acid] : an antibiotic $C_5H_7N_3O_4$ that is used to inhibit the growth of some tumors

aza·thi·o·prine \ˌazə'thīəˌprēn, -əprən\ *n* [*aza-* containing nitrogen in place of carbon + *thio-* containing sulfur + pu*rine*] : a purine antimetabolite $C_9H_7N_7O_2S$ that is used esp. to suppress antibody production

azin·phos·meth·yl \ˌāzᵊn(ˌ)fäs'methəl, ˌaz-\ *n* [*azine* + *phos*phorus + *methyl*] : an organophosphorus pesticide $C_{10}H_{12}N_3O_3PS_2$ used against insects and mites

B

bach·e·lor·ette \ˌbach(ə)lə'ret\ *n* [*bachelor* + *-ette*, fem. dim. suffix] : a young unmarried woman

back·beat \'bakˌbēt\ *n* [*back*ground music + *beat*] : a steady pronounced rhythm that is the characteristic driving force esp. of rock music <using the band to construct a heavy *backbeat* dance pattern to complement the vocalist —Gary Von Tersch>

back·ground·er \'bakˌgrau̇ndə(r)\ *n* : an informal off-the-record news conference in which a government official provides reporters with background information on a particular government policy or action <detailed *backgrounders*. . . a useful tool for informally clarifying policy —*Newsweek*>

back judge *n* : a football official whose duties include keeping the official time and identifying eligible pass receivers

back·lash* \'bakˌlash\ *n* : a strong adverse reaction (as to a recent political or social development) <the white *backlash*. . . to the Black Power movement —Evelyn Geller> <the threat of an "English *backlash*" against the Quebec people —Bruce Hutchison> <a major American involvement could have stirred new *backlashes* of anti-Semitism —J.A. Wechsler>

back of beyond *chiefly Brit* : an extremely remote place; *esp* : the outback of Australia

back–street \ˈbak(ˌ)strēt\ *adj* : done or made surreptitiously <the terror, abuse and loneliness of her *back-street* abortion —Mary F. Hoyt>

back·up* \'bakˌəp\ *n* : one that serves as a substitute or alternative <the second spacecraft would be a *backup* in case of failure>

back·up \ˈbak-\ *adj* **1** : serving as a backup <most systems in the Apollo spacecraft have *backup* systems in case of failure —*Science News*> **2** : serving as an accompaniment <he records as a soloist with *backup* musicians —Ellen Sander>

bac·te·rio·cin \bak'tirēəsən\ *n* [ISV *bacteri*um + connective *-o-* + *-cin* (as in *colicin*)] : an antibacterial agent (as colicin) produced by bacteria

bad-mouth \ˈbad,mau̇th, -th̲\ *vt* : to criticize severely : make disparaging remarks about <New Yorkers who *bad-mouth* their own city —David Butwin>

bad news *n pl but sing in constr* : a troublesome situation or person

bag* *n* **1** : frame or state of mind <when a person acts stupidly, he is "in his stupid *bag*" —Junius Griffin> **2** : something suited to one's taste : something one likes or does well : specialty <hasn't been my *bag* so far, but I'm a very dedicated actor —Dick Van Dyke> **3 a** : an individual's typical way of life <can't expect people who are in another *bag* to accept my *bag*—Jerry Rubin> **b** : a characteristic manner of expression <more than any other singer in the soul *bag* —Albert Goldman> **4** : something that frustrates or impedes : hang-up **5** : a small packet of a narcotic drug (as heroin or marijuana)

Ba·ha·sa In·do·ne·sia \bəˈhäsə,indəˈnēzhə, -ēshə, -ēzēə, -ēsēə\ *n* [Indonesian *bahasa indonésia,* fr. *bahasa* language (fr. Skt *bhāsā,* fr. *bhāsate* he speaks; akin to Gk *phanai* to say) + *indonésia* Indonesian, fr. *Indonesia,* republic in Malay archipelago] : the Malay dialect that is the national language of the Republic of Indonesia

Ba·ker–Nunn camera \,bākə(r)ˈnən-\ *n* [after James G. *Baker* b1914 & Joseph *Nunn,* Am. optical designers] : a large camera for tracking earth satellites

BAL \,bē,āˈel\ *n* [*b*asic *a*ssembly *l*anguage] : a generalized assembly language for programming a computer with a small memory

ball* *vt* [*ball* testis] : to have sexual intercourse with <bachelor who wanders through life *balling* various chicks —Gene Lees> <she was inevitably treated as a high-class groupie and was expected to *ball* visiting dignitaries —William Kloman> — often considered vulgar

ball control *n* : an offensive strategy (as in football or basketball) in which a team tries to maintain possession of the ball for extended periods of time

ball·park \ˈbȯl,pärk, -,pȧk\ *adj* [fr. the phrase *in the ballpark* approximately correct] : approximately correct <a 20 percent increase would be a good *ballpark* figure —H. L. Mac Odrum>

ballsy \ˈbȯlzē, -zi\ *adj* **ball·si·er; -est** [*balls* (pl. of *ball* testis) + *-y,* adj. suffix] : aggressively tough : gutsy <a *ballsy* little guy, and . . . the most perfect writer of my generation —Norman Mailer>

bal·lute \bəˈlüt, ˈba,lüt\ *n* [*ball*oon + parach*ute*] : a small inflatable parachute for stabilization and deceleration of a jumper or object before the conventional parachute opens

Baltimore chop \ˈbȯltə,mō(ə)r-, -,mȯ(ə)r-, -mər-\ *n* [so called fr. its perfection by the Baltimore baseball team of the 1890s] : a batted ball in baseball that usu. bounces too high for an infielder to make a putout at first base

ba·nan·as \bəˈnanəz\ *adj* : crazy <spelling the English language drives everyone *bananas* —G. H. Poteet>

banana seat *n* : an elongated bicycle saddle that often has an upward-curved back

band razor *n* : a safety razor with a cartridge that contains a narrow single-edged band of steel which may be advanced to expose a new surface

bang·er \ˈbaŋə(r)\ *n* **1** [prob. fr. the noise sausages often make while frying] *Brit* : a sausage <*bangers* and mash> **2** *Brit* : a firecracker **3** *Brit* : a noisy dilapidated automobile

banquet lamp *n* : a tall elaborate kerosene table lamp

Ban·tu·stan \ˌban-(,)tüˌstan, ˈbantə,s-, ˌbän-(,)tüˌstän\ *n* [*Bantu* + *-stan* land (as in *Hindustan*)] : an all-black enclave in the Republic of South Africa with a limited degree of self-government

Bar·ce·lo·na chair \ˌbärsəˌlōnə, ˌbȧs-\ *n* [fr. *Barcelona,* Spain, site of the 1929 International Exposition for which the chair was designed] : an armless chair with leather-covered cushions on a stainless steel frame

Bar·do·li·no \,bärdᵊlˈēnō, -dəˈlē-\ *n* [It, fr. *Bardolino,* village on Lake Garda, Italy] : a light dry red Italian wine

barf \ˈbärf, ˈbȧf\ *vi* [origin unknown] : to throw up : vomit — **barf** *n*

bar·gel·lo \bärˈjelō\ *n* [fr. the *Bargello,* museum in Florence, Italy; fr. the use of this stitch in the upholstery of 17th cent. chairs at the Bargello] : a needlepoint stitch that produces a zigzag pattern

bar girl *n* : a prostitute who frequents bars

bar·iat·rics \ˌbarēˈa·triks\ *n pl but sing in constr* [*bar-* weight (fr. Gk *baros*) + *-iatrics*, deriv. of Gk *iatros* physician] : a branch of medicine that deals with the treatment of obesity — **bar·ia·tri·cian** \-ēə·ˈtrishən\ *n*

bar mitz·vah \(ˈ)bärˈmitsvə, (ˈ)bȧˈm-, -(ˌ)vä\ *vt* **bar mitz·vahed; bar mitz·vah·ing** *often cap B&M* : to administer the ceremony of bar mitzvah to

Ba·ro·lo \bäˈrō(ˌ)lō, bə-\ *n* [fr. *Barolo*, village in the Piedmont region, Italy] : a dry red Italian wine

baro·re·cep·tor \ˌbarōrə̇ˌseptə(r), -ōrēˌ-\ *also* **bar·o·cep·tor** \ˈbarōˌs-\ *n* [*baro-* weight, pressure (fr. Gk *baros*) + *receptor*] : a neural receptor sensitive to changes in pressure < *baroreceptors* of the arterial walls >

Bar·tók·ian \ˌbärˈtäkyən, -tȯk-, -kēən\ *adj* [Béla *Bartók* †1945 Hung. composer] : of, relating to, or suggestive of Béla Bartók or his musical compositions < stressing a flowing line rather than the usual *Bartókian* percussiveness —D.J. Henahan >

bary·on \ˈbarēˌän, -ēən\ *n* [ISV *bary-* (fr. Gk *barys* heavy) + *-on* elementary particle, fr. *ion*] : any of a group of elementary particles (as a nucleon or a heavier particle) that obey Fermi-Dirac statistics and satisfy the principle of conservation of baryon number — **bary·on·ic** \ˌbarēˌänik\ *adj*

baryon number *n* : a number equal to the number of baryons minus that of antibaryons in a system of elementary particles

base* *n* : a price level at which a security previously actively declining in price resists further price decline

base exchange *n* : a post exchange on a naval or an air force base

BA·SIC \ˈbāsik, -zik\ *n* [*B*eginner's *A*ll-purpose *S*ymbolic *I*nstruction *C*ode] : a standardized language for programming and interacting with a computer

basi·lect \ˈbazə̇ˌlekt, ˈbāzə̇-, -sə̇-\ *n* [*basi-* base, lower part (fr. L *basis*) + *-lect* (as in *dialect*)] : the least prestigious dialect of a community — compare ACROLECT

basis* *n* : a set of linearly independent vectors in a vector space such that any vector in the vector space can be expressed as a linear combination of them with appropriately chosen coefficients

batch* *n* : a group of jobs to be run on a computer at one time with the same program < *batch* processing >

ba·tracho·tox·in \bə·ˌtrakəˈtäksə̇n, ˌba·trəkō-\ *n* [ISV *batracho-* (fr. Gk *batrachos* frog) + *toxin*] : a very powerful steroid venom $C_{31}H_{42}N_2O_6$ extracted from the skin of a South American frog (*Phyllobates aurotaenia*)

battered child syn·drome \-ˈsinˌdrōm, *also* -ˈsindrəm\ *n* : the complex of grave physical injuries (as fractures, hematomas, and contusions) that results from gross abuse (as by a parent) of a young child

baud* \ˈbȯd, ˈbōd\ *n, pl* **baud** *also* **bauds** : a variable unit of data transmission speed usu. equal to one bit per second

Bayes·ian \ˈbāzēən, ˈbāzhən\ *adj* [Thomas *Bayes* †1761 Eng. mathematician] : being or relating to a theory (as of decision or of statistical inference) in which probabilities are associated with individual events or statements and not merely with sequences of events (as in frequency theories)

BCD \ˌbē(ˌ)sēˈdē\ *n* [*b*inary *c*oded *d*ecimal] : a code for representing alphanumeric information (as on magnetic tape)

B cell *n* [*b*one-marrow-derived *cell*] : a lymphocyte that produces antibodies — compare T CELL

beach bunny *n* : a girl who joins a surfing group but does not engage in surfing

beach·wear \ˈbēchˌwa(ə)r, -ˌwe(ə)r, -ˌwaə, -ˌweə\ *n* : clothing for wear at the beach

beautiful people *n pl, often cap B&P* : people who are identified with high society < to this festival came the stars, the magnates, the *beautiful people*, and the crowds of onlookers —Roland Gelatt > < an audience aglow with *Beautiful People*, in their colorful dress and creamy affluence —Irving Howe >

bed·da·ble \ˈbedəbəl\ *adj* : suitable for taking to bed : sexually attractive < tolerated brains in women who were too old to be *beddable* —Peter Quennell >

bed·so·nia \ˌbedˈsōnēə\ *n, pl* **bedsoni·ae** \-nēˌī\ [NL, fr. Samuel P. *Bedson* †1969 Brit. bacteriologist] : any of a group of microorganisms including the causative agents of psittacosis, lymphogranuloma venereum, and trachoma and now classified in the genus *Chlamydia* of the family Chlamydiaceae

beef Bour·gui·gnon \-¦bu̇r(,)gēn¦yōⁿ\ *n* [part trans. of F *boeuf bourguignon,* lit., Burgundian beef] : chunks of beef cooked with vegetables in burgundy and often cognac

beef Wel·ling·ton \-'weliŋtən\ *n* [prob. fr. the name *Wellington*] : a fillet of beef covered with pâté de foie gras and enclosed in pastry

be·hav·ior·al scientist \bə̇'hāvyərəl-, bē-\ *n* : a specialist in behavioral science

Belgian Ma·li·nois \-,malən'wä\ *n* : any of a breed of squarely built working dogs closely related to the Belgian sheepdog and having relatively short straight hair with a dense undercoat

Belgian Ter·vu·ren \-(,)tər'vyu̇rə̇n, -(,)ter-\ *n* [fr. *Tervuren,* commune in Brabant, Belgium] : any of a breed of working dogs closely related to the Belgian sheepdog but having abundant long straight fawn-colored hair with black tips

bells \'belz\ *n pl* [short for *bell bottoms*] : pants with wide flaring bottoms

bel·ly·board \'belē,bō(ə)rd, -li-, -,bȯ(ə)rd, -ōəd, -ȯəd\ *n* [fr. the prone position of the rider] : a small buoyant board usu. less than three feet long that is used in surf riding

belt·ed–bi·as tire \¦beltə̇d¦bīəs-\ *n* : a pneumatic tire with a hooplike belt of cord or steel around the tire underneath the tread and on top of the ply cords laid at an acute angle to the center line of the tread

be·me·gride \'bemə,grīd, -ēm-\ *n* [*be*ta + *e*thyl + *me*thyl + *g*luta*ri*c acid + im*ide*] : an analeptic drug $C_8H_{13}NO_2$ used esp. to counteract the effect of barbiturates

[1]**benchmark** \'bench,märk, -,mȧk\ *n* : something that serves as a standard by which others may be measured <economic *benchmarks,* including business loans, auto, steel and oil production and the money supply —*Newsweek*> ; *esp* : a standardized problem by which computer systems or programs may be compared

[2]**benchmark** *vt* : to test (as a computer system) by a benchmark problem

Ben·ning·ton \'beniŋtən\ *or* **Bennington ware** *also* **Bennington pottery** *n* : ceramic ware including earthenware, stoneware, and Parian ware produced at Bennington, Vt.; *esp* : earthenware with brown or mottled glaze

Bering time \'bi(ə)riŋ-, 'be(ə)r-\ *n* [*Bering* (*sea*)] : the time of the 11th time zone west of Greenwich that includes western Alaska and the Aleutian islands

Ber·mu·da petrel \bə(r)¦myüdə-, *South also* -müd-\ *n* : a brown-and-white earth-burrowing nocturnal bird (*Pterodroma cahow*) formerly abundant in Bermuda but now nearly extinct

Ber·noul·li trial \bə(r)¦nülē-; (,)ber¦nü(,)ē-, -¦nü,yē-\ *n* [Jacques *Bernoulli* †1705 Swiss mathematician] : a statistical experiment that has two mutually exclusive outcomes each of which has a constant probability of occurrence

best–ef·forts \¦best¦efə(r)ts\ *adj, of security underwriting* : not involving a firm commitment on the part of an underwriter to take up any unsold shares or bonds of an issue being underwritten

be·ta–ad·ren·er·gic \¦bād·ə,adrə¦nərjik, -¦nōj-, *also* ¦bē-\ *adj* : of, relating to, or being a beta-receptor <*beta-adrenergic* blocking action>

beta–adrenergic receptor *n* : BETA-RECEPTOR

beta decay *n* **1** : a radioactive transformation of an atomic nucleus in which the atomic number is increased or decreased by 1 by the simultaneous emission of a beta particle and a neutrino or antineutrino without change in the mass number **2** : the decay of an unstable elementary particle in which an electron or positron is emitted

be·ta–ox·i·da·tion \¦bād·ə,äksə̇¦dāshən, *also* ¦bē-\ *n* : stepwise catabolism of fatty acids in which two-carbon fragments are successively removed from the carboxyl end of the chain

beta particle* *n* : an electron or positron ejected from the nucleus of an atom during beta decay; *also* : a high-speed electron or positron

be·ta–re·cep·tor \'bād·ərə̇,septə(r), *also* 'bē-\ *n* : a receptor that responds strongly to or is activated by epinephrine and isoproterenol but is relatively unresponsive to levarterenol and that is associated with positive cardiac chronotropic and inotropic effects, vasodilation, and inhibition of smooth muscle in the bronchi, myometrium, and intestine — compare ALPHA-RECEPTOR

Bi·a·fran \bē'afrən, bī-, -äf-, -àf-\ *n* [*Biafra*, name assumed by seceding region of Nigeria (1967–1970)] : a native or inhabitant of the onetime secessionist Republic of Biafra — **Biafran** *adj*

bi·aly \bē'alē\ *n, pl* **bialys** [Yiddish, short for *bialystoker*, fr. *bialystoker* of Bialystok, fr. *Białystok*, city in northeast Poland] : a flat breakfast roll that has a depressed center and is usu. covered with onion flakes

bi·as–belt·ed tire \ˌbīəsˌbeltəd-\ *n* : BELTED-BIAS TIRE

biased* *adj* **1** : tending to yield or select one outcome more frequently or less frequently than others in a statistical experiment <a *biased* coin> <a *biased* sample> **2** : having an expected value different from the quantity or parameter estimated <a *biased* estimate> **3** : not having minimum probability of rejecting the null hypothesis when it is true <a *biased* statistical test>

bi·as–ply tire \ˌbīəsˌplī-\ *n* : a pneumatic tire having crossed layers of ply cord set diagonally to the center line of the tread

bi·ath·lon \bī'athlən, -ˌlän \ *n* [*bi-* two (fr. L) + *-athlon* (as in *pentathlon*)] : an athletic contest in which competitors ski over a 20-kilometer cross-country course and stop at designated points to fire a rifle at stationary targets

Bibb lettuce \'bib-\ *n* [Major John *Bibb*, 19th cent. Am. grower] : lettuce of a variety that has a small head and dark green color

bi·cul·tur·al \ˌbīˌkəlch(ə)rəl\ *adj* : of, relating to, or including two distinct cultures <*bicultural* education> — **bi·cul·tur·al·ism** \-(ˌ)lizəm\ *n*

bi·di·a·lec·tal \ˌbīˌdīəˌlektəl\ *adj* : fluent in the use of two dialects of the same language — **bidialectal** *n*

bi·di·a·lec·tal·ism \-təˌlizəm\ *or* **bi·di·a·lect·ism** \(ˌ)bīˌdīəˌlekt(ˌ)izəm\ *n* : facility in using two dialects of the same language

bi·don·ville \ˌbēˌdō^{n}'vē(ə)l\ *n* [F, fr. *bidon* tin can (fr. MF, canteen, fr. OF, prob. fr. —assumed— ON *bidha* milk jug — whence Icel *bidha*) + *ville* city, fr. OF, village] : a settlement of jerry-built dwellings on the outskirts of a city (as in France)

big bang *n* : the cosmic explosion that marked the beginning of the universe according to the big bang theory

big bang theory *n* : a theory in astronomy: the universe originated billions of years ago from the explosion of a single mass of compressed material —compare STEADY STATE THEORY

big beat *n, often cap both Bs* : rock music

big·foot \'bigˌfu̇t\ *n, often cap* [fr. the size of the footprints ascribed to it] : SASQUATCH

big gun *n* : GUN

bike* *n* : a 2-wheeled automotive vehicle (as a motorcycle or motor bicycle)

bike·way \'bīˌkwā\ *n* : a thoroughfare for bicycles

bi·layer \'bīˌlāə(r), -ˌleər, -ˌleə\ *n* : a film or membrane with two molecular layers <a *bilayer* of phospholipid molecules>

bi–lev·el \'bīˌlevəl\ *n* : a two-story house with the first floor beginning below ground level and divided into two areas by a ground-level entry situated between the stories of the adjoining areas

bil·li–bi \ˌbilēˌbē, -liˌ-\ *n* [F, alter. of *Billy B.*, William B. Leeds, Jr. †1972 Am. industrialist; fr. his partiality for it] : a soup made of mussel stock, white wine, and cream and served hot or cold

bi·na·ry* \'bīnərē, -ri, *sometimes* -ˌner-\ *adj* **1** : involving a choice or condition of two alternatives only (as on-off or yes-no) **2** : involving binary notation

binary notation *n* : expression of a number with a base of 2 using only the digits 0 and 1 with each digital place representing a power of 2 instead of a power of 10 as in decimal notation

bio- \'bīō\ *comb form* [*biological*] : being such biologically <the *bio*mother gave up her baby for adoption>

bio·ac·tiv·i·ty \ˌbīō(ˌ)akˌtivəd·ē, -d·i\ *n* [*bio-* life, living organisms (fr. Gk, fr. *bios* mode of life) + *activity*] : the effect (as of an insecticide) on a living organism

bio·as·tro·nau·tics \-ˌastrəˌnȯd·iks, -näd-\ *n pl but sing or pl in constr* : the medical and biological aspect of astronautics — **bio·as·tro·nau·ti·cal** \-ikəl\ *adj*

bio·au·tog·ra·phy \ˌbīōȯˈtägrəfē\ *n* : the identification or comparison of organic compounds separated by chromatography by means of their effect on living organisms and esp. microorganisms — **bio·au·to·graph** \-ˈȯd·əˌgraf\ *n* — **bio·au·to·graph·ic** \¦bīōˌȯd·ə¦grafik\ *adj*

bio·cid·al \¦bīə¦sīdᵊl\ *adj* [*bio-* + *-cidal* killing, deriv. of L *caedere* to cut, kill] : destructive to life < *biocidal* temperature effects > < *biocidal* compounds >

bio·clean \ˈbīōˌklēn\ *adj* : free or almost free of harmful or potentially harmful organisms (as bacteria) < a *bioclean* room >

bio·de·grad·able \¦bīōdə̇¦grādəbəl\ *adj* : capable of being broken down esp. into innocuous products by the action of living beings (as microorganisms) < *biodegradable* detergents > — **bio·de·grad·abil·i·ty** \-ˌgrādə¦biləd·ē\ *n* — **bio·deg·ra·da·tion** \-ˌdegrə¦dāshən\ *n* — **bio·de·grade** \-də̇¦grād, -dē¦-\ *vb*

bio·elec·tro·gen·e·sis \¦bīōə̇ˌlektrəˈjenəsə̇s, -ōēˌl-\ *n* : the production of electricity by living organisms

bio·elec·tron·ics \¦bīōə̇(ˌ)lek¦träniks\ *n pl but sing in constr* **1** : a branch of the life sciences that deals with electronic control of physiological function esp. as applied in medicine to compensate for defects of the nervous system **2** : a branch of science that deals with the role of electron transfer in biological processes

bio·en·gi·neer·ing* \¦bīōˌenjə̇¦ni(ə)riŋ, -rēŋ\ *n* : the application to biological or medical science of engineering principles (as the theory of control systems in models of the nervous system) or engineering equipment (as in the construction of artificial organs) — **bio·en·gi·neer** \-¦ni(ə)r, -iə\ *n*

bio·en·vi·ron·men·tal \¦bīōən¦vīrən¦mentᵊl, -(ˌ)en¦v-, -ī(ə)rn¦-\ *adj* : concerned with the environment and esp. with deleterious factors in the environment of living beings

bio·feed·back \-¦fēdˌbak\ *n* : the technique of making unconscious or involuntary bodily processes (as heartbeat or brainwaves) perceptible to the senses (as by use of an oscilloscope) in order to manipulate them by conscious mental control

bio·geo·ce·nose *or* **bio·geo·coe·nose** \ˌbīō¦jēōsə̇¦nōz, -nōs\ *n* [Russ *biogeotsenoz*, fr. NL *bio-* + *geo-* earth (deriv. of Gk *gē*) + *-coenosis*, deriv. of Gk *koinōsis* sharing, fr. *koinos* common] : BIOGEOCOENOSIS

bio·geo·coe·no·sis *or* **bio·geo·ce·no·sis** \-¦jēōsə̇¦nōsə̇s\ *n, pl* **-no·ses** \-¦nōˌsēz\ : the complex of a community and its environment functioning as an ecological unit in nature : ecosystem — **bio·geo·coe·not·ic** \-¦näd·ik\ *adj*

bio·haz·ard \ˈbīō¦hazə(r)d\ *n* : biological material that constitutes a hazard to man or his environment — used esp. of infective material

bio·in·stru·men·ta·tion \¦bīōˌin(t)strəmən·¦tāshən, -ˌmen-\ *n* : the development and use of instruments for recording and transmitting physiological data (as from astronauts in flight); *also* : the instruments themselves

biological clock *n* : an inherent timing mechanism responsible for various cyclical behaviors and physiological activities of living beings

bio·ma·te·ri·al \¦bīōmə¦tirēəl, -¦tēr-\ *n* : material used for or suitable for use in prostheses that come in direct contact with living tissues

bio·med·i·cal \-medə̇kəl\ *adj* **1** : of or relating to biomedicine < *biomedical* studies > **2** : of, relating to, or involving biological, medical, and physical science < *biomedical* engineering >

bio·med·i·cine \-¦medəsən, *Brit usu* -¦medsə̇n\ *n* : a branch of medical science concerned esp. with the capacity of human beings to survive and function in abnormally stressful environments and with the protective modification of such environments

bi·on·ics \bīˈäniks\ *n pl but sing in constr* [*bio-* + *-onics* (as in *electronics*)] : a branch of science concerned with the application of data about the functioning of biological systems to the solution of engineering problems — **bi·on·ic** \-nik\ *adj*

bio·or·gan·ic \¦bīōˌȯ(r)¦ganik\ *adj* : of or relating to the organic chemistry of biologically significant substances

bio·poly·mer \-¦päləmə(r)\ *n* : a polymeric substance (as a protein or a polysaccharide) formed in a biological system

bio·re·search \-rə̇¦sərch, -¦rēˌs-, -sə̄ch, -səich\ *n* : research in biological science

bio·rhythm \'bīō,rithəm\ *n* : an innately determined rhythmic biological process or function (as sleep behavior); *also* : an innate rhythmic determiner of such a process or function — **bio·rhyth·mic** \,bīō'rithmik\ *adj* — **bio·rhyth·mic·i·ty** \-thmisəd·ē\ *n*

bio·sat·el·lite \,bīō'sad·ᵊl,īt, -atᵊl,īt\ *n* : an artificial satellite for carrying a living human being, animal, or plant

bio·sci·ence \'bīō'sīən(t)s\ *n* : biological science : biology — **bio·sci·en·tif·ic** \,bīō,sīən'tifik\ *adj* — **bio·sci·en·tist** \'bīō'sīəntəst\ *n*

bio·sen·sor \'bīō'sen,sȯ(ə)r, -'sen(t)sə(r)\ *n* : a device sensitive to a physical stimulus (as heat or a particular motion) and transmitting information about a life process (as of an astronaut)

bio·spe·le·ol·o·gy \,bīō,spēlē'äləjē, -,spel-\ *n* : the biological study of cave-dwelling organisms — **bio·spe·le·ol·o·gist** \-əjəst\ *n*

bio·te·lem·e·try \-tə'lemə·trē\ *n* : the remote detection and measurement of a biological function, activity, or condition of a man or animal — **bio·tele·met·ric** \-,telə'me·trik\ *adj*

bio·trans·for·ma·tion \-,tran(t)sfə(r)'māshən, -(,)fȯ(r)-\ *n* : the transformation of a chemical compound into another compound in a living system

bio·tron \'bīə·,trän\ *n* [*bio-* + *-tron* (as in *cyclotron*)] : a climate control chamber used to study the effect of specific environmental factors on living organisms

bi·qui·na·ry \(')bī'kwīnərē, -win-\ *adj* [*bi-* two + *quinary* quintuple] : of, based on, being, or relating to a mixed-base system of numbers in which each decimal digit n is represented as a pair of digits xy where $n = 5x + y$ and x is written in base 2 as 0 or 1 and y is written in base 5 as 0, 1, 2, 3, or 4 <decimal 9 is represented by *biquinary* 14>

Birch·er \'bərchər, 'bəchə(r, 'bəichə(r\ *n* [the John *Birch* Society, ultraconservative political organization] : a member or adherent of the John Birch Society — **Birch·ism** \-,chizəm\ *n* — **Birch·ist** \-chəst\ *or* **Birch·ite** \-,chīt\ *n or adj*

bird* *n* **1** : one that flies (as an airplane, a rocket, a satellite, or a spacecraft) **2** : an obscene gesture of contempt made by pointing the middle finger upward while keeping the other fingers down — usu. used with *the* <some . . . gave the peace sign out of classroom windows, and others gave the *bird* —L.K. Truscott IV>; called also *finger*

birdy·back *also* **bird·ie·back** \'bərdē,bak, -əd-, -əid-, -di-\ *n* [*bird* + *-yback* (as in *piggyback*)] : the movement of loaded truck trailers by airplane

bi·sta·ble \(')bī'stābəl\ *adj* : having two stable states <a *bistable* electrical element> — **bi·sta·bil·i·ty** \,bīstə'biləd·ē\ *n*

bi·stat·ic \(')bī'stad·ik, -ēk\ *adj* [*bi-* two + *static* stationary] : involving the use of a transmitter and receiver at separate locations < *bistatic* radar>

¹bit* *n* **1 a** : a characteristic pattern of behavior <book burning, unless it's an embassy library, is strictly a Fascist *bit* —Gene Williams> **b** : a standardized procedure <the familiar, "testing: 1 . . . 2 . . . 3 . . . 4 . . ." *bit* to check sound level and room acoustics —David Curl> **2 a** : a particular appearance or style <sick of the bouffant *bit* —H.B. Jacobs> **b** : the aggregate of items, situations, or activities appropriate to a given style, genre, or role

²bit* *n* : the physical representation (as in a computer tape or memory) of a bit by an electrical pulse, a magnetized spot, or a hole whose presence or absence indicates data

bite* *vb* — **bite the bullet** : to enter with resignation upon a difficult or distressing course of action <someone finally had to *bite the bullet*, and . . . the decision properly went out over my name —R. D. Wood>

bite plate *n* : a dental appliance that is usu. made of plastic and wire, is worn in the palate or sometimes on the lower jaw, and is used in orthodontics and prosthodontics to assist in therapy and diagnosis

bi·unique \,bīyü'nēk\ *adj* : being a correspondence between two sets that is one-to-one in both directions <the *biunique* correspondence between the points on a straight line and the real numbers> <a phonemic transcription should be *biunique*> — **bi·unique·ness** \-knəs\ *n*

Bi·zen ware \bē'zen-\ *n* [part trans. of Jap *bizen-yaki*, fr. *Bizen*, former province in Japan, where it was made + Jap *yaki* pottery] : a Japanese ceramic ware produced since the 14th century that is typically a dark bronzy stoneware often with smears of natural ash glaze

black* *vt, chiefly Brit* : to declare (as a business or industry) subject to boycott by trade-union members

[1]**black belt** *n* **1** : an area characterized by rich black soil **2** *often cap both Bs*: an area densely populated by blacks

[2]**black belt** *n* [fr. the color of the belt of the uniform worn by the holder of the rating] **1** : a rating of expert in various arts of self-defense (as judo and karate) **2** : one who holds a black belt

blackboard jungle *n* : an urban school whose students are generally belligerent and disorderly

black box *n* **1** : a usu. complicated electronic device (as a radar set) that can be inserted in or removed as a unit from a particular place in an assembly (as a spacecraft) **2** : a usu. electronic device (as a control for a computer) which operates on an input to produce an output but whose internal mechanism is hidden from or mysterious to the user

black comedy *n* [trans. of F *comédie noire*] : comedy that employs black humor

Black English *n* : the nonstandard dialect of English held to be spoken by a majority of American blacks

black hole *n* : a hypothetical celestial body with a small diameter and intense gravitational field that is held to be a collapsed star

black humor *n* [trans. of F *humour noir*] : humor marked by the use of usu. morbid, ironic, grotesquely comic episodes that ridicule human folly — **black–hu·mored** \¦blak¦(h)yümə(r)d\ *adj* — **black humorist** *n*

black·light trap \ˈblakˈlīt·ˌtrap\ *n* : a trap for insects that uses a form of black light to attract them

black lung *n* : a disease of the lungs caused by habitual inhalation of coal dust (as by miners)

black money *n* : income (as from gambling) that is not reported to the government for tax purposes <the country is full of *black money* in hiding from the tax collectors —Alexander Campbell>

Black Muslim *n* : a member of a black group that professes Islamic religious belief and advocates a separate black community

black nationalist *n, often cap B&N* : one of a group of militant blacks who advocate separatism from the whites and the formation of self-governing black communities — **black nationalism** *n, often cap B&N*

blackness* *n* **1** : the aggregate of qualities characteristic of the Negro race **2** : NEGRITUDE

Black Panther *n* : a member of an organization of militant American blacks

black power *n* : the power of American blacks esp. as applied to the achieving of their political and economic rights

black studies *n pl* : studies (as in history and literature) relating to the culture of American blacks

blahs \ˈbläz, -àz\ *n pl* : a feeling of boredom, discomfort, or general dissatisfaction — usu. used with *the* <you're moribund from the late-winter *blahs.* And you feel you must get away for a weekend —Richard Curtis>

blast* *n* **1** : an enjoyably exciting occasion or event; *esp* : a party <great beer *blasts* were held on the mountain —Peter Range> **2** : a home run in baseball <second *blast* into the left centerfield bleachers came with one out in the sixth inning —*Springfield (Mass.) Union*>

blast *n* [*-blast* formative unit, deriv. of Gk *blastos* bud, shoot] : an immature or imperfectly developed cell — **blastic** *also* **blast** *adj*

blax·ploi·ta·tion \¦blakˌsplȯi¦tāshən\ *n* [blend of *blax* (alter. of *blacks*) and *exploitation*] : the exploitation of blacks by producers of black-oriented films

[1]**bleep** \ˈblēp\ *n* [imit.] : a short high-pitched sound (as from electronic equipment)

[2]**bleep** *vt* : BLIP

blind trust *n* : an arrangement by which a person in a sensitive position protects himself from possible conflict of interest charges by placing his financial affairs in the hands of a fiduciary and giving up all right to know about or intervene in their handling

blip* \ˈblip\ *vt* **blipped; blip·ping** : to remove (recorded sound) from a videotape so that in the received television program there is an interruption in the sound <swear-words *blipped* by a censor> <her dialogue is studded with the kind of language that is *blipped* on TV —Louise A. Sweeney>

blitz* \ˈblits\ *n* : a rush on a passer in football by the linebackers or safetymen

blitz* *vt* **1** : to rush (a passer) in football from a position as a linebacker or defensive back **2** : to order (as a linebacker) to blitz **~** *vi, of a linebacker or defensive back* : to make a rush on the passer in football — **blitz·er** \-sə(r)\ *n*

block* *vt* : to work out (as the principal positions and movements) for the performers (as of a play) <spent three hours painstakingly reading and rereading lines while *blocking* their stage movements —Melodie Bowsher>; *also* : to work out the players' positions and movements for (as a scene or play) <*blocked* the play, meticulously moving the characters around the room and through the lines —Mel Gussow> — often used with *out*

block·bust·ing \ˈbläkˌbəstiŋ\ *n* : profiteering by first inducing white property owners to sell hastily and often at a loss by appeals to fears of depressed values because of threatened minority encroachment and then reselling at inflated prices — **block-bust·er** \ˈbläkˈbəstə(r)\ *n*

block·ing* \ˈbläkiŋ\ *n* : the planning and working out of the principal positions and movements of stage performers (as for a play) <camera shots, musical cues, *blocking,* makeup, costumes and the rest were run through —Robert Jacobson>

bloom* *n* : an excessive growth of plankton

blou·son \ˈblau̇ˌzän, -ˌsän, -sᵊn; ˈblüˌzän\ *n* [F, dim. of *blouse* blouse] : a woman's garment (as a dress or blouse) having a close waistband with a blousing of material over it

blow* *vt* **blew; blown; blow·ing** : to consume by smoking <a few had started *blowing* grass in their early teens —Daniel Greene> — **blow one's cool** : to lose one's composure — **blow one's mind** **1** : to affect one with intense emotional excitement <a grand guignol floor show that's guaranteed to *blow your mind* —Foster Hirsch> **2** : to take one by surprise <did *blow my mind* and forced me to think —C.M. Mahon> **3** : to undergo or cause to undergo a psychedelic experience <heroin really *blew my mind* —Joe Eszterhas>

bluegrass* *n* [fr. the *Blue Grass Boys,* performing group, fr. *Bluegrass State,* nickname of Kentucky] : country music played on unamplified stringed instruments (as banjos, fiddles, guitars, and mandolins) and characterized by free improvisation and close usu. high-pitched harmony

blue heaven *n, slang* : amobarbital or its sodium derivative in a blue tablet or capsule

blues·man \ˈblüzmən, -ˌman\ *n* : one who plays or sings the blues

blues–rock \ˈblüzˈräk\ *n* : blues sung to a rock 'n' roll background

blue stellar object \-ˈstelər-\ *n* : any of various blue celestial bodies that do not emit appreciable radio waves

blush·er* \ˈbləshə(r)\ *n* : a cosmetic applied to the face to give a usu. pink color or to accent the cheekbones

B lym·pho·cyte \ˈbēˈlim(p)fəˌsīt\ *n* [*b*one-marrow-derived *lymphocte*] : B CELL

board* *n* **1 boards** *pl* : the low wooden wall enclosing a hockey rink **2** : the rounded or rectangular board behind the basket at the end of a basketball court : backboard — usu. used in pl. **3** : a long narrow buoyant board used in surfing : a surfboard

boa·tel \(ˈ)bōˈtel\ *n* [blend of *boat* and *hotel*] : a waterside hotel equipped with docks to accommodate persons traveling by boat

bo·cage* \bōˈkäzh\ *n* [*bocage* countryside with wooded patches, fr. F] : a supporting and ornamental background (as of shrubbery and flowers) for a ceramic figure

body bag *n* : a zippered bag (as of rubber) in which a human corpse is placed (as for transportation)

body language *n* : the bodily gestures and mannerisms by which a person communicates with others

body shirt *n* **1** : a woman's close-fitting top made with a sewn-in or snapped crotch **2** : a close-fitting shirt or blouse

body stocking *n* : a sheer close-fitting one-piece garment for the torso that often has sleeves and legs

body·suit \ˈbädēˌs(y)üt\ *n* : a close-fitting one-piece garment for the torso

body·surf \-ˌsərf, -ˌsə̄f, -ˌsəif\ *vi* : to ride on a wave without a surfboard by planing on the chest and stomach — **body·surf·er** \-fə(r)\ *n*

bof·fo \ˈbäf(ˌ)ō\ *adj* [*boffo,* n., short for *boffola*] : extraordinarily successful : sensational <we're a *boffo* smash! —Tom Eyen> <should be *boffo* for boating biz —H.D. Whall>

bo·gey* \ˈbu̇gē, ˈbōgē, ˈbügē\ *n, pl* **bogeys** *slang* : an unidentified flying object <on Gemini 7 the crew reported a *bogey*. . . in the sky —Neal Stanford>

boil·off \ˈbȯilˌȯf, *also* -ˌäf\ *n* : the vaporization of a liquid (as liquid oxygen)

Bok·mål \ˈbu̇kˌmȯl, ˈbōk-\ *n* [Norw, fr. *bok* book (fr. ON *bōk*) + *mål* language, fr. ON *māl*] : a literary form of Norwegian developed by the gradual reform of written Danish : Riksmål — compare NYNORSK

bo·lo tie \ˈbō(ˌ)lō-\ *or* **bo·la tie** \ˈbōlə-\ *n* [prob. fr. *bola*] : a cord fastened around the neck with an ornamental clasp and worn as a necktie

bomb* *n* **1** : an inept or unfavorably received performance : a flop or failure <a critical success but a financial *bomb—New York*> **2** : a long pass in football **3** : a shot in basketball made far away from the basket

bomb* *vi* : to be a failure <if I *bomb* in the movies . . . I could always join the Peace Corps —R.G. Goulet>; *esp* : to fail to win audience approval <will not be the first show to seem great in Philadelphia and then to *bomb* in New York —Clive Barnes>

bombed \ˈbämd\ *adj, slang* : affected by alcohol or drugs : drunk, high

bomb·let \ˈbämlət\ *n* [*bomb* + *-let,* dim. suffix] : a small bomb <weapons components such as grenade bodies, *bomblet* cases and explosives —D.D. Darling>

bond·ed* \ˈbändəd\ *adj* : composed of two or more layers of the same or different fabrics held together by an adhesive <*bonded* jersey>

bon·kers \ˈbäŋkə(r)z, ˈbȯŋ-\ *adj* [origin unknown] : out of one's mind : crazy, mad <if I don't work, I go *bonkers* —Zoe Caldwell>

boo \ˈbü\ *n* [origin unknown] : marijuana

boob tube \ˈbübˌt(y)üb\ *n* [fr. the belief that a taste for television viewing indicates stupidity] : a television set <spending weekends at various motels and deftly removing their *boob tubes* —F.A. Tinker>; *also* : the medium of television or the watching of television <if you don't think your family is addicted to the television habit, try doing without the *boob tube* for a few days and see what happens —Harold Hudson> <the role of advertising in managing the *boob tube's* coverage of complex problems —Bill Cutler>

boon·ies \ˈbünēz, -iz\ *n pl* [by shortening and alter. fr. *boondocks*] *slang* : rural backcountry : sticks, boondocks <out in the *boonies,* where bright city distractions are hours away —Jesse Kornbluth>

boot·strap* \ˈbütˌstrap\ *n* : a computer routine consisting of a few initial instructions by means of which the rest of the instructions are brought into the computer

bootstrap *vt* : to enter (a program) into a computer by a bootstrap

borough* *n* : a civil division of the state of Alaska corresponding to a county in other states

bos·sa no·va \ˌbäsəˈnōvə, ˌbȯs-\ *n* [Pg, lit., new trend, fr. *bossa* hump, bump, trend (fr. F *bosse* hump, fr. OF *boce*) + *nova,* fem. of *novo* new, fr. L *novus*] **1** : a Brazilian dance characterized by the sprightly step pattern of the samba and a subtle bounce **2** : music resembling the samba with jazz interpolations

Bos·ton arm \ˈbȯstən-, *sometimes* ˈbäs-, *in rapid speech also* -sᵊn-\ *n* [fr. its development by four institutions in Boston, Mass.] : an artificial arm that is activated by an amputee's nerve impulses which are electrically amplified and transmitted to a motor operating the arm

bot·tle–feed \ˈbäd·ᵊlˌfēd, ˈbätᵊl-\ *vt* **-fed; -feed·ing** : to feed (as an infant) with a bottle

bottleneck* *or* **bottleneck guitar** *n* : a style of guitar playing in which an object (as a metal bar or the neck of a bottle) is pressed against the strings for a glissando effect

bottom out *vi, of a security market* : to decline to a point where demand begins to exceed supply and a rise in prices is imminent

bouque·tière \ˌbük(ə)ˈtye(ə)r, -k(ə)tēˈe(ə)r\ *adj* [F, woman who sells flowers, fem. of *bouquetier* flower seller, fr. *bouquet* bouquet] : garnished with vegetables <rack of lamb *bouquetière*>

bou·zou·ki *also* **bou·sou·ki** \büˈzükē, bəˈ-\ *n, pl* **-kia** \-kēə\ *also* **-kis** [NGk *mpouzouki*] : a long-necked stringed musical instrument of Greek origin

box* *n* : television : a television set : BOOB TUBE

bpi *abbr* bits per inch; bytes per inch

braces *n pl* : wire fastened to teeth to correct irregularities in their position

bra·ci·o·la \bräch(ē)ˈōlə\ *or* **bra·ci·o·le** \-lā\ *n* [*braciola* fr. It, fr. *brace* live coal, fr. OIt *bragia; braciole* fr. It, pl. of *braciola*] : a thin slice of meat (as steak) that is usu. wrapped around a filling of meat, chopped vegetables, and seasonings and often cooked in wine

bra·dy·ki·nin \ˌbrādəˈkīnən\ *n* [*brady-* slow (fr. Gk *bradys*) + *kinin*] : a kinin that is formed in injured tissue, acts in vasodilation of small arterioles, is held to play a part in inflammatory processes, and is composed of a chain of nine amino acids

brain* *n* : an automatic device (as a computer) that performs one or more of the functions of the human brain for control, guidance, or computation <the *brain* of a missile>

brain death *n* : final cessation of activity in the central nervous system as indicated by a flat record on an electroencephalogram

brain drain *n* : the migration of professional people (as scientists, professors, or physicians) from one country to another usu. for higher salaries or better living conditions

brain hor·mone \-ˈhȯrˌmōn, -ˈhȯ(ə)-\ *n* : a hormone that is secreted by neurosecretory cells of the insect brain and that stimulates the prothoracic glands to secrete ecdysone

bra·less \ˈbräləs, -räl-, *sometimes* -rȯl-\ *adj, of a woman* : wearing no bra — **bra·less·ness** \-nəs\ *n*

branch* *n* : a part of a computer program executed as a result of a program decision

branch* *vi* : to follow one of two or more branches (as in a computer program)

bread·board \ˈbredˌbō(ə)rd, -ˌbȯ(ə)rd, -ōəd, -ȯəd\ *vt* : to make an experimental arrangement of (an electronic circuit) on a flat surface

Brecht·ian \ˈbrektēən, -k̲-\ *adj* [Bertolt *Brecht* †1956 Ger. dramatist] : of, relating to, or suggestive of Bertolt Brecht or his writings <the production . . . is coarse in spirit and with no gloss at all on its rendering of the *Brechtian* view of a materialistic society —Irving Kolodin>

bride's basket *n* [so called fr. such bowls' frequently being given as wedding presents in the late 19th century] : an ornate, handled, usu. colored, and often cased glass bowl fitted with a silver-plated base

broad·band \ˈbrȯdˌband\ *adj* : of, having, or involving operation with uniform efficiency over a wide band of frequencies <a *broadband* radio antenna>

broken home *n* : a family of which the parents are not living together

bro·mo·ura·cil \ˌbrōmōˈyu̇rəˌsil, -məˈ-, -əsəl\ *n* [*bromo-* containing bromine + *uracil*] : a mutagenic uracil derivative $C_4H_3N_2O_2Br$ that pairs readily with adenine and sometimes with guanine during bacterial or phage DNA synthesis

brown bag·ging \ˈbrau̇nˈbagiŋ, -gēŋ\ *n* [fr. the brown paper bag used] **1** : the practice of carrying a bottle of liquor into a restaurant or club where setups are available but where the sale of liquor by the drink is illegal **2** : the practice of carrying one's lunch (as to work) usu. in a brown paper bag — **brown–bag** \-ˌbag\ *vb* — **brown bag·ger** \-gə(r)\ *n*

brown fat *n* : a mammalian heat-producing tissue occurring esp. in hibernators

brownie point *n, often cap B* : a credit regarded as earned esp. by currying favor with a superior <a new chance to gain those *Brownie points* so essential to promotion and tenure —Theodore Sturgeon> <must make this kind of scholarship respectable, give *brownie points* for it —G.E. Forsythe>

brown lung disease *n* : a chronic industrial disease associated with the inhalation of cotton dust over a long period of time : byssinosis

brown recluse spider *n* [*recluse* prob. fr. NL *reclusa,* specific epithet, fr. LL, fem. of *reclusus* shut up; fr. its living chiefly in dark corners] : a venomous spider (*Loxosceles reclusa*) introduced into the southern U.S. that has a violin-shaped mark on the cephalothorax and produces a dangerous neurotoxin

brown•ware \ˈbrau̇nˌwa(ə)r, -ˌwe(ə)r\ *n* **1** : a brown-glazed earthenware formerly widely used for utility pottery **2** : typically primitive pottery that fires to a brown or reddish color

brush•back \ˈbrəshˌbak\ *n* : a pitch thrown near the batter's head in baseball in an attempt to make him move back from home plate

bru•tal•ism \ˈbrüd•ᵊlˌizəm, -ütᵊl-\ *n* : a style in art and esp. architecture using exaggeration and distortion to create its effect (as of massiveness or power) — **bru•tal•ist** \-ᵊləst\ *adj or n*

bubble* *n* : something (as a plastic structure) that is more or less semicylindrical or dome-shaped

bubble car *n* : an automobile having a transparent bubble top

bub•ble•gum \ˈbəbəlˌgəm\ *n* [fr. the fact that bubble gum is chewed chiefly by children] : rock music characterized by simple repetitive phrasing and intended esp. for young teenagers

bug off \ˌbəgˈȯf, *also* -äf\ *vi* [short for *bugger*] : to go away : leave, scram <the body's immune system, nature's way of telling foreign substances to *bug off* — Philip Nobile> — usu. used as a command <you'll get your forecast. Now *bug off* — P.B. Benchley>

bum•mer \ˈbəmə(r)\ *n* [*bum* not good] **1** : an unpleasant drug-induced hallucinatory experience; *broadly*: an unpleasant event or situation <people seem to realize that this war is a *bummer*—Arthur Moses> **2** : something that fails : a flop <the book is a *bummer*—Albert Goldman>

bumper sticker *n* : an adhesive strip of paper or plastic bearing a printed message (as a slogan or a candidate's name)

bumper strip *n* : BUMPER STICKER

bunny* *n* [fr. *Bunny,* a service mark used for a waitress whose minimal attire includes a tail and ears resembling those of a rabbit] : a pretty girl esp. considered as an object of sexual desire <those ads, where the hirsute hero struts off with a bikinied *bunny* —Chris Welles>

Bun•ra•ku \bu̇nˈrä(ˌ)kü, ˈbu̇n(ˌ)r-\ *n* [Jap] : Japanese puppet theater featuring large costumed wooden puppets, onstage puppeteers, and a chanter who speaks all the lines

buns \ˈbənz\ *n pl* : the human buttocks

bu•reau•cra•tese \ˌbyu̇rəˌkrad•ˌēz, ˈbyü-, -rō-, -aˈtēz; byüˌräkrəˌtēz, byu̇-, byə-; -ēs\ *n* [*bureaucrat* + *-ese* jargon] : an impersonal style of language typically used by bureaucrats and marked by the prevalence of abstractions, jargon, euphemisms, and circumlocutions <the style is heavy, cliché-ridden, *bureaucratese* at its very worst —A.H. Marckwardt> <even in its original, carefully hedged *bureaucratese* the warning was ominous —*Newsweek*>

Bur•kitt's lym•pho•ma \ˌbərkəts(ˌ)limˌfōmə, ˌbək-\ *or* **Burkitt lymphoma** \-kət-\ *n* [Denis Parsons *Burkitt* b1911 Brit. surgeon] : a malignant lymphoma that affects primarily the upper and lower jaws, orbit, retroperitoneal tissues situated near the pancreas, kidneys, ovaries, testes, thyroid, adrenal glands, heart, and pleura, that occurs esp. in children of central Africa, and that is associated with Epstein-Barr virus

Burkitt's tu•mor *or* **Burkitt tumor** \-ˌt(y)ümə(r)\ *n* : BURKITT'S LYMPHOMA

burn* *n* : the firing of a spacecraft rocket engine in flight

burn bag *n* : a bag for holding classified papers that are to be destroyed by burning

burn•out* \ˈbərnˌau̇t, ˈbən-, ˈbəin-\ *n* **1 a** : the process or an instance of burning out **b** : the cessation of operation of a jet engine as the result of exhaustion of or shutting off of fuel **2** : the point in the trajectory of a rocket engine at which burnout occurs

bush *adj* [prob. short for *bush-league*] : of an inferior class or group of its kind : bush-league, unprofessional, amateurish <the travesty was not that the speedway went the show-business route, but that the execution was so *bush* —J.S. Radosta>

bush hat *n* [*bush* backcountry] : a broad-brimmed hat worn esp. as part of an Australian military uniform

businessman's risk *n* : an investment (as a stock) with a moderately high risk factor that is bought with an eye to growth potential and capital gains or sometimes tax advantages rather than for income

bus·ing *or* **bus·sing** \ˈbəsiŋ\ *n* : the act of transporting by bus; *specif* : the transporting of children to a school outside their residential area as a means of establishing racial balance in the school

bust* *vt* **1** : to put under arrest <was *busted* for running a Baltimore stock swindle —*Newsweek*> **2** : to make a raid on <since her brothel was *busted* —Diana Davenport>

bust* *n* : a police raid <the night the club was raided . . . he was rushed into the kitchen, fitted with a white jacket, and disguised as a waiter until the *bust* was completed —David Butwin>; *also* : an instance of making an arrest <the biggest *bust* of top narcotics dealers ever —Mary P. Nichols>

bu·sul·fan \byüˈsəlfən\ *n* [*but*ane + *sulf*onyl] : an antineoplastic agent $C_6H_{14}O_6S_2$ used in the treatment of chronic myelogenous leukemia

butch* \ˈbu̇ch\ *n* : one who is butch

butch *adj* [prob. fr. *Butch,* a nickname for boys, esp. tough boys] **1** *of a homosexual* : playing the male role in a homosexual relationship **2** : very masculine in appearance or manner

butter pat* *n* : an individual dish for a pat of butter

but·ton–down* *also* **but·toned–down** \ˈbətᵊnˌdau̇n\ *adj* [fr. the fact that button-down shirts are felt to be conservative] : lacking originality and imagination and adhering to conventional standards esp. in dress and behavior <*button-down* minds who want to know about the paper's pension plan rather than what beat is open —*Newsweek*>

button man *n* [earlier *button boy* page, errand boy; fr. the buttons on a page's uniform] : a low-ranking member of an underworld organization who is given disagreeable and often dangerous assignments

bu·tut \ˈbüˌtüt\ *n* [native name in Gambia] **1** : a monetary unit of Gambia equal to $^1/_{100}$ dalasi **2** : a coin representing one butut

buy–in \ˈbīˌin\ *n* : the act or process of buying in to cover a short on a stock or commodity exchange

buzz off *vi* : to leave forthwith : go away : scram — usu. used as a command <he sits down, shoving away — "*Buzz off*! *Buzz off*!" — the cat that occupies his chair —Gerald Clarke>

buzz session *n* : a small informal group discussion <the PTA meeting will be opened to informal *buzz sessions* —*Fallon (Nev.) Eagle-Standard*>

buzz word *n* : an important-sounding and often technical word or phrase that frequently has little meaning and is used chiefly to impress laymen <it is obvious those *buzz words* were used to draw attention to an otherwise somewhat trivial article —T.W. Bryan>

BX \(ˈ)bēˈeks\ *n* : BASE EXCHANGE

BYOB *abbr* bring your own booze; bring your own bottle

byte \ˈbīt\ *n* [perh. alter. of *bite* morsel] : a group of adjacent binary digits often shorter than a word that a computer processes as a unit <an 8-bit *byte*>

Byz·an·tine* \ˈbizᵊn·ˌtēn, *sometimes* ˈbī-, -ˌtīn; *sometimes* bəˈzan·ˌtēn, bī-, -ˌtīn, -ntən\ *adj* **1** : of, relating to, or characterized by a devious and usu. surreptitious manner of operation <the government, with its own *Byzantine* sources of intelligence —Wesley Pruden> **2** : intricately involved : labyrinthine <searching in the *Byzantine* complexity of the record for leads, defenses, and . . . evidence of perjured testimony —B.L. Collier>

BZ \(ˈ)bēˈzē\ *n* [*BZ,* army code name] : a gas that when breathed produces incapacitating physical and mental effects

C

cabana set *n* : a two-piece beachwear ensemble for men consisting of loosely fitting shorts and a short-sleeved jacket

ca·ble·cast \ˈkābəlˌkast\ *vt* **-cast** *also* **-cast·ed; -cast·ing** : to telecast by cable TV — **cablecast** *n* — **ca·ble·cast·er** \-ə(r)\ *n*

cable TV *n* : COMMUNITY ANTENNA TELEVISION

Caer·phil·ly \ke(ə)rˈfilē, kär-, kī(ə)r-, kə(r)-\ *n* [fr. *Caerphilly,* urban district in Wales] : a mild white whole-milk Welsh cheese

Cae·sar salad \ˈsēzə(r)-\ *n* [fr. *Caesar's,* restaurant in Tijuana, Mexico, where it originated] : a tossed salad made typically with romaine, garlic, anchovies, and croutons and served with a dressing of olive oil, coddled egg, lemon juice, and grated cheese

ca·fé filtre \ˈkaˌfāˈfiltə(r), *F* kȧfāfiltr(ᵊ)\ *n* [F] : coffee made by passing hot water through ground coffee and a filter

caff \ˈkaf\ *n* [by shortening and alter. fr. *café*] *Brit* : a small restaurant serving light meals : café

cage* *n* : a sheer one-piece dress that has no waistline, is often gathered at the neck, and is worn over a close-fitting underdress or slip

CAI *abbr* computer-assisted instruction

cal·ci·phy·lax·is \ˌkalsəfəˈlaksəs\ *n, pl* **-lax·es** \-akˌsēz \ [NL, fr. *calci-* calcium + *-phylaxis* (as in *prophylaxis*)] : an adaptive response that follows systemic sensitization by a calcifying factor (as a D-vitamin) and a challenge (as with a metallic salt) and involves local inflammation and sclerosis with calcium deposition — **cal·ci·phy·lac·tic** \ˈkalsəfəˈlaktik\ *adj* — **cal·ci·phy·lac·ti·cal·ly** \-tək(ə)lē, -li\ *adv*

cal·ci·to·nin \ˌkalsəˈtōnən\ *n* [*calci-* + *ton*ic, adj. + *-in* chemical compound] : THYROCALCITONIN

caliper* *n* : a device consisting of two plates lined with a frictional material that press against the sides of a rotating wheel or disk in some brake systems

callback \ˈkȯlˌbak\ *n* : a recall by a manufacturer of a recently sold product (as an automobile) for correction of a defect

cal·li·graph \ˈkaləˌgraf\ *vt* [back-formation fr. *calligraphy*] : to produce or reproduce in a calligraphic style <the pages were some of them printed, some *calligraphed,* some illuminated, some painted —Francis Meynell>

call in* *vb* — **call in sick** : to report by telephone that one will be absent because of illness

call–in \ˈkȯl(ˌ)in\ *adj, of a radio program* : allowing listeners to engage in on-the-air telephone conversations with the host <a constant guest on radio *call-in* shows —*Playboy*>

cam·eo* \ˈkamēˌō\ *n* : a small theatrical role performed by a well-known actor or actress and often limited to a single scene <a neat *cameo* performance as a fifth-columnist butler —Michael Billington>

[1]camp \ˈkamp\ *n* [origin unknown] **1** : exaggerated effeminate mannerisms (as of speech or gesture) exhibited esp. by homosexuals; *also* : a homosexual displaying such mannerisms **2** : something that is so outrageously artificial, affected, inappropriate, or out-of-date as to be considered amusing — **camp·i·ly** \-pəlē, -li\ *adv* — **camp·i·ness** *n* — **campy** *adj*

[2]camp *adj* **1** : of, relating to, or displaying camp <specializing in *camp* send-ups of the songs of the Fifties and Sixties —John Elsom> **2** : of, relating to, or being a camp <loose-limbed sensuality, which was sometimes macho and sometimes *camp* —Jane Margold>

[3]camp *vi* : to engage in camp : exhibit the qualities of camp <he . . . was *camping,* hands on hips, with a quick eye to notice every man who passed by —R. M. McAlmon>

camper* *n* : a portable dwelling (as a collapsible structure folded into a small trailer or a specially equipped automotive vehicle) for use during casual travel and camping

camphor glass *n* : glass with a cloudy white appearance resembling gum camphor in lump form

can* *n, slang* : an ounce of marijuana

C and W *abbr* country and western

candy strip·er \-ˌstrīpə(r)\ *n* [fr. the red and white stripes of her uniform] : a teenage volunteer nurse's aide

cannon net *n* : a net that is left in wait on the ground until birds or mammals are in position and then is spread over them by the simultaneous firing of several projectiles

can of worms : something that presents one problem after another : a source of continuing difficulty : an unpleasant mess <to suggest Washington bureaucracy should determine the circumstances under which any public instrumentality can borrow opens up a new *can of worms* —J.J. Fogarty>

ca·non·i·cal form \kəˈnänəkəl-\ *n* : the simplest form of a matrix; *specif* : the form of a square matrix that has zero elements everywhere except along the principal diagonal

Can·ton china \ˈkan·ˌtän-, kan·ˈtän-\ *n* : porcelain Canton ware esp. when blue-and-white

Canton enamel *n* [fr. *Canton,* China] : Chinese enamelware of Limoges type

ca·pac·i·tate* \kəˈpasəˌtāt\ *vt* **-tat·ed; -tat·ing** : to cause (sperm) to undergo capacitation

ca·pac·i·ta·tion* \kəˌpasəˈtāshən\ *n* : change undergone by sperm in the female reproductive tract which enables them to penetrate and fertilize an egg

capital gains distribution *n* : the part of the payout of an investment company to its shareholders that consists of realized profits from the sale of securities and technically is not income

capital structure *n* : the makeup of the capitalization of a business in terms of the amounts and kinds of equity and debt securities : the equity and debt securities of a business together with its surplus and reserves

ca·po \ˈkä(ˌ)pō, ˈka-, ˈkȧ-\ *n, pl* **capos** [It, head, chief, fr. L *caput*] : the head of a branch of a crime syndicate

cap·puc·ci·no \ˌkäp(y)əˈchēnō, ˌka-, ˌkȧ-, -(y)ü̇ˈ-\ *n* [It, lit., Capuchin; fr. the likeness of its color to that of a Capuchin's habit] : espresso coffee topped with frothed hot milk or cream and often flavored with cinnamon

ca·pri pants \kaˈprē-, kə-; ˈkä(ˌ)prē-, ˈka-\ *n pl, often cap C* [fr. *Capri,* island in the Bay of Naples, Italy] : close-fitting pants that have tapered legs with a slit on the outside of the leg bottom, extend almost to the ankle, and are used for informal wear esp. by women

cap·sid \ˈkapsə̇d\ *n* [L *capsa* case + E *-id* structure, particle] : the outer protein shell of a virus particle — **cap·sid·al** \-dᵊl\ *adj*

cap·so·mere \ˈkapsəˌmi(ə)r\ *n* [*caps*id + connective *-o-* + *-mere* part, segment, deriv. of Gk *meros* part] : one of the subunits making up a viral capsid

car·a·van·eer \ˌkarə(ˌ)vaˈni(ə)r, -əvəˈ-, -niə(r\ *n* : CARAVANNER 1

car·a·van·ner \ˌkarəˌvanə(r), *also* ˈker-, *esp Brit* ˌkarəˈvanə(r)\ *n* **1** *or* **car·a·van·er** : one that travels in a caravan — called also *caravaneer* **2** *Brit* : one that goes camping with a trailer

car·ba·ryl \ˈkärbəˌril, -ərə̇l\ *n* [*carb*amate + *aryl* radical derived from an aromatic hydrocarbon] : a nonpersistent carbamate insecticide $C_{12}H_{11}O_2N$ effective against numerous crop, forage, and forest pests

car bed *n* [fr. its use in carrying infants in cars] : a portable bed for an infant

car·ben·i·cil·lin \ˌkär(ˌ)benə̇ˈsilə̇n\ *n* [*car*boxy *benz*ylpen *icillin*] : a broad-spectrum penicillin that is effective against gram-negative bacteria (as pseudomonas) and that acts esp. by inhibiting cell-wall synthesis

car·bo·line \ˈkärbəˌlēn\ *n* [*carb-*+ind*ole* + pyrid*ine*] : any of various isomers $C_{11}H_8N_2$ the tricyclic structure of which is related to indole and pyridine and which is found in many alkaloids

carbon dating *n* : determination of age (as of an archaeological find) by means of the content of carbon 14 — called also *carbon-14 dating, radiocarbon dating* — **car·bon-date** \ˈkärbənˌdāt, ˈkȧb-\ *vt*

carbon spot* *n* : a small black spot on a coin

carbon star *n* : a reddish star of low surface temperature composed in part of carbon compounds

car·bo·rane \ˈkärbəˌrān\ *n* [blend of *carbon* and *borane*] : any of a class of thermally stable compounds $B_nC_2H_{n+2}$ that are used in the synthesis of polymers and lubricants

car coat *n* : a three-quarter-length overcoat

card-car·ry·ing \ˌkärdˌkarēiŋ, ˌkȧd-, *also* -ˌkerē-\ *adj* [fr. the assumption that such a member carries a membership card] **1** : being a full-fledged member esp. of a Communist party **2** : being strongly identified with a group (as of people with a common interest) < *card-carrying* members of the ecology movement —Richard Neuhaus >

car·di·nal·i·ty \ˌkärdᵊnˈaləd·ē\ *n* : the number of elements in a given mathematical set

cardinal number* *n* : the property that a mathematical set has in common with all sets that can be put into one-to-one correspondence with it

car·dio·ac·cel·er·a·tor \ˌkärdē(ˌ)ōəkˌseləˌrād·ər, -akˌ-\ *or* **car·dio·ac·cel·er·a·to·ry** \-ˌseləraˌtōrē, -ˌtȯr-, -i\ *adj* [*cardio-* heart (fr. Gk *kardia* heart) + *accelerator* or *acceleratory*] : speeding up the action of the heart — **car·dio·ac·cel·er·a·tion** \-ˌselə-ˌrāshən\ *n*

car·dio·gen·ic \ -ˌjenik, -nēk, *also* -jēn-\ *adj* [*cardio-* + *-genic* produced by] : caused by a cardiac condition < *cardiogenic* shock >

car·dio·meg·a·ly \ˌkärdēōˈmegəlē\ *n* [*cardio-* + *-megaly* enlargement, deriv. of Gk *megal-, megas* large, great] : enlargement of the heart

car·dio·my·op·a·thy \ˌkärdēōˌmīˌäpəthē\ *n* [*cardio-* + *myopathy* disorder of muscle tissue] : a typically chronic disorder of heart muscle that may involve hypertrophy and obstructive damage to the heart

car·dio·pul·mo·nary \-ˌpu̇lməˌnerē, -ˌpəl-\ *adj* [*cardio-* + *pulmonary* relating to the lungs] : of or relating to the heart and lungs < *cardiopulmonary* resuscitation >

car·dio·ver·sion \ -ˌvərzhən, -vəzh-, -vəizh-, *also* -shən\ *n* [*cardio-* + *-version*, fr. L *version-, versio* action of turning] : application of an electric shock in order to restore normal heartbeat

car·hop \ˈkärˌhäp, ˌkȧˌ-\ *vi* : to work as a carhop

ca·ri·so·pro·dol \kəˌrīsəˈprōˌdȯl, -īzə-, -dōl\ *n* [*car-* (prob. fr. *carbamate*) + *isopropyl* + *diol* compound with two hydroxyl groups] : a drug $C_{12}H_{24}N_2O_4$ related to meprobamate that is used to relax muscle and relieve pain

carnival glass *n, often cap C* [fr. its frequent use for prizes at carnival booths] : pressed glass with an iridescent finish mass-produced in a variety of colors (as frosty white or deep purple) in the U. S. in the early 20th century

carrier bag *n, Brit* : SHOPPING BAG

carry* *vb* — **carry the can** *Brit* : to bear alone and in full an often hazardous responsibility <in good democratic theory, Ministers are responsible to the people for the miscalculation of Arab intentions and potential. They ought to *carry the can* —Eric Silver >

carry* *n, pl* **carries** : a quantity that is transferred in addition from one number place to the adjacent one of higher place value

car·ry-cot \ˈkarēˌkät\ *n, Brit* : a portable bed for an infant

car·ry·on \ˈkarēˌȯn, -ˌän, *also* ˈker-\ *n* : a piece of luggage suitable for being carried aboard an airplane by a passenger — **carry-on** *adj*

Car·te·sian plane \(ˈ)kärˌtēzhən-, (ˈ)kȧˌ-\ *n* : a plane whose points are labeled with Cartesian coordinates

Cartesian product *n* : a set that is constructed from two given sets and comprises all pairs of elements such that one element of the pair is from the first set and the other element is from the second set

car·top·per \ˈkärˌtäpər; ˈkȧˌ-, -pə(r\ *n* : a small boat that may be transported on top of a car

case·book* \ˈkāsˌbu̇k\ *n* : a compilation of primary and secondary documents relating to a central topic together with scholarly comment, exercises, and study aids that is often designed to serve as a source book for short papers (as in a course in composition) or as a point of departure for a research paper

ca·sette \kəˈset, ka-\ *n* [alter. of *cassette*] **1** : a cassette photographic film **2** : a cassette for magnetic tape

cash bar *n* : a bar (as at a wedding reception) at which drinks are sold — compare OPEN BAR

cash flow *n* : a measure of corporate worth that consists of net income after taxes plus bookkeeping deductions involving no cash outlay and that is usu. figured in dollars per share of common stock outstanding

cas·sette* \kəˈset, ka-\ *n* : a usu. plastic cartridge having two small reels and containing magnetic tape with the tape on one reel passing to the other without having to be threaded

Cas·tro·ism \ˈkas(ˌ)trōˌizəm, *sometimes* -äs-\ *n* [Fidel *Castro* *b*1927 Cuban political leader] : the political, economic, and social principles and policies of Fidel Castro — **Cas·tro·ist** \-ōˌist, -ōəst\ *n or adj* — **Cas·tro·ite** \-ōˌīt\ *n or adj*

CAT *abbr* clear-air turbulence

cat·e·chol·amine \ˌkad·əˈchōləˌmēn, -əˈsh-, -əˈk-, -ōl-, -əmən\ *n* [*catechol* pyrocatechol + *amine*] : any of various substances (as epinephrine, norepinephrine, and dopamine) that function as hormones or neurotransmitters or both and are related to pyrocatechol but have one or more amine side groups

cat·suit \ˈkatˌsüt\ *n* : a one-piece or two-piece formfitting woman's garment with bell-bottomed legs

CATV *abbr* community antenna television

CB *abbr* citizens band

CBW *abbr* chemical and biological warfare

CCTV *abbr* closed-circuit television

ce·di \ˈsādē\ *n* [Akan *sedie* cowrie] **1** : the basic monetary unit of Ghana **2** : a note representing one cedi

cell* *n* : a basic subdivision of a computer memory that is addressable and can hold one basic operating unit (as a word)

center* *n* : the center of the circle inscribed in a regular polygon

cen·ter·fold \ˈsentə(r)ˌfōld\ *n* : a foldout that is the center spread of a magazine

cen·ter–of–mass system* \ˌsentərə(v)ˈmas-\ *n* : a frame of reference in which the center of mass is at rest

cen·ti·sec·ond \ˈsentəˌsekənd, *also* -ənt, *esp before a pause or consonant* -ən, -ᵊŋ\ *n* [ISV *centi-* hundredth (deriv. of L *centum* hundred) + *second*] : one hundredth of a second

central angle *n* : an angle formed by two radii of a circle

central dogma *n* : a theory in genetics and molecular biology subject to several exceptions that genetic information is coded in self-replicating DNA and undergoes unidirectional transfer to messenger RNAs in transcription which act as templates for protein synthesis in translation

central limit the·o·rem \-ˌthēərəm, -ˌthi(ə)rəm\ *n* : any of several fundamental theorems of probability and statistics giving the conditions under which the distribution of a sum of independent random variables is approximated by the normal distribution; *esp* : a special case of the central limit theorem which is much applied in sampling: the distribution of the mean of a sample from a population with finite variance is approximated by the normal distribution as the number in the sample becomes large

central processing unit *n* : PROCESSOR 1b

central tendon *n* : a 3-lobed aponeurosis located near the central portion of the diaphragm caudal to the pericardium and composed of intersecting planes of collagenous fibers

ceph·a·lor·i·dine \ˌsefəˈlōrəˌdēn, -ˈlär-\ *n* [prob. fr. *cephal*osporin + *-idine* chemical compound] : a broad-spectrum antibiotic $C_{19}H_{17}N_3O_4S_2$ derived from cephalosporin and used esp. in the treatment of gonorrhea

ceph·a·lo·spo·rin \ˌsefələˈspōrən, -ˈspȯr-\ *n* [*Cephalosporium* + *-in* chemical compound] : any of several antibiotics produced by an imperfect fungus (genus *Cephalosporium*)

ceph·a·lo·thin \ˈsefələ(ˌ)thin\ *n* [*cephalo*sporin + *thio-* containing sulfur + *-in* chemical compound] : a semisynthetic broad-spectrum antibiotic $C_{16}H_{15}N_2NaO_6S_2$ that is an analogue of a cephalosporin and is effective against penicillin-resistant staphylococci

cereal leaf beetle *n* : a small reddish brown black-headed Old World chrysomelid beetle (*Oulema melanopa*) that feeds on cereal grasses and is a serious threat to U. S. grain crops

ce·re·bral–pal·sied \səˈrēbrəlˈpȯlzēd, ˈserəbrəl-\ *adj* : affected with cerebral palsy

ce·ru·lo·plas·min \səˌrüləˌplazmən, ˌser(y)əl-\ *n* [ISV *cerulo-* (fr. L *caeruleus* dark blue) + *plasma* + *-in* chemical compound; prob. orig. formed in Sw] : a plasma oxidase that is an alpha globulin active in copper storage and transport

ce·si·um clock \ˈsēzēəm-, -zh(ē)əm-\ *n* : an atomic clock regulated by the natural vibration frequency of cesium atoms

cesium 137 *n* : a radioactive isotope of cesium that has the mass number 137 and a half-life of about 12 months and that is present in fallout

CFA *abbr* certified financial analyst

chain printer *n* : a line printer in which the printing element is a continuous chain

chain rule *n* : a mathematical rule concerning the differentiation of a function of a function (as $f[u(x)]$) by which under suitable conditions of continuity and differentiability one function is differentiated with respect to the second considered as an independent variable and then the second function is differentiated with respect to the independent variable <if $v = u^2$ and $u = 3x^2 + 2$ the derivative of v by the *chain rule* is $2u(6x)$ or $12x(3x^2 + 2)$>

chair·one \ˈche(ə)rˌwən, ˈcha(ə)r-, ˈcheəˌ-, ˈchaəˌ-\ *n* : CHAIRPERSON

chair·per·son \-ˌpərsᵊn, -ˌpəs-, -ˌpəis-\ *n* **1** : the presiding officer of a meeting or an organization or a committee <pocket reference handbook provides the *chairperson* of any meeting with a concise summary of parliamentary procedures —*Henry Regnery Co. Catalog*> **2** : the administrative officer of a department of instruction (as in a college) <an opening now exists for *chairperson* of the Department of Oral Surgery at the School of Dentistry —*advt*>

chamberlain* *n* : an often honorary papal attendant; *specif* : a priest having a rank of honor below domestic prelate

Chan·dler's wobble \ˌchandlə(r)z-, -nl-\ *n* [Seth Carlo *Chandler* †1913 Am. astronomer] : an elliptical oscillation of the earth's axis of rotation with a period of 14 months whose cause has not been determined

changing room *n, Brit* : a room where one may change clothes; *esp* : one for use by sports participants : a locker room

channel* *n* : a path along which information passes or an area (as of magnetic tape) on which it is stored

chan·nery \ˈchan(ə)rē, -ri\ *adj* [Sc, gravelly, fr. *channer* gravel, alter. of *channel* gravel, channel; fr. gravel's being a major constituent of the channel of a river] : containing more than 15 percent but less than 90 percent fragments of thin flat sandstone, limestone, or schist up to 6 inches along the longer axis <*channery* soil>

character* *n* : a symbol (as a letter or number) that represents information; *also* : a representation (as by a series of ones and zeros) of such a character that may be accepted by a computer

characteristic* *n* : the smallest positive integer *n* which for an operation in a ring or field yields 0 when any element is used *n* times with the operation

characteristic equation *n* : an equation in which the characteristic polynomial of a matrix is set equal to 0

characteristic poly·no·mi·al \-ˌpäləˌnōmēəl\ *n* : the determinant of a square matrix in which an arbitrary variable (as *x*) is subtracted from each of the elements along the principal diagonal

characteristic root *n* : a scalar associated with a given linear transformation of a vector space and having the property that there is some nonzero vector which when multiplied by the scalar is equal to the vector obtained by letting the transformation operate on the vector <if $T(v) = \lambda v$, where T is a linear transformation, v is a nonzero vector, and λ is a scalar, then λ is a *characteristic root* of T, and v is a characteristic vector

of *T* corresponding to λ > ; *specif* : a root of the characteristic equation of a matrix — called also *characteristic value*

characteristic vector *n* : a nonzero vector that is mapped by a given linear transformation of a vector space onto a vector that is the product of a scalar multiplied by the original vector — called also *eigenvector*

char·broil \'chär,brȯil, 'chȧ,-, *esp before a pause or consonant* -ȯiəl\ *vt* [*char*coal + *broil*] : to broil on a rack over hot charcoal

charge con·ju·ga·tion \-,känjə'gāshən\ *n* : an operation in mathematical physics in which each particle in a system is replaced by its antiparticle

chau·vin·ism* \'shōvə̇,nizəm\ *n* : an attitude of superiority toward members of the opposite sex; *also* : behavior expressive of such an attitude < maintain that it is a sexist fallacy to fight male *chauvinism* with female *chauvinism* —Lynn Z. Bloom >

check off* *vt* : to change (a football play called in the huddle) at the line of scrimmage

checkout \'chek,au̇t\ *n* **1** : the process of examining and testing something as to readiness for intended use < facilities for the manufacture, testing, assembly, and *checkout* of launch vehicles and spacecraft —George E. Mueller > **2** : the process of familiarizing oneself with the operation of a mechanical thing (as an airplane) < training that must include *checkout* on several types of multiengine airplanes —*Plane Talk*>

chef's salad \'shef'saləd\ *n* : a meal-size salad that usu. includes lettuce, tomatoes, celery, hard-boiled eggs, and julienne strips of meat and cheese

che·la·tor \'kē,lād·ə(r)\ *n* : a binding agent that suppresses chemical activity by forming chelates

che·mo·nu·cle·ar \'kemō'n(y)üklēə(r), 'kēmō-, ÷ -kyələ(r)\ *adj* : being or relating to a chemical reaction induced by nuclear radiation or fission fragments

che·mo·sen·so·ry \-'sen(t)s(ə)rē, -ri\ *adj* : related to or involved in the sensory reception of chemical stimuli < *chemosensory* hairs > < *chemosensory* responses >

che·mo·sphere \'kemə,sfi(ə)r, 'kēmə-, -,sfiə\ *n* : a stratum of the upper atmosphere in which photochemical reactions are prevalent and which begins about 20 miles above the earth's surface

che·mo·ster·il·ant \'kemō'sterələnt, 'kēmō-\ *n* : a substance that produces irreversible sterility (as of an insect) without marked alteration of mating habits or life expectancy — see APHOLATE — **che·mo·ster·il·iza·tion** \-,sterələ'zāshən, -,lī'z-\ *n* — **che·mo·ster·il·ize** \-'sterə,līz\ *vb*

che·mo·sur·gery \-'sərj(ə)rē, -'səj-, -'səij-, -ri\ *n* : removal by chemical means of diseased or unwanted tissue — **che·mo·sur·gi·cal** \-jə̇kəl\ *adj*

che·mo·tax·on·o·my \-,tak'sänəmē, -mi\ *n* : the classification of plants and animals based on similarities and differences in biochemical composition — **che·mo·taxo·nom·ic** \-,taksə'nämik\ *adj*— **che·mo·tax·o·nom·i·cal·ly** \-k(ə)lē, -li\ *adv*— **che·mo·tax·on·o·mist** \-,tak'sänəmə̇st\ *n*

cheong·sam \'cheu̇ŋ'säm, 'chȯŋ-\ *n* [Chin (Cant) *ch'eung shaam,* lit., long gown] : a dress with a slit skirt and a mandarin collar worn esp. by Oriental women

chiao \'jau̇\ *n, pl* **chiao** [Chin (Pek) *chiao*^{3}] **1** : a monetary unit of China equal to $^1/_{10}$ yuan **2** : a coin or note representing one chiao

Chi·ca·na \chi'känə, shi-, -kȧn-\ *n* [*Chicano* + -*a* (fr. Sp, fem. ending)] : a female Chicano — **Chicana** *adj*

chi·cane* \shə̇'kān, chə̇-\ *n* : a series of tight turns in opposite directions in an otherwise straight stretch of a road-racing course

chi·ca·nis·mo \chi'kä'niz(,)mō, shi-, -kȧ-, -is(,)mō\ *n, often cap* [*Chicano* + *-ismo* (fr. Sp, -ism)] : strong ethnic pride exhibited by Chicanos

Chi·ca·no \chi'kän(,)ō, shi-, -kȧn-\ *n, pl* **-nos** [modif. of Sp *mejicano* Mexican, fr. *Méjico* Mexico] : an American of Mexican descent — **Chicano** *adj*

chick·en–and–egg \,chik(ə̇)nən(d)'eg, -'āg\ *adj* [fr. the proverbial question of whether the chicken or the egg first came into being] : of, relating to, or being a dilemma of cause and effect or of priority < a *chicken-and-egg* affair: it isn't easy to say which came first, the parts or the boys with the ability to play them —Christopher Ford > < my problem is a *chicken-and-egg* one. To provide the goodies that will interest people, I need money and I don't like to hit people for money unless I can provide services that they need —P.J. Rich >

chicken Ki·ev \-'kē,(y)ef, -,(y)ev, -,(y)əf\ *n* [fr. *Kiev,* U.S.S.R.] : a boned chicken breast that is stuffed with seasoned butter and deep fried

chicken Tet·raz·zi·ni \-,te·trə¦zēnē, -ni\ *n* [Luisa *Tetrazzini* †1940 It. opera singer] : an au gratin dish consisting of chicken meat, noodles, mushrooms, and almonds in a velouté sauce

Chien ware \chē'en,-\ *also* **Chien yao** \-n¦yau̇\ *n* [Chin (Pek) *ch'ien yao²*, fr. *Ch'ien-an,* locality in China where it was first made + Chin (Pek) *yao²* pottery] : a dark Chinese stoneware dating from the Sung period, usu. having a black brown-mottled glaze, and usu. used for tea ware

child·proof \'chīl(d),prüf\ *adj* : designed to prevent tampering by children <a *childproof* door lock> <fences or other *childproof* ramparts —W.E. Homan>

chill factor *n* : WINDCHILL

Chil·tern Hundreds \,chiltə(r)n-\ *n pl* [fr. *Chiltern Hundreds,* three hundreds in the Chiltern hills of England appointment to the stewardship of which is a disqualification for membership in Parliament] : a nominal appointment granted by the British crown that serves as a legal fiction to enable a member of Parliament to relinquish his seat

chi·me·rism \kī'mi(ə)r,izəm, kə̇-, 'kīmə,riz-\ *n* : the state of being a genetic chimera

Chinese fire drill *n* : a state of great confusion or disorder <we had a *Chinese fire drill* here. Pandemonium broke loose. Everybody was running around calling everybody he knew asking for help —Nareid Maxey>

chip* *n* : INTEGRATED CIRCUIT

chi·ral \'kī(ə)rəl\ *adj* [*chir-* hand (deriv. of Gk *cheir*) + *-al* relating to] : of or relating to a molecule that is nonsuperimposable on its mirror image — **chi·ral·i·ty** \kī'ralə̇d·ē, kə̇'-\ *n*

chi–square distribution \'kī¦skwa(ə)r-, -¦skwe(ə)r-\ *n* : a probability density function that gives the distribution of the sum of the squares of a number of independent random variables each having a normal distribution with zero mean and unit variance, that has the property that the sum of two random variables with such a distribution also has one, and that is widely used in testing statistical hypotheses esp. about the theoretical and observed values of a quantity and about population variances and standard deviations

chit·lin circuit \'chitlə̇n-\ *n* [fr. the assumption that chitterlings are eaten chiefly by blacks] : the aggregate of theaters and nightclubs that feature black entertainers

chlor·am·bu·cil \klōr'ambyə,sil, klȯr-\ *n* [*chlor*oethyl + *am*ino + *bu*tyri*c* + *-il* related substance] : a nitrogen mustard derivative $C_{14}H_{19}Cl_2NO_2$ used esp. to treat leukemias and Hodgkin's disease

chlor·di·az·epox·ide \,klōrdī,azə̇'päk,sīd, ,klȯr-\ *n* [*chlor-* containing chlorine + *diaz-* containing the group N_2 + *epoxide*] : a compound $C_{16}H_{14}ClN_3O$ the hydrochloride of which is used as a tranquilizer in the treatment of various psychoneuroses and alcoholism

chlor·mer·o·drin \klōr'merədrə̇n, klȯr-\ *n* [*chlor-* + *mer*cury + connective *-o-* + -hy*drin* chemical compound containing halogen or cyanogen] : a mercurial diuretic $C_5H_{11}ClHgN_2O_2$ used in the treatment of some forms of edema, ascites, and nephritis

chlor·prop·amide \-'präpə,mīd, -prōp-, -əmə̇d\ *n* [*chlor-* + *prop*ane + *amide*] : a sulfonyl urea compound $C_{10}H_{13}ClN_2O_3S$ used to reduce blood sugar in the treatment of mild diabetes

choke* *vi* **choked; chok·ing** : to lose one's composure and fail to perform effectively in a critical situation <but they did lose . . . . Why? Overconfident? Maybe. Peaked too soon? Maybe. Got behind and *choked*? Maybe. —Dan Jenkins> <we *choked,* we made a lot of errors. . . . I think we felt the pressure today —Bill North>

cho·le·sta·sis \,kōlə'stāsə̇s, ,käl-\ *n, pl* **-sta·ses** \-'stā,sēz\ [NL, fr. *chol-* bile, gall (deriv. of Gk *cholē, cholos* gall) + *-stasis* stoppage, deriv. of Gk *stasis* standing, stopping] : a checking or failure of bile flow — **cho·le·stat·ic** \¦kōlə¦stad·ik, ¦käl-\ *adj*

cho·li·no·lyt·ic \¦kōlənō¦lid·ik, ¦käl-\ *adj* [ISV acetyl*choline* + connective *-o-* + *-lytic* of decomposition, fr. Gk *lytikos* able to loose, fr. *lyein* to loose] : interfering with the action of acetylcholine or cholinergic agents — **cholinolytic** *n*

cho·li·no·mi·met·ic \-mə̇¦med·ik, -(ˌ)mī¦-\ *adj* [ISV acetyl*choline* + connective *-o-* + *mimetic*] : resembling acetylcholine or simulating its physiologic action — **cholinomimetic** *n*

Chom·skian *or* **Chom·skyan** \ˈchäm(p)skēən, -ȯm-, -kyən\ *adj* [Avram Noam *Chomsky* b1928 Am. linguist] : of, relating to, or based on the linguistic theories of Noam Chomsky <the applicability of a *Chomskian* transformation is determined by comparison of two syntactic structures —D.G. Hays>

chopper* *n* : a customized motorcycle

chord organ *n* : an electronic or reed organ with buttons for producing simple chords

chrome* \ˈkrōm\ *n* : something plated with an alloy of chromium

chug·a·lug \¦chəgə¦ləg\ *vb* **-lugged; -lug·ging** [imit.] *vt* : to drink a whole container of without pause <*chugalugged* his beer, and . . . called out for another draft —M.J. Bosse> ~ *vi* : to drink a whole container (as of beer) without pause

church key *n* : a can opener with a triangular pointed head for piercing the tops of cans (as of beer) <killed the six-pack, two cans apiece, opening them with a *church key* and drinking right out of the cans —Kay Martin>

churn* *vt* : to subject (a client's security account) to excessive numbers of purchases and sales primarily to generate additional commissions <revoked the registration of several firms which have *churned* the accounts —*Frauds & Quackery Affecting the Older Citizen*>

chutz·pah *also* **chutz·pa** *or* **hutz·pah** *or* **hutz·pa** \ˈk̲u̇tspə, ˈhu̇-, -(ˌ)spä\ *n* [Yiddish, fr. LHeb *ḥuṣpāh*] : supreme self-confidence : nerve, gall <flaunted her newfound grooviness with characteristic *chutzpah* by smoking a joint onstage —Ed McCormack>

ciao \ˈchau̇\ *interj* [It, fr. It dial., alter. of *schiavo* (I am your) slave, fr. ML *sclavus* slave] — used conventionally as an utterance at meeting or parting

ci·lan·tro \sə̇ˈläntrō, -lan-\ *n* [Sp, coriander, fr. LL *coliandrum,* alter. of L *coriandrum*] : leaves of coriander used as a flavoring or garnish

cine·an·gio·car·di·og·ra·phy \¦sinēˌanjēōˌkärdē¦ägrəfē\ *n* [*cine-* motion picture (fr. *cinema*) + *angiocardiography*] : motion-picture photography of a fluoroscopic screen recording passage of a contrasting medium through the chambers of the heart and large blood vessels — **cine·an·gio·car·dio·graph·ic** \-dēə¦grafik, -ēk\ *adj*

cine·an·gi·og·ra·phy \-ˌanjē¦ägrəfē\ *n* : motion-picture photography of a fluorescent screen recording passage of a contrasting medium through the blood vessels — **cine·an·gio·graph·ic** \-ˌanjēə¦grafik, -ēk\ *adj*

cinéma vé·ri·té \-¦verə̇¦tā\ *n* [F *cinéma-vérité* truth cinema] : the art or technique of filming a motion picture (as a documentary) so as to convey candid realism

cine·phile \ˈsinə̇ˌfīl\ *n* [*cine-* + *-phile* lover, deriv. of Gk *philos* beloved, loving] : a devotee of motion pictures

cir·ca·di·an \(ˌ)sərˈkādēən, ¦sərkə¦dēən\ *adj* [L *circa* about + *dies* day + E *-an,* adj. suffix] : being, having, characterized by, or occurring in approximately 24 hour periods or cycles (as of biological activity or function) <*circadian* oscillations> <*circadian* periodicity> <*circadian* rhythm in hatching> <*circadian* leaf movements>

circ·an·nu·al \(ˈ)sər¦kanyə(wə)l\ *adj* [L *circa* about + E *annual*] : having, characterized by, or occurring in approximately yearly periods or cycles (as of biological activity or function) <*circannual* rhythmicity>

cir·cum·plan·e·tary \¦sərkəm¦planəˌterē, ¦sə̄k-, ¦səik-\ *adj* [*circum-* around, about (fr. L, fr. *circum,* fr. *circus* circle) + *planetary*] : surrounding and relatively close to a planet <*circumplanetary* space>

cir·cum·so·lar \-¦sōlə(r), -ˌlär, -ˌlȧ(r\ *adj* : revolving about or surrounding the sun <a *circumsolar* orbit>

cir·cum·stel·lar \-¦stelə(r)\ *adj* : surrounding or occurring in the vicinity of a star <*circumstellar* dust>

cir·cum·ter·res·tri·al \-tə¦rest(r)ēəl, -¦res(h)chəl\ *adj* : revolving about or surrounding the earth <a *circumterrestrial* orbit>

cis·lunar \(ˈ)sis¦lünə(r), -ˌnär, -ˌnȧ(r\ *adj* [*cis* on this side (fr. L) + *lunar*] : of or relating to the space between the earth and the moon or the moon's orbit

cis·ter·na* \sis'tərnə\ *n, pl* **-nae** \-ˌnē\ : one of the interconnected flattened vesicles or tubules comprising the endoplasmic reticulum

cis·tron \'siˌsträn\ *n* [*cis-trans* + *-on* basic hereditary component] : a segment of DNA which specifies a single functional unit (as a protein or enzyme) and within which two heterozygous and closely linked recessive mutations are expressed in the phenotype when on different homologous chromosomes but not when on the same chromosome — compare OPERON — **cis·tron·ic** \si'stränik\ *adj*

citizen's arrest *n* : an arrest made by a citizen who derives his authority from the fact that he is a citizen

citizens band *n* : one of the frequency bands that in the U.S. is allocated officially for private radio communications

citrus red mite *n* : a comparatively large mite (*Panonychus citri*) that is a destructive pest on the foliage of citrus — called also *citrus red spider*

city·bil·ly \'sid·ēˌbilē, -d·iˌ-, -li\ *n, pl* **-bil·lies** [*city* + hill*billy*] : a musician or singer brought up in a city who performs country music

clad* *adj, of a coin* : consisting of outer layers of one metal bonded to a core of a different metal

cla·dis·tic \klə'distik, kla'-, -ēk\ *adj* [*clad-* (fr. Gk *klados* branch) + *-istic,* adj. suffix] : based on shared lines of evolutionary descent < *cladistic* relationships are usually determined from phenetic evidence > — compare PHENETIC — **cla·dis·ti·cal·ly** \-tək(ə)lē, -tēk-, -li\ *adv*

cla·dis·tics \-iks, -ēks\ *n pl but sing in constr* : biological systematics based on cladistic relationships

clado·gen·e·sis \ˌkladə'jenəsəs\ *n* [NL, fr. Gk *klados* branch + *genesis*] : evolutionary change characterized by treelike branching of lines of descent — **clado·ge·net·ic** \ˌkladōjə'ned·ik, -ēk\ *adj* — **clado·ge·net·i·cal·ly** \-k(ə)lē, li\ *adv*

clang·er \'klaŋə(r)\ *n, Brit* : a conspicuous blunder — often used in the phrase *drop a clanger* <the Inland Revenue dropped an outsize *clanger.* It sent an income tax form to Samuel Pepys, the diarist who died in 1703 —Nicholas Holmes>

clapped–out \ˌklap'daủt\ *adj, Brit* : exhausted or worn-out esp. from hard use or hard work <many flights, sometimes in *clapped-out* aircraft —*Times Lit. Supp.*> <they start in slaving . . . at crack of dawn and by the time I get there for dinner, everybody's *clapped-out* —Patrick Ryan>

class* *n* **1** : a group of adjacent and discrete or continuous values of a random variable **2** : a mathematical set

class action *n* : a legal action undertaken by one or more plaintiffs on behalf of themselves and all other persons having an identical interest in the alleged wrong

clath·rate \'klaˌthrāt, 'klathrət\ *n* : a clathrate compound

clath·ra·tion \kla'thrāshən\ *n* : the process of clathrate formation

clean* *adj* **1** : free from drug addiction <an addict's baby is often born addicted; these children were born *clean* —Gertrude Samuels> **2** : having no drugs in one's possession <the severe lack of drugs, since . . . everybody seemed to have come up to New Haven *clean* —*East Village Other*>

clean room \'klēnˌrüm, -ˌrủm\ *n* : a room for the manufacture or assembly of objects (as precision parts) that is maintained at a high level of cleanliness by special means

clear–air tur·bu·lence \ˌkli(ə)r'a(ə)r'tərbyələn(t)s, -'e(ə)r-\ *n* : sudden severe turbulence occurring in cloudless regions that causes violent jarring or buffeting of aircraft passing through

clear·way \'kli(ə)rˌwā, 'kliəˌ-\ *n, Brit* : an expressway with fully controlled access : a freeway

cleaver* *n* : a rock ridge protruding from a glacier or snowfield

cleft sentence *n* : a sentence produced by a transformation which adds *what* to the beginning and a form of the verb *be* to the end of the original sentence and removes a noun phrase from its original position to follow *be* <the sentence "George likes gin" yields the *cleft sentence* "What George likes is gin">

client state *n* : a country that is economically, politically, or militarily dependent on another country <Congress is going to cut back on military aid to *client states* and raise barriers against new military involvement —Tris Coffin>

Clio \'klē(,)ō\ *n* [L *Clio,* the Greek muse of history, fr. Gk *Kleiō*] : any of several statuettes awarded annually by a professional organization for notable achievement in radio and television commercials

clock* *n* : a synchronizing device (as in a computer) that produces pulses at regular intervals

clock radio *n* : a combination clock and radio device in which the clock can be set to turn on the radio at a designated time

clo·fi·brate \klō'fīb,rāt, -'fib-\ *n* [perh. fr. *chlo*rine + *fibr-* fiber + propion*ate*] : a compound $C_{12}H_{15}ClO_3$ used esp. in the treatment of hypercholesterolemia

clo·mi·phene \'kläma̧,fēn, 'klōm-\ *n* [*chlo*rine + a*mi*ne + *-phene* (fr. *phenyl*)] : a synthetic drug $C_{26}H_{28}ClNO$ used in the form of its citrate to induce ovulation

clone \'klōn\ *vt* **cloned; clon·ing** : to culture as or cause to grow as a clone; *specif:* to grow (a genetically identical individual) from a single somatic cell of a given organism

closed* *adj* **1** : traced by a moving point that returns to an arbitrary starting point < *closed* curve > ; *also* : so formed that every plane section is a closed curve < *closed* surface > **2** : characterized by mathematical elements that when subjected to an operation produce only elements of the same set < the set of whole numbers is *closed* under addition and multiplication > **3** : containing all the limit points of every subset < a *closed* set >

closed loop *n* : an automatic control system for an operation or process in which feedback in a closed path or group of paths acts to maintain the output at the desired level

closet* *adj* : being so in private : secret < a *closet* racist > < pretending to be a tough-minded naturalist when he's really a *closet* transcendentalist —J.R. Frakes >

closet queen *n* : one who is a latent or a covert homosexual

closing* *n* : a meeting between parties to a real-estate deal usu. together with their attorneys and interested parties (as a mortgagor) for the purpose of formally transferring title

closing costs *n pl* : expenses (as for appraisal, title search, and title insurance) connected with the purchase of real estate that usu. constitute a charge against the purchaser additional to the cost of the property purchased

closure* *n* **1** : the property that a number system or a set has when it is mathematically closed under an operation **2** : a set that contains a set and all limit points of the set

cloud nine *n* [perh. fr. the ninth and highest heaven of Dante's Paradise, whose inhabitants are most blissful because nearest to God] : a feeling of extreme well-being or elation — usu. used with *on* < was on *cloud nine* after his victory > < the A-flat major Ballade which lifted the body of listeners out of their collective seats and gave them a ride on *cloud nine* —L.I. Snyder >

clout* *n* : ability or power to affect something (as a political decision) : influence, pull < the oil lobby, the labor lobby, the doctors' lobby, the postal lobby, the people with the money and the *clout* again and again exercise undue influence upon the nation's legislators —*Parade Mag.* >

clox·a·cil·lin \ˌkläksəˈsilən\ *n* [*chl*orophenol + is*oxa*zole + peni*cillin*] : a synthetic oral penicillin $C_{19}H_{17}ClN_3NaO_5S$ esp. effective against staphylococci because of resistance to their penicillinases

cloze \'klōz\ *adj* [by shortening & alter. fr. *closure*] : of, relating to, or being a test of reading comprehension that involves having the person being tested supply words which have been systematically deleted from a text

cluster* *n* : a group of buildings and esp. houses built close together on a sizable tract in order to preserve open spaces larger than the individual yard for common recreation

cluster college *n* : a small residential college constituting a semiautonomous division of a university and usu. specializing in one branch of knowledge (as history and the social sciences)

CN* *abbr* chloroacetophenone

co·adapt·ed \ˌkōəˈdaptəd\ *adj* [*co-* with, together (fr. L) + *adapted*] : mutually adapted esp. by natural selection < *coadapted* gene complexes >

Co·an·da effect \kōˈandə-, -än-\ *n* [Henri *Coanda* †1972 Romanian engineer] : the tendency of a jet of fluid emerging from an orifice to follow an adjacent flat or curved surface and to entrain fluid from the surroundings so that a region of lower pressure develops

cobblers \ˈkäblə(r)z\ *n pl* [fr. *cobblers' awls,* rhyming slang for *balls*] *Brit* : foolish or insincere talk : nonsense, bunk <I'll bet he gives them that spiel at every house he goes to — he was word perfect. It was all a load of *cobblers* —Bill Naughton>

CO·BOL \ˈkō,bȯl\ *n* [*co*mmon *b*usiness *o*riented *l*anguage] : a standardized business language for programming a computer

co·chro·mat·o·graph \,kō(,)krōˈmad·ə,graf\ *vi* : to undergo separation out of a mixed sample by cochromatography <a compound that *cochromatographs* with farnesol> ~ *vt* : to subject to cochromatography

co·chro·ma·tog·ra·phy \,kō,krōməˈtägrəfē, -fi\ *n* : chromatography of two or more samples together; *esp* : identification of an unknown substance by chromatographic comparison with a known substance

cock·a·ma·my *or* **cock·a·ma·mie** \ˈkäkə,māmē\ *adj* [prob. fr. *cockamamie* decal, alter. of *decalcomania*] : being ridiculous or unbelievable : absurd <of all the *cockamamy* excuses I ever heard —Leo Rosten> <if you ever bring us a *cockamamie* script like this again we'll ban you from the studio for life —Art Buchwald>

code* *n* : GENETIC CODE

code* *vi* : to specify the genetic code

code–switch·ing \ˈkōd¦swichiŋ\ *n* : the switching from the linguistic system of one language or dialect to that of another

co·dom·i·nant* \(ˈ)kō¦dämənənt\ *adj* : being fully expressed in the heterozygous condition <the blood groups O, A, B, and AB are controlled by *codominant* alleles>

co·don \ˈkō,dän\ *n* [*code* + *-on* basic hereditary component] : a triplet of adjacent nucleotides that is part of the genetic code and that specifies a particular amino acid in a protein or starts or stops protein synthesis

cods·wal·lop \ˈkädz,wäləp, -wȯl-\ *n* [origin unknown] *chiefly Brit* : foolish or worthless talk or writing : nonsense, drivel <from which the author manages to soar sympathetically above his own fuzzy *codswallop* —Mordecai Richler> <shall continue to attack their philosophy for the dangerous *codswallop* that it is —*The People*>

co·en·zy·mat·ic \¦kō,enzə¦mad·ik, *also* -,zī¦-\ *adj* : of or relating to a coenzyme <*coenzymatic* activity> — **co·en·zy·mat·i·cal·ly** \-mad·ək(ə)lē\ *adv*

co·en·zyme Q \(ˈ)kō¦en,zīmˈkyü\ *n* [*Q* prob. fr. *quinone*] : UBIQUINONE

coes·ite \ˈkō,zīt\ *n* [Loring *Coes,* Jr., *b*1915 Am. chemist] : a dense crystalline silica formed from quartz under great heat and pressure and found in meteorite craters

coffee lightener *or* **coffee whit·en·er** \-¦(h)wīt(ᵊ)nə(r)\ *n* : a nondairy product used as a substitute for cream in coffee

cog·ni·tive dissonance \¦kägnəd·iv-\ *n* : internal psychological conflict resulting from incongruous beliefs and attitudes held simultaneously

co·he·sion·less \kōˈhēzhənləs, -,les\ *adj* : composed of particles or granules that tend not to cohere <*cohesionless* soils>

co·in·ci·dent* \kōˈin(t)sədənt, -dᵊnt, -,dent\ *or* **coincident indicator** *n* : an economic indicator (as level of personal income or of retail sales) that more often than not correlates directly with the state of the economy

co·in·sti·tu·tion·al \¦kō,instə¦t(y)üshnəl, -shənᵊl\ *adj* : of, relating to, or being a high school having separate class or activity areas for boys and girls

cold duck *n* [trans. of G *kalte ente,* a drink made of a mixture of fine wines] : a beverage that consists of a blend of sparkling burgundy and champagne

cold weld *vi* : to adhere on contact without application of pressure or heat — used of metals in the vacuum of outer space

col·i·ci·no·ge·nic \¦käləsənə¦jenik, -,sēn-, -jēn-, -ēk\ *adj* [*colicin* + connective *-o-* + *-genic* producing] **1** : producing or having the capacity to produce colicins <*colicinogenic* bacteria> **2** : conferring the capacity to produce colicins <*colicinogenic* genetic material> — **col·i·ci·no·ge·nic·i·ty** \-nəjəˈnis(ə)d·ē, -i\ *n*

col·i·ci·nog·e·ny \,käləsəˈnäjənē, -ni\ *n* : the capacity to produce colicins

co·lin·ear* \(ˈ)kō¦linēə(r)\ *adj* : having corresponding parts arranged in the same linear order <a gene and the protein it determines are *colinear*> — **co·lin·ear·i·ty** \(,)kō,linēˈarəd·ē\ *n*

co·lis·tin \kə'listən, kō-\ *n* [NL *colistinus*, specific epithet of the bacterium producing it] : a polymyxin antibiotic produced by a bacterium (*Bacillus colistinus*) from Japanese soil and used in the treatment of some gastrointestinal infections

col·la·gen·o·lyt·ic \ˌkäləjənə'lid·ik, -ˌjen-, -ēk\ *adj* [*collagen* + connective *-o-* + *-lytic* of decomposition, fr. Gk *lytikos* able to loose, fr. *lyein* to loose] : relating to or having the capacity to break down collagen <*collagenolytic* activity> <*collagenolytic* enzyme>

col·lap·sar \kə'lapˌsär\ *n* [*collapse* + *-ar* (as in *quasar*] : BLACK HOLE

col·le·gi·al·i·ty* \kəˌlējē'aləd·ē\ *n* : the participation of bishops in the government of the Roman Catholic Church in collaboration with the pope

col·or–blind* \'kələ(r)ˌblīnd\ *adj* : not recognizing differences of race <*color-blind* policy which refused to record anything about the race of welfare recipients —D.P. Moynihan>; *esp* : free from racial prejudice <would become, in reality, a white man with an invisible black skin in a *color-blind* community —James Farmer>

col·or·cast·er \-ˌkastə(r), -ȧs-\ *n* [*color* picturesqueness + broad*caster*] : a broadcaster (as of a sports contest) who supplies vivid or picturesque details and often gives statistical or analytical information

color–code \ˈkələ(r)ˌkōd\ *vt* : to color (as wires or pipes) according to a key designed to facilitate identification

color–field \ˈkələ(r)ˌfē(ə)ld\ *adj* : of, relating to, or being abstract painting in which color is emphasized and form and surface are correspondingly de-emphasized <*color-field* abstractionists>

color painting *n* : color-field painting — **color painter** *n*

COM *abbr* computer-output microfilm; computer-output microfilmer

com·bi·na·to·ri·al* \kəmˌbīnə'tōrēəl, ˌkämbənə-, -'tȯr-\ *adj* : of or relating to the arrangement, operation, and selection of mathematical elements within finite or discrete sets or states (as the set of possible states of a digital computer)

combinatorial to·pol·o·gy \-tə'päləjē\ *n* : a study that deals with geometric forms based on their decomposition into combinations of the simplest geometric figures

com·bi·na·to·rics \ˌkämbənə'tōriks, kəmˌbīn-, -'tȯr-\ *n pl but sing in constr* [*combinator*ial mathemat*ics*] : combinatorial mathematics

comb–out* \'kōˌmau̇t\ *n* : the combing of hair into a desired hairdo

come·back·er \'kəmˌbakə(r)\ *n* : a grounder in baseball hit directly to the pitcher

come on* *vi* : to project an indicated personal image <*comes on* gruff and laconic . . . on the telephone —Robert Craft>

command* *n* **1** : an electrical or electronic signal that actuates a device (as a control mechanism in a spacecraft or one step in a computer) **2** : the activation of a device in or the control of a vehicle (as a spacecraft) by means of a command

command mod·ule \-'mäj(ˌ)ü(ə)l\ *n* : a space vehicle module designed to carry the crew, the chief communication equipment, and the equipment for reentry

commentator* *n* : a layman who leads a congregation in prayer at Mass or explains the rituals performed by the priest

common market *n* : an economic unit formed to remove trade barriers among members

common trust fund *n* : a fund which is managed by a bank or trust company and in which the assets of many small trusts are handled as a single portfolio with individual beneficiaries receiving returns proportionate to their share of the principal

communication theory *or* **communications theory** *n* : a theory that deals with the technology of the transmission of information (as in the printed word or a computer) between men, men and machines, or machines and machines

community antenna television *n*: a system of television reception in which signals from distant stations are picked up by a tall or elevated antenna and sent by cable to the individual receivers of paying subscribers

com·mu·ta·tiv·i·ty \kəˌmyüd·ə'tivəd·ē, ˌkämyəd·ə'ti-\ *n* : the property of being commutative <the *commutativity* of a mathematical operation>

com·mu·ta·tor* \'kämyəˌtād·ə(r)\ *n* : an element of a mathematical group that when multiplied by the product of two given elements yields the product of the elements in reverse order

commute* *vi* **commut·ed; commut·ing :** to yield the same result regardless of order — used of two mathematical elements undergoing an operation or of two operations on elements

com·mute \kə'myüt\ *n* **1 :** an act or instance of commuting <his usual morning *commute* to work —*Newsweek*> **2 :** the distance covered in commuting <about an hour's *commute* from the university —*College Composition & Communication*>

comp \'kämp, 'kəmp\ *vi* [short for *accompany*] **:** to play an irregularly rhythmic jazz accompaniment

com·pact·ible \kəm'paktəbəl\ *adj* **:** capable of being compacted < *compactible* soils>

competence* *n* **1 :** readiness of bacteria to undergo genetic transformation **2 :** the knowledge which enables a person to speak and understand a language — contrasted with *performance*

competent* *adj* **:** having the capacity to respond (as by producing an antibody) to an antigenic determinant <immunologically *competent* cells>

competitive* *adj* **:** depending for effectiveness on the relative concentration of two or more substances < *competitive* inhibition of an enzyme>

com·pil·er* \kəm'pīlə(r)\ *n* **:** a computer program that automatically converts instructions written in a higher-level language (as FORTRAN or COBOL) into machine language

complement* *n* **:** the set of all elements that do not belong to a given set and are contained in a particular mathematical set containing the given set

com·ple·men·tar·i·ty* \ˌkämplə(ˌ)men·'tarəd·ē, -ləmən·-\ *n* **:** the capability for precise pairing between complementary strands or nucleotides of DNA or sometimes RNA

com·ple·men·ta·ry* \ˌkämplə'mentərē, -n·trē, -ri\ *adj* **:** characterized by the capacity for precise pairing of purine and pyrimidine bases between strands of DNA and sometimes RNA such that the structure of one strand determines the other

com·ple·men·ta·tion* \ˌkämpləmən·'tāshən, -lə(ˌ)men·-\ *n* **1 :** the determination of the complement of a given mathematical set **2 :** production of normal phenotype in an individual heterozygous for two closely related mutations with one on each homologous chromosome and at a slightly different position

complex con·ju·gate \-'känjəgət, -jēg-, -jəˌgāt\ *n* **1 :** one of two complex numbers (as $a + bi$ and $a - bi$) differing only in the sign of the imaginary part **2 :** a matrix whose elements and the corresponding elements of a given matrix form pairs of conjugate complex numbers

com·plex·om·e·try \ˌkämˌplek'sämə·trē, kəm-, -ri\ *n* [*complex* + connective *-o-* + *-metry* measuring, deriv. of Gk *metron* measure] **:** a titrimetric technique involving the use of a complexing agent (as EDTA) as the titrant — **com·plex·o·met·ric** \(ˌ)kämˌpleksə'me·trik, kəm-\ *adj*

com·po·nent* \kəm'pōnənt, 'kämˌpō-, käm'pō-\ *n* **:** a coordinate of a vector

composite* *adj, of a statistical hypothesis* **:** specifying a range of values for one or more statistical parameters —compare SIMPLE

computation* *n* **:** the use or operation of a computer

com·pu·ta·tion·al linguistics \ˌkämpyu̇'tāshnəl-, -shənᵊl-\ *n pl but usu sing in constr* **:** linguistic research carried out by means of a computer

compute* *vb* **comput·ed; comput·ing** *vt* **:** to determine or calculate by means of a computer ~ *vi* **:** to use a computer

com·put·er·ese \kəmˌpyüd·əˌrēz, -ütə-, -ēs\ *n* [*computer* + *-ese* jargon] **1 :** MACHINE LANGUAGE **2 :** jargon used by computer technologists

com·put·er·ite \-'pyüd·əˌrīt, -ütə-\ *n* **:** COMPUTERNIK

com·put·er·ize \kəm'pyüd·əˌrīz, -ütə-\ *vb* **-ized; -iz·ing** *vt* **1 :** to carry out or control by means of a computer < *computerized* typesetting> <planning to *computerize* their entire accounting systems —*Data Processing Mag.*> **2 :** to equip with computers <getting the rights but not the skills of a modern *computerized* society —J.B. Reston> ~ *vi* **:** to use computers <another advantage of *computerizing* is that the automatic printout virtually eliminated human error in transcribing data —*Consumer Reports*> — **com·put·er·iz·able** \-ˌpyüd·əˌrīzəbəl\ *adj* — **com·put·er·iza·tion** \-ˌpyüd·ərə'zāshən, -ˌrīz-\ *n*

com·put·er·like \-ˌpyüd·ə(r),līk\ *adj* : resembling or characteristic of a computer <handled with *computerlike* impersonality in anonymous offices —D.W. Harding>

com·put·er·nik \-ˈpyüdə(r),nik\ *n* [*computer* + *-nik*] : a person who works with or has a deep interest in computers

Com·sat \ˈkäm,sat\ *service mark* — used for communications services involving an artificial satellite

concave* *n* : a concave line or surface

con·cep·tu·al* \kənˈsepchə(wə)l, kän-, -ˈsepshwəl\ *adj* : of, relating to, or being conceptual art

conceptual art *n*: an art form in which the artist's intent is to convey a concept rather than to create an art object — **conceptual artist** *n*

con·crete* \ˈkän,krēt, känˈkrēt, -äŋ-\ *adj* : of or relating to concrete poetry <a *concrete* poet>

concrete* *n* **1** : CONCRETE POETRY **2** : a concrete poet

concrete poetry *n* : poetry in which the poet's intent is conveyed by the graphic patterns of letters, words, or symbols rather than by the conventional arrangement of words

con·cret·ism* \-ēd·,izəm\ *n* : the theory or practice of concrete poetry — **con·cret·ist** \-ēd·əst\ *n*

conditional* *adj* **1** : involving or yielding values that are conditional probabilities <a *conditional* distribution> **2** : eliciting a conditional response <a *conditional* stimulus> **3** : permitting survival only under special growth or environmental conditions <*conditional* lethal mutations>

conditional probability *n*: the probability that a given event will occur if it is certain that another event has taken place or will take place

conditioned* *adj* : CONDITIONAL 2 <a *conditioned* stimulus>

con·do \ˈkän(,)dō\ *n, pl* **condos** [short for *condominium*] : an individually owned unit in a multi-unit structure (as an apartment house) or complex : a condominium

con·fig·u·ra·tion* \kən,fig(y)əˈrāshən, ,kän-\ *n*: something (as a figure, contour, pattern, or apparatus) that results from a particular arrangement of parts or components; *esp* : a set of interconnected equipment forming a computer system

con·for·ma·tion·al \,kän(,)fó(r)ˈmāshnəl, -nfə(r)-, -shənᵊl\ *adj*: of, relating to, or being molecular conformation <*conformational* studies of proteins> — **con·for·ma·tion·al·ly** \-lē, -li\ *adv*

Cong \ˈkäŋ, ˈkóŋ\ *n, pl* **Cong** [short for *Vietcong*] : a member of the Vietcong

conglomerate* *n* : a widely diversified company; *esp* : a corporation that acquires other companies whose activities are unrelated to the corporation's primary activity

con·glom·er·a·tor \kənˈglämə,rād·ə(r)\ *n* : one who forms or heads a conglomerate

con·gru·ence* \kənˈgrüən(t)s, ˈkäŋgrəwən(t)s\ *n* : a statement that two numbers or mathematical expressions (as polynomials) are congruent with respect to a modulus

congruent *adj* : having the difference divisible by a given modulus <12 is *congruent* to 2 (modulo 5) since $12 - 2 = 2 \times 5$>

con·ju·gate* \ˈkänjəgət, -jēg-, -jə,gāt\ *n* : an element of a mathematical group that is equal to a given element of the group multiplied on the right by another element and on the left by the inverse of the latter element

con·ju·ga·tion* \,känjəˈgāshən\ *n* : the one-way transfer of DNA between bacteria in cellular contact

¹conk \ˈkäŋk, ˈkóŋk\ *vt* [prob. by shortening and alter. fr. *congolene*, a preparation used for straightening hair, prob. fr. *congolene*, a hydrocarbon produced from Congo copal, fr. *Congolese* + *-ene* unsaturated carbon compound] : to treat (as kinky hair) so as to straighten

²conk *n* : a hairstyle in which kinky hair is straightened out and flattened down or lightly waved

conservation of angular momentum : a principle in physics: the total angular momentum of a system free of external torque remains constant irrespective of transformations and interactions within the system

conservation of bary·ons \\-ˈbarēənz, -ˌänz\\ : a principle in physics: the number of baryons in an isolated system of elementary particles remains constant irrespective of transformations or decays

conservation of charge : a principle in physics: the total electric charge of an isolated system remains constant irrespective of whatever internal changes may take place

conservation of lep·tons \\-ˈlepˌtänz\\ : a principle in physics: the number of leptons in an isolated system of elementary particles remains constant irrespective of transformations or decays

conserve* *vt* **conserved; conserv·ing** : to maintain (a quantity) constant during a process of chemical or physical change < *conserve* angular momentum >

consistent* *adj* : tending to be arbitrarily close to the true value of the parameter estimated as the sample becomes large <a *consistent* statistical estimator>

console* *n* : the part of a computer used for communication between the operator and the computer

con·sol·i·da·tion* \\kənˌsäləˈdāshən\\ *n* : a period of backing and filling in a security or commodity market usu. following a strong run-up of prices and typically preceding a further active advance

constituent structure *n* : a formal representation of the grammatical structure of a sentence in terms of its individual constituents; *also* : the structure which such a representation describes

consumer* *n* : an organism requiring complex organic compounds for food which it obtains by preying on other organisms or by eating particles of organic matter — compare PRODUCER

con·sum·er·ism \\kənˈsüməˌrizəm\\ *n* **1** : the promotion of the consumer's interests < *consumerism* is undoubtedly a needed corrective to corporate excesses —L.E. Sissman > **2** : the theory that an increasing consumption of goods is economically desirable < our addiction to the concept of unlimited growth, the promotion of blatant *consumerism*, and the direction of much social and economic energy into frivolous aspects of society —F.H. Borman *et al* > — **con·sum·er·ist** \\-ərəst\\ *n*

con·sum·ma·to·ry* \\kənˈsəməˌtōrē, -ˌtȯr-, -i\\ *adj* : of, relating to, or being a response or act (as eating or copulating) that terminates a period of usu. goal-directed behavior

contact in·hi·bi·tion \\-ˌin(h)əˈbishən\\ *n* : cessation of cellular undulating movements upon contact with other cells with accompanying cessation of cell growth and division

con·tain·er·iza·tion \\kənˌtānərəˈzāshən, -ˌrīˈz-\\ *n* : a method of shipping whereby a considerable amount of material (as merchandise) is packed in large containers for more efficient handling

con·tain·er·ize \\kənˈtānəˌrīz\\ *vt* **-ized; -iz·ing** : to ship by containerization < *containerized* freight >

con·tain·er·ship \\-nə(r)ˌship\\ *n* : a ship esp. designed or equipped for carrying containerized cargo

con·tex·tu·al·ize \\kənˈtekschə(wə)ˌlīz, kän-\\ *vt* **-ized; -iz·ing** : to place (as a word or activity) in a context — **con·tex·tu·al·iza·tion** \\-ˌtekschə(wə)ləˈzāshən, -ˌlī\\ *n*

continental seating *n, often cap C* : theater seating with no center aisle and with room enough between rows to allow easy passage

continuous creation theory *n* : STEADY STATE THEORY

con·toid \\ˈkän-ˌtȯid\\ *n* [*con*sonan*t* + *-oid* resembling] : a speech sound of a phonetic rather than phonemic classification that includes most sounds traditionally treated as consonants and that excludes those (as English \\y\\, \\w\\, \\r\\, and \\h\\) which like vowels are characterized by the escape of air from the mouth over the center of the tongue without oral friction

con·tra·test \\ˈkän-trəˌtest\\ *adj* [*contra-* against (fr. L) + *test*] : of, relating to, or serving as an experimental control

control chart *n* : a chart kept to determine whether or not the number of defectives in a daily industrial operation exceeds reasonable expectation : quality control chart

convenience food *n* : a packaged food designed for quick and easy preparation

con·ver·gent lady beetle \\kənˈvərjənt-, -ˈvəj-, -ˈvəij-\\ *also* **convergent** *n* [fr. the two converging white lines on its prothorax] : a periodically migratory beneficial lady beetle (*Hippodamia convergens*) that feeds on various crop pests (as aphids)

conversation* *n* : an exchange similar to conversation; *esp* : real-time interaction with a computer esp. through a keyboard

conversation pit *n* : a usu. sunken area (as in a living room) with intimate seating that facilitates conversation

converse* *vi* **conversed; con·vers·ing** : to carry on an exchange similar to a conversation; *esp* : to interact with a computer

cookbook* : a book of detailed instructions

cooking top *n* : a built-in cabinet-top cooking apparatus consisting of four heating units for gas or electricity

cook·top \ˈku̇kˌtäp\ *n* : the flat top of a range

cool* *adj* : employing understatement and a minimum of detail to convey information and usu. requiring the listener, viewer, or reader to complete the message <another indication of the very *cool*. . . character of this medium —H.M. McLuhan>

cool* *vb* — **cool it** : to keep or regain control of one's emotions : go easy <everything would be much nearer to being all right if only everybody would *cool it* — get the mind back in tune with the body —*Times Lit. Supp.*>

co–opt* \(ˈ)kōˈäpt\ *vt* : to take in and make part of a group, movement, or culture : absorb <the students are *co-opted* by a system they serve even in their struggle against it —A.C. Danto>

coordinate* *adj* : of, relating to, or being a system of indexing by two or more terms so that documents may be retrieved through the intersection of index terms

coordinates* *n pl* : articles (as of clothing or furniture) designed to be used together and to attain their effect through pleasing contrast (as of color, material, or texture) <the shirt and the tie are color *coordinates*>

cop out* \(ˈ)käpˈau̇t\ *vi* : to back out (as of an unwanted responsibility) : evade — often used with *on* or *of* <young Americans who *cop out* on society —*Christian Science Monitor*> <*copping out* of jury duty through a variety of machinations —H.F. Waters>

cop–out \ˈkäpˌau̇t\ *n* **1** : an excuse for copping out : pretext **2** : the means for copping out **3** : one who cops out **4** : the act or an instance of copping out

coq au vin \ˌkōkōˈva^{n}, ˌkäk-, ˌko̊k-, -ko̊ˈv-, *F* ko̊kōva^{n}\ *n* [F, cock with wine] : chicken cooked in usu. red wine

cor·al·ene \ˈko̊rəˌlēn, ˈkär-\ *n* [irreg. fr. *coral*] **1** : a raised decoration of glass beading on glassware **2** : glassware with coralene decoration

cord·less \ˈko̊(ə)rdləs, -o̊(ə)d-\ *adj* : having no cord; *esp* : powered by a battery <*cordless* tools>

cor·don bleu* \ˌko̊rdō^{n}ˈblœ\ *adj, often cap C & B* **1 a** : of, relating to, or being a cook of great skill **b** : of, relating to, or being the food prepared by such a cook **2** : stuffed with ham and Swiss cheese <veal *cordon bleu*>

core* *n* **1** : a tiny doughnut-shaped piece of magnetic material (as ferrite) used in computer memories — called also *magnetic core* **2** *or* **core memory** *or* **core storage** : a computer memory consisting of an array of cores strung on fine wires

core city *n* : INNER CITY

co·re·pres·sor \ˌkōrəˈpresə(r)\ *n* : a substance that activates a particular genetic repressor by combining with it

corn chip *n* : a piece of a crisp dry snack food prepared from a seasoned cornmeal batter

corner* *adj* : of, relating to, or being a defensive football player who covers one of the flanks <*corner* linebacker> <*corner* positions>

cor·ner·back \ˈko̊rnərˌbak, *sometimes* ˈko̊nər-; ˈko̊(ə)nəˌbak\ *n* : a defensive back in football whose duties include defending the flank and covering a wide receiver

cor·ner·man \-ˌman, -mən\ *n* : one that is in a corner: as **a** : CORNERBACK **b** : a basketball forward

corn·row \ˈko̊(ə)rnˌrō, ˈko̊(ə)n-\ *vt* [fr. the fancied resemblance of the braids to rows of corn] : to style (hair) by dividing into sections that are braided usu. flat to the scalp in rows — **cornrow** *n*

co·ro·tate \(ˈ)kōˈrōˌtāt\ *vi* : to rotate in conjunction with or at the same rate as another rotating body — **co·ro·ta·tion** \ˌkō(ˌ)rōˈtāshən\ *n*

cor·pus al·la·tum \ˌkȯrpəsə'lād·əm, -äd-\ *n, pl* **cor·po·ra al·la·ta** \ˌkȯrpərə·ə'lād·ə, -äd- \ [NL, lit., applied body] : one of a pair of separate or fused bodies in many insects that are sometimes closely associated with the corpora cardiaca and secrete hormones (as juvenile hormone)

corpus car·di·a·cum \-pəskär'dīəkəm\ *n, pl* **cor·po·ra car·di·a·ca** \-pərəkär'dīəkə\ [NL, lit., cardiac body] : one of a pair of separate or fused bodies of nervous tissue in many insects that lie posterior to the brain and dorsal to the esophagus and function in the storage and secretion of brain hormone

co·set \'kōˌset\ *n* : a subset of a mathematical group that consists of all the products obtained by multiplying either on the right or the left a fixed element of the group by each of the elements of a given subgroup

cosmetic* *adj* : lacking in depth or thoroughness : superficial <bought up older homes in declining neighborhoods, fixed them up with *cosmetic* repairs, and sold them at inflated values —M.W. Karmin>

cos·met·i·cize \käz'med·əˌsīz\ *vt* **-cized; -ciz·ing** : to make (something unpleasant or ugly) superficially attractive <saw the singer whole; this is not a flack's *cosmeticized* biography —*Playboy*>

cos·mo·drome \'käzməˌdrōm\ *n* [Russ *Kosmodrom,* fr. *Kosmo*naut cosmonaut + *-drom* racecourse, large specially prepared place, deriv. of Gk *dromos* racecourse, act of running] : a Soviet aerospace center; *esp* : a Soviet spacecraft launching installation

cos·mo·gen·ic \ˌkäzməˌjenik\ *adj* [*cosmic* (*ray*) + connective *-o-* + *-genic* produced by] : produced by the action of cosmic rays <*cosmogenic* carbon 14>

cos·mo·nau·tics \ˌkäzmə'nȯd·iks, -näd-\ *n pl but usu sing in constr* : the science of the construction and operation of vehicles for travel in space beyond the earth's atmosphere : Soviet astronautics — **cos·mo·nau·tic** \-d·ik, -ēk\ *or* **cos·mo·nau·ti·cal** \-d·əkəl, -ēk-\ *adj*

cost–ef·fec·tive \'kȯstə'fektiv, -tēˌ-, *also* 'käst-\ *adj* : economical in terms of tangible benefits produced by money spent — **cost–ef·fec·tive·ness** \ˌkȯstə'fektivnəs, -tē'-, *also* ˌkäst-\ *n*

cost–push \'kȯs(t)ˌpu̇sh, *also* 'käs(t)-\ *n* : an increase or upward trend in production costs (as wages) that tends to result in increased consumer prices irrespective of the level of demand — compare DEMAND-PULL — **cost–push** \ˌkȯs(t)-, *also* ˌkäs(t)-\ *adj*

cot death *n, chiefly Brit* : SUDDEN INFANT DEATH SYNDROME

co·ter·mi·nal \(ˈ)kōˌtərmnəl, -mənᵊl\ *adj* : having different angular measure but with the vertex and sides identical—used of angles generated by the rotation of lines about the same point in a given line whose values differ by an integral multiple of 2π radians or of 360° <*coterminal* angles measuring 30° and 390°>

co·trans·duc·tion \ˌkōˌtran(t)s'dəkshən, -ˌtranz'-\ *n* : transduction involving two or more genetic loci carried by a single bacteriophage

cou·chette \kü'shet\ *n* [F, berth, bunk, dim. of *couche* bed, fr. MF] **1** : a compartment on a European passenger train so arranged that berths can be provided at night **2** : one of the berths in a couchette

cou·lom·bic \(ˈ)küˌläm(b)ik, kəˌl-, -lōm-\ *adj* : of or relating to electrostatic coulomb forces

cou·ma·phos \'küməˌfäs, -fȯs\ *n* [*Couma*rin, a toxic lactone + *phos*phorus] : an organophosphorus systemic insecticide and anthelmintic $C_{14}H_{16}ClO_5PS$ used esp. on cattle and poultry

count·abil·i·ty \ˌkau̇n(t)ə'biləd·ē, -i\ *n* : the quality or state of being countable

count·ably \'kau̇n(t)əblē, -li\ *adv* : in a way that is countable <*countably* infinite sets>

counter* *n* : a football play in which the ballcarrier goes in a direction opposite to the flow of play

coun·ter·con·di·tion·ing \ˌkau̇n(t)ə(r)kənˌdish(ə)niŋ\ *n* [*counter-* contrary, opposite (deriv. of L *contra* against, opposite) + *conditioning*] : conditioning in order to replace an undesirable response (as fear) to a stimulus (as an engagement in public speaking) by a favorable one

coun·ter·cul·ture \ˈkau̇n(t)ə(r),kəlchə(r)\ *n* : a culture esp. of the young with values and mores that run counter to those of established society — **coun·ter·cul·tur·al** \ˌkau̇n(t)ə(r)ˈkəlch(ə)rəl\ *adj* — **coun·ter·cul·tur·ist** \-ch(ə)rist\ *n*

coun·ter·ex·am·ple \ˈkau̇n(t)ərəg,zampəl\ *n* : an example that disproves a theorem or proposition; *broadly* : an example that is inconsistent with or contrary to what is typical or usual

coun·ter·in·sur·gen·cy \ˌkau̇n(t)ərinˈsərjən(t)sē\ *n* : organized activity designed to combat insurgency — **coun·ter·in·sur·gent** \-jənt\ *n*

coun·ter·in·tu·itive \-inˈt(y)üəd·iv\ *adj* : contrary to intuition <complex systems are *counterintuitive.* They behave in ways opposite to what most people expect —J.W. Forrester>

coun·ter·pho·bic \ˌkau̇n(t)ə(r)ˈfōbik\ *adj* : relating to, preferring, or seeking a situation that is feared

coun·ter·pro·duc·tive \-prəˈdəktiv\ *adj* : tending to hinder the attainment of a desired goal <violence as a means to achieve an end is *counterproductive* —W.E. Brock *b*1930>

coun·ter·pro·gram·ming \-ˈprō,gramiŋ, -ˈprōgrəmiŋ\ *n* : the scheduling of programs by television networks so as to attract audiences away from simultaneously telecast programs of competitors

coun·ter·pul·sa·tion \-,pəlˈsāshən\ *n* : a technique for reducing the work load on the heart by the automatic lowering of systemic blood pressure just before or during expulsion of blood from the ventricle and by the automatic raising of blood pressure during diastole

country* *adj* **1** : of or relating to country music <*country* singer> **2** : featuring country music <*country* radio stations>

country and western *adj, sometimes cap C&W* : having or using lyrics, style, or string instrumentation identified with country music of western U.S. origin

country rock *n* : ROCKABILLY

cour·gette \ku̇(ə)rˈzhet, ku̇əˈzhet\ *n* [F dial., dim. of *courge* gourd] *chiefly Brit* : a zucchini squash

courtesy light *n* : an interior automobile light that goes on automatically when a door is opened

cow·boy·ing \ˈkau̇,bȯi(·i)ŋ\ *n* : the work or occupation of a cowboy

CPI *abbr* consumer price index

CPU *abbr* central processing unit

crack·back \ˈkrakˈbak\ *n* : a blind-side block on a defensive back in football by a pass receiver who starts downfield and then cuts back toward the middle of the line

cram·be* \ˈkram(ˌ)bē\ *n* : an annual Mediterranean herb (*Crambe abyssinica*) cultivated as an oilseed crop

cranberry glass *n* : clear ruby glass usu. with a blue-violet tint

cra·nio·pha·ryn·gi·oma \ˌkrānē(ˌ)ōfə,rinjēˈōmə\ *n* [*cranio-* cranium + *pharyng-* pharynx + connective *-i-* + *-oma* tumor] : a neoplasm of the brain near the pituitary gland that occurs esp. in children or young adults and is often associated with increased intracranial pressure

crash* *vi* **1** *slang* : to return to a normal state after a drug-induced experience <the individual *crashing* from high-dose amphetamine abuse appears to be sleeping well a good deal of the time —Lester Grinspoon & Peter Hedblom> **2** *slang* : to go to bed for the night : sleep <sometimes we can't pay the rent and we *crash* around town, sleep in yards or at friends' houses —*East Village Other*>

crash pad* *n* : a place where free temporary lodging is available <storefront medical clinics and *crash pads* for runaway youths —Martin Oppenheimer>

crash·wor·thy \ˈkrash,wərt͟hē, -,wə̄t͟h-, -,wəit͟h-, -i\ *adj* [*crash* + *-worthy* (as in *seaworthy*)] : resistant to the effects of a collision <the ideal *crashworthy* car would have a strong passenger compartment —*Consumer Reports*> — **crash·wor·thi·ness** \-nə̇s\ *n*

crawl·er·way \ˈkrȯlə(r),wā\ *n* [fr. its slow-moving traffic] : a road built esp. for moving heavy rockets and spacecraft

crawl·way \ˌkrȯl-\ *n* : a low passageway (as in a cave) that can be traversed only by crawling

cray·fish·ing \ˈkrāˌfishiŋ\ *n* : the occupation or pastime of catching crayfish

crazy *n, pl* **crazies** : one who is or acts crazy <he said you were a *crazy* and always had been but that he trusted you —Ernest Hemingway>; *esp* : one associated with a radical or extremist political cause <candidates were not the *crazies* of the left but sensible and practical men —R.J. Gleason> <fall into the hands of . . . the right-wing *crazies* —H.S. Thompson>

C–re·ac·tive protein \ˈsē(ˌ)rēˌaktiv-\ *n* [*C*-polysaccharide, a polysaccharide found in the cell wall of pneumococci and precipitated by this protein, fr. *c*arbohydrate] : a protein present in blood serum in various abnormal states (as inflammation or neoplasia)

cre·den·tial·ism \krəˈdenchəˌlizəm, krēˈ-\ *n* : undue emphasis on credentials (as college degrees) as prerequisites to employment <to deemphasize *credentialism* will require that employers make greater efforts to evaluate applicants as individuals —D.L. Wolfle>

cred·i·bil·i·ty gap \ˌkredəˈbilədˌēˌgap\ *n* **1 a** : lack of trust <a special *credibility gap* is likely to open between the generations —Kenneth Keniston> **b** : lack of believability <a *credibility gap* created by contradictory official statements —Samuel Ellenport> **2** : an instance of being discrepant : discrepancy <the *credibility gap* between the professed ideals . . . and their actual practices —Jeanne L. Noble>

cred·it·wor·thy \ˈkredətˌwərthē, -ˌwəth-, -wəith-, -i\ *adj* : being financially sound enough to justify the extension of credit : having an acceptable credit rating — **cred·it·wor·thi·ness** \-nəs\ *n*

creeping* *adj* : developing or advancing slowly over a period of time <*creeping* urbanization> <*creeping* senility>

cre·mains \krəˈmānz, krēˈ-\ *n pl* [blend of *cremated* and *remains*] : the ashes of a cremated human body

crew sock *n* [fr. its use by rowing crews] : a short bulky usu. ribbed sock

crib death *n* : SUDDEN INFANT DEATH SYNDROME <*crib death* is the leading cause of mortality among infants more than a month old —Nicholas Wade>

cri du chat syndrome \ˌkrēdüˈshä-, -dəˈ-\ *n* [*cri du chat* fr. F, cry of the cat] : an inherited condition that is characterized by a mewing cry, mental retardation, physical anomalies, and the absence of part of a chromosome

crisis center *n* : a facility run usu. by nonprofessionals who counsel those who telephone for help in a personal crisis

cris·ta* \ˈkristə\ *n* : any of the inwardly projecting folds of the inner membrane of a mitochondrion

critical region *n* : the set of outcomes of a statistical test for which the null hypothesis is to be rejected

crock* *n* [fr. the phrase *crock of shit*] : insincere, pretentious, or misleading talk : bull — often used in the phrase *that's a crock*

cross–dis·ci·plin·ary \ˈkrȯsˈdisəpləˌnerē, *also* ˈkräs-, *esp Brit* -ˌdisəˈplinərē, -i\ *adj* : of, relating to, or involving two or more disciplines : interdisciplinary <*cross-disciplinary* study>

cross–dress \-ˈdres\ *vi* : to dress in the clothes of the opposite sex

cross multiply *vi* [back-formation fr. *cross multiplication*] : to find the two products obtained by multiplying the numerator of each of two fractions by the denominator of the other

cross–re·ac·tive \-(ˌ)rēˈaktiv\ *adj* : capable of undergoing cross-reaction — **cross–re·ac·tiv·i·ty** \-(ˌ)rēˌakˈtivədˌē, -i\ *n*

crown of thorns *or* **crown–of–thorns starfish** : a starfish (*Acanthaster planci*) of the Pacific region that is covered with long spines and is destructive to the coral of coral reefs

cruise* *vb* **cruised; cruis·ing** *vi* : to search (as in public places) for a sexual partner <to *cruise* for sex requires leisure —Laud Humphreys> ~ *vt* : to search in (a public place) for a sexual partner <*cruises* the singles bars for girls one night and the gay bars for homosexuals the next —A.W. Johnston>

crunch* *n* : a tight or critical situation: as **a** : a critical point in the buildup of pressure between opposing elements <if it came to the *crunch,* the small new states would succumb —*Times Lit. Supp.*> **b** : a severe economic squeeze (as on credit) <a *crunch* would cripple home mortgages, slow down mergers and acquisitions, and ultimately cut employment —Walter Fedor>

cryo·bi·ol·o·gy \ˌkrīō(ˌ)bīˈäləjē\ *n* [*cryo-* cold, freezing (deriv. of Gk *kryos* icy cold) + *biology*] : the study of the effects of extremely low temperature on biological systems (as cells or organisms) — **cryo·bi·o·log·i·cal** \-ˌbīəˈläjəkəl\ *adj* — **cryo·bi·o·log·i·cal·ly** \-k(ə)lē, -li\ *adv* — **cryo·bi·ol·o·gist** \-(ˌ)bīˈäləgəst\ *n*

cryo·chem·is·try \-ˈkeməstrē, -ri\ *n* : chemistry dealing with processes carried out at very low temperatures — **cryo·chem·i·cal** \-ˈkeməkəl\ *adj* — **cryo·chem·i·cal·ly** \-k(ə)lē, -li\ *adv*

cryo·elec·tron·ics \-əˌlekˈträniks\ *n pl but sing in constr* : a branch of electronics that employs cryogenic methods to bring about a desired effect (as superconductivity) — **cryo·elec·tron·ic** \-ˈtränik\ *adj*

cryo·gen·ic* \ˌkrīəˈjenik\ *adj* **1** : being or relating to a very low temperature <a *cryogenic* temperature of −50°C> **2 a** : requiring or involving the use of a cryogenic temperature **b** : requiring cryogenic storage **c** : suitable for the storage of a cryogenic substance <a *cryogenic* container>— **cry·o·gen·i·cal·ly** \-nək(ə)lē\ *adv*

cry·on·ics \krīˈäniks\ *n pl but usu sing in constr* [*cry*obiology + *-onics* (as in *electronics*] : the practice of freezing a dead diseased human being in hopes of bringing him back to life at some future time when a cure for his disease has been developed — **cry·on·ic** \(ˈ)krīˈänik\ *adj*

cryo·pre·cip·i·tate \ˌkrīōprəˈsipəd·ət, -əˌtāt\ *n* : a precipitate that is formed by cooling a solution — **cryo·pre·cip·i·ta·tion** \-prəˌsipəˈtāshən\ *n*

cryo·probe \ˈkrīəˌprōb\ *n* : a blunt instrument used to apply cold to tissues in cryosurgery

cryo·protective \ˌkrīōprəˈtektiv, -(ˌ)prō-\ *adj* : serving to protect from freezing <an extracellular *cryoprotective* agent>

cryo·pump \ˈkrīōˌpəmp\ *n* : a vacuum pump whose operation involves the freezing and absorption of gases on cold surfaces at very low temperatures — **cryopump** *vi*

cryo·sorp·tion \ˌkrīōˈsörpshən\ *n* : the adsorption of gases onto the cold surfaces of a cryopump

cryo·sur·gery \-ˈsərj(ə)rē\ *n* : surgery in which extreme controlled chilling (as by use of liquid nitrogen) produces the desired dissection — **cryo·sur·geon** \-ˈsərjən\ *n* — **cryo·sur·gi·cal** \-jəkəl\ *adj*

cryp·to·bi·o·sis \ˌkrip(ˌ)tōˌbīˈōsəs, -(ˌ)bēˈ-\ *n, pl* **-bi·o·ses** \-ˈōˌsēz \ [NL, fr. *crypto-* hidden, covered (deriv. of Gk *kryptos* hidden) + *-biosis* mode of life, deriv. of Gk *bios* life] : the reversible cessation of metabolism under extreme environmental conditions (as low temperature)

crystal* *n* : powdered methamphetamine

cu·chi·fri·to \ˌküchiˈfrēd·ō, -chēˈ-\ *n, pl* **-tos** [AmerSp, fr. *cuche, cuchi* hog, pig (fr. Sp *cochino*) + Sp *frito* fried, past part. of *freir* to fry, fr. L *frigere*] : a deep-fried cube of pork

Cui·se·naire rod *also* **Cuisenaire colored rod** \ˌkwēzᵊnˈa(ə)r-, -ˈe(ə)r-\ *n* [fr. *Cuisenaire,* a trademark] : any of a set of colored rods that are usu. of 1 centimeter cross section and of ten lengths from 1 to 10 centimeters and that are used for teaching number concepts and the basic operations of arithmetic

culture shock *n* : a sense of confusion and uncertainty sometimes with feelings of anxiety that may affect people exposed to an alien culture without adequate preparation <the *culture shock* often suffered by Americans on work assignments abroad —Kenneth Goodall>

cumulative* *adj* : summing or integrating over all data or values of a random variable less than or less than or equal to a specified value < *cumulative* normal distribution> < *cumulative* frequency distribution>

cumulative distribution function *n* : a function that gives the probability that a random variable is less than or equal to the independent variable of the function

cup* *n* : the symbol ∪ indicating the union of two sets

cup·pa \ˈkəpə\ *n* [fr. *cuppa tea,* pronunciation spelling of *cup of tea*] *chiefly Brit* : a cup of tea <if you're trying to lose weight one of the few comforts left to you is probably a nice sweet *cuppa* —*News of the World*>

cu·pule* \ˈkyüˌp(y)ül\ *n* : an outer integument partially enclosing the seed of some seed ferns

cu·rate's egg \ˌkyu̇rə̇ts'-\ *n* [fr. the story of a curate who was given a stale egg by his bishop and declared that parts of it were excellent] *Brit* : something with both good and bad parts or qualities <this is a bit of a *curate's egg,* very good but spoilt by facetiousness —*Times Lit. Supp.*>

cu·ri·age \ˈkyu̇rēij, kyəˈr-\ *n* : the strength of radioactivity expressed in curies

curl* *n* : a hollow arch of water formed when the crest of a breaking wave spills forward — called also *tube, tunnel*

curve* *vt* **curved; curv·ing** : to throw a curve to (a batter) in baseball

custard glass *n* : opaque glass of creamy buff color

cut* *n* : a single song or musical piece on a phonograph record <the best *cut* in the album>

cut·abil·i·ty \ˌkəd·əˈbilə̇d·ē, -i\ *n* : the proportion of lean salable meat yielded by a carcass

cut·back* \ˈkətˌbak\ *n* : a surfing maneuver in which a surfboard is turned back toward the crest of the wave

cute·sy *also* **cute·sie** \ˈkyütsē, -si\ *adj* **cute·si·er; -est** [*cute* + *-sy* (as in *folksy*)] : self-consciously cute <tries . . . to be bright and often ends up merely *cutesy* —Newgate Callendar> — **cute·sy·ness** \-nə̇s\ *n*

cy·a·no·ac·ry·late \ˌsīənōˈakrəˌlāt, -ələ̇t\ *n* [*cyano-* containing the cyanogen group + *acrylate*] : any of several liquid acrylate monomers that readily undergo anionic polymerization and are used as adhesives in industry and on living tissue in medicine to close wounds as an adjunct to surgery

cy·ber·cul·ture \ˈsībə(r)ˌkəlchə(r)\ *n* [*cyber*netics + *culture*] : a society that is served by cybernated industry — **cy·ber·cul·tur·al** \ˌsībə(r)ˌkəlch(ə)rəl\ *adj*

cy·ber·nat·ed \ˈsībə(r)ˌnād·ə̇d\ *adj* [fr. *cybernation;* after such pairs as E *automation: automated*] : characterized by or involving cybernation <a *cybernated* factory> <a *cybernated* society>

cy·ber·na·tion \ˌsībə(r)ˈnāshən\ *n* [*cyber*netics + *-ation* action or process] : the automatic control of a process or operation (as in manufacturing) by means of computers

cy·borg \ˈsīˌbȯrg, -ȯ(ə)g\ *n* [*cyb*ernetic + *org*anism] : a human being who is linked (as for temporary adaptation to a hostile space environment) to one or more mechanical devices upon which some of his vital physiological functions depend

cy·ca·sin \ˈsīkəsə̇n\ *n* [*cycas* + *-in* chemical compound] : a glucoside $C_8H_{16}N_2O_7$ that occurs in cycads and results in toxic and carcinogenic effects when introduced into mammals

cy·clase \ˈsīˌklās, -āz\ *n* [*cycl-* cyclic + *-ase* enzyme] : an enzyme (as adenyl cyclase) that catalyzes cyclization of a compound

cy·claz·o·cine \sīˈklazəˌsēn, -əsə̇n\ *n* [*cycl-* + *azocine,* a compound C_7H_7N, fr. *benzazocine,* a derivative of azobenzene, prob. irreg. fr. *azobenzene*] : an analgesic $C_{18}H_{25}NO$ that inhibits the effect of morphine and related addictive drugs and is used in the treatment of drug addiction

cycle* *n* : a permutation of a set of ordered elements in which each element takes the place of the next and the last becomes first

cy·cle·ry \ˈsīkəl(ˌ)rē, -klə(ˌ)rē, -ri\ *n, pl* **-ries** : a place where bicycles are sold and serviced

cy·clic aden·o·sine mo·no·phos·phate \ˈsīklikəˌdenəˌsēnˌmänəˈfäsˌfāt, -əsə̇n-, -ˌmōn-, *also* ˈsiklik-\ *n* : CYCLIC AMP

cy·clic AMP \ˌsīklikˌā(ˌ)emˈpē, *also* ˌsik-\ *n* : a cyclic mononucleotide of adenosine that has been implicated in control mechanisms regulating metabolism and function in the nervous system and that is the common mediator within the cell of many hormones and biogenic amines — called also *adenosine monophosphate*

cyclic group *n* : a mathematical group that has an element such that every element of the group can be expressed as one of its powers

cy·clo \ˈsē(ˌ)klō, ˈsik(ˌ)lō\ *n, pl* **cy·clos** [prob. fr. F, short for (assumed) *cyclotaxi,* fr. moto*cycl*ette motorcycle + connective *-o-* + *taxi*] : a 3-wheeled motor-driven taxi

cy·clo·di·ene \ˌsīklōˈdīˌēn, ˌsik-, -ˌdīˈēn\ *n* [*cyclo-* cyclic + *-diene* compound with two double bonds] : an organic insecticide (as aldrin, dieldrin, chlordane, or endosulfan) with a chlorinated methylene group forming a bridge across a 6-membered carbon ring

cy·clo·phos·pha·mide \ˌsīkləˈfäsfəˌmīd, ˌsik-, -əməd\ *n* [prob. fr. *cyclo-* + *phosphorus* + *amide*] : an immunosuppressive and antineoplastic agent $C_7H_{15}Cl_2N_2O_2P$ used esp. against lymphomas and some leukemias

cy·clo·tom·ic* \ˌsīkləˈtämik, ˌsi-, -(ˌ)klō-\ *adj*: relating to, being, or containing a polynomial of the form $x^{p-1} + x^{p-2} + \ldots + x + 1$ where p is a prime number

cy·clo·tron resonance \ˈsīkləˌträn-\ *n* : the absorption of electromagnetic energy by a charged particle orbiting in a magnetic field when the electromagnetic and orbital frequencies are equal

cy·pro·hep·ta·dine \ˌsīprōˈheptəˌdēn\ *n* [*cy*clic + *pro*pyl + *hepta-* seven (fr. Gk *hepta*) + piperi*dine*] : a drug $C_{21}H_{21}N$ that acts antagonistically to histamine and serotonin and is used esp. in the treatment of asthma

cy·prot·er·one \sīˈpräd·əˌrōn\ *n* [prob. fr. *cy*clic + *proges terone*] : a synthetic steroid used in the form of its acetate to inhibit androgenic secretions (as testosterone)

cys·ta·mine \ˈsistəˌmēn, -əmən\ *n* [*cyst*ine + *amine*] : a cystine derivative $C_4H_{12}N_2S_2$ used in the prevention of radiation sickness (as of cancer patients)

cys·ta·thi·o·nine \ˌsistəˈthīəˌnēn, -ənən\ *n* [irreg. fr. *cyst*eine, an amino acid + *methionine,* an amino acid] : a sulfur-containing amino acid $C_7H_{14}N_2O_4S$ formed as an intermediate in the conversion of methionine to cysteine in animals

cys·te·amine \sisˈtēəmən\ *n* [*cyste*ine + *amine*] : a cysteine derivative C_2H_7NS used in the prevention of radiation sickness (as of cancer patients)

cy·to·chi·me·ra \ˌsīd·ōkəˈmirə, -ˌkīˈ-\ *n* [NL, fr. *cyto-* cell (deriv. of Gk *kytos* hollow vessel) + *chimera*] : an individual (as a plant, an organ, or a tissue) having cells of varied genetic constitution and esp. of various ploidy levels

cy·to·dif·fer·en·ti·a·tion \-ˌdifəˌrenchēˈāshən\ *n*: the development of specialized cells (as muscle, blood, or nerve cells) from undifferentiated precursors

cy·to·ecol·o·gy \-əˈkäləjē, -eˈk-, -ēˈk-\ *n* : the study of organismic adaptation at the molecular and cellular level — **cy·to·eco·log·i·cal** \-ˌēkəˈläjəkəl, -ˌekə-\ *adj*

cy·to·ki·nin \-ˈkīnən\ *n* : any of various substituted adenines with an amino group attached at the number six position that are plant growth substances

cy·to·me·gal·ic \ˌsīd·ōməˌgalik, -ēk\ *adj* [NL *cytomegalia* condition of having enlarged cells] : characterized by or causing the formation of enlarged cells <a *cytomegalic* virus>

cy·to·meg·a·lo·vi·rus \ˌsīd·əˌmegəlōˈvīrəs\ *n* [NL, fr. *cytomegalia* + connective *-o-* + *virus*] : any of several viruses that cause cellular enlargement and formation of eosinophilic inclusion bodies esp. in the nucleus and include the causative agent of a severe disease esp. of newborns that usu. affects the salivary glands, brain, kidneys, liver, and lungs

cy·to·mem·brane \ˌsīd·əˈmemˌbrān\ *n* : one of the cellular membranes including those of the plasmalemma, the endoplasmic reticulum, nuclear envelope, and Golgi apparatus

cy·to·mor·phol·o·gy \-ˌmȯ(r)ˈfäləjē\ *n* : the morphology of cells — **cy·to·mor·pho·log·i·cal** \-fəˈläjəkəl\ *adj*

cy·to·patho·gen·ic \-ˌpathəˈjenik\ *adj* : pathologic for or destructive to cells — **cy·to·patho·ge·nic·i·ty** \-jəˈnisəd·ē\ *n*

cy·to·pho·tom·e·ter \-(ˌ)fōˈtäməd·ə(r)\ *n* : a photometer for use in cytophotometry

cy·to·pho·tom·e·try \-(ˌ)fōˌtämə·trē\ *n* : photometry applied to the study of the cell or its constituents — **cy·to·pho·to·met·ric** \-ˌfōd·əˈme·trik\ *also* **cy·to·pho·to·met·ric·al** \-kəl\ *adj* — **cy·to·pho·to·met·ri·cal·ly** \-k(ə)lē\ *adv*

cy·to·sol \'sīd·ə,säl, -,sȯl\ *n* [*cyto-* + *sol* fluid colloidal system, fr. *solution*] : the fluid portion of the cytoplasm exclusive of organelles and membranes that is usu. obtained as the supernatant fraction from high-speed centrifugation of a tissue homogenate

cy·to·stat·ic \¦sīd·ə¦stad·ik\ *adj* [*cyto-* + Gk *statikos* causing to stand] : tending to retard cellular activity and multiplication <*cytostatic* treatment of tumor cells> — **cytostatic** *n* — **cy·to·stat·i·cal·ly** \-ə̇k(ə)lē\ *adv*

cy·to·tech \'sīd·ə,tek\ *n* [by shortening] : CYTOTECHNOLOGIST

cy·to·tech·nol·o·gist \¦sīd·ō(,)tek'näləjə̇st\ *also* **cy·to·tech·ni·cian** \-(,)tek'nishən\ *n* : a medical technician trained to assist a pathologist in the identification of cells and cellular abnormalities (as in cancer)

cy·to·vi·rin \,sīd·ə'vī(ə)rə̇n\ *n* [*cyto-* + *virus* + *-in* chemical compound] : a compound that is produced by a bacterium (*Streptomyces olivochromogenes*) and that is active against some plant viruses (as tobacco mosaic virus)

D

da• *abbr* deka-

DA \,dē'ā\ *n* : a doctor of arts

dal·a·pon \'dalə,pän\ *n* [prob. fr. *di*- two + *alpha* + *propionic* acid] : an herbicide $C_4H_4Cl_2O_2$ that kills monocotyledonous plants selectively and is used esp. on unwanted grasses

da·la·si \dä'läsē, -si\ *n* [native name in Gambia] **1** : the basic monetary unit of Gambia **2** : a coin or note representing one dalasi

dal·ton \'dȯltᵊn\ *n* [John *Dalton* †1844 Eng. chemist and physicist] : a unit of mass for expressing masses of atoms, molecules, or nuclear particles equal to $^1/_{12}$ of the atomic mass of the most abundant carbon isotope $_6C^{12}$: atomic mass unit

damsel bug *n* : any of a family (Nabidae) of small brown or black bugs that feed on pest insects

dan \'dän, 'dan\ *n* [Jap, step, grade] : the expert level in Oriental arts of self-defense (as judo and karate) and games (as shogi)

D & C *abbr* dilatation and curettage

dap·sone \'dap,sōn, -,zōn\ *n* [*di*aminodi*p*henyl *sulfone*] : an antimicrobial agent $C_{12}H_{12}N_2O_2S$ used esp. against leprosy

Dar·win's finches \,därwə̇nz-, ,dȧw-\ *n pl* [Charles *Darwin* †1882 Eng. naturalist] : finches of a subfamily (Geospizinae) characterized by great variation in bill shape and confined mostly to the Galapagos islands

das *abbr* dekastere

da·shi·ki \dä'shēkē, də'-\ *n* [alter. of Yoruba *danshiki*] : a usu. brightly colored loose-fitting one-piece pullover garment worn esp. by men

data bank *n* **1** : a collection of data organized esp. for rapid search and retrieval (as by computer) **2** : an institution whose chief concern is building and maintaining a data bank

da·ta·ma·tion \,dād·ə'māshən, ,da-, ,dȧ-, ,dä-\ *n* [*data* + auto*mation*] : automatic data processing; *also* : the enterprises engaged in manufacturing, selling, and servicing data-processing equipment

data processing *n* : the conversion and subsequent processing of raw data esp. by computer — **data processor** *n*

dating bar *n* : a bar that caters esp. to young unmarried men and women

dau·no·my·cin \,dȯnə'mīsᵊn, ,daů-\ *n* [(assumed) It *daunomicina*, fr. *Dau*nia, ancient region of Apulia, Italy + It *-o-*, connective vowel + *-micina* (as in *streptomicina* streptomycin)] : an antibiotic $C_{27}H_{29}NO_{10}$ that is a nitrogenous glycoside and is used experimentally as an antineoplastic agent

day–care center \ˌdāˌke(ə)r-, -ˌka(ə)r-, -ˌkeə-, -ˌkaə-\ *n* : a center that provides supervision and facilities for preschool children during the day

day·glow \ˈdāˌglō\ *n* [*day* + air*glow*] : airglow seen during the day

day·side* \ˈdāˌsīd\ *n* : the side of a planet in daylight

day trader *n* : a speculator who seeks profit from the intraday fluctuation in the price of a security or commodity and therefore completes double trades of buying and selling or selling and covering in the course of single sessions of the market — **day–trade** \ˈdā-ˌtrād\ *n or vb*

DDE \ˌdē(ˌ)dēˈē\ *n* [*d*ichloro*d*iphenyldichloro*e*thylene] : a persistent organochlorine $C_{15}H_8Cl_4$ that is produced by the metabolic breakdown of DDT

DDVP \ˌdē(ˌ)dēˌvēˈpē\ *n* [*d*imethyl + *d*ichlor- containing two chlorine atoms + *v*inyl + *p*hosphate] : DICHLORVOS

de–ac·ces·sion \ˌdēəkˈseshən, -ˌak-\ *vt* : to remove and sell (a work of art) from a museum's collection esp. to raise funds to purchase other works of art <does not *de-accession* works or dispose of them by sale, unless it owns duplicates — D.L. Shirey> ~ *vi* : to de-accession a work of art <I'm sick of being told museums must *de-accession.* Of course they must —Edmund Carpenter>

de·ac·yl·ate \ˌdēˈasəˌlāt\ *vt* [*de-* remove, do the opposite (deriv. of L *de* from, away) + *acylate* to introduce acyl into] : to remove an acyl group from (a compound) — **de·ac·yl·a·tion** \-ˌasəˈlāshən\ *n*

dead drop *n* [fr. the absence of personal contact between the agents] : a prearranged hiding place for the deposit and pickup of information obtained through espionage

Dear John *n* : a letter (as to a soldier) in which a wife asks for a divorce or a girl friend breaks off an engagement or a friendship <jilted? Recipient of a *Dear John* letter? —Gore Vidal>

de·boost \(ˈ)dēˌbüst, də-\ *n* : the process of slowing down a spacecraft <before *deboost* into low orbit —C.J. Sitomer>

de·bug* \(ˌ)dēˈbəg, dəˈ-\ *vt* : to remove a concealed microphone or wiretapping device from <*debug* a room>; *also* : to make (concealed microphones) ineffective by electronic means — **de·bug·ger** \ˌdēˈbəgə(r), də-\ *n*

deca·met·ric \ˌdekəˌme·trik\ *adj* [fr. the wavelength range being between 1 and 10 dekameters] : of, relating to, or being a radio wave of high frequency

Dec·ca \ˈdekə\ *n* [*Decca* Co., British firm which developed it] : a system of long-range navigation utilizing the phase differences of continuous-wave signals from synchronized ground transmitters

deciding *adj* : having the effect of settling a contest or controversy <the *deciding* run> <the *deciding* vote>

deck* *n* **1** : TAPE DECK 1b **2** : a group of usu. punched data-processing cards

de·clin·ing–bal·ance method \dəˌklīniŋˌbalən(t)s-, dē-\ *n* : a method of calculating periodic depreciation that involves determining at regular (as annual) intervals throughout the expected life of an asset of equal percentage amounts of a cost balance which is progressively decreased by subtraction of each prior increment of depreciation from the original cost of the asset

de·col·late* \dəˈkälˌāt, dēˈ-\ *vt* : to separate the copies of (as a computer printout produced in multiple copies)

de·col·o·nize \(ˈ)dēˈkäləˌnīz, də-\ *vt* : to free from colonial status ~ *vi* : to grant independence to colonies — **de·col·o·ni·za·tion** \(ˌ)dēˌkälənəˈzāshən, -ˌnīˌ-\ *n*

de·com·pos·er* \ˌdēkəmˈpōzə(r)\ *n* : any of various organisms (as many bacteria and fungi) that return constituents of organic substances to ecological cycles by feeding on and breaking down dead protoplasm

de·cou·ple \(ˌ)dēˈkəpəl, dəˈ-\ *vt* **1** : to reduce or eliminate the coupling of (as circuits or mechanical parts) **2** : to decrease the seismic effect of (a nuclear explosion) by explosion in an underground cavity — **de·cou·pler** \-ˈkəp(ə)lə(r)\ *n*

de·crim·i·nal·ize \(ˈ)dēˈkrimənᵊlˌīz, dəˈ-, -m(ə)nəl-\ *vt* **-ized; -iz·ing** : to remove from the purview of statutory criminality <wanted to *decriminalize* the possession of marijuana> — **de·crim·i·nal·iza·tion** \-ˌkrimənᵊləˈzāshən, -mnəl-, -ˌlīˈ-\ *n*

deep* *adv* : near the outer limits of the normal area of play <the shortstop was playing *deep*>

deep space* *also* **deep sky** *n* : space well beyond the limits of the earth's atmosphere including space outside the solar system

deep structure *n* : a formal representation of the underlying semantic content of a sentence; *also* : the structure which such a representation specifies — compare SURFACE STRUCTURE

de–es·ca·late \(ˈ)dēˈeskəˌlāt, ÷ -kyə-\ *vi* : to decrease in extent, volume, number, amount, or scope : diminish <the rhetoric of violence has *de-escalated*—John Cogley> ~ *vt* : to decrease the extent, volume, number, amount, or scope of <my sister . . . tried to *de-escalate* our feud —H.A. Smith> <a tactical step toward *de-escalating* the Vietnamese war —Barbara Raskin> — **de–es·ca·la·tion** \(ˌ)dē-ˌeskəˈlāshən, ÷ -kyə-\ *n*

de–es·ca·la·tor \(ˈ)dēˈeskəˌlād·ə(r), ÷-kyə-\ *n* : an advocate of de-escalation

de–es·ca·la·to·ry \-ələˌtōrē, -ˌtȯr-\ *adj* : of or relating to de-escalation <took the first *de-escalatory* step>

deet \ˈdēt\ *n* [fr. *d. t.* (abbr. of *diethyl toluamide*)] : a colorless oily liquid insect repellent $C_{12}H_{17}NO$

defensive* *adj* : of, relating to, or being industries (as foods, utilities, and insurance) which provide essential needs to the ultimate consumer and in which business activity is relatively insensitive to changes in general business activity

deferred income* *n* : current income forgone to produce a later higher income (as at retirement)

de·fi·bril·late \(ˈ)dēˈfibrəˌlāt, dė-, -ˈfīb-\ *vt* : to restore the rhythm of (a fibrillating heart) — **de·fi·bril·la·tion** \(ˌ)dēˌfibrəˈlāshən, dė-, -ˌfīb-\ *n* — **de·fi·bril·la·tive** \dēˈfibrəˌlād·iv, dėˈ-, -ˈfīb-, -ələd-\ *adj* — **de·fi·bril·la·tor** \-rəˌlād·ə(r)\ *n* — **de·fi·bril·la·to·ry** \-rəˌlād·ərē, -rələˌtōrē, -tȯr-, -ri\ *adj*

¹de·fo·cus \(ˈ)dēˈfōkəs, dė-\ *vt* : to cause (as a beam of radiation or a lens) to deviate from an accurate focus ~ *vi* : to lose accuracy of focus : become defocused

²defocus *n* : a result of defocusing; *esp* : an image (as on motion-picture film) deliberately blurred for dramatic effect

de·fog \(ˈ)dēˈfȯg, dė-, -ˈfäg\ *vt* : to remove fog or condensed moisture from : keep free of fog <defroster couldn't even keep the windshield fully *defogged*—*Consumer Reports*>— **de·fog·ger** \-ə(r)\ *n*

de·fuse* \(ˈ)dēˈfyüz\ *vt* : to make less dangerous, potent, or tense : calm <the means to *defuse* explosive campus racial situations —M.L. Dillon>

de·gen·er·a·cy* \dėˈjen(ə)rəsē, dēˈ-, -si\ *n* : the coding of an amino acid by more than one codon of the genetic code

de·gen·er·ate* \-n(ə)rėt\ *adj* **1** : being mathematically simpler (as by having a factor or constant equal to zero) than the typical case <the graph of a second degree equation yielding two intersecting lines is a *degenerate* hyperbola> **2** : having two or more states or subdivisions <*degenerate* energy level> **3** : having more than one codon representing an amino acid; *also* : being such a codon

de·grad·able \dėˈgrādəbəl, dē-\ *adj*: capable of being chemically degraded <*degradable* detergents>

de·gran·u·la·tion \(ˌ)dēˌgranyəˈlāshən, dėˌ-\ *n* : the process of losing granules <*degranulation* of leukocytes>

de·hy·drase \ dēˈhīˌdrās, -āz\ *n* **1** : DEHYDRATASE **2** : an enzyme that accelerates the removal of hydrogen from metabolites and its transfer to other substances

de·hy·dra·tase \-ˈhīdrəˌtās, -āz\ *n* : an enzyme that catalyzes the removal of oxygen and hydrogen from metabolites in the proportion in which they form water

de·hy·dro·chlo·ri·nase \(ˌ)dēˌhīdrəˈklōrėˌnās, -lȯr-, -āz\ *n* : an enzyme that dehydrochlorinates a chlorinated hydrocarbon (as DDT) and is found esp. in some DDT-resistant insects

de·hy·dro·chlo·ri·nate \-ˌnāt\ *vt* **-nat·ed; -nat·ing** : to remove hydrogen and chlorine or hydrogen chloride from (a compound) — **de·hy·dro·chlo·ri·na·tion** \-ˌklōrėˈnāshən, -lȯr-\ *n*

de·in·dus·tri·al·iza·tion \ˌdēənˌdəstrēələˈzāshən\ *n* : the act or process of reducing or destroying the industrial organization and potential esp. of a defeated nation

deka·gram \ˈdekəˌgram\ *n* [alter. of *decagram*] : 10 grams

deka·li·ter \-ˌlid·ə(r)\ *n* [alter. of *decaliter*] : 10 liters

deka·me·ter \-ˌmēd·ə(r)\ *n* [alter. of *decameter*] : 10 meters

deka·met·ric \ˌdekəˈme·trik\ *adj* [by alter.] : DECAMETRIC

deka·stere \ˈdekəˌsti(ə)r\ *n* [alter. of *decastere*] : 10 cubic meters

delay* *n* : a play in football in which a ballcarrier or potential receiver delays momentarily as if to block and then runs his prescribed route

deli *also* **del·ly** \ˈdelē, -li\ *n, pl* **del·is** *also* **del·lies** [short for *delicatessen*] : a store where ready-to-eat food products (as cooked meats and prepared salads) are sold : delicatessen

delicacy* *n* : the degree of differentiation between subcategories of linguistic categories <by increase in *delicacy,* the primary class is broken down into secondary classes —M.A.K. Halliday>

de·lim·it·er* \dəˈliməd·ə(r), dē-\ *n* : a character that marks the beginning or end of a unit of data (as on a magnetic tape)

deliver* *vi* : to produce the promised, desired, or expected results : come through <failed to *deliver* on their promises> <year after year, he promised salary raises and could almost never *deliver* —John McPhee>

de·lo·cal·ize* \(ˈ)dēˈlōkəˌlīz\ *vt* : to remove (electrons) from a particular position

de·mag·ni·fy \(ˈ)dēˈmagnəˌfī, də-\ *vt* : to reduce the size of (as a photographic image or an electron beam) — **de·mag·ni·fi·ca·tion** \-ˌmagnəfəˈkāshən\ *n*

de·mand–pull \dəˈmandˌpu̇l, dē-\ *n* : an increase or upward trend in spendable money that tends to result in increased competition for available goods and services and a corresponding increase in consumer prices — compare COST-PUSH — **demand–pull** *adj*

de·mas·cu·lin·ize \(ˌ)dēˈmaskyələˌnīz, də-\ *vt* : to remove the masculine character or qualities of <prenatal stress . . . *demasculinizes* the behavior of males —Ingeborg L. Ward> <seems sensitive to women and the need to *demasculinize* society —Brenda F. Fasteau & Bonnie Lobel> — **de·mas·cu·lin·iza·tion** \-ˌmaskyələnəˈzāshən, -ˌnīˈ-\ *n*

dem·e·ton \ˈdeməˌtän\ *n* [prob. fr. *di*ethyl + *mer*captan + *thi*o*n*ate] : a mixture of organophosphorus insecticides used as a systemic on plants

demo* \ˈde(ˌ)mō\ *n, pl* **demos** **1** : a demonstration <gave *demos* of karate and judo during the intermission>; *esp* : a political demonstration : a protest <workers elsewhere staged brief strikes and *demos* —Donald Kirk> **2** : something used for purposes of demonstration: as **a** : a demonstration record or tape <*demos* are cut by song publishers to demonstrate their songs —*Rolling Stone*> **b** : a demonstrator automobile <sale on 1975 factory *demos*>

de·mo·li·tion derby \ˌdeməˈlishən-, ˌdē-\ *n* : a contest in which drivers bang old cars into one another until only one car remains running

de·moth·ball \(ˈ)dēˈmȯthˌbȯl\ *vt* : to remove the preservative covering of in order to reactivate (as ships)

de·mys·ti·fy \(ˈ)dēˈmistəˌfī\ *vt* : to eliminate the mystifying features of <his novels . . . *demystify* death, confronting us with the omnipresent reality of it —Harriet Blodgett>

den·som·e·ter \denˈsäməd·ə(r)\ *n* [ISV *dens-* (fr. L *densus* dense) + connective *-o-* + *-meter* instrument for measuring, deriv. of Gk *metron* measure] **1** : an instrument for measuring the porosity of paper by forcing air through it **2** : an instrument for determining density or specific gravity : densimeter

de·nu·cle·ar·ize \(ˈ)dēˈn(y)üklēəˌrīz, ÷-kyələˌrīz\ *vt* **-ized; -iz·ing** : to remove nuclear arms from : prohibit the use of nuclear arms in <both sides . . . agree that Germany should be *denuclearized* —*Newsweek*> <the proposed *denuclearized* zone in Latin America — H. A. Spalding> — **de·nu·cle·ar·iza·tion** \(ˌ)dēˌn(y)üklēərəˈzāshən, ÷ -kyələr-, -ˌrīˈz-\ *n*

¹de·or·bit \(ˈ)dēˈȯrbət, -ˈȯ(ə)b-\ *vi* : to go out of orbit ~ *vt* : to cause to deorbit <*deorbit* a spacecraft>

[2]**deorbit** *n* : the process of deorbiting
de·oxy·ri·bo·nu·cle·o·tide \(ˌ)dēˈäksēˌrī(ˌ)bōˈn(y)üklēəˌtīd\ *n* [*deoxyribo*se + *nucleotide*] : a nucleotide that contains deoxyribose and is a constituent of DNA
de·po·lit·i·cize \ˈdēpəˈlid·əˌsīz\ *vt* : to remove the political character from : take out of the realm of politics — **de·po·lit·i·ci·za·tion** \-ˌlid·əsəˈzāshən\ *n*
de·pol·lute \-pəˈlüt\ *vt* : to remove the pollution from < *depollute* our rivers and streams > — **de·pol·lu·tion** \-ˈlüshən\ *n*
de·pres·sur·ize \(ˌ)dēˈpreshəˌrīz\ *vt* : to release (as a pressurized aircraft) from pressure — **de·pres·sur·iza·tion** \-ˌpresh(ə)rəˈzāshən, -ˌrīˈ-\ *n*
de·rail·leur \dəˈrālə(r), dē-\ *n* [F *dérailleur,* fr. *dérailler* to throw off the track (fr. *dé-* de- + *rail* rail, fr. E)] : a multiple-speed gear mechanism on a bicycle that involves the moving of the chain from one sprocket to another < 10-speed *derailleur* >
de·reg·u·late \(ˈ)dēˈregyəˌlāt, də-\ *vt* : to remove from regulation : decontrol < proposals to *deregulate* natural-gas prices — *Wall Street Jour.* > — **de·reg·u·la·tion** \-ˌregyəˈlāshən\ *n*
de·repress \ˈdērəˈpres\ *vt* : to activate (a gene) by releasing from a blocked state — **de·re·pres·sion** \-ˈpreshən\ *n*
derm·abra·sion \ˈdərməˈbrāzhən, ˈdəm-\ *n* [*derm-* skin (deriv. of Gk *derma*) + *abrasion*] : surgical removal of skin blemishes or imperfections (as scars or tattoos) by abrasion (as with sandpaper or wire brushes)
derrick* *vt* : to remove (a pitcher) from a baseball game
de·sa·li·nate \(ˈ)dēˈsaləˌnāt, -sā-\ *vt* **-nat·ed; -nat·ing** [*de-* + *salin-* salt (deriv. of L *sal* salt) + *-ate* act on] : to remove salt from < *desalinate* seawater > — **de·sa·li·na·tor** \-ˌnād·ə(r)\ *n*
de·sa·li·nize \-ˌnīz\ *vt* **-nized; -niz·ing** : DESALINATE
de·school \ˈdēˈskül\ *vt* : to eliminate traditional schools from < the movement to *deschool* society —John Holt >
de·scrip·tor* \dəˈskriptə(r), dē-\ *n* : a word or phrase (as an index term) used to identify an item (as a subject or document) esp. in an information retrieval system; *also* : an alphanumeric symbol so used
de·select \ˈdēsəˈlekt\ *vt* : to dismiss (a trainee) from a training program < had been *deselected* because he was "unsuitable" for the work —*N.Y. Times* >
designated hitter *n* : a baseball player designated at the start of the game to bat in place of the pitcher without causing the pitcher to be removed from the game
de·si·pra·mine \ˌdezəˈpramən, dəˈziprə-, -ˌmēn\ *n* [*des*methyl (fr. *des-* having a molecule characterized by the removal of one or more atoms + *methyl*) + im*ipramine*] : a tricyclic drug $C_{18}H_{22}N_2$ used as an antidepressant
des·mo·some \ˈdezməˌsōm\ *n* [*desmo-* bond, ligament (deriv. of Gk *desmos* band, bond) + *-some* body, deriv. of Gk *sōma*] : a specialized local thickening of the cell membrane of an epithelial cell that serves to anchor contiguous cells together
de·spin \(ˈ)dēˈspin\ *vt* **-spun; -spin·ning** : to stop the rotation of or reduce the speed of rotation of (as a satellite)
de·sta·lin·iza·tion \(ˌ)dēˌstälənəˈzāshən, -tal-, -ˌnīˈz-\ *n* : the discrediting of Stalin and his policies
de·struct \ˈdēˌstrəkt, dəˈs-, dēˈs-\ *n* [short for *destruction*] : the deliberate destruction of a rocket after launching esp. during a test; *also* : such destruction of a device or material (as to prevent its falling into enemy hands)
de·ter·rence* \dəˈtərən(t)s, -ˈter-; -ˈtə·rən(t)s\ *n* : the maintaining of vast military power and weaponry in order to discourage war < an official council blessing on the concept of nuclear *deterrence* —*Current Biog.* >
det·o·nate* \ˈdetᵊnˌāt, ˈded·əˌnāt\ *vt* **-nat·ed; -nat·ing** : to set off in a burst of activity : spark < programs that *detonated* controversies >
de·tu·mes·cent \ˌdēt(y)üˈmesᵊnt\ *adj* : characterized by detumescence
deu·ter·ate \ˈd(y)üd·əˌrāt\ *vt* **-at·ed; -at·ing** [*deuter*ium + *-ate* act on] : to introduce deuterium into (a compound)
developing *adj* : not having attained a potential economic level of industrial production and standard of living (as from lack of capital) : underdeveloped < *developing* nations >

de·vol·a·til·ize \(ˈ)dēˈvälətᵊlˌiz, də-, *Brit also* ˌdēvəˈlat-\ *vt* : to remove volatile material from (as coal) — **de·vol·a·til·iza·tion** \-ˌvälətᵊləˈzāshən, *Brit also* -vəˌlat-\ *n*
dex \ˈdeks\ *n* [short for *Dexedrine*] : the sulfate of dextroamphetamine
dexa·meth·a·sone \ˌdeksəˈmethəˌsōn, -ˌzōn\ *n* [perh. fr. *Dexa*myl, a trademark + *meth*yl + *-sone* (as in *cortisone*)] : a synthetic adrenocortical steroid $C_{22}H_{29}FO_5$ used esp. as an anti-inflammatory and antiallergic agent
Dex·e·drine \ˈdeksəˌdrēn, -drən\ *trademark* — used for a preparation of the sulfate of dextroamphetamine
dex·ies \ˈdeksēz\ *n pl* : tablets or capsules of the sulfate of dextroamphetamine
dex·tran·ase \-strəˌnās, -ˌnāz\ *n* : a hydrolase that prevents tooth decay by breaking down dextran and eliminating dental plaque
di·ag·o·nal·ize \(ˈ) dīˈag(ə)nᵊlˌīz, -gnəl-\ *vt* **-ized; -iz·ing** : to put (a matrix) in a form with all the nonzero elements along the diagonal from upper left to lower right — **di·ag·o·nal·iz·able** \-ˈīzəbəl\ *adj* — **di·ag·o·nal·iza·tion** \-ˌag(ə)nᵊləˈzāshən, -gnəl-\ *n*
diagonal ma·trix \-ˈmā·triks\ *n* : a matrix that has all the nonzero elements located along the diagonal from upper left to lower right
di·az·e·pam \dīˈazəˌpam\ *n* [*diaz-* containing the group N_2 + *ep*oxide + *-am* compound related to ammonia] : a tranquilizer $C_{16}H_{13}ClN_2O$ used esp. to relieve anxiety and tension and as a muscle relaxant
DH *abbr* designated hitter
dice* *n* : a close contest between two racing-car drivers for position during a race
dice* *vi* **diced; dic·ing** : to engage in a jockeying for position (as in an automobile race) <had been *dicing* along the road with the driver of another car —*London Daily Telegraph*>
dic·ey \ˈdīsē\ *adj* : having an uncertain outcome : risky <in the best of situations, detoxification is a *dicey* undertaking —J.M. Markham>
di·chlor·vos \(ˈ)dīˈklō(ə)rˌväs, -lȯ(ə)r-, -vəs\ *n* [*dichlor-* containing two atoms of chlorine + *v*inyl + ph*os*phate] : a nonpersistent organophosphorus pesticide $C_4H_7Cl_2O_4P$ that is used esp. against insects and is of low toxicity to man — called also *DDVP*
dich·otic \(ˈ)dīˈkōd·ik, -käd-\ *adj* [*dich-* in two, apart (deriv. of Gk *dicha* in two) + *-otic* of the ear, fr. Gk *ōtikos,* fr. *ōt-, ous* ear] : affecting or relating to the two ears differently in regard to a conscious aspect (as pitch or loudness) or a physical aspect (as frequency or energy) of sound — **dich·oti·cal·ly** \-d·ək(ə)lē\ *adv*
dictionary* *n, pl* **-nar·ies** : a list (as of synonyms or hyphenation instructions) stored in machine-readable form for reference by an automatic system (as for information retrieval or computerized typesetting)
di·eth·yl tolu·amide \ˌdīˌethəlˈtäl(ˌ)yüəˌmīd, -əməd\ *n* [*diethyl* + *tolu-* related to toluene + *amide*] : DEET
difference* *vt* **-enced; -enc·ing** : to compute the difference between <measuring the output and *differencing* this from a desired setting —Andrew St. Johnston>
di·func·tion·al \(ˈ)dīˈfəŋ(k)shnəl, -shənᵊl\ *adj* [*di-* two + *functional*] : of, relating to, or being a compound with two sites in the molecule that are highly reactive — **di·func·tion·al·i·ty** \(ˌ)dīˌfəŋ(k)shəˈnaləd·ē\ *n*
dig·i·tal* \ˈdijəd·ᵊl\ *adj* : providing a readout in numerical digits <a *digital* voltmeter> <a *digital* clock radio>
dig·i·tal·ize \ˈdijəd·ᵊlˌīz\ *vt* **-ized; -iz·ing** : to put (as data) into digital notation
di·glos·sia \(ˈ)dīˈgläsēə, -ˈglȯs-\ *n* [NL, fr. F *diglossie,* fr. *di-* two + *-glossie,* fr. Gk *glōssa* language, tongue] : the use of two languages or dialects for different functions or at different social levels — **di·glos·sic** \-sik, -sēk\ *adj*
di·hy·droxy·ac·e·tone \ˌdīhīˌdräksēˈasəˌtōn\ *n* [*dihydroxy-* containing two hydroxyl groups + *acetone*] : a triose $C_3H_6O_3$ that is used esp. to produce artificial tanning of the skin
dike, dikey *var of* DYKE, DYKEY
di·lu·tive \(ˈ)dīˈl(y)üd·iv, dəˈl-\ *adj* : reducing or involving reduction of per share income of a corporate stock <the *dilutive* effect of stock options and convertible securities>

dimension* *n* : the number of elements in a basis of a vector space

di·meth·o·ate \dī'methə,wāt\ *n* [*dime*thyl + *-thi*o*ic* having a sulfur atom in place of an oxygen atom + *-ate* derivative compound] : an organophosphorus insecticide $C_5H_{12}NO_3PS_2$ used on livestock and various crops

di·meth·yl·hy·dra·zine \ˌdīˌmethəl'hīdrəˌzēn\ *n* [*dimethyl* + *hydrazine*] : either of two flammable corrosive isomeric liquids $C_2H_8N_2$ which are methylated derivatives of hydrazine and of which one is used in rocket fuels

di·meth·yl·ni·tros·amine \-(ˌ)nī·'trōsəˌmēn\ *n* [*dimethyl* + *nitrosamine*] : a carcinogenic nitrosamine that occurs esp. in tobacco smoke

di·meth·yl·sulf·ox·ide \-(ˌ)səl'fäkˌsīd\ *n* [*dimethyl* + *sulfoxide*] : a compound $(CH_3)_2SO$ obtained as a by-product in wood-pulp manufacture and used as a solvent and in experimental medicine — called also *DMSO*

di·meth·yl·tryp·ta·mine \-'triptəˌmēn\ *n* [*dimethyl* + *tryptamine*] : an easily synthesized hallucinogenic drug that is chemically similar to but shorter acting than psilocybin — called also *DMT*

dinch \'dinch\ *vt* [origin unknown] : to extinguish by crushing <looked at his half-smoked cigar, then on his way to the cabaña he *dinched* it in the concrete flowerpot —John O'Hara>

din·er–out \ˌdīnə'rau̇t\ *n, pl* **diners–out** \ˌdīnə(r)'zau̇t \ : one who dines away from home esp. in the course of an active social life <an essential aspect of being a leading writer, in his opinion, was to be a leading *diner-out* —W.G. Rogers>

ding–a–ling* \'diŋəˌliŋ\ *n* : DINGBAT

ding·bat* \'diŋˌbat\ *n* : a silly or crazy person <convinced huge chunks of the electorate . . . that the candidate is a gibbering *dingbat* —H.S. Thompson>

dink \'diŋk\ *n* [origin unknown] *slang* : a Vietnamese — used disparagingly

di·ox·in \dī'äksən\ *n* [*di-* two + *oxygen* + *-in* chemical compound] : any of several heterocyclic hydrocarbons that occur esp. as persistent toxic impurities in herbicides; *esp* : a teratogenic impurity $C_{12}H_4O_2Cl_4$ in 2,4,5,-T

di·phos·pho·gly·cer·ic acid \(ˈ)dīˌfäsfō(ˌ)glis'erik-\ *n* [*di-* two + *phosph-* phosphate + *glyceric acid*] : a diphosphate of glyceric acid that is an important intermediate in photosynthesis and in glycolysis and fermentation

dip·lo·tene \ˌdipləˌtēn\ *adj* : relating to or being the diplotene stage of meiotic prophase

di·pyr·i·dam·ole \(ˈ)dīˌpirə'damˌōl, -ōl\ *n* [*di-* two + *pyrid*ine + *am*ino + *-ol* hydrocarbon of the benzene series] : a drug $C_{24}H_{40}N_8O_4$ used as a coronary vasodilator

di·quat \'dīˌkwät\ *n* [*di-* two + *quat*ernary] : a powerful nonpersistent herbicide $C_{12}H_{12}Br_2N_2$ that has been used to control water weeds (as the water hyacinth)

director's chair *n* [fr. its use by movie directors] : a lightweight usu. folding armchair with a back and seat usu. of cotton duck

dir·ham* \də'ram\ *n* **1 a** : the basic monetary unit of Morocco and the United Arab Emirates **b** : a coin or note representing one dirham **2 a** (1) : a monetary unit of Iraq equal to $^1/_{20}$ dinar (2) : a coin representing one dirham **b** : a monetary unit of Libya equal to $^1/_{1000}$ dinar

dirty pool *n* [*pool* pocket billiards] : underhanded or unsportsmanlike conduct <none of the lawyers . . . seems to have been disturbed by the fact that all the recommended techniques were illegal. It appears that the scheme . . . was rejected not on the ground that it was *dirty pool* but on the ground of impracticality —*New Yorker*>

dis·ag·gre·gate* \(ˈ)dis'agrəˌgāt\ *vi* : to break up or apart <the molecules of a gel *disaggregate* to form a sol> — **dis·ag·gre·ga·tive** \-ˌgād·iv\ *adj*

dis·am·big·u·ate \ˌdis(ˌ)am'bigyəˌwāt, -əwət\ *vt* **-at·ed; -at·ing** [*dis-* reverse, do the opposite (fr. L) + *ambigu*ous + *-ate* act on] : to establish a single semantic or grammatical interpretation for — **dis·am·big·u·ation** \-ˌbigyə'wāshən\ *n*

dis·bound \(ˈ)dis'bau̇nd\ *adj* : no longer having a binding <a *disbound* pamphlet>

disc brake *n* : a brake that operates by the friction of a caliper pressing against the sides of a rotating disc

dis·co·theque \'diskəˌtek, ˌdiskə'tek\ *n* [F *discothèque* collection of phonograph records, discotheque, fr. *disque* disk (fr. L *discus*) + connective *-o-* + *thèque* (as in *bibliothèque* library, fr. L *bibliotheca*)] : a usu. small intimate nightclub for dancing to recorded music; *also* : a nightclub often featuring psychedelic and mixed-media attractions (as slides, movies, and special lighting effects)

dis·cre·tion·ary account \dis'kreshə,nerē-, *chiefly Brit* -'kreshən(ə)ri-\ *n* : a security or commodity market account in which an agent (as a broker) is given power of attorney allowing him to make independent decisions and buy and sell for the account of his principal

discretionary income *n* : the part of personal income left after basic necessities (as food, shelter, and taxes) have been paid for

dis·cret·iza·tion \(,)dis,krēd·ə'zāshən\ *n* : the action of making mathematically discrete

dish·ware \'dish,wa(ə)r, -,we(ə)r, -,waə, -,weə\ *n* : tableware (as of china) used in serving food

dishy \'dishē, -i\ *adj* **dish·i·er; -est** *chiefly Brit* : being good-looking : attractive <kissed and caressed by *dishy* young girls —*Daily Mirror (London)*> <looks *dishier* than he did when he was one of the cinema's favorite romantic heroes —Margaret Forwood>

dis·in·sec·tion \,disən'sekshən, -,in's-\ *n* : removal of insects (as from an aircraft)

dis·in·ter·me·di·a·tion \(,)dis,intə(r),mēdē'āshən\ *n* [fr. the investor's bypassing of the intermediate institution] : diversion of savings from institutions (as savings banks) with governmentally imposed interest ceilings to direct investment in higher-yielding securities

dis·in·tox·i·cate \;disᵊn'täksə,kāt\ *vt* : to subject (as a drug user or an alcoholic) to disintoxication

dis·joint* \(;)dis'joint\ *adj* : lacking common members <*disjoint* mathematical sets>

disk* *or* **disc*** *n* **1** : a round flat plate (as of metal) coated with a magnetic substance on which data for a computer can be stored — called also *magnetic disk* **2** : a circular grid in a phototypesetting machine

disk·ette \'dis,ket, ,dis'ket\ *n* [*disk* + *-ette*, dim. suffix] : FLOPPY DISC

disk pack *n* : a storage device for a computer that consists of a stack of magnetic disks mounted on a central hub and their removable protective cover and that can be handled and stored as a unit

displacement* *n* : the substitution of another form of behavior for what is normal or expected esp. when the normal response is nonadaptive

display* *n* : a device (as a cathode-ray tube) that gives information in visual form in communications <a computer *display*> <a radar *display*>

dis·pos·able \dis'pōzəbəl\ *n* : something (as a paper blanket) that is disposable <returnable containers have been replaced by *disposables* —P.C. Stuart>

dissonance* *n* : inconsistency between the beliefs one holds or between one's actions and one's beliefs : discord

dis·tract·er* *or* **dis·tract·or*** \dis'traktə(r)\ *n* : an incorrect answer given as a choice in a multiple-choice test

distribute* *vi* **-ut·ed; -ut·ing** : to be mathematically distributive

distributed *adj* : characterized by a statistical distribution of a particular kind <a normally *distributed* random variable>

distribution* *n* **1** : an arrangement of statistical data that exhibits the frequency of the occurrence of the values of a variable : frequency distribution **2** : a function of a discrete random variable that gives the probability that a specific value will occur : probability function **3** : a function of a continuous random variable whose integral over an interval gives the probability that its value will fall within the interval : probability density function

distribution function *n* : a function that gives the probability that a random variable is less than or equal to the independent variable of the function

distributive education *n, often cap D & E* : a vocational program set up between schools and employers in which the student receives both classroom instruction and on-the-job training

di·sul·fi·ram \,dī'səlfə,ram\ *n* [tetraethylthiu*ram disulfi*de] : a compound $C_{10}H_{20}N_2S_4$ that causes a severe physiological reaction to alcohol and is used in the treatment of alcoholism

di·sul·fo·ton \dī'səlfə·ˌtän\ *n* [*di*ethyl + *sulfo-* containing sulfur + *-ton* (prob. fr. *thionate*)] : an organophosphorus systemic insecticide $C_8H_{19}O_2PS_3$ used esp. on cultivated plants

di·uron \'dīyəˌrän\ *n* [*di-* two + *urea* + *-on* chemical compound] : a persistent herbicide $C_9H_{10}Cl_2N_2O$ used esp. to control annual weeds

di·verge* \də'vərj, (ˈ)dīˈv-, -vəj-, -vəij-\ *vi* **diverged; diverg·ing** : to be mathematically divergent

divergence* *n* : the state of being mathematically divergent

divide* *vt* **divid·ed; divid·ing** : to use as a divisor — used with *into* < *divide* 14 into 42 >

divide* *n* : an instance of division performed by a computer; *also* : the means for performing division

division sign *n* **1** : the symbol ÷ used to indicate division **2** : a diagonal / used to indicate a fraction

DMSO \ˌdē(ˌ)emˌe'sō\ *n* [*di*methyl *sulf*oxide] : DIMETHYLSULFOXIDE

DMT \ˌdēˌem'tē\ *n* [*di*methyl*t*ryptamine] : DIMETHYLTRYPTAMINE

DMZ *abbr* demilitarized zone

DN·ase \(ˈ)dēˈenˌās, -ˌāz\ *also* **DNA·ase** \(ˌ)dēˌen'āˌās, -ˌāz\ *n* : an enzyme that hydrolyzes DNA to nucleotides

DNF *abbr* did not finish

Do·bro \'dō(ˌ)brō\ *trademark* — used for an acoustic guitar having a metal resonator

dock* *vt* : to maneuver and join mechanically (as two spacecraft) while in space

doggie bag *or* **doggy bag** *n* [fr. the original assumption that such leftovers were destined for the diner's dog] : a bag used for carrying home leftover food and esp. meat from a meal eaten at a restaurant

do–good·ing \'düˈgu̇diŋ\ *n* : the activities of a do-gooder

dogs·body \'do̊gzˌbädē, *sometimes* 'däg-\ *n* [Brit. naval slang, midshipman, fr. slang *dog's body* pease pudding] *chiefly Brit* : one who performs menial tasks <thought it would be grand to have a housekeeper and general *dogsbody* he wouldn't have to pay, and could bully —Georgette Heyer>

do–it–your·self \ˈdüəchə(r)ˈself, -ətyə-\ *adj* : of, relating to, or designed for use in construction, repair, or artistic work done by an amateur or hobbyist <a *do-it-yourself* car model kit>

do–it–your·self·er \-'selfə(r)\ *n* : one who engages in do-it-yourself activities

do·jo \'dō(ˌ)jō\ *n, pl* **dojos** [Jap *dōjō*, fr. *dō* way, art + *-jō* ground] : a school for training in various arts of self-defense (as judo and karate)

Dol·by·ized \'do̊lbēˌīzd, 'dōl-\ *adj* : equipped with or recorded with the use of a Dolby System

Dol·by System \'do̊lbē-, 'dōl-, -bi-\ *trademark* — used for an electronic device that eliminates noise from recorded sound

dol·ce vi·ta \ˌdōlchē'vē(ˌ)tä, -(ˌ)chā-\ *n* [It, lit., sweet life] : a life of indolence and self-indulgence <introduced him to the *dolce vita* of New York's high-society bohemians —*Current Biog.*>

DOM \ˌdē(ˌ)ō'em\ *n* [prob. fr. *d*imeth*o*xy- containing two methoxy groups + *m*ethyl] : STP

dome car *n* : a railroad car with a raised glassed-in seating section

domestic prelate *n* : a priest having permanent honorary membership in the papal household and ranking above a papal chamberlain

domino effect *n* [fr. the fact that if a number of dominoes are stood on end one behind the other with a slight intervening space, a slight push on the first one will result in the toppling of all the others] : a cumulative effect produced when one event initiates a succession of similar events <businessmen, in particular, fear the *domino effect* of an increase that tends to push up the wages of higher-paid workers to keep pace with gains legislated for lower-paid employees —J.N. Erlenborn>

domino theory *n* [*domino* (effect)] **1** : the theory that if one nation in Southeast Asia becomes Communist-controlled the neighboring nations will also become Communist-controlled <the *domino theory* was offered to prove that all Asia, or more, was at stake —A.D. Tussing> **2** : the theory that if one act or event is allowed to take place a succession of similar acts or events will follow <another frequently mentioned fear is the *domino theory*—that if you grant the gays a lounge, all sorts of other deviant and weird groups will demand lounges —Robert Liebert>

done·ness \ˈdənnəs\ *n*: the condition of being cooked to the desired degree <test the meat for *doneness*>

dong \ˈdȯŋ\ *n, pl* **dong** [Annamese] **1** : the basic monetary unit of North Vietnam **2** : a coin or note representing one dong

do·pa·mine \ˈdōpəˌmēn, -əmən\ *n* [*dopa* + *amine*] : a monoamine neurotransmitter that is a decarboxylated form of dopa; *also* : dopa itself

dop·ant \ˈdōpənt\ *n* [*dope* to treat with a foreign substance + *-ant* agent] : an impurity added usu. in minute amounts to a pure substance to alter its properties

Dopp·ler \ˈdäplə(r)\ *adj* : of, relating to, or utilizing a shift in frequency in accordance with the Doppler effect; *also* : of or relating to Doppler radar

Doppler radar *n* : a radar system utilizing the Doppler effect for measuring velocity

dor·min \ˈdȯrmən\ *n* [*dorm*ancy + *-in* chemical compound] : ABSCISIC ACID

double bind *n*: a psychological dilemma in which a usu. dependent person (as a child) receives conflicting interpersonal communications from a single source or faces disparagement no matter what his response to a situation

dou·ble–blind \ˌdəbəlˈblīnd\ *adj* : of, relating to, or being an experimental procedure in which neither the subjects nor the experimenters know the makeup of the test and control groups during the actual course of the experiments — compare SINGLE-BLIND

double–cov·er \-ˈkəvə(r)\ *vt* : to cover (a single offensive player) with two defenders

double knit *n* : a knitted fabric (as wool) made with a double set of needles to produce a double thickness of fabric with each thickness joined by interlocking stitches

double precision *n* : the use of two computer words rather than one to represent a number

dou·ble·speak \ˈdəbəlˌspēk\ *n* : inflated, involved, and often deliberately ambiguous language <the semantic nightmare of Orwellian *doublespeak* where peace means war and love means hate —Stephen Ullmann>

doublet* *n* **1 a** : a pair of atomic, molecular, or nuclear quantum states that are usu. close together in energy and arise from two possible orientations of spin **b** : a pair of spectral frequencies of light arising from transitions to or from such quantum states **2** : a pair of otherwise similar elementary particles (as a proton and a neutron) with different charge

dove* *n* : one who takes a conciliatory attitude (as in a dispute) and advocates negotiations and compromise — compare HAWK — **dov·ish** \ˈdəvish\ *adj* — **dov·ish·ness** *n*

down·er* \ˈdau̇nə(r)\ *n* **1** : a depressant drug and esp. a barbiturate — compare UPPER **2** : something (as an experience, situation, or person) that is depressing <on those paranoid or *downer* days, it is easy to take offense —Sue Critchfield> <but the "Happiness Hour"... proved to be a soggy *downer* —John J. O'Connor>

down–home \ˌdau̇nˈhōm\ *adj* : having the simple, informal, earthy qualities that are characteristic of country people (as of the southern U.S.) <as *down-home* as Abe Lincoln —Seymour Krim> <family-style meals and informal, *down-home* hospitality —*Southern Living*> <the *down-home* quality of the black musical experience —Margo Jefferson> <funky *down-home* blues —Tony Glover>

down·play \ˈdau̇nˌplā\ *vt* : to play down : de-emphasize <government has long sought to *downplay* the reports of terrorism —J.N. Goodsell>

down·range \ˌdau̇nˈrānj\ *adv (or adj)* : away from a launching site and along the course of a test range

Down's syn·drome \ˈdau̇nˈsinˌdrōm, -ˈsindrəm\ *n* [J. L. H. *Down* †1896 Eng physician] : a congenital idiocy in which a child is born with slanting eyes, a broad short skull, and broad hands with short fingers : mongolism

down·tick \ˈdau̇nˌtik\ *n* : a stock market transaction at a price below the last previous transaction in the same security — compare UPTICK 1

dox·y·cy·cline \ˌdäksəˈsīˌklēn, -ˈsīklən\ *n* [*de*oxy- derived by the removal of an oxygen atom + *oxy*-containing oxygen + tetra*cycline*] : a broad-spectrum antimicrobial tetracycline derivative $C_{22}H_{24}N_2O_8$

dozens *n pl* : a game that consists of exchanging often obscene insults usu. about the members of the opponent's family <the real aim of the *dozens* was to get a dude so mad he'd cry —H.R. Brown>— often used in the phrase *play the dozens*

draft* *vi* : to drive close behind another car while racing at high speed in order to take advantage of the reduced air pressure created by the leading car

drag* *n* : something that is boring <their work . . . is a *drag* a good deal of the time —Nora Johnson>

drag queen *n* : a male homosexual who dresses as a woman

draw·down* \ˈdrȯˌdau̇n\ *n* : a lowering of the water level (as in a reservoir)

dream·scape \ˈdrēmzˌkāp, -mˌsk-\ *n* [*dream* + *-scape* (as in *landscape*)] : a dreamlike usu. surrealistic scene <seemed greener than he had remembered any jungle to be: a *dreamscape* out of neverland —Frank Yerby>; *also* : a painting of a dreamscape

drill·ship \ˈdrilˌship\ *n* : a ship equipped for drilling (as for oil) in the ocean floor

drive* *n* : a device including an electric motor and heads for reading or writing a magnetic storage medium (as magnetic tape or disks)

drive·line \ˈdrīvˌlīn\ *n* : the parts including the universal joint and the drive shaft that connect the transmission with the driving axles of an automotive vehicle

drive–up \-ˌəp\ *adj* : designed to allow patrons or customers to be served while remaining in their automobiles <two *drive-up* windows at the bank>

drop* *vt* **dropped; drop·ping** : to take (a drug) through the mouth : swallow <he *drops* acid>

drop–in \ˈdräˌpin\ *n* **1** : one who drops in : a casual visitor **2** : an informal social gathering at which guests are invited to drop in

drop out* *vi* : to withdraw from conventional society because of disenchantment with its values and mores <a kind of guru for the young who were *dropping out*—George Levine>

dropout* *n* **1** : one who drops out of conventional society **2** : a spot on a magnetic tape from which information has disappeared

drop pass *n* : a pass in ice hockey in which the dribbler skates past the puck leaving it for a teammate following close behind

drown·proof·ing \ˈdrau̇nˈprüfiŋ\ *n* : a technique for staying afloat in water for an extended period with minimum effort through the use of a person's natural buoyancy

drum printer *n* : a line printer in which the printing element is a revolving drum

drunk tank *n* : a large detention cell for arrested drunks

dry out *vt* : to detoxify from the effects of excessive drinking of alcoholic beverages ~ *vi* : to undergo detoxification

du·al–pur·pose fund \ˌd(y)üəlˌpərpəs-, -ˌpəp-, -ˌpəip-\ *n* : a closed-end investment company with two classes of shares one of which is entitled to all dividend income and the other to all gains from capital appreciation

duc·ti·bil·i·ty \ˌdəktəˈbilədˑē\ *n* : the quality or state of being ductile

dude* *n* : fellow, guy <jive-talking West Coast *dudes* and their ladies —Roger Greenspun>

du·en·de \düˈen(ˌ)dā\ *n* [Sp dial., charm, fr. Sp, ghost, goblin, fr. *duen de casa,* prob. fr. *dueño de casa* owner of a house] : the power to attract through personal magnetism and charm

dulls·ville \ˈdəlzˌvil\ *n, slang* : something or some place that is dull or boring <mostly it was one teacher speaking to one camera, and *dullsville* —M.P. Mayer> <that long-ago summer when he decided San Diego was *dullsville* —Guy Flatley>; *also* : the state of being bored : boredom <together, these American prototypes ought to spell *dullsville* —*Playboy*>

dummy variable *n* : an arbitrary mathematical symbol or variable that can be replaced by another without affecting the value of the expression in which it occurs <the variable of integration in a definite integral is a *dummy variable*>

dump* *vt* : to copy (data in a computer's internal storage) onto an external storage medium

dump* *n* : an instance of dumping data stored in a computer

dump on *vt* : to speak disparagingly of : BAD-MOUTH <made it a practice to . . . *dump on* . . . religious leaders —Faubion Bowers>

dune buggy *n* : a motor vehicle with oversize tires for driving on sand beaches

dunk shot *n* : a shot in basketball made by jumping high into the air and throwing the ball down through the basket

duplicate* *vi* **-cat·ed; -cat·ing** : to become duplicate : replicate <DNA in chromosomes *duplicates*>

du·pli·ca·tion* \ˌd(y)üplə̇ˈkāshən\ *n* : a chromosomal aberration in which a segment of genetic material is repeated

durable press *n* **1** : the process of treating a fabric with a chemical (as a resin) and heat for setting the shape and for aiding wrinkle resistance **2** : a material treated by durable press **3** : the condition of material treated by durable press — **du·ra·ble–press** \ˈd(y)u̇rəbəlˈpres\ *adj*

dust·off \ˈdəstˌȯf\ *n* [fr. the dust raised by a helicopter in landing or taking off] : a helicopter used to evacuate the dead and wounded from a combat area

dyke *or* **dike** \ˈdīk\ *n* [origin unknown] : a female homosexual; *esp* : one assuming an aggressively masculine role — **dy·key** *or* **di·key** \-kē\ *adj*

dy·nap·o·lis \dīˈnapələ̇s\ *n* [NGk, fr. *dyna*mikos dynamic (fr. Gk, powerful) + *polis* city, fr. Gk] : a city planned for orderly growth along a main traffic artery by means of self-contained communities

dys·au·to·no·mia \(ˌ)disˌȯd·əˈnōmēə, -ˌäd·-\ *n* [*dys-* abnormal, difficult (deriv. of Gk *dys-* bad, difficult) + *autonom*ic + *-ia* pathological condition] : a familial disorder of the nervous system characterized esp. by multiple sensory deficiency (as of taste and pain) and by excessive sweating and salivation — **dys·au·to·nom·ic** \-ˈnämik, -ēk\ *adj*

dys·ba·rism \ˈdisbəˌrizəm\ *n* [*dys-* + *bar-* weight, pressure (deriv. of Gk *barys* heavy) + *-ism* state, condition] : the complex of symptoms (as bends, headache, or mental disturbance) that accompanies exposure to excessively low or rapidly changing environmental air pressure

dys·gen·e·sis \(ˈ)disˈjenəsə̇s\ *n* : defective development esp. of the gonads (as in Klinefelter's syndrome or Turner's syndrome)

dys·to·pia \diˈstōpēə\ *n* [*dys-* + *-topia* (as in *utopia*)] : an imaginary place which is depressingly wretched and whose people lead a fearful existence <an Orwellian *dystopia* working away full blast —John Simon> — **dys·to·pi·an** \-pēən\ *adj*

E

earth·rise \ˈərthˌrīz, ˈə̄th-, ˈəith-\ *n* : the rising of the earth above the horizon of the moon as seen from the moon

EBCDIC \ˈepsə̇ˌdik, ˈebs-\ *n* [*e*xtended *b*inary *c*oded *d*ecimal *i*nterchange *c*ode] : a code for representing alphanumeric information (as on magnetic tape)

eb·ul·lism \ˈeb(y)əˌlizəm\ *n* [L *ebullire* to come bubbling out] : the formation of bubbles in body fluids under sharply reduced environmental pressure

ec·cle·si·al \ə̇ˈklēzēəl, eˈk-, -zhəl\ *adj* : of or relating to a church esp. as a formal and established institution : ecclesiastical <these differences of *ecclesial* belief . . . are not an absolute prohibition of intercommunion —W.M. Bassett>

ec·dy·sone \ˈekdə̇ˌsōn\ *n* [*ecdysis* + horm*one*] : any of several arthropod hormones that in insects are produced by the prothoracic gland and that trigger molting and metamorphosis

echo·en·ceph·a·log·ra·phy \ˌe(ˌ)kōənˌsefəˈlägrəfē, -fi\ *n* [ISV, fr. L *echo* + ISV *encephalography*] : the use of ultrasound in the examination and measurement of internal structures (as the ventricles) of the skull and in the diagnosis of abnormalities

echo·lo·cate \ˌekōˈlōˌkāt\ *vt* : to find by echolocation <a bat *echolocates* food> ~ *vi* : to utilize or have the capacity for echolocation

echo·vi·rus \ˈe(ˌ)kōˌvīrəs\ *n* [*e*nteric *c*ytopathogenic *h*uman *o*rphan + *virus*] : any of a group of picornaviruses that are found in the gastrointestinal tract, that cause cytopathic changes in cells in tissue culture, and that are sometimes associated with respiratory ailments and meningitis

eco·ca·tas·tro·phe \ˌekōkəˈtastrə(ˌ)fē, ˌēkō-\ *n* [*eco-* environment, habitat (deriv. of Gk *oikos* house) + *catastrophe*] : a major destructive upset in the balance of nature esp. when caused by the intervention of man

eco·cide \ˈekōˌsīd, ˈēkō-\ *n* [*eco-* + *-cide* killing, deriv. of L *caedere* to cut, kill] : the destruction and esp. the deliberate destruction (as in war) of large areas of the natural environment <herbicides, insecticides, bulldozers, and nuclear weapons now give humanity a greatly enhanced capability to commit *ecocide* —P.R. Ehrlich & J.P. Holdren>

eco·geo·graph·ic \ˌekōˌjēəˈgrafik, ˌēkō-\ *or* **eco·geo·graph·ic·al** \-əkəl\ *adj* : of or relating to both ecological and geographical aspects of the environment — **eco·geo·graph·i·cal·ly** \-k(ə)lē\ *adv*

economy *adj* : designed to save the buyer money <*economy* cars>

eco·phys·i·ol·o·gy \ˌēkōˌfizēˈäləjē, ˌekō-\ *n* : the science of the interrelationships between the physiology of organisms and their environment — **eco·phys·i·o·log·ic·al** \-ēəˈläjəkəl\ *adj* — **eco·phys·i·ol·o·gist** \-ēˈäləjəst\ *n*

eco·sphere \ˈēkōˌsfi(ə)r, ˈekō-, -ˌsfiə\ *n* : the parts of the universe (as the biosphere) habitable by living organisms — **eco·spher·ic** \-ˌsfi(ə)rik, -ˌsfer-\ *adj*

ec·to·crine \ˈektəkrən; -ˌkrin, -rīn, -rēn\ *n* [*ecto-* outside, external + *-crine* (as in *endocrine*)] : a metabolite produced by an organism of one kind and utilized by one of another kind

ec·to·hor·mone \ˌektəˈhorˌmōn, -ˌho(ə)ˌ-\ *n* : PHEROMONE — **ec·to·hor·mon·al** \ˌektəˌho(r)ˈmōnᵊl\ *adj*

ecu·me·nop·o·lis \ˌekyəməˈnäpələs, eˌkyüm-\ *n* [NGk *oikoumenopolis*, fr. Gk *oikoumenē* the inhabited world (deriv. of *oikos* house) + *polis* city] : a single city encompassing the whole world that is held to be a possibility of the future

ed·it \ˈedət\ *n* : an instance or the result of editing <had to stay up late to do the final *edit* on the CIA report —Robert Scheer>

EDP *abbr* electronic data processing

educational park *n* : a large centralized educational complex of elementary and secondary schools

educational psychologist *n* : a specialist in educational psychology

educational television *n* **1** : PUBLIC TELEVISION **2** : television that provides instructional material esp. for students sometimes by closed circuit

ed·u·ca·tion·ese \ˌejəˌkāshəˈnēz, -ēs\ *n* [*education* + *-ese* jargon] : the jargonistic language used esp. by educational theorists <the faults of *educationese* are excessive abstraction and intentional vagueness —Wilson Follett> <leads to their being "retained" (*educationese* for left back) in the first grade at least once —C.E. Silberman>

EEC *abbr* European Economic Community

egg* *n* — **with egg on one's face** : in a state of embarrassment or humiliation <after putting up a competent job of defending the indefensible, cheerfully confided that the Government was sure to change its mind and he only hoped they didn't do it too soon and leave him *with egg on his face* —Austin Mitchell>

egg cream *n* : a drink consisting of milk, a flavoring syrup, and soda water

ego–trip \ˈēgōˌtrip\ *vi* **-tripped; -trip·ping** : to behave in a self-seeking manner <never overplayed, never *ego-tripped*, never grabbed the spotlight —Bob Palmer> — **ego–trip·per** \-ə(r)\ *n*

ego trip *n* : something that enhances and satisfies one's ego <think that a woman is . . . on an *ego trip* if she wants to run for political office —Betty Friedan>

EHV *abbr* extra high voltage

ei·gen·vec·tor \ˈīgənˌvektə(r)\ *n* [ISV *eigen-* (fr. G *eigen* own, peculiar, characteristic) + *vector*] : CHARACTERISTIC VECTOR

eight·fold way \ˈāt,fōldˈwā\ *n* [fr. the *Eightfold Way*, the Buddhist teaching of the means of attaining Nirvana through rightness of belief, resolve, speech, action, livelihood, effort, thought, and meditation; fr. the fact that the most common grouping contains eight interacting particles] : a unified theoretical scheme for classifying the relationship among strongly interacting elementary particles on the basis of isospin and hypercharge

ekis·tics \əˈkistiks, ēˈk-\ *n pl but sing in constr* [NGk *oikistikē*, fr. fem. of *oikistikos* relating to settlement, fr. Gk, fr. *oikizein* to settle, colonize, fr. *oikos* house] : a science dealing with human settlements and drawing on the research and experience of professionals in various fields (as architecture, engineering, city planning, and sociology) — **ekis·tic** \-tik\ *adj* — **ekis·ti·cian** \ə,kiˈstishən, (,)ē,k-\ *n*

Ek·man dredge \ˌekmən-\ *n* [prob. fr. V.W. *Ekman* †1954 Swed. oceanographer] : a dredge that has opposable jaws operated by a messenger traveling down a cable to release a spring catch and that is used in ecology for sampling the bottom of a body of water

ekt·ex·ine \(ˈ)ekˌtek,sēn, -,sīn\ *n* [Gk *ekto-* outside + E *exine*] : a structurally variable outer layer of the exine

elec·tro·cor·ti·cog·ra·phy \əˌlektrō,kōrtəˌkägrəfē, ēˌl-, -kȯr-, -fi\ *n* [*electro-* electric + *cortico-* cortex + *-graphy* writing, deriv. of Gk *graphein* to write] : the process of recording electrical activity in the brain by placing electrodes in direct contact with the cerebral cortex — **elec·tro·cor·ti·co·graph·ic** \-təkəˌgrafik, -ēk\ *adj* — **elec·tro·cor·ti·co·graph·i·cal·ly** \-k(ə)lē, -li\ *adv*

elec·tro·der·mal \-ˌdərməl, -ˌdəm-, -ˌdəim-\ *adj* : of or relating to electrical activity in or electrical properties of the skin

elec·tro·fish·ing \əˈlektrō,fishiŋ, ēˈl-\ *n* : the taking of fish by a system based on their tendency to respond positively to a source of direct electric current

elec·tro·gas·dy·nam·ics \ə,lektrəˌgas(,)dīˈnamiks, ē,l-, -ēks\ *n pl but sing in constr* : a method of generating electrical energy that is based on the conversion of the kinetic energy of the flow of a high pressure charged combustion gas — **elec·tro·gas·dy·nam·ic** \-ik, -ēk\ *adj*

elec·tro·gen·e·sis \ə,lektrəˈjenəsəs, ēˌl-\ *n* : the production of electrical activity esp. in living tissue

elec·tro·gen·ic \əˌlektrəˌjenik, ēˌl-, -ēk\ *adj* : of or relating to the production of electricity in living tissue <an *electrogenic* pump causing movement of sodium ions across a membrane>

elec·tro·hy·drau·lic \əˌlektrō(,)hīˌdrȯlik, ēˌl-, -ēk\ *adj* **1** : of, relating to, or involving a combination of electric and hydraulic mechanisms <an *electrohydraulic* elevator> **2** : involving or produced by the action of very brief but powerful pulse discharges of electricity under a liquid resulting in the generation of shock waves and highly reactive chemical species <an *electrohydraulic* effect> — **elec·tro·hy·drau·li·cal·ly** \-k(ə)lē, -li\ *adv*

elec·tro·hy·drau·lics \-iks, -ēks\ *n pl but usu sing in constr* : the production of shock waves by electrohydraulic means

electromagnetic interaction *n* : a fundamental interaction experienced by most elementary particles that is responsible for the emission and absorption of photons and for electric and magnetic forces

electronic music *n* : music that consists of sounds electronically captured or originated, taped, and played through a loudspeaker

electron spin resonance *n* : the magnetic resonance of electrons that are either free or bound in atoms

electron transport *n* : the sequential transfer of electrons esp. by cytochromes in cellular respiration from an oxidizable substrate to molecular oxygen by a series of oxidation-reduction reactions

elec·tro·oc·u·lo·gram \əˌlektrōˌäkyələ,gram, ēˌl-\ *n* [*electro-* + *oculo-* eye (deriv. of L *oculus*) + *-gram* drawing, writing, record, deriv. of Gk *gramma* letter, writing] : a record of the standing voltage between the front and back of the eye that is correlated with eyeball movement (as in REM sleep) and obtained by electrodes suitably placed on the skin near the eye

elec·tro·pho·rese \ə͵lektrəfə'rēs, ē͵l-, -'träfə͵-, -ēz\ *vt* **-resed; -res·ing** [back-formation fr. *electrophoresis*] : to subject to electrophoresis

elec·tro·pho·reto·gram \ə͵lektrəfə'red·ə͵gram, ē͵l-\ *n* [*electrophoretic* + connective *-o-* + *-gram*] : a record that consists of the separated components of a mixture (as of proteins) produced by electrophoresis in a supporting medium (as filter paper)

elec·tro·ret·i·no·graph \ə¦lektrō¦ret(ᵊ)nə͵graf, ē¦l-\ *n* [*electro-* + *retino-* retina + *-graph* recording instrument, deriv. of Gk *graphein* to write] : an instrument for recording electrical activity in the retina — **elec·tro·ret·i·no·graph·ic** \-͵ret(ᵊ)nə¦grafik, -ēk\ *adj* — **elec·tro·ret·i·nog·ra·phy** \-(ᵊ)n'ägrəfē, -fi\ *n*

elec·tro·sen·si·tive \ə¦lektrō¦sen(t)səd·iv, -¦sen(t)stiv, ē¦l-, -ēv\ *adj* : being or using sensitive paper on which an image is produced by the passage of electric current through it

elec·tro·sleep \ə'lektrō͵slēp, ē'l-\ *n*: profound relaxation or a state of unconsciousness induced by the passage of a very low voltage electric current through the brain

elec·tro·stat·ic printing \ə¦lektrə¦stad·ik-, ē¦l-, -ēk-\ *n*: a process (as xerography) for printing or copying in which electrostatic forces are used to form the image (as with powder or ink) directly on a surface

el·e·doi·sin \͵elə'dȯisᵊn\ *n* [irreg. fr. NL *Eledone* + *-in* chemical compound] : a small protein $C_{54}H_{85}N_{13}O_{15}S$ from the salivary glands of several octopuses (genus *Eledone*) that is a powerful vasodilator and hypotensive agent

elementary particle* *n* : OXYSOME

el·hi \¦el͵hī\ *adj* [*el*ementary school + *hi*gh school] : of, relating to, or designed for use in grades 1 through 12 <*elhi* students> <*elhi* textbook publishers>

em·bour·geoise·ment \əm'bu̇rzh͵wäzmənt, äm-, em-, -u̇əzh-, -͵mänt, *F* äⁿbu̇rzhwȧzmäⁿ\ *n* [F, fr. *embourgeoiser* to make bourgeois] : the shift to bourgeois values and practices <the *embourgeoisement* of the working class since World War II —Alden Whitman>

emic \'ēmik\ *adj* [phon*emic*] : of, relating to, or having characteristics which are significant to the structure of a language or other behavioral system <a phonemic transcription . . . is an *emic* description of speech —John Algeo> — compare ETIC

em·pa·na·da \(͵)empə'nädə\ *n* [Sp, fr. *empanada* breaded, fem. of *empanado*, past part. of *empanar* to bread, fr. *em-* in + *pan* bread, fr. L *panis*] : a pastry turnover stuffed esp. with a savory meat filling

emulate* *vt* **-lat·ed; -lat·ing** : to imitate (a different computer system) by means of an emulator

emulation* *n* : the use of or technique of using an emulator

em·u·la·tor* \'emyə͵lād·ə(r)\ *n* : a hardware device or a combination of hardware and software that permits programs written for one computer to be run on another usu. newer computer

emul·si·ble \ə'məlsəbəl, ē'm-\ *adj* : capable of being emulsified <*emulsible* mixtures> <*emulsible* oils>

en·amine \'enə͵mēn, e'na͵m-\ *n* [*en-* having one double bond + *amine*] : an amine containing the double bond linkage C=C–N

en·cap·su·lant \ən'kapsələnt, en-, *also* -syə-\ *n* : a material used for encapsulating

en·ceph·a·lo·myo·car·di·tis \en'sefəlō͵mīə(͵)kär'dīd·əs\ *n* [*encephalo-* brain (deriv. of Gk *enkephalos*) + *myocarditis*] : an acute febrile virus disease characterized by degeneration and inflammation of skeletal and cardiac muscle and lesions of the central nervous system

encounter group *n* : a usu. leaderless and unstructured group that seeks to develop the capacity of the individual to express human feelings openly and to form close emotional ties by more or less unrestrained confrontation of individuals (as by physical contact, uninhibited verbalization, or nudity)

endangered *adj* : threatened with extinction <the California condor, one of our country's most *endangered* species of birds —R.C.B. Morton>

end around *n* : a football play in which an offensive end comes behind the line of scrimmage to take a handoff and attempts to carry the ball around the opposite flank

end·ar·ter·ec·to·my \͵en͵därd·ə'rektəmē\ *n* [*endarter*ium inner layer of an artery + *-ectomy* surgical removal, deriv. of Gk *ektemnein* to cut out] : surgical removal of the inner layer of an artery when thickened and atheromatous or occluded (as by intimal plaques)

end•exine \(ˈ)enˌdekˌsēn, -ˌsīn\ *n* [*end-* within, inside (deriv. of Gk *endon*) + *exine*] : an inner membranous layer of the exine

en•do•cyt•ic \ˈendəˈsid•ək, -ˈsīd•-\ *adj* : of or relating to endocytosis : ENDOCYTOTIC

en•do•cy•to•sis \ˌendōˌsīˈtōsəs\ *n, pl* **-to•ses** \-ˈtōˌsēz\ [NL, fr. *endo-* within, inside + *cyt-* cell (deriv. of Gk *kytos* hollow vessel) + *-osis* condition] : incorporation of substances into a cell by phagocytosis or pinocytosis — **en•do•cy•tot•ic** \ˌendōˌsīˌtäd-ik\ *adj*

end–of–day glass \ˌendə(v)ˈdāˌglas\ *n* [from its resemblance to objects made by glassblowers at the end of the day's work to use up various odds and ends of glass left over] : glass of various colors (as red, blue, green, and white) mixed together

en•do•gen•ic* \ˌendəˈjenik, -ēk\ *adj* **1 a** : growing from or on the inside : developing within the cell wall **b** : originating within the body **2** : constituting or relating to metabolism of the nitrogenous constituents of cells and tissues

en•do•mor•phism* \ˌendəˈmȯrˌfizəm\ *n* : a homomorphism that maps a mathematical set into itself — compare ISOMORPHISM

en•do•nu•cle•ase \ˌendōˈn(y)üklēˌās, -āz\ *n* : an enzyme that breaks down a chain of nucleotides (as a nucleic acid) at points not adjacent to the end and thereby produces two or more shorter nucleotide chains — compare EXONUCLEASE

en•do•phil•ic \ˌendəˌfilik\ *adj* [*endo-* within + *-philic* loving, deriv. of Gk *philos* beloved, loving] : ecologically associated with man and his domestic environment — compare EXOPHILIC — **en•doph•i•ly** \enˈdäfəlē\ *n*

en•do•plas•mic re•tic•u•lum \ˌendəˌplazmikrəˈtikyələm\ *n* : a system of interconnected vesicular and lamellar cytoplasmic membranes that functions esp. in the transport of materials within the cell and that is studded with ribosomes in some places

en•do•ra•dio•sonde \ˌendōˈrādēōˌsänd\ *n* : a microelectronic device introduced into the body to record physiological data

en•do•sul•fan \ˌendōˈsəlfən, -ˌfan\ *n* [perh. fr. *end*rin + connective *-o-* + *sulf-* sulfur + *-an* unsaturated carbon compound] : a brownish crystalline insecticide $C_9H_6Cl_6O_3S$ that is used in the control of numerous crop insects and some mites

en•do•tes•ta \ˈendōˌtestə\ *n* : an inner layer of the testa in various seeds — compare SCLEROTESTA

end•point \ˈen(d)ˌpȯint\ *n* : either of two points or values that mark the ends of a line segment or interval; *also* : a point that marks the end of a ray

en•duro \ənˈd(y)u̇(ə)r(ˌ)ō, en-\ *n, pl* **-dur•os** [irreg. fr. *endurance*] : a long race (as for automobiles or motorcyles) stressing endurance rather than speed

en•er•get•ics* \ˌenə(r)ˈjed•iks, -ēks\ *n pl but sing in constr* : the total energy relations and transformations of a system (as a chemical reaction or an ecological community) < *energetics* of muscular contraction >

en•er•giz•er* \ˈenə(r)ˌjīzə(r)\ *n* : ANTIDEPRESSANT

energy* *n* : usable power (as heat or electricity) < urgent need for more large supplies of gas to meet growing *energy* requirements —*Annual Report Atlantic Richfield Co.* >; *also* : the resources for producing such power < the global search for new *energy* sources >

energy budget *n* : an accounting of the income, use, and loss of energy in an ecosystem < the sun's contribution to the *energy budget* of the earth —M. K. Hubbert >

en•ga•gé \ˌäŋgäˈzhā, ˌeŋ- , *F* äⁿgȧzhā\ *adj* [F, fr. past part. of *engager* to engage, pledge] : committed to or supportive of a cause < a man of devout pacifism . . . making even his art *engagé* —E. M. Yoder, Jr. >

English cock•er spaniel \-ˌkäkə(r)-\ *n* : any of a breed of spaniels that have square muzzles, wide well-developed noses, and distinctive heads which are ideally half muzzle and half skull with the forehead and skull arched and slightly flattened

en•tero•bac•te•ri•um \ˌentə(ˌ)rō(ˌ)bakˈtirēəm\ *n* : a bacterium of the family Enterobacteriaceae — **en•tero•bac•te•ri•al** \-ēəl\ *adj* — **en•tero•bac•te•ri•ol•o•gist** \-(ˌ)bakˌtirēˈäləjəst\ *n*

en·tero·path·o·gen·ic \-ˌpathəˈjenik\ *adj* [*entero-* intestine (deriv. of Gk *enteron*) + *pathogenic*] : tending to produce disease in the intestinal tract < *enteropathogenic* bacteria >

en·ter·op·a·thy \ˌentəˈräpəthē\ *n* [*entero-* + *-pathy* disease] : a disease of the intestinal tract

en·tero·vi·rus \ˈentərōˈvīrəs\ *n* [NL, fr. *entero-* + *virus*] : any of a group of picornaviruses (as a Coxsackie virus) that typically occur in the gastrointestinal tract but may be involved in respiratory ailments, meningitis, and neurological disorders — **en·tero·vi·ral** \-rəl\ *n*

en·train* \ənˈtrān, en-\ *vt* : to determine or modify the phase or period of < circadian rhythms *entrained* by a light cycle >

en·ven·om·ation \ənˌvenəˈmāshən, enˌv-\ *n* : an act or instance of impregnating with a venom (as of a snake or spider)

en·ven·om·iza·tion \-əməˈzāshən, -(ˌ)mīˈzā-\ *n* : a poisoning caused by a bite or sting

environment* *n* : an artistic or theatrical work that involves or encompasses the spectator : an instance of environmental art or theater

en·vi·ron·men·tal* \ənˈvīrə(n)ˈmen(t)ᵊl, (ˌ)en-, -ˈvī(ə)r(n)-\ *adj* : involving or encompassing the spectator rather than simply facing him < *environmental* art > < *environmental* theater >

en·vi·ron·men·tal·ist \-ˌvīrə(n)ˈmen(t)ᵊləst, -ˌvī(ə)r(n)-\ *n* : one concerned about the quality of the human environment; *specif* : a specialist in human ecology

epi·fau·na \ˈepəˈfȯnə, ˈepē-, -ˈfänə\ *n* [NL, fr. *epi-* upon (deriv. of Gk *epi* on, upon) + *fauna*] : benthic fauna living on the substrate and esp. on a hard sea floor — compare INFAUNA — **epi·fau·nal** \-nᵊl\ *adj*

epis·co·pal vicar \əˈpiskəpəl-, -əbəl-\ *n* : a bishop assigned to the pastoral supervision of a part of a Roman Catholic diocese

epi·some \ˈepəˌsōm\ *n* [*epi-* + *-some* body, deriv. of Gk *sōma*] : a genetic determinant (as the DNA of some bacteriophages) that can replicate either autonomously in bacterial cytoplasm or as an integral part of the chromosomes — **epi·som·al** \ˈepəˈsōməl\ *adj* — **epi·som·al·ly** \-lē, -li\ *adv* — **epi·som·ic** \-ōmik\ *adj*

EPN \ˌē(ˌ)pēˈen\ *n* [*e*thyl *p*ara-*n*itro-phenyl] : an organophosphorus miticide and insecticide $C_{14}H_{14}NO_4PS$ used esp. on cotton and orchard crops that enhances the toxicity of malathion to vertebrates

ep·oxy \əˈpäksē, eˈp-, (ˌ)ēˈp-, -si\ *vt* **ep·ox·ied** *or* **ep·oxyed; ep·oxy·ing** : to glue with epoxy

Ep·stein–Barr virus \ˌepˌstīnˈbär-\ *n* [Michael Anthony *Epstein* and Y. M. *Barr*, 20th cent. Eng. pathologists, its discoverers] : a herpes virus that causes infectious mononucleosis and that is associated with Burkitt's lymphoma and nasopharyngeal carcinoma

equiv·a·lence class \əˈkwiv(ə)lən(t)s-, ēˈ-\ *n* : a set for which an equivalence relation holds between every pair of elements

equivalence relation *n* : a relation (as equality) between elements of a set (as the real numbers) that is symmetric, reflexive, and transitive and for any two elements either holds or does not hold

equivalent *adj* **1** : having the same solution set < *equivalent* equations > **2** : related by an equivalence relation

ER *abbr* emergency room

erase* *vt* **erased; eras·ing** : to delete from a computer storage device

er·go·met·ric \ˌərgəˈme·trik, -ēk\ *adj* : relating to, obtained by, or being an ergometer < *ergometric* investigations > < *ergometric* findings > < an *ergometric* bicycle >

er·gon·o·mist \(ˌ)ərˈgänəməst\ *n* [fr. *ergonomic* biotechnological, fr. *ergo-* work (fr. Gk *ergon*) + *economic*] : a specialist in biotechnology

er·o·tol·o·gy \ˌerəˈtäləjē\ *n* [Gk *erōt-*, *erōs* sexual love + *-logy* oral or written expression, theory, science, deriv. of Gk *logos* word] : erotic description or literature — **er·o·to·log·i·cal** \ˈerəd·ᵊlˈäjəkəl\ *adj*

er·y·thor·bate \ˌerəˈthȯrˌbāt\ *n* [*erythorbic (acid)* + *-ate* derivative compound] : a salt of erythorbic acid that is used in foods as an antioxidant

er·y·thor·bic acid \ˌerəˈthȯrbik-, -bēk-\ *n* [prob. fr. *erythrose* + asc*orbic acid*] : an optical isomer of ascorbic acid

eryth·ro·leu·ke·mia \əˌrithrō(ˌ)lüˈkēmēə\ *n* [NL, fr. *erythro-* red (deriv. of Gk *erythros*) + *leukemia*] : a malignant disorder that is marked by proliferation of erythroblastic and myeloblastic tissue and in later stages by leukemia

eryth·ro·poi·e·tin \əˌrithrəˈpȯiətᵊn\ *n* [*erythropoietic* producing red blood cells + *-in* chemical compound] : a hormonal substance that is prob. formed in the kidney and stimulates red blood cell formation

es·bat \ˈesˌbat\ *n* [OF, esbat, diversion, blow, fr. *esbatre* to divert, amuse, beat, fr. (assumed) VL *exbattuere*, fr. L *ex-*, intensive prefix + *battuere* to beat] : a meeting of a coven of witches

es·ca·late* \ˈeskəˌlāt, ÷-kyə-\ *vb* **-lat·ed; -lat·ing** *vi* : to increase in extent, volume, number, amount, or scope : expand <any limited nuclear war would rapidly *escalate* into full-scale disaster —*Sat. Eve. Post*> **~** *vt* : to increase the extent, volume, number, amount, or scope of < *escalated* the case from a political crisis to an epic constitutional collision —*Newsweek*>

es·ca·la·tion* \ˌeskəˈlāshən, ÷ -kyə-\ *n* : an increasing in extent, volume, number, amount, or scope — **es·ca·la·to·ry** \ˈeskələˌtōrē, -ˌtȯr-, ÷ -kyə-\ *adj*

ESL *abbr* English as a second language

establishment* *n, often cap* **1** : a group of social, economic, and political leaders who form a ruling class (as of a nation) <by *them* he meant not the English, but the governing classes, the *Establishment*—A.J.P. Taylor> **2** : a controlling group <the Welsh literary *Establishment*. . . kept him out of everything —Keidrych Rhys> <the high-strung gladiators of the cookbook *establishment*. . . who are forever plunging verbal forks into each other's orange soufflés —Marcia Seligson>

estimate* *n* : a numerical value obtained from a statistical sample and assigned to a population parameter

es·ti·ma·tor* \ˈestəmād·ə(r)\ *n* : ESTIMATE; *also* : a statistical function whose value for a sample furnishes an estimate of a population parameter

es·tro·ge·nic·i·ty \ˌestrəjəˈnisəd·ē\ *n* : capacity for estrogenic action or effect

ET* *abbr* elapsed time

eta particle \ˈād·ə-, ˈēd·ə-\ *n* [*eta*, the seventh letter in the Greek alphabet] : an uncharged and spinless elementary particle that has a mass 1074 times the mass of an electron and that decays rapidly into pions or gamma rays

eth·a·cryn·ic acid \ˌethəˌkrinik-, -nēk-\ *n* [fr. *eth*ane + *a*cetic + buty*ryl* + phe*n*ol] : a diuretic $C_{13}H_{12}Cl_2O_4$ used esp. in the treatment of edema

eth·am·bu·tol \ethˈambyu̇ˌtȯl, -ˌtōl\ *n* [*eth*ylene + *am*ine + *bu*tan*ol*] : a compound $C_{10}H_{24}N_2O_2$ used esp. in the treatment of tuberculosis

etha·mi·van \eˈthaməˌvan, ˌethəˈmīvən\ *n* [di*eth*yl + *am*ide + *van*illic acid] : an analeptic drug and central nervous stimulant $C_{12}H_{17}NO_3$ that is related to vanillic acid and is used as a respiratory stimulant for intoxication with central nervous depressants (as barbiturates) and for chronic lung diseases

eth·i·on \ˈethēˌän\ *n* [blend of *ethyl* and *thion-* sulfur, fr. Gk *theion*] : an organophosphate $C_9H_{22}O_4P_2S_4$ used as a pesticide

eth·i·on·amide \ˌethēˈänəˌmīd, əˈthīən-, -əməd\ *n* [ethyl + *thion-* + *amide*] : a compound $C_8H_{10}N_2S$ used against mycobacteria (as in tuberculosis and leprosy)

ethnic* *n* : a member of an ethnic group; *esp* : one who retains the customs, language, or social views of his group

eth·no·mu·si·col·o·gy \ˌeth(ˌ)nōˌmyüzəˈkäləjē, -ji\ *n* [*ethno-* ethnic (deriv. of Gk *ethnos* nation) + *musicology*] : a study of the music chiefly of non-European cultures esp. in relation to the culture that produces it — **eth·no·mu·si·co·log·i·cal** \-əkəˈläjəkəl\ *adj* — **eth·no·mu·si·col·o·gist** \-əˈkäləjəst\ *n*

eth·no·sci·ence \ˈethnōˌsīən(t)s\ *n* : the nature lore (as folk taxonomy of plants and animals) of primitive people

eth·o·sux·i·mide \ˌethōˈsəksəˌmīd, -əməd\ *n* [*eth*yl + connective *-o-* + *-suximide* (by shortening and alter. fr. *succinimide*)] : an antidepressant drug $C_7H_{11}NO_2$ derived from succinic acid and used to relieve epilepsy

et·ic \ˈed·ik\ *adj* [phon*etic*] : of, relating to, or having linguistic or behavioral characteristics considered without regard to their structural significance <a sound spectrogram is a good example of *etic* description —John Algeo> — compare EMIC

etio·patho·gen·e·sis \ˌēd·ēōˌpathəˈjenəsə̇s, *also* ˌe-\ *n* [*etio-* cause (deriv. of Gk *aitia*) + *pathogenesis* development of a disease] : the cause and development of a disease or abnormal condition

ETV *abbr* educational television

eu·phen·ics \yüˈfeniks, -nēks\ *n pl but sing in constr* [*eu-* good, well (deriv. of Gk *eys* good) + *phen-* (fr. *phenotype*); after E *genotype: eugenics*] : a science that deals with the biological improvement of human beings after birth — **eu·phen·ic** \-ik, -ēk\ *adj*

Eu·ro·bond \ˈyu̇rōˌbänd\ *n* [*Euro*pe + *bond*] : a bond sold outside its country of origin; *esp* : a bond of a U.S. corporation that is sold outside the U.S. and that is denominated and paid for in dollars and yields interest in dollars

Eu·ro·crat \ˈyu̇rəˌkrat\ *n* [*Euro*pe + *-crat* member of a class or faction, deriv. of Gk *kratos* strength, power] : a staff member of the administrative commission of the European Common Market

Eu·ro·cur·ren·cy \ˈyu̇rōˌkər·ənsē, -ˌkə·rənsē\ *n* [*Euro*pe + *currency*] : moneys (as of the U.S. and Japan) held outside their countries of origin and used in the money markets of Europe

Eu·ro·dol·lar \-ˌdälə(r)\ *n* [*Euro*pe + *dollar*] : a U.S. dollar held outside the U.S. and esp. in Europe

Eu·ro·po·cen·tric \yəˌrōpəˌsen·trik, ˌyürəpə-\ *adj* : centered on Europe and the Europeans <both [China and the United States] remained outside the *Europocentric* power politics of the 19th century —J.K. Fairbank> <the ethnocentric, or *Europocentric,* view that has been held for so long a time in the West —C.V. Woodward> — **Euro·po·cen·trism** \-ˌsen·trizəm\ *n*

EVA *abbr* extravehicular activity

even per·mu·ta·tion \-ˌpərmyu̇ˈtāshən\ *n* : a permutation that is produced by the successive application of an even number of interchanges of pairs of elements — compare ODD PERMUTATION

event* *n* : a subset of the possible outcomes of a statistical experiment <7 is an *event* in the throwing of two dice>

ev·er·glade \ˈevə(r)ˌglād\ *n* [fr. the *Everglades,* Fla.] : a swampy grassland esp. in southern Florida usu. containing sawgrass and at least seasonally covered by slowly moving water — usu. used in pl.

ex·ac·ta \igˈzaktə, eg-\ *n* [AmerSp *quiniela exacta* exact quiniela] : PERFECTA

exchange force *n* : a force between two elementary particles (as a neutron and a proton) arising from the continuous interchange between them of other particles (as pions)

ex·ci·mer \ˈeksə̇(ˌ)mə(r)\ *n* [*exci*ted di*mer*] : a dimer existing in an excited state

ex·ci·ton \ˈeksə̇ˌtän\ *n* [*excit*ation + *-on* elementary particle] : a mobile bound electron-hole pair that is produced in a solid by the absorption of a photon — **ex·ci·ton·ic** \ˌeksə̇ˌtänik\ *adj*

ex·ci·ton·ics \ˌeksə̇ˈtäniks\ *n pl but sing in constr* : a branch of solid-state physics that deals with excitons and their behavior in semiconductors and dielectrics

ex·clu·sion·ary rule \ə̇ksˈklüzhəˌnerē-, eks-\ *n* : a legal rule that bars any unlawfully obtained evidence from being used in court proceedings

exclusive dis·junc·tion \-disˈjəŋ(k)shən\ *n* : a statement of a logical proposition expressing alternatives usu. taking the form $p + q$ meaning p or q but not both

ex–di·rec·to·ry \ˌeksdə̇ˌrekt(ə)rē, *rapid* -ˌdrek-\ *adj* [L *ex* out of] *Brit* : not listed in a telephone directory : unlisted < *ex-directory* number>

exo·bi·ol·o·gy \ˌek(ˌ)sōbīˈäləjē\ *n* [*exo-* outside (fr. Gk *exō*) + *biology*] : extraterrestrial biology — **exo·bi·o·log·i·cal** \-ˌbīəˌläjə̇kəl\ *adj* — **exo·bi·ol·o·gist** \-bīˈäləjə̇st\ *n*

ex·o·cri·nol·o·gy \ˌeksəkrə̇ˈnäləjē, -ˌkrī-, -ˌkrē-\ *n* [*exocrine* secreting externally (fr. *exo-* + *-crine,* fr. Gk *krinein* to separate) + connective *-o-* + *-logy* theory, science, deriv. of Gk *logos* word] : the study of external secretions (as pheromones) that serve an integrative function

exo·cy·clic \¦ek(ˌ)sō¦sīklik, -¦sik-\ *adj* : situated outside of a ring in a chemical structure

exo·nu·cle·ase \ˌeksō'n(y)üklēˌās, -ˌāz\ *n* : an enzyme that breaks down a nucleic acid by removing nucleotides one by one from the end of a chain — compare ENDONUCLEASE

exo·nu·mia \ˌeksə'n(y)ümēə\ *n pl* [NL, fr. *exo-* + E *numismatic* + NL *-ia* related things] : numismatic items (as tokens, medals, or scrip) other than coins and paper money

exo·nu·mist \ˌeksə'n(y)ümə̇st, 'eksəˌn(y)ü-\ *n* **1** : a specialist in exonumia **2** : a collector of exonumia

exo·phil·ic \¦eksə¦filik\ *adj* [*exo-* + *-philic* loving, deriv. of Gk *philos* beloved, loving] : ecologically independent of man and his domestic environment — compare ENDOPHILIC — **ex·oph·i·ly** \ek'säfəlē\ *n*

exotic* *adj* : of or relating to striptease < *exotic* dancing >

exotic* *n* : a dancer who performs a striptease

explosive* *adj* : done by the force of a controlled explosion < *explosive* welding > < *explosive* forming of metal parts >

ex·po \'ek(ˌ)spō\ *n, pl* **ex·pos** [short for *exposition*] : a public exhibition or show : an exposition

ex·po·nence \ik'spōnən(t)s, ek's-, 'ekˌs-\ *n* [fr. *exponent,* after such pairs as E *dependent: dependence*] : the correlation between an abstract linguistic category and its exponents < by moving towards the data within abstractions one is considered to be moving down the scale of *exponence* —R.H. Robins >

ex·po·nent* \-nənt\ *n* : a specific element of a linguistic category < *eat* is an *exponent* of the class 'verb' >

ex·po·nen·ti·a·tion \ˌekspəˌnenchē'āshən, *sometimes* -n(t)sē-\ *n* [*exponent* + *-iation* (as in *differentiation*)] : the act or process of raising a quantity to a power

extension* *n* : a mathematical set (as a field or group) that includes a given and similar set as a subset

ex·tra·chro·mo·som·al \¦ekstrəˌkrōmə¦sōməl, -¦zō-\ *adj* [*extra-* outside, beyond (deriv. of L *extra*) + *chromosomal*] : situated or controlled by factors outside the chromosomes < *extrachromosomal* inheritance >

ex·tra·cor·po·re·al \-kȯ(r)¦pōrēəl, -¦pȯr-\ *adj* : occurring or based outside the living body < heart surgery employing *extracorporeal* circulation > — **ex·tra·cor·po·re·al·ly** \-ēəlē\ *adv*

ex·tra·cra·ni·al \-¦krānēəl\ *adj* : situated or occurring outside the cranium < *extracranial* arterial occlusion >

ex·tra·mi·to·chon·dri·al \-ˌmīd·ə¦kändrēəl\ *adj* : situated or occurring in the cell outside the mitochondria < *extramitochondrial* synthesis of fatty acids >

ex·tra·ne·ous* \(')ek¦strānēəs, ik's-\ *adj*: being a number obtained in solving an equation that is not a solution of the equation < *extraneous* roots >

ex·tra·nu·cle·ar* \¦ekstrə'n(y)üklēə(r), ÷-kyələ(r)\ *adj* : situated outside the nucleus of an atom < *extranuclear* electrons >

ex·traor·di·naire \(ˌ)ekˌstrȯrdᵊn'e(ə)r, ˌekstrəˌȯrd-\ *adj* [F] : markedly exceptional : remarkable, extraordinary — used postpositively < jazz artist *extraordinaire* and composer of more than 50 film scores —Barbara Wilkins > < this bathroom *extraordinaire* is the size of most people's living rooms —Lisa Hammel >

ex·tra·re·nal \¦ekstrə¦rēnᵊl\ *adj* : situated or occurring outside the kidneys < *extrarenal* action of diuretics >

ex·tra·so·lar \-¦sōlə(r), -ˌlär, -ˌlȧ(r\ *adj* : originating or existing outside the solar system < *extrasolar* life >

ex·tra·ve·hic·u·lar \-vē'hikyələ(r)\ *adj* **1** : taking place outside a vehicle (as a spacecraft) < *extravehicular* activity > < an *extravehicular* assignment >

eye chart *n* : a chart that is read at a fixed distance for purposes of testing sight; *esp* : one with rows of letters or objects of decreasing size

eye contact *n*: visual contact with another person's eyes < a handbook . . . put out by one of those new nudist camps . . . which advised beginners to practice *eye contact* —W.K. Zinsser >

eye doctor *n* : a specialist (as an optometrist or ophthalmologist) in the examination, treatment, or care of the eyes

eye·lin·er \ˈī,līnə(r)\ *n* : makeup used to emphasize the contour of the eyes

F

f* *abbr* femto-

fab·ri·ca·ble \ˈfabrəkəbəl\ *adj* [LL *fabricabilis*, fr. L *fabricari* to fabricate] : capable of being shaped <*fabricable* alloys> — **fab·ri·ca·bil·i·ty** \,fabrəkəˈbiləd·ē\ *n*

Fa·bry's disease \ˈfäbrēz-, -riz-\ *n* [Johannes *Fabry* †1930 Ger. dermatologist] : a sex-linked inherited disorder of lipid catabolism characterized esp. by renal dysfunction, a rash in the inguinal, scrotal, and umbilical regions, and corneal defects

face fly *n* : a European fly (*Musca autumnalis*) that is similar to the housefly, is widely established in No. America, and causes great distress to livestock by clustering about the face

face–off* \ˈfās,ȯf\ *n* : a face-to-face confrontation : a showdown <swaggered down cattletown streets, pistols waggling dangerously on their hips as though ready for a *face-off* with any man —W.H. Forbis> <had avoided *face-offs* with the militants —Benjamin DeMott>

fag·got·ry \ˈfagə·trē\ *n* : male homosexuality <why is *faggotry* okay, but the imputation of it discreditable? —W.F. Buckley *b*1925>

fail* *n* : a failure (as by a security dealer) to deliver or receive securities within a prescribed period after a purchase or sale

[1]**fail–safe** \ˈfā(ə)l,sāf\ *adj* **1** : incorporating some feature for automatically counteracting the effect of an anticipated possible source of failure <a *fail-safe* drive train that cannot lock up the rear wheel —*Consumer Reports*> **2** : being or relating to a safeguard that prevents continuing on a bombing mission according to a preconceived plan

[2]**fail–safe** *vi* : to counteract the effect of a malfunction automatically ~ *vt* : to equip with a fail-safe device

fake book \ˈfāk,bu̇k\ *n* [*fake* to improvise + *book*] : a book that contains the melody lines of popular copyrighted songs without accompanying harmonies and that is published without the permission of the copyright owners

fallout* *n* : an incidental result or product <the war . . . produced its own literary *fallout* — a profusion of books —*Newsweek*>

family* *n* : a group constituting a unit of a crime syndicate (as the Mafia) and engaging in underworld activities within a defined geographical area <was made head of one of New York's five large Mafia *families* at the age of twenty-six —Joseph Epstein>

family planning *n* : planning of the number and spacing of one's children by effective methods of birth control

family room *n* : a large room designed as a recreation center for members of a family

fan–jet \ˈfan,jet\ *n* **1** : a jet engine having a ducted fan in its forward end that draws in extra air whose compression and expulsion provide extra thrust **2** : an airplane powered by a fan-jet engine

fantasy* *n, pl* **-sies** : a coin usu. not intended for circulation as currency and often issued by a dubious authority (as a government-in-exile)

Far·a·day rotation \ˈfarə,dā-, -ədē-\ *n* **1** : optical rotation of a beam of polarized light due to the Faraday effect **2** : rotation of a beam of polarized microwaves traversing an isotropic medium along the lines of force of a magnetic field

far–out \ˈfärˈau̇t\ *adj* [*far out* (adverbial phrase), fr. ME *fer oute*, fr. *fer* far + *out, oute* out] : marked by a considerable departure from the conventional or traditional : extreme <a small, *far-out,* but fervent religious sect —Joseph Alsop> — **far–out** \ˈfär,au̇t\ *n* — **far–out·er** \fär,au̇d·ə(r)\ *n* — **far–out·ness** \-ˈau̇tnəs\ *n*

far–red \ˈfä(r)ˈred\ *adj* **1** : lying in the part of the infrared spectrum farthest from the red — used of radiations with wavelengths between 30 and about 1000 microns **2** : lying in the part of the infrared spectrum nearest to the red — used of radiations with wavelengths starting at about .8 micron

fast·back *n* **1** \ˈfas(t)ˈbak\ : a back roof on a closed passenger automobile sloping in a long unbroken line toward the rear bumper **2** \-,bak\ : an automobile having a fastback

fast–breed·er reactor \ˈfas(t)ˈbrēdə(r)-\ *n* : a breeder reactor that depends on high-energy neutrons to produce fissionable material

fast–food \-ˈfüd\ *adj* : specializing in the rapid preparation and service of food (as hamburgers or fried chicken) <a *fast-food* restaurant chain>

fatal *n* : a fatal outcome; *esp* : a fatal automobile accident <had 11 *fatals* at three spots on Interstate 610 —Dexter Jones>

fat city *n* : an extremely comfortable situation or condition of life : the state of being well-off

fat deposit *n* : connective tissue in which fat is stored and which has the cells distended by droplets of fat

fate* *n* : the expected result of normal development <prospective *fate* of embryonic cells>

fat farm *n* : HEALTH SPA

Faulk·ner·ian \(ˈ)fȯkˈnirēan, -ˈner-\ *adj* [William Cuthbert *Faulkner* †1962 Am. novelist] : of, relating to, or suggestive of William Faulkner or his writings <style is rather *Faulknerian,* skillfully handled, a pastiche of past and present, memories and fantasies —John Leonard>

fa·ve·la *also* **fa·vel·la** \fəˈvelə\ *n* [Pg *favela*] : a settlement of jerry-built shacks lying on the outskirts of a Brazilian city

fax \ˈfaks\ *n* [by shortening and alter. fr. *facsimile*] : the transmission of graphic matter (as printing or still pictures) by wire or radio and its reproduction : facsimile

FDC* *abbr* fleur de coin

federal funds *n pl* : uncommitted reserves of a Federal Reserve member bank available for interbank loans esp. to enable other banks to maintain their legally required reserves

feed·back in·hi·bi·tion \ˈfēd,bak,in(h)əˈbishən\ *n* : inhibition of an enzyme controlling an early stage of a series of biochemical reactions by the end product when it reaches a critical concentration

feed·through \ˈfēd,thrü\ *n* : a conductor that connects two circuits on opposite sides of a surface

fel·late \ˈfel,āt, fəˈlāt\ *vb* **-lat·ed; -lat·ing** [L *fellatus,* past part. of *fellare* to suck] *vt* : to perform fellatio on ~ *vi* : to fellate someone — **fel·la·tor** \ˈfel,ād·ə(r), fəˈlā-\ *n*

femme* \ˈfem\ *n* : a lesbian who plays the female role in a homosexual relationship

fem·to- \ˈfem(p)(,)tō\ *comb form* [ISV, fr. Dan or Norw *femten* fifteen (fr. ON *fimmtān*) + connective *-o-*] : one quadrillionth (10^{-15}) part of <*femto*ampere>

fence–mend·ing \ˈfen(t)sˈmendiŋ\ *n* : the rehabilitating of a deteriorated political relationship <governmental employees have spent their time and energy on political *fence-mending* to keep their party in power —S.H. Patterson & A.W.S. Little>

fen·tan·yl \fenˈtanᵊl, ˈfentᵊn,il\ *n* [alter. of *phentanyl,* fr. *phen-* phenyl + *et*hyl + *an*iline + *-yl* chemical radical, fr. Gk *hylē* wood, matter] : a compound $C_{22}H_{28}N_2O$ used esp. as an analgesic

fen·thi·on \fenˈthī,än, -īən\ *n* [*fen-* (alter. of *phen-* phenyl) + *-thion* sulphur-containing compound] : an organophosphorus insecticide $C_{10}H_{15}O_3PS_2$

fer·mi \ˈfer(,)mē\ *n* [Enrico *Fermi* †1954 Ital. physicist] : a unit of length equal to 10^{-13} centimeter

fer·re·dox·in \,ferəˈdäksən\ *n* [L *fer*rum iron + E *redox* + *-in* chemical compound] : an iron-containing plant protein that functions as an electron carrier in photosynthetic organisms and in some anaerobic bacteria

FET \ˌef(ˌ)ēˈtē\ *n* : FIELD-EFFECT TRANSISTOR

FET *abbr* federal excise tax

fe·tal hemoglobin \¦fēd·ᵊl-\ *n* : a hemoglobin variant that predominates in the blood of a newborn and persists in increased proportions in some forms of anemia (as thalassemia)

fetal position *n* [fr. the similar position of the fetus in the womb] : a resting position in which the body is curved, the legs and arms are bent and drawn toward the chest, and the head is bowed forward and which is assumed esp. in some forms of psychic regression

fe·tol·o·gy \fēˈtäləjē\ *n* [*feto-* fetus + *-logy* theory, science, deriv. of Gk *logos* word] : a branch of medical science concerned with the study and treatment of the fetus in the uterus — **fe·tol·o·gist** \-jə̇st\ *n*

fet·tuc·ci·ne Al·fre·do \ˌfed·əˈchēnē(ˌ)alˈfrā(ˌ)dō, -ȧl-, -äl-\ *or* **fet·tuc·ci·ne all' Al·fre·do** \-ˌal(ˌ)alˈfrā(ˌ)dō, -ˌȧl(ˌ)ȧl-, -ˌäl(ˌ)äl-\ *n* [*Alfredo all' Augusteo,* restaurant in Rome, where it originated] : a dish consisting of butter, fettuccine, Parmesan cheese, cream, and seasonings

Feul·gen \ˈfȯilgən\ *adj* : of, relating to, utilizing, or staining by the Feulgen reaction <positive *Feulgen* mitochondria>

fi·ber·fill \ˈfībə(r)ˌfil\ *n* : man-made fibers (as of polyester) used as a filling material (as for cushions, sleeping bags, or winter jackets)

fiber op·tics \-ˈäptiks\ *n pl* **1** : thin transparent fibers of glass or plastic that are enclosed by material of a lower index of refraction and that transmit light throughout their length by internal reflections; *also* : a bundle of such fibers used in an instrument (as for viewing body cavities) **2** *sing in constr* : the technique of the use of fiber optics — **fi·ber–op·tic** \¦fībər¦äptik\ *adj*

fi·ber·scope \ˈfībə(r)ˌskōp\ *n* [*fiber* + *-scope* instrument for observing, deriv. of Gk *skeptesthai* to watch, look at] : a flexible instrument utilizing fiber optics and used for examination of inaccessible areas (as the interior of the stomach)

Fi·bo·nac·ci number \ˌfibə¦nächē-, ˌfēb-\ *n* [Leonardo *Fibonacci* (Leonardo Pisano) †*ab* 1250 Ital. mathematician] : a number in the infinite sequence 1, 1, 2, 3, 5, 8, 13, . . . of which the first two terms are 1 and 1 and each succeeding term is the sum of the two immediately preceding

fiche \ˈfēsh, *also* ˈfish\ *n, pl* **fiche** *also* **fiches** [short for *microfiche*] : a sheet of microfilm containing rows of microimages of pages of printed matter : microfiche

fiddle* *n* [Brit. slang *fiddle* to cheat] *Brit* : an illegal or dishonest transaction or one of doubtful legality or honesty : a dodge, swindle, or fraud <the lorry driver instigated a *fiddle* whereby a smaller amount was put in the tank than shown on the invoice —*London Times*> <a 1967 capital gains *fiddle*—Peter Jenkins> <one of the legitimate tax *fiddles* —Alisdair Fairley>

fi·do \ˈfīd(ˌ)ō\ *n, pl* **fidos** [*f*reaks + *i*rregulars + *d*efects + *o*ddities] : a coin having a minting error

fi·du·ci·ary* \fə̇d(y)üshēˌerē, fīˈ-, -ri\ *adj* : being a mark or set of marks in the reticle of an optical instrument used as a point of reference or for a measure

field* *n* : a particular area (as a column on a punched card) in which the same type of information is regularly recorded

field* *vt* : to answer or respond to extemporaneously <*fielded* the questions with ease> <tactfully *field* the numerous phone calls that came in from anxious models night and day —Peter Maas>

field–ef·fect transistor \ˈfē(ə)ldə̇ˌfekt-, -ēˌf-\ *n* : a nonrectifying transistor in which the output current is controlled by a variable electric field

field ion microscope *n* : a high-magnification microscope in which an image of the atoms of a metal surface is formed on a fluorescent screen by means of usu. helium ions formed in a high-voltage electric field

field judge *n* : a football official whose duties include covering action on kicks and forward passes and timing intermission periods and time-outs

fighting chair *n* : a chair attached to the deck of a boat from which a salt-water angler plays a hooked fish

film·card \ˈfilm,kärd, ˈfiu̇m-, -ˌkȧd\ *n* : FICHE

film·og·ra·phy \filˈmägrəfē, fiu̇ˈm-\ *n, pl* **-phies** [*film* + connective *-o-* + *-graphy* writing, deriv. of Gk *graphein* to write] : a list of motion pictures featuring the work of a prominent film figure (as an actor or director) or relating to a particular topic <the present volumes each have a complete *filmography* of the stars —Henry Halpern>

film·set·ting \ˈfilm,sed·iŋ, ˈfiu̇m-\ *n* : text composition done directly on film — **film·set** \-ˌset\ *adj* — **filmset** *vt* — **film·set·ter** \-ˌsed·ə(r)\ *n*

finance company* *n* : a company that specializes in making loans usu. to individuals

financial service *n* : an organization that studies the business situation and security market and makes investment recommendations usu. in a regularly issued publication

finder's fee *n* : a fee paid to a financial finder often in the form of a percentage of the sum involved

fine structure *n* **1** : a multiplet occurring in an atomic spectrum as a result of electron interaction **2** : microscopic structure of a biological entity or one of its parts esp. as studied in preparations for the electron microscope — **fine structural** *adj*

finger* *n* : BIRD 2 <secretaries in Hartford, Connecticut, give the *finger* to ribald construction workers —Richard Woodley>

finger food *n* : a food (as a radish or carrot) that can be conveniently eaten with the fingers

fingerprint* *n* : the chromatogram or electrophoretogram obtained by cleaving a protein by enzymatic action and subjecting the resulting collection of peptides to two-dimensional chromatography or electrophoresis

fink* \ˈfiŋk\ *n* : one who is disapproved of or is held in contempt <I was the very model of a well-adjusted old *fink*, spending my working hours selling out and my leisure time up against the wall —Lou D'Angelo>

fink out *vi* **1** : to fail miserably **2** : to back out : cop out <others from his roots as anxious to change the world have cracked under the pressure or *finked out* in the fat of middle-age —Seymour Krim>

fire·flood \ˈfī(ə)r,fləd, ˈfīə,-\ *or* **fire·flood·ing** \-iŋ\ *n* : the process of injecting compressed air into a petroleum reservoir and burning some of the oil so as to drive the rest of the oil into producing wells

firm·ware \ˈfərm,wa(ə)r, -ˌwe(ə)r, ˈfə̄m-, ˈfəim-, -ˌwaə, -ˌweə\ *n* : software functions (as a computer program) implemented through a small special-purpose computer memory unit (as a read-only memory)

first blood *n* **1** : the first drawing of blood in a contest (as boxing) **2** : an initial advantage over an opponent <drew *first blood* when they won the pole and the third spot on the starting grid —Kim Chapin>

fish–eye \ˈfish,ī\ *adj* [fr. the resemblance of the lens to the protruding eye of a fish] : being, having, or produced by a wide-angle photographic lens that has a highly curved protruding front, that covers an angle of about 180 degrees, and that gives a circular image with barrel distortion <a *fish-eye* view> <a *fish-eye* camera>

fish protein concentrate *n* : flour made of pulverized dried fish

five–o'clock shadow \ˌˈfīvə,kläk-\ *n* [fr. the resemblance of a dark beard's stubble to a shadow] : the growth of beard present late in the afternoon on the face of a man who has not shaved since morning

fixed–point \ˈfiks(t)ˌˈpȯint\ *adj* : involving or being a mathematical notation (as in a decimal system) in which the point separating whole numbers and fractions is fixed — compare FLOATING-POINT

flag football *n* : a variation of football in which a player must pull off a flag attached to a ballcarrier's clothing to stop the play

flagship* *n* : the finest, largest, or most important one of a series or group <the company's *flagship* store> <the *flagships* of its computer line —*Newsweek*> <presenting the Boston Symphony Orchestra as the *flagship* of its cultural programs —Jonathan Price>

flak* \ˈflak\ *n* **1** : abusive criticism <I've taken *flak* from newsmen who think I've sold out —Chet Huntley> **2** : heated discussion : opposition <this modest proposal ran into *flak* —Charles MacDonald>

flake* *n* : one (as a professional athlete) that is flaky : a screwball or nut <he is, in the snowfall of sports conformity, a self-designated refreshing *flake—Springfield* (*Mass.*) *Union*>

flakeboard \ˈflāk͵bō(ə)rd, -͵bȯ(ə)rd, -͵bōəd, -͵bȯəd\ *n* : a composition board made of flakes of wood bonded with synthetic resin

flaky* *also* **flak·ey** *adj* **flak·i·er; -est** : markedly odd or unconventional : crazy <they used to call me *flaky*. . . but now that I'm a millionaire they'll be calling me an eccentric —Derek Sanderson> <the *flakiest* things sometimes happen around the world, unwilled by man or nature —A.J. Large>

flame stitch *n* : a needlepoint stitch that produces a pattern resembling flames

flanker* *or* **flanker back** *n* : a football player stationed wide of the formation; *esp* : an offensive halfback who lines up on the flank slightly behind the line of scrimmage and serves chiefly as a pass receiver

flap·pa·ble \ˈflapəbəl\ *adj* : lacking self-assurance and self-control : easily upset <his resonant voice is friendly, yet decisive; constructive and reassuring to . . . the *flappable* chef —Doris Tobias>

flare* *n* **1** : a short pass in football thrown to a back who is running toward the sideline **2 flares** *pl* : trousers that flare toward the bottoms

flash* *vi* : to expose one's genitals usu. suddenly and briefly in public

flash* *n* : RUSH

flash·cube \ˈflash͵kyüb\ *n* : a plastic cube containing four flashbulbs that fits into the top of a camera and revolves after each shot

flashed glass *n* : glass in which a very thin layer of colored glass or of a metallic oxide is flashed to clear glass

flash–for·ward \ˈflashˈfȯrwərd, -ˈfȯ(ə)wəd, *sometimes* -ˈfȯrəd, *South also* -ˈfärwərd, -ˈfäwəd\ *n* [*flash* (as in *flashback*) + *forward*] : a literary or theatrical technique used esp. in motion pictures and television that involves interruption of the chronological sequence of events by interjection of events or scenes of future occurrence; *also* : an instance of a flash-forward

flash pho·tol·y·sis \-fōˈtäləsəs\ *n* : the process of decomposing a chemical with an intense flash of light and observing spectroscopically the transient molecular fragments produced

flea collar *n* : a collar for animals that contains insecticide for killing fleas

fleur de coin \͵flərdə͵kwa^{n}, -lǝd-\ *adj* [F *à fleur de coin,* lit., with the bloom of the die] : being in the preserved mint condition

flex·a·gon \ˈfleksə͵gän, -əgən\ *n* [*flex* + *-agon* (as in *hexagon*)] : a folded paper figure that can be flexed along its folds to expose various arrangements of its faces

flex·time \ˈfleks͵tīm\ *n* [*flex*ible + *time*] : a system that allows employees to choose their own times for starting and finishing work within a broad range of available hours

flick–knife \ˈflik͵nīf\ *n, Brit* : a pocketknife with a spring-loaded blade that will fly open upon pressing a release catch : a switchblade knife

flight bag *n* **1** : a traveling bag usu. with zippered outside compartments for use esp. in air travel; *esp* : one that fits under an airplane seat **2** : a small thin lightweight canvas satchel decorated with the name of an airline

flip* *vi* **flipped; flip·ping** **1** : to lose self-control <when he *flips* it takes three men to hold him —Eddie Krell> — often used with *out* <mother was *flipping* out, drinking more each day —Wayne Ross> **2** : to become extremely enthusiastic <I *flipped* for that man's music —Melissa Hayden>

flip chart *n* : a series of hinged sheets (as of cardboard) that can be flipped over the top and out of view in presenting information sequentially

flip side *n* [*flip* to turn over] : the reverse and usu. less popular side of a phonograph record

floating decimal *n* : a system of decimal point placement in an electronic calculator in which the decimal point is free to move automatically across the display board in order to allow the maximum number of decimal places in the readout

float·ing–point \ˈflōd·iŋ͵pȯint\ *adj* : involving or being a mathematical notation in which a quantity is denoted by one number multiplied by a power of the number base

<the fixed-point value 99.9 could be expressed in a *floating-point* system as .999 × 10^2> — compare FIXED-POINT

flo·ka·ti \flō'kätē\ *n, pl* **flokati** *or* **flo·ka·tes** \-ä,tes\ [NGk *phlokatē*, fr. *phloko* strand of wool, prob. fr. G *flocke* flock of wool (fr. MHG *vlocke*)] : a hand-woven Greek rug with a thick shaggy pile

floor exercise *n* : an event in gymnastics competition consisting of various ballet and tumbling movements (as jumps, somersaults, and handstands) performed without apparatus

floor partner *n* : a member of a brokerage firm who owns a seat on an exchange and acts as floor broker for his firm

floppy disc *n* : a small flexible plastic disk coated with magnetic material on which data for a computer can be stored

floss *vi* : to use dental floss <everyone knows you should brush, but few know they should *floss* —Robert Brackett>

flower bug *n* : any of various small mostly black-and-white predaceous bugs (family Anthocoridae) that frequent flowers and feed on pest insects (as aphids and thrips)

flower child *n* : a hippie who indicates his belief in love, beauty, and peace by wearing or displaying flowers

flower people *n pl* : FLOWER CHILDREN <smiling, mild-mannered *flower people* sang, chanted, tinkled bells, handed out flowers, blew bubbles and danced —D.A. Schmidt>

flu·er·ic \(')flü¦erik\ *adj* [irreg. fr. L *fluere* to flow] : FLUIDIC

flu·er·ics \flü'eriks\ *n pl but usu sing in constr* : FLUIDICS

flu·id·ic* \flü'idik, -ēk\ *adj* : of, relating to, or being a device (as an amplifier or control) that depends for operation on the pressures and flows of a fluid in precisely shaped channels — **fluidic** *n*

flu·id·ics \-iks, -ēks\ *n pl but usu sing in constr* : the technology of fluidic devices

flu·id·on·ics \,flüə'däniks, -ēks\ *n pl but usu sing in constr* [*fluid* + *-onics* (as in *electronics*)] : FLUIDICS

flu·o·cin·o·lone ac·e·to·nide \,flüə¦sinᵊl,ōn,asə'tō,nīd\ *n* [*fluo*rine + *cin*ene, a terpene (fr. *cin*eole + *-ene* unsaturated carbon compound) + prednis*olone* + *acetone* + *-ide* derivative compound] : a steroid $C_{24}H_{30}F_2O_6$ used esp. as an anti-inflammatory agent in the treatment of skin diseases

flu·o·ri·diz·er \'flu̇(ə)rə,dīzə(r), -lōr-, -lȯr-\ *n* **1** : one that fluoridizes **2** : a fluorine-containing water and oil repellent finish for textiles

flu·o·ro·plas·tic \¦flu̇(ə)(,)rō'plastik, ¦flōr(,)ō-, ¦flȯ(,)rō-\ *n* [*fluoro-* fluorine + *plastic*] : any of various fluoropolymers that are used chiefly for cast and molded parts and as coatings

flu·o·ro·poly·mer \-'päləmə(r)\ *n* : any of various homopolymers or copolymers that consist mainly of fluorine and carbon and that are characterized by chemical inertness, thermal stability, and a low coefficient of friction

flu·o·ro·ura·cil \-'yu̇rə,sil, -əsəl\ *n* : a fluorine-containing pyrimidine base $C_4H_3FN_2O_2$ used to treat some kinds of cancer

fly* *n, pl* **flies** : a football pass pattern in which the receiver runs straight downfield

flying crane *n* : a helicopter equipped with a crane and used esp. for lifting and transporting heavy cargoes

FMN \,ef(,)e'men\ *n* [*f*lavin *mono**n*ucleotide] : a yellow crystalline mono-phosphoric ester $C_{17}H_{21}N_4O_9P$ of riboflavin

FOBS *abbr* fractional orbital bombardment system

foil* *n* : a body similar to an airfoil but designed for action in or on water : a hydrofoil

fo·late \'fō,lāt\ *n* [*fol*ic (acid) + *-ate* derivative compound] : a crystalline pteroylglutamic acid $C_{19}H_{19}N_7O_6$ that is a vitamin of the B complex and is used in the treatment of nutritional anemias and sprue : folic acid <the uptake of *folate* by the mutant —*Biol. Abstracts*>

folk mass *n* : a mass in which traditional liturgical music is replaced by folk music

folk–rock \'fōk¦räk\ *n* : folk songs sung to a rock 'n' roll background — **folk–rock** *adj* — **folk–rock·er** \-¦räkə(r)\ *n*

fon·due fork \(ˈ)fän¦d(y)ü-\ *n* : a long slender usu. 2-tined fork used in cooking or eating fondue

food pyramid *n* : an ecological hierarchy of food relationships esp. when expressed quantitatively (as in mass, numbers, or energy) in which a chief predator is at the top, each level preys on the next lower level, and green plants are usu. at the bottom

food stamp *n* : a government-issued stamp that is sold at little cost or given to low-income persons and is redeemable for food

foot·pad* \ˈfu̇tˌpad\ *n* : a flattish foot on the leg of a spacecraft for distributing weight to minimize sinking into a surface

for·mat \ˈfȯ(ə)rˌmat, -ȯ(ə)ˌm-\ *vt* **for·mat·ted; for·mat·ting** [*format*, n.] : to produce (as a book, printed matter, or data) in a specified form (as print) or style <get complete reports of your experiment, *formatted* as you like them and prepared automatically during the experiment —*advt*> <assigned to teach freshman composition from a trendily *formatted* collection of contemporary materials —Samuel McCracken>

formula *adj* [*formula*, n.] *of a racing car* : conforming to prescribed specifications of size, weight, and engine displacement and usu. having a long narrow body, open wheels, a single-seat open cockpit, and an engine in the rear

formula investing *n* : investing according to a plan (**formula plan**) under which more funds are invested in equity securities when the market is low and more are put into fixed-income securities when the market advances

FOR·TRAN \ˈfȯr·ˌtran, ˈfȯ(ə)-\ *n* [*for*mula *tran*slation] : an algebraic and logical language for programming a computer

fortune cookie *n* : a thin folded cookie containing a slip of paper on which a fortune, proverb, or humorous statement is printed

found object *n* [trans. of F *objet trouvé*] : a natural or discarded object (as a piece of driftwood or junk) found by chance and held to have aesthetic value esp. through the working of natural forces on it

found poem *n* : a poem consisting of words found in a nonpoetic context (as a product label) and usu. rearranged by the poet into poetic form

Fou·ri·er trans·form \ˌfu̇rē¦āˈtran(t)sˌfȯrm, fu̇rˈyā-, -ˌfȯ(ə)m\ *n* [Baron Jean Baptiste Joseph *Fourier* †1830 Fr. geometrician and physicist] : a function (as $F(u)$) that under suitable conditions can be obtained from a given function (as $f(x)$) by multiplying by e^{iux} and integrating over all values of x

four·plex \ˈfō(ə)rˌpleks, ˈfȯ(ə)rˌ-, ˈfōəˌ-, ˈfȯ(ə)ˌ-\ *n* [*four* + *-plex* (as in *duplex*)] : a building that contains four separate apartments

foxy* *adj* **fox·i·er; -est** : being good-looking : attractive, sexy <*foxy* chicks>

FPC* *abbr* fish protein concentrate

fractional orbital bom·bard·ment system \-bämˈbärdmənt-, -bəmˈ-\ *n* : a system for delivering a nuclear warhead from orbit by slowing it down by a retrorocket before completion of an orbit

frag \ˈfrag\ *vt* **fragged; frag·ging** [*frag* fragmentation grenade] : to injure or kill (one's military leader) deliberately by means of a fragmentation grenade <officers and NCO's who insist on ordering troops into the field are commonly *fragged*— hit by a grenade rolled under their tent flaps —Fred Gardner>— **frag·ger** \-ə(r)\ *n* — **frag·ging** \-iŋ, -ēŋ\ *n*

frame* *n* : a minimal unit of instruction or stimulus in a programmed instruction routine : a unit of programmed instruction calling for a response by the student

frame·shift \ˈfrāmˌshift\ *n* : a mutation in which a number of nucleotides not divisible by three is inserted or deleted so that some triplet codons are read incorrectly during genetic translation — called also *frameshift mutant, frameshift mutation*

fran·chi·see \ˌfranchə¦zē, -ˌchī¦-, *sometimes* -¦sē\ *n* [*franchise* + *-ee* recipient of an action] : one who is granted a franchise to operate a unit in a chain of business establishments

Fran·co–American \ˌfraŋ(ˌ)kōə¦merəkən\ *n* [*Franco-* French (fr. ML, fr. *Francus* Frenchman) + *American*] : an American of French or esp. French-Canadian descent — **Franco–American** *adj*

fran·co·phone \'fraŋkə,fōn\ *adj, often cap* [F, fr. *franco-* French + Gk *phōnē* voice, speech] : having or belonging to a French-speaking population esp. in a country where two or more languages are spoken

Francophone *n* : a French-speaking person esp. in a country where two or more languages are spoken

fran·glais \frän^{n}'glā, -äŋ'g-\ *n, often cap* [F, blend of *français* French and *anglais* English] : French marked by a considerable number of borrowings from English

freak* *n* **1** : one who uses illicit drugs <a mescal *freak*> <a needle *freak*> **2** : a highly individualistic critic or rebel; *esp*: a hippie <how to raise a child who will not be a *freak*. . . or a man-in-the-gray-flannel-suit —Aline Willbur> **3** : an ardent enthusiast <a horror film we chiller *freaks* can recommend —Liz Smith> <fungus *freaks* have been flocking to the woods in record numbers —*Newsweek*>

freak out *vi* **1** : to withdraw from reality and society esp. by taking drugs <learns she enjoys *freaking out* on drugs —Hollis Alpert> **2** : to experience nightmarish hallucinations as a result of taking drugs : have a bad trip <one or two participants *freaked out* and had a very hard time of it —Warren J. Hinckle *b*1938> **3** : to behave irrationally or unconventionally under or as if under the influence of drugs <she is *freaking out* as the birth of her child approaches —Sara Blackburn> **4** : to become disturbed, upset, or angry <*freaked out* immediately and sent a platoon of detectives after the guy —Ed Ward> ~ *vt* **1** : to put under the influence of a psychedelic drug **2** : to put into a state of intense excitement <one of the ideas that *freaks* me *out* and which I'd like to do —Frank Gillette> **3** : to disturb the composure of : upset or anger <what he saw *freaked* him *out* so much that he still gets shaken when he remembers it —*Berkeley Barb*> — **freaked–out** \,frēk'daůt\ *adj*

freak–out \'frē,kaůt\ *n* **1** : a withdrawal from reality esp. by means of drugs <those who wanted a day-long or all-night *freak-out* could choose LSD —R.D. Lyons> **2 a** : a drug-induced state of mind characterized by terrifying hallucinations : a bad trip <a murderer who is convinced he killed a girl while on a *freak-out* —*advt*> **b** : an irrational act by one who freaks out **3** : a gathering of hippies <the local hippies' social event of the season, the Easter Sunday *freak-out* in Elysian Park —*Springfield (Mass.) Union*> **4** : one who freaks out <unconvincing composite of guerrilla fighters, *freak-outs,* and Hottentots —W.J.J. Sheed>

free agent *n* : a professional athlete (as a football player) who is free to negotiate a contract with any team

free–as·so·ci·ate \,frēə'sos(h)ē,āt\ *vi* [back-formation fr. *free association*] : to engage in free association <asked to *free-associate* about his dream —Maya Pines>

free·bie *or* **free·bee** \'frēbē, -bi\ *n* [by alter. fr. earlier slang *freeby* gratis, irreg. fr. *free*] : something (as a theater ticket) given or received without charge <a season *freebie* to the Giants —Frank Deford>

freedom ride *n, often cap F&R* : a ride made by civil rights workers through states of the southern U.S. to ascertain whether public facilities (as bus terminals) are desegregated — **freedom rider** *n, often cap F&R*

free–fire zone \'frē'fī(ə)r-\ *n* : an area (as in South Vietnam) where any moving thing is a legitimate target

free safety *n* : a safetyman in football who has no specific pass receiver to guard in a man-to-man defense and who usu. helps wherever needed on defense

free university *n* : an unaccredited autonomous free institution established within a university by students to present and discuss subjects not usu. dealt with in the academic curriculum

freeze–etch·ing \'frē,zechiŋ\ *n* : preparation of a replica (as by simultaneous vapor deposition of carbon and platinum) for electron microscopic examination of the exposed surface of quick-frozen material (as a tissue) after fracture along natural structural lines — **freeze–etch** \'frē,zech\ *or* **freeze–etched** \-,zecht\ *adj*

freeze–frame \'frēz,frām\ *n* : a frame of a motion-picture film that is repeated so as to give the illusion of a static picture

fret* *vt* **fret·ted; fret·ting** : to depress (the strings of a musical instrument) against the frets ~ *vi* : to fret the strings of a musical instrument

Fried·man·ite \ˈfrēdmə͵nīt\ *n* [Milton *Friedman* *b*1912 Am. economist] : a monetarist who adheres to the theory of economist Milton Friedman that economic regulation should be through direct governmental manipulation of the money supply

fri·jo·les re·fri·tos \frēˈhōlēz(͵)rāˈfrē(͵)tōz, -ˈhō͵lās-, -ˈhȯ͵lās-, -ōs\ *n pl* [Sp, lit., refried beans] : frijoles cooked with seasonings, fried, then mashed and fried again

frit·to mis·to \͵ˈfrēd·ōˈmistō, ͵ˈfrētō-\ *n* [It, lit., fried mixture] : small pieces of seafood, meat or vegetables that are dipped in batter and fried

frog* *n* : a small holder with perforations or spikes that is placed in a bowl or vase to keep cut flowers in position

front–end load \frənt͵end-\ *n* : the part of the total load taken out of early payments under a contract plan for the periodic purchase of investment-company shares

fron·te·nis \͵ˈfrən͵ˈtenəs, (ˈ)frän-\ *n* [AmerSp, blend of Sp *frontón* pelota court and *tenis* tennis, fr. E *tennis*] : a game of Mexican origin played with rackets and a rubber ball on a 3-walled court

front·lash \ˈfrənt͵lash\ *n* [*front* + *-lash* (as in *backlash*)] : a counterreaction to a political backlash

front money *n* : money that is paid in advance for a promised service or product

frosting* *n* : the lightening (as by chemicals) of small strands of hair throughout the entire head to produce a two-tone effect — compare STREAKING

fruit machine *n* [fr. the use of pictures of various fruits as symbols to be matched] *Brit* : a coin-operated machine for gambling : a slot machine

fuel cell *n* : a device that continuously converts the chemical energy of a fuel (as hydrogen) directly into electrical energy

fu·el·er \ˈfyü(ə)lə(r), -yu̇-\ *n* : a dragster that uses specially blended fuel rather than gasoline

fun fur *n* : relatively inexpensive or synthetic fur for casual wear

funk* \ˈfəŋk\ *n* : funky music

funky* \ˈfəŋkē, -ki\ *adj* **funk·i·er; -est** [fr. *funky* musty, foul, fr. *funk* offensive smell] **1** : having an earthy unsophisticated style and feeling; *specif* : having the style and feeling of early blues <*funky* piano playing> **2** : odd or quaint in appearance or style <expected a *funky*. . . type, and instead I met this beautiful, gracious lady —Laura Cunningham>

funny car *n* : a specialized dragster that has a one-piece molded body resembling the body of a mass-produced car

funny farm *n* : a psychiatric hospital <Edith, at least, sometimes appears to be in touch with reality; Amy seems like a candidate for the *funny farm* —Judy Klemesrud>

fu·ra·zol·i·done \͵fyu̇rəˈzälə͵dōn, -zȯl-\ *n* [*fur-* related to furan + *azole* compound with a five-membered ring containing nitrogen + *-ide* derivative compound + *-one* ketone or analagous compound] : an antimicrobial drug $C_8H_7N_3O_5$ used esp. against parasitic infections

fu·ro·se·mide \f(y)əˈrōsə͵mīd\ *also* **fur·se·mide** \ˈfərsə-, ˈfəsə-\ *n* [*fur-* + *sulfur* + *-emide,* prob. alter. of *amide*] : a powerful diuretic $C_{12}H_{11}ClN_2O_5S$ used esp. in the treatment of edema

future shock *n* : the physical and psychological distress suffered by one who is unable to cope with the rapidity of societal and technological changes

fu·tu·rol·o·gy \͵fyüchəˈräləjē\ *n* [G *futurologie,* fr. *futur* future + connective *-o-* + *-logie* theory, science, deriv. of Gk *logos* word] : a study that deals with future possibilities based on current trends — **fu·tu·ro·log·i·cal** \͵ˈfyüchərə͵ˈläjəkəl\ *adj* — **fu·tu·rol·o·gist** \͵fyüchəˈräləjəst\ *n*

fuzz tone *or* **fuzz box** *n* : an electronic device (as on an electric guitar) which by distorting the sound gives it a fuzzy quality

G

G \ˈjē\ *adj* [general] *of a motion picture* : of such a nature that persons of all ages may be allowed admission — compare PG, R, X

G* *abbr* giga-

ga·ga·ku \gäˈgä(ˌ)kü\ *n, often cap* [Jap. fr. *ga* elegance + *gaku* music] : the ancient court music of Japan

Gal·braith·ian \(ˌ)galˈbrāthēən, -thyən\ *adj* [John Kenneth *Galbraith* *b*1908 Am. economist] : of or relating to the economic theories or programs of John Kenneth Galbraith <taking a *Galbraithian* attitude toward the gross national product —E.M. Harrington>

gal·li·um ar·se·nide \ˈgalēəmˈärsᵊnˌīd\ *n* : a synthetic compound GaAs used esp. as a semiconducting material

gallows humor *n* : humor that makes fun of very serious or terrifying situations <the two last survivors in a dying world are whiling away their desolation with somber *gallows humor*—wit and sobriety yielding a combined swan song and hyena laughter —John Simon>

Ga·lois theory \(ˈ)galˈwä-\ *n* [Evariste *Galois* †1832 Fr. mathematician] : a part of the theory of mathematical groups concerned esp. with the conditions under which a solution to a polynomial equation with coefficents in a given mathematical field can be obtained in the field by the repetition of operations and the extraction of nth roots

game ball* *n* : a ball (as a football) presented by the members of a team to a player or coach in recognition of his contribution to the team's victory

game plan *n* [fr. the use of a strategy or plan in a game like football] : a strategy for achieving an objective <the unsettling impact of the fuzzy *game plan* for wage-and-price controls —C.J. Rolo>

gamma decay *n* **1** : a radioactive transformation of an atomic nucleus in which the nucleus loses energy by emitting a gamma ray without change of mass number or atomic number **2** : the decay of an unstable elementary particle in which one or more photons are emitted

gamma ray* *n* : a high-energy photon

gam·ma-ray astronomy \ˈgaməˌrā-\ *n* : astronomy dealing with the properties of celestial bodies deduced from gamma rays they emit

gang bang *n* : copulation by several persons in succession with the same passive partner — **gang-bang** \ˈgaŋˌbaŋ\ *vb*

gan·gle \ˈgaŋgəl\ *vi* **gan·gled; gan·gling** \-g(ə)liŋ\ [back-formation fr. *gangling*] : to move in an awkward ungraceful manner <the models came out and *gangled* down the catwalk —Germaine Greer> <there was no traffic; five minutes ago a couple tractors . . . *gangled* by —Elizabeth Enright> — **gangle** *n*

gang·sa \ˈgäŋ(ˌ)sä\ *n* [Indonesian *gampang gangsa,* fr. *gampang* musical instrument consisting of bars struck by hammers + *gangsa* brass] : a Balinese metallophone with bamboo resonators

gantry* *n, pl* **gantries** : a movable scaffold with platforms at different levels for use in erecting and servicing rockets before launching

garage sale *n* : a sale of used household or personal articles (as furniture, tools, or clothing) held on the seller's own premises — called also *tag sale, yard sale*

garbage* *n* : inaccurate or useless data <no system is better than the information which it receives. In fact, data processing people refer to this common phenomenon as "GIGO" or "*garbage* in—*garbage* out" —Bob Donovan>

gar·çon·nière \ˌgärsᵊnˈye(ə)r, -(ˌ)sȯn-\ *n* [F, fr. *garçon* boy, bachelor] : a bachelor apartment

garment bag *n* : a traveling bag that folds in half and has a center handle for easy carrying

Gar·vey·ism \'gärvē,izəm, 'gȧv-\ *n* [Marcus *Garvey* †1940 Jamaican Black Nationalist] : a 20th century racial and political doctrine advocating black separation and the formation of self-governing black nations in Africa — **Gar·vey·ite** \-ē,īt\ *n*

gas chro·mato·graph \-krō'mad·ə,graf, -krə-\ *n* : an instrument used to separate a sample into components in gas chromatography

gas chro·ma·tog·ra·phy \-,krōmə'tägrəfē, -fi\ *n* : chromatographic analysis in which the sample is carried in vapor form through a column of absorbing material usu. along with a carrier gas (as nitrogen or helium) — **gas chro·mato·graph·ic** \-krō,mad·ə-'grafik, -ēk\ *adj*

gas·dy·nam·ics \,gas(,)dī'namiks, -ēks\ *n pl but sing in constr* : a branch of dynamics that deals with gaseous fluids including products of combustion and plasmas — **gas·dy·nam·ic** \-ik, -ēk\ *adj* — **gas·dy·nam·i·cist** \-'naməsəst\ *n*

gas·ket·ed \'gaskəd·əd\ *adj* : furnished with a gasket <a *gasketed* screw-cap can>

gate* *n* : a device (as in a computer) that outputs a signal when specified input conditions are met <logic *gate*>

gaudy iron·stone \-'ī(ə)rn,stōn, -'īən-\ *n* : a polychrome-decorated mid-19th century English ironstone ware

Gauss·ian integer \'gaùsēən-\ *n* [Karl Friedrich *Gauss* †1855 Ger. mathematician] : a complex number $a + bi$ where a and b are integers and $i = \sqrt{-1}$

gay·ola \gā'olə\ *n* [blend of *gay* homosexual and *payola*] : an undercover or indirect payment made (as to a crime syndicate) by establishments catering to homosexuals

ga·zump \gə'zəmp\ *vt* [origin unknown] *Brit* : to swindle or cheat; *specif* : to demand a higher price from (the buyer of a house) than that agreed on <the practice of raising the price of a house after an agreement with a buyer on what the price would be. The buyer would find he had been *gazumped* when he showed up for the closing —Norman Gelb>

GB \(')jē'bē\ *n* [code name] : an extremely toxic chemical warfare agent $C_4H_{10}FO_2P$: sarin

GED *abbr* general educational development

gee–whiz \(')jē'(h)wiz\ *adj* **1** : designed to arouse wonder or excitement or to amplify the merits or significance of something esp. by the use of clever or sensational language <*gee-whiz* journalism> **2** : marked by spectacular or astonishing qualities or achievement <the Andes are a *gee-whiz* mountain range. The highest, the longest, the driest —Jeanne A. Davis> **3** : characterized by wide-eyed enthusiasm, excitement, and wonder <a *gee-whiz* approach to politics that wears a little thin —*Business Week*>

ge·müt·lich \gə'mu̅e̅tlik\ *adj* [G, fr. MHG *gemüetlich,* fr. *gemüete* spirit, heart (fr. *ge-*, perfective, associative and collective prefix — fr. OHG *gi-* + *muot* mood, spirit, mind, fr. OHG) + *-lich* -ly, adj. suffix fr. OHG *-lih*] : agreeably pleasant : comfortable <easy, natural and *gemütlich* in her writing —*Times Lit. Supp.*>

ge·müt·lich·keit \gə'mu̅e̅tlik,kīt\ *n* [G, fr. *gemütlich* pleasant + *-keit* state, condition, fr. MHG, alter. of *-heit,* fr. OHG] : the quality or state of being gemütlich : cordiality, friendliness

gene pool *n* : the collection of genes in an interbreeding population that includes each gene at a certain frequency in relation to its alleles : the genetic information of a population of interbreeding organisms

general obligation bond *n* : a municipal of which payment of interest and principal is backed by the taxing power and credit of the issuing governmental unit

general term *n* : a mathematical expression composed of variables and constants that yields the successive terms of a sequence or series when integers are substituted for one of the variables often denoted by k <x^k is the *general term* of the series $1 + x + x^2 + x^3 + \ldots$>

gen·er·a·tive grammar \'jenə,rād·iv-, -n(ə)rəd·iv-\ *n* **1** : a description of a language in the form of an ordered set of rules for producing the grammatical sentences of that language **2** : TRANSFORMATIONAL GRAMMAR

generator* *n* : a mathematical entity that when subjected to one or more operations yields another mathematical entity or its elements; *specif* : a point, line, or surface whose motion generates a line, surface, or solid : a generatrix

ge·ner·ic* \jə'nerik, -ēk\ *n* : a generic drug <the consumer's desire to buy low-cost *generics* instead of more expensive brand name drugs —Barbara J. Culliton>

ge·net·ic code \jə̇ned·ik-, -ēk-\ *n* : the biochemical basis of heredity consisting of codons in DNA and RNA that determine the specific amino acid sequence in proteins and that are essentially uniform for the forms of life studied so far

genetic engineering *n* : alteration of hereditary defects by intervention in gene-controlled bodily processes and when practicable by directed changes in the genetic material

genetic map *n* : MAP 1

genetic marker *n* : a usu. dominant gene or trait that serves esp. to identify genes or traits linked with it

gen·ta·mi·cin \ˌjentə'mīsᵊn\ *n* [alter. of earlier *gentamycin,* fr. *genta-* (prob. irreg. fr. *gentian violet;* fr. the color of the organism from which it is produced) + *-mycin,* fr. *streptomycin*] : a broad-spectrum antibiotic that is derived from an actinomycete (*Micromonospora purpurea* or *M. echinospora*)

geo·co·ro·na \ˌjēəkə'rōnə, ˌjēō-\ *n* [*geo-* earth, ground (deriv. of Gk *gē*)] : the outermost part of the earth's atmosphere consisting primarily of hydrogen

geology* *n* : the study of the solid matter of a celestial body <lunar *geology*> <the *geology* of Mars>

geomagnetic storm *n* : a marked temporary disturbance of the earth's magnetic field that is held to be related to sunspots : a magnetic storm

geometric* *or* **geometrical*** *adj* : increasing in a geometric progression <*geometric* population growth>

geo·probe \'jēəˌprōb, 'jēō-\ *n* : a rocket designed for space exploration near the earth but at distances of more than 4000 miles

geo·sta·tion·ary \ˌjē(ˌ)ō'stāshəˌnerē, *sometimes* -sh(ə)nərē\ *adj* : of, relating to, or being an artificial satellite that travels from west to east at an altitude of over 22,000 miles above the equator and at the same speed as that of the earth's rotation so that the satellite seems to remain in the same place

geo·syn·chro·nous \-'siŋkrənəs, -'sin-\ *adj* : GEOSTATIONARY — **geo·syn·chro·nous·ly** \-lē, -li\ *adv*

German wire·haired pointer \-'wī(ə)rˌha(ə)rd-, -ˌhe(ə)rd-\ *n* : any of a German breed of liver or liver and white hunting dogs that have a flat-lying wiry coat composed of hairs one and one-half to two inches in length

germ·free \ˌjərm'frē, ˌjəm-, ˌjəim-\ *adj* : free of microorganisms

Ge·samt·kunst·werk \gə'zämtˌku̇nstˌverk\ *n* [G, fr. *gesamt* whole, entire + *kunst* art + *werk* work, production] : an art work produced by a synthesis of various art forms (as music and drama)

get* *vb* — **get it on** **1** : to become enthusiastic, energetic, or excited <when they get with a rock group they just really *get it on*—John Von Ohlen> **2** : to engage in sexual intercourse — **get one's rocks off** **1** : to experience orgasm **2** : to become pleasurably excited — **get on the stick** : to begin functioning energetically <worrying what might happen if we didn't *get on the stick* pretty fast —Tim Findley>

get off* *vi* **1** : to get high on a drug — usu. used with *on* <*get off* on heroin> **2** : to experience orgasm **3** : to become pleasurably excited — usu. used with *on* <for a long while, if I heard somebody play a piece that was really hard to play, I *got off* more on that than the melody —Alvin Lee> ~ *vt* : to cause to get off

giga·bit \'jigəˌbit, 'gigə-\ *n* [*giga-* billion (deriv. of Gk *gigas* giant) + *bit*] : one billion bits

giga·cy·cle \-ˌsīkəl\ *n* : a unit of frequency equal to one billion hertz

giga·watt \-ˌwät\ *n* : a unit of power equal to one billion watts

GI·GO \'gīˌgō, 'gē-\ *abbr* garbage in, garbage out

give–up* *n* [fr. the giving up by the first broker of part of the commission to the second] **1** : a security or commodity market order which one broker executes for a client of a second broker and the commission for which is shared by the two brokers **2** : the part of a commission due a broker from a major client (as a mutual fund) that he is directed by the client to turn over to another broker who has provided special services (as research or sale of fund shares) to the client

glas·phalt \'gla,sfȯlt\ *n* [blend of *glass* and *asphalt*] : a mixture of asphalt and crushed glass used to surface roads

glitch \'glich\ *n* [prob. fr. G *glitschen* to slip, slide, fr. MHG, intensive of *glīten* to glide, fr. OHG *glītan*] **1** : an unwanted brief surge of electric power : a false or spurious electronic signal **2 a** : a failure to function properly : a malfunction <a *glitch* in the fuel cell of a spacecraft> **b** : a minor mishap; *also*: a minor technical problem **3** : a sudden change in the period of rotation of a neutron star

glitter rock *n*: rock music performed by male musicians who are made up to look grotesquely feminine

glop \'gläp\ *n* [prob. imit.] **1 a** : a thick semiliquid food or mixture of foods that is usu. unappetizing in appearance <got himself full of whatever *glop* it was the child was supposed to eat —James Thurber> **b** : a thick sticky liquid <freakishly shaving the top of their heads to demonstrate some new aerosol *glop*—Charles Hollander> **2** : tasteless or worthless stuff <clothing its rhetoric with gooey slabs of prose *glop* —Pete Hamill> — **glop·py** \-pē\ *adj*

glu·tar·al·de·hyde \,glüd·ə'raldə,hīd\ *n* [*glutar*yl + *aldehyde*] : a compound $C_5H_8O_2$ that contains two aldehyde groups and is used esp. in leather tanning, disinfection, and fixation of biological tissues

glu·teth·i·mide \glü'tethə,mīd, -əməd\ *n* [*glut*aryl + *eth*yl + *imide* compound derived from ammonia] : a sedative-hypnotic drug $C_{13}H_{15}NO_2$ chemically and physiologically related to phenobarbital

glyph* \'glif\ *n* [short for *hieroglyph*] : a symbol (as a curved arrow on a road sign) that carries information nonverbally

gno·to·bi·ol·o·gy \¦nōd·ə(,)bī¦äləjē\ *n* [Gk *gnōtos* known + E *biology*] : GNOTOBIOTICS — **gno·to·bi·ol·o·gist** \-əjəst\ *n*

gno·to·bi·ot·ic \¦nōd·ə(,)bī¦äd·ik, *also* -bē¦ä-\ *adj* [Gk *gnōtos* known (fr. *gignōskein* to know) + E *biotic* relating to life] : of, relating to, living in, or being a controlled environment containing one or a few kinds of organisms; *also*: free from other living organisms : axenic <*gnotobiotic* mice> — **gno·to·bi·ote** \,nōd·ə'bī,ōt\ *n* — **gno·to·bi·ot·i·cal·ly** \¦nōd·ə(,)bī¦äd·ək(ə)lē, *also* -bē¦ä-\ *adv*

gno·to·bi·ot·ics \'nōd·ə(,)bī¦äd·iks\ *n pl but sing in constr* : the raising and study of animals under gnotobiotic conditions

go* *vb* — **go public** *of a close corporation*: to offer stock for sale to the general public

go *adj*: functioning properly : being in good and ready condition <declared all systems *go*>

goal·mouth \'gōl,mau̇th\ *n* : the area directly in front of the goal (as in soccer or hockey)

goal·tend·ing \-¦tendiŋ\ *n* **1** : the action of guarding a goal (as in hockey) **2** : a violation of the rules that involves touching or deflecting a basketball which is on its downward path toward the basket or which is on or within the rim of the basket

go down* *vi*: to take place : happen <I'll tell you everythin' that *went down* —V.E. Smith>

go·fer *also* **go·pher** \'gōfə(r)\ *n* [alter. of *go for;* fr. his being required to go for or go after things] : an employee whose duties include running errands <the office *gofer,* who is sent out to buy coffee, cigarettes, and the like —*Time*>

go–go \'gō(,)gō\ *adj* [by shortening] **1** : A-GO-GO <*go-go* dancers> **2** : being active or lively : spirited <play *go-go* baseball> <a decisively quiet turn from the eight *go-go* years of the . . . administration that preceded it —Maurice Carroll> **3** : using such tools of speculation as leverage and short selling : speculative <a *go-go* mutual fund>

gold·en–ag·er \¦gōldə¦nājə(r)\ *n* [fr. *Golden Age clubs,* organizations for recreational activities of the elderly] : an elderly person; *esp* : one who has retired

golden old·ie \-'ōldē, -i\ *n* : a phonograph recording or a song that was a hit in the past <rock and roll is a field in which last month's No. 1 hit is today's *golden oldie* —*New Yorker*>

gold point* *n* : a fixed point on the international temperature scale equal to the melting point of gold or 1064.43°C

gold record *n* : a gold phonograph record awarded to a singer or group whose single record has sold at least one million copies or whose album has sold at least 500,000 copies

golf cart *n* **1** : a small cart for wheeling a golf bag around a golf course **2** : a motorized cart for carrying a golfer and his equipment around a golf course

gondola* *n* : an enclosed car suspended from a cable and used for transporting passengers; *esp* : one used as a ski lift

go–no–go \ˈgōˈnō͵gō\ *adj* **1** : being or relating to a required decision to continue or stop a course of action <one of the toughest parts of a spaceman's job is making *go-no-go* decisions —Russell Baker> **2** : being or relating to a point at which a go-no-go decision must be made <*go-no-go* decision points when ground controllers or the astronauts themselves can elect not to take the next step —*Science News*>

goof–off \ˈgü͵ȯf\ *n* : one who evades work or responsibility <an all-round *goof-off* heavily in debt —John Simon>

goofy–foot \ˈgüfē͵fu̇t\ *or* **goofy–foot·er** \-u̇d·ə(r)\ *n, pl* **goofy–foots** *or* **goofy–footers** : a surfer who rides a surfboard with the right foot forward

goose* *vt* **goosed; goos·ing** : to spur to action or accelerated growth : push, prod <an effort to *goose* newstand sales>

gox \ˈgäks\ *abbr* gaseous oxygen

GPA *abbr* grade-point average

grab* *vt* **grabbed; grab·bing** : to seize the attention of : impress, strike <the technique of *grabbing* an audience —Pauline Kael>

grade point *n* : a numerical value assigned to each letter grade (as F = 0, D = 1, C = 2, B = 3, A = 4) received in a school or college course that is multiplied by the number of credits for the course

grade–point average \ˌgrādˌpȯint-\ *n* : the average obtained by dividing the total number of grade points by the total number of credits earned

grammar* *n* : a system of rules that defines the grammatical structure of a language

gram·mat·i·cal·i·ty \grə͵mad·əˈkaləd·ē\ *n* : the quality or state of being grammatical

Gram·my \ˈgramē, -mi\ *n, pl* **Grammys** *or* **Grammies** [*gram*ophone + *-my* (as in *Emmy*)] : any of several gold-plated statuettes awarded annually by a professional organization for notable achievement in phonograph recording

grand touring car *n* : a usu. 2-passenger coupe — called also *GT*

granny glasses *n pl* : spectacles with usu. small oval, round, or square lenses and metal frames

gra·no·la \grəˈnōlə\ *n* [fr. *Granola*, a former trademark] : rolled oats mixed with other ingredients (as brown sugar, raisins, coconut, or nuts) and used esp. as a breakfast food and health food

grants·man·ship \ˈgran(t)smən͵ship\ *n* : the art of obtaining grants of money (as for research projects) <the only kinds of *grantsmanship* that . . . officials concede are effective are the literary virtues of clarity and succinctness. The art is more usually understood to mean dressing up an idea —Nicholas Wade> — **grants·man** \-mən\ *n*

gra·num \ˈgrānəm\ *n, pl* **gra·na** \-nə\ [NL, fr. L, grain] : one of the lamellar stacks of chlorophyll-containing material in plant chloroplasts

graphic* *n* **1** : a graphic representation displayed by a computer (as on a cathode-ray tube) **2 graphics** *pl but sing or pl in constr* : the process whereby a computer displays graphics and an operator can manipulate them (as with a light pen)

grass* *n* : marijuana

grass carp *n* : an herbivorous fish (*Ctenopharyngodon idella*) of Russia and mainland China that has been introduced elsewhere to control aquatic weeds — called also *white amur*

gravi·sphere \ˈgravə͵sfi(ə)r, -iə\ *n* [*grav*ity + *sphere*] : the sphere of space in which the gravitational influence of a particular celestial body is predominant

grav·i·ta·tion·al collapse \͵gravəˈtāshnəl-, -shənᵊl-\ *n* : the tendency of matter to move rapidly toward a common center of gravity that results in the formation of stars, star clusters, and galaxies from the dilute gas of interstellar space

gravitational interaction *n*: a weak fundamental interaction that is hypothesized to occur between elementary particles but that has been observed only on a scale larger than that hypothesized

gravitational wave *n*: a hypothetical wave held to travel at the speed of light and to propagate the gravitational field

grav·i·ton \ˈgravə̇ˌtän\ *n* [ISV *gravity* + *-on* elementary particle]: a hypothetical particle with zero charge and rest mass that is held to be the quantum of the gravitational field

gravity wave* *n*: GRAVITATIONAL WAVE

Gray Panther *n* [*gray* + *Panther* (as in *Black Panther*); fr. the fact that many elderly people have gray hair]: a member of an organization of militant elderly people

Green Beret *n* [fr. the green beret worn as part of his uniform]: a member of the U.S. Army Special Forces

green goddess dressing *n* [fr. *The Green Goddess* (1921) play by William Archer †1924 Scot. dramatist and critic]: a green salad dressing consisting of mayonnaise, sour cream, anchovies, chives, parsley, tarragon vinegar, and seasonings

greenhouse effect *n*: a warming of the earth's surface and the lower layers of the atmosphere that tends to increase with increasing atmospheric carbon dioxide and that is caused by conversion of solar radiation into heat in a process involving selective transmission of short wave solar radiation by the atmosphere, its absorption by the earth's surface, and reradiation as infrared which is absorbed and partly reradiated back to the surface by carbon dioxide and water vapor in the air

green revolution *n*: the great increase in production of food grains (as rice, wheat, and maize) due to the introduction of high-yielding varieties, to the use of pesticides, and to better management techniques

gremlin* *n*: GREMMIE

grem·mie *also* **grem·my** \ˈgremē, -mi\ *n, pl* **gremmies** [*grem*lin + *-ie*, dim. suffix] : a young or inexperienced surfer; *esp*: one whose behavior is objectionable — called also *gremlin*

grid* *n* **1**: a network of conductors for the distribution of electric power; *also*: a network of radio or television stations **2**: the starting positions of cars on a racecourse **3** : a device (as of glass) in a phototypesetting machine on which are located the characters to be exposed as the text is composed

groove* *vb* **grooved; groov·ing** [fr. the phrase *in the groove*] *vt* **1**: to enjoy appreciatively <some dopey gals in the Village who would have *grooved* this combination of paint shop, cookery, and baby crap —Alexander King> **2**: to excite pleasurably <*grooving* their minds with cannabis —Stephen Nemo> ~ *vi* **1**: to enjoy oneself intensely : experience keen pleasure <self-perception that informs you how and when to *groove* in your own way —Al Calloway> **2**: to interact harmoniously <contemporary minds and rock *groove* together —Benjamin De Mott>

groove* *n*: an enjoyable, pleasurable, or exciting experience <I found the theater a *groove* and a gas —Lee Marvin>

gross out *vt*: to offend or insult by gross speech or action — **gross–out** \ˈgrōˌsau̇t\ *n*

ground* *vt*: to throw (a football) intentionally to the ground to avoid being tackled for a loss

ground–ef·fect machine \ˌgrau̇ndə̇ˌfekt-, -ēˌfekt-\ *n* [fr. the support provided by the cushion of air as if the vehicle rode on the ground]: an air-cushion vehicle for traveling over land or water

ground·out \ˈgrau̇nˌdau̇t\ *n* [*ground*er + *out*]: a play in baseball in which a batter is put out after hitting a grounder to an infielder <retired on a *groundout* to second base>

group* *n*: a mathematical set that is closed under a binary associative operation and that has an identity element and an inverse for every element

group grope *n, slang*: a sex orgy <live out their sexual fantasies in either single encounters or *group gropes* —*Newsweek*>

group·ie \ˈgrüpē, -pi\ *n* [*group* + *-ie*, n. suffix] **1 a**: a female fan of a rock musician or group who hangs around esp. in hopes of a sexual liaison <*groupies*, who follow rock stars not to get their autographs but to get them into bed —Fred Sparks> **b**: a fan and esp. a female fan of someone other than a rock celebrity whose motivation is similar <stock-car *groupies*> <some male *groupies* who try to attach themselves to their entourage —Martha Duffy> **2** : a follower or hanger-on of a celebrity or group of celebrities <political *groupies*> <a 19-year-old quiz show *groupie* —Robert Hurwitz> <accompanying contingents of press *groupies* and journalism students —*Playboy*>

group theory *n* : a branch of mathematics concerned with the properties of groups

group·think \ˈgrüpˌthiŋk\ *n* [*group* + *think* (as in *doublethink*)] : conformity to group values and ethics <a product of *groupthink* and the bureaucrat's instinct to keep programs running no matter what the cost —Robert Gillette>

growth* *n* : anticipated progressive growth in capital value and income <younger investors may prefer *growth* to immediate income>

growth company *n* : a company that grows at a greater rate than the economy as a whole

grun·gy \ˈgrənjē, -ji\ *adj* **grun·gi·er; -est** [origin unknown] : being in a dirty or uncared-for condition <*grungy* old boots> <*grungy* bars> <every little town was clean and electrified and civilized—nothing like the *grungy* outposts —P.D. Young>

grunt* *n* : a U.S. army or marine foot soldier esp. in the Vietnam war <officers often relied upon artillery strikes to do the killing and the *grunts* to do the counting after death —John Larsen>

GT \ˌjēˈtē\ *n* [*g*rand *t*ouring (car)] : GRAND TOURING CAR

gua·neth·i·dine \gwäˈnethəˌdēn, -ədən\ *n* [*guanidine* + *eth*yl] : a synthetic guanidine derivative $C_{10}H_{22}N_4$ used esp. in treating severe high blood pressure

guerrilla theater *n* : drama dealing with controversial social and political issues that is usu. performed outdoors (as on streets or in parks) <*guerrilla theater* by Vietnam veterans who tried to express in a dramatic way what they had done and seen in South Vietnam —Noam Chomsky> — called also *street theater*

gun* *n* : a heavy surfboard that is usu. longer than a Malibu board, has a round nose and a tapered tail, and is usu. used in surf over 15 feet in height — called also *big gun*

gunboat diplomacy *n* : diplomacy backed by the use or threat of military force <the restraints of nuclear deterrence, and of world public opinion, seem to have ended the effectiveness of *gunboat diplomacy* —H.S. Ashmore>

Gunn effect \ˈgən-\ *n* [J. B. *Gunn* *b* 1928 Brit. physicist] : the production of rapid fluctuations of current when the voltage applied to a semiconductor device exceeds a critical value with the result that microwave power is generated

gun·ship \ˈgənˌship\ *n* : an armed helicopter used esp. for protecting troop transport helicopters against ground fire <hovering . . . *gunships* laced the weeds with rockets and .50-cal. bullets —*Time*>

gus·sy up \ˌgəsēˈəp\ *vt* **gus·sied up; gus·sy·ing up** \ˌgəs(ē)iŋ\ [origin unknown] : to dress up : prettify <women were thought to be more provocative of sinful deliberation if *gussied up* in snaps, bows and frills —Russell Baker> <the emphasis is on visual effect, and in *gussying up* form many architects sacrifice function —W.H. Whyte>

gut *adj* **1** : arising from one's inmost self : visceral <a *gut* reaction to the misery he has seen —J.A. Lukas> **2** : having strong impact or immediate relevance <*gut* issues>

gut course *n* [prob. fr. its being likened in softness to the belly] : a course (as in college) that is easily passed <had planned to major in English because it is usually an innocuous, gentlemanly major which is made up of *gut courses* —*Williams Alumni Rev.*>

gyp·lure \ˈjipˌlu̇(ə)r, -lu̇ə\ *n* [*gyp*sy (moth) + *lure*] : a synthetic sex attractant used in trapping male gypsy moths

gyp·sum board \ˈjipsəm-\ *n* : wallboard with a center of gypsum plaster : plasterboard

gy·ro·cop·ter \ˈjīrəˌkäptə(r)\ *n* [auto*gyro* + heli*copter*] : a usu. one-passenger rotary-wing aircraft that is driven forward by a conventional propeller

gy·ro·dy·nam·ics \ˌjī(ˌ)rō(ˌ)dīˈnamiks, -ēks\ *n pl but sing in constr* [*gyro*scope + *dynamics*] : a branch of dynamics that deals with rotating bodies and esp. gyroscopes

H

ha·bit·u·ate* \hə'bichə,wāt, ha-\ *vi* **-at·ed; -at·ing** : to cause habituation <marijuana may be *habituating*>

hack·ing pocket \'hakiŋ-\ *n* [fr. its use on hacking coats] : a slanted coat pocket usu. with a flap

ha·dal \'hādᵊl\ *adj* [F, fr. *Hadès* Hades + *-al,* adj. suffix] : of, relating to, or being the parts of the ocean below 6000 meters

had·ron \'ha,drän\ *n* [ISV *hadr-* thick, heavy (fr. Gk *hadros*) + *-on* elementary particle] : any one of a class of elementary particles which includes the pion and all heavier particles and each member of which takes part in the strong interaction — **ha·dron·ic** \ha'dränik, -ēk\ *adj*

haf·nia \'hafnēə\ *n* [NL, fr. *hafnium* + *-a* oxide] : a white refractory crystalline oxide HfO_2 of hafnium

hail·er* \'hālə(r)\ *n* [short for *loud-hailer*] : a hand-held combined microphone and loudspeaker : a bullhorn

hair spray *n* : a preparation that is sprayed on the hair to keep it in place

hair·weav·ing \'ha(ə)r,wēviŋ, 'he(ə)r-\ *n* : the process of covering a bald spot with human hair and nylon thread woven into the wearer's own hair — **hair·weave** \-,wēv\ *n* — **hair weaver** *n*

ha·la·la *also* **ha·la·lah** \hə'lälə\ *n, pl* **halala** *or* **halalas** [Ar] **1** : a monetary unit of Saudi Arabia equal to $^1/_{100}$ riyal **2** : a coin representing one halala

halfway house* *n* : a center for formerly institutionalized individuals (as mental patients or drug addicts) that is designed to facilitate their readjustment to private life

hal·lu·ci·nate* \hə'lüsᵊn,āt\ *vt* **-nat·ed; -nat·ing** : to perceive or experience as an hallucination <the child tends to objectify strong but insubstantial experiences, as when he *hallucinates* an imaginary companion —Joseph Church>

halo·car·bon \¦halə¦kärbən, -¦kȧb-\ *n* [*halo*gen + *carbon*] : any of various compounds (as fluorocarbon) of carbon and one or more halogens

halo·cline \'halə,klīn\ *n* [*halo-* salt (deriv. of Gk *hals*) + *-cline* slope, deriv. of Gk *klinein* to lean] : a usu. vertical gradient in salinity

halo·per·i·dol \,halō'perə̇,dȯl, -,dōl\ *n* [*halo*gen + pi*perid*ine + *-ol* compound containing hydroxyl] : a depressant $C_{21}H_{23}ClFNO_2$ of the central nervous system used esp. as a tranquilizer

halo·thane \'halə,thān\ *n* [*halo*gen + e*thane*] : a nonexplosive inhalational anesthetic $C_2HBrClF_3$

ha·mate \'hā,māt\ *n* [*hamate* shaped like a hook, fr. L *hamatus,* fr. *hamus* hook] : a bone on the inner side of the second row of the carpus in mammals

hamstring* *or* **hamstring muscle** *n* : any of three muscles at the back of the thigh that function to flex and rotate the leg and extend the thigh

handjob \'han,jäb\ *n, slang* : an act of stimulating the genitals manually usu. to orgasm

handprint \'han(d),print\ *n* : an impression of a hand on a surface

hands–on \'han(d)¦zȯn, -¦zän\ *adj* [*hands-* (as in *hands-off*) + *on*] : including or devoted to individual involvement in practical occupational activities <combines fast-paced academic work with *hands-on* training for real jobs — Peter Janssen>

hang* *vb* **hung; hang·ing** *vt* : to throw (a breaking pitch) so that it fails to break properly < *hung* a curve out there like an apple on a tree, and Shannon picked it off. The drive was a mile high and hit against the beer sign above the scoreboard —Ray Fitzgerald> ~ *vi, of a thrown ball* : to fail to break or drop as intended <the pass *hung,* as the football buffs say, and [a defender] intercepted —W. N. Wallace> — **hang five** : to ride a surfboard with the weight of the body forward and the toes of one foot turned over the front edge of the board — **hang loose** : to remain calm : relax — **hang ten** : to ride a surfboard with the weight of the body forward and the toes of both feet turned over the front edge of the board

hang glider *n* : a kitelike glider from which a harnessed rider hangs while gliding down from a cliff or hill — **hang gliding** *n*

hang–loose \ˌhaŋˈlüs\ *adj* [fr. the verb phrase *hang loose*] : being highly informal, relaxed, unstructured, or uninhibited <adherence to the hedonistic *hang-loose* ethic —Geoffrey Semmon & Grafton Trout> <it's a *hang-loose* outfit. Totally disorganized. Nobody knows which end is up —Beatrice Berg>

hanging curve *n* : an intended curve ball that fails to break <hit a *hanging curve* for a home run in the sixth —Jim Brosnan>

hang–up* \ˈhaŋˌəp\ *n* : a source of mental or emotional difficulty <people were honest about their fears . . ., their *hang-ups,* their panic, their prejudices —Kate Millett>

ha·ni·wa \ˈhänəˌwä\ *n, pl* **haniwa** [Jap] : a large baked clay figure usu. in the form of a hollow cylinder or a crude human figure customarily placed on early Japanese grave mounds

happening* *n* : an event or series of events designed to evoke a spontaneous audience reaction to sensory, emotional, or spiritual stimuli: as **a** : the activities concurrent with or involved in the creation or presentation of a nonrepresentational art object (as an action painting) **b** : a usu. unrehearsed staged performance utilizing art objects and sound effects for chance and impromptu results

happy hour *n* : a period of time during which the prices of drinks at a bar or lounge are reduced or hors d'oeuvres are served gratis

hap·to·glo·bin \ˈhaptəˌglōbən\ *n* [Gk *haptein* to fasten, bind + E connective *-o-* + hemo*globin*] : a carbohydrate-containing serum alpha globulin that can combine with free hemoglobin in the plasma

hard* *adj* **1** : being at once addictive and gravely detrimental to health <such *hard* drugs as heroin> **2** : resistant to biodegradation <*hard* detergents> <*hard* pesticides like DDT>

hard copy *n* : copy (as that produced in connection with a computer or produced from microfilm) that is readable without use of a special device

hard–core \ˌhärdˈkō(ə)r, -ˈkȯ(ə)r; ˌhädˈkōə(r, -ˈkȯ(ə)(r\ *adj* **1** : of, relating to, or being persons whose economic position and educational background are substandard and who experience chronic unemployment <the major ills of our nation—rampant crime, inadequate educational systems, *hard-core* unemployment —G.R. Ford> **2** *of pornography* : containing explicit descriptions of sex acts or scenes of actual sex acts — compare SOFT-CORE

hard–edge \ˈhärdˌej, ˈhäd-\ *adj* : of or relating to abstract painting characterized by geometric forms with clearly defined boundaries

hardened* *adj* : protected from possible danger from blast or heat by means of concrete or earth or by being situated underground <a *hardened* missile launching site> <a *hardened* missile>

hard·hat \ˈhärdˌhat, ˈhäd-\ *n* **1** [fr. the fact that construction workers wear protective hard hats] : a construction worker **2** [fr. the fact that some construction workers are outspokenly opposed to nonconformists] : a conservative who is strongly opposed to nonconformists <a *hardhat* type, mouthing prejudices about the young and the blacks and the freeloaders on welfare —*New Yorker*>

hard–line \-ˈlīn\ *adj* : advocating a persistently firm course of action <a *hard-line* policy toward polluters> <ran on a *hard-line* segregationist platform —*Current Biog.*>

hard–lin·er \-ˈlīnə(r)\ *n* : an advocate of a hard-line policy <accused of being simplistic *hard-liners* against even the most moderate demands —Jack Rosenthal>

hard rock *n* : rock 'n' roll in its original style marked by loudness and a steady insistent beat

hardware* *n* **1** : the physical components (as electronic and electrical devices) of a vehicle (as a spacecraft) or an apparatus (as a computer) **2** : devices (as tape recorders, phonographs, and closed-circuit television) used as instructional equipment — compare SOFTWARE

hard·wired \ˌhärdˈwī(ə)rd; ˌhädˈwīəd\ *adj* : being in the form of permanent electronic circuits <an instruction repertoire . . . implemented in 400 *hardwired* specifics —*Datamation*>

Har·dy–Wein·berg \ˌhärdēˈwīnˌbərg\ *adj* : of, relating to, or governed by the Hardy-Weinberg law <*Hardy-Weinberg* equilibrium>

Hardy–Weinberg law *n* [G.H. *Hardy* †1947 Eng. mathematician and W. *Weinberg*, 20th cent. Ger. scientist] : a fundamental principle of population genetics: population gene frequencies and genotype frequencies remain constant from generation to generation if mating is random and if mutation, selection, immigration, and emigration do not occur — called also *Hardy-Weinberg principle*

hash \ˈhash\ *n* [short for *hashish*] : the unadulterated resin from the flowering tops of the female hemp plant (*Cannabis sativa*) : hashish

hassle* *vt* **has·sled; has·sling** : to subject to persistent or acute annoyance : harass <we're still being *hassled* by male officials, and we still have to fight twice as hard as the men do to get fair treatment —Billie Jean King>

hatchback \ˈhachˌbak\ *n* **1** : a back on a closed passenger automobile (as a coupe) having an upward-opening hatch **2** : an automobile having a hatchback

haute cuisine \ˌ(h)ōtkwəˈzēn, -kwē-\ *n* [F, lit., high cuisine] : a refined style of cooking marked by artful or elaborate methods of preparation <a hotel dining room doesn't expect to be judged in terms of *haute cuisine* —*New York*>; *also* : food prepared in this style <an artful combination of the crudest country food plus whatever *haute cuisine* he could obtain by cajolery rather than a large outlay of money —J.A. Michener>

hawk* *n* : one who takes a militant attitude (as in a dispute) and advocates immediate vigorous action — compare DOVE — **hawk·ish** \ˈhȯkish\ *adj* — **hawk·ish·ly** \-lē, -li\ *adv* — **hawk·ish·ness** \-nəs\ *n*

Haw·thorne effect \ˈhȯˌthȯrn-\ *n* [fr. the *Hawthorne* Works of the Western Electric Co., Cicero, Ill., where its existence was established by experiment] : the stimulation to increase output or accomplishment (as in an industrial or educational methods study) that results from the mere fact of being under concerned observation; *also* : such an increase in output or accomplishment

hay·lage \ˈhālij\ *n* [*hay* + si*lage*] : stored forage that is essentially grass silage wilted to 35 to 50 percent moisture

HC* *abbr* hard copy

head* *n* [short for *pothead* or *acidhead*] : one who uses a drug (as LSD or marijuana)

head dip *n* : a surfing feat in which a surfer squats on the board, leans forward, and dips his head into the wave

head·er* \ˈhedə(r)\ *n* **1** : a mounting plate through which electrical terminals pass from a sealed device (as a transistor) **2** : a fall or dive head foremost <took a *header* down the stairs> **3** : a shot or pass in soccer made by heading the ball

head·rest* \ˈhedˌrest\ *n* : a resilient pad at the top of the back of an automobile seat esp. for preventing whiplash injury

head restraint *n* : HEADREST

head shop *n* [*head* drug user] : a shop that specializes in articles (as hashish pipes, incense, posters, and beads) of interest to drug users

health food *n* : a food held to be highly conducive to health

health spa \-ˌspä, -ˌspȯ, -ˌspa\ *n* : a commercial establishment with facilities for assisting its patrons to lose weight — called also *fat farm*

heat* *n, slang* : the police <didn't even know that the *heat* had busted a friend of mine until I read about it —Robert Courtney>

heat island *n* : an urban area in which significantly more heat is absorbed and retained (as by buildings and streets) than in surrounding areas

heat pipe *n* : a closed container in which a continuing cycle of evaporation and condensation of a fluid takes place with the heat being given off at the condenser end and which is more effective in transferring heat than a metallic conductor

heat pol·lu·tion \-pəˈlüshən\ *n* : THERMAL POLLUTION

heat sink *n* : a substance or device for the absorption or dissipation of unwanted heat (as from a process or an electronic device)

heavy* *n, pl* **heavies** **1** : a large wave **2** *slang* : a person of consequence : big shot <aren't bold enough to match wits with the pedagogical *heavies*—Nancy B. Evans & Susan D. Fernandez>

heavy chain *n* : either of the two larger of the four polypeptide chains that comprise antibodies — compare LIGHT CHAIN

hedge fund *n* : an investing group usu. in the form of a limited partnership that employs speculative techniques (as short selling and leverage) in the hope of obtaining large capital gains

heliborne \ˈhelə̇ˌbō(ə)rn, ˈhēl-, -ˌbȯ(ə)rn\ *adj* [*heli*copter + *borne*] : transported by helicopter < *heliborne* troops>

he·lic·i·ty \heˈlisəd·ē, hə̇-\ *n, pl* **-ties** [*helic-* helix + *-ity* state, quality] **1** : the motion of a particle about an axis parallel to its direction of motion **2** : the component of the spin of a particle in its direction of motion measured in quantum units of spin

heli·lift \ˈhelə̇ˌlift, ˈhēl-\ *vt* [*heli*copter + *lift*] : to transport (troops) by helicopter

heli·pad \-ˌpad\ *n* [*heli*copter + *pad*] : a landing and takeoff surface for helicopters

heli·spot \-ˌspät\ *n* [*heli*copter + *spot*] : a temporary landing surface for helicopters

heli·stop \-ˌstäp\ *n* [*heli*copter + *stop*] : a place to land helicopters : heliport

he·li·um–4 \ˌhēlēəmˈfō(ə)r, -ˈfȯ(ə)r, -ˈfōə, -ˈfȯə\ *n* : the most common isotope of helium having the mass number four

helium–3 \-ˈthrē\ *n* : the isotope of helium having the mass number three

Hem·ing·way·esque \ˌhemiŋˌwāˌesk\ *adj* [Ernest Miller *Hemingway* †1961 Am. writer] : of, relating to, or suggestive of Ernest Hemingway or his writings <striving for a kind of *Hemingwayesque* elemental truth amid the sun-drenched walls and deep interior shadows of an endlessly picturesque Spain —Roger Greenspun> <evolved what we thought was a *Hemingwayesque* fatalism—this mainly involved consuming a lot of beer, as I recall —R.R. Lingeman>

he·mo·di·al·y·sis \ˌhēmōdīˌaləsə̇s, ˌhemō-\ *n* [*hemo-* blood (deriv. of Gk *haima*) + *dialysis*] : the process of removing blood (as of a kidney patient) from an artery, purifying it by dialysis, adding vital substances, and returning it to a vein

hemoglobin S *n* [*s*ickle cell] : a hemoglobin that occurs in the red blood cells in sickle-cell anemia and sickle-cell trait

he·pa·to·cyte \hə̇ˈpad·əˌsīt, ˈhepəd·ə-\ *n* [*hepato-* liver (deriv. of Gk *hēpat-*, *hēpar*) + *-cyte* cell, deriv. of Gk *kytos* hollow vessel] : an epithelial parenchymatous cell of the liver

hep·a·top·a·thy \ˌhepəˈtäpəthē\ *n, pl* **-thies** [*hepato-* + *-pathy* disease] : an abnormal or diseased state of the liver

hep·a·to·tox·ic·i·ty \ˌhepəd·ōˌtäkˈsisə̇d·ē\ *n, pl* **-ties** **1** : a state of toxic damage to the liver **2** : capacity to cause hepatotoxicity

hep·a·to·tox·in \ˌhepəd·ōˈtäksə̇n\ *n* [*hepato-* + *toxin*] : a substance toxic to the liver

her·ma·typ·ic \ˌhərməˈtipik, -ēk\ *adj* [Gk *herma* prop, reef + E *typ-* (fr. Gk *typtein* to strike, coin) + *-ic* relating to] : building reefs < *hermatypic* corals>

Her·mi·tian matrix \erˌmēshən-, (ˌ)hərˌmish-\ *n* [Charles *Hermite* †1901 Fr. mathematician] : a square matrix having the property that each pair of elements comprised of one in the *i*th row and *j*th column and the other in the *j*th row and *i*th column are conjugate complex numbers

her·pes·vi·rus \ˌhər(ˌ)pēzˌvīrəs\ *n* : any of a group of DNA-containing viruses that replicate in cell nuclei and produce herpes

¹het·ero \ˈhed·ə(ˌ)rō\ *adj* [short for *heterosexual*] : being heterosexual <find that homosexual marriages are as miserable as *hetero* ones —Rosalyn Regelson>

²hetero *n, pl* **-eros** : one who is heterosexual <no more of a security risk than the *heteros* around him —Tom Wicker>

het·ero·at·om \ˌhed·ərōˌad·əm\ *n* [*hetero-* different (deriv. of Gk *heteros*) + *atom*] : an atom other than carbon in the ring of a heterocyclic compound

het·ero·sex \ˈhed·ərōˌseks\ *n* [short for *heterosexuality*] : the quality or state of being heterosexual : heterosexuality

heu·ris·tic* \hyu̇ˈristik, -ēk\ *n* : a heuristic method or procedure

hexa·dec·i·mal \ˌheksəˌdes(ə̇)məl\ *adj* [alter. (influenced by *hexa-* six, fr. Gk *hex*) of *sexadecimal*] : of, relating to, or being a number system with a base of 16

hexa·meth·y·lene·tet·ra·mine \ˌheksəˈmethəˌlēnˈte·trəˌmēn, -əmən\ *n* [ISV, fr. *hexa-* + *methylene* + *tetramine*] : a crystalline compound $C_6H_{12}N_4$ used esp. as an accelerator in vulcanizing rubber, as an absorbent for phosgene, and as a diuretic

hick·ey* \ˈhikē, -ki\ *n, pl* **hickeys** [*hickey* pimple, of unknown origin] : a temporary red mark produced in lovemaking by biting and sucking the skin

hidden tax *n* : a tax exacted from a person other than the one on whom the ultimate burden of the tax is expected to fall : an indirect tax

high–energy \ˌhīˈenə(r)jē, -ji\ *adj* **1 a** : having such speed and kinetic energy as to exhibit relativistic departure from classical laws of motion — used esp. of elementary particles whose velocity has been imparted by an accelerator **b** : of or relating to high-energy particles <a *high-energy* reaction> **2** : yielding a relatively large amount of energy when undergoing hydrolysis <*high-energy* phosphate bonds in ATP>

high energy physics *n* : physics that deals with the constitution, properties, and interactions of elementary particles as revealed by experiments involving particle accelerators

high·light·er \ˈhīˌlīd·ə(r)\ *n* : a cosmetic for highlighting facial features

1**high–rise** \ˈhīˈrīz\ *adj* **1** : being multistory and equipped with elevators <*high-rise* buildings> **2** : of, relating to, or characterized by high-rise buildings <a *high-rise* district>

2**high–rise** *n* : a high-rise building

high–riser \-ə(r)\ *n* : HIGH-RISE

Hil·bert space \ˌhilbə(r)t-\ *n* [David *Hilbert* †1943 Ger. mathematician] : a vector space for which a scalar product is defined and which has the property that if a sequence of elements is such that any two members are arbitrarily close together when the members are chosen far enough along in the sequence, the sequence converges to a limit belonging to the vector space

hip* *n* : HIPNESS <a spiritual hustler, the Elmer Gantry of *hip* —Tim Cahill>

hip–hug·gers \ˈhipˌhəgə(r)z\ *n pl* : low-slung usu. close-fitting trousers that rest on the hips

hip·ness \ˈhipnəs\ *n* : the quality or state of being hip <remarks intended to show his *hipness* —Jack Kerouac>

hip·pie *or* **hip·py** \ˈhipē, -pi\ *n, pl* **hippies** [*hip* + *-ie,* n. suffix] : a young person who rejects the mores of established society (as by dressing unconventionally or favoring communal living), adheres to a nonviolent ethic, and often uses marijuana or psychedelic drugs; *broadly* : a long-haired unconventionally dressed young person

hip·pie·dom \ˈhipēdəm, -pid-\ *n* [*hippie* + *-dom* realm, area, group of people] : the world of hippies <a tribal rock 'n' roll musical about *hippiedom* —Lewis Funke>

hip·ster·ism \ˈhipstəˌrizəm\ *n* **1** : HIPNESS **2** : the way of life characteristic of hipsters

his·to·com·pat·i·bil·i·ty \ˌhi(ˌ)stōkəmˌpad·əˈbiləd·ē\ *n* [*histo-* tissue (deriv. of Gk *histos* mast, loom, beam, web) + *compatibility*] : a state of mutual tolerance between tissues that permits one to be grafted effectively to the other — **his·to·com·pat·i·ble** \-kəmˈpad·əbəl\ *adj*

his·to·phys·i·o·log·i·cal \-ˌfizēəˈläjəkəl\ *or* **his·to·phys·i·o·log·ic** \-ˈläjik\ *adj* : of or relating to histophysiology

hit* *n* **1** : a single dose of a narcotic drug <the junkie is relatively cool between *hits* —Jonathan Black> **2** : a premeditated murder usu. committed by a member of a crime syndicate <setting up *hits*. . . during the family wars of Prohibition —*Newsweek*>

Hitch·cock·ian \(ˈ)hichˈkäkēən, -kyən\ *adj* [Alfred Joseph *Hitchcock* *b*1899 Am. (Eng.-born) motion-picture director] : of, relating to, or suggestive of the cinematic style or technique of Alfred Hitchcock <production has just the right escalating *Hitchcockian* panic —Michael Billington>

hit man *n* [*hit* murder] : a professional assassin who works for a crime syndicate <reported that the shootings were done by professional mob *hit men* —Buddy Nevins>

hoa·gie *also* **hoa·gy** \'hōgē\ *n, pl* **hoagies** [origin unknown] : a large sandwich made from a long roll split and generously filled (as with cold cuts, cheese, onion, lettuce, and tomato)

ho·dad \'hō,dad\ *n* [perh. alter. of *hodag*, a mythical animal noted for its ugliness] : a nonsurfer who frequents surfing beaches and pretends to be a surfer

hold* *n* : a delay in a countdown (as in launching a missile)

holding pattern *n* : a usu. oval course flown (as over an airport) by aircraft awaiting clearance to land <New York is a multi-layered traffic tangle: in the air (a two-hour *holding pattern*) —Robert Craft>

ho·lid·ic \hä'lidik, hō'-\ *adj* [*hol-* complete, total (deriv. of Gk *holos* whole) + *-idic* (as in *meridic*)] : having the active constituents chemically defined <*holidic* diets> — compare MERIDIC, OLIGIDIC

Hol·ler·ith \'hälə,rith\ *n* [Herman *Hollerith* †1929 Am. engineer] : code for representing alphanumeric information on punch cards — called also *Hollerith code*

Hollerith card *n* : a punch card for data processing

ho·lo·gram \'hälə,gram, 'hōl-\ *n* [*holo-* complete, total (deriv. of Gk *holos* whole) + *-gram* drawing, writing, record, deriv. of Gk *gramma* letter, writing] : a three-dimensional picture produced in the form of an interference pattern on a photographic film or plate without use of a lens by two beams of coherent light (as from a laser) so that for reconstruction of the image the pattern is viewed by coherent light passing through the film or plate

ho·lo·graph \-,graf\ *n* [*holo-* + *-graph* something written, deriv. of Gk *graphein* to write] : HOLOGRAM

ho·log·ra·phy \hə'lägrəfē, hō-, -fi\ *n* : the process of making or using a hologram — **holograph** *vt* — **ho·lo·graph·ic** \,hälə'grafik, ,hō-, -ēk\ *adj* — **ho·lo·graph·i·cal·ly** \-k(ə)lē, -li\ *adv*

home free \'hōm'frē\ *adj* : having attained a comfortable position usu. after considerable effort <knew . . . that he had a hit and was *home free* —Martin Kasindorf>

home stand *n* : a series of baseball games played at a team's home field

hom·i·ni·za·tion \,hämənəzāshən, -,nī-\ *n* [*homin-* human (fr. L *homin-*, *homo* human being) + *-ization* making] **1** : the evolutionary development of human characteristics that differentiate man from his primate ancestors **2** : the progressive taking over and adapting of the world to his needs by man

hom·i·nized \'hämə,nīzd\ *adj* : characterized by hominization

ho·mo·ge·ne·ity* \,hōməjə'nēəd·ē, ,hä-, -(,)mōj-, -'nāə-, ÷-'nīə-\ *n* : the state of having identical distribution functions or values <a test for *homogeneity* of variances> <*homogeneity* of two statistical populations>

Ho·mo ha·bi·lis \'hō(,)mō'habələs\ *n* [NL, fr. L *homo* man + *habilis* skillful, handy] : an extinct primate that is known from eastern African fossil remains associated with crude tools, is believed to have flourished some two million years ago, and is variously interpreted as the earliest true man or an australopithecine

ho·mo·mor·phism* \,hōmə'mȯr,fizəm, ,häm-\ *n* : a mapping of a mathematical group, ring, or vector space onto another in such a way that the result obtained by applying an operation to elements of the domain is mapped onto the result obtained by applying the operation to their images in the range

1ho·mo·phile \'hōmə,fīl\ *adj* [*homo*sexual + *-phile* loving, deriv. of Gk *philos* beloved, loving] : oriented toward and concerned with the rights or welfare of the homosexual; *also* : being homosexual

2homophile *n* : one who is homosexual

ho·mo·pho·bia \,hōmə'fōbēə\ *n* [*homo*sexual + *phobia*] : irrational fear of homosexuality or homosexuals — **ho·mo·pho·bic** \-bik, -bēk\ *adj*

ho·mo·sex \'hōmə,seks\ *n* [short for *homosexuality*] : the quality or state of being homosexual : homosexuality

hon·cho \'hän(,)chō\ *n, pl* **honchos** [Jap *hanchō* squad leader, fr. *han* squad + *chō* head, chief] : someone in charge : a boss or leader <the Democrats' big *honchos* believe they need a woman on the ticket this year —Michael Kramer>

honey bucket *n* : a bucket for collecting human excrement

honey wagon *n* **1 :** a vehicle for transporting human excrement **2 :** a portable outdoor toilet

hon·ky *or* **hon·kie** *also* **hon·key** \ˈhȯŋkē, ˈhä-, -ki\ *n, pl* **honkies** [origin unknown] : a white man — usu. used disparagingly

hootch *or* **hooch** \ˈhüch\ *n* [modif. of Jap *uchi* house] : a thatched hut esp. in Vietnam; *broadly* : a house, dwelling, or barracks

hopefully* *adv* : it is hoped : we hope <procedures which would *hopefully* lead to the resolution of the more important substantive issue —*AAUP Bull.*> <to get good or (*hopefully*) rave reviews —H.C. Schonberg> <this mask might, *hopefully,* become indistinguishable from what one actually was —S.N. Behrman> <*hopefully* better coordinated and more effective programs may result —N.M. Pusey>

HO scale \(ˈ)āˌchō-\ *n* [fr. its fitness for rails of HO gage] : a scale of $^{1}/_{8}$ inch to one foot used esp. for model toys (as automobiles or trains)

host plant *n* : a plant upon which an organism (as an insect or mildew) lodges and subsists

hot* *adj* **hot·ter; hot·test :** being full of detail and information and requiring little or no involvement of the listener, viewer, or reader <distinguishes a *hot* medium like radio . . . from a cool one like TV —H.M. McLuhan>

hot·dog \ˈhätˌdȯg, *sometimes* -däg\ *vb* **-dogged; -dog·ging** [prob. fr. *hot dog,* exclamation of approval or gratification] *vi* : to show off by performing fancy maneuvers (as when surfing or skiing) ~ *vt* : to hotdog while surfing on (a wave) — **hot·dog·ger** \-ə(r)\ *also* **hotdog** *n* — **hotdogging** *n*

hotel china *n* [fr. its capacity to withstand the hard use typically met with in hotels] : a high-fired well-vitrified American ceramic ware approaching hard-paste porcelain in composition

hot line *n* **1 :** a direct telephone line in constant readiness to operate so as to facilitate immediate communication (as between heads of two governments) **2 :** a telephone service by which usu. unidentified callers can talk confidentially about personal problems to a sympathetic listener <drug-counseling services, some with around-the-clock "crisis" *hot lines* —R.D. McFadden>

hot pants* *n pl* : very short shorts

hots \ˈhäts\ *n pl* : strong sexual desire — used with *the* <a not very pretty ninny with the *hots* for gypsy-dark men —H.C. Veit>

hot shoe *n* : a receptacle on a camera that provides a point of attachment for an electronic flashgun and that effects synchronization of the flashgun and shutter

hot–wire \ˈhätˌwī(ə)r, -ˌwīə\ *vt* : to short-circuit the wires of (an automotive vehicle or its ignition system) in order to start the engine without using a key

Hub·ble constant \ˌhəbəl-\ *n* [Edwin P. *Hubble* †1953 Am. astronomer] : a proportionality constant used in relating the apparent velocity of recession of a distant galaxy and its distance so that a greater rate of recession indicates a greater distance

Hu·go \ˈ(h)yügō\ *n, pl* **Hugos** [*Hugo* Gernsback †1967 Am. (Luxembourg-born) author, inventor, and publisher] : any of several trophies awarded annually by a professional organization for notable achievement in science-fiction writing

hung \ˈhəŋ\ *adj* : having a large penis

hung up* *adj* **1 :** having a hang-up <sometimes I'm so *hung up* I can't function —*New Yorker*> **2 :** being much involved with: as **a :** infatuated <they get *hung up* on some fellow here —Jeff Brown> **b :** enthusiastic <people who are *hung up* on French Provincial —Walter Goodman> **c :** obsessed <*hung up* on winning>

hunting* *n* **1 :** a periodic variation in speed of a synchronous electrical machine from that of the true synchronous speed **2 :** a self-induced and undesirable oscillation of a variable above and below the desired value in an automatic control system **3 :** a continuous attempt by an automatically controlled system to find a desired equilibrium condition

hutzpah *or* **hutzpa** *var of* CHUTZPAH

hybrid computer *n* : a computer system consisting of a combination of analog and digital computer systems

hy·dro* \'hī(,)drō\ *n, pl* **hydros** [short for *hydroplane*] : a speedboat with hydrofoils or a stepped bottom so that the hull will rise wholly or partly out of the water as the boat attains speed : a hydroplane

hy·dro·acous·tic \¦hī(,)drōə¦küstik\ *adj* [*hydro-* water (deriv. of Gk *hydōr*) + *acoustic*] **1** : of or relating to the production of acoustic energy from the flow of fluids under pressure **2** : of or relating to the transmission of sound in water

hy·dro·bi·ol·o·gist \-(,)bī'äləjəst\ *n* : a specialist in hydrobiology

hy·dro·chlo·ro·thi·a·zide \,hīdrə,klōrə'thīə,zīd\ *n* [*hydro*gen + *chlor*ine + *thiazide*] : a diuretic and antihypertensive drug $C_7H_8O_4N_3ClS_2$

hy·dro·crack \'hī(,)drō¦krak\ *vt* [*hydro*gen + *crack*] : to crack (hydrocarbons) in the presence of hydrogen

hy·dro·crack·er \-ə(r)\ *n* : an apparatus for hydrocracking

hy·dro·dy·nam·i·cist \,hīdrōdī'naməsəst\ *n* : one who specializes in hydrodynamics

hy·dro·foil* \'hīdrə,fȯil\ *n* : a motorboat that has metal plates or fins attached by struts fore and aft so that they act in water as airplane wings do in air and lift the hull a short distance above the water

hy·dro·gas·i·fi·ca·tion \¦hīdrō,gasəfə'kāshən\ *n* [*hydro*gen + *gasification*] : the process of reacting hydrogen or a mixture of steam and hydrogen with coal at high temperature and high pressure so that the carbon in the coal reacts directly or indirectly to produce methane used for fuel — **hy·dro·gas·i·fi·er** \-'gasə,fī(ə)r\ *n*

hy·dro·mag·net·ic \-(,)mag'ned·ik, -ēk\ *adj* [*hydro-* water, liquid + *magnetic*] **1** : of or relating to phenomena arising from the motion of electrically conducting fluids in the presence of electric and magnetic fields **2** : being a wave in an electrically conducting fluid immersed in a magnetic field

hy·dro·mag·net·ics \-iks, -ēks\ *n pl but sing in constr* : a branch of physics that deals with hydromagnetic phenomena

hy·dro·naut \'hīdrə,nȯt, -nät\ *n* [*hydro-* water + *-naut* (as in *astronaut*)] : a member of the crew of a deep-sea vehicle (as a bathyscaphe) other than a submarine

hy·dro·nau·tics \(')hīdrə¦nȯd·iks, -¦näd·-\ *n pl but sing in constr* [*hydro-* + *-nautics* (as in *aeronautics*)] : the science of constructing and operating marine craft and instruments designed to explore the ocean environment

hy·dron·ic \hī'dränik\ *adj* [*hydro-* + *-onic* (as in *electronic*)] : of, relating to, or being a system of heating or cooling that involves transfer of heat by a circulating fluid in a closed system of pipes — **hy·dron·i·cal·ly** \-nək(ə)lē\ *adv*

hy·dron·ics \-niks\ *n pl but usu sing in constr* : a hydronic system

hydroplane* *vi, of a vehicle or tire* : to ride supported by a film of water on a wet surface when a critical speed is reached and when the lift between the tire and the pavement exceeds the weight riding on the tire with a resultant loss of directional stability and braking effectiveness

hy·dro·skim·mer \'hīdrō,skimə(r)\ *n* [*hydro-* + *skimmer*] : an air-cushion vehicle for use over water

hy·dro·space \-,spās\ *n* [*hydro-* + *space*] : the regions beneath the surface of the ocean

hy·dro·treat \-,trēt\ *vt* [*hydro*gen + *treat*] : to subject to hydrogenation < *hydrotreat* lube oil > — **hy·dro·treat·er** \-,trēd·ə(r)\ *n*

hy·dro·trope \'hīdrə,trōp\ *n* [back-formation fr. *hydrotropic*] : a hydrotropic substance

hy·droxo·co·bal·amin \hī¦dräksə(,)kō'baləmən, -(,)sō-\ *n* [*hydroxyl* + connective *-o-* + *cobalamin* member of the vitamin B_{12} group] : a member $C_{62}H_{89}CoN_{13}O_{15}P$ of the vitamin B_{12} group used in treating and preventing B_{12} deficiency

hy·droxy·urea \(¦)hī,dräksēyu̇'rēə, -si-\ *n* [*hydroxyl* + *urea*] : a compound $CH_4N_2O_2$ used as an antineoplastic agent in some forms of leukemia

hype* \'hīp\ *n* [*hype* hypodermic] **1** : something intended to deceive : a deception < had come upon some way I could work a *hype* on the penal authorities —Malcolm X > **2** : extravagant promotional advertising < the premier . . . ended weeks of calculated frenzy, hoopla and *hype* —Judy Klemesrud > < *hype* was artfully elevated by Barnum to the level of entertainment —James Childs >

hype *vt* **hyped; hyp·ing** **1** : to put on : mislead, deceive <no hustler could have it known that he'd been *hyped*—Malcolm X> **2 a** : to rouse or stimulate — usu. used with *up* <his assignment is to *hype* up the crowd —J.S. Radosta> **b** : to cause to increase <there are no cut-rate subscriptions to *hype* the figures —James Brady> **3** : to promote or publicize extravagantly <*hype* youth-oriented products to young people —Nancy McCarthy> — **hyped–up** \ˌhīpˌdəp\ *adj*

hyper-* *prefix* : that is or exists in a space of more than three dimensions <*hyper*cube> <*hyper*space>

hy·per·al·do·ste·ron·ism \ˌhīpəˌralˈdästəˌrōˌnizəm, -ˌraldōstəˈrō-\ *n* [*hyper-* above, beyond, excessive (deriv. of Gk *hyper* over) + *aldosteronism*] : ALDOSTERONISM

hy·per·bar·ic* \ˌhīpə(r)ˈbarik\ *adj* : of, relating to, or utilizing greater than normal pressure esp. of oxygen <*hyperbaric* medicine> <*hyperbaric* chamber> — **hy·per·bar·i·cal·ly** \-rək(ə)lē\ *adv*

hy·per·bol·ic* \ˌhīpə(r)ˈbälik, -ēk\ *adj* : of, relating to, or being a space in which more than one line parallel to a given line passes through a point <*hyperbolic* geometry>

hy·per·charge \ˈhīpərˌchärj, ˈhīpəˌchåj\ *n* : a quantum characteristic of a closely related group of strongly interacting particles represented by a number equal to twice the average value of the electric charge of the group

hy·per·com·plex \ˌhīpə(r)(ˌ)kämˌpleks, -ə(r)kəmˌpleks\ *adj* : of, relating to, or being a general form of number that can be expressed as a vector of *n* dimensions in the form $x_1e_1 + x_2e_2 + \dots + x_ne_n$ where the coefficients $x_1, x_2, \dots x_n$ range over a given number field and $e_1 = (e, 0, 0, \dots 0), e_2 = (0, e, 0, \dots 0), \dots e_n = (0, 0, \dots e)$ where e is the multiplicative identity of the field <*hypercomplex* variable>

hy·per·dip·loid \-ˌdipˌlȯid\ *adj*: having slightly more than the diploid number of chromosomes — **hy·per·dip·loi·dy** \-ˌlȯidē\ *n*

hy·per·ex·cit·abil·i·ty \-əkˌsīd·əˈbiləd·ē, -i\ *n* : the state or condition of being unusually or excessively excitable — **hy·per·ex·cit·able** \-ˌsīd·əbəl\ *adj*

hy·per·fine structure \ˈhīpə(r)ˌfīn-\ *n* : a fine structure multiplet occurring in an atomic spectrum that is due to interaction between electrons and nuclear spin

hy·per·geo·met·ric distribution \ˌhīpə(r)ˌjēəˌme·trik-\ *n* : a probability function of the form

$$f(x) = \frac{\binom{M}{x}\binom{N-M}{n-x}}{\binom{N}{n}} \quad \text{where} \quad \binom{M}{x} = \frac{M!}{x!(m-x)!}$$

that gives the probability of obtaining exactly x elements of one kind and $n - x$ elements of another if n elements are chosen at random without replacement from a finite population containing N elements of which M are of the first kind and $N - M$ are of the second kind

hy·per·lip·id·emia \ˌhīpə(r)ˌlipəˈdēmēə\ *n* [NL, fr. ISV *hyper-* + *lipid* + *-emia* blood condition, deriv. of Gk *haima* blood] : the presence of excess fats or lipids in the blood — **hy·per·lip·id·emic** \-mik, -mēk\ *adj*

hy·per·mar·ket \ˈhīpərˌmärkət, ˈhīpəˌmåkət\ *n, Brit* : a very large department store that includes a supermarket

hy·per·pha·gic \ˌhīpə(r)ˈfājik\ *adj* : relating to or affected with hyperphagia <*hyperphagic* rats>

hy·per·po·lar·ize \ˌhīpə(r)ˈpōləˌrīz\ *vt* : to produce an increase in potential difference across (a biological membrane) <a *hyperpolarized* nerve cell> — **hy·per·po·lar·iza·tion** \-ˌpōlərəˈzāshən, -ˌrīˈz-\ *n*

hy·per·sexual \-ˌseksh(ə)wəl, -ˌsekshəl\ *adj*: characterized by excessive sexual arousal or overindulgence in sexual activity — **hy·per·sex·u·al·i·ty** \ˌhīpə(r)ˌsekshəˈwaləd·ē\ *n*

hy·per·ve·loc·i·ty \-vəˈläsəd·ē, -ˈlästē\ *n* : a high or relatively high velocity; *esp* : one greater than 10,000 feet per second

hy·po·der·mis* \ˌhīpəˈdərməs, -ˈdəm-, -ˈdəim-\ *n* : the thin layer of loose fatty connective tissue underlying the skin and binding it to the parts beneath

hy·po·dip·loid \ˌhīpōˈdipˌlöid\ *adj* [*hypo-* under, down, less than normal (deriv. of Gk *hypo* under) + *diploid*] : having slightly fewer than the diploid number of chromosomes — **hy·po·dip·loi·dy** \-ˌlöidē\ *n*

hy·po·ther·mic \ˌhīpəˈthərmik, ˌthəm-, -ˌthəim-\ *adj* : relating to, utilizing, or characterized by hypothermia <*hypothermic* cardiovascular surgery> <*hypothermic* dogs>

hy·pox·emic \ˌhīˌpäkˈsēmik\ *adj* : relating to, characterized by, or affected with hypoxemia

I

IC \ˌīˈsē\ *n* : INTEGRATED CIRCUIT

ice* *n* : an undercover premium paid to a theater employee for choice theater tickets

ice–cream chair \ˈīˌskrēm-\ *n* [fr. its use in ice-cream parlors] : a small armless chair with a circular seat for use at a table

ice·kha·na \ˈīsˌkänə, -kan-, -kȧn-, ˌīsˈk-\ *n* [*ice* + gym*khana*] : an automobile gymkhana held on a frozen lake or river

ice–out \ˈīsˌau̇t\ *n* : the melting of ice from the surface of a body of water (as a lake) in the spring

ICU *abbr* intensive care unit

ID \ˌīˈdē\ *n* [*id*entification] : a pause in a radio or television broadcast for announcement of the identity of the station or network

IDDD *abbr* international direct distance dialing

idem·po·tent \īˈdempəd·ənt, ə̇ˈdem-; ˌīdəmˈpōtᵊnt, ˌīˌdem-\ *adj* [ISV *idem-* same (fr. L *idem*) + L *potent-, potens* having power] : relating to or being a mathematical quantity which is not zero and every positive power of which equals itself — **idem·po·ten·cy** \-ən(t)sē, -ᵊn(t)sē\ *n* — **idempotent** *n*

identification parade *n, Brit* : a line of persons arranged by the police esp. for the identification of a suspected criminal by a victim or an eyewitness : a lineup

identity crisis *n* : psychosocial conflict or confusion in an individual concerning his social role that may be accompanied by loss of feelings of sameness and continuity of the personality and that occurs esp. during adolescence in response to changes in internal drives and to external pressures to adopt new roles

identity ma·trix \-ˈmā·triks\ *n* : a square matrix with numeral 1's along the principal diagonal and 0's elsewhere

IDP *abbr* **1** inosine diphosphate **2** integrated data processing **3** international driving permit

ike·ba·na \ˌikə̇ˈbänə, ˌēk-, -kēˈ-\ *n* [Jap, fr. *ikeru* to keep alive, arrange + *hana* flower] : the Japanese art of flower arranging that emphasizes form and balance

illuminate* *vt* **-nat·ed; -nat·ing** : to subject to radiation <warning system . . . would alert the pilot when his plane was being *illuminated* by hostile radar —*Technical Survey*>

image* *n* : a set of values of a mathematical function (as a homomorphism) that corresponds to a particular subset of the domain

im·bal·anced \(ˈ)imˈbalən(t)st\ *adj* : not balanced; *esp* : having a disproportionately large number of members of one racial or ethnic group <*imbalanced* schools>

imip·ra·mine \ə̇ˈmiprəˌmēn, ˈim-, -əmən, ˌimə̇ˈpra-\ *n* [*imi*de + *pr*opyl + *amine*] : an antidepressant drug $C_{19}H_{24}N_2$

imitation milk *n* : a dietary whole-milk substitute: as **a** : milk with the natural fat replaced by a vegetable oil **b** : a wholly artifical product made with carbohydrate, fat, and protein of plant or synthetic origin

im·mit·tance \i'mitᵊn(t)s\ *n* [*im*pedance + ad*mittance*] : electrical admittance or impedance — used of transmission lines, networks, and measuring instruments

immune* *adj*: concerned with or involving immunity < *immune* globulins > <an *immune* response> < *immune* surveillance mechanisms >

immuno-* *comb form* : immunologic < *immuno*hematology >

im·mu·no·as·say \ˌimyənō'asˌā, əˌmyünō-, -(ˌ)a'sā\ *n* [*immuno-* immune, immunity + *assay*] : the identification of a substance (as a protein) through its capacity to act as an antigen — **im·mu·no·as·say·able** \-aˌsāəbəl\ *adj*

im·mu·no·com·pe·tence \-'kämpəd·ən(t)s\ *n* : the capacity for normal immune response <altered the *immunocompetence* of the lymphocytes> — **im·mu·no·com·pe·tent** \-pəd·ənt\ *adj*

im·mu·no·cy·to·chem·is·try \-ˌsīd·ō'keməstrē\ *n* : the biochemistry of cellular immunology — **im·mu·no·cy·to·chem·i·cal** \-'keməkəl\ *adj* — **im·mu·no·cy·to·chem·i·cal·ly** \-ək(ə)lē\ *adv*

im·mu·no·de·fi·cien·cy \-də'fishənsē\ *n*: failure to produce an immune system with a normal complement of immunocompetent B cells and T cells

im·mu·no·dif·fu·sion \-də'fyüzhən\ *n*: the separation of an antigen complex into discrete parts through differences in ability to pass through a semipermeable membrane or migrate through a medium

im·mu·no·elec·tro·pho·re·sis \ˌimyənōəˌlektrəfə'rēsəs, əˌmyünō-\ *n, pl* **-re·ses** \-'rēˌsēz\ : electrophoretic separation of proteins followed by identification through specific immunologic reactions — **im·mu·no·elec·tro·pho·ret·ic** \-'red·ik\ *adj* — **im·mu·no·elec·tro·pho·ret·i·cal·ly** \-ək(ə)lē\ *adv*

im·mu·no·flu·o·res·cence \-(ˌ)flü(ə)r'esᵊn(t)s, -flōr-, -flȯr-\ *n* : a labeling of antigen or antibody with fluorochrome dyes esp. for the purpose of demonstrating the presence of corresponding antibodies or antigens in a tissue preparation or a smear

im·mu·no·glob·u·lin \-'gläbyələn\ *n* : a protein (as an antibody) made up of light chains and heavy chains usu. linked by disulfide bonds

im·mu·no·he·ma·tol·o·gy \-ˌhēmə'täləjē\ *n*: a branch of immunology that deals with the immunologic properties of blood — **im·mu·no·he·ma·to·log·ic** \-ˌhēməd·ᵊl'äjik\ *adj* — **im·mu·no·he·ma·to·log·i·cal** \-jəkəl\ *adj* — **im·mu·no·he·ma·tol·o·gist** \-ˌhēmə'täləjəst\ *n*

im·mu·no·his·to·chem·i·cal \-ˌhistō'keməkəl\ *adj* : of or relating to the application of histochemical and immunologic methods to chemical analysis of living cells and tissues — **im·mu·no·his·to·chem·i·cal·ly** \-ək(ə)lē, -li\ *adv* — **im·mu·no·his·to·chem·is·try** \-'keməstrē, -ri\ *n*

im·mu·no·his·tol·o·gy \ˌimyənō(ˌ)his'täləjē, əˌmyünō-\ *n* : a branch of immunology that deals with the application of immunologic methods to histology — **im·mu·no·his·to·log·ic** \-ˌhistə'läjik, -ēk\ *adj* — **im·mu·no·his·to·log·i·cal** \-'läjəkəl\ *adj* — **im·mu·no·his·to·log·i·cal·ly** \-ək(ə)lē\ *adv*

im·mu·no·pa·thol·o·gy \-pə'thäləjē, -pa'-\ *n* : a branch of medicine that deals with immunologic abnormalities and disease — **im·mu·no·path·o·log·ic** \-ˌpathə'läjik, -ēk\ *adj* — **im·mu·no·path·o·log·i·cal** \-jəkəl\ *adj* — **im·mu·no·pa·thol·o·gist** \-pə'thäləjəst, -pa'-\ *n*

im·mu·no·re·ac·tive \-rē'aktiv\ *adj* : reacting to particular antigens or haptens <serum *immunoreactive* insulin> — **im·mu·no·re·ac·tiv·i·ty** \-(ˌ)rēˌak'tivəd·ē, -i\ *n*

im·mu·no·sup·pres·sion \-sə'preshən\ *n*: suppression (as by drugs) of natural immune responses — **im·mu·no·sup·pres·sant** \-sə'presᵊnt\ *n* — **im·mu·no·sup·pres·sive** \-sə'presiv\ *adj*

im·mu·no·ther·a·peu·tic \-ˌtherə'pyüd·ik, -ēk\ *adj* : of, relating to, or characterized by immunotherapy < *immunotherapeutic* strategies for treating cancer —Jean L. Marx>

im·pact·ed area \əm'paktəd-\ *n*: an area in which a large number of public school students are from families living or working on nontaxable federal property

implicit differentiation *n*: the process of finding the derivative of a dependent variable in an implicit function by differentiating each term separately, by expressing the derivative of the dependent variable as a symbol, and by solving the resulting expression for the symbol

im·plode* \əm'plōd\ *vi* **im·plod·ed; im·plod·ing :** to undergo violent compression <massive stars which *implode*>

imported fire ant *n* **:** a small brown South American fire ant (*Solenopsis saevissima richteri*) that is a destructive pest in the southeastern U.S.

im·pres·sion·ist* \əm'presh(ə)nəst\ *n* **:** an entertainer who does impressions of noted personalities

in* *adj* **1 :** keenly aware of and responsive to what is new and smart <the *in* crowd> **2 :** highly approved by those who are au courant <became an *in* place for fashionable people —N.T. Kenney> — **in–ness** \'innəs\ *n*

-in \ˌin\ *n comb form* [*in* (as in *sit-in*)] **1 :** organized public protest by means of or in favor of : demonstration <teach-*in*> <love-*in*> **2 :** public group activity <swim-*in*>

in–and–out* \ˈinəˈnau̇t\ *adj* **:** involving purchase and sale of the same security within a short period <*in-and-out* trading>

in·bounds \ˈinˈbau̇n(d)z\ *adj* **:** of or relating to putting a basketball in play by passing it onto the court from out of bounds <an *inbounds* pass>

in·ca·pac·i·tant \ˌinkə'pasətənt, -səd·ə-\ *n* **:** an incapacitating agent <a chemical *incapacitant*>

in·ca·pac·i·ta·tor \-əˌtād·ə(r)\ *n* **:** INCAPACITANT

inconsistent* *adj* **:** not satisfiable by the same set of values for the unknowns <*inconsistent* equations> <*inconsistent* inequalities>

independent* *adj* **1 :** having linear independence <an *independent* set of vectors> **2 :** having the property that the joint probability (as of events or samples) or the joint probability density function (as of random variables) equals the product of the probabilities or probability density functions of separate occurrence

independent assortment *n* **:** formation of combinations of chromosomes in meiosis with one of each diploid pair of homologous chromosomes passing at random into each gamete independently of each other pair; *also* : the similar process when genes on different pairs of homologous chromosomes are considered

in·dex·ation \ˌinˌdek'sāshən\ *n* **:** a system of economic control in which certain variables (as wages and interest) are tied to a cost-of-living index so that both rise or fall at the same rate and the detrimental effect of inflation is theoretically eliminated — called also *indexing*

indicator* *n* **:** any of a group of statistical values (as level of employment and change in the price of industrial raw materials) that taken together give an indication of the health of the economy — compare COINCIDENT, LAGGER, LEADER

in·do·cy·a·nine green \ˈində'sīəˌnēn-, -'sīənən-\ *n* [*indo-* indigo + *cyanine*] **:** a green tricarbocyanine dye $C_{43}H_{47}N_2NaO_6S_2$ used esp. in testing liver blood flow and cardiac output

in·do·meth·a·cin \ˌindō'methəsən\ *n* [*indo*le + *meth*yl + *a*cetic acid + *-in* chemical compound] **:** a nonsteroid analgesic anti-inflammatory agent $C_{19}H_{16}ClNO_4$ used esp. in treating arthritis

in·duc·er* \in'd(y)üsə(r)\ *n* **:** a substance capable of activating a structural gene by combining with and inactivating a genetic repressor

in·dus·tri·al–rev·e·nue bond \ənˈdəstrēəlˈrevən(y)ü-\ *n* **:** a revenue bond issued to provide industrial facilities for lease and dependent on the lease revenue for amortization and interest payments

inertial platform *n* **:** an assemblage of devices used in inertial guidance together with the mounting

inertial space *n* **:** a part of space away from the earth assumed to have fixed coordinates so that the trajectory of an object (as a spacecraft or missile) may be calculated in relation to it

inertia welding *n* **:** the welding of metals by means of the heat produced by friction when one metallic piece is pressed while spinning against another

in·fau·na \'inˌfȯnə, -ˌfän-\ *n* [NL, fr. *in-* within + *fauna*] **:** benthic fauna living in the substrate and esp. in a soft sea bottom—compare EPIFAUNA — **in·fau·nal** \-nᵊl\ *adj*

in–flight \(ˌ)inˌflīt\ *adj* **1 :** made or carried out while in flight <*in-flight* calculations> **2 :** provided for use or enjoyment while in flight <*in-flight* movies>

in·for·mat·ics \ˌinfə(r)ˈmad·iks\ *n pl but sing in constr* [ISV *informa*tion + *-ics* study, knowledge] : INFORMATION SCIENCE

information retrieval *n*: the techniques of storing and recovering and often disseminating recorded data esp. through the use of a computerized system

information science *n*: the collection, classification, storage, retrieval, and dissemination of recorded knowledge treated both as a pure and as an applied science — **information scientist** *n*

in·fra·sound \ˈinfrəˌsau̇nd\ *n* [*infra-* below (fr. L *infra*) + *sound*] : a wave phenomenon of the same physical nature as sound but with frequencies below the range of human hearing

in–house \ˈinˈhau̇s\ *adj*: of, relating to, or carried on within a group or organization <reform of the judicial system must be *in-house* —Tim Murphy> <*in-house* industrial psychologists employed by some large companies —Caroline Donnelley>

ini·tial·ism \əˈnishəˌlizəm\ *n* : an acronym formed from initial letters

ini·tial·ize \-ˌlīz\ *vt* **-ized; -iz·ing** : to set (as a computer program counter) to a starting position or value — **ini·tial·iza·tion** \əˌnish(ə)ləˈzāshən\ *n*

initial teaching alphabet *n* [fr. the fact that it is used only in the initial stages of teaching reading] : a 44-symbol alphabet designed esp. for children who are learning to read English

injection* *n* **1** : the placing of an artificial satellite or a spacecraft into an orbit or on a trajectory—called also *insertion* **2** : the time or place at which injection occurs

in·ject·or razor \ənˈjektə(r)-\ *n* : a safety razor with a narrow single-edged blade that is forced into place by a blade dispenser

in–line \(ˈ)inˈlīn\ *adj (or adv)* : having the parts or units arranged in a straight line; *also* : being so arranged

inner city *n* : the usu. oldest and most densely populated central section of a city <decided to keep its plant in the *inner city* instead of fleeing to the suburbs —Carol G. Kleiman> — **in·ner–city** \ˈinə(r)ˈsid·ē, -i\ *adj*

input \ˈinˌpu̇t\ *vt* **in·put·ted** *or* **input; in·put·ting** [*input*, n.] : to enter (as data) into a computer or data processing system <a large volume of data . . . will be *input* to the file —R.L. Venezky> <could employ a typewriter keyboard to *input* questions to a computer —Harrison Bryan>

insertion* *n* : INJECTION

instant* *adj* : produced or occurring with or as if with astonishing rapidity and ease <this 15,000-pound concussion weapon clears an area the size of a football field to make an *instant* landing zone for helicopters —P.R. Ehrlich & J.P. Holdren> <what the technology of communications now offers us—*instant* knowledge on the one hand, and *instant* boredom . . . on the other —Arlene Croce> <became an *instant* celebrity> <does not offer the *instant* answers of closed ideologies —Warren Taylor>

instant re·play \-ˈrēˌplā\ *n* : a videotape recording of an action (as a play in football) that can be played back (as in slow motion) immediately after the action has been completed

instruction* *n* : a code that tells a computer to perform a particular operation

instrumental* *adj* : based on or involving reward or avoidance of distress <*instrumental* learning> <*instrumental* conditioning>

insurance *adj* : increasing the winning team's lead while making it impossible for the other team's next score to tie the game <an *insurance* run> <grabbed the next rebound and, after a foul, sank two *insurance* free throws with one second left —*N.Y. Times*>

integral domain *n* : a mathematical ring in which multiplication is commutative, which has a multiplicative identity element, and which contains no pair of nonzero elements whose product is zero <the integers under the operations of addition and multiplication form an *integral domain*>

integrated circuit *n* : a tiny complex of electronic components (as transistors, resistors, and capacitors) and their interconnections produced in or on a single small slice of material (as silicon) — called also *chip* — **integrated circuitry** *n*

in·te·gro·dif·fer·en·tial \ˌintə̇(ˌ)grōˌdifə'renchəl, inˌte-, inˌtē-\ *adj* [*integr*al + connective *-o-* + *differential*] : involving both mathematical integration and differentiation < *integrodifferential* equations >

intelligent* *adj* : able to perform some of the functions of a computer <an *intelligent* terminal >

intensive care *adj* : having special medical facilities, services, and monitoring devices to meet the needs of gravely ill patients <an *intensive care* unit > — **intensive care** *n*

in·ter·cep·tion* \ˌintə(r)'sepshən\ *n* : an intercepted forward pass <threw three *interceptions* in one game >

in·ter·cru·ral \ˌintə(r)ˌkrů(ə)rəl\ *adj* [*inter-* between (deriv. of L *inter*) + *crural*] : situated or taking place between two crura and esp. in the region of the groin < *intercrural* intercourse >

in·ter·face* \'intə(r)ˌfās\ *n* **1** : the place at which two independent systems meet and act upon or communicate with each other <the *interface* between engineering and science > <the man-machine *interface*> ; *broadly*: an area in which diverse things interact on each other < *interface* between the known and unknown > <the high school-college *interface*> **2** : the means by which interaction or communication is effected at an interface <an *interface* between a computer and a typesetting machine >

interface *vb* **-faced; -fac·ing** *vt* **1** : to connect by means of an interface < *interface* a machine with a computer > **2** : to serve as an interface for ~ *vi* **1** : to become interfaced <a system that *interfaces* with a computer > **2** : to interact or coordinate harmoniously <the computer technicians . . . *interface* with the flight controllers —H.S.F. Cooper, Jr. >

in·ter·fer·on \ˌintə(r)'fi(ə)ˌrän\ *n* [*interfer*ence + *-on* chemical compound] : a heat-stable soluble basic antiviral protein of low molecular weight produced usu. by cells exposed to the action of a virus, sometimes to that of another intracellular parasite (as a brucella), or experimentally to that of certain chemicals

in·ter·in·di·vid·u·al \ˌintə(r)ˌində̇ˌvij(ə)wəl, -jəl\ *adj* : involving or taking place between individuals < *interindividual* conflicts >

in·ter·lab·o·ra·to·ry \-'lab(ə)rəˌtōrē, -ˌtȯr-, *Brit usu* lə'bärət(ə)rē, -i\ *adj* : of, relating to, or engaged in by more than one laboratory < *interlaboratory* measurements > < *interlaboratory* study >

in·ter·leave* \-ˌlēv\ *vt* **-leaved; -leav·ing** : to arrange in or as if in alternate layers

[1]in·ter·me·dia \ˌintə(r)ˌmēdēə\ *adj* [*inter-* between + *media*] : of, relating to, or involving the use or effect of several media <an *intermedia* discotheque > <the *intermedia* show, with slides and movies and dancers and electronic music —R.R. Lingeman >

[2]in·ter·me·dia *n* : an art form involving the simultaneous use of several media <the mixing of genres in *intermedia* that makes use of dance, films, painting, electronics —Roger Shattuck >

intermediate* *n* : an automobile larger than a compact but smaller than a full-sized automobile

in·ter·mod·al \ˌintə(r)ˌmōdᵊl\ *adj* [*inter-* between + *mode* + *-al*, adj. suffix] **1** : being or involving transportation by more than one form of carrier during a single journey **2** : used for intermodal transportation

interpreter* *n* : a computer program that translates an instruction into machine language and executes it before going to the next instruction

in·ter·ro·bang *also* **in·tera·bang** \in'terəˌbaŋ\ *n* [*interro*gation (point) + *bang* printers' slang for *exclamation point*] : a punctuation mark ‽ designed for use esp. at the end of an exclamatory rhetorical question

interrogate* *vt* **-gat·ed; -gat·ing** : to give or send out a signal to (as a transponder or computer) for triggering an appropriate response

interrupt *n* : a signal to a computer that stops the execution of an ongoing program while a higher priority program is executed <computer switches to a different set of registers whenever an *interrupt* occurs > ; *also* : a circuit that conveys such a signal <communication between the machine and the telescope is through 16 *interrupts* and an elaborate digital input-output system —R.B. Dunn >

in·ter·sen·so·ry \ˌintə(r)ˈsen(t)s(ə)rē, -ri\ *adj* : involving two or more sensory systems < *intersensory* factors in memory loss >

in·ter·stock \ˈintə(r)ˌstäk\ *n* : a piece inserted between scion and stock in grafting (as to allow union of incompatible varieties or to induce dwarfing)

into* *prep* : strongly involved with or deeply interested in <her two children . . . are both *into* art —*New York*> <is *into* carved ivory rings and pale-green jade bracelets —*McCall's*> <the perfect book for anyone who's deeply *into* plants —C.H. Simonds>

in·tra–ar·te·ri·al \ˌin·trə(ˌ)ärˈtirēəl, ˌin·(ˌ)trä-\ *adj* [*intra-* within (deriv. of L *intra*) + *arterial*] : situated within, introduced into, or involving entry by way of an artery < *intra-arterial* chemotherapy > < *intra-arterial* catheters > < *intra-arterial* injection > — **in·tra–ar·te·ri·al·ly** \-ēəlē\ *adv*

in·tra·car·di·ac \-ˌkärdēˌak, -ˌkȧd-\ *also* **in·tra·car·di·al** \-dēəl\ *adj* : situated within, introduced into, or involving entry into the heart < *intracardiac* puncture > < *intracardiac* surgery > <an *intracardiac* catheter > — **in·tra·car·di·al·ly** \-dēəlē\ *adv*

in·tra·day \ˌin·trəˌdā\ *adj* : occurring in the course of a single day <the market showed wide *intraday* fluctuations >

in·tra·der·mal test \ˌin·trəˌdərməl-, -(ˌ)trä-, -ˌdəm-, -dəim-\ *n* : a test for immunity or hypersensitivity made by injecting a minute amount of diluted antigen into the skin

in·tra·ga·lac·tic \-gəˌlaktik, -ēk\ *adj* : situated or occurring within the confines of a single galaxy <if radio engineers on a planet with a technology more advanced than ours wanted to establish an *intragalactic* communication network —*Scientific American*>

in·tra·op·er·a·tive \-ˌäp(ə)rəd·iv, -ˌäpəˌrād·iv\ *adj* : occurring, carried out, or encountered in the course of surgery < *intraoperative* irradiation > < *intraoperative* infarction > — **in·tra·op·er·a·tive·ly** \-lē, -li\ *adv*

in·tra·per·son·al \-ˌpərs(ᵊ)nəl, -ˌpə̄s-, -ˌpəis-\ *adj* : occurring within the individual mind or self < *intrapersonal* concerns of the aged >

in·tra·pop·u·la·tion \-ˌpäpyəˈlāshən\ *adj* : occurring within or taking place between members of a population < *intrapopulation* variation >

in·tra·uter·ine device \-ˈyüd·ərə̇n-, -ˌrīn-\ *n* : a device (as a spiral of plastic or a ring of stainless steel) inserted and left in the uterus to prevent effective conception — called also *intrauterine contraceptive device, IUD*

in·tra·vas·cu·lar \-ˌvaskyələ(r)\ *adj* : relating to the interior of, occurring within, or situated within a vessel and esp. a blood vessel < *intravascular* thrombosis > < *intravascular* observations > — **in·tra·vas·cu·lar·ly** *adv*

in·tro·gres·sant \ˌin·trəˈgresᵊnt, -trō-\ *n* : an individual resulting from and exhibiting evidence of introgression — **introgressant** *adj*

inverse* *n* : a set element that is related to another element in such a way that the result of applying a given binary operation to them is an identity element of the set

investment letter stock *n* : LETTER STOCK

I/O *abbr* input/output

ion·ic propulsion \īˈänik-, -ēk-\ *n* : ION PROPULSION

ion·o·mer \īˈänəmə(r)\ *n* [*ion* + connective *-o-* + poly*mer*] : any of a class of tough synthetic ethylene-based thermoplastic resins consisting of a long-chain polymer

ion·o·sonde \īˈänəˌsänd\ *n* [ISV *iono*sphere + *sonde*] : a device for determining and recording the heights of ionized layers in the ionosphere by means of shortwaves reflected from them

ion propulsion *n* : propulsion of a body by the forces resulting from the rearward discharge of a stream of ionized particles

ion rocket *n* : a reaction engine deriving thrust from the ejection of a stream of ionized particles : an ion engine

irreducible* *adj* : incapable of being factored into polynomials of lower degree with coefficients in some given field (as the rational numbers) or integral domain (as the integers) < *irreducible* polynomials >

ISBN *abbr* International Standard Book Number

iso•en•zyme \ˌīsō'enˌzīm, *also* ˌīzō-\ *n* [*iso-* equal, uniform (deriv. of Gk *isos* equal) + *enzyme*] : ISOZYME — **iso•en•zy•mat•ic** \-ˌenzəˈmad•ik, -zīˈ-\ *adj* — **iso•en•zy•mic** \-(ˌ)en'zīmik\ *adj*

iso•ge•ne•ic \ˌīsōjə'nēik, *also* ˌīzō-\ *adj* [*iso-* + *-geneic* (as in *syngeneic*)] : SYNGENEIC <an *isogeneic* graft>

isolated camera *n* [fr. its focusing on isolated activities] : a television camera used to videotape an ongoing activity (as a play in football) for immediate replay

iso•la•to \ˌīsə'lād•ō, *also* ˌīzə-\ *n, pl* **-toes** [It, adj., isolated] : one who is physically or spiritually isolated from his fellowman

iso•met•rics \ˌīsə'me•triks, *also* ˌīzə-\ *n pl but sing or pl in constr* : exercise or a system of exercises involving isometric contraction of muscles

isom•e•try \ī'sämə•trē\ *n, pl* **-tries** [*iso-* + *-metry* measuring, deriv. of Gk *metron* measure] : a mapping of a metric space onto another or onto itself so that the distance between any two points in the original space is the same as the distance between their images in the second space <rotation and translation are *isometries* of the plane>

isomor•phic* \ˌīsə'mȯ(r)fik, *also* ˌīzə-\ *adj* : related by an isomorphism <*isomorphic* mathematical rings> — **iso•mor•phi•cal•ly** \-fək(ə)lē\ *adv*

iso•mor•phism* \-'mȯ(r)ˌfizəm\ *n* : a one-to-one correspondence between two mathematical sets; *esp* : a homomorphism that is one-to-one — compare ENDOMORPHISM

iso•spin \'īsəˌspin, *also* 'īzə-\ *n* [*iso*topic *spin*] : a quantum characteristic of a group of closely related elementary particles (as a proton and a neutron) handled mathematically like ordinary spin with the possible orientations in a hypothetical space specifying the number of particles of differing electric charge comprising the group

iso•to•pic spin \ˌīsə'täpik-, -'tōp-, *also* ˌīzə-\ *n* : ISOSPIN

iso•zyme \'īsəˌzīm, *also* 'īzə-\ *n* [*iso-* + *-zyme* enzyme, fr. Gk *zymē* leaven] : one of two or more chemically distinct but functionally similar enzymes — **iso•zy•mic** \ˌīsəˈzīmik, *also* ˌīzə-\ *adj*

ITA *abbr* initial teaching alphabet

Italian sandwich *n* : HOAGIE

it•er•a•tive* \'id•əˌrād•iv, -ərəd•-\ *adj* : relating to or being a computational procedure in which replication of a cycle of operations produces results which approximate the desired result more and more closely <an *iterative* procedure in computer programming>

IUD \ˌīyü'dē, ˌīˌyü-\ *n* : INTRAUTERINE DEVICE

J

jam* *n* : a round in roller derby in which a jammer from each team attempts to circle the course and pass members of the opposing team in order to score points

jam•mer* \'jamə(r)\ *n* : a player on a roller derby team who attempts to circle the course and pass members of the opposing team in order to score points

jams \'jamz\ *n pl* [prob. short for *pajamas*] : knee-length loose-fitting swim trunks usu. having a drawstring waist and large brightly colored patterns

Japanese quail *n* : any of a subspecies (*Coturnix coturnix japonica*) of Old World quail from China and Japan used extensively in laboratory research

jaw•bone \'jȯˌbōn\ *vt* **-boned; -bon•ing** [*jawbone*, n.] : to attempt to influence by jawboning <use the Presidential power to *jawbone* prices and profits into line — Nicholas Von Hoffman>

jawboning *n* : a strong appeal by a chief of state to national business and labor leaders for price and wage restraints <guidelines and presidential *jawboning* were used to deter wage and price leapfrogging —J.R. Walsh>

jazz* *n* : similar but unspecified things : stuff <I *love* sailing . . . all that wind, and the waves, and all that *jazz* —John Updike>

jazz–rock \ˈjaz¦räk\ *n* : a blend of jazz and rock music

Jesus freak *n, often cap F* [*Jesus* Christ] : a member of a fundamentalist youth group whose life-style includes communal living, Bible study, street preaching, and abstinence from illicit drugs

jet·ava·tor \ˈjed·ə,vād·ə(r)\ *n* [irreg. fr. *jet* + el*evator*] : a control surface for deflecting a rocket's exhaust stream so as to change the direction of thrust

jet boat *n* : a boat propelled by an engine which expels a powerful jet of water

jet lag *n* : a group of mental and physical symptoms (as fatigue and irritability) following rapid travel through several time zones that prob. result from disruption of circadian rhythms in the human body

jet set *n* [fr. the fact that jet-setters frequently travel by jet] : an international social group of wealthy individuals who frequent fashionable resorts <she glides easily from Washington society to the international *jet set* —Susanna McBee> — **jet–set·ter** \ˈjet,sed·ə(r)\ *n*

jive \ˈjīv\ *adj, slang* [*jive* deceptive or foolish talk] : being misleading, deceitful, or phony <if you are late getting to heaven, you will give Saint Peter some *jive* excuse —Langston Hughes> <you could tell that these cats were *jive* by the way they went around saying, "Yeah, man, do you shoot stuff?" and all this sort of nonsense —Claude Brown>

job action *n* : a temporary action (as a slowdown) by workers as a protest and means toward forcing compliance with demands <massive sick calls, mass rallies, demonstrations and other *job actions* —*Boston Sunday Advertiser*>

job–hop·ping \ˈjäb,häpiŋ\ *n* : the practice of moving (as for immediate financial gain) from job to job — **job–hop·per** \-pə(r)\ *n*

jock* *n* [fr. the wearing of jockstraps by male athletes] : an athlete and esp. a school or college athlete <old scrapbooks that testify to his glory as a high school *jock* —Chris Chase> <longstanding lack of opportunities for women *jocks* —Grace Lichtenstein>

jogging *n* : running at a slow even pace; *also* : exercise consisting of walking and jogging

John Birch·er \ˈjänˈbərchər, -bə̄chə(r, -bəichə(r\ *n* : BIRCHER

join* *n* : UNION 1

joint* *adj* : being a function of or involving two or more variables and esp. random variables <a *joint* probability density function>

jo·mon \ˈjō,män\ *adj, often cap* [Jap *jōmon* straw rope pattern; fr. the characteristic method of forming designs on pottery of the period] : of, relating to, or typical of a Japanese neolithic cultural period extending from about 3000 B.C. or earlier to about 200 B.C. and characterized esp. by elaborately ornamented hand-formed unglazed pottery (**Jomon ware**)

Jor·dan curve the·o·rem \¦jȯrdᵊn¦kərvˈthēərəm, -ˈthi(ə)rəm\ *n* [*Jordan curve* simple closed curve, after Camille *Jordan* †1922 Fr. mathematician] : a fundamental theorem of topology: every simple closed curve divides the plane into two regions and is the common boundary between them

Jo·seph·son effect \ˈjōzəfsən-, *also* -ōsə̇-\ *n* [B.D. *Josephson*, 20th cent. Eng. physicist] : the passage of electrons at superconductivity temperatures through a thin insulator separating two superconductors so that when the electrons are accelerated through the barrier by application of a voltage the energy they gain is emitted as electromagnetic radiation

jou·al \zhüˈäl, -ˈal, -ˈäl\ *n, often cap* [CanF, fr. Joual *joual* horse, fr. F *cheval*] : a French patois spoken esp. by uneducated French Canadians

joy·stick* \ˈjȯi,stik\ *n* : a manual control for any of various devices (as a computer display) that resembles an airplane's joystick esp. in being capable of motion in two or more directions

ju·do·ist \ˈjü(,)dōə̇st, ˈjüdəwə̇st\ *n* : one who is trained or skilled in judo

jug band *n* : a band that uses usu. crude improvised instruments (as jugs, washboards, and stovepipes)

juice* *n* **1** : alcoholic liquor <travelers . . . who are into *juice* value the advantage of being able to drink at any café or wayside inn . . . a glass of these excellent vintages —Eugene Fodor> **2** *slang* : exorbitant interest exacted of a borrower under the threat of violence

juice·head \ˈjüsˌhed\ *n, slang* : a heavy or habitual drinker of alcoholic beverages

juke \ˈjük\ *vt* **juked; juk·ing** [prob. alter. of E dial. *jouk* to cheat, deceive] : to fake out of position (as in football) <I beat my man, every time. Sometimes I *juke* him right out of his shoes and he's lying on the ground in his socks —Gail Cogdill>

jump* *vi* : to go from one sequence of instructions in a computer program to another <*jump* to a subroutine>

jump* *n* : a transfer from one sequence of instructions in a computer program to a different sequence <a conditional *jump*>

jump cut *n* : a discontinuity or acceleration in the action of a filmed scene brought about by removal of medial portions of the shot — **jump–cut** \ˈjəmpˌkət\ *vb*

jumper* *n* : a shot in basketball made while jumping <hit a *jumper* from the top of the key>

jumping–jack \ˈjəmpiŋˌjak\ *n* : a conditioning exercise performed while standing by jumping from a position with the feet together and arms at the sides to a position with legs spread and hands touching overhead and then to the original position — called also *side-straddle hop*

jump suit* *n* : a one-piece garment consisting of a blouse or shirt with attached trousers or shorts

jun \ˈjün\ *n, pl* **jun** [Korean] **1** : a monetary unit of North Korea equal to $^{1}/_{100}$ won **2** : a coin representing one jun

junk art *n* : three-dimensional art made from discarded material (as of metal, mortar, glass, or wood) — **junk artist** *n*

ju·ri·me·tri·cian \ˌju̇rəməˈtrishən\ *n* : a specialist in jurimetrics

ju·ri·met·rics \ˌju̇rəˈme·triks\ *n pl but usu sing in constr* [L *juri-, jus* law + E *-metrics* (as in *econometrics*)] : the application of scientific methods to legal problems

juvenile hor·mone \-ˈhō(ə)rˌmōn, -ˈhȯ(ə)rˌ-, -ˈhōəˌ-, -ˈhȯəˌ-\ *n* : an insect hormone used experimentally to control pest insects by disrupting their life cycles that is secreted by the corpora allata, inhibits maturation to the imago, and controls maturation of eggs and yolk deposition in the imago

ju·ve·nil·ize \ˈjüvənᵊlˌīz, -vnəl-\ *vt* **-ized; -iz·ing** [*juvenile* + *-ize* make] : to restrain from normal development and maturation : prolong the immaturity of <chemicals that *juvenilize* insect larvae> — **ju·ve·nil·iza·tion** \ˌjüvənᵊləˈzāshən, -vnəl-, -lˌīˈz-\ *n*

K

k* *n, often cap* [*kilo-* thousand, deriv. of Gk *chilioi*] **1** : thousand <a salary of $14*K*> **2** [fr. the fact that 1024 (2^{10}) is the power of 2 closest to 1000] : a unit of computer storage capacity equal to 1024 bytes <a computer memory of 64*K*>

k* *abbr* kindergarten

Kaf·ka·esque \ˌkäfkəˈesk, ˌkaf-\ *adj* [Franz *Kafka* †1924 Austrian writer] : of, relating to, or suggestive of Franz Kafka or his writings <pathetically reveal her gradual disintegration . . . to a pale wreck trapped in a *Kafkaesque* nightmare —John Ardagh>

ka·lim·ba \kəˈlimbə, kä-\ *n* [of African origin; akin to Bemba *akalimba* zanza, Kimbundu *marimba* xylophone] : an African thumb piano that is derived from the zanza or mbira

kal·li·din \ˈkalədən\ *n* [G, fr. *kalli*krein + *-d-* (prob. fr. *dekapeptid* peptide having 10 amino acids, fr. *deka-* ten + *peptid* peptide) + *-in* chemical compound] : any of several kinins formed from blood plasma globulin by the action of kallikrein

kal·li·kre·in \ˌkaləˈkrēən, kəˈlik-\ *n* [G, fr. *kalli-* beautiful, white (deriv. of Gk *kallos* beauty) + pan*kre*as pancreas (fr. Gk) + *-in* chemical compound; prob. fr. its therapeutic use in pancreatic disorders] : an enzyme that liberates kinins from blood plasma

ka·na·my·cin \ˌkanəˈmīsᵊn, ˌkän-\ *n* [NL *kanamyceticus* (specific epithet of *Streptomyces kanamyceticus*) + E *-in* chemical compound] : a broad-spectrum antibiotic from a Japanese soil actinomycete (*Streptomyces kanamyceticus*)

ka·on \ˈkāˌän\ *n* [ISV *ka* (fr. *K-meson*) + *-on* elementary particle] : an unstable meson produced in high-energy particle collisions that has charged forms 966.3 times more massive than the electron and a neutral form 974.6 times more massive than the electron

Ka·ra·tsu ware \kəˈrät(ˌ)sü-\ *n* [fr. *Karatsu,* city in Japan] : a Japanese ceramic ware traditionally made from the 7th century at Karatsu on Kyushu island that is probably the earliest glazed Japanese ceramic ware, includes both earthenware and stoneware, and comprises chiefly vessels for chanoyu

kar·ma* \ˈkärmə, ˈkȧmə, *also* ˈkərmə\ *n* : a characteristic emanation, aura, spirit, or atmosphere that can be sensed : vibrations < enthusiastic ease was the predominating *karma* at Rainbow Party headquarters —Stu Werbin >

kart \ˈkärt\ *n* [prob. fr. *GoKart,* a trademark] : a miniature motorcar used esp. for racing

kart·ing \ˈkärd·iŋ\ *n* : the sport of racing miniature motorcars

kbar *abbr* kilobar

keeper* *n* : an offensive football play in which the quarterback runs with the ball

kel·vin \ˈkelvən\ *n* : a unit of temperature equal to $^1/_{273.16}$ of the Kelvin scale temperature of the triple point of water

Ken·ya·pi·the·cus \ˌkenyəpəˈthēkəs, ˌkēnyə-, -ˈpithək-\ *n* [NL, genus name, fr. *Kenya,* country in Africa + *-pithecus* ape, deriv. of Gk *pithēkos*] : an ancient prehuman African primate that is held to belong to the human ancestral line and that is placed in a distinct genus (*Kenyapithecus*) or included in *Ramapithecus*

kernel* *n* **1** : a subset of the elements of one set (as a group) that a function (as a homomorphism) maps onto an identity element of another set **2** : KERNEL SENTENCE

kernel sentence *n* : a sentence (as "John is big" or "John is a man") exemplifying in a language one of a very small group of grammatically simple sentence types or patterns (as noun phrase + be + adjective phrase or noun phrase + be + noun phrase) which cannot be broken down into simpler sentence types and which in transformational grammar are the basic stock or source from or according to which all sentences in that language are formed or derived and in terms of which all sentences of the language can ultimately be described — called also *kernel*

ke·to·glu·ta·rate \ˌkēd·ō(ˌ)glüˈtäˌrāt\ *n* [*ketoglutar*ic (acid) + *-ate* salt or ester of an acid] : a salt or ester of ketoglutaric acid

key* *vi* **keyed; key·ing** : to observe the position or movement of an opposing player in football in order to anticipate the play — usu. used with *on* < the middle linebacker was *keying* on the halfback >

key \ˈkē\ *n, pl* **keys** [by shortening and alter. fr. *kilo* kilogram] *slang* : a kilogram esp. of marijuana or heroin

key club *n* [fr. the fact that each member is provided with a key to the premises] : an informal private club serving liquor and providing entertainment

key·set \ˈkēˌset\ *n* : a set of systematically arranged keys for operating a machine (as a typewriter) : a keyboard

keystroke \ˈkēˌstrōk\ *n* : the act or an instance of depressing a key on a keyboard — **keystroke** *vb*

kick out* *vi* : to turn a surfboard around and drive it over the top of a wave by pushing down on the rear of the board with the foot

kicky* \ˈkikē\ *adj* **kick·i·er; -est** : providing a kick or thrill < *kicky* violent scenes, carefully estranging you from the victims so that you can enjoy the rapes and beatings —Pauline Kael > — often used as a generalized term of approval < *kicky* clothes >

ki·lo·bar \ˈkēlə͵bär, ˈkilə-, -͵bȧ(r\ *n* [ISV *kilo-* thousand (deriv. of Gk *chilioi*) + *bar*] : a unit of pressure equal to 1000 bars — abbr. *kbar*
ki·lo·baud \-͵bȯd, -͵bōd\ *n* : 1000 baud
ki·lo·bit \-͵bit\ *n* : 1000 bits
kilo·mega·cy·cle \¦kēlə¦megə͵sīkəl, ¦kilə-\ *n* : 1000 megacycles : one billion cycles
ki·lo·oer·sted \¦kēlō¦ərstəd, ¦kilō-, -¦ȯr-\ *n* : 1000 oersteds
ki·lo·rad \ˈkēlō͵rad, ˈkilō-\ *n* : 1000 rads
ki·net·ic art \kəˈned·ik-, kīˈ-\ *n* : art in which movement (as of a motor-driven part or a changing electronic image) is a basic element — **kinetic artist** *n*
ki·net·i·cism \kə̇ˈned·ə͵sizəm, kīˈ-\ *n* : KINETIC ART
ki·net·i·cist \-əsə̇st\ *n* **1** : a specialist in kinetics **2** : KINETIC ARTIST
ki·ne·tin \ˈkīnətə̇n\ *n* [*kinet-* motion (fr. Gk *kinētos* moving) + *-in* chemical compound] : a plant growth substance $C_{10}H_9N_5O$ that increases mitosis and callus formation
ki·neto·some \kə̇ˈned·ə͵sōm, kīˈ-\ *n* [*kineto-* motion (fr. Gk *kinētos* moving) + *-some* body, deriv. of Gk *sōma*] : a minute distinctively staining granule typically found at the base of every flagellum or cilium
king·side \ˈkiŋ͵sīd\ *n* : the side of a chessboard containing the file on which both kings sit at the beginning of the game
ki·nin \ˈkīnə̇n\ *n* [Gk *kinein* to move, stimulate + E *-in* chemical compound] **1** : any of various polypeptide hormones that are formed locally in the tissues and have their chief effect on smooth muscle **2** : any of various plant growth factors that are related to adenine and play a part in fundamental growth processes
ki·nin·o·gen \kīˈninəjə̇n\ *n* [*kinin* + connective *-o-* + *-gen* producer, deriv. of Gk *-genēs* born] : an inactive precursor of a kinin — **ki·nin·o·gen·ic** \(¦)kī¦ninə¦jenik\ *adj*
kinky* \ˈkiŋkē, -ki\ *adj* **kink·i·er; -est** **1** : relating to, having, or appealing to bizarre or unconventional tastes esp. in sex <an egregious attempt to exploit both sentimental and *kinky* appetites —Mark Goodman> <every *kinky* weirdo thing you want to do —Philip Roth> <delicious tangles may ensue, a bit of *kinky* sex, a jolly murder —Mary E. Barrett>; *also* : being sexually deviant <a *kinky* baron in leg irons, begging for another spanking —Diana Davenport> **2** : outlandish, strange, odd, far-out <likes to dress in . . . *kinky* clothes, and he does appear to be flamboyant —Rosemary Brown> <one of the *kinkiest* divisions in the army of culinary skeptics, the health-food addicts —*Time*> — **kink·i·ness** \-nə̇s\ *n*
Ki·run·di \kə̇ˈründē, -di\ *n* : the Bantu language of the central African republic of Burundi
kissing disease *n* [fr. the belief that it is frequently transmitted by kissing] : the disease infectious mononucleosis
kiss of life **1** *Brit* : artificial respiration by the mouth-to-mouth method **2** *Brit* : something that restores vitality <manages some trick of timing that gives clichés the *kiss of life* —Irving Wardle>
Kis·wa·hi·li \(͵)ki͵swäˈhēlē, -li\ *n* : the Swahili language
kiwi fruit *also* **kiwi berry** *n* [fr. the fact that it is usu. imported to America from New Zealand] : the fruit of the Chinese gooseberry
Kline·fel·ter's syndrome \¦klīn͵feltə(r)¦sin͵drōm, *also* -¦sindrəm\ *n* [Harry F. *Klinefelter* *b*1912 Am. physician] : an abnormal condition characterized by two X and one Y chromosomes and an infertile male phenotype with small testicles
kludge *also* **kluge** \ˈklüj\ *n* [origin unknown] : a system and esp. a computer system made up of components that are poorly matched or were orig. intended for some other use
klutz \ˈkləts\ *n* [Yiddish *klotz, klutz,* fr. G *klotz,* lit., wooden block, fr. MHG *kloz* lumpy mass] : a clumsy and awkward person <is such a *klutz* you have to laugh as he slinks across a sumptuous Texas lawn accidentally turning on the sprinklers —Liz Smith> — **klutzy** \ˈklətsē, -si\ *adj*
K–me·son \ˈkā¦mez͵än, -¦mes͵än, -¦mā-, -¦mē-\ *n* : KAON
knee–jerk \¦nē͵jərk, -͵jək, -͵jəik\ *adj* : readily predictable : automatic <the latest response of public officials to mounting crime in the streets amounts to nothing more than another *knee-jerk* reaction —J.F. Ahern>; *also* : reacting in a readily

predictable way < *knee-jerk* liberals > <seeming to be your own man, rather than a *knee-jerk* reactor to events —Benjamin DeMott >

knockoff \ˈnäkˌȯf\ *n* : a copy (as of a dress design) that sells for less than the original

ko·bo \ˈkȯˌbȯ\ *n, pl* **kobo** [alter. of *copper*] **1** : a monetary unit of Nigeria equal to $^1/_{100}$ naira **2** : a coin representing one kobo

kook \ˈkük\ *n* [by shortening and alter. fr. *cuckoo*] : one whose ideas or actions are eccentric, fantastic, or insane <must listen to the deviants of our society before pronouncing them all *kooks* —H.G. Cox >

kooky *also* **kook·ie** \ˈkükē, -ki\ *adj* **kook·i·er; -est** : having the characteristics or being characteristic of a kook : crazy, offbeat < *kooky,* lovable characters who look like everyone's zany brother —Rex Reed > < *kooky* . . . adventure of a couple of romantic iconoclasts —William Fadiman > — **kook·i·ly** \ˈkükəlē, -li\ *adv* — **kook·i·ness** \ˈkükēnəs, -kin-\ *n*

ko·ra \ˈkōr(ˌ)ä, ˈkȯr-, -rə\ *n* [native name in Senegal] : a 21-string musical instrument of African origin that resembles a lute

K particle *n* : KAON

krad \ˈkāˌrad\ *n, pl* **krad** *also* **krads** [*kilo rad*] : KILORAD

Krem·lin·ol·o·gy \ˌkremləˈnäləjē\ *n* [*Kremlin* + connective *-o-* + *-logy* theory, science, deriv. of Gk *logos* word] : the study of the policies and practices of the Soviet Russian government <prognostications here are subject to all the usual pitfalls of *Kremlinology* —Robert Gillette > — **Krem·lin·olog·i·cal** \ˌkremlənᵊlˈäjəkəl\ *adj* — **Krem·lin·ol·o·gist** \ˌkremləˈnäləjəst\ *n*

Kro·neck·er delta \ˈkrōˌnekə(r)-\ *n* [Leopold *Kronecker* †1891 Ger. mathematician] : a function of two variables that is 1 when the variables have the same value and is 0 when they have different values

ku·do \ˈk(y)üd(ˌ)ō\ *n, pl* **kudos** [back-formation fr. *kudos* (taken as a pl.)] **1** : an award or honor <a score of honorary degrees and . . . other *kudos* —*Time*> **2** : a compliment or tribute <to all three should go some kind of special *kudo* for refusing to succumb —Al Hine >

kun·da·li·ni \ˌkündᵊlˈēnē, -däˈlē-\ *n, often cap* [Skt *kuṇḍalinī,* fr. fem. of *kuṇḍalin* circular, coiled, fr. *kuṇḍala* ring] : the yogic life-force that is held to lie coiled at the base of the spine until it is aroused and sent to the head to trigger enlightenment

kung fu \ˌkəŋˈfü, ˌküŋ-\ *n* [Chin dial.; akin to Chin (Pek) *ch'üan² fa³*, lit., boxing principles] : a Chinese art of self-defense resembling karate

ku·ru \ˈkü(ˌ)rü\ *n* [native name in New Guinea, lit., trembling] : a fatal disease of the nervous system that is caused by a slow virus, resembles scrapie in sheep, and occurs among tribesmen of eastern New Guinea

Ku·ta·ni \küˈtänē\ *or* **Kutani ware** *n* [fr. *Kutani,* village in Japan] : a Japanese porcelain produced in and about the village of Kutani on Honshu island since the mid-17th century and esteemed for originality of design and coloring

kvetch \kəˈvech, ˈkve-, ˈkfe-\ *vi* [Yiddish *kvetshn,* lit., to squeeze] : to complain habitually : GRIPE < *kvetches* constantly about being 33 years old —H.F. Waters >

kwa·cha \ˈkwächə\ *n, pl* **kwacha** [native name in Zambia, lit., dawn] **1 a** : the basic monetary unit of Zambia **b** : the basic monetary unit of Malawi **2** : a note representing one kwacha

KWIC \ˈkwik\ *n* [*key word in context*] : a computer-generated index alphabetized on a keyword that appears within a portion of its context

KWOC \ˈkwäk\ *n* [*key word out of context*] : a computer-generated index in which the keyword is followed by its context

L

La·combe \lə'kōm\ *n* [*Lacombe* Experiment Station, Lacombe, Alberta, Canada, where the breed was developed] **1** : a breed of white bacon-type swine developed in Canada from Landrace, Chester White, and Berkshire stock **2** *often not cap*: an animal of the Lacombe breed

laggard* *n*: a security whose price has lagged for no obvious reason behind the average of its group or of the market

lag·ger* \'lagə(r)\ *n* : an economic indicator (as spending on new plants and equipment) that more often than not maintains an existent trend for some time after the state of the economy has turned onto an opposite trend — called also *lagging index*

laid–back \ˌlādˌbak\ *adj*: being relaxed in style or character : easygoing, unhurried <an insinuating kind of country rock, so *laid-back* that it almost falls asleep —John Rockwell>

lamb·da \'lamdə\ *or* **lambda particle** *n*: an uncharged elementary particle that has a mass 2183 times that of an electron, is an unstable baryon, and decays typically into a nucleon and a pion with an average lifetime of 2.6×10^{-10} second

lame \'lām\ *n, slang*: a person who is not in the know : a square <one either knows what's happening on the street, or he is a *lame* —John Horton>

land·er* \'landə(r)\ *n*: one that lands; *esp*: a space vehicle that is designed to land on a celestial body (as the moon or a planet)

landmark* *n*: a structure (as a building) of unusual historical and usu. aesthetic interest; *esp* : one that is officially designated and set aside for preservation

language* *n* : MACHINE LANGUAGE

Lan·tian man \ˌlanˌtyan-\ *or* **Lan–t'ien man** \-ˌtyen-\ *n* [fr. *Lan-t'ien,* district in Shensi province, China] : an extinct man known from parts of a skull excavated in China and held to be an extremely primitive example of modern man

lap belt *n* : a seat belt that fastens across the lap

La·place trans·form \lə'pläsˌtran(t)sˌfȯrm, -'plas-\ *n* [Pierre Simon de *Laplace* †1827 Fr. astronomer and mathematician] : a transformation of a function $f(x)$ into the function $g(t) = \int_0^\infty e^{-xt} f(x)\,dx$ that is useful esp. in reducing the solution of an ordinary linear differential equation with constant coefficients to the solution of a polynomial equation

lase \'lāz\ *vi* **lased; las·ing** [back-formation fr. *laser*] : to emit coherent light

L–as·par·a·gi·nase \ˌela'sparəjəˌnās, -āz\ *n* [*L-* levorotatory + *asparagine* + *-ase* enzyme] : an enzyme that breaks down the physiologically commoner form of asparagine, is obtained esp. from bacteria, and is used esp. to treat leukemia

last hurrah *n* [*The Last Hurrah* (1956) by Edwin O'Connor †1968 Am. novelist] : a last effort or attempt <his unsuccessful Senate run was his *last hurrah*—R.W. Daly>

latent root *n* : a characteristic root of a matrix

lath·y·rit·ic \ˌlathə'rid·ik\ *adj*: of, relating to, affected with, or characteristic of lathyrism < *lathyritic* rats> < *lathyritic* cartilage> < *lathyritic* collagen>

la·tic·i·fer \lā'tisəfə(r)\ *n* [ISV *latici-* (fr. NL *latic-, latex*) + *-fer* bearing, one that bears, deriv. of L *ferre* to carry] : a plant cell or vessel that contains latex

launder* *vt* : to cause (illegally obtained money) to appear legitimate by channelization through a third party so as to conceal the true source <banks were used to *launder* money illegally skimmed from casinos —*Private Eye*> <involved in bugging, surveillance, collecting and *laundering* campaign funds —B.J. Wattenberg>

laundry list *n* [fr. the listing of articles of clothing sent to a laundry] : a usu. long list of items <the *laundry list* of new consumer-protection bills —N.C. Miller>

law of par·si·mo·ny \-'pärsəˌmōnē, -'pȧs-\ : a scientific and philosophic rule that entities should not be multiplied unnecessarily which is interpreted as requiring that the simplest of competing theories be preferred to the more complex and that explanations of unknown phenomena be sought first in terms of known quantities

law·ren·cium \lȯˈren(t)sēəm, ləˈ-, -nch(ē)əm\ *n* [NL, fr. Ernest O. *Lawrence* †1958 Am. physicist + NL *-ium* chemical element] : a short-lived radioactive element of atomic number 103 that is produced artificially from californium — symbol *Lr*

lay·about \ˈlāə,bau̇t\ *n* [fr. the phrase *lay about,* nonstandard alter. of *lie about*] *chiefly Brit* : one who spends his time in idleness : idler, loafer <equating all those in need of relief with the hard core of professional beggars, spongers and *layabouts — Times Lit. Supp.*>

lay–by* \ˈlāˌbī\ *n* : the final operation (as a last cultivating) in the growing of a field crop

lazy eye *n* [fr. the fact that a person suffering from this condition uses only one eye] : dimness of sight without apparent change in the eye structures that is associated esp. with toxic effects or dietary deficiencies

LDH *abbr* **1** lactate dehydrogenase **2** lactic dehydrogenase

L–do·pa \(ˈ)elˈdōpə\ *n* [*l-* levorotatory + *dopa*] : the levorotatory form of dopa found esp. in broad beans or prepared synthetically and used in treating Parkinson's disease

leader* *n* : an economic indicator (as the level of corporate profits or of stock prices) that more often than not shows a change in direction before a corresponding change in the state of the economy — called also *leading indicator*

LED *n* [*l*ight-*e*mitting *d*iode] : a semiconductor diode that emits light when subjected to an applied voltage and that is usu. used in an electronic display (as for a pocket calculator or a digital watch)

leisure suit *n* : a suit consisting of a shirt jacket and matching trousers for informal wear

lek·var \ˈlek,vär, -,vå(r\ *n* [Hung] : a prune butter used as a pastry filling

LEM \ˈlem\ *n* : LUNAR EXCURSION MODULE

le·one \lēˈōn\ *n* [fr. Sierra *Leone,* Africa] **1** : the basic monetary unit of Sierra Leone **2** : a note representing one leone

Leo·nid \ˈlēənəd\ *n, pl* **Leonids** *or* **Le·on·i·des** \lēˈänə,dēz\ [L *Leon-, Leo,* a constellation, lit., lion + E *-id* meteor; fr. their appearing to radiate from a point in the constellation Leo] : one of the shooting stars constituting the meteor shower that recurs near the 14th of November

lep·ton·ic \(ˈ)lepˌtänik\ *adj* : of, relating to, or producing a lepton <*leptonic* decay of a hyperon>

lep·ton number \ˈlep,tän-\ *n* : a number equal to the number of leptons minus that of antileptons in a system of elementary particles

lep·to·spire \ˈleptə,spī(ə)r, -īə\ *n* : a spirochete of the genus *Leptospira*

lesion *vt* : to produce lesions in

letter bomb *n* : an explosive device concealed in an envelope and mailed to the intended victim

let·ter·form \ˈled·ər,fȯrm, -ə,fȯ(ə)m\ *n* : the shape of a letter of an alphabet esp. from the standpoint of design or development <squared *letterforms* came into use for Greek inscriptions long before Roman engravers adopted them —Richard Olson>

let·ter·set \-,set\ *n* [*letter*press + off*set*] : offset printing in which an image on a letterpress plate is transferred to a rubber roller and offset onto the paper

letter stock *n* [fr. the letter signed by the purchaser stating that the stock is acquired for investment and not for public sale] : restricted and unregistered stock that may not be sold to the general public without undergoing registration

leu·ke·mic \lüˈkēmik, -mēk\ *n* : a person suffering from leukemia

leu·ko·dys·tro·phy \,lükōˈdistrəfē\ *n* [*leuko-* white (deriv. of Gk *leukos*) + *dystrophy*] : any of several genetically determined diseases characterized by progressive degeneration of the white matter of the brain

lev·al·lor·phan \,levəˈlȯr,fan, -fən\ *n* [*lev-* levorotatory + *all*yl + m*orph*ine + *-an* unsaturated carbon compound] : a drug related to morphine that is used to counteract morphine poisoning

level of significance : the probability of rejecting the null hypothesis in a statistical test when it is true — called also *significance level*

le·ver·age* \ˈlev(ə)rij, ˈlēv-, -rēj\ *n* : the use of credit to enhance one's speculative capacity <buying stocks on margin is a simple example of *leverage*>

leverage *vt* **-aged; -ag·ing** : to provide (as a corporation) or supplement (as money) with leverage <mismanaged, unwisely *leveraged*, and highly illiquid corporations . . . reap the whirlwind of bankruptcy —N.A. Bailey> <margin may *leverage* the speculator too much —D.W. Kelly>

lex·is \ˈleksəs\ *n, pl* **lex·es** \-kˌsēz\ [Gk, speech, word] : the words of a language : vocabulary

lib \ˈlib\ *n* [by shortening] : LIBERATION

lib·ber \ˈlibə(r)\ *n* : one who advocates liberation <a women's *libber*>

lib·er·a·tion* \ˌlibəˈrāshən\ *n* : a movement seeking equal rights and status for a group <women's *liberation*> <gay *liberation*>

licensed practical nurse *n* : a trained person authorized by license (as from a state) to provide routine care for the sick —abbr. *LPN*

licensed vocational nurse *n* : a licensed practical nurse authorized by license to practice in the states of California or Texas — abbr. *LVN*

lid* *n* : an ounce of marijuana

li·dar \ˈlīˌdär\ *n* [*li*ght + ra*dar*] : a device or system for locating an object that is similar in operation to radar but emits pulsed laser light instead of microwaves

lif·er* \ˈlīfə(r)\ *n* : a career member of the armed forces <professional soldiers, *lifers* who believe in the military and its mission —S.V. Roberts>

life science *n* : a branch of science (as biology, medicine, anthropology, or sociology) that deals with living organisms and life processes — usu. used in pl. — **life scientist** *n*

life–sup·port system \ˈlīfsəˌpō(ə)rt-, -ˌpȯ(ə)rt-\ *n* : a system that provides all or some of the items (as oxygen, food, water, control of temperature and pressure, disposition of carbon dioxide and body wastes) necessary for maintaining the life and health of a person (as in a spacecraft or on the surface of the moon)

lifting body *n* : a maneuverable rocket-propelled wingless vehicle that is capable of travel in aerospace or in the earth's atmosphere where its lift is derived from its shape and that can be landed on the ground

li·gase \ˈlīˌgās, -ˌgāz\ *n* [ISV *lig-* (fr. L. *ligare* to bind, tie) + *-ase* enzyme] : an enzyme that catalyzes the linking together of two molecules usu. with concurrent splitting off of a pyrophosphate group from ATP

light–adapt·ed \ˈlīd·əˌdaptəd, ˈlīt-\ *adj* : adjusted for vision in bright light : having undergone light adaptation

light chain *n* : either of the two smaller of the four polypeptide chains that comprise antibodies — compare HEAVY CHAIN

light pen *n* : a hand-held photosensitive device that is connected to a computer and used with the cathode-ray tube display for direct communication with the computer by adding, deleting, manipulating, or altering information

light show *n* : a kaleidoscopic display of colored lights, slides, and films suggestive of the hallucinogenic effects of psychedelic drugs

light water *n* : ordinary water as distinguished from heavy water

lig·no·caine \ˈlignəˌkān\ *n* [*ligno-* lignin (deriv. of L *lignum* wood) + *-caine* synthetic alkaloid anesthetic, deriv. of G *kokain* cocaine] : a crystalline compound that is used in the form of its hydrochloride as a local anesthetic

li·ku·ta \ləˈkütə, (ˈ)lēˌk-\ *n, pl* **ma·ku·ta** \(ˈ)mäˌkütə\ [of Niger-Congo origin; prob. akin to obs. Nupe *kuta* stone] **1** : a monetary unit of Zaire equal to $^1/_{100}$ zaire **2** : a coin representing one likuta

lim·bic* \ˈlimbik\ *adj* : of, relating to, or being the limbic system of the brain

limbic system *n* : a group of subcortical structures (as the hypothalamus, the hippocampus, and the amygdala) of the brain that are concerned esp. with emotion and motivation

lim·bo \ˈlim(ˌ)bō\ *n, pl* **limbos** [native name in West Indies] : a West Indian acrobatic dance orig. for men that involves bending over backward and passing under a horizontal pole which is lowered slightly for each successive pass

limit point *n* : a point that is related to a set of points in such a way that every neighborhood of the point no matter how small contains another point belonging to the set — called also *point of accumulation*

limo \ˈlim(ˌ)ō\ *n, pl* **limos** [short for *limousine*] **:** a limousine <they rode *limos* to the airport with groupies in the glove compartment and a tax man riding shotgun —Richard Boeth>

limp·en \ˈlimpən\ *vi* **:** to become limp <few heard the blow, but Grown Boy *limpened* instantly and fell —Carson McCullers>

lin·ac \ˈlinˌak\ *n* [*lin*ear *ac*celerator] **:** a device in which charged particles are accelerated in a straight line by successive impulses from a series of electrical fields **:** linear accelerator

lin·co·my·cin \ˌliŋkəˈmīsᵊn\ *n* [*linco-* (fr. *Streptomyces lincolnensis,* an actinomycete) + *-mycin* substance obtained from a fungus, fr. *streptomycin*] **:** an antibiotic obtained from an actinomycete (*Streptomyces umbrinus* var. *cyaneoniger*) and found effective esp. against cocci

linear* *adj* **1 :** composed of simply drawn lines with little attempt at pictorial representation <*linear* script> **2 :** relating to, concerned with, or psychologically influenced by the sequential structure of the printed line <those rare remaining *linear,* word-oriented people who feel restive at being cut off from the great, younger majority of visual, media-message unthinkers —Roy Bongartz>

Linear A *n* **:** a linear form of writing used in Crete from the 18th to the 15th centuries B.C.

linear algebra *n* **1 :** a branch of mathematics that is concerned with mathematical structures closed under the operation of addition and scalar multiplication and with their applications and that includes the theory of systems of linear equations, matrices, determinants, vector spaces, and linear transformations **2 :** a mathematical ring which is also a vector space with scalars from an associated field and whose multiplicative operation is such that $(aA)(bB) = (ab)(AB)$ where a and b are scalars and A and B are vectors — called also *algebra*

linear alkylate sulfonate \-ˌalkəˌlātˌsəlfəˌnāt\ *n* **:** a biodegradable salt of sulfonic acid used in detergents as a surface-active agent

Linear B *n* **:** a linear form of writing employing syllabic characters used at Knossos on Crete and on the Greek mainland from the 15th to the 12th centuries B.C. for documents in the Mycenaean language

linear combination *n* **:** a mathematical entity (as 4x + 5y + 6z) which is composed of sums and differences of elements (as variables, matrices, or equations) whose coefficients are not all zero

linear dependence *n* **:** the property of one set (as of matrices or vectors) with coefficients taken from a given set of having at least one linear combination equal to zero when at least one of the coefficients is not equal to zero — **lin·ear·ly dependent** \ˈlinēə(r)lē-, ˈlinyə(r)lē-\ *adj*

linear independence *n* **:** the property of a set (as of matrices or vectors) of having no linear combination of the elements equal to zero when coefficients are taken from a given set unless the coefficient of each element is zero — **lin·ear·ly independent** \ˈlinēə(r)lē-, ˈlinyə(r)lē-\ *adj*

linear motor *n* **:** a motor that produces thrust in a straight line by direct induction rather than with the use of gears

linear transformation *n* **1 :** a transformation in which the new variables are linear functions of the old variables **2 :** a function that maps the vectors of one vector space onto the vectors of the same or another vector space with the same field of scalars in such a way that the image of the sum of two vectors equals the sum of their images and the image of a scalar product equals the product of the scalar and the image of the vector

line judge *n* **:** a football linesman whose duties include keeping track of the official time for the game

line printer *n* **:** a high-speed printing device (as for a computer) that prints each line as a unit rather than character by character — **line printing** *n*

line score *n* **:** a printed score of a baseball game giving the runs, hits, and errors made by each team

lin·gui·ne \liŋˈgwēnē, -(ˌ)nā\ *also* **lin·gui·ni** \-nē, -ni\ *n* [It, pl. of *linguina,* dim. of *lingua* tongue, fr. L] **:** pasta in flat narrow strips

link* *n* : an identifier attached to an element (as an index term) in a system in order to indicate or permit connection with other similarly identified elements

linked* *adj* : having or provided with links

lin·u·ron \ˈlinyə,rän\ *n* [prob. fr. *lin*dane, an insecticide + *ur*ea + *-on* chemical compound] : a selective herbicide $C_9H_{10}O_2Cl_2N_2$ used esp. to control weeds in crops of soybeans or carrots

lip* *n* : a limb of a labiate corolla

lip cell *n* : one of the narrow thin-walled cells of the sporangia in some ferns that mark the point at which dehiscence begins

li·pid·ic \ləˈpidik\ *adj* : of or relating to lipids < *lipidic* antigens > < *lipidic* inclusions >

li·po·poly·sac·cha·ride \ˌlīpō,päliˈsakə,rīd, ˌlipō-\ *n* [ISV *lipo-* fat, lipid (deriv. of Gk *lipos* fat) + *polysaccharide*] : a large molecule consisting of lipids and sugars joined by chemical bonds

li·po·tro·pin \ˌlipəˈtrōpən, ˌlī-\ *n* [*lipotrop*ic promoting the utilization of fat + *-in* chemical compound] : a hormone of the anterior pituitary held to function in the mobilization of fatty reserves

Lip·pes loop \ˌlipəs-, *also* ˈlips-\ *n* [Jack *Lippes*, 20th cent. Am. physician] : an S-shaped plastic intrauterine contraceptive device

lit–crit \ˌlitˈkrit\ *n* [*lit*erary *crit*icism] : literary criticism < responsiveness, in a first-rate patch of *lit-crit*, to a great writer —Benjamin DeMott > < knows every *lit-crit* cliché in the book —R.A. Sokolov >

litmus test *n* : a test in which a single indicator (as an attitude, event, or fact) is decisive < in Soviet intellectual circles the name Osip Mandelstam . . . could be used as a *litmus test* to determine people's loyalties —*Times Lit. Supp.* >

lit·ter·bag \ˈlid·ə(r),bag\ *n* : a bag used (as in an automobile) for disposal of refuse

living will *n* : a written declaration in which a person requests that if he becomes disabled beyond reasonable expectation of recovery he be allowed to die rather than be kept alive by artificial means

LM* *abbr* lunar module

load* *n* : the decrease in capacity for survival of the average individual in a population due to the presence of deleterious genes in the gene pool < the mutational *load* is the genetic *load* caused by mutation >

locked–in* \ˌläkˌdin\ *adj* : unable or unwilling to shift invested funds because of the tax effect of realizing capital gains

logic* *n* : the fundamental principles and applications of truth tables and of the interconnection of circuit elements and gates necessary for computation in a computer; *also* : the circuits themselves

log·nor·mal \(ˈ)lȯgˌnȯrməl, (ˈ)läg-\ *adj* : of, relating to, or being a logarithmic function (as the logarithm of a random variable) that has a normal distribution — **log·nor·mal·i·ty** \ˌlȯgnȯrˈmaləd·ē, ˌläg-\ *n* — **log·nor·mal·ly** \(ˈ)lȯgˌnȯrməlē, (ˈ)läg-\ *adv*

long–term* \ˈlȯŋˌtərm, -ˌtəm, -ˌtəim\ *adj* : generated by assets held for longer than six months < *long-term* capital gains >

look–in* \ˈlu̇k,in\ *n* : a quick pass in football to a receiver running diagonally toward the center of the field

look·up \ˈlu̇k,əp\ *n* : the process or an instance of looking something up; *esp* : the process of matching by computer the words of a text with material stored in memory < an automatic hyphenation system using logic and dictionary *lookup* >

loop* *n* **1** : a series of instructions (as for a computer) that is repeated until a terminating condition is reached **2** : INTRAUTERINE DEVICE; *esp* : LIPPES LOOP

Lo·rentz force \ˈlōr,en(t)s-, ˌlȯr-\ *n* [Hendrik A. *Lorentz* †1928 Du. physicist] : the force exerted on a moving charged particle in a magnetic field

LOS *abbr* **1** line of scrimmage **2** line of sight

love beads *n pl* : a necklace of beads; *esp* : beads worn as a symbol of love and peace

love·bug \ˈləvˌbəg\ *n* [fr. the fact that it is usually seen copulating] : a small black bibionid fly (*Plecia nearctica*) with a red thorax that is often a nuisance esp. while copulating along highways in states of the U.S. bordering the Gulf of Mexico where it is attracted to photochemical breakdown products of motor vehicle exhaust and tends to clog radiators and tarnish paint if the crushed bodies are not removed from vehicle surfaces

lowball \ˈlō,bȯl\ *vt* : to give (a customer) a deceptively low cost estimate that one has no intention of honoring <request that the statement be signed by an official of the firm. That way, a salesman won't be able to *lowball* you —*Consumer Reports*>

lowest terms *n pl* : the numerator and denominator of a fraction that have no factor in common <reduce a fraction to *lowest terms*>

low profile *n* : an inconspicuous mode of operation or behavior <avoid publicity, keep a *low profile,* and let Washington handle everything —Joan Silver & Linda Gottlieb>

low–rise \ˈlōˌrīz\ *adj* [*low* + *-rise* (as in *high-rise*)] **1** : being one or two stories and not equipped with elevators <a *low-rise* classroom building> **2** *of trousers* : low-slung and usu. close-fitting

LPM *abbr, often not cap* lines per minute

LPN *abbr* licensed practical nurse

Lr *symbol* lawrencium

lunar excursion mod·ule \-ˌmäj(ˌ)ü(ə)l\ *or* **lunar module** *n* : a space vehicle module designed to carry astronauts from the command module to the surface of the moon and back

lu·nar·naut \ˈlünə(r)ˌnȯt, -ˌnät\ *n* [*lunar* + astro*naut*] : an astronaut who explores the moon

LVN *abbr* licensed vocational nurse

ly·ase \ˈlī,ās, -,āz\ *n* [Gk *lyein* to loosen, release + E *-ase* enzyme] : an enzyme (as a decarboxylase) that forms double bonds by removing groups from a substrate other than by hydrolysis or that adds groups to double bonds

lym·phan·gi·og·ra·phy \ˌlim,fanjēˈägrəfē\ *n* [*lymphangio-* lymphatic vessels (fr. NL *lymphangion* lymphatic vessel, fr. *lympha* lymph + Gk *angeion* vessel, blood vessel) + *-graphy* writing, recording, deriv. of Gk *graphein* to write] : LYMPHOGRAPHY — **lym·phan·gio·gram** \limˈfanjēə,gram\ *n* — **lym·phan·gio·graph·ic** \(ˌ)limˌfanjēəˈgrafik\ *adj*

lym·pho·gran·u·lo·ma·tous \ˌlim(p)fə,granyəˈlōməd·əs\ *adj* [NL *lymphogranulomat-, lymphogranuloma* + E *-ous,* adj. suffix] : of, relating to, or characterized by lymphogranulomas <*lymphogranulomatous* skin diseases>

lym·phog·ra·phy \limˈfägrəfē\ *n* [*lympho-* lymph + *-graphy* writing, recording, deriv. of Gk *graphein* to write] : X-ray depiction of lymph vessels and nodes after use of a radiopaque material — **lym·pho·gram** \ˈlim(p)fə,gram\ *n* — **lym·pho·graph·ic** \ˌlim(p)fəˈgrafik\ *adj*

lym·pho·sar·co·ma·tous \ˌlim(p)fəsärˈkōməd·əs\ *adj* [NL *lymphosarcomat-, lymphosarcoma* + E *-ous,* adj. suffix] : being, affected with, or characterized by lymphosarcomas <large *lymphosarcomatous* masses> <*lymphosarcomatous* cows> <human *lymphosarcomatous* disease>

ly·oph·i·liz·er \(ˌ)līˈäfə,līzə(r)\ *n* [*lyophilize* to freeze-dry + *-er,* agent suffix] : a device used to carry out the process of freeze-drying

ly·si·me·tric \ˌlīsəˈme·trik\ *adj* : relating to or involving the use of a lysimeter <*lysimetric* observations>

ly·so·gen* \ˈlīsəgən\ *n* : a lysogenic bacterium or bacterial strain

ly·so·gen·ic* \ˌlīsəˈjenik, -ēk\ *adj* : not virulent : temperate <*lysogenic* viruses>

ly·sog·e·nize \līˈsäjə,nīz\ *vt* **-nized; -niz·ing** : to make lysogenic — **ly·sog·e·ni·za·tion** \-,säjənəˈzāshən, -,nīˈ-\ *n*

ly·sog·e·ny \līˈsäjənē\ *n* : the state of being lysogenic

ly·so·some \ˈlīsə,sōm\ *n* [ISV *lyso-* lysis + *-some* body, deriv. of Gk *sōma;* orig. formed in F] : a saclike cellular organelle that contains various hydrolytic enzymes — **ly·so·som·al** \ˌlīsəˈsōməl\ *adj* — **ly·so·som·al·ly** \-məlē\ *adv*

ly·so·staph·in \ˌlīsəˈstafən\ *n* [*lyso-* lysis + *staph* staphylococcus + *-in* chemical compound] : an antimicrobial enzyme that is obtained from a strain of staphylococcus and is effective against other staphylococci

M

MABE *abbr* master of agricultural business and economics

mac·chi·net·ta \ˌmäkəˈnetə, -ed·ə\ *n* [It *macchinetta* (*da caffè*) coffee machine, fr. dim. of *macchina* machine, fr. L *machina*] : a drip-coffee maker in which water is heated in the upper part which is then inverted to allow the water to run through the coffee into the lower part

mace \ˈmās\ *vt* **maced; mac·ing** : to spray with the liquid Mace <grabbed a policeman's whistle and got *maced* in the face —*Rolling Stone*>

Mace \ˈmās\ *trademark* — used for a temporarily disabling liquid that when sprayed in the face of a person (as a rioter) causes tears, dizziness, immobilization, and sometimes nausea

machine language *n* **1** : a code closely corresponding to a computer's internal representation of information <a program written in *machine language*> **2** : a physical form of information that can be used by a computer : machine-readable form <a list of literary works already converted to *machine language* —Gary Carlson>

ma·chine–read·able \məˌshēnˌrēdəbəl\ *adj* : directly usable by a computer <*machine-readable* text>

machine translation *n* : automatic translation from one language to another

ma·chis·mo \mäˈchēz(ˌ)mō, mə-, -ˈkē-, -ˈki-, -ˈchi-, -s(ˌ)mō\ *n* [MexSp, fr. Sp *macho* male + *-ismo* action, state] : a strong sense of masculine pride : an exaggerated awareness and assertion of masculinity <in its origins *machismo* is the sexual and familial ideology or value-system of the Mediterranean world —Frederic Hunter> <sadly he realized the rioters were asserting their manhood, just as he once had to prove his *machismo* by the self-defeating act of shooting a policeman —J.B. Lane>

¹ma·cho \ˌmä(ˌ)chō\ *adj* [Sp, male, fr. L *masculus*] : aggressively virile : markedly or exaggeratedly masculine <all their *macho* swagger and bravado —Burr Snider> <the kind of *macho* humor football players find so appealing —Gary Cartwright> <his skintight stage armor of *macho* black leather —Ed McCormack>

²ma·cho \ˈmä(ˌ)chō\ *n, pl* **machos** **1** : MACHISMO <a compulsion to prove the collective *macho* by consenting to another bloody misadventure —L. L. King> **2** : one who exhibits machismo <pride leads *machos* into betting sums they cannot afford —Evelyn P. Stevens>

Mac·lau·rin's series \məˌklȯrən(z)-\ *n* [Colin *Maclaurin* †1746 Scot. physician] : a Taylor's series of the form

$$f(x) = f(0) + \frac{f'(0)}{1!}x + \frac{f''(0)}{2!}x^2 + \ldots + \frac{f^{[n]}(0)}{n!}x^n + \ldots$$

in which the expansion is about the reference point zero — called also *Maclaurin series*

Mc·Lu·han·esque \məˌklüəˌnesk\ *adj* [Herbert Marshall *McLuhan* b1911 Canad. educator] : of, relating to, or suggestive of Marshall McLuhan or his theories <the *McLuhanesque* mosaic of the TV screen —E. A. Kosner>

mac·ro \ˈmak(ˌ)rō\ *n, pl* **macros** [short for *macroinstruction*] : a single computer instruction that stands for a sequence of operations

mac·ro·ag·gre·gate \ˌmakrōˈagrəgət\ *n* [*macro-* long, large (deriv. of Gk *makros* long) + *aggregate*] : a relatively large particle (as of soil or a protein) — **mac·ro·ag·gre·gat·ed** \-ˌagrəˌgād·əd\ *adj*

mac·ro·bi·ot·ic* \-bīˈäd·ik, -bē-\ *adj* : of, relating to, or being an extremely restricted diet (as one containing chiefly whole grains) that is usu. undertaken by its advocates to promote health and well-being although it may actually be deficient in essential nutrients (as fats)

ma·cro·bi·ot·ics* \-iks\ *n pl but sing in constr* : a macrobiotic dietary system

mac·ro·glob·u·lin \ˌmakrōˈgläbyələn\ *n* [ISV] : a highly polymerized globulin of high molecular weight

mac·ro·glob·u·lin·emia \ˌmakrōˌgläbyələ'nēmēə\ *n* [NL, fr. ISV *macroglobulin* + NL *-emia* blood condition, deriv. of Gk *haima* blood] : a disorder characterized by increased blood serum viscosity and by macroglobulins in the serum — **mac·ro·glob·u·lin·emic** \-'nēmik\ *adj*

mac·ro·in·struc·tion \ˌmakrōin'strəkshən\ *n* : MACRO

mac·ro·lide \'makrəˌlīd\ *n* [*macro*cyclic + *l*actone + *-ide* derivative compound] : any of several antibiotics that contain a lactone ring and are produced by actinomycetes of the genus *Streptomyces*

mac·ro·or·gan·ism \ˌmakrō'örgəˌnizəm, -'ö(ə)g-\ *n* : an organism large enough to be seen by the normal unaided human eye

ma·fia* \'mäfēə, 'maf-\ *n, often cap* : a group of people of similar interests or backgrounds prominent or powerful in a particular field or enterprise <protesting the presumptions of the mental-health *mafia* —R.J. Neuhaus> <the most churlish of his detractors — which is to say most of the contemporary literary *Mafia* —Richard Boeth>

ma·fi·o·so \ˌmäfē'ō(ˌ)sō, ˌmaf-, -'ō(ˌ)zō\ *n, pl* **ma·fi·o·si** \-sē, -zē\ *often cap* [It, fr. *mafioso,* adj., belonging to the Mafia, fr. *Mafia* + *-oso,* adj. suffix] : a member of the Mafia or a mafia <key witness against alleged *Mafioso* is feared slain —*N.Y. Times*> <among . . . literary *mafiosi,* even violence has to be sandwiched between drinks —Lois B. Gould>

magic number *n* **1** : one of a set of numbers for which an atomic nucleus exhibits a high degree of stability when either the proton or neutron count is equal to the number **2** : a number that represents a combination of wins for a leader (as in a baseball pennant race) and losses for a contender which mathematically guarantees the leader's winning the championship

mag·i·cube \'majəˌkyüb\ *n* [blend of *magic* and *cube*] : a flashcube that for its firing depends only on the mechanical ignition of a primer within the device

magnetic* *n* : a magnetic substance

magnetic bottle *n* : a magnetic field for confining plasma for experiments in nuclear fusion

magnetic core *n* **1** : a mass of iron (as in an electromagnet or transformer) that serves to intensify the magnetic field resulting from current carried in a surrounding coil **2** : CORE 1

magnetic disk *n* : DISK 1

mag·ne·to·car·dio·gram \magˌnēd·ō'kärdēəˌgram, -ˌned-\ *n* [*magneto-* magnetic field, magnetism + *cardiogram*] : a recording of a magnetocardiograph

mag·ne·to·car·dio·graph \-'kärdēəˌgraf\ *n* : an instrument for recording the changes in the magnetic field around the heart that is used to supplement information given by an electrocardiograph — **mag·ne·to·car·dio·graph·ic** \-ˌkärdēəˌgrafik, -ēk\ *adj* — **mag·ne·to·car·di·og·ra·phy** \-ˌkärdē'ägrəfē\ *n*

mag·ne·to·flu·id·dy·nam·ic \-ˌflüə(d)dīˌnamik, -ēk\ *adj* : HYDROMAGNETIC 1 — **mag·ne·to·flu·id·dy·nam·ics** \-iks, -ēks\ *n pl but sing or pl in constr*

mag·ne·to·flu·id·me·chan·ic \-ˌflüədməˌkanik, -ēk\ : HYDROMAGNETIC 1 — **mag·ne·to·flu·id·me·chan·ics** \-iks, -ēks\ *n pl but sing or pl in constr*

mag·ne·to·gas·dy·nam·ics \-ˌgasdī'namiks, -ēks\ *n pl but sing in constr* : HYDROMAGNETICS — **mag·ne·to·gas·dy·nam·ic** \-ˌgasdīˌnamik, -ēk\ *adj*

mag·ne·to·pause \mag'nēd·əˌpöz, -'ned-\ *n* [*magneto*sphere + *pause*] : the outer boundary of a magnetosphere

mag·ne·to·plas·ma·dy·nam·ic \magˌnēd·ōˌplazmədīˌnamik, -ˌned-, -ēk\ *adj* : HYDROMAGNETIC 1 — **mag·ne·to·plas·ma·dy·nam·ics** \-iks, -ēks\ *n pl but sing or pl in constr*

mag·ne·to·sphere \mag'nēd·əˌsfi(ə)r, -'ned-, -ˌsfiə\ *n* **1** : a region of the upper atmosphere that surrounds the earth, extends out for thousands of miles, and is dominated by the earth's magnetic field so that charged particles are trapped in it **2** : a region that surrounds a celestial body (as a planet) and is comparable to the earth's magnetosphere in trapping charged particles — **mag·ne·to·spher·ic** \-ˌnēd·əˌsfi(ə)rik, -ˌned-, -ˌsferik, -ēk\ *adj*

mag·non \ˈmagˌnän\ *n* [*mag*netic + *-on* elementary particle, quantum] : one of the quanta into which a spin wave is divided

Mah·ler·ian \mäˈlerēən, -ˈlir-\ *adj* [Gustav *Mahler* †1911 Austrian composer] : of, relating to, or suggestive of Gustav Mahler or his music <a symphony only in the *Mahlerian* sense of a song cycle with orchestra —Irving Kolodin>

mail cover *n* : a postal monitoring and recording of information (as return address and postmark) on all mail going to a designated addressee

Mail·gram \ˈmā(ə)lˌgram\ *trademark* — used for a message that is transmitted by wire to a post office which delivers it to the addressee

main·frame \ˈmānˌfrām\ *n* : a computer and esp. the computer itself and its cabinet as distinguished from peripheral devices connected to it

mai tai \ˈmīˌtī\ *n, pl* **mai tais** [Tahitian *maitai* good] : a cocktail made with rum, curaçao, orgeat, lime, and fruit juices, shaken with shaved ice, and often garnished with fruit (as pineapple and a maraschino cherry)

ma·jol·i·ca* \məˈjäləkə, *sometimes* -ˈyäl-\ *n* : a 19th century earthenware modeled in naturalistic shapes and glazed in bright colors

major–medical \ˌmājə(r)ˌmedəkəl\ *adj* : of, relating to, or being a form of insurance designed to pay all or part of the medical bills of major illnesses usu. after deduction of a fixed initial sum

make* *vb* — **make it** **1** : to be successful <trying to *make it* as writer-in-residence at the university —Gershon Legman> **2** : to have sexual intercourse <one young couple who would . . . *make it* in a rear seat —Thomas Pynchon> — **make waves** : to disturb the status quo <unimaginative, traditional career man who does not *make waves* —Henry Trewhitt>

make out* *vi* **1** : to engage in sexual intercourse <an insecure, homely kid who wanted to get laid and couldn't *make out* —Rona Jaffe> **2** : to engage in amorous kissing and caressing : neck <he started *making out* with Kathy . . . kissing her, putting his hands all over her —John Reid>

makuta *pl of* LIKUTA

Mal·i·bu board \ˌmaləˌbü-\ *n* [*Malibu* Beach, California] : a lightweight surfboard 9 to 10 feet long with a round nose, square tail, and slightly convex bottom

ma·lic \ˈmalək, ˈmāl-\ *adj* : involved in and esp. catalyzing a reaction in which malic acid participates <*malic* dehydrogenase> <*malic* enzyme>

ma·lo·lactic \ˌmalōˌlaktik, ˌmālō-\ *adj* [*malo-* malic acid + *lactic*] : relating to or involved in the bacterial conversion of malic acid to lactic acid in wine <*malolactic* fermentation>

mam·mo·gram \ˈmaməˌgram\ *n* [*mamma* breast + connective *-o-* + *-gram* drawing, writing, record, deriv. of Gk *gramma* letter, writing] : a photograph of the breasts made by X rays

mam·mog·ra·phy \maˈmägrəfē\ *n* [*mamma* + connective *-o-* + *-graphy* writing, deriv. of Gk *graphein* to write] : X-ray examination of the breasts (as for early detection of cancer) — **mam·mo·graph·ic** \ˌmaməˈgrafik\ *adj*

Man* *n* **1** : the police <when I heard the siren, I knew it was the *Man* —*Amer. Speech*> **2** : the white establishment : white society <surprise that any black man . . . should take on so about the *Man* —Peter Goldman>

man·eb \ˈmaˌneb\ *n* [*man*ganese + *e*thylene + *b*is- twice, fr. L *bis*] : a carbamate agricultural fungicide $C_4H_6MnN_2S_4$

ma·ni·cot·ti \ˌmanəˈkäd·ē\ *pl* **manicotti** [It, lit., muff, fr. *manica* sleeve, fr. L] : tubular pasta shells stuffed esp. with ricotta

manifold* *n* **1** : a mathematical set **2** : a topological space such that every point has a neighborhood which is homeomorphic to the interior of a sphere in euclidean space of the same number of dimensions

-man·ship \mənˌship\ *n suffix* [sports*manship*] : art or practice of maneuvering to gain a tactical advantage <games*manship*> <one-up*manship*> <grants*manship*>

many–val·ued \ˌmenēˌval(ˌ)yüd, -ni-, -ˌvalyəd\ *adj* : MULTIPLE-VALUED

Mao \ˈmau̇\ *adj* [*Mao* Tse-tung *b*1893 Chin. communist leader] : having a long narrow cut and a mandarin collar <*Mao* jacket> <designers are showing mandarin collars, kimono sleeves, *Mao* suits —*McCall's*>

MAO *abbr* monoamine oxidase

Mao·ism \ˈmau̇ˌizəm\ *n* : the theory and practice of Marxism-Leninism developed in China chiefly by Mao Tse-tung — **Mao·ist** \ˈmau̇əst\ *n or adj*

map* *n* **1** : the arrangement of genes on a chromosome — called also *genetic map* **2** : MAPPING

map* *vt* **mapped; map·ping** : to locate (a gene) on a chromosome <mutants which have been genetically *mapped*> ~ *vi, of a gene* : to be located <a repressor *maps* near the corresponding structural gene>

map·ping \ˈmapiŋ\ *n* : a mathematical correspondence that assigns exactly one element of one set to each element of the same or another set <a one-to-one continous *mapping*>

mar·ag·ing steel \ˌmärˌājiŋ-\ *n* [*mar*tensite + *aging*] : a strong tough low-carbon martensitic steel which contains up to 25 percent nickel and in which hardening precipitates are formed by aging

Mar·ek's disease \ˈmarəks-, ˈmer-\ *n* [J. *Marek* †1952 Ger. veterinarian] : a cancerous disease of poultry that is characterized esp. by proliferation of lymphoid cells and is caused by a virus resembling a herpes virus

Mar·fan's syndrome *or* **Mar·fan syndrome** \ˌmärˌfanˌsinˌdrōm, -ˌsindrəm\ *n* [Antonin Bernard Jean *Marfan* †1942 Fr. pediatrician] : a hereditary disorder characterized by abnormal elongation of the long bones and often by ocular and circulatory defects

mar·ga·ri·ta \ˌmärgəˈrēd·ə\ *n* [MexSp, prob. fr. the name *Margarita* Margaret] : a cocktail consisting of tequila, lime or lemon juice, and an orange-flavored liqueur

mar·gin·al* \ˈmärjnəl, -jənᵊl\ *adj* : relating to or being a function of a random variable that is obtained from a function of several random variables by integrating or summing over all possible values of the other variables <a *marginal* probability function>

mari·cul·ture \ˈmarəˌkəlchə(r)\ *n* [*mari-* sea (fr. L *mare*) + *culture*] : the cultivation of marine organisms by exploiting their natural environment — **mari·cul·tur·ist** \-chərəst\ *n*

mar·i·na·ra \ˌmarəˈnarə, ˌmerəˈnerə, -när-\ *adj* [It (*alla*) *marinara* in sailor style, fr. *marinara,* fem. of *marinaro* of sailors, fr. *marino* marine] : made with tomatoes, onion, garlic, and spices < *marinara* sauce>

marker* *or* **marker gene** *n* : GENETIC MARKER

Mar·ko·vi·an \märˈkōvēən, -kȯ-, -fēən\ *or* **Mar·kov** \ˈmärˌkȯf, -ȯv\ *also* **Mar·koff** \-ȯf\ *adj* : of, relating to, or resembling a Markov process or Markov chain esp. by having probabilities defined in terms of transition from the possible existing states to other states < *Markovian* models> < *Markovian* properties>

Markov process *also* **Markoff process** *n* [Andrei Andreevich *Markov* †1922 Russ. mathematician] : a stochastic process (as Brownian movement) that resembles a Markov chain except that the states are continuous; *also* : a Markov chain with discrete states

martial art *n* : one of several arts of combat (as karate, judo, or kung fu) of Oriental origin that are widely practiced as sport

Mary Gre·go·ry \ˌmerēˈgreg(ə)rē, ˌmār-, ˌmar-, -riˈ-, -ˈgrāg-, -ri\ *n* [*Mary Gregory,* thought to have been a late 19th cent. Am. glass painter] : colored glassware of a popular 19th century style marked by white enamel decoration usu. including figures of children

Mary Jane *n* [by folk etymology (influenced by Sp *Juana* Jane)] *slang* : marijuana

mas·con \ˈmasˌkän\ *n* [*mass* + *con*centration] : one of the concentrations of large mass under the surface of the moon's maria whose gravitational effect is held to cause perturbations of the paths of spacecraft orbiting the moon

mash* *n, Brit* : mashed potatoes <bangers and *mash*>

mass·cult \ˈmasˌkəlt\ *n* [*mass cult*ure] : the artistic and intellectual culture associated with and disseminated through the mass media : mass culture

mass·less \ˈmasləs, *sometimes* ˈmäs-\ *adj* : having no mass < *massless* particles> — **mass·less·ness** *n*

Mass of the Resurrection : a mass for the dead in which the celebrant wears white vestments to symbolize the joyous resurrection of the dead

MAT* *abbr* master of arts in teaching

matching funds *n pl*: funds provided (as by a government) that match funds provided by the recipient

ma·ter·ni·ty \mə'tərnəd·ē, -'tən-, -'təin, -i\ *adj* **1** : designed for wear during pregnancy < a *maternity* dress > **2** : effective for the period close to and including childbirth < *maternity* leave >

mathematical biology *n* : a branch of biology concerned with the construction of mathematical models to describe and solve biological problems — **mathematical biologist** *n*

ma·tri·fo·cal \ˌma·trəˈfōkəl, ˌmā-\ *adj* [*matri-* mother (deriv. of L *mater*) + *focal*] : gravitating toward or centered upon the mother : matricentric < a *matrifocal* family structure >

ma·trix al·ge·bra \ˌmā·triksˈaljəbrə\ *n* : generalized algebra that deals with the operations and relations among matrices

ma·trix sentence \ˌmā·trik(s)-\ *n* : that one of a pair of sentences joined by means of a transformation that keeps its essential external structure and syntactic status < in "the book that I want is gone," "the book is gone" is the *matrix sentence*>

ma·ven *also* **ma·vin** *or* **may·vin** \'māvən\ *n* [Yiddish *meyvn*, fr. LHeb *mēbhīn*, perh. fr. Heb *mēbhī* one who has brought in] : one who is experienced or knowledgeable : an expert < committed enough malapropian misdemeanors to keep the *mavens* at Oxford busy for a generation —Leo Rosten >

maxi \'maksē, -si\ *n* [fr. *maxi-*] : a long skirt or coat that usu. extends to the ankle — called also respectively *maxiskirt, maxicoat*

maxi- \'maksē, -si\ *comb form* [fr. *maximum*, after E *minimum: mini-*] **1** : extra long < *maxi*-dress > < *maxi*-kilt > **2** : extra large < *maxi*-sculpture > < *maxi*-problems >

max·il·lo·facial \makˌsi(ˌ)lō'fāshəl\ *adj* [*maxillo-* maxilla + *facial*] : of, relating to, or affecting the maxilla and the face < *maxillofacial* lesions >

maxi·min \'maksəˌmin\ *n* [*maxi*mum + *min*imum] : the maximum of a set of minima; *esp* : the largest of a set of minimum possible gains each of which occurs in the least advantageous outcome of a strategy followed by a participant in a situation governed by the theory of games — compare MINIMAX

maximum likelihood *n* : a statistical method for estimating population parameters (as the mean and variance) from sample data that selects as estimates those parameter values maximizing the probability of obtaining the observed data

ma·yo \'mā(ˌ)ō\ *n* [by shortening] : mayonnaise < hold the *mayo* and lettuce but lay on the mustard —Don Imus >

mbi·ra \em'birə, əm-, -bēr-\ *n* [native word in southern Africa; of Bantu origin] : an African musical instrument that consists of a gourd resonator, a wooden box, and a varying number of tuned metal or wooden strips that vibrate when plucked with the thumb or fingers

MCS *abbr* **1** master of commercial science **2** master of computer science **3** missile control system

mean value theorem *n* : a theorem in calculus: if a function of one variable is continuous on a closed interval and differentiable on the interval minus its end points there is at least one point where the derivative of the function is equal to the slope of the line joining the end points of the curve representing the function on the interval

meat-and-potatoes \ˌmētᵊnpəˈtād·(ˌ)ōz, -ᵊnbəˈ-, -ēd·ᵊn-, -ˈtād·əz\ *adj*: of fundamental importance : basic < the *meat-and-potatoes* problems of everyday living and loving —D.J. Heckman >

mec·a·myl·amine \ˌmekə'miləˌmēn, -əmən\ *n* [*meth*yl + *cam*phane, a crystalline terpene + *amine*] : a drug that in the hydrochloride $C_{11}H_{21}N.HCl$ is used orally as a ganglionic blocking agent to effect a rapid lowering of severely elevated blood pressure

mechanical bank *also* **mechanical*** *n* : a toy bank in which operation of a lever activates a mechanism that goes through some amusing or absurd routine and deposits a coin

mech·a·no·chem·is·try \ˌmekənōˈkeməstrē\ *n* [*mechano-* mechanical + *chemistry*] : chemistry that deals with the conversion of chemical energy into mechanical work (as in the contraction of a muscle) — **mech·a·no·chem·i·cal** \-ˈkemə̇kəl\ *adj*

mech·a·no·re·cep·tor \ˌmekə(ˌ)nōrə̇ˈseptə(r)\ *n* : a neural end organ (as a tactile receptor) that responds to a mechanical stimulus (as a change in pressure) — **mech·a·no·re·cep·tion** \-rə̇ˈsepshən\ *n* — **mech·a·no·re·cep·tive** \-rə̇ˈseptiv\ *adj*

mech·lor·eth·amine \ˌmeˌklōrˈethəˌmēn, -lȯr-, -əmə̇n\ *n* [*me*thyl + *chloro*ethyl + *amine*] : a nitrogen mustard $C_5H_{11}Cl_2N$ used as an insect chemosterilant, as a war gas, and in palliative treatment of some neoplastic diseases

me·dia·ge·nic \ˌmēdēəˈjenik, -jēn-, -nēk\ *adj* [*media,* pl. of *medium* + *-genic* (as in *photogenic*] : likely to appeal to the audiences of the mass media and esp. television < *mediagenic* politicians >

media mix *n* : a presentation (as in a theater) in which several media (as films, tapes, and slides) are employed simultaneously

me·di·an* \ˈmēdēən\ *n* **1** : a vertical line that divides the histogram of a frequency distribution into two parts of equal area **2** : a value of a random variable for which all greater values make the distribution function greater than one half and all lesser values make it less than one half

med·ic·aid \ˈmedə̇ˌkād, -dē-\ *n* [*medic*al + *aid*] : a program of medical aid designed for those unable to afford regular medical service and financed by the state and federal governments

medi·care \ˈmedə̇ˌke(ə)r, -ˌka(ə)r, -ˌkeə, -ˌkaə\ *n* [blend of *medical* and *care*] : a government program of medical care esp. for the aged

me·di·og·ra·phy \ˌmēdēˈägrəfē, -fi\ *n* [*medi*um + connective *-o-* + *-graphy* writing, deriv. of Gk *graphein* to write] : a list of multimedia materials relating to a particular subject

me·dul·lin \məˈdələ̇n, me-; ˈmedᵊlə̇n, ˈmejəl-\ *n* [NL *medulla* + E *-in* chemical compound; fr. its isolation from the medulla of the kidney] : a renal prostaglandin effective in reducing blood pressure

mef·e·nam·ic acid \ˌmefəˌnamik-\ *n* [di*me*thyl + *fen-* (by shortening and alter. fr. *phenyl*) + *am*inobenzo*ic acid*] : a crystalline compound $C_{15}H_{15}NO_2$ used esp. to relieve pain or inflammation

mega·bar \ˈmegəˌbär, -ˌbȧ(r\ *n* [ISV *mega-* large, million (deriv. of Gk *megas* large) + *bar*] : a unit of pressure equal to one million bars

mega·bit \-ˌbit\ *n* : one million bits

mega·buck \-ˌbək\ *n* : one million dollars < beyond the foundations . . . stood the feds and the *megabucks* from Washington —Peter Schrag >

mega·death \-ˌdeth\ *n* : one million deaths — used as a unit in reference to atomic warfare < the estimate that the Kremlin can now destroy 40 per cent of our industry and take a toll of 13 *megadeaths* —Joseph Alsop >

mega·ma·chine \-məˌshēn\ *n* : a social system that functions impersonally like a gigantic machine < through the army, in fact, the standard model of the *megamachine* was transmitted from culture to culture —Lewis Mumford >

mega·rad \-ˌrad\ *n* : one million rads

mega·struc·ture \-ˌstrəkchə(r), -ksh-\ *n* : a very large multistory building < a seven-block *megastructure* . . . of shops, parking garages, offices, and hotels, connected by plazas, walkways, and glass-enclosed arcades —Anthony Bailey >

mega·unit \-ˌyünə̇t\ *n* : one million units

mega·vi·ta·min \ˌmegəˈvīd·əmə̇n, *Brit also* -ˈvitəmə̇n\ *adj* : relating to or consisting of very large doses of vitamins < *megavitamin* therapy >

me·gil·lah *also* **me·gil·la** \məˈgilə\ *n* [Yiddish *megillah,* fr. Heb. *mĕgillāh* scroll, volume (used esp. of the Book of Esther, read aloud at the Purim celebration)] *slang* : a long involved story or account < the whole *megillah* > < he'd had a lot of stuff patented over the years, but people had robbed him or swiped his ideas; the usual inventor's *megillah* —Alexander King >

me·la·no·cyte–stim·u·lat·ing hor·mone \məˈlanəˌsītˈstimyəˌlād·iŋˈhȯrˌmōn, ˈmelənōˌsīt-\ *n* : a vertebrate hormone of the pituitary gland that darkens the skin by stimulating melanin dispersion in pigment-containing cells — called also *melanophore-stimulating hormone*

mel·a·to·nin \ˌmeləˈtōnən\ *n* [prob. fr. *mela*nocyte + sero*tonin*; fr. its power to lighten melanocytes] : a vertebrate hormone of the pineal gland that produces lightening of the skin by causing contraction of melanin-containing cells and that plays a role in sexual development and maturation

mem·bran·al \ˌmemˈbrānᵊl\ *adj* : relating to or characteristic of cellular membranes

memory* *n* : capacity for storing information <a computer with 16K words of *memory*>

memory trace *n* : an alteration that is held to take place within the central nervous system and to constitute the physical basis of learning

men·a·zon \ˈmenəˌzän\ *n* [perh. fr. di*me*thyl + diami*no*- + tri*az*ine + thi*on*ate] : an organophosphate insecticide $C_6H_{12}N_5O_2PS_2$ used esp. against parasitic insects of warm-blooded animals

me·nin·go·en·ceph·a·lit·ic \məˌniŋ(ˌ)gōənˌsefəˈlid·ik, -in(ˌ)jō-\ *adj* : relating to or characteristic of meningoencephalitis <*meningoencephalitic* lesions>

meno·tax·is \ˌmenəˈtaksəs\ *n* [NL, fr. *meno-* remaining, persisting (deriv. of Gk *menein* to remain) + *taxis*] : a taxis involving a constant reaction (as movement at a constant angle to a light source) but not a simple movement toward or away from the directing stimulus

mercy killing *n* : the act or practice of killing individuals (as persons or domestic animals) that are hopelessly sick or injured for reasons of mercy : euthanasia

me·rid·ic \məˈridik\ *adj* [Gk *merid-*, *meris* part + E *-ic*, adj. suffix] : having some but not all active constituents chemically defined <insects reared on a *meridic* diet> — compare HOLIDIC, OLIGIDIC

mer·i·toc·ra·cy \ˌmerəˈtäkrəsē\ *n* [*merit* + connective *-o-* + *-cracy* government, dominant class, deriv. of Gk *kratos* strength, power] **1** : an educational system whereby the talented are chosen and moved ahead on the basis of their achievement (as in competitive examinations) **2** : leadership by the talented — **mer·it·o·crat·ic** \ˌmerəd·əˈkrad·ik\ *adj*

mer·it·o·crat \ˈmerəd·ōˌkrat\ *n* [*merit* + *-crat* member of a dominant class, deriv. of Gk *kratos* strength, power] : one who advances through a meritocratic system

mero·my·o·sin \ˌmerəˈmīəsən\ *n* [*mero-* part, partial (deriv. of Gk *meros* part) + *myosin*] : either of two structural subunits of myosin that are obtained esp. by tryptic digestion

me·son* \ˈmezˌän, ˈmesˌän, ˈmā-, ˈmē-\ *n* : any of a group of strongly interacting particles that can be created and annihilated in arbitrary numbers, that have a mass between that of an electron and a proton, and that obey the Bose-Einstein statistics

me·so·pe·lag·ic \ˌmezōpəˈlajik, ˌmesō-, ˌmē-\ *adj* [*meso-* mid, middle (deriv. of Gk *mesos*) + *pelagic*] : of, relating to, or inhabiting oceanic depths from about 600 feet to 3000 feet <*mesopelagic* fish>

me·so·scale \ˈmezəˌskāl, ˈmes-, ˈmē-\ *adj* : of or relating to a meteorological phenomenon approximately 1 to 100 kilometers in horizontal extent <*mesoscale* cloud pattern> <*mesoscale* wind circulation>

me·so·some* \-ˌsōm\ *n* : a cell organelle that appears in electron micrographs as an invagination of the plasma membrane and is a site of localization of respiratory enzymes

messenger RNA *n* : an RNA that carries the code for a particular protein from the nuclear DNA to the ribosome and acts as a template for the formation of that protein — compare TRANSFER RNA

mes·tra·nol \ˈmestrəˌnȯl, -ˌnōl\ *n* [*m*ethyl + *estr*ogen + pregn*ane*, a crystalline steroid hormone + *-ol* chemical compound] : a synthetic estrogen $C_{21}H_{26}O_2$ used in oral contraceptives

meta·cen·tric \ˌmed·əˈsen·trik\ *n* : a metacentric chromosome

met·al·lide \ˈmed·ᵊlˌīd\ *vt* **-lid·ed; -lid·ing** [obs. *metallide*, n., a binary compound of metals, fr. *metall-* metal + *-ide* derivative compound] : to diffuse (atoms of a metal or metalloid) into the surface of a metal by electrolysis in order to impart a desired surface property (as hardness) to the bulk metal

me·tal·lo·en·zyme \mə¦talō¦en,zīm\ *n* [*metallo-* metal + *enzyme*] : an enzyme consisting of a protein linked with a specific metal

meta·mer·ic* \,med·ə'merik, -'mi(ə)r-\ *adj* : of, relating to, or being color metamers <a *metameric* pair> — **me·tam·er·ism*** \mə'tamə,rizəm\ *n*

meta·ram·i·nol \,med·ə'ramə̇,nȯl, -,nōl\ *n* [perh. fr. *meta-* after, change, isomeric, derivative (deriv. of Gk *meta* with, among, after) + hyd*r*oxyl + *amine* + *-ol* chemical compound] : a sympathomimetic drug $C_9H_{13}NO_2$ used esp. as a vasoconstrictor

meta·rho·dop·sin \¦med·ərō'däpsə̇n\ *n* : either of two intermediate compounds formed in the bleaching of rhodopsin by light

me·te·or·oi·dal \¦mēd·ēə¦rȯidᵊl\ *adj* : of or relating to meteoroids

me·te·pa \mə'tēpə, me'-\ *n* [*me*thyl + *tepa*] : an insect chemosterilant $C_9H_{18}N_3OP$ that is a methyl derivative of tepa

meter maid *n* : a female member of a police force who is assigned to write tickets for parking violations

Meth·e·drine \'methə,drēn, -ədrə̇n\ *trademark* — used for methamphetamine

meth·i·cil·lin \¦methə¦silə̇n\ *n* [*meth*yl + pen*icillin*] : a synthetic penicillin esp. effective against penicillinase-producing staphylococci

Method* *n* : a dramatic technique by which an actor seeks to gain complete identification with the inner personality of the character being portrayed so that all thoughts, feelings, and actions expressed in the portrayal are those of the character and not of the actor

meth·o·trex·ate \,methə·'trek,sāt, -ksə̇t\ *n* [*meth*yl + connective *-o-* + *-trex-* (arbitrary infix) + *-ate* derivative compound] : a toxic anticancer drug $C_{20}H_{22}N_8O_5$ that is an analogue of folic acid and an antimetabolite

me·thoxy·flu·rane \me,thäksē'flu̇(ə)r,ān\ *n* [*meth*yl + *oxy-* containing oxygen + *fluor-* containing fluorine + eth*ane*] : a nonexplosive gaseous general anesthetic $C_3H_4Cl_2F_2O$ related to chloroform

meths \'meths\ *n pl but sing in constr* [contr. of *methylated spirits*] *Brit* : ethyl alcohol denatured with methanol

meth·yl·ase \'methə,lās, -āz\ *n* [*methyl* + *-ase* enzyme] : an enzyme that catalyzes methylation (as of RNA or DNA)

meth·yl·do·pa \¦methəl'dōpə\ *n* [*methyl* + *dopa*, an amino acid] : a drug $C_{10}H_{13}NO_4$ used to lower blood pressure

meth·yl para·thi·on \¦methəl,parə'thīən, -'thī,än\ *n* : a potent synthetic organophosphate insecticide $C_8H_{10}NO_5PS$ that is more toxic than parathion

meth·yl·phe·ni·date \,methəl'fenə,dāt, -'fēn-\ *n* [*methyl* + *phen*yl + piper*id*ine + acet*ate*] : a mild stimulant $C_{14}H_{19}NO_2$ of the central nervous system used in the form of the hydrochloride to treat narcolepsy and hyperkinetic behavior disorders in children

meth·yl·pred·nis·o·lone \¦methəlpred'nisə,lōn\ *n* [*methyl* + *prednisolone*] : any of several corticoids used as anti-inflammatory agents

meth·y·ser·gide \,methə'sər,jīd\ *n* [*methy*l + ly*serg*ic acid + am*ide*] : a drug $C_{21}H_{27}N_3O_2$ used in the form of its maleate in the treatment and prevention of vascular headache

metric* *n* : a mathematical function that associates with each pair of elements of a set a real nonnegative number constituting their distance and satisfying the conditions that the number is zero only if the two elements are identical, the number is the same regardless of the order in which the two elements are taken, and the number associated with one pair of elements plus that associated with one member of the pair and a third element is equal to or greater than the number associated with the other member of the pair and the third element

met·ri·cate \'me·trə̇,kāt\ *vt* **-cat·ed; -cat·ing** *Brit* : METRICIZE

met·ri·ca·tion \,me·trə̇'kāshən\ *n* : the act or process of metricizing

met·ri·cize* \'me·trə̇,sīz\ *vt* **-cized; -ciz·ing** : to change into or express in the metric system

metric space *n* : a mathematical set for which a metric is defined for any pair of elements

¹met·ro \ˈme·(ˌ)trō\ *n* [fr. the phrase *metropolitan government*] : metropolitan regional government

²metro *adj* : of, relating to, or constituting a region including a city and the surrounding suburban areas that are socially and economically integrated with it : metropolitan < *metro* government > < major *metro* markets > < branch libraries in *metro* Atlanta —*Library Jour.* >

met·ro·ni·da·zole \ˌme·trəˈnīdəˌzōl\ *n* [*me*thyl + *-tron-* (prob. fr. *nitro*) + im*ide* + *azole*] : a drug $C_6H_9N_3O_3$ used in treating vaginal trichomoniasis

me·tyr·a·pone \məˈtirəˌpōn\ *n* [perh. fr. *meth*y*l* + *-rapone* (perh. alter. of *propanone*)] : a metabolic hormone $C_{14}H_{14}N_2O$ that inhibits biosynthesis of cortisol and is used to test for normal functioning of the hypothalamus and pituitary

MIA \ˌe(ˌ)mīˈā\ *n* [*m*issing *i*n *a*ction] : a member of the armed forces whose whereabouts following a combat mission are unknown and whose death cannot be established beyond reasonable doubt

Mi·chae·lis constant \mīˌkāləˈ-, mə-\ *n* [Leonor *Michaelis* †1949 Am. biochemist] : a constant that is a measure of the kinetics of an enzyme reaction and that is equivalent to the concentration of substrate at which the reaction takes place at one half its maximum velocity

mick·ey–mouse \ˌmikēˌmau̇s, -ki-\ *vt* [fr. *Mickey Mouse,* a trademark] : to provide (a film) with accompanying music that closely describes or mimics the action

¹Mickey Mouse *adj* [fr. *Mickey Mouse,* a trademark used for a cartoon character] : petty: as **a** : lacking importance : trivial, insignificant < switch to *Mickey Mouse* courses, where you don't work too hard —Willie Cager > **b** : annoyingly petty : small-minded < directives did away with *Mickey Mouse* Navy regs —*Newsweek* > **c** : small-time, second-rate, bush-league < running a race in two stages . . . is bad enough; two days for a 226-mile race is *Mickey Mouse* —J.S. Radosta >

²Mickey Mouse *n* : something that is Mickey Mouse < eliminating the *Mickey Mouse* from the soldier's routine —L.J. Binder >

MICR *abbr* magnetic ink character recognition

mi·cro·an·a·tom·i·cal \ˌmī(ˌ)krōˌanəˈtäməkəl\ *adj* [*microanatomy* + *-ical,* adj. suffix] : of or relating to the microscopic structure of the tissues of organisms : histological

mi·cro·beam \ˈmīkrōˌbēm\ *n* [*micro-* small, one millionth (deriv. of Gk *mikros* small) + *beam*] : a beam of radiation of small cross section < a focused laser *microbeam* > < a *microbeam* of electrons >

micro·body \-ˌbädē, -di\ *n* : PEROXISOME

mi·cro·cap·sule \-ˌkapsəl, -(ˌ)sül, *also* -ps(ˌ)yül *or* -psyəl\ *n* : a tiny capsule containing material (as an adhesive or a medicine) that is released when the capsule is broken, melted, or dissolved

mi·cro·cir·cuit \-ˌsərkət, -ˌsək-, -ˌsəik-\ *n* : a compact electronic circuit consisting of elements of small size — **mi·cro·cir·cuit·ry** \-kə·trē\ *n*

mi·cro·cir·cu·la·tion \ˌmīkrōˌsərkyəˈlāshən\ *n* **1** : the part of the circulatory system made up of very fine channels (as capillaries or venules) **2** : circulation through very fine channels — **mi·cro·cir·cu·la·to·ry** \-ˈsərkyələˌtōrē, -ˌtȯrē\ *adj*

mic·ro·coc·cal \-ˌkäkəl\ *adj*: relating to or characteristic of micrococci < *micrococcal* enzymes >

mi·cro·code \ˈmīkrəˌkōd\ *n* : code used in microprogramming

mi·cro·com·put·er \ˌmī(ˌ)krōkəmˈpyüd·ə(r)\ *n* : a very small computer

mi·cro·culture \ˈmīkrōˌkəlchə(r)\ *n* **1** : the culture of a small group of human beings with limited perspective < those who have been eduated by experience or by learning to a broader view may escape the *microculture* of the specific group with which they are identified —H.L. Shapiro > **2** : a microscopic culture of cells or organisms — **mi·cro·cul·tur·al** \ˌmīkrōˌkəlch(ə)rəl\ *adj*

mi·cro·dis·tri·bu·tion \ˌmīkrōˌdistrəˈbyüshən\ *n* : the precise distribution of one or more kinds of organisms in a microhabitat or in part of an ecosystem < *microdistribution* of soil mites >

mi·cro·dot \ˈmīkrōˌdät\ *n* : a photographic reproduction of printed matter reduced to the size of a dot for ease or security of transmittal

mi·cro·ecol·o·gy \ˌmīkrōə̇ˈkäləjē, -eˈkäl-, -ēˈkäl-\ *n* : ecology of all or part of a small community (as a microhabitat or a housing development) — **mi·cro·eco·log·i·cal** \-ˌēkəˈläjə̇kəl, -ˌekəˈläj-\ *adj*

mi·cro·elec·trode* \ˌmīkrōə̇ˈlekˌtrōd\ *n* : a minute electrode; *esp* : one that is inserted in a living biological cell or tissue to study its electrical characteristics

mi·cro·elec·tron·ics \ˌmīkrōə̇ˌlekˈträniks, -ēks\ *n pl but sing in constr* : a branch of electronics that deals with the miniaturization of electronic circuits and components — **mi·cro·elec·tron·ic** \-ik, -ēk\ *adj* — **mi·cro·elec·tron·i·cal·ly** \-ə̇k(ə)lē, -li\ *adv*

mi·cro·en·cap·su·late \-ə̇nˈkapsəˌlāt\ *vt* : to enclose in a microcapsule < *microencapsulated* aspirin > — **mi·cro·en·cap·su·la·tion** \-ə̇nˌkapsəˈlāshən\ *n*

mi·cro·form* \ˈmīkrəˌfȯrm, -ˌfȯ(ə)m\ *n* **1** : a process or medium for reproducing printed matter in a much reduced size < store information in *microform* > < microfilm, microfiche, and other *microforms* > **2** : matter reproduced by microform or a copy of such matter < companies now producing *microforms* >

mi·cro·fun·gus \ˌmīkrōˈfəŋgəs\ *n* : a fungus (as a mold) with a microscopic fruiting body — **mi·cro·fun·gal** \-gəl\ *adj*

mi·cro·gauss \ˈmīkrōˌgau̇s\ *n* : one millionth of a gauss

mi·cro·graph·ics \ˌmīkrəˈgrafiks, -ēks\ *n pl but sing in constr* : the industry concerned with the manufacture and sale of graphic material in microform; *also* : the production of graphic material in microform — **mi·cro·graph·ic** \-ik, -ēk\ *adj*

mi·cro·im·age \ˈmīkrōˌimij, -ˌimēj\ *n* : an image (as on a microfilm) that is of greatly reduced size

mi·cro·in·struc·tion \ˌmīkrōə̇nˈstrəkshən\ *n* : a computer instruction corresponding to a single machine operation

mi·cro·ma·chin·ing \ˈmīkrōməˌshēniŋ, -ēŋ\ *n* : the removing (as in drilling, planing, or shaping) of small amounts of metal by action other than that of a sharp-edged tool < *micromachining* with an electron beam >

mi·cro·me·te·or·ite* \ˌmīkrōˈmed·ēəˌrīt\ *n* : a meteoritic particle of very small size — **mi·cro·me·te·or·it·ic** \ˌmīkrōˌmēd·ēəˈrid·ik\ *adj*

mi·cro·me·te·or·oid \ˌmīkrōˈmēd·ēəˌrȯid\ *n* : MICROMETEORITE

mi·cro·min·ia·ture \-ˈminēəˌchu̇(ə)r, -ˈminə̇ˌchu̇(ə)r, -ˈminyə-, -ə̇chər, -ˌt(y)u̇(ə)r\ *adj* **1** : MICROMINIATURIZED **2** : suitable for use with microminiaturized parts

mi·cro·min·ia·tur·iza·tion \-ˌminēəˌchu̇rə̇ˈzāshən, -ˌminə̇ˌ-, -ˌminyə-, -ə̇chər-, -ˌt(y)u̇r-\ *n* : the process of producing microminiaturized things

mi·cro·min·ia·tur·ized \-ˈminēəchəˌrīzd, -ˈminə̇chə-, -nyəchə-, -ˌtyu̇ˌrīzd\ *adj* : reduced to or produced in a very small size and esp. in a size smaller than one considered miniature < *microminiaturized* electronic circuit >

mi·cro·mod·ule \ˌmīkrōˈmäj(ˌ)ü(ə)l\ *n* : a microminiaturized module

mi·cro·mor·phol·o·gy \-mȯrˈfäləjē, -mȯ(ə)ˈf-\ *n* **1** : the microscopic structure of a material — used esp. with reference to soils **2** : minute morphological detail esp. as determined by electron microscopy; *also* : the study of such detail — **mi·cro·mor·pho·log·ic** \-ˌmȯrfəˈläjik\ *adj* — **mi·cro·mor·pho·log·i·cal** \-jə̇kəl\ *adj* — **mi·cro·mor·pho·log·i·cal·ly** \-jə̇k(ə)lē\ *adv*

mi·cro·pop·u·la·tion \-ˌpäpyəˈlāshən\ *n* **1** : a population of microorganisms **2** : the population of organisms within a small area

mi·cro·probe \ˈmīkrəˌprōb\ *n* : a device for microanalysis that operates by exciting radiation in a minute area or volume of material so that the composition may be determined by means of the emission spectrum

mi·cro·pro·ces·sor \ˌmīkrōˈpräsˌesə(r), prōs-\ *n* : a very small computer (as one on an IC chip)

mi·cro·pro·gram·ming \-ˈprōˌgramiŋ, -ˈprōgrəmiŋ\ *n* : the use of routines stored in memory rather than specialized circuits for controlling a device (as a computer) — **mi·cro·pro·gram** \-ˈprōˌgram, -ˈprōgrəm\ *n or vt*

mi·cro·pub·li·ca·tion \-ˌpəblə̇ˈkāshən\ *n* **1** : MICROPUBLISHING **2** : something published in microform

mi·cro·publishing \-ˈpəblə̇shiŋ\ *n* : the publishing of new or previously published material in microform — **mi·cro·pub·lish** \-ˈpəblish, -ēsh\ *vt* — **mi·cro·pub·lish·er** \-shə(r)\ *n*

mi·cro·punc·ture \-ˈpəŋ(k)chə(r)\ *n*: an extremely small puncture <a *micropuncture* of the nephron>

mi·cro·spo·ran·gi·ate \ˌmī(ˌ)krōspəˈranjēət\ *adj* : bearing or being microsporangia

mi·cro·state \ˈmīkrōˌstāt\ *n*: an independent nation of very small area and population <visiting statesmen get equal treatment, whether they represent a super power or a *microstate — Christian Science Monitor*>

mi·cro·sur·gery \ˌmīkrōˈsərj(ə)rē, -ˈsəj-, -ˈsəij-\ *n* : minute dissection or manipulation (as by a micromanipulator or laser beam) of living structures (as cells) for surgical or experimental purposes — **mi·cro·sur·gi·cal** \-jə̇kəl\ *adj*

mi·cro·teaching \ˈmīkrōˌtēchiŋ\ *n* : practice teaching in which a student teacher's teaching of a small class for a short time is videotaped for subsequent evaluation

mi·cro·text \-ˌtekst\ *n* : text in microform

mi·cro·tubule \ˌmīkrōˈt(y)ü(ˌ)byü(ə)l\ *n*: any of the minute cylindrical structures that are widely distributed in protoplasm and are made up of longitudinal fibrils — **mi·cro·tu·bu·lar** \-ˈt(y)übyələ(r)\ *adj*

mi·cro·vas·cu·lar \-ˈvaskyələ(r)\ *adj* : of, relating to, or constituting the part of the circulatory system made up of minute vessels (as venules or capillaries) that average less than 0.3 millimeter in diameter — **mi·cro·vas·cu·la·ture** \-ˈvaskyələˌchu̇(ə)r, -ˌt(y)u̇(ə)r\ *n*

mi·cro·vil·lus \-ˈviləs\ *n* : a microscopic projection of a tissue, a cell, or a cell organelle; *esp*: one of the fingerlike outward projections of some cell surfaces — **mi·cro·vil·lar** \-ˈvilər\ *adj* — **mi·cro·vil·lous** \-ləs\ *adj*

microwave oven \ˌmīkrəˌwāv-\ *n* : an oven in which food is cooked by the heat produced as a result of microwave penetration of the food

mid·course \ˌmidˌkō(ə)rs, -ˌkȯ(ə)rs, -ˌkōəs, -ˌkȯ(ə)s\ *adj* : being or relating to the part of a course (as of spacecraft) that is between the initial and final phases <a *midcourse* correction> — **mid·course** \ˈmidˈk-\ *n*

mid·cult \ˈmidˌkəlt\ *n* [*mid*dlebrow *cult*ure] : the artistic and intellectual culture that is neither highbrow culture nor lowbrow culture : middlebrow culture <fastidious literary people disdainful even of *midcult* —H.J. Muller>

middle America *n, often cap M* : the middle-class segment of the U.S. population <persuade *Middle America* to reduce its level of energy consumption —A.F. Buchan>; *esp* : the traditional or conservative element of the middle class <appealed to *Middle America* with his emphasis on such traditional middle-class values as patriotism, social stability, and individual initiative — *Current Biog.*> — **middle American** *n, often cap M*

midi \ˈmidē, -di\ *n* [*mid* + *-i* (as in *mini*)] : a dress, skirt, or coat that usu. extends to the mid-calf — called also respectively *midi dress, midi skirt, midi coat*

mil* \ˈmil\ *n* : thousand <found a salinity of 38.4 per *mil*>

millimicro- *comb form* [*milli-* thousandth (deriv. of L *mille* thousand) + *micro-* millionth, deriv. of Gk *mikros* small] : billionth <*millimicro*second>

mil·li·ra·di·an \ˌmiləˈrādēən\ *n* : one thousandth of a radian

mil·li·rem \ˈmiləˌrem\ *n* : one thousandth of a rem

mim·eo \ˈmimē(ˌ)ō\ *n* [short for *mimeographed*] : a mimeographed publication

mim–mem \ˈmimˈmem\ *adj* [*mim*icry + *mem*orization] : of, relating to, or being a drill pattern in which students repeat usu. in chorus a foreign language phrase supplied by their instructor

mind–blow·ing \ˈmīn(d)ˈblōiŋ\ *adj* **1** : PSYCHEDELIC 1a, 1b <some 400 *mind-blowing* experiences . . . initiated by sacred mushrooms, psilocybin, LSD or DMT —Howard Junker> **2** : mentally or emotionally exciting : overwhelming <on the third martini, a *mind-blowing* and terrible idea comes straight out of the glass into your head —James Dickey> — **mind·blow·er** \-ˈblō(ə)r, -ˈblōə\ *n*

mind–ex·pand·ing \ˈmīndə̇kˌspandiŋ\ *adj* : PSYCHEDELIC 1a <*mind-expanding* drugs>

mini \ˈminē, -ni\ *n* [*mini-*] **1** : a very small automobile : minicar **2** : a short skirt or dress that usu. extends to the mid-thigh — called also respectively *miniskirt* or *minidress*

mini- *comb form* [*mini*ature] : very small : miniature

miniature pin·scher \-ˈpinchə(r)\ *n* : a toy dog that suggests a small Doberman pinscher and measures 10 to 12½ inches in height at the withers

miniature schnau·zer \-ˈs(h)naüzə(r), -ˈshnaütsə(r)\ *n* : a schnauzer of a breed that is 12 to 14 inches in height and is classified as a terrier

mini·bike \ˈminē,bīk, -nə̇-\ *n* : a small one-passenger motorcycle having a low frame and elevated handlebars

mini·bus \-,bəs\ *n* : a small bus used esp. for short trips

mini·cab \-,kab\ *n* : a small car used as a taxicab

mini·com·put·er \ˈminēkəmˈpyüd·ə(r), -nə̇k-\ *n* : a small comparatively inexpensive computer

min·i·mal* \ˈminəməl\ *adj, often cap* : of, relating to, or being minimal art < *minimal* aluminum pieces —Grace H. Glueck >

minimal art *n* : abstract art (as painting or sculpture) consisting primarily of simple geometric forms executed in an impersonal style — **minimal artist** *n*

min·i·mal·ism \ˈminəmə,lizəm\ *n* : MINIMAL ART

min·i·mal·ist* \ˈminəmələ̇st\ *n* : MINIMAL ARTIST

minimalist *adj* : MINIMAL

mini·max \ˈminə̇,maks, -nē,m-\ *n* [*mini*mum + *max*imum] : the minimum of a set of maxima; *esp* : the smallest of a set of maximum possible losses each of which occurs in the most unfavorable outcome of a strategy followed by a participant in a situation governed by the theory of games — compare MAXIMIN

minimax principle *n* : a principle of choice for a decision problem: one should choose the action which minimizes the loss that he stands to suffer even under the worst circumstances

minimax the·o·rem \-ˈthēərəm, -ˈthi(ə)rəm\ *n* : a theorem in the theory of games: the lowest maximum expected loss equals the highest minimum expected gain

minimum* *n* : the lowest speed allowed on a highway

mini·pig \ˈminē,pig, -nə̇-\ *n* : a miniature pig bred for use in scientific research

mini·ski \-,skē\ *n* **1** : a short ski worn esp. by beginners **2** : a miniature ski worn by a skibobber

mini·state \-,stāt\ *n* : MICROSTATE

mini·sub \-,səb\ *n* : a very small submarine used esp. in research (as on the ocean bottom)

Min·ne·so·ta Mul·ti·pha·sic Personality Inventory \,minəˈsōd·ə,məltə̇ˈfāzik-, -tē-, -,tī-\ *n* [fr. the University of *Minnesota,* where it was developed] : a test of personal and social adjustment based on a complex scaling of the answers to an elaborate true or false test

miracle fruit *n* [fr. the fact that its fruit causes foods eaten after it to taste sweet] : a small shrubby tree (*Synsepalum dulcificum*) of the family Sapotaceae having a fruit that is a fleshy single-seeded berry; *also* : its fruit

mi·rex \ˈmī,reks\ *n* [prob. fr. pis*mire* + *ex*terminator] : a chlorinated-hydrocarbon insecticide $C_{10}Cl_{12}$ used esp. against ants

MIRV \ˈmərv\ *n* [*m*ultiple *i*ndependently targeted *r*eentry *v*ehicle] : a missile with two or more warheads that are designed to reenter the atmosphere on the way to separate enemy targets; *also* : any of the warheads of such a missile

mis·com·mu·ni·ca·tion \(ˌ)miskə,myünə̇ˈkāshən\ *n* [*mis-* bad, badly, not, opposite + *communication*] : failure to communicate clearly

mis·di·ag·nose \-ˈdīəg,nōs, -,nōz\ *vt* : to diagnose incorrectly — **mis·di·ag·no·sis** \-,dīəgˈnōsə̇s\ *n*

mis·ori·ent \-ˈōrē,ent, -ˈȯr-\ *vt* : to orient improperly or incorrectly — **mis·ori·en·ta·tion** \-,ōrēənˈtāshən, -,ȯr-, -ē,en-\ *n*

mis·sense \ˈmis,sen(t)s\ *n* [*mis-* + *-sense* (as in *nonsense*)] : genetic mutation involving alteration of one or more codons so that different amino acids are determined — compare NONSENSE

missionary position *n* [perh. so-called fr. the insistence of some missionaries that the traditional Western coital position is the only acceptable one] : a coital position in which the female lies on her back with the male on top of her

mist* *n* : a drink of alcoholic liquor (as Scotch) served over cracked ice and garnished with a twist of lemon peel

mi·to·gen \ˈmīd·əjən\ *n* [*mito-* mitosis + *-gen* producer] : a substance that induces mitosis

mi·to·gen·ic \ˌmīd·əˈjenik\ *adj* : producing mitosis — **mi·to·ge·nic·i·ty** \ˌmīd·əjə-ˈnisəd·ē\ *n*

mi·to·my·cin \ˌmīd·əˈmīsᵊn\ *n* [prob. fr. ISV *mito-* + *-mycin* substance obtained from a fungus, fr. *streptomycin*] : a complex of antibiotic substances which is produced by a Japanese streptomyces (*Streptomyces caespitosus*) and one form of which acts directly on DNA and is an effective antineoplastic agent

mi·to·spore \ˈmīd·əˌspō(ə)r, -ˌspȯ(ə)r, -ˌspōə, -ˌspȯ(ə)\ *n* : a haploid or diploid spore produced by mitosis

mix* *n* : a commercially prepared nonalcoholic mixture of ingredients for a mixed drink <mai tai *mix*>

mixed–me·dia \ˈmikstˈmēdēə\ *adj* : MULTIMEDIA

mixed media *n* : MULTIMEDIA

MLD *abbr* median lethal dose

MMPI *abbr* Minnesota Multiphasic Personality Inventory

¹mod \ˈmäd\ *adj, often cap* [short for *modern*] : modern, up-to-date; *esp* : bold, free, and unconventional in style, behavior, or dress <*mod* suits> <the *mod* look in clothes> <the world's most *mod* Prime Minister —*Forbes*>

²mod *n, often cap* : someone or something that is mod <dresses of white organza with skirts that miss the floor by six or eight inches await the *Mods* among us; the faint at heart may have them full length —*New Yorker*>

model* *n* : a system of postulates, data, and inferences presented as a mathematical description of an entity or state of affairs <a mathematical *model* of the physical world>

model* *vt* : to produce a representation or simulation of <using a computer to *model* a problem>

mo·dem \ˈmōˌdem\ *n* [*mo*dulator + *dem*odulator] : a device that converts signals from one form to a form compatible with another kind of equipment <a *modem* for transmitting computer data over telephone lines>

modesty panel *n* : a panel that fits across the front of a desk or table to conceal the legs of a person sitting there

modified American plan *n* : a hotel rate whereby guests are charged a fixed sum (as by the day or week) for room, breakfast, and dinner

mod·u·lar arithmetic \ˈmäjələ(r)-\ *n* : arithmetic that deals with whole numbers where the numbers are replaced by their remainders after division by a fixed number <5 hours after 10 o'clock is 3 o'clock because clocks follow a *modular arithmetic* with modulus 12>

mod·u·lar·i·ty \ˌmäjəˈlarəd·ē, -ler-\ *n* : the use of discrete functional units in building an electronic or mechanical system

mod·u·lar·ized \ˈmäjələˌrīzd\ *adj* : constructed of modules <*modularized* electronic equipment>

mod·ule* \ˈmäj(ˌ)ü(ə)l\ *n* **1** : any of a series of standardized units intended for use together <furniture *modules*> <instructional *modules*> **2** : an assembly of components that are packaged or mounted together and constitute a functional unit for an electronic or mechanical system <a *module* for a computer> **3** : an independent unit that constitutes a part of the total structure of a space vehicle <a propulsion *module*> **4 a** : a subset of an additive group that is also a group under addition **b** : a mathematical set that is a commutative group under addition and that is closed under multiplication which is distributive from the left or right or both by elements of a ring and for which $a(bx) = (ab)x$ or $(xb)a = x(ba)$ or both where a and b are elements of the ring and x belongs to the set

mod·u·lus* \ˈmäjələs\ *n* **1** : the factor by which a logarithm of a number to one base is multiplied to obtain the logarithm of the number to a new base **2** : the length of the radius vector from the origin to the point representing the number in the complex plane **3** : the number of different numbers used in a system of modular arithmetic

mo·gul \ˈmōgəl\ *n* [prob. of Scand origin; akin to Norw dial. *muge* heap, pile, fr. ON *mūgi*] : a bump in a ski run

mois·tur·ize \ˈmȯischəˌrīz\ *vt* **-ized; -iz·ing** : to add moisture to < *moisturize* the air > — **mois·tur·iz·er** \-ə(r)\ *n*

moldy fig *n* **1** : a devotee of traditional jazz **2** : one that is old-fashioned

mom–and–pop \ˌmämən(d)ˈpäp\ *adj, of a business* : small in size and owned or operated by one person or family < a *mom-and-pop* candy store >

moment of truth **1** : the final sword thrust in a bullfight **2** : a moment of crisis on the outcome of which much or everything depends < the lift-off of a . . . space vehicle with three men aboard is an awesome *moment of truth* —R.A. Petrone >

mon·e·ta·rism \ˈmänətəˌrizəm, ˈmən-, *also* ˈmōn-\ *n* [*monetary* + *-ism,* n. suffix] : a theory in economics: changes in the price level tend to vary directly and in the value of money inversely with the amount of money in circulation and the velocity of its circulation : quantity theory

mon·e·ta·rist \-tərəst, -ˌrist\ *n* : an adherent of monetarism

money* *n* — **on the money** : at exactly the right place or time

mon·go \ˈmäŋ(ˌ)gō\ *n, pl* **mongo** [Mongolian] **1** : a monetary unit of Outer Mongolia equal to $^1/_{100}$ tugrik **2** : a coin representing one mongo

monitor* *n* : software or hardware that monitors the operation of a system and esp. a computer system

[1]**mono** \ˈmän(ˌ)ō\ *adj* [short for *monophonic*] : of or relating to sound transmission, recording, or reproduction involving a single transmission path : monophonic < a *mono* phonograph record >

[2]**mono** *n, pl* **monos** **1** : a mono phonograph record **2** : mono reproduction < recorded in both *mono* and stereo >

[3]**mono** \ˈmän(ˌ)ō, *also* ˈmōn-\ *n* [short for *mononucleosis*] : the disease mononucleosis

mono·amine* \ˌmänōəˈmēn, *also* ˌmōnō-\ *n* : an amine RNH_2 having one organic substituent attached to the nitrogen atom; *esp* : one (as serotonin) that is functionally important in neural transmission

monoamine ox·i·dase \-ˈäksəˌdās, -ˌdāz\ *n* : an enzyme that deaminates monoamines and that affects the nervous system by breaking down monoamine neurotransmitters oxidatively

mono·am·i·ner·gic \ˌmänōˌaməˈnərjik, *also* ˌmōn-\ *adj* [*monoamine* + *erg-* work (fr. Gk *ergon*) + *-ic,* adj. suffix] : liberating or involving monoamines (as serotonin or norepinephrine) in neural transmission < *monoaminergic* neurons > < *monoaminergic* mechanisms >

mono·cha·sial \ˌmänəˈkāzh(ē)əl, ˌmōn-, -zēəl\ *adj* : of, relating to, or being a monochasium

mono·chrome* \ˈmänəˌkrōm, *also* ˈmōn-\ *adj* : characterized by reproduction or transmission of visual images in tones of gray rather than in colors : black-and-white < *monochrome* motion pictures >

mono·con·tam·i·nate \ˌmän(ˌ)ōkənˈtaməˌnāt, *also* ˌmōn(ˌ)ō- *or* -nə-\ *vt* [*mono-* one, single (deriv. of Gk *monos* single, alone) + *contaminate*] : to infect (a germ-free organism) with one kind of pathogen — **mono·con·tam·i·na·tion** \-kənˌtaməˈnāshən\ *n*

mono·func·tion·al \-ˈfəŋ(k)shnəl, -shənᵊl\ *adj* : of, relating to, or being a compound with one highly reactive site in the molecule (as in polymerization) < formaldehyde is a *monofunctional* reagent >

mono·germ \-ˌjərm, -ˌjəm, -ˌjəim\ *adj* [prob. fr. *mono-* + *germ*inate] : producing or being a fruit that gives rise to a single plant < a *monogerm* variety of sugar beet > — compare MULTIGERM

mono·ki·ni \ˌmänəˈkēnē\ *n* [*mono-* + *-kini* (as in *bikini*)] **1** : a topless bikini **2** : extremely brief shorts for men — **mono·ki·nied** \-nēd\ *adj*

mono·lith·ic* \ˌmänᵊlˈithik, ˌmōn-, -thēk\ *adj* **1** : formed from a single crystal < a *monolithic* silicon chip > **2** : produced in or on a monolithic chip < a *monolithic* circuit > **3** : consisting of or utilizing a monolithic circuit or circuits

mono·ploid* \ˈmänəˌplȯid, ˈmōn-\ *adj* : having or being the basic haploid number of chromosomes in a polyploid series of organisms

mono·pole \-ˌpōl\ *n* **1** : a single positive or negative electrical charge; *also* : a hypothetical north or south magnetic pole existing alone **2** : a radio antenna in the form of a single often straight radiating element

mono·sex·u·al \ˌmän(ˌ)ōˈseksh(ə)wəl, -shəl, *also* ˌmōn- *or* -nə-\ *adj* **1** : being or relating to a male or a female rather than a bisexual **2** : composed of or intended for individuals of one sex < *monosexual* schools > — **mono·sex·u·al·i·ty** \-ˌsekshəˈwaləd·ē, -i\ *n*

mono·some* \ˈmänəˌsōm, ˈmōn-\ *n* : a single ribosome

mon·ta·gnard* \ˌmōⁿˌtänˈyär(d), -ˌtan-; ˌmäntᵊnˈyärd, -tən-\ *n, often cap* : a member of a people inhabiting a highland region in southern Vietnam bordering on Cambodia — **montagnard** *adj, often cap*

Mon·te Car·lo \ˌmäntēˈkär(ˌ)lō-, -tə̇ˈk-\ *adj* [*Monte Carlo,* Monaco, city noted for its gambling casino] : of, relating to, or involving the use of random sampling techniques and often the use of computer simulation to obtain approximate solutions to mathematical or physical problems esp. in terms of a range of values each of which has a calculated probability of being the solution < *Monte Carlo* methods > < *Monte Carlo* calculations >

Mon·te·zu·ma's revenge \ˌmäntəˈzüməz-\ *n* [*Montezuma* II †1520 last Aztec ruler of Mexico] : diarrhea contracted in Mexico esp. by tourists

mon·uron \ˈmänyəˌrän, ˈmōn-\ *n* [*mono-* + *urea* + *-on* chemical compound] : a persistent herbicide $C_9H_{11}ClN_2O$ used esp. to control mixed broad-leaved weeds

moon·craft \ˈmünˌkraft\ *n* : MOONSHIP

moon·fall \-ˌfȯl\ *n* [*moon* + *-fall* (as in *landfall*)] : a landing on the moon

moon·flight \-ˌflīt\ *n* : a flight to the moon

moon·ing \ˈmüniŋ\ *n* [fr. E slang *moon* buttocks] : the practice of exposing one's buttocks (as through the window of a moving vehicle)

moon·port \ˈmünˌpō(ə)rt, -pȯ(ə)rt, -pōət, -pȯ(ə)t\ *n* : a place on earth equipped for sending spacecraft to the moon

moon·ship \-ˌship\ *n* : spacecraft for travel to the moon

moonshot \-ˌshät\ *or* **moon shoot** *n* : the act or an instance of launching a spacecraft on a course to the moon

moon·walk \-ˌwȯk\ *n* : an instance of walking on the moon — **moon·walk·er** \-ˌwȯkə(r)\ *n*

mo·ped \ˈmōˌped\ *n* [Sw, fr. *mo*tor motor + *ped*al pedal] : a lightweight low-powered motorbike that can be pedaled

MOR *abbr* middle of the road

morn·ing–af·ter pill \ˌmȯrniŋˈaftər-, ˌmȯ(ə)niŋˈaftə-\ *n* [fr. its being taken after rather than before intercourse] : an oral drug that blocks implantation of a fertilized egg in the human uterus and thereby interferes with pregnancy

morph \ˈmȯ(ə)rf, ˈmȯ(ə)f\ *n* [Gk *morphē* form] **1** : a local population of a species that consists of interbreeding organisms and is distinguishable from other populations by morphology or behavior though capable of interbreeding with them **2** : a phenotypic variant of a species

morph- *or* **morpho-*** *comb form* : relating to form and < *morpho*functional >

mor·phac·tin \mȯrˈfaktə̇n\ *n* [prob. fr. *morph-* form (deriv. of Gk *morphē*) + *act-* (fr. L *actus* motion) + *-in* chemical compound] : any of several synthetic fluorine-containing compounds that tend to produce morphological changes and suppress growth in plants

mor·pho·phys·i·ol·o·gy \ˌmȯr(ˌ)fōˌfizēˈäləjē\ *n* [ISV *morpho-* form (deriv. of Gk *morphē*) + *physiology*] : a branch of biology that deals with the interrelationships of structure and function — **mor·pho·phys·i·o·log·i·cal** \-ˌfizēəˈläjə̇kəl\ *adj*

Möss·bau·er effect \ˌmə(r)sˌbau̇(ə)r-, ˌməs-, ˌmœs-, ˌmes-\ *n* [Rudolph L. *Mössbauer* *b*1929 Ger. physicist] : the emission and absorption of gamma rays without recoil by various radioactive nuclei embedded in solids — compare NUCLEAR RESONANCE

mo·to·cross \ˈmōd·ōˌkrȯs\ *n* [*motor* + *cross*-country] : a motorcycle race on a tight closed course over natural terrain that includes steep hills, sharp turns, and often mud

motor home *n* : an automotive vehicle built on a truck or bus chassis and equipped as a self-contained traveling home

motor inn *or* **motor hotel** *n* : a usu. multistory urban motel

mous·sa·ka \müˈsäkə, ˈmüˌs-, ˌmüsäˈkä\ *n* [NGk *mousakas*] : a dish of ground meat (as lamb) and sliced eggplant often topped with a seasoned sauce

mouth hook *n* : one of a pair of hooked larval mouthparts of some two-winged flies that function as jaws

mox·i·bus·tion \¦mäksə¦bəschən\ *n* [*moxa* + connective *-i-* + *-bustion* (as in *combustion*)] : medical use of a moxa

mri·dan·ga \mrēˈdäŋgə, ˌmərē-\ *or* **mri·dan·gam** \-gəm\ *n* [Skt *mṛdaṅga*, prob. of imit. origin] : a drum of India that is shaped like an elongated barrel and has tuned heads of different diameters

mRNA *abbr* messenger RNA

Ms. \(ˈ)miz, *sometimes* (ˈ)mis\ *n* [prob. blend of *miss* and *Mrs.*] — used instead of *Miss* or *Mrs.* (as when the marital status of a woman is unknown or irrelevant) < *Ms.* Mary Smith >

MSW *abbr* **1** master of social welfare **2** master of social work

mule* *n, slang* : an individual who smuggles or delivers illicit drugs

mul·ti·cen·tric \¦məlˌtī¦sen·trik, -ltē-, -ltə̇-\ *adj* [*multi-* many, two or more (deriv. of L *multus* much, many) + *-centric* centered] : having multiple centers of origin <a *multicentric* tumor> — **mul·ti·cen·tri·cal·ly** \-trik(ə)lē\ *adv* — **mul·ti·cen·tric·i·ty** \-senˈtrisə̇d·ē\ *n*

mul·ti·com·pa·ny \-ˈkəmp(ə)nē, -ni\ *n* : a large corporate enterprise with interests in two or more separate industries

mul·ti·fac·to·ri·al* \-fakˈtōrēəl, -ˈtȯr-\ *or* **mul·ti·fac·tor** \-¦faktə(r)\ *adj* : having or involving a variety of elements <a *multifactorial* study>

mul·ti·germ \-¦jərm, -¦jəm, -¦jəim\ *adj* [prob. fr. *multi-* + *germ*inate] : producing or being a fruit cluster capable of giving rise to several plants <a *multigerm* variety of sugar beet> — compare MONOGERM

mul·ti·hull \-¦həl\ *adj* : having more than one hull <a *multihull* boat>; *also* : of or relating to multihull boats

mul·ti–in·dus·try \-¦indəstrē, -ri\ *adj* : active in or concerned with two or more separate industries < *multi-industry* companies >

mul·ti·lay·ered \-¦lāə(r)d, -¦le(ə)rd, -¦leəd\ *or* **mul·ti·lay·er** \-¦lāə(r), -¦le(ə)r, -¦leə\ *adj* : having or involving several distinct layers, strata, or levels < *multilayered* epidermis > < *multilayered* tropical rain forest > < *multilayered* insights >

mul·ti·mar·ket \¦məlˌtī¦märkə̇t, -ltē-, -ltə̇-, -¦mȧk-\ *adj* : MULTI-INDUSTRY

¹mul·ti·me·dia \-¦mēdēə\ *adj* : using, involving, or encompassing several media < *multimedia* kits for teachers > <a *multimedia* presentation> <just sat there — through movies on a triptych of screens, voices over microphones, and other *multimedia* distractions —Edith Oliver>

²multimedia *n pl but sing or pl in constr* : communication, entertainment, or art in which several media are employed

¹mul·ti·na·tion·al \-¦nashnəl, -shənᵊl\ *adj* **1 a** : of, relating to, or involving more than two nations <a *multinational* nuclear force> **b** : having divisions in more than two countries <a *multinational* corporation> **c** : of or relating to a multinational corporation <a *multinational* executive> **2** : of or relating to more than two nationalities <the attractive young Americans in the Islands are all proud of their *multinational* ancestry and mixed blood —*Amer. Labor*>

²multinational *n* : a multinational corporation

mul·ti·na·tion·al·ism \-ˈnashnəˌlizəm, -shənᵊlˌizəm\ *n* : the establishment or operation of multinational corporations

multiple re·gres·sion \-rə̇ˈgreshən, -rē-\ *n* : regression in which one variable is estimated by the use of more than one other variable

multiple store *n, chiefly Brit* : a chain store

mul·ti·plet* \ˈməltəplə̇t\ *n* **1** : any of two or more atomic, molecular, or nuclear quantum states that are usu. close together in energy and that arise from different relative orientations of angular momenta **2** : a group of spectral frequencies arising from transitions to or from a multiplet quantum state **3** : a group of elementary particles that are different in charge but similar in other properties (as mass)

mul·ti·ple–val·ued \ˌməltəpəlˈval(ˌ)yüd, -lyəd\ *adj* : having at least one and sometimes more of the values of the range associated with each value of the domain <a *multiple-valued* function>

mul·ti·pli·ca·tive identity \ˌməltəˈplikəd·iv-, ˌməltəpləˈkād·iv-\ *n* : an identity element (as 1 in the group of rational numbers without 0 under the operation of multiplication) that in a given mathematical system leaves unchanged any element by which it is multiplied

multiplicative inverse *n* : an element of a mathematical set that when multiplied by a given element yields the identity element — called also *reciprocal*

multiplier effect *n* : the effect of a relatively minor factor in precipitating a great change; *esp* : the effect of a relatively small change in one economic factor (as rate of saving or level of consumer credit) in inducing a disproportionate increase or decrease in another (as gross national product)

mul·ti·ply \ˈməltəˌplī\ *n, pl* **-plies** : an instance of multiplication performed by a computer; *also* : the means for performing multiplication

mul·ti·pro·cess·ing \ˌməlˌtīˈpräsˌesiŋ, -ltē-, -ltə-, -ˈpräsəs-, -ˈprōs-\ *n* : the processing of several computer programs at the same time esp. by a computer system with several processors sharing a single memory — **mul·ti·pro·ces·sor** \-sˌesə(r), -səs-\ *n*

mul·ti·pro·gram·ming \-ˈprōˌgramiŋ, -ˈprōgrəm-\ *n* : the technique of utilizing several interleaved programs concurrently in a single computer system — **mul·ti·pro·grammed** \-ˌprōˌgramd, -ˌprōgrəmd\ *adj*

mul·ti·pronged \-ˌprȯŋd\ *adj* **1** : having several prongs <*multipronged* fishing spears> **2** : having several distinct aspects or elements <a *multipronged* attack on the problem>

mul·ti·re·sis·tant \-rəˌzistənt, -rē-\ *adj* : biologically resistant to several toxic agents <*multiresistant* falciparum malaria> — **mul·ti·re·sis·tance** \-tən(t)s\ *n*

mul·ti·sen·so·ry \-ˌsen(t)s(ə)rē, -ri\ *adj* : relating to or involving perception by several physiological senses <*multisensory* teaching methods> <*multisensory* experience>

mul·ti·ver·si·ty \ˌməltəˈvərsəd·ē, -tēˌv-, -stē\ *n, pl* **-ties** [*multi-* + *-versity* (as in *university*)] : a very large university with many component schools, colleges, or divisions, with widely diverse functions (as the teaching of freshmen and the carrying on of advanced research), and with a large staff engaged in activities other than instruction and esp. in administration

mu–me·son* \ˈm(y)üˌmezˌän, -ˈmesˌän, -ˈmā-, ˈmē-\ *n* : MUON

mu·on* \ˈmyüˌän\ *n* : an unstable lepton that is common in the cosmic radiation near the earth's surface, has a mass 206.77 times the mass of the electron and an average lifetime of 2.20×10^{-6} second, and exists in negative and positive forms related as particle and antiparticle — **mu·on·ic** \myüˈänik\ *adj*

mu·ram·ic acid \myu̇ˌramək-\ *n* [*mur-* (fr. L *murus* wall) + glucos*am*ide + *-ic*, adj. suffix] : an amino sugar $C_9H_{17}NO_7$ that is a lactic acid derivative of glucosamine and is found esp. in bacterial cell walls and in blue-green algae

mu·rein \ˈmyu̇rēən, ˈmyu̇(ə)rˌēn\ *n* [*mur*amic acid + *-ein* chemical compound] : a polymer that is composed of alternating units of muramic acid and glucosamine bearing an acetyl group and that is characteristic of the cell walls of prokaryotic cells

Murphy's Law \ˌmərfēz-, ˌməf-, ˌməif-\ *n* [fr. the name *Murphy*] : an observation: anything that can go wrong will go wrong <it has been established that computers are followers of *Murphy's Law* —P.H. Dorn>

Muslim* *n* : BLACK MUSLIM

mu·ta·ge·nic·ity \ˌmyüd·əjəˈnisəd·ē\ *n* [*mutagenic* + *-ity*, n. suffix] : the capacity to induce mutations

mu·ta·ro·tase \ˌmyüd·əˈrōˌtās, -āz\ *n* [*mutarot*ation + *-ase* enzyme] : an isomerase found esp. in mammalian tissues that catalyzes the interconversion of anomeric forms of certain sugars

mu·ta·tor gene \ˌmyüˌtād·ə(r)-\ *also* **mutator** \ˈmyüˌtād·ə(r), myüˈtād·ə(r)\ *n* [L *mutator* one that changes, fr. *mutatus*, past part. of *mutare* to change] : a gene that increases the mutability of one or more other genes

Mu·zak \ˈmyüˌzak\ *trademark* — used for recorded background music

MV* *abbr* main verb
MVP *abbr* most valuable player
MY *abbr, often not cap* million years
my·co·plas·ma \ˌmīkōˈplazmə\ *n, pl* **my·co·plasmas** *or* **my·co·plas·ma·ta** \-məd·ə\ : a microorganism of the genus *Mycoplasma* — **my·co·plas·mal** \-məl\ *adj*
my·co·tox·in \-ˈtäksən\ *n* [*myco-* fungus (deriv. of Gk *mykēs*) + *toxin*] : a poisonous substance produced by a fungus and esp. a mold — compare AFLATOXIN — **my·co·tox·ic** \-ˌtäksik\ *adj* — **my·co·tox·ic·i·ty** \-ˌtäkˈsisəd·ē\ *n* — **my·co·tox·i·co·sis** \-ˌtäksəˈkōsəs\ *n*
my·elo·fi·bro·sis \ˌmīəlōfīˈbrōsəs\ *n* [NL, fr. *myelo-* marrow, spinal cord (fr. NL, fr. Gk *myelos* marrow, fr. *mys* mouse, muscle) + *fibrosis*] : an anemic condition in which bone marrow becomes fibrotic and the liver and spleen usu. exhibit development of blood cell precursors — **my·elo·fi·bro·tic** \-ˈbräd·ik\ *adj*
my·e·lo·pro·lif·er·a·tive \-prəˈlifəˌrād·iv, -ˈlif(ə)rəd·-\ *adj* : of, relating to, or being a disorder (as leukemia) marked by excessive proliferation of bone marrow elements and esp. blood cell precursors
My·lar \ˈmīˌlär\ *trademark* — used for a polyester film
myo·elec·tric \ˌmīōəˌlek·trik, -ēˌl-\ *also* **myo·elec·tri·cal** \-kəl\ *adj* [*mys-* muscle (deriv. of Gk *mys* mouse, muscle) + *electric*] : of, relating to, or utilizing electricity generated by muscle — **myo·elec·tri·cal·ly** \-k(ə)lē-, -li\ *adv*
myo·fil·a·ment \-ˈfiləmənt\ *n* : one of the individual filaments of actin or myosin that make up a myofibril
mys·te·ri·um \məˈstirēəm, -tēr-\ *n* [NL, fr. E *mystery* + NL *-ium* chemical radical] : a source of fluctuating radio emissions in the Milky Way galaxy held to be excited hydroxyl radicals
myxo·vi·rus \ˈmiksəˌvīrəs\ *n* [NL, fr. *myxo-* mucus, slime (deriv. of Gk *myxa* lampwick, nasal slime) + *virus*; fr. its affinity for certain mucins] : any of a group of rather large RNA-containing viruses that includes influenza and mumps viruses — **myxo·vi·ral** \ˌmiksəˌvīrəl\ *adj*

N

n* *abbr* nano-
Nab·o·kov·ian \ˌnabəˈkōvēən, -ˈkȯv-, -ˈkȯfēən\ *adj* [Vladimir Vladimirovich *Nabokov* *b*1899 Am. (Russ.-born) novelist & poet] : of, relating to, or suggestive of Vladimir Nabokov or his writings < *Nabokovian* marginal people inhabiting interims and delusions —Guy Davenport >
NAD \ˌe(ˌ)nāˈdē\ *n* : NICOTINAMIDE-ADENINE DINUCLEOTIDE
NADP \ˌeˌnā(ˌ)dēˈpē\ *n* : NICOTINAMIDE-ADENINE DINUCLEOTIDE PHOSPHATE
nai·ra \ˈnī(ə)rə\ *n* [alter. of *Nigeria*, country in West Africa] **1** : the basic monetary unit of Nigeria **2** : a coin or note representing one naira
naive* *adj* : not previously subjected to experimentation or to a particular experimental situation < experimentally *naive* rats > ; *also* : not having previously used a particular drug (as marijuana)
na·led \ˈnāˌled\ *n* [origin unknown] : a short-lived insecticide $C_4H_7O_4PBr_2Cl_2$ of relatively low toxicity to warm-blooded animals that is used esp. to control crop pests and mosquitoes
na·li·dix·ic acid \ˌnāləˌdiksik-\ *n* [perh. fr. *na*phthyr*idi*ne, $C_8H_6N_2$ (fr. *naphth*alene + p*yridine*) + carbo*xy lic acid*] : an antibacterial agent $C_{12}H_{12}N_2O_3$ that is used esp. in the treatment of genitourinary infections

nal·ox·one \'naləkˌsōn\ *n* [*N-al*lyl + hydr*oxyl* + *-one* oxygen compound] : a potent antagonist $C_{19}H_{21}NO_4$ of narcotic drugs and esp. morphine
name of the game : the necessary thing to do, have, or strive for : the essential quality or matter <patience is the *name of the game* in coastal duck hunting —Dick Beals> <in bicycle design, weight reduction is the *name of the game* —Harlan Meyer>
NAND \'nand\ *n* [*not AND*] : a computer logic circuit that produces an output which is the inverse of that of an AND circuit
nan·no·fos·sil \ˌnanō'fäsəl\ *n* [*nanno-* dwarf (deriv. of Gk *nannos, nanos*) + *fossil*] : a fossil of nannoplankton
nano·me·ter \'nanəˌmēd·ə(r)\ *n* [ISV *nano-* billionth (fr. L *nanus* dwarf, fr. Gk *nannos, nanos*) + *meter*] : one billionth of a meter
nano·sec·ond \-ˌsekənd, -ənt\ *n* : one billionth of a second — abbr. *nanosec, nsec*
narc *or* **nark** \'närk, 'nȧk\ *n* [short for *narcotics agent*] : one (as a government agent) who investigates narcotics violations
narcotic* *n* : a drug (as marijuana or LSD) that is subject to restriction similar to that of addictive narcotics whether in fact it is physiologically narcotic and addictive or not
national seashore *n* : a recreational area adjacent to a seacoast and maintained by the federal government
Native American* *adj* **1** : of or relating to Native Americans <*Native American* languages> **2** : of American Indian descent <*Native American* students>
Native American* *n* : an American Indian
na·tri·ure·sis \ˌnā·trē(y)əˌrēsəs, ˌna·-\ *also* **na·tru·re·sis** \-trəˌrē-\ *n* [NL, fr. *natri*um sodium + *uresis* urination] : excessive loss of cations and esp. sodium in the urine — **na·tri·uret·ic** \-trē(y)əˌred·ik\ *adj or n*
natural* *adj* : AFRO — **natural** *n*
natural food *n* : food that contains no additives (as preservatives and artificial flavorings)
natural language* *n* : the language of ordinary speaking and writing — distinguished from *machine language*
natural scientist *n* : a specialist in natural science
nature trail *n* : a trail (as through a woods) for facilitating the enjoyment or study of natural surroundings
NEB *abbr* New English Bible
neb·bish \'nebish\ *n* [Yiddish *nebach, nebech* poor thing (used interjectionally), of Slav origin; akin to Czech *neboh* wretched, Pol *nieboże* poor creature] : a timid, meek, or ineffectual person <always plays *nebbishes* named Claude — in fantasies, Claude is a tiger; in life, old ladies have to help him across the street —Chris Chase>
negative income tax *n* : a system of federal subsidy payments to families with incomes below a stipulated level proposed as a substitute for or supplement to welfare payments
negative transfer *n* : the impeding of learning or performance in a situation by the carry-over of learned responses from another situation — called also *negative transfer effect*
ne·gri·tude \'nēgrəˌtüd, 'neg-, -ˌtyüd\ *n* [F *négritude,* fr. *nègre* Negro + connective *-i-* + *-tude,* n. suffix] **1** : a consciousness of and pride in the cultural and physical aspects of the African heritage **2** : the state of being a Negro
Ne·gro·ness \'nē(ˌ)grōnəs; *esp South* 'ni(ˌ)-, 'nigrə-, 'nēgrə-\ *n* : the quality or state of being Negro : NEGRITUDE
ne·gro·ni \nə'grōnē, -ni\ *n, often cap* [prob. fr. the name *Negroni*] : a cocktail consisting of sweet vermouth, bitters, and gin
Neh·ru \'ne(ə)r(ˌ)ü, 'nā(ˌ)rü\ *adj* [Jawaharlal *Nehru* †1964 Indian nationalist] : MAO <a *Nehru* jacket>
neo·co·lo·nial·ism \ˌnē(ˌ)ōkə'lōnyəˌlizəm, -nēə-\ *n* [*neo-* new (fr. Gk *neos*) + *colonialism*] : the economic and political policies by which a Great Power indirectly maintains or extends its influence over other areas or peoples — **neo·co·lo·nial·ist** \-nyələst, -nēə-\ *n or adj*

neo·cor·ti·cal \ˌnēōˈkȯrtəkəl, -ˈkȯ(ə)d-, -ēkəl\ *adj* : of or relating to the neocortex

neo–Da·da \ˈnēōˈdä(ˌ)dä, -ˈdȧ(ˌ)dȧ\ *n* : an anti-art movement esp. of the late 1950s and the 1960s based on tenets similar to those of Dada but having more interest in the object than Dada claimed to have; *broadly* : JUNK ART — **neo–Da·da·ism** \-ˌizəm; -ˈdäˌdizəm, -ˈdȧˌdizəm\ *n* — **neo–Da·da·ist** \-ˌist; -ˈdäˌdäəst, -ˈdȧˌdȧəst, -ˌdəst\ *adj or n*

neur·amin·i·dase \ˌn(y)ürəˈminəˌdās, -ü-, -āz\ *n* [*neuramin*ic acid + *-idase* (as in *glucosidase*)] : a hydrolytic enzyme that is found esp. in microorganisms of the respiratory or intestinal tract and that splits mucoproteins by breaking a glucoside link

neu·ris·tor \n(y)üˈristə(r)\ *n* [*neur*on + trans*istor;* fr. its functioning like a neuron and not requiring the use of transistors] : a usu. electronic device along which a signal propagates with uniform velocity and without attenuation

neu·ro·ac·tive \ˈn(y)ürōˈaktiv, -ü-\ *adj* [*neuro-* nerve, neural (deriv. of Gk *neuron* nerve, sinew) + *active*] : stimulating neural tissue < *neuroactive* substances >

neu·ro·bi·ol·o·gy \-bīˈäləjē\ *n* : a branch of the life sciences that deals with the anatomy, physiology, and pathology of the nervous system — **neu·ro·bio·log·i·cal** \-ˌbīəˈläjəkəl\ *adj* — **neu·ro·bio·log·i·cal·ly** \-k(ə)lē\ *adv* — **neu·ro·bi·ol·o·gist** \-bīˈäləjəst\ *n*

neu·ro·chem·is·try \-ˈkeməstrē\ *n* : the study of the chemical makeup and activities of nervous tissue — **neu·ro·chem·i·cal** \-ˈkeməkəl\ *adj* — **neu·ro·chem·ist** \-ˈkeməst\ *n*

neu·ro·en·do·crine* \-ˈendəkrən, -ˌkrīn, -ˌkrēn\ *adj* : of, relating to, characterized by, or being a neurosecretion or the process of neurosecretion

neu·ro·en·do·crin·ol·o·gy \-ˌendəkrəˈnäləjē\ *n* : a branch of the life sciences dealing with neurosecretion and the physiological interaction between the central nervous system and the endocrine system — **neu·ro·en·do·crin·o·log·i·cal** \-ˌendəkrənəˈläjəkəl\ *adj*

neu·ro·he·mal organ *also* **neu·ro·hae·mal organ** \ˌn(y)ürōˌhēməl-, -ü-\ *n* [*neuro-* + *hem-* blood (deriv. of Gk *haima*) + *-al,* adj. suffix] : an organ (as a corpus cardiacum of an insect) that releases stored neurosecretory substances into the blood

neu·ro·hy·po·phy·se·al *or* **neu·ro·hy·po·phy·si·al** \ˈn(y)ürō(ˌ)hīˈpäfəˈsēəl, -ü-, -ˈhīpə-, -ˈzē-, -ˈhīpəˈfiz-\ *adj* : of, relating to, or secreted by the neurohypophysis < *neurohypophyseal* hormones >

neu·ro·ki·nin \-ˈkīnən\ *n* : a vasodilator kinin that may be a cause of migraine headaches

neu·ro·lept·an·al·ge·sia \ˈn(y)ürōˌlepˌtanᵊlˈjēzhə, -ü-, -z(h)ēə\ *or* **neu·ro·lep·to·an·al·ge·sia** \ˌn(y)ürōˈleptōˌan-, -ü-\ *n* [NL, fr. ISV *neurolept-* or *neurolepto-* (fr. *neuroleptic*) + *analges*ic + NL *-ia* (as in *analgesia*)] : joint administration of a tranquilizing drug and an analgesic esp. for relief of surgical pain — **neu·ro·lept·an·al·ge·sic** \ˈn(y)ürōˌlepˌtanᵊlˈjēzik\ *adj*

neu·ro·lep·tic \ˌn(y)ürōˈleptik, -ü-\ *n* [ISV *neuro-* + psycho*leptic;* orig. formed as F *neuroleptique*] : a drug used to reduce mental disturbance (as anxiety and tension) in people and animals : tranquilizer — **neuroleptic** *adj*

neu·ro·phar·ma·col·o·gy \ˈn(y)ürōˌfärməˈkäləjē, -ü-\ *n* : a branch of medical science dealing with the action of drugs on and in the nervous system — **neu·ro·phar·ma·co·log·ic** \-ˌfärməkəˈläjək\ *adj* — **neu·ro·phar·ma·co·log·i·cal** \-ˌfärməkəˈläjəkəl\ *adj* — **neu·ro·phar·ma·col·o·gist** \-ˈkäləjəst\ *n*

neu·ro·psy·chic \-ˈsīkik\ *also* **neu·ro·psy·chi·cal** \-ˈsīkəkəl\ *adj* : of or relating to both the mind and the nervous system as affecting mental processes

neu·ro·sci·ence \-ˈsīən(t)s\ *n* : a branch (as neurology or neurophysiology) of the life sciences that deals with the anatomy, physiology, biochemistry, or molecular biology of nerves and nervous tissue and esp. with their relation to behavior and learning — **neu·ro·sci·en·tist** \-əntəst\ *n*

neu·ro·sen·so·ry \-ˈsen(t)s(ə)rē\ *adj* : of or relating to afferent nerves < *neurosensory* control of feeding behavior >

neu·ros·po·ra \n(y)üˈräspərə\ *n* : a fungus of the genus *Neurospora*

neu·ro·trans·mit·ter \ˈn(y)ürōˈtran(t)smid·ə(r), -ü-, -tranz-\ *n* : a chemical substance (as norepinephrine or acetylcholine) that transmits nerve impulses across a synapse

neu·ter·cane \ˈn(y)üd·ə(r),kān\ *n* [L *neuter* neither + E *-cane* (as in hurricane); from the difficulty of classifying it as either hurricane or frontal storm] : a subtropical cyclone that is usu. less than 100 miles in diameter and that draws energy from sources common to both the hurricane and the frontal cyclone

neutron star *n* [fr. the hypothesis that the cores of such stars are composed entirely of neutrons] : any of various hypothetical very dense celestial objects that consist of closely packed nuclear particles resulting from the collapse of a much larger stellar body and that may be detectable through their emission of X rays

new drug *n* : a drug that has not been declared safe and effective by qualified experts under the conditions prescribed, recommended, or suggested on the label and that may be a new chemical formula or an established drug prescribed for use in a new way

new economics *n pl but usu sing in constr* : an economic concept that is a logical extension of Keynesianism and that holds that appropriate fiscal and monetary maneuvering can maintain healthy economic growth and prosperity indefinitely

new issue *n* : a new security or an additional amount of a security made available for the first time to the general public

New Left *n* : a political movement originating in the U.S. in the 1960s that is composed chiefly of students and various militant groups and that actively advocates (as by demonstrations) radical changes in prevailing political, social, and educational practices — **new leftist** *n, often cap N&L*

new math *or* **new mathematics** *n* : mathematics that is based on set theory esp. as taught in elementary and secondary schools

new·speak \ˈn(y)ü,spēk\ *n, often cap* [*Newspeak*, a language "designed to diminish the range of thought" in the novel *Nineteen Eighty-Four* (1949) by George Orwell †1950 Eng. author] : propagandistic language characterized by euphemism, circumlocution, and the inversion of customary meanings <specializes in "outplacement"; that is, helping a company get rid of people it doesn't want and finding new jobs for them . . . the "terminating executive" or "candidate," as he is called in the *newspeak* of the trade —Jeremy Main>

new town* *n* : an urban development comprising a small to medium-size city with a broad range of housing and planned industrial, commercial, and recreational facilities

new wave *n, often cap N&W* [trans. of F *nouvelle vague*] : a cinematic movement that is characterized by improvisation, abstraction, and subjective symbolism and that often makes use of experimental photographic techniques

ngwee \eŋˈgwē, en-\ *n, pl* **ngwee** [native name in Zambia, lit., bright] **1** : a monetary unit of Zambia equal to $^1/_{100}$ kwacha **2** : a coin representing one ngwee

ni·al·amide \nīˈalə,mīd, -əməd\ *n* [*ni*cotinic acid + *a*myl + *amide*] : an antidepressant drug $C_{16}H_{18}N_4O_2$ that is an inhibitor of monoamine oxidase

nic·o·tin·amide–ad·e·nine di·nu·cle·o·tide \,nikəˌtēnə,mīdˌadᵊn,ēn,dīˌn(y)üklēə,tīd, -ˌtin-, -əməd-, -ᵊnən-\ *n* : a coenzyme $C_{21}H_{27}N_7O_{14}P_2$ of numerous dehydrogenases that occurs in most cells and plays an important role in all phases of intermediary metabolism as an oxidizing agent or when in the reduced form as a reducing agent for various metabolites

nicotinamide–adenine dinucleotide phos·phate \-ˌfäs,fāt\ *n* : a coenzyme $C_{21}H_{28}N_7O_{17}P_3$ of numerous dehydrogenases (as that acting on glucose-6-phosphate) that occurs esp. in red blood cells and plays a role in intermediary metabolism similar to nicotinamide-adenine dinucleotide but acting often on different metabolites

nig·ger* \ˈnigə(r)\ *n* : a member of a socially disadvantaged class of persons <it's time for somebody to lead all of America's *niggers*. . . . And by this I mean the Young, the Black, the Brown, the Women, the Poor—all the people who feel left out of the political process —R.V. Dellums>

night·glow \ˈnīt,glō\ *n* [*night* + air*glow*] : airglow seen during the night

-nik \(,)nik\ *n suffix* [Yiddish, fr. Pol & Russ] : one connected with or characterized by being <peace*nik*> <neat*nik*>

nil·po·tent \ˌnil,pōtᵊnt\ *adj* [L *nil* nothing + *potent-, potens* having power] : equal to zero when raised to some power <*nilpotent* matrices>

nit \ˈnit\ *n* [ISV, fr. L *nitēre* to shine] : a unit of brightness equal to one candle per square meter of cross section perpendicular to the rays

nit·pick \ˈnit,pik\ *vi* [back-formation fr. *nit-picking*] : to engage in nit-picking <the program was so unusual and adventurous . . . that nobody was inclined to *nitpick* —H.C. Schonberg> — **nit·pick·er** \-ə(r)\ *n*

nit–pick·ing \-iŋ\ *n* [fr. *nit* louse egg, young louse] : minute and usu. petty criticism <an impish parody of the pretensions and *nit-picking* of academic scholarship —*Current Biog.*>

ni·tro·fu·ran·to·in \ˌnī·(ˌ)trōfyəˈrantəwən\ *n* [*nitrofuran* + hydan*toin* a crystalline compound $C_3H_4N_2O_2$] : a nitrofuran derivative $C_8H_6N_4O_5$ that is a broad-spectrum antimicrobial agent esp. valuable in urinary tract infections

ni·tro·ge·nase \ˌnī·ˈträjəˌnās, ˈnī·trəj-, -āz\ *n* [*nitrogen* + *-ase* enzyme] : an enzyme that contains iron and molybdenum and that catalyzes the conversion of molecular nitrogen into ammonia in nitrogen fixation

nitrogen nar·co·sis \-närˈkōsəs, -näˈk-\ *n* : a state of euphoria and exhilaration that occurs when nitrogen in normal air enters the bloodstream at approximately seven times atmospheric pressure (as in deep-water diving) — called also *rapture of the deep*

nit·ty–grit·ty \ˌnid·ēˌgrid·ē\ *n* [origin unknown] : what is essential or basic : specific practical details <getting down to the *nitty-gritty*> <has kept the *nitty-gritty* of politics as background for what is essentially a novel of character —Patrick Anderson> — **nitty–gritty** *adj*

nob·ble* \ˈnäbəl\ *vt* **nob·bled; nob·bling** \-b(ə)liŋ\ *Brit* : to get hold of : catch, nab <say the lion had caught the Admiral, and the General was trying to rescue his brother and got *nobbled*, too —Peter Dickinson>

node* *n* : the termination or intersection of lines or curves : vertex

no–fault \ˌnōˌfȯlt\ *adj* **1** : of, relating to, or being a motor vehicle insurance plan under which an accident victim is compensated usu. up to a stipulated limit for actual losses (as medical bills and lost wages) but not for nuisance claims (as of pain or suffering) by his own insurance company regardless of who is responsible for the accident **2** : of, relating to, or being a divorce law according to which neither party is held responsible for the breakdown of the marriage

noise* *n* **1** : electromagnetic radiation (as light or radio waves) that is composed of several frequencies and that involves random changes in frequency or amplitude **2** : irrelevant or meaningless bits or words occurring along with desired information (as in a documentary search or a computer output) <retrieving a small subset of high-relevance documents with very little *noise* —*Amer. Documentation*>

noise pol·lu·tion \-pəˌlüshən\ *n* : environmental pollution consisting of annoying or harmful noise (as of automobiles or jet airplanes) — called also *sound pollution*

no–knock \ˌnōˌnäk\ *adj* : of, relating to, or being the entry by police into private premises without knocking and without identifying themselves (as to make an arrest) <suggests that the name of the *no-knock* law be changed to something more felicitous, like "quick-entry" —Elizabeth B. Drew> — **no–knock** *n*

no–load \ˌnōˌlōd\ *adj* : sold at net asset value <*no-load* mutual funds>

nominal* *adj* : being according to plan : falling within a range of acceptable planned limits : satisfactory <everything was *nominal* during the spacecraft launch> <the satellite had a *nominal* orbit>

nominal* *n* **1** : a linguistic form (as English *boy* or *he*) that inflects for number or case or for both **2** : a word or word group functioning as a noun normally functions

non·ad·di·tive \(ˈ)nänˌadəd·iv, -tiv\ *adj* [*non-* not (deriv. of L *non*) + *additive*] **1** : not having a numerical value equal to the sum of values for the component parts **2** : of, relating to, or being a genic effect that is not additive — **non·ad·di·tiv·i·ty** \-ˌadəˈtivəd·ē\ *n*

non·aligned \ˌnänᵊlˌīnd\ *adj* : not allied with other nations and esp. with either the Communist or the non-Communist blocs <*nonaligned* countries>

non·align·ment \ˌnänᵊlˈīnmənt\ *n* : the condition of a state or government that is nonaligned

non·book \ˈnänˌbu̇k, *sometimes* ˈnən-\ *n* : a book which has little literary merit or factual information and which is often a compilation (as of pictures or press clippings) <a new *nonbook* (transcribed from a series of TV interviews) —William Brandon>

non·can·di·date \(ˈ)nänˈkan(d)əˌdāt, -ədət\ *n* : one who is not a candidate; *esp* : one who has declared himself not a candidate for a particular political office < the Republican Party's most insistent *noncandidate* for the presidential nomination —David Holstrom > — **non·can·di·da·cy** \-ˈkan(d)ədəsē, -si\ *n*

non·chro·mo·so·mal \ˌnänˌkrōməˈsōməl, *sometimes* ˌnən-\ *adj* **1** : not situated on a chromosome **2** : not involving chromosomes

non·cross·over \(ˈ)nänˈkrȯˌsōvə(r)\ *adj* : having or being chromosomes that have not participated in genetic crossing-over < *noncrossover* offspring >

non·dairy \ˌnänˈde(ə)rē, -ˈda(ə)rē, *sometimes* ˌnən-\ *adj* : containing no milk or milk products < *nondairy* coffee lightener >

non·de·struc·tive \-dəˈstrəktiv\ *adj* : not destructive; *specif* : not causing destruction of material being investigated or treated < *nondestructive* testing of metal > — **non·de·struc·tive·ly** \-lē, -li\ *adv*

non·di·a·bet·ic \-ˌdīəˈbed·ik\ *adj* : not affected with diabetes — **nondiabetic** *n*

non·dia·paus·ing \-ˈdīəˌpȯziŋ\ *adj* **1** : not having a diapause **2** : not being in a state of diapause

non·dis·crim·i·na·tion \-dəˌskriməˈnāshən\ *n* : the absence or avoidance of discrimination < *nondiscrimination* in employment > — **non·dis·crim·i·na·to·ry** \-dəˈskrimənəˌtōrē, -ˌtȯrē\ *adj*

non·di·vid·ing \-dəˈvīdiŋ\ *adj* : not undergoing cell division

non·drink·er \(ˈ)nänˈdriŋkə(r)\ *n* : one who abstains from alcoholic beverages

non·drink·ing \-ˈdriŋkiŋ\ *adj* : abstaining from alcoholic beverages <a *nondrinking* family >

non·empty \ˌnänˈem(p)tē, *sometimes* ˌnən-\ *adj* : not empty; *specif* : containing at least one element < *nonempty* sets >

non·en·zy·mat·ic \-ˌenzəˈmad·ik\ *or* **non·en·zy·mic** \-(ˌ)enˈzīmik\ *also* **non·en·zyme** \-ˈenˌzīm\ *adj* : not involving the action of enzymes < *nonenzymatic* cleavage of protein > — **non·en·zy·mat·i·cal·ly** \-ˌenzəˈmad·ək(ə)lē\ *adv*

non·event \ˈnänəˈvent, -ēˈv-\ *n* **1** : a highly publicized event of little intrinsic interest <the . . . press giggled and yawned as it went through the motions of covering that dreaded occupational bane, the *nonevent* —Burr Snider > **2** : an occurrence that is officially ignored <this week's anniversary of his death is a Soviet *nonevent* —*Newsweek*>

non·flu·en·cy \(ˌ)nänˈflüən(t)sē\ *n* **1** : lack of fluency **2** : an instance of nonfluency — **non·flu·ent** \-ˈflüənt\ *adj*

non·graded \-ˈgrādəd\ *adj* : having no grade levels < *nongraded* schools >

non·green \-ˈgrēn\ *adj* : not green; *specif* : containing no chlorophyll <fungi and other *nongreen* saprophytes >

non·he·ro \ˈnänˈhē(ˌ)rō, -ˈhi(ə)r(ˌ)ō\ *n* : ANTIHERO

non·hi·ber·nat·ing \(ˈ)nänˈhībə(r)ˌnād·iŋ\ *adj* **1** : not being in hibernation **2** : not capable of hibernation <a *nonhibernating* strain of hamster >

non·histone \-ˈhistˌōn\ *adj* : rich in aromatic amino acids and esp. tryptophan < *nonhistone* proteins >

non·host \ˈnänˈhōst\ *n* : a plant that is not attacked or parasitized by a particular organism

non·iden·ti·cal \ˌnän(ˌ)īˈdentəkəl, ˌnänəˈd-, *sometimes* ˌnən-\ *adj* : not identical: **a** : different < *nonidentical* terms > **b** : derived from two ova : fraternal < *nonidentical* twins >

non·in·sec·ti·ci·dal \-(ˌ)inˌsektəˈsīdᵊl\ *adj* **1** : lacking an insecticidal action **2** : not involving the use of an insecticide

non·neg·a·tive \-ˈnegəd·iv\ *adj* : not negative : being either positive or zero <a *nonnegative* integer >

non·neo·plas·tic \-ˌnēəˈplastik, -ˌnēō-\ *adj* : not being or not caused by neoplasms < *nonneoplastic* diseases >

non·nu·cle·ar \-ˈn(y)üklēə(r), ÷ -kyələ(r)\ *adj* **1** : not producing or involving a nuclear explosion <a *nonnuclear* bomb > <a *nonnuclear* mining blast > **2** : not operating by or involving atomic energy <a *nonnuclear* propulsion system > **3** : not having developed or not having the atom bomb <a *nonnuclear* country> **4** : not involving the use of atom bombs < *nonnuclear* war>

no–no \ˈnō,nō\ *n, pl* **no–no's** *or* **no–nos** : something that is unacceptable or forbidden <using halves of stamps is a *no-no* —*Postal Life*> <a list of *no-no's* about language usage —C.C. Revard>

non·per·sis·tent \¦nänpə(r)¦sistənt, *sometimes* ¦nən-\ *adj* : not persistent: as **a** : decomposed rapidly by environmental action < *nonpersistent* insecticides> **b** : capable of being transmitted by a vector for only a relatively short time < *nonpersistent* viruses>

non·per·son \ˈnän¦pərsᵊn, -¦pōsᵊn, -¦pəisᵊn, *sometimes* ˈnən-\ *n* : a person regarded as nonexistent: as **a** : one regarded as never having existed : UNPERSON <became a *nonperson* in the bureaucracy, a ghost —Robert Sherrill> **b** : one having no social or legal status <servants are . . . *nonpersons;* the English upper classes have always recognised this —Michael Grosvenor-Myer>

non·pol·lut·ing \¦nänpə¦lüd·iŋ, *sometimes* ¦nən-\ *adj* : causing little or no pollution < *nonpolluting* sources of power>

non·pro·lif·er·a·tion \-prə,lifə¦rāshən\ *adj* : providing for the stoppage of the world-wide spread of nuclear arms production < *nonproliferation* treaty> — **nonproliferation** *n*

non·re·com·bi·nant \-(,)rē¦kämbənənt\ *adj* : not exhibiting the results of genetic recombination < *nonrecombinant* progeny> — **nonrecombinant** *n*

non·re·pro·duc·tive \-,rēprə¦dəktiv\ *adj* : not reproducing; *esp* : not capable of reproducing <a *nonreproductive* caste of colonial insects> — **nonreproductive** *n*

non·sed·i·ment·able \-,sedə¦men(t)əbəl\ *adj* : not capable of being sedimented under specified conditions (as of centrifugation)

nonsense* *n* : genetic mutation involving formation of one or more codons that do not code for any amino acid and usu. cause termination of the molecular chain in protein synthesis — compare MISSENSE

nonsense* *adj* : consisting of one or more codons that are genetic nonsense

non·sig·nif·i·cant* \¦nän(,)sig¦nifəkənt, *sometimes* ¦nən-\ *adj* : having or yielding a value lying within limits between which variation is attributed to chance <a *nonsignificant* statistical test> — **non·sig·nif·i·cant·ly** \-lē, -li\ *adv*

non·ste·roid \¦nän¦sti(ə)r,ȯid, *also* -¦ste(ə)r-, *sometimes* ¦nən-\ *or* **non·ste·roi·dal** \-stə¦rȯidᵊl\ *adj* : of, relating to, or being a compound and esp. a drug that is not a steroid — **nonsteroid** *n*

non·tar·get \-¦tärgət, -¦täg-\ *adj* : not being the intended object of action by a particular agent <effect of insecticides on *nontarget* organisms>

non·triv·i·al \(ˈ)nän¦trivēəl\ *adj* **1** : not trivial <stress the importance of an extremely large file in the construction of *nontrivial* inferences —Christine A. Montgomery> **2** : having the value of at least one variable not equal to zero < *nontrivial* solutions to linear equations>

non–U \¦nän¦yü\ *adj* : not upper-class : of, relating to, or typical of the lower classes <a thoughtful, *non-U* escapee from a technical college —Timothy Foote>

non·vec·tor \(ˈ)nän¦vektə(r), *sometimes* (ˈ)nən-\ *n* : an organism (as an insect) that does not transmit a particular pathogen (as a virus)

non·vo·coid \-¦vō,kȯid\ *n* : CONTOID

noo·sphere \ˈnōə,sfi(ə)r, -,sfiə\ *n* [ISV *noo-* mind (fr. Gk *noos, nous*) + *sphere;* prob. orig. formed as Russian *noosfera*] **1** : the biosphere as altered consciously or unconsciously by human activities **2** : the sum of human intellectual activities

NOR \ˈnȯ(ə)r\ *n* [*not OR*] : a computer logic circuit that produces an output that is the inverse of that of an OR circuit

Nor·dic* \ˈnȯrdik, -ēk\ *adj* : of or relating to competitive ski events consisting of ski jumping and cross-country racing — compare ALPINE

nor·eth·in·drone \nȯˈrethən,drōn\ *n* [*nor*mal + *ethin*yl (var. of *ethynyl*) + *-dr-* (perh. fr. *androgen*) + testoster*one*] : a synthetic progestational hormone $C_{20}H_{26}O_2$ used in oral contraceptives

nor·ethyn·o·drel \,nȯrəˈthinə,drel\ *n* [*nor*mal + *ethyn*yl + connective *-o-* + *-dr-* (perh. fr. *androgen*) + *-el* (perh. alter. of *-al* pharmaceutical product)] : a progesterone derivative $C_{20}H_{26}O_2$ used in oral contraceptives and clinically in the treatment of abnormal uterine bleeding and the control of menstruation

norm* *n* **1** : a real-valued nonnegative function defined on a vector space and satisfying the conditions that the function is zero if and only if the vector is zero, that the function of the product of a scalar and a vector is equal to the product of the absolute value of the scalar and the function of the vector, and that the function of the sum of two vectors is less than or equal to the sum of the functions of the two vectors; *specif*: the square root of the sum of the squares of the absolute values of the elements of a matrix or of the components of a vector **2** : the greatest distance between two successive points of a set of points that partition an interval into smaller intervals

normal* *adj* **1** *of a subgroup* : having the property that every coset produced by operating on the left with a given element is equal to the coset produced by operating on the right with the same element **2** : relating to, involving, or being a normal curve or normal distribution < *normal* approximation to the binomial distribution > **3** *of a matrix*: having the property of commutativity under multiplication by the transpose of a matrix each of whose elements is a conjugate complex number with respect to the corresponding element of the given matrix

normal divisor *n* : a normal subgroup

nor·mal·ize* \ˈnȯrmə͵līz, ˈnȯ(ə)m-\ *vt* **-ized; -iz·ing** : to make mathematically or statistically normal (as by a transformation of variables) — **nor·mal·iz·able** \-͵lī-zə-bəl\ *adj*

nor·mal·iz·er* \-͵līzə(r)\ *n* **1** : a subgroup consisting of those elements of a group for which the group operation with regard to a given element is commutative **2** : the set of elements of a group for which the group operation with regard to every element of a given subgroup is commutative

normal or·thog·o·nal \-ȯrˈthägənᵊl, -ȯ(ə)ˈth-\ *adj* : ORTHONORMAL

normed \ˈnȯ(ə)rmd, ˈnȯ(ə)md\ *adj* : being a mathematical entity upon which a norm is defined <a *normed* vector space>

nor·mo·ther·mia \͵nȯrməˈthərmēə\ *n* [NL, fr. *normo-* normal + *-thermia* state of heat, deriv. of Gk *thermē* heat] : normal body temperature — **nor·mo·ther·mic** \-ˈthərmik\ *adj*

northern corn root·worm \-ˈrüt͵wərm, -ˈru̇t-, -wə̄m, -͵wəim\ *n* : a corn rootworm (*Diabrotica longicornis*) often destructive to maize in the northern parts of the central and eastern U.S.

nor·trip·ty·line \nȯrˈtriptə͵lēn\ *n* [*nor*mal + *tript-* (alter. of *trypt-* — as in *tryptophan*) + *-yl* chemical radical + *-ine* chemical substance] : a tricyclic drug $C_{19}H_{21}N$ that is used as an antidepressant

nose–ride \ˈnōz͵rīd\ *vi*: to ride or perform stunts on the nose of a surfboard — **nose–rid·er** \-ə(r)\ *n*

¹nosh \ˈnäsh\ *vb* [Yiddish *nashn,* fr. MHG *naschen* to eat on the sly] *vi*: to eat between meals : snack < *noshing* on a chili dog and coke —Lyn Tornabene> ~ *vt*: to snack on : eat <the cost of food *noshed* by the assembled multitude —Beatrice Berg> — **nosh·er** \-shə(r)\ *n*

²nosh *n* **1** : a light snack <bring her something to eat, just a little *nosh,* anything at all —Ed McCormack> **2** *chiefly Brit*: a meal : food <a slap-up Christmas *nosh* for 100 stray cats and dogs —*Sunday Mirror* (*London*)> <recipes for some of the world's niftiest *nosh* —*Daily Mirror* (*London*)>

nosh–up \-͵əp\ *n, chiefly Brit*: a meal and esp. a large or elaborate meal <a demo outside the Town Hall protested against a *nosh-up* for 250 inside — *Wolverhampton Express & Star*>

NOT \ˈnät\ *n* [*not*] : a logical operator that produces a statement that is the inverse of an input statement

notch·back \ˈnäch͵bak\ *n* **1** : a back on a closed passenger automobile having a distinct deck — compare FASTBACK **2** : an automobile having a notchback

no–till \(ˈ)nōˈtil\ *n* : NO-TILLAGE

no–till·age \-ij, -ēj\ *n* : a system of farming that consists of planting a narrow slit trench without tillage and with the use of herbicides to suppress weeds

nou·velle vague \(ˌ)nüˌvelˈväg, -ˈvåg\ *n* [F, lit., new wave, fr. *nouvelle* (fem. of *nouveau* new, fr. L *novellus*) + *vague* wave, fr. OF *wage*, fr. ON *vāgr;* akin to OE *wǣg* wave, *wegan* to move] : NEW WAVE

NP* *abbr* noun phrase

nsec *abbr* nanosecond

nuclear force *n* **1** : the powerful force between nucleons that holds atomic nuclei together **2** : STRONG INTERACTION

nuclear magnetic resonance *n* : the magnetic resonance of an atomic nucleus

nuclear resonance *n* : the resonance absorption of a gamma ray by a nucleus identical to the nucleus that emitted the gamma ray — compare MÖSSBAUER EFFECT

nu·cleo·cap·sid \ˌn(y)ükleōˈkapsəd\ *n* [*nucleo-* nucleus, nucleic acid + *capsid*] : the nucleic acid and surrounding protein coat in a virus

nu·cleo·gen·e·sis \-ˈjenəsəs\ *n* : NUCLEOSYNTHESIS

nu·cle·o·lo·ne·ma \(ˌ)n(y)üˌklēələˈnēmə\ *also* **nu·cle·o·lo·neme** \-ˈklēələˌnēm\ *n* [NL *nucleolonema* fr. *nucleolus* + connective *-o-* + Gk *nēma* thread] : a filamentous network consisting of small granules in some nucleoli

nu·cle·on* \ˈn(y)ükləˌän\ *n* : a hypothetical single entity with one-half unit of isospin capable of manifesting itself as either a proton or a neutron and of making transitions between these two states

nu·cleo·phile \ˈn(y)ükleōˌfīl\ *n* [*nucleo-* nucleus, nucleic acid + *-phile* lover, deriv. of Gk *philos* beloved, loving] : a nucleophilic substance (as an electron-donating reagent)

nu·cleo·syn·the·sis \ˌn(y)ükleōˈsin(t)thəsəs\ *n* : the production of a chemical element in nature from hydrogen nuclei or protons (as in stellar evolution) — **nu·cleo·syn·thet·ic** \-sənˌthed·ik\ *adj*

[1]nud·ie \ˈn(y)üdē, -di\ *n* **1** : SKIN FLICK **2** : a publication that features photographs of nudes

[2]nudie *adj* : featuring nudes < *nudie* films > < *nudie* magazines >

null* *adj* **1** : having zero as a limit < *null* sequence > **2** *of a matrix* : having all elements equal to zero

nullity* *n* : the number of elements in a basis of a null-space

null–space \ˈnəlˌspās\ *n* : a subspace of a vector space consisting of vectors that under a given linear transformation are equal to zero

number line *n* : a line of infinite extent whose points correspond to the real numbers according to their distance in a positive or negative direction from a point arbitrarily taken as zero

nu·mer·a·cy \ˈn(y)ümərəsē\ *n* [L *numer*us number + E *-acy* (as in *literacy*)] : the capacity for quantitative thought and expression

nu·mer·ate \-rət\ *adj* [L *numer*us number + E *-ate* (as in *literate*)] : marked by numeracy : having or showing the ability to think quantitatively < designers in this country tend to be more literate than *numerate* —Paul Reilly >

nu·mer·ic \n(y)üˈmerik\ *n* [*numeric*, adj.] : a number or numeral

numerical analysis *n* : the study of quantitative approximations to the solutions of mathematical problems including consideration of the errors and bounds to the errors involved

numerical control *n* : automatic control (as of a machine tool) by a digital computer — **nu·mer·i·cal·ly controlled** \n(y)üˌmerək(ə)lē-\ *adj*

numerical taxonomy *n* : taxonomy that applies the quantitative measurement of many characters to the determination of taxa and to the construction of diagrams indicating systematic relationships — **numerical tax·o·nom·ic** \-ˌtaksəˌnämik\ *adj* — **numerical tax·on·o·mist** \-takˈsänəməst\ *n*

nur·tur·ance \ˈnərchərən(t)s\ *n* : affectionate care and attention — **nur·tur·ant** \-rənt\ *adj*

nut* *n, slang* : a bribe given to a policeman

nuts–and–bolts \ˌnəts(ə)n(d)ˌbōlts\ *adj* : of, relating to, or dealing with specific practical details < *nuts-and-bolts* studies of . . . enrollment projections, space needs, and work loads —J.G. Gaff & R.C. Wilson >

nuts and bolts *n pl* **1 :** the working parts or elements **2 :** the practical workings of a machine or enterprise as opposed to theoretical considerations or speculative possibilities <the *nuts and bolts* of municipal government>

Ny·norsk \ˈn(y)üˈnȯ(ə)rsk, ˈnüē-\ *n* [Norw, lit., new Norwegian, fr. *ny* new (fr. ON *nȳr*) + *norsk* Norwegian] : a literary form of Norwegian based on the spoken dialects of Norway : Landsmål —compare BOKMÅL

O

Obie \ˈōbē\ *n* [*O.B.*, abbr. for *off-Broadway*] : any of several prizes awarded annually by a newspaper for excellence in off-Broadway theater

object language *n* : TARGET LANGUAGE

ob·jet trou·vé \ˌȯbˌzhā(ˌ)trüˈvā\ *n, pl* **objets trouvés** *same*\ [F, lit., found object] : FOUND OBJECT

ocea·naut \ˈōshəˌnȯt, -ˌnät\ *n* [blend of *ocean* and *-naut* (as in *aquanaut*)] : AQUANAUT

ocean engineering *n* : engineering that deals with the application of design, construction, and maintenance principles and techniques to the ocean environment

oce·an·ics \ˌōshēˈaniks\ *n pl but usu sing in constr* : a group of sciences that deal with the ocean

ocean·o·log·ic \ˌōshənəˈläjik\ *or* **ocean·o·log·i·cal** \-jəkəl\ *adj* : of or relating to oceanology : oceanographic — **ocean·o·log·i·cal·ly** \-nəˈläjək(ə)lē\ *adv*

ocean·ol·o·gist \ˌōshəˈnäləjəst\ *n* : a specialist in oceanology : oceanographer

och·ra·tox·in \ˌōkrəˈtäksən\ *n* [NL *ochraceus* (specific epithet of *Aspergillus ochraceus*) + E *toxin*] : a mycotoxin produced by an aspergillus (*Aspergillus ochraceus*)

oc·ta·pep·tide \ˌäktəˈpepˌtīd\ *n* [*octa-* eight (fr. Gk *oktō* & L *octo*) + *peptide*] : a protein fragment or molecule (as oxytocin or vasopressin) that consists of eight amino acids linked in a polypeptide chain

¹OD \ˌōˈdē\ *n* [*over*d*ose*] **1 :** an overdose of a narcotic <some junkie croaks in the Bronx, right? He takes an *OD*—Richard Woodley> **2 :** one who has taken an overdose of a narcotic <died at his home . . . an apparent smack *OD*—*Rolling Stone*>

²OD *vi* **OD'd** *or* **ODed** \ˌōˈdēd\ **OD'ing** \ˌōˈdē(i)ŋ\ : to become ill or die from an OD <ragged girls would stumble across the room, *OD'd* on pills — Lair Mitchell> <twenty-three kids . . . had been killed in drug- or pimp-related murders, and this doesn't include the minors who *OD'd* —Larry Zicht>

odd–lot·ter \ˈädˈläd·ə(r)\ *n* : a speculator or an investor who habitually buys and sells stock in less than round lots

odd per·mu·ta·tion \-ˌpərmyu̇ˈtāshən, -ˌpə̄m-, -ˌpəim-, -yəˈtā-\ *n* : a permutation that is produced by the successive application of an odd number of interchanges of pairs of elements — compare EVEN PERMUTATION

odont·o·log·i·cal \(ˌ)ōˌdäntᵊlˈäjəkəl\ *adj* : of or relating to odontology

off \ˈȯf, *also* ˈäf\ *vt, slang* : to kill or murder <if you want to *off* a pig, *off* him. Don't rap about it —*Berkeley Barb*> <*offed* over 20 souls, none of them with a machine gun, that being the chief difference between him and Dillinger —Molly Ivins>

off Broad·way \-ˈbrȯdˌwā\ *n* [fr. its usu. being produced in smaller theaters outside of the Broadway theatrical district] : a part of the New York professional theater stressing fundamental and artistic values and formerly engaging in experimentation — **off–Broadway** *adj*

off–cam·era \ˌȯfˈkam(ə)rə, *also* ˈäf-\ *adv or adj* **1 :** out of the range of a motion-picture or television camera <chided me *off-camera* during a commercial break —W.H.

Manville> **2** : in private life <if she won critical kudos on the entertainment pages, her performances *off-camera* were met with less enthusiasm on the front pages —Arthur Knight & Hollis Alpert>

offering price* *n*: the price at which an open-end mutual fund is sold consisting of its asset value usu. plus a specified load

of·fi·ci·a·lis \ə,fishē'äləs, -'al-\ *n, pl* **of·fi·ci·a·les** \-'ä(,)lās, -'a(,)lēz \ [NL, fr. ML, official] : the presiding judge of the matrimonial court of a Roman Catholic diocese

off–line \'ȯf¦līn, *also* 'äf-\ *adj* **1 a** : not being in continuous direct communication with a computer <an *off-line* scanner> **b** : operating or done independently of a computer <*off-line* storage of data> **2** : of, relating to, or being a cryptographic system in which encryption and decryption are accomplished independently of telecommunication machines — compare ON-LINE 3 — **off–line** *adv*

off–off–Broad·way \(')ȯf¦ȯf,brȯd,wā, *also* (')äf¦äf-\ *n* [fr. its relation to off-Broadway being analogous to the relation of off-Broadway to Broadway] : an avant-garde theatrical movement in New York that stresses untraditional techniques and radical experimentation — **off–off–Broadway** *adj*

off–putting \'ȯf,pu̇d·iŋ, *also* 'äf-\ *adj* : that puts one off : repellent, disagreeable <anything new is always *off-putting* and upsetting —Dwight Macdonald>

offshore fund *n* : an investment fund based outside the U.S., not subject to registration with the Security and Exchange Commission, and barred by law from selling its shares within the U.S.

off–the–peg \,ȯfthə¦peg, *also* ,äf-\ *adj, chiefly Brit* : not made to order : ready-made, ready-to-wear <*off-the-peg* clothes —*The People*>

off–the–rack \-¦rak\ *adj* : ready-made, ready-to-wear <*off-the-rack* suits>

off–the–shelf \-¦shelf, -¦sheu̇f\ *adj* : available as a stock item : not specially designed or custom-made <*off-the-shelf* computer peripherals>

off·track betting \¦ȯf¦trak-, *also* ¦äf-\ *n* : pari-mutuel betting that is carried on away from the racetrack

old–mon·ey \¦ōl(d),mənē, -ni\ *adj* : possessing wealth that has been inherited through several generations <insists on protecting the names of his clients, a large number of whom are *old-money* and sensitive to publicity —Joanne Winship>

ole·an·do·my·cin \,ōlē,andə'mīsᵊn\ *n* [prob. fr. *oleand*er + connective *-o-* + *-mycin* substance obtained from a fungus, fr. *streptomycin*] : an antibiotic $C_{35}H_{61}NO_{12}$ produced by a streptomyces (*Streptomyces antibioticus*)

ol·fac·tron·ics \,äl,fak'träniks, ,ōl-\ *n pl but sing in constr* [*olfac*tion + *-tronics* (as in *electronics*)] : a branch of physical science dealing with the detection and identification of odors

ol·i·gid·ic \,älə'gidik, ,ōl-, -'ji-\ *adj* [*olig-* few (deriv. of Gk *oligos*) + *-idic* (as in *meridic*)] : having the active constituents with the exception of water undefined chemically <*oligidic* growth medium> — compare HOLIDIC, MERIDIC

oligo·mer \ō'ligəmə(r), ə'l-\ *n* [*oligo-* few (deriv. of Gk *oligos*) + *-mer* member of a class, fr. Gk *meros* part] : a polymer or polymer intermediate that contains relatively few structural units — **oligo·mer·ic** \ō¦ligə¦merik, ə¦l-, ¦äləgō¦merik, -mir-\ *adj* — **oligo·mer·iza·tion** \-,ligə,merə'zāshən, -mir-\ *n*

oli·go·my·cin \,äligō'mīsᵊn, ,ōli-\ *n* [*oligo-* + *-mycin* substance obtained from a fungus, fr. *streptomycin*] : any of several antibiotic substances produced by an actinomycete

oli·go·nu·cle·o·tide \¦äləgō'n(y)üklēə,tīd, ə¦ligə-\ *n* : a chain of usu. from 2 to 10 nucleotides

olin·go \ō'liŋ,gō\ *n, pl* **-gos** [AmerSp, howling monkey] : any of a genus (*Bassaricyon*) of long-tailed slender-bodied carnivores of Central and South America that are related to the raccoon

omah \'ō(,)mä\ *n, often cap* [origin unknown] : SASQUATCH

om·buds·man \'äm,bu̇dzmən, 'ȯm-, -(,)bəd-, äm'b-, ȯm'b-, -,man\ *n, pl* **ombudsmen** \-mən, -,men\ [Sw, lit., representative, commissioner, fr. ON *umbothsmathr*, fr. *umboth* commission (fr. *um* around + *bjōtha* to command) + *mathr* man] **1** : a government official (as in Sweden or New Zealand) appointed to receive and investigate complaints made by individuals against abuses or capricious acts of public officials **2** : one that investigates complaints (as from students or customers), reports findings, and helps to achieve equitable settlements — **om•buds•man•ship** \-mən-ˌship\ *n*

om•buds•wom•an \-zˌwu̇mən\ *n, pl* **om•buds•wo•men** \-ˌwimə̇n\ : a female ombudsman

ome•ga* \ōˈmegə, ōˈmēgə, ōˈmāgə\ *n* **1** *or* **omega particle** : a negatively charged elementary particle that has a mass 3280 times the mass of an electron and that is an unstable baryon decaying into a xi and a pion with an average lifetime of about 10^{-10} second **2** *or* **omega me•son** \-ˈmezˌän, -ˈmesˌän, -ˈmā-, -ˈmē-\ : a very short-lived unstable meson with mass 1532 times the mass of an electron

om•ni•fo•cal \ˌämnə̇ˈfōkəl, -nē-\ *adj* [*omni-* all (fr. L *omnis*) + *focal*] : of, relating to, or being a bifocal eyeglass that is so ground as to permit smooth transition from one correction to the other

-on \ˌän\ *n suffix* [fr. *-on* (in *ion*)] : basic hereditary component <cistr*on*> <oper*on*>

on•board \ˈänˈbō(ə)rd, -ˈbȯ(ə)rd, -ˈbōəd, -ˈbȯ(ə)d\ *adj* : carried within a vehicle (as a rocket, satellite, or spacecraft) <an *onboard* computer>

on–camera \-ˈkam(ə)rə\ *adv or adj* : within the range of a motion-picture or television camera <is eager to do it *on-camera* —Robert Kotlowitz>

on•co•gen•e•sis \ˌäŋkōˈjenəsə̇s\ *n* [NL, fr. *onco-* tumor (fr. Gk *onkos* bulk, mass) + *genesis*] : the induction or formation of tumors

on•co•ge•nic•i•ty \ˌäŋkōjə̇ˈnisə̇d•ē\ *n* : the capacity to induce or form tumors

one–lin•er \ˈwənˈlīnə(r)\ *n* : a very succinct joke or witticism <turns away hard questions with easy *one-liners* —Andy Logan>

[1]**one–on–one** \ˈwənänˈwən\ *adv or adj* : directly against a single opposing player <everyone tends to go *one-on-one* because he thinks he can do it all by himself —Dave Cowens> <broke away cleanly and came waltzing in *one-on-one* at the utterly exposed Ranger goalie —J.S. Radosta> <pro basketball's most spectacular *one-on-one* player —Steve Cady>

[2]**one–on–one** *n* : a game or an aspect of a game which pits one offensive player against a single defender; *esp* : an informal basketball game between two players who alternate at offense and defense

one–tailed test \ˈwənˌtā(ə)l(d)-\ *n* : a statistical test for which the critical region consists of all values of the test statistic greater than a given value or less than a given value but not both — called also *one-sided test, one-tail test;* compare TWO-TAILED TEST

one–time pad \ˈwənˌtīm-\ *n* [prob. fr. its original form's being a pad of keys whose sheets were torn off and discarded after a single use] : a random-number additive or mixed keying sequence to be used for a single coded message and then destroyed

one–up \ˈwənˈəp\ *vt* **-upped; -up•ping** [back-formation fr. *one-upmanship*] : to practice one-upmanship on <intellectual argument is a serious business in our day and age; hopefully, we are trying to do something other than *one-up* each other —Nicholas Thompson>

onion dome *n* : a dome (as of a church) having the general shape of an onion — **onion–domed** \ˈənyənˌdōmd\ *adj*

on–line \ˈȯnˈlīn, ˈän-, *South sometimes* ˈōn-\ *adj* **1** : located at a point served directly by a particular railroad <*on-line* industry> **2 a** : being under the direct control of or in continuous direct communication with a computer <*on-line* memory devices> **b** : operating or done in real time <*on-line* analysis of data> **3** : of, relating to, or being a cryptographic system whose telecommunication machines automatically encipher, transmit, receive, and decipher messages in a single instantaneous operation — compare OFF-LINE 2 — **on–line** *adv*

onto* *prep* — used as a function word which precedes a word or phrase denoting a set each element of which is the image of at least one element of another set <a function mapping the set *S* *onto* the set *T*>

on•to \ˈȯn(ˌ)tü, ˈän-\ *adj* : mapping in such a way that every element in one set is the image of at least one element in another set <a function that is one-to-one and *onto*>

OOB \ˌōˌōˈbē\ *n* [*o*ff-*o*ff-*B*roadway] : OFF-OFF-BROADWAY

op \ˈäp\ *or* **op art** *n* [by shortening] : OPTICAL ART — **op artist** *n*

op–ed page \ˌäpˌed-\ *n* [*op*posite + *ed*itorial] : the page opposite the editorial page of a newspaper that features by-lined articles (as by columnists) reflecting individual points of view

open* *adj* **1** : being a mathematical interval that contains neither of its endpoints **2** : being a set each point of which has a neighborhood all of whose points are contained in the set <the interior of a sphere is an *open* set>

open admissions *n pl but sing or pl in constr* : OPEN ENROLLMENT 2

open bar *n* : a bar (as at a wedding reception) at which drinks are served free — compare CASH BAR

open–cir·cuit \ˌōpənˌsərkət, ˌōpᵊmˌ-, -ˌsək-, -ˌsəik-\ *adj* : of or relating to an open circuit; *specif* : being or relating to television in which programs are broadcast so that they are available to all receivers within range

open classroom *n* : an informal flexible system of elementary education in which open discussions and individualized activities replace the traditional subject-centered studies

open enrollment *n* **1** : the voluntary enrollment of a student in a public school other than the one he is assigned to on the basis of his residence **2** : enrollment on demand as a student in an institution of higher learning irrespective of formal qualifications

open–heart \ˌōpənˌhärt, ˌōpᵊmˌ-, -ˌhät\ *adj* : of, relating to, or performed on a heart temporarily relieved of circulatory function and laid open for inspection and treatment <*open-heart* surgery>

open loop *n* : a control system for an operation or process in which there is no self-correcting action

open sentence *n* : a statement (as in mathematics) that contains at least one blank or unknown and that becomes true or false when the blank is filled or a quantity is substituted for the unknown

op·er·and* \ˌäpəˌrand\ *n* : the part of a computer instruction that indicates the quantities to be operated on; *also* : one of these quantities

operating system *n* : software that supports or complements the hardware of a computer system (as by keeping track of the different programs in multiprogramming)

operation* *n* : a single step performed by a computer in the execution of a program

op·er·a·tion·al·is·tic \ˌäpəˌrāshnəlˌistik, -shənᵊl-\ *adj* : of or relating to operationalism

op·er·a·tion·a·lize \ˌäpəˈrāshnəlˌīz, -shənᵊl-\ *vt* **-lized; -liz·ing** : to make operational <*operationalize* a program> — **op·er·a·tion·al·iza·tion** \äp(ə)ˌrāshnələˈzāshən, -shənᵊl-, -lˌīˈzāshən\ *n*

op·er·a·tion·ist \ˌäpəˈrāsh(ə)nəst\ *n* : an advocate or adherent of operationalism

operator* *or* **operator gene** *n* : a chromosomal region that triggers formation of messenger RNA by one or more structural genes and is itself subject to inhibition by a genetic repressor — compare OPERON

opera window *n* : a small window on each of the rear side panels of an automobile

op·er·on \ˈäpəˌrän\ *n* [ISV *oper*ator + *-on* basic hereditary component; prob. orig. formed in F] : the closely linked combination of an operator and the structural genes it regulates

optical* *adj* **1** : visible <an *optical* galaxy> **2 a** : of, relating to, or utilizing light <an *optical* emission> <an *optical* telescope> <*optical* microscopy> **b** : involving the use of light-sensitive devices to acquire information for a computer <*optical* character recognition> **3** : of or relating to optical art <*optical* painting>

optical art *n* : nonobjective art characterized by the use of straight or curved lines or geometric patterns often for an illusory effect (as of perspective or motion)

op·to·elec·tron·ic \ˌäp(ˌ)tōəˌlekˈtränik, -ēˌlek-, -ēk\ *adj* [*opt*ical + connective *-o-* + *electronic*] : being or related to a device in which light energy and electrical energy are coupled — **op·to·elec·tron·ics** \-iks, -ēks\ *n pl but sing in constr*

OR \ˈȯ(ə)r, ˈȯ(ə)\ *n* : a logical operator equivalent to the sentential connective *or* <*OR* gate in a computer>

or·a·cy \ˈōrəsē, ˈȯr-, ˈär-, -si\ *n* [*or*al + *-acy* (as in *literacy*)] : the capacity for oral expression and for understanding spoken language <has accomplished its only pur-

pose—that of teaching literacy in the conventional form, and *oracy* with as acceptable an accent as may happen to have been spoken into the teaching tapes —James Pitman>

oral history *n* : tape-recorded historical information obtained in interviews with persons who have led significant lives; *also* : the study of such information — **oral historian** *n*

order* *n* **1** : the number of elements in a finite mathematical group **2** : a class of mutually exclusive linguistic forms any and only one of which may occur in a fixed definable position in the permitted sequence of items forming a word

ordered* *adj* **1** : having elements succeeding according to rule; *specif* : having the property that every pair of different elements is related by a transitive relationship that is not symmetric **2** : having a specified first element <a set of *ordered* pairs>

ordinal number* *n* : a number that designates both the order of the elements of an ordered set and the cardinal number of the set

or·ga·no \ˈȯrgə(ˌ)nō, ȯrˈga(ˌ)nō\ *adj* [short for *organometallic*] : of, relating to, or being an organic compound that usu. contains a metal or metalloid bonded directly to carbon <an *organo* derivative of mercury>

or·gano·chlo·rine \ȯrˌganəˈklōrˌēn, -ˈklȯr-, ˌȯrgənō-, -rən\ *adj* [*organo-* organic + *chlorine*] : of, relating to, or belonging to the chlorinated hydrocarbon pesticides (as aldrin, DDT, or dieldrin) — **organochlorine** *n*

or·gano·phos·phate \-ˈfäsˌfāt\ *n* : an organophosphorus pesticide — **or·gano·phosphate** *adj*

or·gano·phos·pho·rus \-ˈfäsf(ə)rəs\ *also* **or·gano·phos·pho·rous** \-ˈfäsf(ə)rəs; -fäsˈfōrəs, -ˈfȯr-\ *adj* : of, relating to, or being a phosphorus-containing organic compound and esp. a pesticide (as malathion) that acts by inhibiting cholinesterase — **organophosphorus** *n*

ori·en·teer·ing \ˌōrēən·ˈti(ə)riŋ, -ē(ˌ)en-\ *n* [prob. modif. (influenced by *-eer*, n. suffix) of Sw *orientering*, fr. *orientera* to orient, fr. F *orienter*] : a cross-country race in which each participant uses a map and compass to navigate his way between checkpoints along an unfamiliar course

or·thog·o·nal* \ȯrˈthägənᵊl, ȯ(ə)ˈth-\ *adj* **1** : having a sum of products or an integral that is zero or sometimes one under specified conditions: as **a** *of real-valued functions* : having the integral of the product of each pair of functions over a specific interval equal to zero **b** *of vectors* : having the scalar product equal to zero **c** *of a square matrix*: having the sum of products of corresponding elements in any two rows or any two columns equal to one if the rows or columns are the same and equal to zero otherwise : having a transpose with which the product equals the identity matrix **2** *of a linear transformation* : having a matrix that is orthogonal : preserving length and distance **3** : composed of mutually orthogonal elements <an *orthogonal* basis of a vector space>

or·thog·o·nal·iza·tion \ȯ(r)ˌthägənᵊ ləˈzāshən, -gnəl-, -lˌīˈz-\ *n* : the replacement of a set of vectors by a linearly equivalent set of orthogonal vectors

or·tho·mo·lec·u·lar \ˌȯ(r)thəməˌlekyələ(r), -thō-\ *adj* [*ortho-* straight, right, perpendicular (deriv. of Gk *orthos* straight) + *molecular*] : relating to or being a theory according to which disease and esp. mental illness may be cured by restoring the optimum amounts of substances normally present in the body <*orthomolecular* psychiatry> <*orthomolecular* therapy>

or·tho·nor·mal \-ˈnȯrməl, -ˈnȯ(ə)m-\ *adj* **1** *of real-valued functions* : orthogonal with the integral of the square of each function over a specified interval equal to one **2** : being or composed of orthogonal elements of unit length <*orthonormal* basis of a vector space>

or·thot·ics \ȯrˈthäd·iks\ *n pl but sing in constr* [fr. Gk *orthōsis* straightening; after such pairs as E *prosthesis: prosthetics*] : a branch of mechanical and medical science dealing with the support and bracing of weak or ineffective joints or muscles — **orthot·ic** \-ik\ *adj* — **or·tho·tist** \ˈȯrthətəst\ *n*

or·tho·tropic* \ˌȯ(r)thəˌträpik, -ˌtrō-\ *adj* **1** : being, having, or relating to properties (as strength, stiffness, and elasticity) that are symmetric about two or three mutually perpendicular planes <a piece of straight-grained wood is an *orthotropic* mate-

rial> **2** *of a bridge* : designed so that the roadway serves as an orthotropic structural member : constructed with a steel-plate deck as an integral part of the support structure

Or·well·ian \ȯ(r)ˈwelēən\ *adj* [George *Orwell*, pseudonym of Eric Blair †1950 Eng. writer] : of, relating to, or suggestive of George Orwell or his writings <almost an example of *Orwellian* newspeak; revolution is transformed, at least for propaganda purposes, from a beginning into an end —Richard Schickel> <an *Orwellian* dystopia working away full blast —John Simon>

or·zo \ˈȯr(ˌ)zō\ *n* [prob. modif. of NGk *oryza* rice, fr. Gk] : rice-shaped pasta

os·cu·lat·ing circle \ˌäskyəˌlād·iŋ\ *n* : a circle which is tangent to a curve at a given point, which lies in the limiting plane determined by the tangent to the curve and a point moving along the curve to the point of tangency, which has its center situated on the normal to the curve at the given point and also on the concave side of the projection of the curve onto the limiting plane, and which has a radius equal to the radius of curvature

os·mol \ˈäzˌmōl, ˈäˌsmōl\ *n* [blend of *osmosis* and *mol*] : a standard unit of osmotic pressure based on a one molal concentration of an ion in a solution — **os·mo·lal** \(ˈ)äzˌmōləl, (ˈ)äˌsmō-\ *adj* — **os·mo·lal·i·ty** \ˌäzmeˈlaləd·ē, ˌäsm-\ *n*

os·mo·lar \(ˈ)äzˌmōlə(r), (ˈ)äˌsm-\ *adj* : of, relating to, or having the properties of osmosis : osmotic — used chiefly of biological fluids — **os·mo·lar·i·ty** \ˌäzməˈlarəd·ē, ˌäsm-\ *n*

os·mot·ic shock \äzˌmäd·ik-, äsˌm-\ *n* : a rapid change in the osmotic pressure (as by transfer to a medium of different concentration) affecting a living system

os·so bu·co \ˌōsōˈbü(ˌ)kō\ *n* [It *ossobuco* marrowbone] : a dish of veal shanks braised with vegetables, white wine, and seasoned stock

ost·mark \ˈȯstˌmärk, ˈäs-\ *n* [G, lit., East mark] : the mark of East Germany

os·to·my \ˈästəmē\ *n, pl* **-mies** [col*ostomy*] : an operation (as a colostomy) to create an artificial passage for bodily elimination

OTC *abbr* over-the-counter

oto·tox·ic \ˌōd·əˈtäksik\ *adj* [*oto-* ear (fr. Gk *ōt-, ous*) + *toxic*] : adversely affecting organs or nerves involved in hearing or balance <*ototoxic* drugs> — **oto·tox·i·ci·ty** \-(ˌ)täkˈsisəd·ē, -i\ *n*

out* *adj* : not approved of or accepted by those who are keenly aware of and responsive to what is new and smart : not in <for many business executives, the gray-flannel suit is *out* and sideburns are in —C. K. Aldrich>

out·reach* \ˈau̇tˌrēch\ *n* : the extending of services or activities beyond current or conventional limits <to provide what is called community *outreach*, new facilities were needed —Ada L. Huxtable>; *also* : the extent of such services or activities <the international communications systems . . . are going to continue to expand their *outreach* —Harold Taylor>

outside* *adj* : made or done from the outside or from a distance <borrowed a basketball and practiced his *outside* shot all day>

ovals of Cas·si·ni \-kəˈsēnē, -ka-, -kȧ-\ [G. D. *Cassini* †1712 Fr. astronomer] : a curve that is the locus of points of the vertex of a triangle whose opposite side is fixed and the product of whose adjacent sides is a constant and that has the equation $[(x + a)^2 + y^2][(x - a)^2 + y^2] - k^4 = 0$ where k is the constant and a is one half the length of the fixed side

over·achiev·er \ˌōvərəˌchēvər, ˌōvə(r)əˌchēvə(r\ *n* : one who achieves success over and above a standard or expected level <tended to be *overachievers*, doing better in school than their IQs would indicate —*The Sciences*> — **over·achieve** \-əˌchēv\ *vi*

over·book \ˌōvə(r)ˈbu̇k\ *vt* : to issue reservations for (as an airplane flight) in excess of the space available ~ *vi* : to issue reservations in excess of the space available

over·dom·i·nance \ˌōvə(r)ˈdäm(ə)nən(t)s\ *n* : the property of having a heterozygote that produces a phenotype more extreme or better adapted than that of the homozygote — **over·dom·i·nant** \ˌōvə(r)ˌdäm(ə)nənt\ *adj*

[1]**over·dub** \ˈōvə(r)ˌdəb\ *vt* : to transfer (recorded sound) onto a recording that bears sound recorded earlier in order to produce a combined effect <what we did then was

to put down all the tracks first and then I would *overdub* the vocal later —Carly Simon >

[2]**overdub** *n* **1** : the act or an instance of overdubbing < the last big album it took them eight months of *overdubs* to produce —Lester Bangs > **2** : recorded sound that is overdubbed < vocal *overdubs*>

over·kill \ˈōvə(r)ˌkil\ *n* [*overkill*, v.] **1** : the capability of destroying an enemy or target with a nuclear force larger than is required < thirty more Poseidons are to follow in this insane race for *overkill*—I. F. Stone > **2** : an excess of something (as a quantity or an action) beyond what is required or suitable for a particular purpose < an *overkill* in weaponry > < the failures of that tone—the satirical *overkill* in Dickens, the facetiousness of Thackeray —John Fowles > < the *overkill* was unbearable: none of the recipes seemed to contain one cup of sugar when two would do — Nora Ephron > **3** : killing in excess of what is intended or required : excessive killing < the overlong seasons and punishing *overkill* that brought ducks to the thin edge of extinction —Zack Taylor > — **overkill** \ˈōvə(r)ˌkil, ˌōvə(r)ˈkil\ *vb*

over·nu·tri·tion \ˌōvə(r)n(y)üˈtrishən\ *n* : excessive food intake esp. when viewed as a factor in pathology

overshoot \ˈōvə(r)ˌshüt\ *n* : the action or an instance of overshooting; *esp* : a going beyond an intended point < a pinpoint landing instead of another off-the-mark touchdown like the four-mile *overshoot* experienced on Apollo 11 —Richard Witkin >

oversteer \-ˌsti(ə)r, -ˌstiə\ *n* : the tendency of an automobile to steer into a sharper turn than the driver intends sometimes with the result that the vehicle's rear end swings to the outside; *also* : the action or an instance of oversteer

over·win·ter \ˌōvə(r)ˌwintə(r)\ *adj* : occurring during the period spanning the winter < *overwinter* mortality of small game >

Ovon·ic \ōˈvänik\ *n* [short for *ovonic device*] : a device that operates in accordance with the Ovshinsky effect

Ovon·ics \-iks\ *n pl but usu sing in constr* [*Ov*shinsky effect + electr*onics*] : a branch of electronics that deals with applications of the Ovshinsky effect — **ovonic** *adj, often cap*

Ov·shin·sky effect \ävˈshin(t)skē-, ȯv-\ *n* [Stanford R. *Ovshinsky b*1923 Am. inventor] : the change from an electrically nonconducting state to a semiconducting state shown by glasses of special composition upon application of a certain minimum voltage

ox·a·cil·lin \ˌäksəˌsilən\ *n* [is*oxa*zole, a compound C_3H_3NO + peni*cillin*] : a semisynthetic penicillin that is esp. effective in the control of infections caused by penicillin-resistant staphylococci

ox·az·e·pam \äkˈsazəˌpam\ *n* [hydr*ox*yl + di*azepam*] : a tranquilizing drug $C_{15}H_{11}ClN_2O_2$

Ox·bridge \ˈäks(ˌ)brij\ *adj* [*Ox*ford University, England + Cam*bridge* University, England] : of, relating to, or characteristic of Oxford and Cambridge universities < exacted an *Oxbridge* degree in order to ensure that its members had had the education of gentlemen —*Times Lit. Supp.* > — compare PLATEGLASS, REDBRICK

ox·i·da·tive phos·phor·y·la·tion \ˈäksəˌdād·iv,fäsfərəˈlāshən\ *n* : the synthesis of ATP by phosphorylation of ADP for which energy is obtained by electron transfer from reduced carbon compounds to oxygen

oxo·trem·o·rine \ˌäksōˈtreməˌrēn, -ərən\ *n* [*oxo-* oxygen + *tremor* + *-ine* chemical substance] : a cholinergic agent $C_{12}H_{18}N_2O$ that induces tremors and is used to screen drugs for activity against Parkinson's disease

oxy·ac·id \ˈäksēˌasəd\ *n* [*oxy-* oxygen + *acid*] : an acid (as sulfuric acid) that contains oxygen — called also *oxygen acid*

ox·y·gen·ase \ˈäksəjəˌnās, -ˌnāz\ *n* [*oxygen* + *-ase* enzyme] : an enzyme that catalyzes the reaction of an organic compound with molecular oxygen

oxygen cycle *n* : the cycle whereby atmospheric oxygen is converted to carbon dioxide in animal respiration and regenerated by green plants in photosynthesis

oxy·some \ˈäksəˌsōm\ *n* [*oxy-* + *-some* body, deriv. of Gk *sōma*] : one of the structural units of mitochondrial cristae that are observed by the electron microscope usu.

as spheres or stalked spheres and that are prob. sites of fundamental energy-producing reactions

oysters Rocke•fel•ler \-ˈräk(ə),felə(r)\ *n pl* [John Davison *Rockefeller* †1937 Am. oil magnate] : a dish of oysters baked with chopped spinach and a seasoned sauce

ozone•sonde \ˈō,zōn,sänd\ *n* : a balloon-borne instrument that measures the concentration of ozone at various altitudes and broadcasts the data by radio

P

p* *abbr* pico-

p* *symbol* **1** momentum of a particle **2** *often cap* the probability of obtaining a result as great as or greater than the observed result in a statistical test if the null hypothesis is true

pa* *abbr* pascal

pa•'anga \pä•ˈäŋ(g)ə\ *n, pl* **pa'anga** [Tongan, lit., seed] **1** : the basic monetary unit of Tonga **2** : a coin or note representing one pa'anga

pace car *n* : an automobile that leads the field of competitors through a pace lap but does not participate in the race

pace lap *n* : a lap of an auto racecourse made by the entire field of competitors before the start of a race to allow the engines to warm up and to permit a flying start

page* *n* : a sizable subdivision of computer memory; *also* : a block of information that fills a page and can be transferred as a unit between the internal and external storage of a computer

page* *vi* **paged; pag•ing** : to proceed through matter displayed on a CRT display as if turning pages

paging* *n* : the movement of blocks of information between the internal and external storage of a computer

pair–bond \ˈpa(ə)r,bänd, ˈpe(ə)r-, ˈpaə,-, ˈpeə,-\ *n* : an exclusive union with a single mate at any one time : a monogamous relationship — **pair–bond•ing** \-iŋ\ *n*

paired–as•so•ci•ate learning \ˌpa(ə)rdəˌsōs(h)ēət-, ˌpe(ə)rd-, -shət-, -s(h)ē,āt-\ *n* : the learning of syllables, digits, or words in pairs (as in the study of a foreign language) so that one member of the pair evokes recall of the other

pa•laz•zo pants \pəˈlät(,)sō-\ *n pl* : extremely wide-legged pants for women

pa•leo•mag•ne•tism \ˌpālēōˈmagnə,tizəm, *chiefly Brit* ˌpal-\ *n* [*paleo-* ancient (fr. Gk *palaios* ancient, fr. *palai* long ago)] **1** : the intensity and direction of residual magnetization in ancient rocks **2** : a study that deals with paleomagnetism — **pa•leo•mag•net•ic** \-(,)magˈned•ik\ *adj* — **pa•leo•mag•net•i•cal•ly** \-ək(ə)lē\ *adv* — **pa•leo•mag•ne•tist** \-(,)magnəd•əst\ *n*

pa•leo•tem•per•a•ture \-ˈtempə(r),chu̇(ə)r, -p(ə)rə-, -chə(r), -,t(y)u̇(ə)r, -,chu̇ə, -,t(y)u̇ə; *rapid* -ˈtem(p)chə(r)\ *n* : the temperature (as of the ocean) during a past geological age

Pan–Af•ri•can•ism \ˌpanˈafrəkə,nizəm\ *n* : a movement for the political union of all the African nations — **Pan–Af•ri•can** \-kən\ *adj*— **Pan–Af•ri•can•ist** \-kənəst\ *n or adj*

pan•chres•ton \panˈkrestən, -,tän\ *n* [Gk *panchrēston* panacea, fr. neut. of *panchrēstos* good for all work, fr. *pan-* all (fr. *pan,* neut. of *pant-, pas* all, every) + *chrēstos* good] : a broadly inclusive thesis that is intended to cover all possible variations within an area of concern and that in practice usu. proves to be an unacceptable oversimplification

pan·gram \ˈpangrəm, -aŋg-, -ˌgram\ *n* [*pan-* all + Gk *grammat-, gramma* letter] : a short sentence (as "The quick brown fox jumps over the lazy dog") containing all 26 letters of the English alphabet — **pan·gram·mat·ic** \ˌpangrəˈmad·ik, -aŋg-\ *adj*

pant·dress \ˈpantˌdres\ *n* **1** : a garment having a divided skirt **2** : a dress worn over matching shorts

Panther* *n* : BLACK PANTHER

pant·suit *or* **pants suit** \ˈpantˌsüt\ *n* : a woman's ensemble consisting usu. of a long jacket and tailored pants of the same material

panty hose *also* **panti·hose** \ˈpantēˌhōz\ *n* : a one-piece undergarment for women consisting of hosiery combined with a panty

panty raid *n* : a raid on a women's dormitory by male college students to obtain panties as trophies

pa·pa·raz·zo \ˌpäpəˈrät(ˌ)sō\ *n, pl* **pa·pa·raz·zi** \-sē\ [It, fr. It dial., a buzzing insect] : a free-lance photographer who aggressively pursues celebrities for the purpose of taking candid photographs <the New York *paparazzi* were out in great numbers, and their flashbulbs were going off in flickering succession —John Corry>

paper factor *n* : a substance orig. isolated from pulpwood of the balsam fir that is a selectively effective insecticide with activity like that of juvenile hormone

paper gold *n* : SDRS

pa·per–train \ˈpāpə(r)ˌtrān\ *vt* : to train (as a dog) to defecate and urinate on paper in the house

pa·po·va·vi·rus \pəˈpōvəˌvīrəs\ *n* [*pa*pilloma + *po*lyoma + *va*cuolation + *virus*] : any of a group of viruses that have a capsid with 42 protuberances resembling knobs and that are associated with or are responsible for various neoplasms (as some warts) of mammals

Pap smear *also* **Pap test** \ˈpap-\ *n* [*Pap* short for *Papanicolaou,* fr. George N. *Papanicolaou* †1962 Am. medical scientist] : a method for the early detection of cancer employing exfoliated cells and a special staining technique that differentiates diseased tissue

par·a·dox·i·cal sleep \ˌparəˈdäksəkəl-\ *n* : a state of sleep that recurs cyclically several times during a normal period of sleep and that is characterized by increased neuronal activity of the forebrain and midbrain, by depressed muscle tone, and esp. in man by dreaming, rapid eye movements, and vascular congestion of the sex organs — called also *REM sleep*

para·foil \ˈparəˌfȯil\ *n* [*para*chute + *-foil* (as in *airfoil*)] : a self-inflating fabric device that resembles a parachute, behaves in flight like an airplane wing, is maneuverable, is capable of landing a payload at slow speed, and can be launched from the ground in a high wind like a kite

para·glid·er \ˈparəˌglīdə(r)\ *n* [*para*chute + *glider*] : a triangular device on a spacecraft or rocket that consists of two flexible sections, that resembles a kite, and that is deployed when needed for guiding and landing a spacecraft after reentry or for recovering a launching rocket

para·in·flu·en·za virus \ˌparəˌinflüˈenzə-\ *n* [*para-* beside, closely related to (deriv. of Gk *para* beside) + *influenza*] : any of several myxoviruses that are associated with or are responsible for some respiratory infections in children

para·jour·nal·ism \-ˈjərnᵊlˌizəm, -ˈjən-, -ˈjəin-\ *n* : journalism that is heavily colored by the opinions of the reporter <a mini-epoch of ego-tripping *parajournalism* —Herbert Gold> — **para·jour·nal·ist** \-ᵊləst\ *n* — **para·journalistic** \-ᵊlˌistik\ *adj*

para·kite \ˈparəˌkīt\ *n* [*para*chute + *kite*] : a parachute with slits that is towed against the wind by an automobile or motorboat so that a person harnessed to the parachute is lifted and pulled along through the air — **para·kit·ing** \-ˌkīd·iŋ\ *n*

para·lan·guage \-ˌlaŋgwij, -wēj, *sometimes* -ŋw-\ *n* : optional vocal effects (as tone of voice) that accompany or modify the phonemes of an utterance and may communicate meaning

para·le·gal \-ˌlēgəl\ *adj* : of, relating to, or being a paraprofessional who assists a lawyer <a *paralegal* counselor> — **paralegal** *n*

para·lin·guis·tics \ˌparəˌliŋˈgwistiks, -ēks\ *n pl but usu sing in constr* : the study of paralanguage — **para·lin·guis·tic** \-ik, -ēk\ *adj*

para·mag·net·ic resonance \ˌparə(ˌ)magˌned·ik-, -ēk-\ *n* : ELECTRON SPIN RESONANCE

para·med·ic \ˌparəˈmedik, -ēk\ *n* : one who assists a physician (as by giving injections and taking X rays)

pa·ram·e·ter* \pəˈramәd·ә(r)\ *n* **1** : any of a set of physical properties whose values determine the characteristics or behavior of a system <*parameters* of the atmosphere such as temperature, pressure, and density> **2** : something represented by a parameter; *broadly* : characteristic, element, factor <still, by the *parameters* that count, I am among the more liberated women in my zip code —Gael Greene>

pa·ram·e·ter·ize \pəˈramәd·ә,rīz, ˈpram-\ *or* **pa·ram·e·trize** \-mә·ˌtrīz\ *vt* **-ter·ized** *or* **-trized; -ter·iz·ing** *or* **-triz·ing** : to express in terms of parameters — **pa·ram·e·ter·iza·tion** \-ˌramәd·ərəˈzāshən, ˌpram-, -mә·trә-, -ˌīˈzā-\ *or* **pa·ram·e·tri·za·tion** \-mә·trә-\ *n*

para·met·ric amplifier \ˌparəˈme·trik-, -ēk-\ *n* : a high-frequency amplifier whose operation is based on time variations in a parameter (as reactance) and which converts the energy at the frequency of an alternating current into energy at the input signal frequency in such a way as to amplify the signal

parametric equation *n* : any of a set of equations that express the coordinates of the points of a curve as functions of one parameter or that express the coordinates of the points of a surface as functions of two parameters

para·my·o·sin \ˌparəˈmīəsən\ *n* : a fibrous protein that is found in molluscan muscle

para·po·lit·i·cal \-pəˈlid·əkəl\ *adj* : existing alongside a political structure or group in a professedly nonpolitical capacity <*parapolitical* jobs like university presidencies —Adam Hochschild>

para·pro·fes·sion·al \-prəˈfeshnəl, -ənᵊl\ *n* : a trained aide who assists a professional person (as a teacher or physician) <numbers of *paraprofessionals* serving more of the population at a lower technical level —E.Z. Friedenberg> — **paraprofessional** *adj*

para·pro·tein \-ˈprō,tēn, -ˈprōd·ēən\ *n*: any of various abnormal serum globulins with unique physical and electrophoretic characteristics

para·pro·tein·emia \ˌparə,prō,tēˈnēmēə, -ōd·ēəˈn-\ *n* [*paraprotein* + *-emia* blood condition, deriv. of Gk *haima* blood] : the abnormal presence of a paraprotein in the blood

para·quat \ˈparə,kwät\ *n* [*para-* + *qua*ternary] : an herbicide containing a salt of a cation $C_{12}H_{14}N_2$ that is used esp. as a weed killer

para·sex·u·al \ˌparəˈseksh(ə)wəl, -shəl\ *adj* : relating to or being reproduction that results in recombination of genes from different individuals but does not involve meiosis and formation of a zygote by fertilization as in sexual reproduction <the *parasexual* cycle in some fungi>

para·sex·u·al·i·ty* \-ˌsekshəˈwaləd·ē, -i\ *n* : the state of being parasexual

para·wing \ˈparə,wiŋ\ *n* [*para*chute + *wing*] : PARAGLIDER

par·gy·line \ˈpärjə,lēn\ *n* [pro*pargyl,* an alcohol + *-ine* chemical substance] : a monoamine oxidase inhibitor $C_{11}H_{13}N$ whose hydrochloride is used as an antihypertensive and antidepressant agent

pa·ri·etals \pəˈrīəd·ᵊlz\ *n pl* : the regulations governing the visiting privileges of members of the opposite sex in campus dormitories

par·i·ty* \ˈparəd·ē, -i, *also* ˈper-\ *n* **1 a** : the property of an integer with respect to being odd or even <3 and 7 have the same *parity*> **b** : the property of oddness or evenness of an odd or even function (as certain functions in quantum mechanics) **c** (1) : the state of being odd or even used as the basis of a method of detecting errors in binary-coded data (2) : PARITY BIT **2** : the property of an elementary particle or physical system that indicates whether or not its mirror image occurs in nature

parity bit *n* : a bit added to an array of bits (as on magnetic tape) to provide parity

parking orbit *n* : the orbit of an artificial satellite or a space vehicle traveling around a body (as the earth) in such a way as to serve as a station from which another vehicle is launched or as to be itself propelled later into a new trajectory

Par·kin·son's Law \ˌpärkənsənz-, ˌpȧk-\ *n* [C. Northcote *Parkinson* b1909 Eng. historian] **1** : an observation in office organization: the number of subordinates increases at a fixed rate regardless of the amount of work produced **2** : an observation in office organization: work expands so as to fill the time available for its completion

par·o·mo·my·cin \ˌparəmōˈmīsᵊn\ *n* [Gk *paromoios* closely resembling (fr. *para-* beside + *homoios* like) + E connective *-o-* + *-mycin* substance obtained from a fungus, fr. *streptomycin;* fr. its similarity to neomycin] : a broad-spectrum antibiotic that is obtained from a streptomyces (*Streptomyces rimosus*) and is used esp. against intestinal amebiasis

Parsons table *n* [prob. fr. the name *Parsons*] : a rectangular table having straight legs that form the four corners

partially ordered *adj* : having some but not all mathematical elements connected by a relation that is transitive and not symmetric

partial product *n* : a product obtained by multiplying a multiplicand by one digit of a multiplier with more than one digit

par·ti·cle·board \ˈpärd·əkəlˌbō(ə)rd, -ˌbȯ(ə)rd; ˈpȧd·-, -ˌbōəd, -ˌbȯ(ə)d\ *n* : a composition board made of very small pieces of wood bonded together (as with a synthetic resin)

particle physics *n* : HIGH-ENERGY PHYSICS

partition* *n* : the separation of a set (as the points of a line) into subsets such that every element belongs to one set and no two subsets have an element in common

par·ton \ˈpärˌtän\ *n* [*part* + *-on* elementary particle] : a hypothetical particle that is held to be a constituent of nucleons

party poop·er \-ˌpüpə(r)\ *n* : one who refuses to join in the fun at a party; *broadly* : one who refuses to go along with everyone else <I hate to be a *party pooper* but I did not find it "dazzling" or "a smash" or "a milestone in TV entertainment"—Goodman Ace>

par·y·lene \ˈparəˌlēn\ *n* [contr. of *paraxylene*] : any of several thermoplastic crystalline materials that are polymers of paraxylene and are used esp. as electrical insulation coating

pas·cal \pasˈkal, pȧskȧl\ *n* [after Blaise *Pascal* †1662 Fr. scientist and philosopher] : a unit of pressure in the mks system equivalent to one newton per square meter

pass–fail \ˈpasˈfā(ə)l\ *n* : a system of grading whereby the grades "pass" and "fail" replace the traditional letter grades — **pass–fail** *adj*

passive* *adj* **1** : not involving expenditure of chemical energy <*passive* transport across a cell membrane> **2 a** : exhibiting no gain or control — used of an electronic device (as a capacitor or resistor) **b** : operating solely by means of the power of an input signal <a *passive* communication satellite that reflects television signals> **c** : relating to the detection of or to orientation by means of an object through its emission of energy <a *passive* microwave radiometer>

passive immunization *n* : the process of conferring passive immunity

pasteurization* *n* : partial sterilization of perishable food products (as fruit or fish) with radiation (as gamma rays)

past·ies \ˈpāstēz\ *n pl* [*paste* to stick + *-ie,* dim. suffix] : small usu. round coverings for a woman's nipples <she popped out of a birthday cake, wearing only *pasties* and a black garter —Timothy Ferris>

pas·tis \paˈstis, -ēs\ *n* [F] : a French licorice-flavored liqueur

pata·phys·ics \ˌpad·əˈfiziks\ *n pl but sing in constr* [F *pataphysique*] : intricate and whimsical nonsense intended as a parody of science — **pata·phys·i·cal** \-əkəl\ *adj* — **pata·phy·si·cian** \-fəˈzishən\ *n*

patch* *n* : a temporary correction in a faulty computer program

patch* *vt* **1** : to make a patch in (a computer program) **2** : to connect (as circuits) by a patch cord

patch·board \ˈpachˌbō(ə)rd, -ˌbȯ(ə)rd, -ˌbōəd, -ˌbȯ(ə)d\ *n* : a plugboard in which circuits are interconnected by patch cords

patch panel *n* : PATCHBOARD

path* *n* : a sequence of arcs in a network that can be traced continuously without retracing any arc

patho·mor·phol·o·gy \ˌpathō(ˌ)mȯr¦fäləjē\ *n* [*patho-* disease (deriv. of Gk *pathos,* lit., suffering) + *morphology*] : morphology of abnormal conditions — **patho·mor·pho·log·i·cal** \-ˌmȯrfə¦läjəkəl\ *or* **patho·mor·pho·log·ic** \-jik, -jēk\ *adj*

pa·tri·fo·cal \ˌpa·trə¦fōkəl, ¦pä-\ *adj* [*patri-* father (fr. L *pater*) + *focal*] : gravitating toward or centered upon the father : patricentric <a *patrifocal* family structure>

patterning* *n* : physiotherapy that is designed to improve malfunctioning nervous control by means of feedback from muscular activity imposed by an outside source or induced by other muscles

pau·piette \pō'pyet, (ˌ)pōpē'et\ *n* [F] : a thin slice of meat or fish wrapped around a forcemeat filling

pay·load* \'pāˌlōd\ *n* : the load that is carried by a spacecraft and that consists of things (as passengers or instruments) which relate directly to the purpose of the flight as opposed to things (as fuel) which are necessary for operation; *also* : the weight of such a load

pay·out ratio \'pāˌau̇t-\ *n* : a ratio relating dividend payout of a company to its earnings or cash flow

pazazz *var of* PIZZAZZ

PBS *abbr* Public Broadcasting Service

PCB \ˌpē(ˌ)sē'bē\ *n* [*p*oly*c*hlorinated *b*iphenyl] : POLYCHLORINATED BIPHENYL

PCP \ˌpē(ˌ)sē'pē\ *n* [prob. fr. *p*hen*c*yclidine + *p*ill] : PHENCYCLIDINE

PCV valve *n* [*p*ositive *c*rankcase *v*entilation] : an automotive-emission control valve that recirculates gases (as from blow-by) through the combustion chambers to permit more complete combustion

peaceful co·ex·is·tence \-ˌkōəg'zistən(t)s\ *n* : a living together in peace rather than in constant hostility <the *peaceful coexistence* of states with different social systems —A.P. Mendel>

peace·nik \'pē(ˌ)snik\ *n* [*peace* + *-nik*] : an opponent of war <nor are all the *peaceniks* in Israel young —Georgiana G. Stevens>; *specif* : one who participates in antiwar demonstrations <pictures of protesting social workers, schoolteachers, *peaceniks* or whoever marching around carrying signs — *Wall Street Jour.*>

peace sign *n* : a sign made by holding the palm outward and forming a V with the index and middle fingers that is used to indicate the desire for peace or as a greeting or farewell

peace symbol *n* : the symbol ☮ used to signify peace

pearl* *vi, of a surfboard* : to make a nose dive into the trough of a wave

peat·land \'pētˌland\ *n* : land rich in peat

Peck's bad boy \ˌpeks-\ *n* [fr. the book *Peck's Bad Boy and his Pa* (1883) by George Wilbur Peck †1916 Am. journalist, humorist, and politician] : one whose bad behavior is a source of embarrassment or annoyance <industry, the *Peck's bad boy* of environmentalism —*Newsweek*>

pe·do·phile \'pēdəˌfīl\ *n* [back-formation fr. *pedophilia*] : one affected with pedophilia

peek-a-boo \'pēkəˌbü\ *adj* : of, relating to, or being a document retrieval system in which desired documents are identified by light shining through matching holes in index cards

Pe·king·ol·o·gy \ˌpē(ˌ)kiŋ'äləjē, pē¦kiŋ-\ *n* [*Peking,* capital of Communist China + connective *-o-* + *-logy* theory, science, deriv. of Gk *logos* word] : the study of the policies and practices of Communist China — **Pe·king·ol·o·gist** \-jəst\ *n*

pel·o·ton \ˌpelə'tän, *F* plōtō^{n}\ *or* **peloton glass** *n* [prob. fr. F *peloton* ball, ball of string] : a European ornamental glass often with a variegated metallized and satinized surface and usu. overlaid with strands of contrasting color

pem·o·line \'peməˌlēn, -ələn\ *n* [perh. fr. *ph*enyl + i*m*ino + oxaz*oli*dino*ne,* a derivative of oxazolidine] : a synthetic organic drug $C_9H_8N_2O_2$ that is usu. mixed with magnesium hydroxide, is a mild stimulant of the central nervous system, and is used experimentally to improve memory

pen·ta·gas·trin \¦pentə¦gastrən\ *n* [*penta*peptide + *gastrin,* a hormone that induces secretion of gastric juice] : a pentapeptide that stimulates secretion of gastric acid

pen·ta·pep·tide \¦pentə¦pepˌtīd\ *n* [*penta-* five (deriv. of Gk *pente*) + *peptide*] : a polypeptide that contains five amino acid residues

pen·taz·o·cine \pen'tazə,sēn, -əsən\ *n* [*pent-* five + *-azocine* (as in *phenazocine*)] : an analgesic drug $C_{19}H_{27}NO$ that does not have the strong addictive properties of morphine

pen·to·bar·bi·tone \ˌpentō'bärbə,tōn\ *n* [*pent-* five + connective *-o-* + *barbitone*] *Brit* : a granular barbiturate $C_{11}H_{18}N_2O_3$ used esp. in the form of its sodium or calcium salt as a sedative, hypnotic, and antispasmodic : pentobarbital

pepper steak *n* **1** : thin-sliced steak cooked with green peppers, onions, tomatoes, and soy sauce **2** : STEAK AU POIVRE

per·cen·tile* \pə(r)'sen,tīl\ *n* : a value on a scale of one hundred that indicates the percent of a distribution that is equal to or below it (as in performance) <a score in the 95th *percentile* is a score equal to or better than 95 percent of the scores>

pe·re·on·ite \pə'rēə,nīt\ *n* [*pereon* (var. of *pereion*) + *-ite* segment] : any of the segments of a pereion

per·fec·ta \pə(r)'fektə\ *n* [AmerSp *quiniela perfecta* perfect quiniela] : a betting pool in which the bettor must pick the first and second finishers in a specified race or contest in the correct order in order to win — called also *exacta*

performance* *n* : linguistic behavior — contrasted with *competence*

per·for·ma·tive \pər'fȯrməd·iv, -'fȯ(ə)m-\ *n* [*perform* + *-ative* (as in *imperative*)] : an expression that serves to effect a transaction or that constitutes the performance of the specified act by virtue of its utterance <many *performatives* are *contractual* ("I bet") or *declaratory* ("I declare war") utterances —J.L. Austin> — **performative** *adj*

peri·ap·sis \ˌperē'apsəs\ *n, pl* **peri·ap·si·des** \-'apsə,dē\ [NL, fr. *peri-* around, near (deriv. of Gk *peri*) + *apsis*] : the apsis least distant from the center of attraction

peri·cyn·thi·on \ˌperə'sin(t)thēən\ *n* [NL, fr. *peri-* + *Cynthia*, goddess of the moon (fr. Gk *Kynthia*) + *-on* (as in *aphelion*)] : PERILUNE

peri·lune \'perə,lün\ *n* [*peri-* + L *luna* moon] : the point in the path of a body orbiting the moon that is nearest to the center of the moon

peri·nu·cle·ar \ˌperə'n(y)üklēə(r), ÷ -kyələ(r)\ *adj* : situated around or surrounding the nucleus of a cell

pe·riph·er·al* \pə'rif(ə)rəl\ *adj* : auxiliary, supplementary <a computer's *peripheral* equipment>; *also* : of or relating to computer peripherals

peripheral *n* : a device connected to a computer to provide communication (as input and output) or auxiliary functions (as additional storage)

peri·se·lene \'perəsə,lēn\ *n* [ISV *peri-* + *-selene*, fr. Gk *selēnē* moon] : PERILUNE

peri·se·le·ni·um \ˌperəsə'lēnēəm\ *n* [NL, fr. Gk *peri-* peri- + *selēnē* moon + NL *-ium*, alter. of *-ion* (as in *aphelion*)] : PERILUNE

pe·ri·tus \pə'rēd·əs\ *n, pl* **pe·ri·ti** \-ēd·ē, -ē,tē\ [NL, fr. L *peritus*, adj., skilled, experienced] : an expert (as in theology or canon law) who advises and assists the hierarchy (as in the drafting of schemata) at a Vatican council

permanent press *n* : DURABLE PRESS — **permanent-press** *adj*

per·me·ase \'pərmē,ās, 'pəm-, 'pəim-, -āz\ *n* [ISV *perme-* (fr. *permeate*) + *-ase* enzyme] : an enzyme that catalyzes the transport of another substance across a cell membrane

per·oxi·some \pə'räksə,sōm\ *n* [*peroxide* + *-some* body, deriv. of Gk *sōma*] : a cytoplasmic cell organelle containing enzymes for the production and decomposition of hydrogen peroxide — **per·oxi·som·al** \-ˌräksə'sōməl\ *adj*

per·phe·na·zine \(ˌ)pə(r)'fēnə,zēn, -'fen-\ *n* [blend of *piperazine* and *phenyl*] : a tranquilizing drug $C_{21}H_{26}ClN_3OS$ that is used to control tension, anxiety, and agitation esp. in psychotic conditions

persistent* *adj* **1** : degraded only slowly by the environment <*persistent* pesticides> **2** : remaining infective for a relatively long time in a vector after an initial period of incubation <*persistent* viruses>

personality inventory *n* : any of several tests that attempt to characterize the personality of an individual by objective scoring of replies to numerous questions concerning his own behavior and attitudes — compare MINNESOTA MULTIPHASIC PERSONALITY INVENTORY

personal tax *n* : a tax exacted directly from the person on whom the ultimate burden of the tax is expected to fall : a direct tax

PERT \ˈpərt\ *n*[*p*rogram *e*valuation and *r*eview *t*echnique] : a technique for planning, scheduling, and monitoring a complex project esp. by graphically displaying the separate tasks and showing how they are interconnected

pe·se·wa \pəˈsäwə\ *n*[native name in Ghana] **1** : a monetary unit of Ghana equal to $^{1}/_{100}$ cedi **2** : a coin representing one pesewa

Pe·ter Principle \ˈpēd·ə(r)-\ *n* [Laurence Johnston *Peter b*1919 Am. (Canad.-born) educator, its formulator] : an observation: in a hierarchy every employee tends to rise to his level of incompetence

pe·tit bour·geois \ˌped·ē¦bu̇(ə)rzh¦wä, pə¦tē(t)-; -¦bu̇(ə)zh¦wä, -¦wȧ; *sometimes* -ˈbüzh,-\ *adj* : of, relating to, or characteristic of the petite bourgeoisie

pet·nap·ping \ˈpet,napiŋ\ *n* [*pet* + *-napping* (as in *kidnapping*)] : the act of stealing a pet (as a cat or dog) usu. for profit

pet·ro·dol·lars \ˈpe·trō,däl̇ə(r)z\ *n pl* [*petro*leum + *dollars*] : foreign exchange obtained by petroleum-exporting countries by sales abroad; *esp* : the part in excess of domestic needs that constitutes a pool of potential foreign investment

PG \(ˌ)pēˈjē\ *adj*[*p*arental *g*uidance] *of a motion picture* : of such a nature that persons of all ages may be allowed admission but parental guidance is suggested — compare G,R,X

phago·some \ˈfagə,sōm\ *n* [*phago-* eating, feeding (fr. Gk *phagein* to eat) + *-some* body, deriv. of Gk *sōma*] : a membrane-surrounded vesicle that encloses materials taken into the cell by endocytosis

phal·lic* \ˈfalik, -ēk\ *adj* : of, relating to, or being the stage of psychosexual development in psychoanalytic theory during which a child becomes interested in his own sexual organs — **phal·li·cal·ly** \ˈfalə̇k(ə)lē\ *adv*

phase·out \ˈfā,zau̇t\ *n* : a gradual stopping of operations or production : a closing down by phases

phe·naz·o·cine \fə̇ˈnazə,sēn, -əsə̇n\ *n*[*phen*yl + *-azocine* (perh. irreg. fr. *azoic* containing an azo group + *-ine* chemical substance)] : a drug $C_{22}H_{27}NO$ related to morphine that has greater pain-relieving and slighter narcotic effect

phen·cy·cli·dine \(ˈ)fenˈsiklə̇,dēn, -ˈsīk-, -ədə̇n\ *n* [*phen*yl + *cycl*ic + *-idine* related compound] : a piperidine derivative $C_{17}H_{25}N$ used medicinally as an anesthetic and sometimes illicitly as a psychedelic drug to induce vivid mental imagery — called also *PCP*

phen·el·zine \ˈfenᵊl,zēn\ *n* [*phen*yl + ethy*l* + hydra*zine*] : a monoamine oxidase inhibitor $C_8H_{12}N_2$ used esp. as an antidepressant drug

phe·neth·i·cil·lin \fə̇¦nethə¦silə̇n\ *n*[*phen*yl + *eth*yl + pen*icillin*] : a synthetic penicillin administered orally and used esp. in the treatment of less severe infections caused by bacteria that do not produce penicillinase

phe·net·ic \fə̇ˈned·ik, -ēk\ *adj* [*phen*otype + *-etic* (as in *genetic*)] : of, relating to, or being classificatory systems and procedures that are based on overall similarity usu. of many characters without regard to the evolutionary history of the organisms involved — compare CLADISTIC

phe·net·ics \-iks, -ēks\ *n pl but sing in constr* : a biological systematics based on phenetic relationships — **phe·net·i·cist** \-ˈned·əsə̇st\ *n*

phen·for·min \fenˈfȯrmə̇n, -fȯ(ə)m-\ *n*[*phen*yl + *form*amide + *-in* chemical compound] : a somewhat toxic drug $C_{10}H_{15}N_5$ that is administered orally to lower blood sugar in some cases of diabetes

phen·met·ra·zine \(ˈ)fenˈme·trə,zēn\ *n*[*phen*yl + *me*thyl + te*tra-* four + oxa*zine*] : a sympathomimetic stimulant $C_{11}H_{15}NO$ that tends to cause loss of appetite

phe·no·thi·azine* \ˌfēnōˈthīə,zēn\ *n* : any of various phenothiazine derivatives (as chlorpromazine) that are used as tranquilizing agents esp. in the treatment of schizophrenia

phen·tol·amine \fen'tälə,mēn, -əmən\ *n*[*phen*yl + *tol*uidine + *amine*] : an adrenergic blocking agent $C_{17}H_{19}N_3O$ that is used esp. in the diagnosis of hypertension due to pheochromocytoma

phe·ren·ta·sin \fə'rentəsən\ *n* [Gk *pherein* to carry + *entasis* tension, stretching + E *-in* chemical compound] : a pressor amine present in the blood in severe hypertension

pher·o·mone \'ferə,mōn\ *n* [ISV *phero-* (fr. Gk *pherein* to carry) + *-mone* (as in *hormone*); orig. formed as G *pheromon;* fr. its conveying information from one individual to another] : a chemical substance that is produced by an animal and serves as a specific stimulus to other individuals of the same species for one or more behavioral responses — **pher·o·mon·al** \-nᵊl\ *adj*

Phil·lips curve \,filəps-\ *n* [A.W.H. *Phillips b*1914 Brit. economist] : a graphic representation of the relation between inflation and unemployment which indicates that as the rate of either increases that of the other declines

phil·lu·men·ist \fə'lümənəst\ *n* [*phil-* loving (deriv. of Gk *philos* beloved, loving) + L *lumen* light + E *-ist*, n. suffix] : one who collects matchbooks or matchbox labels

phle·bol·o·gy \flə'bäləjē\ *n* [ISV *phlebo-* vein (deriv. of Gk *phleb-, phleps*) + *-logy* theory, science, deriv. of Gk *logos* word] : a branch of medicine concerned with the veins

phone–in \'fō,nin\ *n* : a call-in radio program

pho·no·car·dio·graph \,fōnə'kärdēə,graf\ *n* : a recording instrument used in phonocardiography

pho·no·rec·ord \'fōnō,rekə(r)d, *also* -k,ȯ(ə)rd *or* -k,ȯ(ə)d\ *n* [*phono*graph + *record*] : a phonograph record

pho·no·tac·tics \,fōnə'taktiks, -ēks\ *n pl but sing in constr* [*phono-* sound, voice (deriv. of Gk *phōnē*) + *tactics*] : the area of phonology concerned with the analysis and description of the permitted phoneme sequences of a language — **pho·no·tac·tic** \,fōnə,taktik, -ēk\ *adj*

phor·ate \'fō(ə)r,āt, 'fȯ(ə)r-\ *n* [phos*phor*us + thion*ate*] : a very toxic organophosphate systemic insecticide $C_7H_{17}O_2PS_3$ that is used esp. to treat seeds

phos·pham·i·don \fäs'famə,dän\ *n* [*phospho*rus + *amide* + *-on* chemical compound] : a contact and systemic organophosphorus insecticide and miticide $C_{10}H_{19}ClNO_5P$

phos·pho·enol·pyr·uvate \'fäs,fōə,nȯlpī'rü,vāt, -,nōl-, -,pī(ə)r'yü-\ *n* [*phosphoenolpyru*vic (acid) + *-ate* salt or ester] : a salt or ester of phosphoenolpyruvic acid

phos·pho·fruc·to·ki·nase \'fäs(,)fō,frəktō'kī,nās, -frük-, -frůk-, -,nāz\ *n* [*phospho*rus + *fructo*se + *kinase*] : an enzyme that catalyzes the transfer of a second phosphate (as from ATP) to fructose in carbohydrate metabolism

phos·pho·glyc·er·al·de·hyde \,fäs(,)fō,glisə'raldə,hīd\ *n* : a phosphate of glyceraldehyde $C_3H_5O_3(H_2PO_3)$ that is formed esp. in anaerobic metabolism of carbohydrates by the splitting of a diphosphate of fructose

phos·pho·ki·nase \-,kī,nās, -,nāz\ *n* : an enzyme that catalyzes the transfer of phosphate groups from ATP or ADP to a substrate

phos·pho·pyr·uvate \-pī'rü,vāt, -(,)pī(ə)r'yü-\ *n* : PHOSPHOENOLPYRUVATE

pho·to·bi·ol·o·gist \,fōd·(,)ōbī'äləjəst\ *n* : a specialist in photobiology

¹pho·to·chro·mic \,fōd·ə,krōmik, -ēk\ *adj* [*photo-* light (fr. Gk *phōt-, phōs*) + *chrom-* color (deriv. of Gk *chrōma*) + *-ic*, adj. suffix] **1** : capable of changing color on exposure to radiant energy (as light) <*photochromic* glass> <*photochromic* proteins> **2** : of, relating to, or utilizing the change of color shown by a photochromic substance <a *photochromic* process> — **pho·to·chro·mism** \-,mizəm\ *n*

²photochromic *n* : a photochromic substance

pho·to·co·ag·u·la·tion \,fōd·ə(,)kō,agyə'lāshən\ *n* : surgical coagulation of tissue by means of a precisely oriented high-energy light source (as a laser beam) — **pho·to·co·ag·u·la·tive** \-kō,agyə,lād·iv, -ēv\ *adj* — **pho·to·co·ag·u·la·tor** \-kō,agyə,lād·ə(r)\ *n*

pho·to–es·say \,fōd·ō'es,ā\ *n* : an analytic or interpretive photographic presentation usu. dealing with its subject from a personal point of view

pho·to·fab·ri·ca·tion \ˌfōd·(ˌ)ō,fabrəˈkāshən\ *n* [*photo-* light, photograph + *fabrication*] : a process for manufacturing components (as microcircuits) in which a design is photographed, reduced, and chemically etched on a surface (as of a semiconductor)
pho·to·in·duced \-ənˈd(y)üst\ *adj* : induced by the action of light <*photoinduced* color changes>
pho·to·isom·er·i·za·tion \ˌfōd·ō(ˌ)ī,sämərəˈzāshən, -ˌrīˈzā-\ *n* : the light-initiated process of change from one isomeric form of a compound, radical, or ion to another
pho·to·mor·pho·gen·e·sis \ˌfōd·ə,mȯrfəˈjenəsəs\ *n* : plant morphogenesis controlled by radiant energy (as light) — **pho·to·mor·pho·gen·ic** \-ˈjenik, -ēk\ *adj*
pho·to·phos·phor·y·la·tion \ˌfōd·ō,fäs,fȯrəˈlāshən\ *n* : the conversion of AMP and ADP to ATP in photosynthesis using radiant energy
pho·to·poly·mer \ˌfōd·ōˈpäləmə(r)\ *n* : a photosensitive plastic used esp. in the manufacture of printing plates
pho·to·re·ac·ti·va·tion \-rē,aktəˈvāshən\ *n* : repair of DNA (as of a bacterium) esp. by a light-dependent enzymatic reaction after damage by ultraviolet irradiation — **pho·to·re·ac·ti·vat·ing** \-ˈaktə,vād·iŋ\ *adj*
pho·to–re·al·ism \ˌfōd·ōˈrēə,lizəm, -ˈriə-\ *n* [*photo-* photographic + *realism*] : realism in painting characterized by the meticulous unidealized depiction esp. of the vulgar or sordid aspects of life — **pho·to–re·al·ist** \-ələst\ *n or adj*
pho·to·re·sist \-rəˈzist\ *n* : a photosensitive resist that polymerizes when exposed to ultraviolet light and that is used in chemical etching
pho·to·res·pi·ra·tion \-ˌrespəˈrāshən\ *n* : oxidation involving production of carbon dioxide during photosynthesis
pho·to·scan \ˈfōd·ō,skan\ *n* [*photoscan*, v.] : a photographic representation of variation in tissue state (as of the kidney) determined by gamma ray emission from an injected radioactive substance — **photoscan** *vb* — **pho·to·scan·ner** \-ˌskanə(r)\ *n*
phrase marker *n* : a representation of the immediate constituent structure of a linguistic construction
phrase structure *n* : the arrangement of the constituents of a sentence
phy·tane \ˈfī,tān\ *n* [*phyt-* plant (deriv. of Gk *phyton*) + *-ane* saturated carbon compound] : an isoprenoid hydrocarbon $C_{20}H_{42}$ that is found esp. associated with fossilized plant remains from the Precambrian and later eras
phy·to·alex·in \ˌfīd·ōəˈleksən\ *n* [*phyto-* plant + *alexin*] : a chemical substance produced by a plant to combat infection by a pathogen (as a fungus)
phy·to·chem·i·cal \-ˈkeməkəl\ *adj* : of, relating to, or being phytochemistry — **phy·to·chem·i·cal·ly** \-k(ə)lē, -li\ *adv*
phy·to·chem·is·try \-ˈkeməstrē\ *n* : the chemistry of plants, plant processes, and plant products — **phy·to·chem·ist** \-ˈkeməst\ *n*
phy·to·chrome \ˈfīd·ə,krōm\ *n* [*phyto-* + *-chrome* coloring matter, deriv. of Gk *chrōma* color] : a chromoprotein that is present in traces in many plants and that plays a role in initiating floral and developmental processes when activated by red or far-red radiation
phy·to·he·mag·glu·ti·nin *also* **phy·to·hae·mag·glu·ti·nin** \ˌfīd·ō,hēməˈglütᵊnən\ *n* : a proteinaceous hemagglutinin of plant origin used esp. to induce mitosis
phy·to·tron \ˈfīd·ə·,trän\ *n* [*phyto-* + *-tron* (as in *cyclotron*)] : a laboratory with facilities for growing plants under various combinations of strictly controlled environmental conditions
PI* *abbr* programmed instruction
piano bar *n* : a cocktail bar that features live piano music
pi·clo·ram \ˈpiklə,ram, ˈpīk-\ *n* [*pic*oline + ch*lor*ine + *am*ine] : a systemic herbicide $C_6H_3Cl_3N_2O_2$ that breaks down only very slowly in the soil
pi·co·farad \ˌpēkōˈfar,ad, -ˈfarəd\ *n* [ISV *pico-* one trillionth, very small (perh. fr. It *piccolo* small) + *farad*] : one trillionth of a farad
pi·co·gram \ˈpēkə,gram\ *n* : one trillionth of a gram
pi·cor·na·vi·rus \pəˈkȯrnəˈvīrəs\ *n* [*pico-* + *RNA* + *virus*] : any of a group of RNA-containing viruses that includes the enteroviruses and rhinoviruses
pi·co·sec·ond \ˌpēkōˈsekənd, -ənt\ *n* : one trillionth of a second

piece* *n* — **piece of the action :** a share in activity or profit <guys in tight-fitting hip-looking suits rubbing their hands slowly together with dollar signs in their eyes. They were . . . managers and agents and producers and all the others that had a *piece of the action* —Charlie Frick>

piece·wise \'pē,swīz\ *adv* : with respect to a number of discrete intervals, sets, or pieces <*piecewise* continuous functions>

pig* *n* : a policeman — usu. used disparagingly

piggyback* *adj* **1** : of, relating to, or being something (as a capsule or package) carried into space as an extra load by a vehicle (as a spacecraft or rocket) **2** : of, relating to, or being a radio or television commercial that is presented in addition to other commercials during one commercial break — **piggyback*** *adv*

Pil·i·pi·no \,pilə'pē(,)nō\ *n* [Pilipino, fr. Sp *Filipino* Philippine] : the Tagalog-based official language of the Republic of the Philippines

pill* *n, often cap* : an oral contraceptive — usu. used with *the* <all the forces believed responsible for the present low and still-falling birthrate are still at work—legal abortion, the *pill,* and a conviction among young people that large families are both socially undesirable and financially burdensome —Paul Woodring>

pillhead \'pil,hed\ *n* : a person who takes pills or capsules (as of amphetamines) for nonmedicinal reasons

pillow talk *n* : intimate conversation between lovers in bed

pill pool *n* [fr. the drawing of small numbered balls from a bottle to determine order of play] : a pocket billiards game in which each player before playing draws from a bottle little numbered balls that are essential to the scoring of the game : Kelly pool

pi·ña co·la·da \,pēnyəkō'lädə\ *n* [Sp, lit., strained pineapple] : a tall drink made of rum, coconut cream, and pineapple juice mixed with ice

pin·hold·er \'pin,hōldə(r)\ *n* : a flower holder that consists of a substantial base topped with projecting pins

pi·no·cy·tot·ic \,pinō(,)sī'täd·ik, ,pīn-, -ōsə't-\ *adj* : of, relating to, or being pinocytosis — **pi·no·cy·tot·i·cal·ly** \-ək(ə)lē\ *adv*

pinta \'pīntə\ *n* [*pint* + *-a* (as in *cuppa*)] *Brit* : a pint of milk <if you want to reduce your chance of becoming intoxicated . . . then get down to your *pinta* before the party —*News of the World*>

pi·sci·cide \'pīsə,sīd, 'pisə-, 'piskə-\ *n* [*pisci-* fish (fr. L *piscis*) + *-cide* killer, deriv. of L *caedere* to cut, kill] : a substance used to kill fish — **pi·sci·ci·dal** \-'sīdᵊl\ *adj*

piss off \'pis'äf, -'ȯf\ *vi, Brit* : to leave forthwith : get out — usu. used as a command <"How's it going, Michael?" "*Piss off,*" he says. He was losing —Spike Milligan>

pivot* *n* : a key player or position; *specif* : an offensive player position in basketball that is occupied by a player (as a center) who stands usu. with his back to his own basket to relay passes, shoot, or provide a screen for teammates

piv·ot·man \'pivət,man, 'pivətmən\ *n* : one who plays the pivot; *specif* : a center on a basketball team

piz·zazz *or* **pi·zazz** *also* **pa·zazz** \pə'zaz\ *n* [origin unknown] : the quality of being exciting or attractive: as **a** : glamour, showiness <bemoans the lack of color and provocative *pizzazz* in today's stars —Vernon Scott> **b** : spirit, vitality <we had four numbers with *pizzazz* and the rest of the show died around them —Gower Champion>

PKU *abbr* phenylketonuria

pla·ce·bo effect \plə'sē(,)bō-\ *n* : improvement in the condition of a sick person that occurs in response to treatment but cannot be considered due to the specific treatment used

place value *n* : the value of the location of a digit in a numeral <in 425 the location of the digit 2 has a *place value* of ten while the digit itself indicates that there are two tens>

¹plane·side \'plān,sīd\ *n* : the area adjacent to an airplane <speaking briefly at *planeside* —*Christian Science Monitor*>

²planeside *adj* : engaged in or made at planeside <paused first for a *planeside* interview —*Time*> <his *planeside* remark —*Newsweek*>

plan·e·tol·o·gy \ˌplanəˈtäləjē\ *n* [*planet* + connective *-o-* + *-logy* science, theory, deriv. of Gk *logos* word] : a study that deals with the condensed matter (as the planets, natural satellites, comets, and meteorites) of the solar system — **plan·e·to·logi·cal** \-ətᵊlˈäjəkəl\ *adj* — **plan·e·tol·o·gist** \-ˈtäləjəst\ *n*

plaque* *n* : a clear area in a bacterial culture produced by destruction of cells by a virus

plasma* *n* : a collection of charged particles (as in a metal) containing about equal numbers of positive ions and electrons that is a good conductor of electricity

plasma jet *n* **1** : a stream of very hot gaseous plasma; *also* : a device for producing such a stream **2** *or* **plasma engine** : a rocket engine designed to derive thrust from the discharge of a magnetically accelerated plasma

plasma torch *n* : a device that heats a gas by electrical means to form a plasma for high-temperature operations (as melting metal)

plas·mid \ˈplazməd\ *n* [*plasma* + *-id* structure, particle] : a cellular element that exists and replicates autonomously in the cytoplasm : plasmagene

plas·mon \ˈplazˌmän\ *n* [*plasma* + *-on* elementary particle] : a quantum of energy that propagates through a plasma as a result of charge density fluctuation

plastic* *adj* : not genuine or sincere : artificial, phony <this is the *plastic* age, the era of the sham and the bogus —Logan Gourlay> <having a speech writer would be definitely too *plastic* —Mark Spitz> — often used as a generalized term of disapproval <takes a positive effort of will . . . to avoid *plastic* food, *plastic* living, and *plastic* entertainment —L.E. Sissman>

plas·to·qui·none \ˌplastōkwəˈnōn, -ˈkwinˌōn\ *n* [*plasto-* formation, development (fr. Gk *plastos* formed, molded) + *quinone*] : a plant substance that is related to vitamin K and plays a role in photosynthetic phosphorylation

plate* *n* : any of the large movable segments into which the earth's crust is divided according to the theory of plate tectonics

plate* *vt* **plat·ed; plat·ing** [fr. the crossing of home plate by the scoring runner] : to cause (as a run) to score in baseball <hit his triple and *plated* two runs —*Sporting News*>

plated am·ber·i·na \-ˌambəˈrēnə\ *n* : an ornamental glass consisting of an amberina casing over a fiery opalescent or white lining

plate·glass \ˈplātˈglas, *in attributive position also* ˌplātˌglas\ *adj* [fr. the common use of plate glass in constructing the buildings of modern British universities] : of, relating to, or being the British universities founded in the latter half of the twentieth century — compare OXBRIDGE, REDBRICK

plate tec·ton·ics \-tekˈtäniks, -ēks\ *n pl but sing in constr* : a theory that the lithosphere of the earth is divided into a small number of plates which float on and travel independently over the mantle and that much of the earth's seismic activity occurs at the boundaries of these plates as a result of frictional interaction; *also* : the process and dynamics of plate movement

platform tennis *n* : a variation of paddle tennis that is played on a wooden platform enclosed by a wire fence

platoon* *n* : two or more players (as in baseball) who alternate in playing the same position

platoon* *vt* : to alternate (one player) with another player in the same position <if I can't play him every day, I'll *platoon* him in left field —Leo Durocher> ~ *vi* **1** : to alternate with another player in the same position **2** : to use alternate players at the same position

play–ac·tion pass \ˌplāˈakshən-\ *n* : a pass play in football in which the quarterback fakes a hand-off before passing the ball

play·book* \ˈplāˌbu̇k\ *n* : a notebook containing diagramed football plays

play·list \-ˌlist\ *n* : a list of recordings to be played on the air by a radio station

plea bargaining *n* : the negotiation of an agreement between a prosecutor and a defendant whereby the defendant is permitted to plead guilty to a reduced charge <sometimes the prisoner helps delay his own trial because he realizes that the longer he is in prison the greater are the chances for *plea bargaining* and a reduced sentence —*Encore*>

plench \\'plench\\ *n* [*pl*iers + wr*ench*] : a combination pliers and wrench operated by squeezing the handle and used to make pulling and turning motions under zero gravity

PL/1 \\(ˌ)pēˌel'wən\\ *n* [*p*rogramming *l*anguage (version) *1*] : a general purpose language for programming a computer

plot* *vi* **plot·ted; plot·ting** : to be located by means of coordinates <the data *plot* at a single point>

plug·ola \\ˌplə'gōlə\\ *n* [*plug* + pay*ola*] **1** : payola given to broadcasters for favorably mentioning or displaying a product other than that of the sponsor of the program aired **2** : bias in news reporting <unlike most of the smoothies that transmit the news, he unwittingly telegraphs his *plugola* —Philip Nobile>

plume* *n* : a hypothetical column of molten rock rising continuously from the earth's lower mantle that is held to be the driving force in plate movement in the theory of plate tectonics

P marker *n* [*P*, symbol for *phrase*] : PHRASE MARKER

pocket* *n* : an area formed by blockers from which a football quarterback attempts to pass

pod* *n* : a detachable compartment (as for personnel, a power unit, or an instrument) on a spacecraft

po·go·noph·o·ran \\ˌpōgə'näfərən\\ *n* : a marine worm belonging to the phylum or class Pogonophora — **pogonophoran** *adj*

point estimate *n* : the single value assigned to a parameter in point estimation

point estimation *n* : estimation in which a single value is assigned to a parameter

point of accumulation : LIMIT POINT

point of no return **1** : the point in the flight of an aircraft beyond which the remaining fuel will be insufficient for a return to the starting point with the result that the craft must proceed **2** : a critical point (as in development or a course of action) at which turning back or reversal is not possible

point-of-sale *or* **point-of-sales** *adj* : of or relating to the place (as a check-out counter) where an item is purchased <*point-of-sale* advertising> <electronic *point-of-sale* terminals>

points *n pl* : a percentage of the face value of a loan often added as a placement fee or service charge

point set *n* : a collection of points in geometry or topology

point set to·pol·o·gy \\-tə'päləjē, -tō-, -tä-\\ *n* : a branch of topology concerned with the properties and theory of topological spaces and metric spaces developed with emphasis on set theory

Pois·son distribution \\pwä'sōⁿ-\\ *n* [Siméon D. *Poisson* †1840 Fr. mathematician] : a probability density function that is often used as a mathematical model of the number of outcomes (as traffic accidents, atomic disintegrations, or organisms) obtained in a suitable interval of time and space, that has the mean equal to the variance, that is used as an approximation to the binomial distribution, and that has the form

$$f(x) = \frac{e^{-\mu}\mu^{x}}{x!} \quad \text{where } \mu$$

is the mean and x takes on nonnegative integral values

polar* *adj* **1 a** : passing over a planet's north and south poles <a satellite in a *polar* orbit> **b** : traveling in a polar orbit <a *polar* satellite> **2** : of, relating to, or expressed in polar coordinates <*polar* equations>; *also* : of or relating to a polar coordinate system

pole* *or* **pole position** *n* : the front-row position nearest the infield in the starting lineup of an automobile race

pole* *n* : the point of origin of two tangents to a conic section that determine a polar

pole lamp *n* : a lamp that consists of a pole to which light fixtures are attached and that usu. extends from floor to ceiling

po·le·mol·ogy \\(ˌ)pōlə'mäləjē\\ *n* [Gk *polemos* war + E *-logy* science, theory, deriv. of Gk *logos* word] : the study of war

po·lio·vi·rus \\ˌpōlē(ˌ)ōˌvīrəs\\ *n* [NL, fr. *polio*myelitis + *virus*] : an enterovirus that occurs in several antigenically distinct forms and is the causative agent of human poliomyelitis

po·lit·i·ci·za·tion \pə,lid·əsə'zāshən\ *n* : the act or process of politicizing <the *politicization* of art is typical of totalitarian tyranny —B.W. Garfield> <*politicization* of campus leaders>

poly·acryl·amide \,pälēə'krilə,mīd\ *n* [*poly-* many, much (deriv. of Gk *polys*) + *acrylamide*] : a polyamide $(–CH_2CHCONH_2–)_x$ of acrylic acid

polyacrylamide gel \-'jel\ *n* : hydrated polyacrylamide that is used esp. for electrophoresis

poly·al·co·hol \,pälē,alkə,hól, -,aůk-\ *n* : an alcohol (as ethylene glycol) that contains more than one hydroxy group

poly·car·bo·nate \,pälē'kärbə,nāt, -lə-, -'kab-\ *n* : any of various tough thermoplastics characterized by high impact strength and high softening temperature

poly·cen·trism \,pälē'sen·,trizəm, -lə-\ *n* [ISV *poly-* + *centric* + *-ism,* n. suffix; prob. orig. formed in It] : the existence of a plurality of centers of Communist thought and leadership — **poly·cen·trist** \-n·trəst\ *n or adj*

poly·chlo·ri·nat·ed bi·phe·nyl \,pälē'klōrə,nād·əd,bī'fenᵊl, ,pälə-, -'klór-, -'fēn-\ *n* : any of several compounds that are produced by replacing hydrogen atoms in biphenyl with chlorine, have various industrial applications, and are poisonous environmental pollutants which tend to accumulate in animal tissues

poly·chro·mat·ic* \-krō'mad·ik, -ēk\ *adj* : being or relating to radiation that is composed of more than one wavelength

poly·cis·tron·ic \-sis'tränik, -ēk\ *adj* : containing the genetic information of a number of cistrons <*polycistronic* messenger RNA>

poly·ether \,pälē,ēthə(r)\ *n* **1** : a polymer in which the repeating unit contains a carbon-oxygen bond derived esp. from an aldehyde or an epoxide **2** : a polyurethane foam made by use of a polyether

poly·imide \,pälē,im,īd\ *n*: any of a class of polymeric synthetic resins resistant to high temperatures, wear, and corrosion and used esp. for coatings and films

poly I.poly C \,pälē'ī,pälē'sē\ *also* **poly I:C** \-,ī'sē\ *n* [*poly-* + *i*nosinic acid + *poly-* + *c*ytidylic acid] : a synthetic RNA that is held to induce interferon formation and that has been used experimentally as an anticancer and antiviral agent

poly·mer·ase \'päləmə,rās, -āz\ *n* [*polymer* + *-ase* enzyme] : any of several enzymes that catalyze the formation of DNA or RNA from precursor substances in the presence of preexisting DNA or RNA acting as a template

poly·oma \,pälē'ōmə\ *or* **polyoma virus** *n* [NL *polyoma,* fr. *poly-* + *-oma* tumor] : a papovavirus of rodents that is associated with various kinds of tumors

poly·ri·bo·some \,pälē,rībə,sōm, -lə-\ *n* : a cluster of ribosomes held together by a molecule of messenger RNA and forming the site of protein synthesis — **poly·ri·bo·som·al** \-,rībə'sōməl\ *adj*

poly·some \'pälē,sōm, -lə-\ *n* [*poly-* + ribo*some*] : POLYRIBOSOME

poly·sor·bate \,pälē'sór,bāt, -lə-\ *n* : any of several emulsifiers used in the preparation of some pharmaceuticals and foods

poly·syn·aptic \-sə'naptik\ *adj* : involving two or more synapses in the central nervous system <*polysynaptic* reflexes> — **poly·syn·ap·ti·cal·ly** \-ək(ə)lē\ *adv*

poly·un·sat·u·rat·ed \,pälē,ən'sachə,rād·əd\ *adj, of a fat or oil* : rich in unsaturated bonds — **poly·un·sat·u·rate** \-,ən'sachə,rāt, -ərət\ *n*

pony car *n* [fr. the fact that the trade names for several such cars come from the names of small breeds of horses] : one of a group of 2-door hardtops of different makes that are similar in sporty styling, high performance characteristics, and price range

poor·boy \'pů(ə)r,bói, 'půə,-, *esp South, NE, & Brit* 'pōə,- *or* 'pó(ə),-\ *n* [prob. fr. its resemblance esp. in fit to the sort of outgrown sweater a poor child might wear] : a close-fitting ribbed sweater

poor-mouth \-,maůth, -th\ *vi* : to plead poverty as a defense or excuse <usually *poor-mouths* when it's his turn to contribute> ~ *vt*: to speak disparagingly of <likes to *poor-mouth* his candidate's chances so that the candidate will appear to have pulled an astonishingly strong victory —Timothy Crouse>

pop* *vt* **popped; pop·ping** : to take (drugs) orally or by injection <keeps *popping* pills>

pop* *adj* : of, relating to, or constituting popular mass culture <*pop* culture> <*pop* clothes> <users of *pop* forms like nightclub comedy and folk-rock preaching —Seymour Krim> <a *pop* journalist carrying the aromas of discotheque and boutique —Irving Howe>

pop* *or* **pop art** *n* : art in which commonplace objects (as road signs, hamburgers, comic strips, or soup cans) are used as subject matter and are often physically incorporated in the work — **pop artist** *n*

pop·ster \'päpstə(r)\ *n* : a pop artist

pop–top \¦päp,täp\ *adj* : having a tab that can be pulled off to make an opening <a *pop-top* beer can> — **pop–top** \'päp'täp\ *n*

population explosion *n* : a pyramiding of numbers of a biological population; *esp* : the recent great increase in human numbers resulting from both increased survival and exponential population growth

pop wine *n* [perh. fr. *pop* carbonated beverage] : a sweet wine and esp. a fruit wine or a fruit-flavored wine

porn \'pȯ(ə)rn, 'pȯ(ə)n\ *or* **por·no** \'pȯr(,)nō, 'pȯ(ə)(,)nō\ *n* [by shortening] : PORNOGRAPHY <countless sex offenders, when caught, turn out to possess large libraries of *porn* —E.A. Roberts, Jr.> <grudgingly admits that there is no evidence to show that *porno* incites the viewer to anything but erotic feelings and expressions —P.M. McGrady, Jr.> — **porn** *or* **porno** *adj*

por·nog·ra·phy* \pȯ(r)'nägrəfē, -fi\ *n* **1** : material (as a book) that is pornographic **2** : the depiction or portrayal of acts in a sensational manner so as to arouse (as by lurid details) a quick intense emotional reaction <the *pornography* of violence>

porny \'pȯrnē, 'pȯ(ə)n-, -ni\ *adj* : pornographic <*porny* films>

po·ro·mer·ic \¦pōrə¦merik, ¦pȯr-\ *n* [*poro-* pore (fr. Gk *poros*) + poly*meric*] : any of a class of tough porous synthetic materials used as a substitute for leather (as in shoe uppers)

POS *abbr* point-of-sale

posi·grade \'päzə,grād\ *adj* [*posi*tive + *-grade* (as in *retrograde*)] : being an auxiliary rocket used for imparting additional thrust to a spacecraft in the direction of motion

po·si·tion·al notation \pə¦zishnəl-, -shənᵊl-\ *n* : a system of expressing numbers in which the digits are arranged in succession, the position of each digit has a place value, and the number is equal to the sum of the products of each digit by its place value

position paper *n* : a detailed report that recommends a course of action on a particular issue <new *position papers,* press releases and speeches came out in an unfocused mass telling of corruption, bad police-community relations, pollution and the other standards of a reform campaign today —R.L. Maullin>

post code *n, Brit* : a code of numbers and letters that identifies each postal delivery area in the United Kingdom

post–de·ter·min·er \'pōs(t)də̇¦tərmə̇nər, -dē-; -¦tēm-, -¦təim-, -ə(r\ *n* [*post-* after (deriv. of L *post*) + *determiner*] : a limiting noun modifier (as *first* or *few*) characterized by occurrence after the determiner in a noun phrase

post·ir·ra·di·a·tion \-ir,ādē'āshən\ *adj* : occurring after irradiation <mutations in *postirradiation* cell divisions>

post·test \'pōs(t),test\ *n* : a test given to students after the completion of an instructional program to measure their achievement and the effectiveness of the program

post·treat·ment \(')pōs(t)¦trētmənt\ *adj* : relating to, typical of, or occurring in the stage following treatment <*posttreatment* examinations> — **posttreatment** *adv*

po·tas·si·um–ar·gon \pə¦tasēəm¦är,gän, -¦á,gän\ *adj* : of, relating to, or being a method of dating archaeological or geological materials based on the radioactive decay of potassium to argon that has taken place in a specimen

pot·head \'pät,hed\ *n* : one who smokes marijuana

pow·der–puff \¦paủdə(r),pəf\ *adj* : intended or designed for females <she played *powder-puff* football —*Sports Illustrated*> <the home-and-husband syndrome of the *powder-puff* press —*New York*>

power* *n* : the probability of rejecting the null hypothesis in a statistical test when a particular alternative hypothesis happens to be true

power broker *n* : a person (as in politics) able to exert strong influence because of votes or individuals that he controls < the party's real *power brokers,* the county bosses —Michael Kramer >

power function *n* : a function of a parameter under statistical test whose value for a particular value of the parameter is the probability of rejecting the null hypothesis if that value of the parameter happens to be true

power series *n* : an infinite series whose terms are successive integral powers of a variable multiplied by constants

power structure *n* **1** : a group of persons having control of a political entity (as a country) or an organization : establishment < the white *power structure* > < how the *power structure* in your local school district operates —R.N. Sheridan > **2** : the hierarchial interrelationships existing within a controlling group < the *power structure* of the American educational establishment —Paul Woodring >

power sweep *n* : an end run in football in which one or more linemen pull back and run interference for the ballcarrier

pox·vi·rus \\'päks¦vīrəs\\ *n* : any of a group of relatively large round, brick-shaped, or ovoid animal viruses (as the causative agent of smallpox) that have a fluffy appearance caused by a covering of tubules and threads

PPLO \\¦pē(ˌ)pēˌel'ō\\ *n, pl* **PPLO** [*p*leuro*p*neumonia-*l*ike *o*rganism] : any of a genus (*Mycoplasma*) of minute pleomorphic gram-negative nonmotile microorganisms without cell walls that are intermediate in some respects between viruses and bacteria and are mostly parasitic usu. in mammals : mycoplasma

pre·ag·ri·cul·tur·al \\¦prēˌagrə'kəlch(ə)rəl\\ *adj* [*pre-* before (deriv. of L *prae*) + *agricultural*] : existing or occurring before the practice of agriculture < *preagricultural* domestication of mammals >

pre·bi·o·log·i·cal \\-ˌbīə'läjəkəl\\ *also* **pre·bi·o·log·ic** \\-jik\\ *adj* : of, relating to, or being chemical or environmental precursors of the origin of life < *prebiological* molecules > < *prebiological* chemical evolution >

pre·bi·ot·ic \\-(ˌ)bī¦äd·ik, -ēk\\ *adj* : PREBIOLOGICAL

pre·cap·il·lary \\(')prē¦kapəˌlerē, *Brit usu* ¦prēkə'pilərē, -ri\\ *adj* : being on the arterial side of and immediately adjacent to a capillary

precision* *n* **1** : the accuracy (as in binary or decimal places) with which a number can be represented usu. expressed in terms of computer words < double *precision* arithmetic permits the representation of an expression by two computer words > **2** : RELEVANCE

pre·cop·u·la·to·ry \\(')prē¦käpyələˌtōrē, -ˌtȯr-\\ *adj* : preceding copulation < *precopulatory* behavior >

pre·de·ter·min·er \\¦prēdə¦tərmənər, -dē-; -¦təm, -¦təim-, -ə(r\\ *n* : a limiting noun modifier (as *both* or *all*) characterized by occurrence before the determiner in a noun phrase

pre·di·a·be·tes \\-ˌdīə'bēd·ēz, -'bēd·əs\\ *n* : an inapparent abnormal state that precedes the development of clinically evident diabetes — **pre·di·a·bet·ic** \\-'bed·ik, -ēk\\ *adj or n*

pre·emer·gent \\-ə¦mərjənt, -ē¦m-, -¦məj-, -¦məij-\\ *adj* : used or occurring before emergence of seedlings aboveground < a *preemergent* crabgrass control >

pre·emp·tive* \\prē'em(p)tiv\\ *adj* : marked by the seizing of the initiative : initiated by oneself < a *preemptive* strike against Chinese nuclear installations —A.F. Buchan >

pre–en·gi·neered \\¦prēˌenjə¦ni(ə)rd, -¦niəd\\ *adj* : constructed of or employing prefabricated modules < a *pre-engineered* building >

prehistoric* *adj* : of or relating to a language in a period of its development from which contemporary records of its actual sounds and forms have not been preserved

pre·his·to·ry* \\(')prē¦hist(ə)rē, -ri\\ *n* : the prehistoric period of man's evolution

pre·in·cu·ba·tion \\¦prēˌiŋkyə¦bāshən, -ˌink-\\ *n* : incubation (as of a biochemical) prior to a process (as a reaction)

prelate nul·li·us \\-nu̇'lēəs\\ *n, pl* **prelates nullius** [part translation of NL *praelatus nullius dioecesis* prelate of no diocese] : a Roman Catholic prelate having ordinary jurisdiction over a district independent of any diocese

pre·launch \(ˈ)prēˌlȯnch, -ˌlänch\ *adj* : preparing for or preliminary to launch (as of a spacecraft) <the *prelaunch* countdown>

pre·mei·ot·ic \ˌprēmīˈäd·ik, -ēk\ *adj* : of, occurring in, or typical of a stage prior to meiosis <*premeiotic* DNA synthesis> <*premeiotic* tissue>

pre·ovi·po·si·tion \ˌprēˌōvəpəˈzishən\ *adj* : of or being the period before oviposition of the first eggs by an adult female (as of an insect)

pre·plant \ˈprēˌplant, ˌprēˌplant\ *also* **pre·plant·ing** \-iŋ\ *adj* : occurring or used before the planting of a crop <*preplant* soil fertilization>

pre·preg \ˈprēˌpreg\ *n* [*pre-* + im*preg*nated] : a reinforcing or molding material (as paper or glass cloth) already impregnated with a synthetic resin

pre·process \(ˈ)prēˌpräsˌes, -ˌprōs-, -əs\ *vt* : to do preliminary processing of (as data) — **pre·pro·ces·sor** \-sˌesə(r), -səsə(r), -səˌsȯ(ə)r, -səˌsȯ(ə)\ *n*

pre·pro·gram \-ˌprōˌgram, -ˌprōgrəm\ *vt* : to program in advance of some anticipated use <*preprogram* a computer>

pre·punch \(ˈ)prēˌpənch\ *vt* : to punch in advance of some anticipated use <paper *prepunched* for a 3-ring binder>

1**pre·soak** \(ˈ)prēˌsōk\ *vt* : to soak beforehand <*presoak* stained clothes> <*presoaked* seeds>

2**pre·soak** \ˈprēˌsōk\ *n* **1** : a cleaning agent used in presoaking clothes **2** : an instance of presoaking

pre·sort \(ˈ)prēˌsȯ(ə)rt, -ˌsȯ(ə)t\ *vt* : to sort (outgoing mail) by zip code usu. before delivery to a post office

press kit *n* : a collection of promotional material for distribution to the press

pre·stress \ˈprēˌstres\ *n* **1** : the process of prestressing **2** : the stresses introduced in prestress **3** : the condition of being prestressed

pre·syn·ap·tic \ˌprēsəˌnaptik\ *adj* : situated or occurring just before a nerve synapse <a *presynaptic* nerve ending> — **pre·syn·ap·ti·cal·ly** \-tək(ə)lē\ *adv*

pre·tax \(ˈ)prēˌtaks\ *adj* : existing before provision for taxes <*pretax* earnings>

1**pre·teen** \ˈprēˌtēn\ *adj* **1** : being less than 13 years old <*preteen* youngsters> <*preteen* drug addicts> **2** : relating to or produced for preteen children <*preteen* fashions> <*preteen* fan magazines>

2**preteen** *n* : a preteen child

pre·treat·ment \(ˈ)prēˌtrētmənt\ *adj* : occurring in or typical of the period prior to treatment <*pretreatment* population estimates made prior to spraying>

pre·vent de·fense \ˈprēˌventˈdēˌfen(t)s; prēˈvent-, prəˈ-, *also* -dəˈfen(t)s\ *n* : a football defense in which linebackers and backs play deeper than usual in order to prevent the completion of a long pass

pre·ven·tive detention* \prəventiv-, prē-\ *n* : imprisonment without the right to bail of an arrested person awaiting trial for a felony who is considered dangerous to society

price–earn·ings ratio \ˈprīsˈərniŋz-\ *n* : a measure of the value of a common stock determined as the ratio of its market price to its earnings per share and usu. expressed as a simple numeral (**price–earnings multiple**)

primary* *adj* **1** : of, relating to, or being the amino acid sequence in proteins <*primary* protein structure> **2** : of, relating to, involving, or derived from primary meristem <*primary* tissue> <*primary* growth> **3** : of, relating to, or involved in the production of organic substances by green plants <*primary* productivity>

primary consumer *n* : a plant-eating organism : herbivore

primary derivative *n* : a word (as *telegram*) whose immediate constituents are bound forms

primary structure *n* : sculpture in the idiom of minimal art — **primary struc·tur·ist** \-ˌstrəkchərəst, -ksh(ə)rəst\ *n*

pri·ma·to·log·i·cal \ˌprīməd·ᵊlˈäjəkəl\ *adj* : of or relating to primatology <*primatological* research>

prim·er* \ˈprīmə(r)\ *n* : a molecule (as of DNA) whose presence is required for formation of more molecules of the same kind

prime rate *n* : an interest rate at which preferred customers can borrow from banks and which is the lowest commercial interest rate available at a particular time and place

principal diagonal *n* : the diagonal in a square matrix that runs from upper left to lower right

print out *vt* : to make a printout of : produce in the form of a printout <I could just punch the right buttons on my computer, and it would *print out* the material I needed —Joseph Napolitan>

print·out \ˈprint,au̇t\ *n* [*print out,* v.] : a printed record produced automatically (as by a computer)

pri·or·i·tize \,prīˈȯrə-,tīz, ˈprīər-\ *vt* **-tized; -tiz·ing** : to list or rate (as projects or goals) in order of priority <expects his underlings to *prioritize* their work and their personal goals —*Newsweek*>

pri·va·tism \ˈprīvə,tizəm\ *n* : the attitude of being uncommitted to or avoiding involvement in anything beyond one's immediate interests <these values, with their strong emphasis on personal self-fulfillment, are reminiscent of the mood of *privatism* that prevailed among students a generation ago —Daniel Yankelovich & Ruth Clark> — **pri·va·tis·tic** \,prīvəˈtistik, -ēk\ *adj*

pro·ac·tive \(ˈ)prōˈaktiv, -ēv\ *adj* [L *pro-* forward (fr. *pro* before, for) + E *active*] : involving modification by a factor which precedes that which is modified <*proactive* inhibition of memory>

probability density *n* : DISTRIBUTION 3; *also* : a particular value of a probability density function

probability distribution *n* : DISTRIBUTION 2, 3

pro·ben·e·cid \prōˈbenəsəd\ *n* [*pro*pyl + *ben*zoic + connective *-e-* + a*cid*] : a drug $C_{13}H_{19}NO_4S$ that acts on renal tubular function and is used to inhibit the excretion of some drugs (as penicillin) and to increase the excretion of urates in gout

pro·ces·sor* \ˈpräs,esə(r), ˈprō-\ *n* **1 a** : a computer **b** : the part of a computer system that operates on data — called also *central processing unit* **2** : a computer program (as a compiler) that puts another program into a form acceptable to the computer

producer* *n* : any of various organisms (as a green plant) which produce their own organic compounds from simple precursors (as carbon dioxide and inorganic nitrogen) and many of which are food sources for other organisms — compare CONSUMER

pro·duc·tiv·i·ty* \(,)prō,dəkˈtivəd·e, ,präd(,)ək-, prə,dək-\ *n* : rate of production esp. of food by fixation of solar energy by producer organisms

pro·ges·to·gen \prōˈjestəjən, -,jen\ *n* [*progest*ational + *-ogen* (as in *estrogen*)] : any of several progestational steroids (as progesterone)

program* *n* : a sequence of coded instructions that is part of an organism <the animal does have a *program* of reactions to stimuli arising in its external and internal worlds —W. G. Van der Kloot>

program* *vt* **-grammed** *or* **-gramed; -gram·ming** *or* **-gram·ing** **1** : to code in an organism's program <the death of cells and the destruction of tissues, organs, and organ systems are *programmed* as normal morphogenetic events in the development of multicellular organisms —J. W. Saunders, Jr.> **2** : to provide with a biological program <cells that have been *programmed* to synthesize hemoglobin>

pro·gram·ma·ble *or* **pro·gram·able** \ˈprōˈgraməbəl\ *adj* : capable of being programmed <a *programmable* calculator> — **pro·gram·ma·bil·i·ty** \,prō,graməˈbiləd·ē\ *n*

programmed instruction *n* : instruction through information given in small steps with each requiring a correct response by the learner before going on to the next step

pro·gram·mer* *or* **pro·gram·er** \ˈprō,gramə(r), ˈprōgrəm-\ *n* : one that prepares an educational program

pro·gram·ming* *or* **program·ing*** \-,gramiŋ, -grəmiŋ\ *n* **1** : the process of instructing or learning by means of an instructional program **2** : the process of preparing an instructional program

progressive rock *n* : rock music characterized by relatively complex phrasings and improvisations and intended for a sophisticated audience

projection* *n* : the process or technique of reproducing a spatial object upon a plane or curved surface by projecting its points; *also* : the graphic reproduction so formed

pro·jec·tu·al \prəˈjekchəwəl, prōˈ-\ *n* [*project* + *-ual* (as in *visual*)] : a usu. instructional material (as a transparency) to be projected (as onto a screen) by a projector

pro·kary·ote *or* **pro·cary·ote** \(ˈ)prōˈkarē,ōt\ *n* [*pro-* before, for + *kary-* cell nucleus (deriv. of Gk *karyon* nut, kernel) + *-ote* (as in *zygote*)] : a cellular organism (as a bacterium or a blue-green alga) that does not have a distinct nucleus — **pro·kary·ot·ic** *or* **pro·cary·ot·ic** \(,)prō,karēˈäd·ik, -ēk\ *adj*

[1]**pro·mo** \ˈprō(,)mō\ *adj* [short for *promotional*] : serving to advertise : promotional < *promo* leaflets >

[2]**promo** *n, pl* **promos** : a promotional announcement, film, recording, blurb, or appearance < shot some *promos* for his syndicated TV show —*New Yorker*>

pro·nase \ˈprō,nās, -āz\ *n* [perh. fr. *protein* + *-ase* enzyme] : a protease from an actinomycete (*Streptomyces griseus*)

pro·neth·a·lol \prōˈnethə,lȯl, -,lōl\ *n* [*pro*pyl + ami*ne* + m*eth*yl + naphth*al*ene + methan*ol*] : a drug $C_{15}H_{19}NO$ that is a beta-adrenergic blocking agent

pro·pa·nil \ˈprōpə,nil\ *n* [*prop*ionic + *anil*ide] : an herbicide $C_9H_9Cl_2NO$ used esp. to control weeds in rice fields

pro·phase* \ˈprō,fāz\ *n* : the initial stage of meiosis in which the chromosomes become visible, homologous pairs of chromosomes undergo synapsis and become shortened and thickened, individual chromosomes become visibly double as paired chromatids, chiasmata occur, and the nuclear membrane disappears

pro·pran·o·lol \prōˈpranə,lȯl, -,lōl\ *n* [prob. alter. of earlier *propanolol,* fr. *propanol* + *-ol* chemical compound] : a beta-adrenergic blocking agent $C_{16}H_{21}NO_2$ used in the treatment of abnormal heart rhythms and angina pectoris

pros·ta·glan·din \,prästəˈglandən\ *n* [ISV *prosta*te *gland* + *-in* chemical compound; fr. its occurrence in the sexual glands of mammals] : any of various oxygenated unsaturated cyclic fatty acids of animals that may perform a variety of hormonelike actions (as in controlling blood pressure or smooth muscle contraction)

pro·tein·oid \ˈprō,tē,nȯid, ˈprōtᵊn,ȯid, ˈprōd·ēə,nȯid\ *n* [*protein* + *-oid* something similar] : any of various polypeptides which can be obtained by suitable polymerization of mixtures of amino acids and some of which may represent an early stage in the evolution of proteins

Protestant ethic *n* : an ethic that stresses the virtue of hard work, thrift, and self-discipline < the *Protestant ethic,* which holds that work is the way to salvation and worldly achievement the sign of God's favor —J.A. Lukas >

pro·the·tel·ic \,prōthəˈtelik\ *adj* : of, relating to, or characterized by prothetely < a *prothetelic* larva > < *prothetelic* malformations >

pro·tho·rac·ic gland \,prōthəˈrasik-\ *n* : one of a pair of thoracic endocrine organs in some insects that control molting

pro·to·con·ti·nent \ˈprōd·ōˈkäntᵊnənt, -ˈkäntnənt\ *n* [*proto-* first, beginning (deriv. of Gk *prōtos*) + *continent*] : SUPERCONTINENT

pro·to·por·ce·lain \ˈprōd·(,)ōˈpōrs(ə)lən, -ˈpȯr-\ *n* [*proto-* + *porcelain;* prob. trans. of G *urporzellan*] : a porcelaneous ware lacking some of the qualities of a true porcelain; *specif* : a hard-fired gray kaolinic Chinese stoneware known since Han times

protract* *vt* : to extend forward or outward < the mandible is *protracted* and retracted in chewing >

pro·vi·ral \ˈprōˈvīrəl\ *adj* : of, relating to, or being a provirus < *proviral* DNA >

prox·e·mics \präkˈsēmiks\ *n pl but sing in constr* [*prox*imity + *-emics* (as in *phonemics*)] : the study of man's personal and cultural need for space and his interaction with his environing space

pseu·do·cho·lin·es·ter·ase \ˈsüdō,kōləˈnestə,rās, -,rāz\ *n* [*pseudo-* false (deriv. of Gk *pseudēs*) + *cholinesterase*] : an enzyme that hydrolizes choline esters and that is found esp. in blood plasma

pseu·do·ran·dom \,südōˈrandəm\ *adj* : being or involving entities (as numbers) that are selected by a definite computational process (as one involving a computer) but that satisfy one or more standard tests for statistical randomness

psi·lo·cin \ˈsīləsən\ *n* [NL *Psilocybe mexicana,* fungus from which it is obtained + E *-in* chemical compound] : a hallucinogenic tertiary amine $C_{12}H_{16}N_2O$ obtained from a fungus (*Psilocybe mexicana*)

psi·lo·cy·bin \\ˌsīlə'sībən\\ *n* [NL *Psilocybe mexicana,* fungus from which it is obtained + E *-in* chemical compound] : a hallucinogenic indole $C_{12}H_{17}N_2O_4P$ obtained from a fungus (*Psilocybe mexicana*)

psi·lo·phyt·ic \\ˌsīlə'fid·ik\\ *adj* : of, relating to, or being plants of the order Psilophytales

psych* *also* **psyche** \\'sīk\\ *vt* **psyched; psych·ing** **1** : to make (oneself) psychologically ready for performance — usu. used with *up* <*psyched* himself up for the race> **2** : to make psychologically uneasy : intimidate, scare <pressure doesn't *psych* me —Jerry Quarry> — often used with *out* <the enemy are completely *psyched* out by this unorthodox move —Kathleen Karr>

psy·che·de·lia \\ˌsīkə'dēlyə\\ *n* [NL, fr. E *psychedelic* + L *-ia,* n. suffix] : the world of people, phenomena, or items associated with psychedelic drugs

[1]**psy·che·del·ic** \\ˌsīkəˌdelik, *also* -ˌdil- *or* -ˌdēl-\\ *adj* [Gk *psychē* soul + *dēloun* to show, revel (fr. *dēlos* evident) + E *-ic,* adj. suffix] **1 a** : of, relating to, or causing an exposure of normally repressed psychic elements <*psychedelic* drugs> **b** : of, relating to, involving, or resulting from the use of psychedelic drugs <*psychedelic* indulgences> <a *psychedelic* experience> <experimental *psychedelic* therapy> **c** : of, relating to, or concerned with psychedelics <hippies escaping to their *psychedelic* lairs —T.E. Mullaney> <*psychedelic* medicine designed to help LSD users> **2 a** : imitating or reproducing the effects (as distorted or heightened sense perception) of psychedelic drugs <*psychedelic* light show> <*psychedelic* art> **b** (1) : brightly colored <ferryboats soon will take on a *psychedelic* look, with an overall coat of international orange and touches of red and yellow —*N.Y. Times*> (2) *of colors* : fluorescent **c** : making use of electronically distorted sounds <*psychedelic* rock> **3** : of, relating to, dealing in, or being the culture associated with psychedelic drugs <*psychedelic* shops> — **psy·che·del·i·cal·ly** \\-ək(ə)lē\\ *adv*

[2]**psychedelic** *n* **1** : a psychedelic drug (as LSD) **2 a** : a user or an advocate of psychedelic drugs **b** : a person with psychedelic social and cultural interests and orientation

psy·che·del·i·cize \\ˌsīkə'deləˌsīz\\ *vt* **-cized; -ciz·ing** : to make psychedelic <the general reluctance of suburbia to be *psychedelicized* —Hendrik Hertzberg>

psy·chic en·er·giz·er \\ˌsīkik'enə(r)ˌjīzə(r)\\ *n* : an antidepressant drug

psy·cho·ac·tive \\ˌsīkō'aktiv\\ *adj* [*psycho-* soul, spirit, mind, psychological (fr. Gk *psychē* breath, life, soul) + *active*] : affecting the mind or behavior <*psychoactive* drugs>

psy·cho·bi·og·ra·phy \\ˌsī(ˌ)kōbī'ägrəfē, -fi\\ *n* : a character analysis : a biography written from a psychodynamic point of view <chilling *psychobiographies* of sadists Stalin and Himmler —*Time*> — **psy·cho·bio·graph·i·cal** \\-ˌbīəˌgrafəkəl\\ *adj*

psy·cho·chem·i·cal \\ˌsīkō'keməkəl\\ *n* : a psychoactive chemical; *esp* : a chemical warfare agent (as a war gas) that acts on nervous centers and makes affected individuals temporarily helpless — **psychochemical** *adj*

psy·cho·his·to·ry \\'sīkōˌhist(ə)rē, -ri\\ *n* : an analysis of an historical person or issue by psychoanalytic methods <everybody these days is writing *psychohistory* (which has the great blessing of being both irrefutable and unprovable) —John P. Roche> — **psy·cho·his·to·ri·an** \\ˌsīkō(h)isˌtōrēən, -'tór-, -'tär-\\ *n* — **psy·cho·his·tor·i·cal** \\-(h)is'tórəkəl, -'tär-\\ *adj*

psy·cho·phar·ma·ceu·ti·cal \\ˌsīkōˌfärmə'süd·əkəl\\ *n* : a drug having an effect on the mental state of a person

psy·cho·phar·ma·col·o·gist \\-mə'käləjəst\\ *n* : a specialist in psychopharmacology

psy·cho·quack \\'sīkōˌkwak\\ *n* : an unqualified psychologist or psychiatrist — **psy·cho·quack·ery** \\ˌsīkō'kwak(ə)rē-, -ri\\ *n*

psy·cho·sur·geon \\'sīkōˌsərjən, -ˌsəj-, -ˌsəij-\\ *n* : a surgeon specializing in psychosurgery

psy·chot·o·gen \\sī'käd·əjən\\ *n* [*psychotic* + connective *-o-* + *-gen* producer] : a chemical agent (as a drug) that induces a psychotic state — **psy·choto·gen·ic** \\(ˌ)sīˌkäd·əˌjenik\\ *adj*

psy·choto·mi·met·ic \\sīˌkäd·ōməˌmed·ik, -mīˌm-\\ *adj* [*psychotic* + connective *-o-* + *mimetic*] : of, relating to, or involving psychotic alteration of behavior and personality <*psychotomimetic* drugs> — **psychotomimetic** *n* — **psy·choto·mi·met·i·cal·ly** \-ək(ə)lē, -li\ *adv*

psy·cho·tox·ic \ˌsīkəˈtäksik\ *adj* : of, relating to, or being an habituating drug (as amphetamine) which is not a true narcotic but the abuse of which may be correlated with deleterious personality and behavioral changes

psych–out \ˈsīkˌau̇t\ *n* : an act or an instance of psyching out <in a *psych-out* you always make a show of confidence, while you work to undermine the confidence of your competition —Don Schollander & Duke Savage>

PTV *abbr* public television

public access *n* : the provision of access by the public to television broadcasting facilities (as a cable television channel) for the presentation of programs

public television *n* : television that provides cultural, informational, and instructional programs for the public and that does not promote the sale of a product or service but does identify the donors of program funds : noncommercial television

puff* *n* : an enlarged region of a chromosome that is associated with intensely active genes involved in RNA synthesis

pull* *vi, of an offensive lineman in football* : to move back from the line of scrimmage toward one flank to provide blocking for a ballcarrier

pull date *n* : a date stamped on perishable products (as baked goods or dairy products) after which they should not be sold

pul·sar \ˈpəlˌsär\ *n* [*pulse* + *-ar* (as in *quasar*)] : a celestial source of pulsating radio waves characterized by a short relatively invariable interval (as .033 second) between pulses that is held to be a rotating neutron star

pump* *n* **1** : electromagnetic radiation for pumping atoms or molecules **2** : the process of pumping atoms or molecules **3** : a mechanism (as the sodium pump) for pumping atoms, ions, or molecules

pump* *vt* **1** : to transport (as ions) against a concentration gradient by the expenditure of energy **2 a** : to raise (atoms or molecules) to a higher energy level by exposure to usu. electromagnetic radiation at one of the resonant frequencies so that reemission may occur at another frequency resulting in amplification or sustained oscillation **b** : to expose (as a laser, semiconductor, or crystal) to radiation in the process of pumping

pumped storage *n* : a hydroelectric system in which electricity is generated during periods of greatest consumption by the use of water that has been pumped into a reservoir at a higher altitude during periods of low consumption

punch–up \ˈpənˌchəp\ *n, Brit* : a fight <take your children to the park and try to get them a turn on the swings. Do not get involved in *punch-ups* with other fathers —*Punch*>

purse crab *n* [fr. the resemblance of the abdomen to a purse] : any of the family Leucosiidae of crabs characterized by a granular carapace and long claws and by an adult female having the abdomen formed into a hemispherical cup that snaps shut against the sternum to form a brood chamber for the eggs; *esp* : one (*Persephona mediterranea*) that occurs in shallow water along the Atlantic coast of Mexico and of the U.S. as far north as New Jersey

push·down \ˈpu̇shˌdau̇n\ *n* : a store of data (as in a computer) from which the most recently stored item must be the first retrieved — called also *pushdown list, pushdown stack*

put* *vb* — **put the make on** : to make sexual advances toward <on a trip to the . . . Naval Station, the men spent most of their time *putting the make on* a cute young Wave who was their guide —David Wellman>

put down* *vt* **1 a** : to belittle or disparage <many writers want to *put down* not only their interviewers but their critics —Melvin Maddocks> **b** : to disapprove or criticize <*put down* for the way he dressed> **2** : to deflate or squelch <a legendary step-parent: rigid, oppressive, untrue, ever ready to *put down* the honest feeling and sound thought that arise within the individual —R.B. Heilman>

put–down \ˈpu̇tˌdau̇n\ *n* : an act or instance of putting down; *esp* : a deflating remark <the bright quips and devasting *put-downs* they wish they'd thought of on the air —Max Gunther>

put–on* \\-ˌȯn, -ˌän\\ *n*: an instance of putting someone on <couldn't decide whether the question was serious or just a *put-on*>; *also*: a parody or spoof <a kind of *put-on* of every pretentious film ever made —C.A. Ridley>

py·re·throid \\pīˈrēˌthrȯid, -ˈreˌ-\\ *n*[*pyrethr*in + *-oid* something similar]: any of various synthetic compounds related to and resembling in insecticidal properties the pyrethrins — **pyrethroid** *adj*

py·ri·meth·amine \\ˌpīrəˈmethəˌmēn, -əmən\\ *n* [*pyrim*idine + *eth*yl + *amine*] : a folic acid antagonist $C_{12}H_{13}ClN_4$ used in the treatment of malaria and of toxoplasmosis

Q

qi·vi·ut \\ˈkēvēət, -vēˌüt\\ *n*[Esk] : the wool of the undercoat of the musk-ox <has successfully domesticated musk-oxen and is attempting to develop techniques for the commercial use of their wool, *qiviut,* a wool finer than cashmere —F.F. Wright>

QSO \\ˌkyü(ˌ)eˈsō\\ *n* [*q*uasi-*s*tellar *o*bject] : QUASI-STELLAR OBJECT

¹Q–switch \\ˈkyüˌswich\\ *n*[*q*uantum + *switch*]: a shutter device (as a filter or chemical-filled cell) that prevents a laser from emitting radiation until the desired internal energy is reached in order that a short high-energy pulse is obtained

²Q–switch *vt*: to control (a laser or laser medium) with a Q-switch

quad·plex \\ˈkwädˌpleks\\ *n*[*quad*ri- four (fr. L) + *-plex* (as in *duplex*)]: FOURPLEX

Qua·dran·tid \\kwäˈdrantəd\\ *n*[NL *Quadrant-, Quadrans* (*Muralis*) mural quadrant, a group of stars in the constellation Draco from which the shower appears to radiate + E *-id* meteor]: one of the shooting stars constituting the meteor shower that recurs annually near the 3d of January

qua·dra·pho·ny \\kwäˈdräfənē, -ˈdraf-; ˈkwädrəˌfänē, -ˌfōnē; -ni\\ *n* [irreg. fr. *quadri-* four (fr. L) + *-phony* sound, deriv. of Gk *phōnē* sound]: the transmission, recording, or reproduction of sound by techniques that utilize four transmission channels — **quad·ra·phon·ic** \\ˌkwädrəˈfänik\\ *adj*

quan·ta·some \\ˈkwäntəˌsōm\\ *n* [prob. fr. *quanta,* pl. of *quantum* + *-some* body, deriv. of Gk *sōma*]: one of the chlorophyll-containing spheroids found in the grana of chloroplasts

quan·tized \\ˈkwänˌtīzd\\ *adj* : characterized by the property of taking on only discrete values <*quantized* angular momentum>

quan·tum electronics \\ˌkwäntəm-\\ *n pl but sing in constr* : a branch of physics that deals with the interaction of radiation with discrete energy levels in substances (as in a maser or laser)

quark \\ˈkwärk, ˈkwȯrk\\ *n* [coined by Murray Gell-Mann *b*1929 Am. physicist] : a hypothetical particle that carries a fractional electric charge and that is held to be a constituent of known elementary particles

quartz–io·dine lamp \\ˌkwȯ(ə)rtsˈīəˌdīn-, -ədᵊn-, -əˌdēn-\\ *n* : an incandescent lamp that has a quartz bulb and a tungsten filament and that contains iodine which reacts with the vaporized tungsten to prevent excessive blackening of the bulb

qua·sar \\ˈkwāˌzär, *also* -ˌsär\\ *n* [*quasi*-stell*ar* radio source] : QUASI-STELLAR RADIO SOURCE

Qua·si·mo·do \\ˌk(w)äzəˈmō(ˌ)dō, -äsə-, -ēˈm-\\ *n, pl* **-dos** [after *Quasimodo,* hunchback in Victor Hugo's novel *Notre-Dame de Paris* (1831)] : a surfing feat in which a surfer squats on the board, leans forward, and extends one arm straight forward and the other straight back

qua·si·par·ti·cle \ˌkwāˌzīˌpärtəkəl, ˌkwāˌsī-, ˌkwäzē-, ˌkwäsē-, ˌkwāzē-\ *n* [*quasi-* as if, in some sense (fr. L *quasi* as if) + *particle*] : a composite entity (as a vibration in a solid) that is analogous in its behavior to a single particle

qua·si–stel·lar object \-ˌstelər-\ *n* : QUASI-STELLAR RADIO SOURCE

quasi–stellar radio source *n* : any of various very distant celestial objects that resemble stars but emit usually bright blue and ultraviolet light and powerful radio waves

quas·qui·cen·ten·ni·al \ˌkwäskwē(ˌ)sen'tenēəl, -skwə-\ *n* [fr. L *quadrans* quarter, after L *semis* half: E *sesquicentennial*] : a 125th anniversary — **quasquicentennial** *adj*

queen·side \'kwēnˌsīd\ *n*: the side of the chessboard containing the file on which both queens sit at the beginning of the game

queen size *adj* **1** : having dimensions of approximately 60 inches by 80 inches — used of a bed **2** : of a size that fits a queen size bed <a *queen size* bedspread>

queen substance *n* : a pheromone that is secreted by queen bees, is consumed by worker bees, and inhibits the development of their ovaries; *also* : the same or a similar substance secreted by termites

queue* *n*: a sequence of messages or jobs held in auxiliary storage awaiting transmission or processing

queue* *vt* **queued; queu·ing** *or* **queue·ing** : to send to or place in a queue

quick kick *n*: a punt in football made on first, second, or third down from a running or passing formation and designed to take the opposing team by surprise

quotient group *n*: a group whose elements are the cosets of a normal subgroup of a given group

quotient ring *n* : a ring whose elements are the cosets of an ideal in a given ring

R

R *adj* [*r*estricted] *of a motion picture* : of such a nature that admission is restricted to persons over a specified age (as 17) unless accompanied by a parent or guardian — compare G, PG, X

rabbit* *n* : a runner on a track team who sets a fast pace for a teammate in the first part of a long-distance race

rabbit ears *n pl* : an indoor dipole television antenna consisting of two usu. extensible rods connected to a base to form a V shape

rack car* *n* : a railroad flatcar equipped with a 2-level or 3-level framework for transporting motor vehicles

radar astronomy *n* : astronomy dealing with investigations of celestial bodies in the solar system by analyzing radar waves directed toward and reflected from the object being studied

radar telescope *n*: a radar transmitter-receiver with an antenna for use in radar astronomy

ra·di·al* \'rādēəl\ *n* : RADIAL TIRE

ra·di·al·ly symmetrical \ˌrādēəlē-\ *adj* : of, relating to, or characterized by radial symmetry

radial tire *or* **radial–ply tire** \ˌrādēəlˌplī-\ *n*: a pneumatic tire in which the ply cords that extend to the beads are laid at right angles to the center line of the tread

ra·di·es·the·sia \ˌrādē(ˌ)es'thēzh(ē)ə\ *n* [NL, fr. L *radius* ray + NL *esthesia* feeling, sensitiveness] **1** : sensitiveness held to enable a person with the aid of divining rod or pendulum to detect things (as the presence of underground water, the nature of an illness, or the guilt of a suspected person); *also* : dowsing, divining **2** : a study that deals with radiesthesia

ra·dio·car·bon dating \ˌrādēōˌkärbən-, -ˌkȧb-\ *n* : CARBON DATING

ra·dio·chro·ma·tog·ra·phy \ˌrādē(ˌ)ōˌkrōməˈtägrəfē\ *n* [*radio-* radiation, radioactive + *chromatography*] : the process of making a quantitative or qualitative determination of a radioisotope-labeled substance by measuring the radioactivity of the appropriate zone or spot in the chromatogram — **ra·dio·chro·mato·graph·ic** \-ˌmad·əˈgrafik\ *adj*

ra·dio·ecol·o·gy \-əˈkäləjē, -ēˈk-\ *n* : the study of the effects of radiation and radioactive substances on ecological communities — **ra·dio·eco·log·i·cal** \-ˌēkəˈläjəkəl, -ˌek-\ *adj* — **ra·dio·ecol·o·gist** \-əˈkäləjəst, -ēˈk-\ *n*

radio galaxy *n* : a galaxy that includes a source from which radio energy is detected

ra·dio·im·mu·no·as·say \ˈrādēˌōˌimyənōˈasˌā, -imˌyü-, -ˌnōaˈsā\ *n* : immunoassay of a substance (as insulin) that has been radioactively labeled

ra·dio·iso·to·pic \ˌrādē(ˌ)ōˌīsəˈtäpik, -ˈtō-\ *adj* : of, relating to, or being a radioisotope < *radioisotopic* techniques > — **ra·dio·iso·to·pi·cal·ly** \-ək(ə)lē\ *adv*

ra·dio·phar·ma·ceu·ti·cal \-ˌfärməˈsüd·əkəl, -ˌfȧm-\ *n* : a radioactive drug used for diagnostic or therapeutic purposes

ra·dio·pro·tec·tive \-prəˈtektiv\ *adj* : serving to protect or aiding in protecting against the injurious effect of radiations < *radioprotective* drugs > — **ra·dio·pro·tec·tion** \-prəˈtekshən\ *n*

ra·dio·pro·tec·tor \-ˈtektə(r)\ *n* : a radioprotective chemical agent

ra·dio·re·sis·tance \-rəˈzistən(t)s\ *n* : resistance (as of a cell or a mutation) to the effects of radiant energy

ra·dio·ster·il·ized \-ˌsterəˌlīzd\ *adj* : sterilized by irradiation (as with X rays or gamma rays) < *radiosterilized* mosquitoes > < *radiosterilized* syringes > — **ra·dio·ster·il·iza·tion** \-ˌsterələˈzāshən, -ˌlī-\ *n*

ra·dio·te·lem·e·try \-təˈleməˑtrē\ *n* **1** : TELEMETRY 1 **2** : BIOTELEMETRY — **ra·dio·tele·met·ric** \-ˌteləˌme·trik\ *adj*

ra·dio–ul·na \-ˈəlnə\ *n* [NL, fr. *radius* (fr. L) + connective *-o-* + *ulna*] : a single bone in the forelimb of an amphibian (as a frog) that represents fusion of the separate radius and ulna of higher forms

rainbow* *or* **rainbow pill** *n, slang* : a drug in a tablet or capsule of several colors; *esp* : a combination of the sodium derivatives of amobarbital and secobarbital in a blue and red capsule

ral·ly·mas·ter \ˈralēˌmastə(r), -li-\ *n* : one who organizes and conducts an automobile rally

ranch·ette \ˌranˈchet\ *n* : a small ranch

rand \ˈrand, *in So. Africa usu* ˈrȧnd *or* ˈrȧnt *or* ˈränt (*the last is usual in Afrikaans*)\ *n, pl* **rand** *or* **rands** [fr. the *Rand* (*Witwatersrand*), gold-producing district in South Africa] **1 a** : the basic monetary unit of the Republic of So. Africa established in 1961 **b** : the basic monetary unit of Botswana, Lesotho, and Swaziland **2** : a coin or note representing one rand

R and B *n* : RHYTHM AND BLUES

R and D *n* : research and development — usu. written *R&D* < pharmaceutical houses decided the *R&D* of cancer drugs wouldn't pay its way in profits —Philip Nobile >

ran·dom–ac·cess \ˌrandəmˌakˌses\ *adj* : permitting access to stored data in any order the user desires < *random-access* computer memory >

ran·dom·iz·er \ˈrandəˌmīzə(r)\ *n* : a device or procedure used for randomization < a spinner with 10 positions can be used as a *randomizer* for the 10 digits >

rank* *n* : the number of linearly independent rows in a matrix

¹rap \ˈrap\ *n* [perh. by shortening & alter. fr. *repartee*] : talk, conversation, chat < has long, disjointed philosophical *raps* with his closest friend —Chandler Brossard >

²rap *vi* **rapped; rap·ping** : to talk freely and frankly < down at the corner bar *rapping* —*Newsweek* > — **rap·per** \ˈrapə(r)\ *n*

rapid eye movement *n* : rapid conjugate movement of the eyes associated esp. with paradoxical sleep

rap session *n* : a small usu. informal group discussion < *rap sessions* in college dorms —J.S. Bruner >
rapture of the deep : NITROGEN NARCOSIS
rate of change : a value that results from dividing the change of a function of a variable by the change in the variable < velocity is the *rate of change* of distance with respect to time >
rat fink \ˈratˌfiŋk\ *n* : FINK < a hypocritical *rat fink* who hasn't for a moment believed in the . . . sermons that he's preached for years —Thomas Meehan >
ratio *vt* **1** : to express as a ratio **2** : to enlarge or reduce the size of (a photograph) in accordance with a ratio
rational* *adj* : relating to, consisting of, or being one or more rational numbers
raunch \ˈrȯnch, ˈrän-\ *n* [back-formation fr. *raunchy*] : vulgarity, bawdiness, smuttiness < Rabelais without the *raunch* would be a drag —Milton Mayer >
RBE *abbr* relative biological effectiveness
read* *vt* **1** : to sense the meaning of (information) in recorded and coded form (as in storage) : acquire (information) from storage — used of a computer or data processor **2** : to read the coded information on (as tape or a punch card)
read–only memory \ˌrēdˈōnlē-, -li-\ *n* : a small computer memory that cannot be changed by the computer and that contains a special-purpose program
read·out* \ˈrēdˌau̇t\ *n* **1** : the process of reading **2 a** : the process of removing information from an automatic device (as an electronic computer) and displaying it in an understandable form **b** : the information removed from such a device and displayed or recorded (as by magnetic tape or printing device) **c** : a device used for readout **3** : the radio transmission of data or pictures from a space vehicle either immediately upon acquisition or later by means of playback of a tape recording
ready·made \ˈredēˌmād, -di-\ *n* : an artifact (as a comb or a pair of ice tongs) selected and displayed as a work of art < what the objet trouvé was to Dada: a perfect *ready-made* —John Simon >
re·ag·gre·gate \(ˈ)rēˈagrəˌgāt\ *vt* : to reform into an aggregate or a whole < *reaggregate* the subunits of a macromolecule > — **reaggregate** \-ˈagrəˌgāt, -əgət\ *n* — **re·ag·gre·ga·tion** \ˌrēˌagrəˈgāshən\ *n*
real* *adj* : REAL-VALUED < functions of a *real* variable >
real time *n* : the actual time during which something takes place < the computer may partly analyze the data in *real time* (as it comes in) —R.H. March > < here's how it looked in *real time* and in slow motion —J.W. Chancellor > — **real–time** *adj*
real–valued \ˌrē(ə)lˈval(ˌ)yüd, -ˈvalyəd\ *adj* : taking on only real numbers for values < a *real-valued* function >
re·branch \(ˈ)rēˈbranch\ *vi* : to form secondary branches
recall* *n* **1** : a public call by a manufacturer for the return of a product that may be defective or contaminated **2** : the ability (as of an information retrieval system) to retrieve stored material
re·can·a·li·za·tion \(ˌ)rēˌkanᵊləˈzāshən, -ˌīˈz-\ *n* : the process of reuniting an interrupted channel of a bodily tube (as a vas deferens)
receptor* *n* : a cellular entity (as a beta-receptor or alpha-receptor) that is a postulated intermediary between a chemical agent (as a neurohumor) acting on nervous tissue and the physiological or pharmacological response
re·char·ter \(ˈ)rēˈchärtər, -ˈchȧd·ə(r\ *vt* : to grant a new charter to < *rechartered* the national bank > — **recharter** *n*
reciprocal* *n* : MULTIPLICATIVE INVERSE
re·cur·sion* \rəˈkərzhən, rēˈ-, -ˈkəzh-, -ˈkəizh-, *chiefly Brit* -ˈkəshən\ *n* : the determination of a succession of elements (as numbers or functions) by operation on one or more preceding elements according to a rule or formula involving a finite number of steps
re·cur·sive \rəˈkərsiv, rēˈ-, -ˈkəs-, -ˈkəis-\ *adj* [*recursion* + *-ive*, adj. suffix] **1** : of, relating to, or involving mathematical recursion **2** : of, relating to, or constituting a procedure that can repeat itself indefinitely or until a specified condition is met < a *recursive* rule in a grammar > — **re·cur·sive·ly** \-lē, -li\ *adv* — **re·cur·sive·ness** \-nəs\ *n*

re·cy·cle* \(ˈ)rēˈsīkəl\ *vt* **1** : to process (as liquid body waste, glass, or cans) in order to regain material for human use <automobiles should be *recycled* by melting and manufacturing into new products —J.S. Poliskin> **2** : to cause (as an electric generator) to accelerate gradually in bringing up to full power production ~ *vi* **1** : to stop the counting and return to an earlier point in a countdown **2** : to return to an original condition so that operation can begin again — used of an electronic device — **re·cy·cla·ble** \-k(ə)ləbəl\ *adj*

red·brick \ˈredˈbrik, *in attributive position also* ˌredˌbrik\ *adj, sometimes cap* [fr. the common use of red brick in constructing the buildings of relatively modern British universities] : of, relating to, or being the British universities founded in modern times — compare OXBRIDGE, PLATEGLASS

red devil *n, slang* : secobarbital or its sodium derivative in a red capsule

re·describe \ˌrēdəˈskrīb\ *vt* : to describe anew or again; *esp* : to give a new and more complete description to (as a biological taxon)

re·de·scrip·tion \-dəˈskripshən\ *n* : a new and more complete description (as of a biological taxon)

Red Guard *n* [*red* communist + *guard*] : a member of a teenage activist organization in China serving the Maoist cause

red·shirt* \ˈredˌshərt, -ˌshə̄t, -ˌshəit\ *n* [fr. the red jersey commonly worn by such a player in practice scrimmages against the regulars] : a college athlete who is kept out of varsity competition for a year in order to extend the period of his eligibility — **redshirt** *vb* — **red·shirt·ing** \-ˌshərd·iŋ, -ˌshə̄d·iŋ, -ˌshəid·iŋ\ *n*

re·duc·tion·ism* \rəˈdəkshəˌnizəm\ *n* : the attempt to explain all biological processes by the same explanations (as by physical laws) that chemists and physicists use to interpret inanimate matter; *also* : the theory that complete reductionism is possible

redundant* *adj* : serving as a duplicate for preventing failure of an entire system (as a spacecraft) upon failure of a single component

re·du·pli·cate* \rəˈd(y)üpləˌkāt, (ˈ)rē-\ *vi* : to undergo reduplication <chromosomes *reduplicate*>

reel–to–reel \ˌrē(ə)ltəˌrē(ə)l, -dəˌ-\ *adj* : of, relating to, or utilizing magnetic tape that requires threading on a take-up reel <a *reel-to-reel* tape recorder>

reflection* *n* **1** : a transformation of a figure in which each point is replaced by a point symmetric with respect to a line **2** : a transformation that involves reflection in more than one axis of a rectangular coordinate system

re·fried beans \(ˈ)rēˈfrīd-\ *n pl* [trans. of Sp *frijoles refritos*] : FRIJOLES REFRITOS

reg·gae \ˈrā(ˌ)gā, ˈre-; reˈgā, rā-; ˈregē, -gi\ *n* [origin unknown] : popular music of West Indian origin that combines elements of the blues with a strong pulsating rhythm

region* *n* : an open connected set together with none, some, or all of the points on its boundary <a simple closed curve divides the plane into two *regions*>

register* *n* **1** : a device in a computer or calculator for storing small amounts of data; *esp* : one in which data can be both stored and operated on **2** : a variety of a language that is appropriate to a particular subject or occasion

regulator gene *or* **regulatory gene** *n* : a gene controlling the production of a genetic repressor

reinforce* *vb* **-forced; -forc·ing** *vt* : to stimulate (as an experimental animal or a student) with a reinforcer following a correct or desired performance — **re·in·force·able** \ˌrēənˈfō(ə)rsəbəl, -ˈfȯ(ə)r-, -ˈfōəs-, -ˈfȯ(ə)s-\ *adj*

re·in·forc·er* \-sə(r)\ *n* : a stimulus (as a reward or the removal of discomfort) that is effective esp. in operant conditioning because it regularly follows a desired response

rejection* *n* : the immunological process of sloughing off foreign tissue or an organ (as a transplant) by the recipient organism

re·jec·tive art \rəˈjektiv-\ *n* : MINIMAL ART

relative biological effectiveness *n* : the relative capacity of a particular ionizing radiation to produce a response in a biological system — abbr. *RBE*

rel·a·tiv·is·tic* \ˌreləd·əˈvistik, -ēk\ *adj* **1** : moving at a velocity such that there is a significant change in mass and other properties in accordance with the theory of relativity <a *relativistic* electron> **2** : of or relating to a relativistic particle

relevance* *n* : the ability (as of an information retrieval system) to retrieve material that satisfies the needs of the user

REM \ˌär(ˌ)ē'em, 'rem\ *n* : RAPID EYE MOVEMENT

remote* *adj* : acting, acted on, or controlled indirectly or from a distance <time-sharing and other *remote* computing services —*GT&E Annual Report*>

REM sleep *n* : PARADOXICAL SLEEP

re·new·able* \rə'n(y)üəbəl, rē'-\ *adj* : capable of being replaced by natural ecological cycles or sound management practices <a *renewable* natural resource>

re·no·gram \'rēnəˌgram\ *n* [*reno-* kidney, renal (fr. L *renes* kidneys) + *-gram* drawing, writing, record, deriv. of Gk *gramma* letter, writing] : a photographic depiction of the course of renal excretion of a radioactively labeled substance — **re·no·graph·ic** \ˌrēnə'grafik\ *adj* — **re·nog·ra·phy** \rē'nägrəfē, rə'-\ *n*

re·no·vas·cu·lar \¦rēnō¦vaskyələ(r)\ *adj* : of, relating to, or involving the blood vessels of the kidneys <*renovascular* hypertension>

rent strike *n* : a refusal by a group of tenants to pay rent (as in protest against poor service)

reo·vi·rus \¦rēō¦vīrəs\ *n* [*r*espiratory *e*nteric *o*rphan *virus*] : any of a group of rather large, widely distributed, and possibly tumorigenic viruses with double-stranded RNA

repertoire* *n* : a list or supply of capabilities <the instruction *repertoire* of a computer>

rep·li·ca·ble \'repləkəbəl\ *adj* [LL *replicabilis* worth repeating, fr. *replicare* to repeat, reply + L *-abilis* capable of] : capable of replication <*replicable* experimental results>

rep·li·case \'repləkās, -āz\ *n* [*replic*ation + *-ase* enzyme] : a polymerase that promotes synthesis of a particular RNA in the presence of a suitable template

rep·li·cate* \'repləˌkāt\ *vi* **-cat·ed; -cat·ing** : to undergo replication : produce a replica of itself <*replicating* virus particles>

rep·li·ca·tive \'repləˌkād·iv\ *adj* : of, relating to, or characterized by replication <the *replicative* form of tobacco mosaic virus>

repress* *vt* : to inactivate (a gene) by allosteric combination at a DNA binding site

re·press·ible \rə'presəbəl\ *adj* : capable of being repressed <*repressible* enzymes controlled by their end products> — **re·press·ibil·i·ty** \-ˌpresə'biləd·ē\ *n*

re·pres·sor* \rə'presə(r)\ *n* : a product of the action of a regulator gene that interacts with a genetic operator and inhibits its function

re·pro·gram \(ˌ)rē¦prōˌgram, -¦prōgrəm\ *vt* : to program anew; *esp* : to write new programs for (as a computer) ~ *vi* : to rewrite a computer program

re·prog·ra·phy \rə'prägrəfē, rē'p-\ *n* [ISV *repro*duction + *-graphy* writing, representation, deriv. of Gk *graphein* to write] : the facsimile reproduction (as by photocopying) of graphic matter (as books or documents) — **re·prog·ra·pher** \-fə(r)\ *n* — **re·pro·graph·ic** \¦rēprə¦grafik, ¦rep-\ *adj*

re–re·fine \¦rērə'fīn, -rē'-\ *vt* : to refine (used motor oil) in order to produce a clean usable lubricant — **re–re·fin·er** \-ə(r)\ *n*

re·seg·re·ga·tion \(¦)rēˌsegrə'gāshən\ *n* : a return (as of a school) to a state of segregation after a period of desegregation

re·ser·pi·nized \rə'sərpəˌnīzd, rē-\ *adj* : treated or medicated with reserpine or a reserpine derivative <*reserpinized* animals> — **re·ser·pin·iza·tion** \-ˌsərpənə'zāshən, -ˌnī'z-\ *n*

reserve clause *n* : a clause in a professional athlete's contract that reserves for the club the exclusive right automatically to renew the contract and that binds the athlete to the club for his entire playing career or until he is traded or released

re·sid \rə'zid\ *n* [by shortening] : RESIDUAL OIL

residence* *n* : the persistence of a substance that is suspended or dissolved in a medium <the *residence* time of a pollutant>

residual* *n* : a payment (as to an actor or writer) for each rerun esp. of a commercial

residual oil *n* : fuel oil that remains after the removal of valuable distillates (as gasoline) from petroleum and that is used esp. by industry — called also *resid*

residual security *n* : common stock or a security convertible into common stock

residue* *n* : the remainder after subtracting a multiple of a modulus from an integer or a power of the integer : the second of two terms in a congruence <2 and 7 are *residues* of 12 modulo 5> <9 is a quadratic *residue* of 7 modulo 5 since $7^2-8\times5 = 9$>

residue class *n* : the set of elements (as integers) that leave the same remainder when divided by the same modulus

resilience* *n* : an ability to recover from or adjust easily to misfortune or change <marvellous *resilience* and courage in recovering from setbacks —*Times Lit. Supp.*>

resistance* *n* : RESISTANCE LEVEL

resistance level *or* **resistance area** *n* : a price level on a rising market at which a security resists further advance because of increased attractiveness of the price to potential sellers

re·sis·to·jet \rə̇'zistō,jet, rē'z-\ *n* [*resist*ance + connective *-o-* + *jet*] : a small reaction engine that uses electrically heated hydrogen or ammonia as a propellant and that produces small thrust (as for satellite control)

resonance* *n* **1 a** : the enhancement of an atomic, nuclear, or particle reaction or a scattering event by excitation of internal motion in the system **b** : magnetic resonance **2** : an extremely short-lived elementary particle

res·pi·ro·met·ric \,respərō'me·trik, rə̇,spīrə'-\ *adj* : of or relating to respirometry or to the use of a respirometer < *respirometric* studies >

re·spon·dent* \rə̇'spändənt\ *n* : a reflex that occurs in response to a specific external stimulus <the knee jerk is a typical *respondent*>

respondent* *adj* : relating to or being behavior or responses to a stimulus that are followed by a reward < *respondent* conditioning >

res·sen·ti·ment \rə,sä^{n}tē'mä^{n}\ *n* [G, fr. F, resentment] : resentment expressed indirectly esp. by belittling the values esteemed by the hated individual

re·start·able \(')rē'stärtəbəl, -'stȧd·əbəl\ *adj* : capable of being restarted < *restartable* rocket engines >

ret·i·nal \'ret^{ə}n,al, -,ȯl\ *n* [*retina* + *-al* aldehyde] : a yellowish to orange aldehyde $C_{20}H_{28}O$ derived from vitamin A that in combination with proteins forms the visual pigments of the retinal rods and cones

ret·i·nol \'ret^{ə}n,ȯl, -,ōl\ *n* [*retina* + *-ol* chemical compound; fr. its chemical the source of retinal] : vitamin A_1

ret·ro–en·gine \'re·trō,enjən, *sometimes* 'rē-·\ *n* [*retro-* backward, back (fr. L *retro*) + *engine*] : a rocket engine on a spacecraft that produces thrust in the direction opposite to the motion of the spacecraft and that is used to reduce speed

ret·ro·fire \-,fī(ə)r\ *vi, of a retro-engine or retro-rocket* : to become ignited ~ *vt* : to cause to retrofire

ret·ro·fit \,re·trō'fit, 're·trō,fit\ *vt* [*retrofit* modification of equipment to include changes made in later models] : to furnish (as an aircraft) with new parts or equipment not available at the time of manufacture

ret·ro·grade* \'re·trə,grād\ *adj* : being or relating to the rotation of a satellite in a direction opposite to that of the body being orbited

ret·ro·pack \'re·trō,pak, *sometimes* 'rē-·\ *n* : a system of auxiliary rockets on a spacecraft that produces thrust in the direction opposite to the motion of the spacecraft and that is used to reduce speed

ret·ro·re·flec·tion \¦re·trōrə̇¦flekshən, *sometimes* ¦rē-·\ *n* : the action or use of a retroreflector

ret·ro·re·flec·tor \-rə̇¦flektə(r)\ *n* : a device that reflects radiation (as light) so that the paths of the rays are parallel to those of the incident rays

Reu·ben sandwich \¦rübən-, *in rapid speech also* ¦rüb^{ə}m-\ *n* [fr. the name *Reuben*] : a grilled sandwich consisting of corned beef, Swiss cheese, and sauerkraut usu. on rye bread

re·vanch·ism \rə̇'vä^{n},shizəm\ *n* : a usu. political policy designed to recover lost territory or status : revanche <a policy of nationalistic *revanchism* —Bernard Fall>

re·vas·cu·lar·iza·tion \(¦)rē,vaskyələrə̇'zāshən, -,rī'z-\ *n* : a surgical procedure for the provision of a new, additional, or augmented blood supply to a body part or organ

revenue sharing *n* : the dispensing of a portion of federal tax revenue to state and local governments to assist in meeting their monetary needs

re·verb \rə'vərb, 'rē,-, -vəb, -vəib\ *n* [short for *reverberation*] : an electronically produced echo effect in recorded music; *also* : a device for producing reverb

reverse osmosis *n* : the flow of fresh water through a semipermeable membrane when pressure is applied to a solution (as seawater) on one side of it

reverse tran·scrip·tase \-,tran'skrip(,)tās, -āz\ *n* [*transcription* + *-ase* enzyme] : a polymerase that catalyzes the formation of DNA using RNA as a template and that is found in many tumor-producing viruses containing RNA

re·ver·tant \rə'vərtᵊnt, rē'-, -vət-, -vəit-\ *n* : an individual or strain that has mutated back to an ancestral form (as the wild type) — **revertant** *adj*

R factor *n* [*r*esistance] : a factor that is present in some bacteria, is a basis of resistance to antibiotics, and can be transferred from cell to cell by conjugation

rheu·ma·toid factor \'rümə,tȯid, 'rụm-\ *n* : a gamma globulin of high molecular weight that is usu. present in rheumatoid arthritis and that behaves like an autoantibody

rhi·no·vi·rus \ˌrīnō'vīrəs\ *n* [NL, fr. *rhino-* nose (fr. Gk *rhin-, rhis*) + *virus*] : any of a group of picornaviruses that are related to the enteroviruses and associated with upper respiratory tract disorders

RHIP *abbr* rank has its privileges; rank hath its privileges

rho* \'rō\ *or* **rho particle** *n* : a very short-lived unstable meson with mass 1490 times the mass of an electron

rhythm and blues *n* : blues orig. performed by black musicians for a black audience and marked by a strong simple beat and often an electronically amplified accompaniment

ri·bo·nu·cle·o·side \ˌrī(,)bō'n(y)üklēə,sīd\ *n* [*ribo*se + *nucleoside*] : a nucleoside that contains ribose

ri·bo·nu·cle·o·tide \-,tīd\ *n* [*ribo*se + *nucleotide*] : a nucleotide that contains ribose and occurs esp. as a constituent of RNA

ribosomal RNA \-,ä(,)re'nā\ *n* : RNA that is a fundamental structural element of the ribosome

ri·bo·some \'rībə,sōm\ *n* [*ribo*nucleic acid + *-some* body, deriv. of Gk *sōma*] : any of the RNA-rich cytoplasmic granules that are sites of protein synthesis — **ri·bo·som·al** \ˌrībə'sōməl\ *adj*

Rich·ter scale \ˌriktə(r)-\ *n* [Charles F. *Richter* b1900 Am. seismologist] : a logarithmic scale for expressing the magnitude of a seismic disturbance (as an earthquake) in terms of the energy dissipated in it with 1.5 indicating the smallest earthquake that can be felt, 4.5 an earthquake causing slight damage, and 8.5 a very devastating earthquake

ricky–tick \ˌrikē'tik, -ki'-\ *n* [imit.] : sweet jazz of a style reminiscent of the 1920s — **ricky–ticky** \-'tikē\ *adj*

ride* *vb* — **ride shotgun** **1** : to guard someone or something while in transit <the armed security forces that have *ridden shotgun* on every Israeli civilian flight since the Athens raid —*Newsweek*> **2** : to ride in the front passenger seat of a motor vehicle <a front-seat passenger *riding shotgun* and calling out road conditions ahead —P.J.C. Friedlander>

rid·er·ship \'rīdə(r),ship\ *n* : the number of persons who ride a particular system of public transportation <total transit *ridership* in the United States has declined since World War II —Tom Wicker>

Rie·mann integral \ˌrē,män-, ˌrēmən-\ *n* [G.F.B. *Riemann* †1866 Ger. mathematician] : a number that is the difference between the values of the indefinite integral of a given function for two values of the independent variable : definite integral

ri·fam·pi·cin \rī'fampəsən\ *n* [*rif*amycin (from which it is derived) + *ampic*ill*in* (which it resembles in efficacy)] : a semisynthetic antibiotic that acts against some viruses and bacteria esp. by inhibiting RNA synthesis

ri·fa·my·cin \ˌrīfə'mīsᵊn\ *n* [alter. of earlier *rifomycin*, fr. *rif-* (fr. *r*eplication *i*nhibiting *f*ungus) + connective *-o-* + *-mycin* substance obtained from a fungus, fr. *streptomycin*] : any of several antibiotics that are derived from cultures of a bacterium (*Streptomyces mediterranei*)

right on *interj* — used to express agreement or to give encouragement <and if you live communally, well, *right on*! —*Great Speckled Bird*>

right–on \ˌrīd·ˈȯn, -ˈän\ *adj* **1** : exactly correct <the *right-on* naturalism of a writer with a perfect pitch for dialogue —L.E. Sissman> **2** : attuned to the spirit of the times <rather than not be considered avant-garde, with it, *right-on,* or gung ho, I improvise several reasons for not having seen any of the new films —Goodman Ace>

right–to–work law \ˌrī(t)təˈwərk, -ˈwək-, -ˈwəik-\ *n* : any of various state laws banning the closed shop and the union shop

¹rinky–dink \ˌriŋkēˌdiŋk, -kiˌ-\ *adj* [origin unknown] **1** : not modern or up-to-date : backward, old-fashioned, out-of-date <a *rinky-dink* town with its shacks and shanties —D.M. Milligan> <old-timers say it was truly a *rinky-dink* railroad in those days —Jules Loh> **2** : small-time <he was a *rinky-dink* dope dealer mostly —V.E. Smith>

²rinky–dink *n* **1** : one who is rinky-dink <if the Senate Majority Leader's blood brother couldn't get through, how was a *rinky-dink* to make connections? —L.L. King> **2** : RICKY-TICK

rinky–tink \-ˌtiŋk\ *n* [perh. by alter.] : RICKY-TICK — **rinky–tinky** \-ˌtiŋkē, -ki\ *adj*

rip off *vt* **1** : to rob <assume that the visitor is more interested in *ripping off* the store than in quietly browsing —Janet Malcolm>; *also* : to steal <$5-million worth of goods *ripped off* at various merchandise-loading . . . spots —*New York*> **2** : to exploit esp. financially : cheat <being *ripped off* by . . . bakers who give us zero nutritional value for our money —Mary Daniels>

rip–off \ˈripˌȯf\ *n* **1** : an act or an instance of stealing : theft <site of a famous gem theft, among other *rip-offs*—R.R. Lingeman>; *also*: an instance of financial exploitation : gyp <don't waste your money on this book . . . it's a *rip-off* —Peter Stollery> **2** : something (as a story or motion picture) that is obviously based on or imitative of something else <this kaleidoscopic fantasy, a *rip-off* on everything from spy novels to the Oedipus complex —Barbara A. Bannon>

rise·time \ˈrīzˌtīm\ *n* : the time required for a pulse on an electronic display (as of an oscilloscope) to increase from one specified value (as 10 percent) of its amplitude to another (as 90 percent)

RNase \ˌäˈrenˌās, -āz\ *or* **RNAase** \ˌä(ˌ)reˈnāˌās, -ˌāz\ *n* [*RNA* + *-ase* enzyme] : an enzyme that catalyzes the hydrolysis of RNA : ribonuclease

road·ie \ˈrōdē\ *n* : one who manages the activities of entertainers on the road <hid out down below in back of the stage, guarded by managers, *roadies* and security people —Eric Sauter> — called also *road manager*

road racing *n* : racing (as in automobiles or on motorcycles) over public roads or over a closed course designed to simulate public roads (as with left and right turns, sharp corners, and hills)

ro·bot·ics \rōˈbäd·iks\ *n pl but sing in constr* : technology dealing with the design, construction, and operation of robots in automation

rock·a·bil·ly \ˈräkəˌbilē, -li\ *n* [*rock and* roll + hill*billy*] : pop music marked by features of rock and country and western styles

rocker* *n* : a rock singer, musician, or song <not a shred of the showman about him, none of the erotic frenzy of the *rockers* —Herb Russcol> <shifting into a nice laid-back *rocker* —Loraine Alterman>

ro·la·mite \ˈrōləˌmīt\ *n* [*rol*l + *-amite,* ending coined by Donald Fancher Wilkes *b*1931 Am. engineer, inventor of the rolamite] : a nearly frictionless elementary mechanism consisting of two or more rollers inserted in the loops of a flexible metal or plastic band with the band acting to turn the rollers whose movement can be directed to perform various functions

roll bar *n* : an overhead metal bar on an automobile designed to protect an occupant in case of a turnover

roll cage *n* : a protective framework of metal bars encasing the driver of a racing car

roller hockey *n* : a variation of ice hockey played on roller skates

Rolle's theorem \ˈrȯlz-, ˈrōlz-\ *n* [Michel *Rolle* †1719 Fr. mathematician] : a theorem in mathematics: if a curve is continuous, crosses the x-axis at two points, and has a tangent at every point between the two intercepts, its tangent is parallel to the x-axis at some point between the intercepts

roll out* *vi* : to run toward one flank usu. parallel to the line of scrimmage esp. before throwing a pass < the quarterback would either hand off to the fullback or fake to him and *roll out* —Arthur Sampson >

roll·out \'rō,lau̇t\ *n* : a football play in which the quarterback rolls out

ROM *abbr* read-only memory

Ror·schach \'rȯ(ə)r,shäk, 'rȯ(ə),shäk\ *adj* : of, relating to, used in connection with, or resulting from the Rorschach test < *Rorschach* blots >

rose* *n* : a plane curve which consists of three or more loops meeting at the origin and whose equation in polar coordinates is of the form $\rho = a \sin n\theta$ or $\rho = a \cos n\theta$ where n is an integer greater than 1

rose medallion *n* : a chiefly 19th century enamel-decorated Chinese porcelain with medallions of oriental figures surrounded and separated by panels of flowers and butterflies

RPG \,är(,)pē'jē\ *n* [*r*eport *p*rogram *g*enerator] : a computer language that generates programs from the user's specifications esp. to produce business reports

running dog *n* [trans. of Chin (Pek) *tsou*^{2} *kou*^{3} hunting dog, lackey, lit., running dog, fr. *tsou*^{3} to go, walk, run + *kou*^{3} dog] : one who does someone else's bidding : lackey < charge the missionaries with being *running dogs* for the imperialistic foreign powers —*Living Age* >

rush* *n* : the immediate pleasurable feeling produced by a drug (as heroin or amphetamine) — called also *flash*

RV \,är'vē\ *n* : a recreational vehicle

rya \'rēə, 'rīə\ *n* [*Rya*, village in southwest Sweden] : a Scandinavian handwoven rug with a deep resilient comparatively flat pile; *also* : the weave typical of this rug

S

s* *abbr* siemens

sac·cade* \sa'käd, sə'-\ *n* [*saccade* a quick check of a horse by a twitch of the reins, fr. F, lit., jerk, twitch] : a small rapid jerky movement of the eye esp. as it jumps from fixation on one point to another (as in reading)

sacred mushroom *n* : any of various New World hallucinogenic fungi (as genus *Psilocybe*) used esp. in some Indian ceremonies

saddled prominent *n* [fr. the hump or prominence on the back of the larva] : a moth (*Heterocampa guttivitta*) whose larva is a serious defoliator of hardwood trees in the eastern and midwestern U.S.

Sa·hel \sə'hā(ə)l, -'hē(ə)l\ *n* [F, fr. Ar *sāḥil* coast, shore] : a savanna or steppe region bordering a desert — **Sa·hel·ian** \-'hālēən, -'hēl-\ *adj*

sail·board \'sā(ə)l,bō(ə)rd, -,bȯ(ə)rd, -,bōəd, -,bȯ(ə)d\ *n* : a small flat sailboat that is designed for one or two passengers

sal·uret·ic \,salyə'red·ik\ *n* [L *sal* salt + E di*uretic*] : a drug that facilitates the urinary excretion of salt and esp. of sodium ion — **saluretic** *adj* — **sal·u·ret·i·cal·ly** \-¦red·ək(ə)lē\ *adv*

SAM \'sam, ,e(,)sā'em\ *n* : SURFACE-TO-AIR MISSILE

sam·bo \'sam(,)bō, 'säm-\ *n* [Russ, fr. *sam*ozashchita *b*ez *o*ruzhiya self-defense without weapons] : an international style of wrestling employing judo techniques

sa·miz·dat \'sämēz,dät\ *n* [Russ, fr. *sam* self + *izdat*el'stvo publisher, fr. *izdat'* to publish, fr. *iz* out, from + *dat'* to give; akin to L *dare* to give] : the system in the U.S.S.R. by which government-suppressed literature is clandestinely printed and distributed; *also* : such literature

sampling distribution *n* : the distribution of a statistic (as a sample mean)

San·da ware \ˈsandə-, ˈsän-\ *n* [fr. *Sanda,* town in western Honshu, Japan, where it originated] : a Japanese pottery and esp. porcelain ware produced since the late 17th century and noted for its celadons

S and M *abbr* sadism and masochism; sadist and masochist

sandwich shop *n* : a restaurant serving light meals : luncheonette

san·gria \ saŋˈgrēə, san-, säŋ-, sän-\ *n* [Sp *sangría,* lit., bleeding, fr. *sangre* blood, modif. of L *sanguin-, sanguis* blood] : a punch made of red wine, fruit juice, sugar, and usu. brandy, sliced fruit, and soda water

san·i·tize* \ˈsanə̇ˌtīz\ *vt* **-tized; -tiz·ing** **1** : to make more acceptable by removing unpleasant or undesired features <the heroine became a dance-hall hostess and she and her milieu have been further *sanitized* for the movies so that not even the properest Bostonian would suspect that dance-hall floozies aren't Radcliffe girls —Judith Crist> **2** : to remove identifying or sensitive material from (as a document) <classified paper (which was later *sanitized* and published . . .) —Deborah Shapley>

Sapir–Whorf hypothesis \səˌpi(ə)rˈ(h)wȯ(ə)rf-\ *n* [Edward *Sapir* †1939 and Benjamin Lee *Whorf* †1941 Am. anthropologists] : WHORFIAN HYPOTHESIS

sa·ran·gi \ˈsärənˌgē, -əŋˌg-\ *n* [Skt *sāraṅgī*] : a stringed musical instrument of India that is played with a bow and that has a tone similar to that of the viola

SASE *abbr* self-addressed stamped envelope

Sas·quatch \ˈsasˌkwach, -ˌkwäch\ *n* [prob. fr. some Amerindian language of British Columbia] : a large hairy manlike animal that is reported as existing in the Pacific Northwest — called also *bigfoot, omah*

satellite* *n* : a usu. independent urban community situated on the outskirts of a large city

saturated diving *n* : SATURATION DIVING — **saturated diver** *n*

sat·u·ra·tion diving \ˌsachəˈrāshən-\ *n* : diving in which a person remains underwater at a certain depth breathing a mixture of gases under pressure until his body becomes saturated with the gases so that decompression time remains the same regardless of how long he remains at that depth — **saturation dive** *n*

Saturday night special *n* : an inexpensive easily concealed handgun

saxi·tox·in \ˌsaksə̇ˈtäksən\ *n* [NL *Saxidomus giganteus,* species of butter clam from which it is isolated + E *toxin*] : a potent nonprotein poison $C_{10}H_{17}N_7O_4.2HCl$ that originates in a causative agent (*Gonyaulax catenella*) of red tide and sometimes occurs in normally edible mollusks

SBN *abbr* Standard Book Number

scag *or* **skag** \ˈskag\ *n* [prob. fr. earlier slang *scag, skag* cigarette butt, cigarette, of unknown origin] *slang* : heroin

sca·lar* \ˈskālə(r), -ˌlär, -ˌlȧ(r\ *adj* : of or relating to a scalar or scalar product <*scalar* multiplication>

scam \ˈskam\ *n* [origin unknown] *slang* : a method or an instance of obtaining money fraudulently : swindle <insurance swindles, credit-card rackets, and practically every *scam* devised by man —Joe Flaherty>

scam·pi \ˈskampē, -pi\ *n, pl* **scampi** [It, pl. of *scampo* Norway lobster] : shrimp; *esp* : large shrimp prepared with a garlic-flavored sauce

scan* *vt* **scanned; scan·ning** : to make a detailed examination of (as a human body) for the presence or localization of radioactive material

scan* *n* **1** : a depiction (as a photograph) of the distribution of radioactive material in something (as a body organ) **2** : the usu. bright line or spot that moves across the screen of a cathode-ray tube (as in a radar set); *also* : the path taken by such a line or spot

scanning electron microscope *n* : an electron microscope in which a beam of focused electrons moves across the object with the secondary electrons produced by the object and the electrons scattered by the object being collected to form a three-dimensional image on a cathode-ray tube — called also *scanning microscope*

scattering matrix *n* : S MATRIX

sce·nar·io* \sə̇ˈnarē(ˌ)ō, -ˈner-, -ˈnär-, *sometimes* shə̇ˈnär- *or* shə̇ˈnȧr-\ *n* : a sequence of events esp. when imagined <pry . . . into the mind of the rapist, tune in on the ob-

scene *scenarios* unreeling inside his head —W.H. Manville> <if you've been busted, then you know the *scenario* all too painfully —Joe Eszterhas>; *esp* : an account or synopsis of a projected course of action or events <had drawn up a number of possible *scenarios* in which nuclear weapons would be used —Martin Mayer>

scene* *n* : a sphere of activity : a way of life <the social *scene*> <the drug *scene*> <thinks the performing arts *scene* here is great —Ellen Phillips> <leading figures of the German porno *scene* —*Times Lit. Supp.*>

schizy *or* **schiz·zy** \ˈskitsē\ *adj* [*schiz*oid + *-y*, adj. suffix] : schizoid <the gap between his private and public selves was making him feel *schizy* —Peter Schjeldahl>

schlepp* *or* **schlep** *or* **shlep** *vi* **schlepped** *or* **shlepped; schlep·ping** *or* **shlep·ping** : to proceed or move slowly, tediously, or awkwardly <*schlepped* through ridiculous crosstown traffic and arrived an hour late —Philip Nobile>

schlepp \ˈshlep\ *or* **schlep·per** *or* **shlep·per** \ˈshlepə(r)\ *n* [Yiddish *shlep, shleper,* fr. *shlepen* to drag, pull, jerk, fr. MHG *sleppen, slēpen,* fr. MLG *slēpen*] : an awkward or incompetent person : jerk <I'm really quite helpless at a cocktail party, a real *schlepper* —G.L. Rogin>

schlock *also* **shlock** \ˈshläk\ *adj* [Yiddish *shlak,* lit., blow, apoplectic stroke, curse, fr. MHG *slag, slac,* fr. OHG *slag,* fr. *slahan* to strike] : of low quality or little worth <*schlock* merchandise> <more *schlock* suburbs, maybe dolled up with a few fountains —Jack Rosenthal> <he was no longer scorned as a *schlock* artist: instead he was celebrated —Mordecai Richler> — **schlock** *n*

schlock·meis·ter \-ˈmīstə(r)\ *n* [*schlock* + G *meister* master] : one who makes or sells schlock products <Hollywood's *schlockmeisters,* meanwhile, are busily grinding out a dozen cookie-cutter copies —*Newsweek*>

schmear *also* **schmeer** *or* **shmear** \ˈshmi(ə)r, -iə\ *n* [Yiddish *shmir* smear, fr. *shmiren* to smear, fr. MHG *smiren, smirwen,* fr. OHG *smirwen*] : an aggregate of related things — usu. used in the phrase *the whole schmear*

schmuck *or* **shmuck** \ˈshmək\ *n* [Yiddish *shmok* penis, fool, fr. G *schmuck* adornment, fr. MLG *smuck;* akin to OE *smoc* smock] : a stupid, naïve, or foolish person <the all-American fan, the downtrodden *schmuck* who slumps in his $10 seat behind an immutable support column, quaffing overpriced beer and cold hot dogs —Charles Farley>; *also* : one who is mean or nasty <sometimes, sure, I am too hard on somebody. Afterward I think, 'Povich, you are such a *schmuck*' —Maury Povich>

schtick *var of* SHTICK

schuss·boom·er \ˈshu̇s͵bümə(r), ˈshüs-\ *n* [*schuss* straight high-speed run on skis (fr. G, lit., shot) + *boomer* one that booms] : one who skis usu. straight downhill at high speed

Schwarz·schild radius \ˈs(h)wȯ(ə)rts͵chīld-; ˈshfärt͵shilt-, ˈshvä-\ *n* [Karl *Schwarzschild* †1916 Ger. astronomer] : the value of the radius of a collapsing celestial body beyond which gravitational forces are so strong that they prevent the escape of matter and energy with the result that the body becomes a black hole

sci–fi \ˌsīˈfī\ *adj* [*sci*ence *fi*ction] : of, relating to, or being science fiction <*sci-fi* writers> <*sci-fi* stories>

scin·ti·scan \ˈsintə͵skan\ *n* [*scinti*llation + *scan*] : a two-dimensional representation of radioisotope radiation from a bodily organ (as the spleen or kidney)

scin·ti·scan·ning \-͵skaniŋ\ *n* : the action or process of making a scintiscan

scle·ro·tes·ta \ˌsklirōˈtestə, ˌsklerō-\ *n* [NL, fr. *sclero-* hard (deriv. of Gk *sklēros*) + *testa*] : the middle stony layer of the testa in various seeds — compare ENDOTESTA

score* *vi* **scored; scor·ing** : to succeed in having sexual intercourse <college roommates who . . . *score* with the same girl —L.H. Lapham>

Scouse \ˈskau̇s\ *n* [back-formation fr. *Scouser*] **1** : a dialect of English spoken in Liverpool **2** : SCOUSER

Scous·er \ˈskau̇sə(r)\ *n* [*scouse* lobscouse + *-er,* n. suffix; fr. the popularity of lobscouse in Liverpool] : a native or inhabitant of Liverpool

scramble* *vi* **scram·bled; scram·bling** *of a football quarterback* : to run with the ball after the pass protection breaks down

scramble* *n* : a motorcycle race over a rough hilly course

scram·jet \ˈskramˌjet\ *n* [*s*upersonic *c*ombustion *ramjet*] : a ramjet airplane engine in which thrust is produced by burning fuel in a supersonic airstream after the airplane has attained supersonic speed by other means of propulsion

scratch·pad \ˈskrachˌpad\ *n* : a small fast auxiliary computer memory

screening test *n* : a preliminary or abridged test intended to eliminate the less probable members of an experimental series

scu·ba diver \ˈsk(y)übə-\ *n* : one who swims under water with the aid of scuba gear — **scuba dive** *vi*

scum·bag \ˈskəmˌbag\ *n* **1** *slang* : a condom **2** *slang* : a dirty or unpleasant person — used as a generalized term of abuse <hearing how I was no good and rotten, that I was a *scumbag* and the most disgusting, slimy being who ever lived —Art Pepper>

SDRs \ˌes(ˌ)dēˈärz, -ˈäz\ *n pl* [*s*pecial *d*rawing *r*ight*s*] : an international means of exchange created under the auspices of the International Monetary Fund for use by governments in settling their international indebtedness

sea–grant college \ˈsēˌgrant-\ *n* : an institution of higher learning that receives federal grants for research in oceanography

seat* *n* : a precise or accurate contact between parts or surfaces

secondary* *or* **secondary offering** *n* : the sale of a large block of an already outstanding stock through dealers but off the floor of an exchange : secondary distribution

secondary derivative *n* : a word (as *teacher*) whose immediate constituents are a free form and a bound form

secondary recovery *n* : the process of obtaining oil (as by waterflood) from a well that has stopped producing

security blanket *n* **1** : a blanket carried by a child as a protection against anxiety **2** : a usu. familiar object or person whose presence dispels anxiety <he's America's old shoe. He's the national *security blanket* —Nicholas Von Hoffman>

seed money *n* : money used for setting up a new enterprise <has supplied six hundred thousand dollars of *seed money* for a combination land-planning and urban-renewal project —L.B. Sager>

sel·e·nod·e·sy \ˌseləˈnädəsē\ *n* [*selen-* moon (deriv. of Gk *selēnē*) + *-odesy* (as in *geodesy*)] : a branch of physical science that deals with determination of the shape and size of the moon and of the exact positions of points on it and with variations of lunar gravity — **sel·e·no·det·ic** \¦selənō¦ded·ik\ *adj*

self–ac·tu·al·ize \¦selˈfakch(əw)əˌlīz, ¦seu̇ˈ-, -ˈfakshwəˌ-\ *vi* : to realize fully one's potential <use it as a feedback to help students *self-actualize* —H.C. Lindgren> — **self–ac·tu·al·iza·tion** \-ˌfakch(əw)ələˈzāshən, -ˌfakshwə-, -ˌlīˈz-\ *n* — **self–ac·tu·al·iz·er** \-ˈfakch(əw)əˌlīzə(r), -ˈfakshwə-\ *n*

self–con·cept \ˈselfˈkänˌsept, ˈseu̇f-, *South often* ˈse(ə)f-\ *n* : the mental image one has of oneself <helped the boy revise his *self-concept* so that he would no longer consider himself defenseless against his acquisitive impulses —C.K. Aldrich>

self–dealing \-ˈdēliŋ\ *n* : financial dealing that is not at arm's length; *esp* : borrowing from or lending to a company by a controlling individual primarily to his own advantage

self–destruct \¦selfdə¦strəkt, ¦seu̇f-, *South often* ¦se(ə)f-\ *vi* : to destroy itself <the endless opportunites have *self-destructed* —W.H. McAllister>

self–rep·li·cat·ing \-ˈreplə̇ˌkād·iŋ\ *adj* : reproducing itself autonomously <DNA is a *self-replicating* molecule>

self–re·pro·duc·ing \-(ˌ)rēprəˈd(y)üsiŋ, *sometimes* -(ˌ)rep-\ *adj* : SELF-REPLICATING

self–stim·u·la·tion \-ˌstimyəˈlāshən\ *n* : stimulation of oneself as a result of one's own activity or behavior <electrical *self-stimulation* of the brain in rats>

selling climax *n* : a sharp decline in stock prices for a short time on very heavy trading volume followed by a rally

semi·au·to·mat·ed \¦semē¦ȯd·əˌmād·əd, ¦seˌmī-, ¦semi-\ *adj* [*semi-* half, partly, partial (fr. L, half) + *automated*] : partly automated <a *semiautomated* process>

semi·axis \-ˈaksə̇s\ *n* : a line segment that has one endpoint at the center of a geometric figure (as an ellipse) and that forms half of an axis

semi·co·ma·tose \¦semē¦kōməˌtōs, ¦seˌmī-, ¦semə̇-\ *adj* : lethargic and disoriented but not completely comatose

semi·con·ser·va·tive \\-kən¦sərvəd·iv, -¦sə̄v-, -¦səiv-\\ *adj* : relating to or being replication (as of DNA) in which the original separates into parts each of which is incorporated into a new whole and serves as a template for the formation of the missing parts — **semi·con·ser·va·tive·ly** \\-də̇vlē-, -li\\ *adv*

semi·group \\ˈsemē,grüp, ˈse,mī-, ˈsemə̇-\\ *n* : a mathematical set that is closed under an associative binary operation

semi·le·thal \\¦semēˈlēthəl, ¦se,mī-, ¦semə̇-\\ *n* : a mutation that in the homozygous condition produces more than 50 percent mortality but not complete mortality — **semilethal** *adj*

sen \\ˈsen\\ *n, pl* **sen** [prob. fr. Indonesian *sén,* prob. from E *cent*] **1** : a monetary unit of Brunei equal to $^1/_{100}$ dollar **2** : a coin representing one sen

send–up \\ˈsen,dəp\\ *n* [Brit. slang *send up* to take off, parody] : a parody or takeoff <many of the scenes . . . are parodies, *send-ups* of history —*Times Lit. Supp.*> <mixes suspense and mystery with some puckish *send-ups* of the genre —Hollis Alpert>

sene \\ˈsenē, -nə̇\\ *n, pl* **sene** *or* **senes** [Samoan, fr. E *cent*] **1** : a monetary unit of Western Samoa equivalent to $^1/_{100}$ tala **2** : a coin representing one sene

sen·gi \\ˈseŋgē, -gi\\ *n, pl* **sengi** [native name in the Congo] : a monetary unit of Zaire equal to $^1/_{100}$ likuta or $^1/_{10,000}$ zaire

senior citizen *n* : an elderly person <one more indignant *senior citizen* penning complaints about the universal decay of virtue —John Updike>; *esp*: one who has retired <now that I am a *senior citizen* and retired from routine daily business —F.P. Sherry>

sen·i·ti \\ˈsenətē, -ti\\ *n, pl* **seniti** [Tongan, modif. of E *cent*] **1** : a monetary unit of Tonga equal to $^1/_{100}$ pa'anga **2** : a coin representing one seniti

sensitivity training *n* : training in a small interacting group that is designed to increase each individual's awareness of his own feelings and the feelings of others and to enhance interpersonal relations through the exploration of the behavior, needs, and responses of the individuals making up the group

sen·so·ri·neu·ral \\¦sen(t)s(ə)rē¦n(y)u̇rəl\\ *adj* [*sensory* + *neural*] : of, relating to, or involving the aspects of sense perception mediated by nerves <*sensorineural* hearing loss>

sen·ti \\ˈsentē, -ti\\ *n, pl* **senti** [Swahili, modif. of E *cent*] : the cent of Tanzania

sen·ti·mo \\ˈsentə̇,mō\\ *n, pl* **-mos** [Pilipino, fr. Sp. *céntimo,* a monetary unit, modif. of F *centime,* fr. *cent* hundred, fr. L *centum*] **1** : a monetary unit of the Republic of the Philippines equal to $^1/_{100}$ peso : centavo **2** : a coin representing one sentimo

se·quen·tial \\sə̇ˈkwenchəl, (ˈ)sē¦k-\\ *n* : an oral contraceptive in which the pills taken during approximately the first three weeks contain only estrogen and those taken during the rest of the cycle contain both estrogen and progestogen

se·ri·al·ism \\ˈsirēə,lizəm, ˈsēr-\\ *n* : serial music; *also* : the theory or practice of composing serial music

service break *n* : a game won on an opponent's serve (as in tennis)

service mod·ule \\-¦mäj(,)ü(ə)l\\ *n* : a space vehicle module containing propellant tanks, fuel cells, and the main rocket engine

set back *n* : an offensive back in football who usu. lines up behind the quarterback

Se·to ware \\ˈsā,tō-, ˈse-\\ *also* **Seto** *n* [*Seto,* city in central Honshu, Japan, where it originated] : a Japanese ceramic ware traditionally produced since the 10th century comprising in its earlier period earthenwares often based on contemporaneous Chinese and Korean porcelains, later high-fired stonewares sometimes with notable brown, black, yellow, or celadon glazes, and from the end of the 18th century chiefly porcelain often decorated with underglaze blue

sex* *n* : the external genital organs of a human being

sexi·dec·i·mal \\¦seksə̇¦des(ə)məl, -ksē-\\ *adj* [*sexi-* six (fr. L *sex*) + *-decimal* (as in *duodecimal*)] : HEXADECIMAL

sex·ism \\ˈsek,sizəm\\ *n* [*sex* + *-ism* (as in *racism*)] : prejudice or discrimination based on sex <she liked to beat boys but not girls in an early version of sadistic *sexism* —Richard Fuller>; *esp*: discrimination against women <trains female students to

deal with the chauvinism and *sexism* of most of their teachers and fellow students —Ruth C. Benson > — **sex·ist** \'seksəst\ *adj or n*

Sey·fert galaxy \ˌsēfə(r)t-, ˌsī-\ *n* [Carl K. *Seyfert* †1960 Am. astronomer] : any of a class of spiral galaxies that have small compact bright nuclei exhibiting variability in light intensity, emission of radio waves, and spectra which indicate hot gases in rapid motion

shades \shādz\ *n pl* : tinted glasses : sunglasses < looks the way Ben Franklin would look if Franklin had worn bangs and purple *shades* —Catherine Breslin >

sha·ku·ha·chi \ˌshäkə'hächē\ *n, pl* **shakuhachi** [Jap (fr. *shaku* measure, foot + *hachi* eight), trans. of a word in some Chin dial.; akin to Chin (Pek) *ch'ih*^{3} *pa*^{1}, an ancient flute, fr. *ch'ih*^{3} measure, foot, the note sol in the pentatonic scale + *pa*^{1}, lit., eight, prob. fr. *pa*^{1} *yin*^{1}, the eight categories of instruments in an ancient Chinese orchestra, fr. *pa*^{1} eight + *yin*^{1} sound, voice, tone, pitch] : a Japanese bamboo flute

sham·a·teur·ism \'shaməˌtərˌizəm, -əd·əˌri-, -əˌt(y)u̇(ə)rˌi-, -əˌchu̇(ə)rˌi-, -əchəˌri-\ *n* [blend of *sham* and *amateurism*] : the practice of treating certain athletes as amateurs so that they will be eligible for amateur competition while subsidizing them with illegal payments or with excessive expense money

shape* *vt* **shaped; shap·ing** : to modify (behavior) by rewarding changes that tend toward a desired response

shatter cone *n* : a conical fragment of rock that has striations radiating from the apex and that is formed by high pressure (as from volcanism or meteorite impact)

shell* *n* : a plain usu. sleeveless overblouse

shell* *vt* : to score heavily against (as an opposing pitcher in baseball)

shield law *n* : a law that protects journalists from forced disclosure of confidential news sources

shift* *n* **1** : a movement of bits in a computer register a specified number of places to the right or left **2** : the act or an instance of depressing the shift key (as on a typewriter)

Shih Tzu \'shēd'zü\ *n* [Chin (Pek) *shih*^{1} *tzŭ*^{3} *kou*^{3} Pekingese dog, fr. *shih*^{1} lion + *tzŭ*^{3} son + *kou*^{3} dog] : a small alert active dog of an old Chinese breed that has a square short unwrinkled muzzle, short muscular legs, massive amounts of long dense hair, and a face that is sometimes compared to a chrysanthemum esp. because of hair that grows upward on the muzzle

shilingi \'shiliŋgē, -gi\ *n, pl* **shilingi** [Swahili, fr. E *shilling*] **1** : the basic monetary unit of Tanzania **2** : a coin representing one shilling

ship* *n* : a spacecraft < the separation system for the Apollo command and lunar *ships* —*Springfield (Mass.) Daily News*>

shirt·dress \'shərtˌdres, 'shət-, 'shəit-\ *n* : a dress that is patterned after a shirt and has buttons down the front and a collar

shirt jacket *n* : a jacket having an open shirtlike collar and usu. long sleeves with cuffs

shlepper *var of* SCHLEPP

shlock *var of* SCHLOCK

shmear *var of* SCHMEAR

shmuck *var of* SCHMUCK

shoot* *vt* : to inject (an illicit drug) esp. into the bloodstream — **shoot from the hip** : to act or speak hastily without consideration of the consequences < second thoughts about letting their man *shoot from the hip* quite as much as his nature prompted him to —R.L. Maullin > — **shoot the curl** *or* **shoot the tube** : to surf into or through the curl of a wave — **shoot the pier** : to surf between the pilings of an ocean pier

shoot down* *vt* : to put an end to esp. by suppression, rejection, or severe criticism < *shoot down* these fraudulent schemes —H.S. Ashmore >

shoot–'em–up \'shüd·əˌməp\ *n* : a movie or television show with much gunfire and bloodshed

shopping bag *n* : a bag (as of strong paper or plastic) that has handles and that is used for carrying small articles

short fuse *n* : a tendency to become angry quickly : a quick temper < had a *short fuse* and would be the most likely to confront the President directly —Pierre Salinger >

short position* *n* : the market position of a trader who has made but not yet covered a short sale

short–term* \'shȯrt¦tərm; 'shȯ(ə)t¦tə̄m, -¦təim\ *adj* : generated by assets held six months or less < *short-term* capital gains >

shotgun* *n* : an offensive football formation in which the quarterback plays a few yards behind the line of scrimmage and the other backs are scattered as flankers or slot-backs

showboat* *n* : one who tries to attract attention by conspicuous behavior

showboat *vi* : to show off

shrink* \'shriŋk\ *n* **1** [short for *headshrinker*] : a psychiatrist <the personae are just those who would patronize a *shrink* —John Thompson> **2** : a woman's short usu. sleeveless sweater often worn over a long-sleeved blouse or sweater

shrink–wrap \-¦rap\ *vt* : to wrap (as a book or meat) in tough clear plastic film that is then shrunk (as by heating) to form a tightly fitting package

shtick *or* **schtick** \'shtik\ *n* [Yiddish *shtik,* lit., piece, fr. MHG *stücke,* fr. OHG *stucki*] : a theatrical routine : bit <his familiar *shticks* — his comic shuffle, his stream-of-consciousness mumble, his mournful sheepdog glances — Stephen Farber>; *also* : something similar to a theatrical shtick <that instant-masterpiece *schtick* is the curse of the critic —Judith Crist> <yet another group in the educational bureaucracy dedicated to the preservation of its own *schtick* —Richard De Lone>

[1]**shuck** \'shək\ *n* [origin unknown] : a wily deception : fraud, sham <a public relations *shuck*> <a Return to Elegance . . . the latest clothing industry *shuck* —Tom Wolfe>

[2]**shuck** *vi* : to use verbal deception to produce a desired appearance (as of sincerity, diligence, or success) < *shucking* it with a judge . . . would be to feign repentance in the hope of receiving a lighter or suspended sentence —Thomas Kochman> **~** *vt*: to deceive, mislead, or swindle <was trundled out at cocktail parties . . . to *shuck* the moneyed liberals —John Leonard>

shun·pik·er \'shən¦pīkə(r)\ *n* : one who engages in shunpiking

shun·pik·ing \-kiŋ\ *n* : the practice of avoiding superhighways esp. for the pleasure of driving on back roads — **shunpike** \-¦pīk\ *vi*

shunt* *n* : an accident (as a collision between two cars) in auto racing

sick–out \'sik,au̇t\ *n* : an organized absence from work by workers on the pretext of sickness in order to apply pressure to management without an actual strike <plan to stage mass *sick-outs* today in their contract dispute with the city —Emanuel Perlmutter>

side·dress \'sī(d),dres\ *n* **1** : plant nutrients used to side-dress a crop **2** : the act or process of side-dressing a crop

side–strad·dle hop \'sīd,stradᵊl-\ *n* : JUMPING-JACK

SIDS *abbr* sudden infant death syndrome

sie·mens \'sēmənz, 'zē-\ *n, pl* **siemens** [Werner von *Siemens* †1892 Ger. electrical engineer and inventor] : a unit of conductance in the mks system equivalent to one ampere per volt

sig·ma* \'sigmə\ *or* **sigma particle** *n* : an unstable elementary particle of the baryon family existing in positive, negative, and neutral charge states with masses respectively 2328, 2343, and 2333 times the mass of an electron

significance level *n* : LEVEL OF SIGNIFICANCE

sign on* *vi* : to announce the start of broadcasting for the day — **sign–on** \'sī,nȯn, -,nän\ *n*

silky terrier *also* **silky** *n* : a low-set toy terrier that weighs 8 to 10 pounds, has a flat silky glossy coat colored blue with tan on the head, chest, and legs, and is derived from crosses of the Australian terrier with the Yorkshire terrier

sil·vex \'sil,veks\ *n* [prob. fr. L *silva* wood + E *ex*terminator] : a selective herbicide $C_6H_7O_3Cl_3$ that is esp. effective in controlling woody plants

sil·vi·chem·i·cal \¦silvə̇'kemə̇kəl\ *n* [L *silva* wood + E connective *-i-* + *chemical*] : any of numerous chemicals derived from a part of a tree

si·ma·zine \'sīmə,zēn\ *n* [*sim-* (prob. alter. of *sym-* symmetrical) + tri*azine*] : a selective herbicide $C_7H_{12}N_5Cl$ used to control weeds among crop plants

simple* *adj, of a statistical hypothesis* : specifying exact values for one or more statistical parameters — compare COMPOSITE

simple closed curve *n* : a closed plane curve (as a circle or an ellipse) that does not intersect itself : Jordan curve

simply connected *adj* : being or characterized by a surface which is divided into two separate parts by every closed curve it contains

simply ordered *adj* : having any two elements equal or connected by a relationship that is not symmetric and any three elements transitively related

simulate* *vt* **-lat·ed; -lat·ing** : to make a simulation of (as a physical system) — **sim·u·la·tive** \ˈsimyə͵lād·əv\ *adj*

sim·u·la·tion* \͵simyəˈlāshən\ *n* **1** : the imitative representation of the functioning of one system or process by means of the functioning of another <a computer *simulation* of an industrial process> **2** : examination of a problem often not subject to direct experimentation by means of a simulator (as a programmed computer)

single* *n* : an unmarried person — usu. used in pl. <swinging *singles*> <the New York *singles* scene> <a way of life for young *singles* —Norman Mailer>

sin·gle–blind \ˈsiŋgəl͵blīnd\ *adj* : of, relating to, or being an experimental procedure in which the experimenters but not the subjects know the makeup of the test and control groups during the actual course of an experiment — compare DOUBLE–BLIND

singles bar *n* : DATING BAR

sin·glet* \ˈsiŋglət\ *n* : an elementary particle not part of a multiplet

sin·gle·ton* \ˈsiŋgəltən\ *n* : a mathematical set that contains exactly one element

singular* *adj* **1** *of a matrix* : having a determinant equal to zero **2** *of a linear transformation* : having the property that the matrix of coefficients of the new variables has a determinant equal to zero

sin·gu·lar·i·ty* \͵siŋgyəˈlarəd·ē, *also* -ˈler-\ *n* **1** : a point at which the derivative of a given function of a complex variable does not exist but every neighborhood of which contains points for which the derivative exists **2** : BLACK HOLE

singular point *n* : SINGULARITY 1

sis·sy bar \ˈsisē-, -si-\ *n* : a narrow inverted U-shaped bar rising from behind the seat of a motorcycle or bicycle that is designed to support a driver or passenger

sit·com \ˈsit͵käm\ *n* [*sit*uation *com*edy] : SITUATION COMEDY

situation comedy *n* : a radio or television comedy series that involves a continuing cast of characters in a succession of unconnected episodes

situation ethics *n pl but sing or pl in constr* [trans. of G *situationsethik*] : a system of ethics which is based on love and by which acts are judged within their contexts instead of by categorical principles

skag *var of* SCAG

skate·board \ˈskāt͵bō(ə)rd, -͵bȯ(ə)rd, -͵bōəd, -͵bȯ(ə)d\ *n* : a narrow board about two feet long mounted on roller-skate wheels — **skate·board·er** \-ə(r)\ *n* — **skate·board·ing** \-iŋ\ *n*

skew field \ˈskyü-\ *n* : a mathematical field in which multiplication is not commutative

skew lines *n pl* : straight lines that do not intersect and are not in the same plane

skibob \ˈskē͵bäb\ *n* [*ski* + *bob* bobsled] : a vehicle that has two short skis one behind the other, a steering handle attached to the forward ski, and a low upholstered seat over the rear ski and that is used for gliding downhill over snow by a rider wearing miniature skis for balance — **ski·bob·ber** \-ə(r)\ *n* — **ski·bob·bing** \-iŋ\ *n*

skid pad *n* : a large usu. circular area of asphalt that is oiled to make it slick and that is used for testing automobiles and motorcycles with controlled skids and spins

skif·fle \ˈskifəl\ *n* [perh. imit.] : jazz or folk music played by a group all or some of whose members play nonstandard instruments or noisemakers (as jugs, washboards, or jew's harps)

skim* *vt* **skimmed; skim·ming** : to remove or conceal (as income) to avoid payment of taxes <indicted by a Federal grand jury on charges they *skimmed* casino money to avoid full tax payment to the Federal Government —*Wall Street Jour.*>

skim·mer* \ˈskimə(r)\ *n* : a fitted sleeveless usu. flaring sheathlike dress

skim·ming* \'skimiŋ\ *n* : the concealing and fraudulent reporting of income (as of a casino) to avoid full tax payments

skin flick *n* : a motion picture characterized by nudity and explicit sexual situations

Skin·ner·ian \skə'nirēən, -'ner-\ *adj* [Burrhus Frederick *Skinner b* 1904 Am. psychologist] : of, relating to, or suggestive of the behavioristic theories of B.F. Skinner < *Skinnerian* behaviorism > <a *Skinnerian* world filled with conditioned people —Caryl Rivers > — **Skinnerian** *n*

[1]**skin·ny–dip** \'skinē,dip\ *vi* [*skin* + *-y*, adj. suffix + *dip*] : to swim in the nude <a male preserve surrendered last winter when a group of nude women invaded a swimming pool where men traditionally *skinny-dipped* alone —*Newsweek* > — **skin·ny–dip·per** \-ə(r)\ *n* — **skin·ny–dip·ping** \-iŋ\ *n*

[2]**skinny–dip** *n* : a swim in the nude

skin–pop \'skin,päp\ *vt* : to inject (a drug) subcutaneously rather than into a vein <I started *skin-popping* heroin, and then I started mainlining —*Amazon Quarterly* >

ski touring *n* : cross-country skiing for pleasure

ski·wear \'ski,wa(ə)r, -,we(ə)r, -,waə, -,weə\ *n* : clothing suitable for wear while skiing

sky·div·ing \'skī,dīviŋ\ *n* : the sport of jumping from an airplane at a moderate altitude (as 6000 feet) and executing various tumbles and dives before pulling the rip cord of a parachute — **sky diver** *n*

sky·jack \'skī,jak\ *vt* [*sky* + *jack* (as in *hijack*)] : to commandeer (an airplane) by the threat of violence — **sky·jack·er** \-ə(r)\ *n* — **sky·jack·ing** \-iŋ\ *n*

sky·lounge \'skī,laùnj\ *n* : a vehicle that picks up passengers and is then carried by a helicopter between a downtown terminal and an airport

sky marshal *n* : an armed federal plainclothesman assigned to prevent skyjackings

slam dunk *n* : DUNK SHOT

slam·mer \'slamə(r)\ *n* : a jail or prison <the penalty for interstate real estate fraud can now send perpetrators to the *slammer* —Carter Shorr >

slap shot *n* : a shot in ice hockey that is made with a swinging stroke so that the puck often leaves the ice

sleep around *vi* : to engage in sex promiscuously <suggesting that, in order to gain her information, she had *slept around* with several politicians —Robert Brustein >

sleeping pill *also* **sleeping tablet** *n* : a drug and esp. a barbiturate that is taken as a tablet or capsule to induce sleep

slim·nas·tics \,slim'nastiks\ *n pl but sing in constr* [blend of *slim* and *gymnastics*] : exercises designed to reduce one's weight

slingshot* *n* **1** : a maneuver in auto racing in which a drafting car accelerates past the car in front by taking advantage of reserve power **2** : a dragster in which the driver sits behind the rear wheels

slip·stream* \'slip,strēm\ *n* : an area of reduced air pressure and forward suction immediately behind a rapidly moving racing car

slipstream *vi* : to drive in the slipstream of a racing car

slope* *n* **1** : the slope of the line tangent to a plane curve at a point **2** [fr. the slanting eyes] *slang* : an Oriental and esp. a Vietnamese — used disparagingly

sloppy joe* \-'jō\ *n* : ground beef cooked in a seasoned sauce (as chili) and usu. served over a bun

slot* *n* : a gap between an end and a tackle in an offensive line in football

slotback \'slät,bak\ *n* : an offensive halfback in football who lines up just behind the slot between an offensive end and tackle

slot car *n* : an electric toy racing automobile that has an arm underneath fitting into a groove for guidance and metal strips alongside the groove for supplying electricity and that is remotely controlled by the operator's hand-held rheostat

slot racing *n* : the racing of slot cars — **slot racer** *n*

slow–pitch *also* **slo–pitch** \'slō,pich\ *n* : softball which is played with 10 men on each side, in which each pitch must travel in an arc from 3 to 10 feet high in order to be legal, and in which base stealing is not permitted

slow virus *n* : a virus with a long incubation period between infection and development of the degenerative disease (as multiple sclerosis, rheumatoid arthritis, or kuru) associated with it

slugging average *n* : the ratio of the total number of bases reached on base hits to official times at bat for a baseball player expressed as a 3-place decimal

slum·lord \ˈsləm,lȯ(ə)rd, -,lȯ(ə)d\ *n* [*slum* + land*lord*] : a landlord who receives inflated rents from substandard neglected properties

slump·fla·tion \,sləm(p)ˈflāshən\ *n* [*slump* + in*flation*] : a state or period of combined economic decline and rising inflation

slurb \ˈslərb\ *n* [*sl-* (as in *sloppy, sleazy, slovenly, slip-shod*) + sub*urb*] : a suburb characterized by wearisomely uniform and usu. poorly constructed houses <the aerospace *slurb* that stretches through the ghosts of fruit groves from the L.A. basin toward the Mexican border —Herbert Gold> <blighting the whole northwestern corner of the state with sprawling *slurbs* —John Fischer>

Slur·vian \ˈslərvēən, ,slə̄v-, ˈsləiv-\ *n* [irreg. fr. *slur* + *-ian,* n. suffix] : speech characterized by slurring

smack *n* [perh. fr. Yiddish *shmek* sniff, whiff, pinch (of snuff)] *slang* : heroin

smaller European elm bark beetle *n* : a European beetle (*Scolytus multistriatus*) that is established in eastern North America

smart bomb *n* : a bomb that can be guided (as by a laser beam) to its target

smashed *adj, slang* : drunk, intoxicated

S ma·trix \ˈes¦mā·triks\ *n* [*s*cattering *matrix*] : a unitary matrix in quantum mechanics the absolute values of the squares of whose elements are equal to probabilities of transition between different states — called also *scattering matrix*

smog·less \ˈsmägləs, *also* ˈsmȯg-\ *adj* **1** : marked by the absence of smog <a *smogless* city> **2** : emitting no fumes that would contribute to the production of smog <*smogless* cars of the future>

SNG *abbr* substitute natural gas; synthetic natural gas

SNO·BOL \ˈsnō,bȯl\ *n* [*S*tri*n*g *O*riented Sym*bo*lic *L*anguage] : a computer programming language for manipulating strings of symbols

snort* *vt* : to take in (as a drug) by inhalation <*snorts* coke> <*snorts* snuff>

snow* *n* : heroin

snow·mak·er \ˈsnō,mākə(r)\ *n* : a device for making snow artificially

snow·mak·ing \-kiŋ\ *adj* : used for the production of artificial snow usu. for ski slopes <*snowmaking* machines>

snow·mo·bil·ing \ˈsnō(,)mō,bēliŋ\ *n* : the sport of driving or racing a snowmobile — **snow·mo·bil·er** \-lə(r)\ *also* **snow·mo·bil·ist** \-ləst\ *n*

Soa·ve \ˈswävā, səˈw-, -ve\ *n* [*Soave,* village near Verona, Italy] : a dry white wine from the area about Soave, Italy

so·cial·ist realism \¦sōsh(ə)ləst-\ *n* [trans. of Russ *sotsialicheskiĭrealizm*] : a theory of Soviet art, music, and literature that calls for the didactic use of artistic work to develop social consciousness in an evolving socialist state — **socialist re·al·ist** \-ˈrēələst\ *n*

so·cio·lin·guis·tic \¦sōs(h)ē(,)ōliŋ¦gwistik\ *adj* [*socio-* society, social, sociological + *linguistic*] **1** : of or relating to the social aspects of language **2** : of or relating to sociolinguistics

so·cio·lin·guis·tics \-tiks\ *n pl but usu sing in constr* : the study of linguistic behavior as determined by sociocultural factors (as social class or educational level)

so·cio·re·li·gious \¦sōs(h)ēōrə¦lijəs, -rē¦l-\ *adj* : of, relating to, or involving a combination of social and religious factors

sodium pump *n* : the process by which sodium ions are actively transported across a cell membrane; *esp* : the process by which the appropriate internal and external concentrations of sodium and potassium ions are maintained in a nerve fiber and which involves the active transport of sodium ions outward with movement of potassium ions to the interior

sodium stea·rate \-ˈstēə,rāt, -ˈsti(ə)r,āt\ *n* : a white powdery salt $C_{17}H_{35}COONa$ that is soluble in water, is the chief constituent of some laundry soaps, and is used esp. in cosmetics and toothpaste

soft* *adj* **1** : occurring at such a speed and under such circumstances as to avoid destructive impact <*soft* landing of a spacecraft on the moon> **2** : not protected against enemy attack <a *soft* aboveground launching site> **3** *of a detergent* : BIO-

DEGRADABLE **4** *of a drug* : considered less detrimental than a hard narcotic <marijuana is usually regarded as a *soft* drug>

softbound \\'sȯf(t)¦bau̇nd\\ *adj* : not bound in hard covers <*softbound* books>

soft–core \\'sȯf(t)¦kō(ə)r, -¦kȯ(ə)r, -¦kōə, -¦kȯ(ə)\\ *adj* [*soft* + *-core* (as in *hard-core*)] *of pornography* : containing descriptions or scenes of sex acts that are less explicit than those in hard-core material

soft–land \\'sȯft¦land\\ *vb* [back-formation fr. *soft landing*] *vi* : to make a soft landing on a celestial body (as the moon) ~ *vt* : to cause to soft-land — **soft–land·er** \\-ə(r)\\ *n*

soft paste* *n* **1** : a fine-grained opaque Chinese ceramic ware related to true porcelain but having part of the kaolin replaced by pegmatite and usu. being fired twice **2** : a lightweight soft opaque clay body (as of early Staffordshire)

soft rock *n* : rock music that is less driving and gentler sounding than hard rock

soft·ware \\'sȯft,wa(ə)r, -,we(ə)r, -,waə, -,weə\\ *n* **1** : the entire set of programs, procedures, and related documentation associated with a system and esp. a computer system; *specif* : computer programs **2** : something used or associated with and usu. contrasted with hardware; *esp* : materials for use with audiovisual equipment

soil·borne \\¦sȯi(ə)l,bō(ə)rn, -,bȯ(ə)rn, -,bōən, -,bȯ(ə)n\\ *adj* : transmitted by or in soil <*soilborne* fungi> <*soilborne* diseases>

So·ka Gak·kai \\,sōkə¦gä¦kī\\ *n* [Jap *Sōka Gakkai*, fr. *sōka* value-creation + *gakkai* learned society] : a Japanese sect of Buddhism that emphasizes active proselytism and the use of prayer for the solution of all human problems

solar cell *n* : a photovoltaic cell (as one including a junction between two types of silicon semiconductors) that is able to convert sunlight into electrical energy and is used (as in artificial satellites) as a power source

solar panel *n* : a battery of solar cells (as in a spacecraft)

solar sail *n* : a propulsive device that consists of a flat material (as aluminized plastic) designed to receive thrust from solar radiation pressure and that can be attached to a spacecraft

solar wind *n* : plasma continuously ejected from the sun's surface into and through interplanetary space

sol·id–state \\¦säləd,stāt\\ *adj* **1** : relating to the properties, structure, or reactivity of solid material; *esp* : relating to the arrangement or behavior of ions, molecules, nucleons, electrons, and holes in the crystals of a substance (as a semiconductor) or to the effect of crystal imperfections on the properties of a solid substance **2 a** : utilizing the electric, magnetic, or photic properties of solid materials <a *solid-state* component> **b** : utilizing solid-state circuitry as opposed to electron tubes <a *solid-state* stereo system>

solution set *n* : the set of values that satisfy an equation; *also* : TRUTH SET

so·mato·sen·so·ry \\¦sōməd·ə¦sen(t)s(ə)rē\\ *adj* [*somato-* body, soma (deriv. of Gk *sōmat-*, *sōma* body) + *sensory*] : of, relating to, or being sensory activity having its origin elsewhere than in the special sense organs (as eyes or ears) and conveying information about the state of the body proper and its immediate environment <neuromuscular spindles and touch receptors are typical of the systems making *somatosensory* inputs to the brain>

so·mato·ther·a·py \\-'therəpē, -pi\\ *n* : psychological therapy that uses physical methods (as drugs or surgery) to modify behavior — **so·mato·ther·a·pist** \\-pəst\\ *n*

so·mato·tro·phic hor·mone \\-,trōfik'hȯr,mōn, -'hȯ(ə),-\\ *n* : a vertebrate polypeptide hormone that is secreted by the anterior lobe of the pituitary gland and regulates growth

son et lumière \\sōnālu̇emyer\\ *n* [F, lit., sound and light] : an outdoor spectacle at an historic site consisting of recorded narration with light and sound effects

son·i·cate \\'sänə,kāt\\ *vt* **-cat·ed; -cat·ing** : to disrupt (as bacteria) by treatment with high-frequency sound waves — **son·i·ca·tion** \\,sänə'kāshən\\ *n* — **son·i·cat·or** \\-ād·ə(r)\\ *n*

so·no·chem·is·try \\¦sänō'keməstrē, ¦sōnō-\\ *n* [*sono-* sound (fr. L *sonus*) + *chemistry*] : a branch of chemistry that deals with the chemical effects of ultrasound — **so·no·chem·i·cal** \\-¦keməkəl, -mēk-\\ *adj*

sorghum web·worm \-ˈweb,wərm, -,wə̄m, -,wəim\ *n* : a noctuid moth (*Celama sorghiella*) whose hairy greenish larva is sometimes a destructive pest of the seed heads of sorghum

sort* *n* : an instance of sorting <an alpha *sort* done by computer>

soul* *n* **1** : a strong positive feeling (as of intense sensitivity and emotional fervor) conveyed esp. by American Negro performers <feel that white rock singers lack *soul* —Rita Kramer> **2** : NEGRITUDE **3** : SOUL MUSIC **4** : SOUL FOOD **5** : SOUL BROTHER

soul *adj* **1** : of, relating to, or characteristic of American Negroes or their culture <vocals are delivered in a raspy, *soul* style —Ellen Sander> **2** : designed for or controlled by Negroes <*soul* radio stations>

soul brother *n* : a male Negro — used esp. by Negroes

soul food *n* : food (as chitterlings, hogs' jowls, ham hocks, collard greens, catfish, and cornbread) traditionally eaten esp. by southern American Negroes

soul music *n* : music that originated with American Negro gospel singing, is closely related to rhythm and blues, and is characterized by intensity of feeling and earthiness

soul sister *n* : a female Negro — used esp. by Negroes

sound pollution *n* : NOISE POLLUTION

soup* *n* : the fast-moving white water that moves shoreward after a wave breaks

source language *n* : a language which is to be translated into another language — compare TARGET LANGUAGE 2

southern house mosquito *n* : a mosquito (*Culex pipiens quinquefasciatus*) that is an important vector of St. Louis encephalitis

southern pea *n* : cowpea, black-eyed pea

southwestern corn borer *n* : a pyralid moth (*Diatraea grandiosella*) whose larva causes serious damage esp. to corn crops by boring in the stalks

soybean cyst nem·a·tode \-ˈnemə,tōd\ *n* : a nematode (*Heterodera glycines*) that is a pest of soybeans causing stunting and yellowing of the plants and reduction in yield

soy·milk \ˈsȯi,milk, -,miu̇k\ *n* : a milk substitute based on soybeans esp. as a protein source and usu. supplemented (as with calcium and vitamins)

spa* \ˈspä, ˈspȯ, ˈspȧ\ *n* : HEALTH SPA

space* *n* : a set of mathematical entities with a set of axioms of geometric character — compare METRIC SPACE, TOPOLOGICAL SPACE, VECTOR SPACE

space·borne \ˈ,spās,bō(ə)rn, -,bȯ(ə)rn, -,bōən, -,bȯ(ə)n\ *adj* **1** : carried in or moving through space external to the atmosphere <*spaceborne* satellites> **2** : involving the use of spaceborne equipment <*spaceborne* television>

spaced–out \ˈ,spāsˈdau̇t\ *adj* : dazed or stupefied by or as if by a narcotic substance <a *spaced-out* addict dances by, bumping into people —Marcia Chambers>

space sickness *n* : unpleasant physiological effects occurring under the conditions of sustained spaceflight

space walk *n* : an extravehicular venture made by an astronaut in space — **space walk** *vi* — **space·walk·er** \ˈspā,swȯkə(r)\ *n* — **space·walk·ing** \-kiŋ\ *n*

space·wom·an \ˈspā,swu̇mən\ *n, pl* **space·wom·en** \ˈspā,swimən \ : a female astronaut

spaghetti western *n, often cap W* : a western motion picture produced by Italians

span* *vt* **spanned; span·ning** : to be capable of forming any element of under given operations <a set of vectors that *spans* a vector space>

Span·glish \ˈspaŋ(g)lish\ *n* [blend of *Spanish* and *English*] : Spanish marked by a considerable number of borrowings from English

spark chamber *n* : a device usu. used to detect the path of a high-energy particle that consists of a series of charged metal plates or wires separated by a gas (as neon) in which observable electric discharges follow the path of the particle

spatial sum·ma·tion \-(,)səˈmāshən\ *n* : sensory summation that involves stimulation of several spatially separated neurons at the same time

spatter glass *n* : END-OF-DAY GLASS

speak·er·phone \ˈspēkə(r),fōn\ *n* : a combination microphone and loudspeaker device for two-way communication by telephone lines

spear·ing \'spi(ə)riŋ\ *n* : an illegal check in hockey in which one player jabs another in the body with the end of a hockey stick

special drawing rights *n pl* : SDRS

special situation *n* : an exceptional corporate condition or prospect that offers unusual chances for capital gains

speed* *n* : methamphetamine or a related drug

speed freak *n* : one who habitually misuses amphetamines and esp. methamphetamine

speed–read·ing \'spēd,rēdiŋ\ *n* : a method of reading rapidly by skimming — **speed–read** \-,rēd\ *vt* — **speed–read·er** \-ə(r)\ *n*

speed shop *n* : a shop that sells custom automotive equipment esp. to hot rodders

sphe·ro·plast \'sfirə,plast, 'sfer-\ *n* [*sphero-* sphere, spherical + *-plast* particle, granule, cell, deriv. of Gk *plastos* molded] : a modified gram-negative bacterium that is characterized by major alteration and partial loss of the cell wall and by increased osmotic sensitivity and that can result from various nutritional or environmental factors or be induced artificially by use of a lysozyme

spider hole *n* : a camouflaged foxhole

spike* *n* : ACTION POTENTIAL

spin·ner* \'spinə(r)\ *n* : a surfing feat in which a standing surfer makes a complete turnaround while the board continues to move straight ahead

spin–off* \'spin,ȯf\ *n* **1** : the distribution by a business to its stockholders of particular assets and esp. of stock of another company **2** : a collateral or derived product or effect : by-product <new household products that are *spin-offs* from missile research>; *also* : a number of such by-products <the *spin-off* from defense research>

spin·out \-,au̇t\ *n* : a rotational skid by an automobile that usu. causes it to leave the roadway

spin resonance *n* : ELECTRON SPIN RESONANCE

spin·to \'spēn·(,)tō, 'spin·-\ *adj* [It, lit., pushed, fr. past part. of *spingere* to push] *of a singing voice* : having both lyric and dramatic qualities <her sumptuous *spinto* soprano has never sounded so firmly under control —D.J. Henahan> — **spinto** *n*

spin wave *n* : a wave of quantized energy that propagates through a substance as a result of magnetic field shifts within an atom in response to an outside stimulus (as a variable magnetic field or radio waves)

spiny–head·ed worm \¦spīnē,hedəd-\ *n* : a parasitic worm belonging to the taxon Acanthocephala

spi·ro·no·lac·tone \spī¦ränə'lak,tōn, spə¦rōnō-\ *n* [*spiro-* chemical compound with one or more two-ring systems (deriv. of L *spira* coil) + *-no-* (prob. arbitrary infix) + *lactone*] : an aldosterone antagonist that promotes diuresis and sodium excretion and is sometimes used to relieve ascites

splash·down \'splash,dau̇n\ *n* : the landing of a manned spacecraft in the ocean — **splash down** *vi*

split–brain \¦split¦brān\ *adj* : having the optic chiasma and corpus callosum severed < behavior in *split-brain* animals >

split end *n* : an offensive end in football who lines up usu. several yards to the side of the formation

spo·do·sol \'spädə,sȯl, 'spōd-\ *n* [Gk *spodos* wood ash + L *solum* ground, soil] : any of various podzols esp. of cool humid regions that have a horizon below the surface composed of an illuvial accumulation of humus with iron or aluminum or both

spoil·er* \'spȯilə(r)\ *n* : an air deflector on the front or on the rear deck of an automobile and esp. a racer for reducing the tendency to lift off the road at high speeds

spokes·per·son \'spōk,spərsᵊn, -pās-, -pəis-\ *n* [*spokes-* (as in *spokesman*) + *person*] **1** : one who speaks as the representative of another; *esp* : one delegated by others to express or present their views or opinions publicly <a frequent State House *spokesperson* —J.R. Dorsey> **2** : one that is or becomes an interpreter (as of an era) or an outstanding advocate (as of a cause) <an effective *spokesperson* for higher education —Paul Lacey> <an especially powerful and influential *spokesperson* for what had become a cultural change in attitudes toward female relationships —Janet Cooper>

sponge·ware \'spənj,wa(ə)r, -,we(ə)r, -,waə, -,weə\ *n* : a typically 19th century earthenware with background color spattered or dabbed (as with a sponge) and usu. a freehand central design

spook* *n* : an undercover agent : spy < the feeling persists that there's no such thing as a former intelligence officer . . . once a *spook,* always a *spook* —H.E. Meyer >

spoon·er \'spünə(r)\ *n* : a container that is designed to hold extra teaspoons and forms part of a 19th century table service

spo·ro·pol·len·in \,spōrə'pälənən, ,spȯr-\ *n* [ISV *sporo-* seed, spore + *pollen* + *-in* chemical compound] : a chemically inert polymer that makes up the outer layer of pollen grains and spores of higher plants

spotted alfalfa aphid *n* : a highly destructive Old World aphid (*Therioaphis maculata*) that is established in the U.S. from coast to coast in warmer areas and that injects a toxic saliva in feeding esp. on alfalfa and causes yellowing and stunting of affected plants

spread end *n* : SPLIT END

sprech·stim·me \'shprek,shtimə, -ek,-\ *n, often cap* [G, lit., speaking voice] : a vocal passage or performance in which a declamation is delivered with rhythmic inflections

sprint car *n* : a rugged racing automobile that is midway in size between midget racers and ordinary racers, has about the same horsepower as the larger racers, and is usu. raced on a dirt track

square out *n* : a pass pattern in football in which a receiver runs downfield a short distance and then breaks at a 90-degree angle for the sideline

squib kick \'skwib-\ *n* : a kickoff in football in which the ball bounces along the ground

sr* *abbr* steradian

Sri Lan·kan \(')srē'läŋkən\ *n* : a native or inhabitant of Sri Lanka — **Sri Lankan** *adj*

sRNA \'es,är(,)en'ā\ *n* [*s*oluble *RNA*] : TRANSFER RNA

SST \,e(,)se'stē\ *n* : SUPERSONIC TRANSPORT

stack* *n* **1** : a memory or a section of memory in a computer for temporary storage **2** : a computer memory consisting of arrays of memory elements stacked one on top of another

stacked heel *n* : a shoe heel made of layers of leather

stag·fla·tion \'stag'flāshən\ *n* [blend of *stagnation* and *inflation*] : persistent inflation combined with stagnant consumer demand and relatively high unemployment

staging* *n* : the disengaging and discarding of a burned-out rocket unit from a space vehicle during flight

stand–alone *adj, of a computer peripheral* : capable of independent operation < a *stand-alone* tape drive > < a *stand-alone* line printer >

standing crop* *n* : the total amount or number of living things (as an uncut farm crop, the fish in a pond, or the organisms in an ecosystem) in a particular situation at any given time

stand·off* \'stan,dȯf\ *n* : a standoff insulator

stan·nous flu·o·ride \'stanəs'flu̇(ə),rīd\ *n* : a white compound SnF_2 of tin and fluorine used in toothpaste to combat tooth decay

sta·pe·dec·to·my \,stāpə'dektəmē, -pē'd-\ *n, pl* **-mies** [ISV *staped-* (fr. NL *staped-, stapes* stapes) + *ectomy* surgical removal] : surgical removal and prosthetic replacement of the stapes to relieve deafness — **sta·pe·dec·to·mized** \-tə,mīzd\ *adj*

stark·ers \'stärkərz, 'stȧkəz\ *adj* [*stark* stark-naked + *-ers* (Oxford University slang suffix)] *chiefly Brit* : completely unclothed : nude < a red flannel nightdress which would bring surrogate dignity to his otherwise *starkers* consort —John Taylor >

star·quake \'stär,kwāk, 'stȧ,-\ *n* : a seismic event on a star

station* *n* : a pocket with its automatic signature-feeding equipment in a gathering machine in a book bindery

sta·tis·tic* \stə'tistik, -ēk\ *n* : a random variable that takes on the possible values of a statistic

stave church *n* : a church of medieval Nordic origin that is made of wooden staves and has gables, a cupola, and often a series of pitched roofs

steady state theory *n* : a theory in astronomy: the universe has always existed and has always been expanding with hydrogen being created continuously and spontaneously — compare BIG BANG THEORY

steak au poivre \-(ˌ)ō'pwävr(ᵊ), -v(rə)\ *n* [F *au poivre* with pepper] : a steak that has had coarsely ground black pepper pressed into it before cooking, is served with a seasoned sauce, and is often flambéed with cognac — called also *pepper steak*

steak Diane \-(')dīˌan\ *n* [prob. fr. the name *Diane*] : a steak that is served with a seasoned butter sauce and is often flambéed with cognac

stel·lar·ator \'steləˌrād·ə(r)\ *n* [*stellar* + *-ator* (as in *generator*); fr. its use of temperatures approaching those occurring in some stars] : a toroidal device for producing controlled nuclear fusion that involves the confining and heating of a gaseous plasma by means of an externally applied magnetic field

stel·lar wind \ˌstelə(r)-\ *n* : plasma ejected at varying rates from a star's surface into interstellar space

ste·re·ol·o·gy \ˌsterē'äləjē, ˌstir-\ *n* [ISV *stereo-* solid, stereoscopic, dealing with three dimensions (deriv. of Gk *stereos* solid) + *-logy* theory, science, deriv. of Gk *logos* word] : a branch of science concerned with inferring the three-dimensional properties of objects or matter ordinarily observed two-dimensionally — **ste·reo·log·i·cal** \-rēə'läjəkəl\ *adj* — **ste·reo·log·i·cal·ly** \-k(ə)lē\ *adv*

ste·reo·phone \'sterēəˌfōn, 'stir-\ *n* [*stereo* stereophonic + *phone*] : a stereophonic headphone

ste·reo·tape \-ˌtāp\ *n* : a stereophonic magnetic tape

ste·reo·tax·ic \ˌsterēəˈtaksik, ˌstir-\ *adj* [NL *stereotaxis* stereotaxic technique (fr. *stereo-* solid, dealing with three dimensions + Gk *taxis* arrangement) + E *-ic,* adj. suffix] : of, relating to, involving, or being a technique or apparatus used in neurological research or surgery for directing the tip of a delicate instrument (as a needle or an electrode) in three planes in attempting to reach a predetermined locus in the nervous system — **ste·reo·tax·i·cal·ly** \-ək(ə)lē\ *adv*

ste·roido·gen·e·sis \stəˌrȯidə'jenəsəs, ˌstirˌȯidə-, *also* ˌster-\ *n* [NL, fr. *steroid* + connective *-o-* + *genesis*] : synthesis of steroids

ste·roido·gen·ic \stəˌrȯidə'jenik, ˌstirˌȯidə-, *also* ˌster-\ *adj* : of, relating to, or involved in steroidogenesis <*steroidogenic* cells> <*steroidogenic* response of ovarian tissue>

Ste·ven·graph \'stēvənˌgraf\ *or* **Ste·vens·graph** \-nzˌg-\ *n* [Thomas *Stevens,* 19th cent. Am. weaver + E *-graph* something written, recording instrument, deriv. of Gk *graphein* to write] : a picture woven in silk

stick shift *n* : a manually operated gearshift mounted esp. on the floor of an automobile

stiletto heel *n* : a high thin heel on women's shoes that is narrower than a spike heel

still bank \'stilˌbaŋk\ *n* [*still* stationary] : a bank (as in the shape of an animal or a ship) with a slot for inserting coins — compare MECHANICAL BANK

stish·ov·ite \'stishəˌvīt\ *n* [S.M. *Stishov,* 20th cent. Russ. mineralogist] : a dense tetragonal mineral SiO_2 consisting of silicon dioxide that is a polymorph of quartz and that is formed under great pressure

sto·chas·tic* \stə'kastik\ *adj* **1** : involving a random variable <a *stochastic* process> **2** : involving chance or probability : probabilistic <a *stochastic* model of radiation-induced mutation>

STOL *abbr* short takeoff and landing

stone·wall* \'stōnˈwȯl\ *vi* : to be uncooperative, obstructive, or evasive <possible that the Soviet Union will gradually abandon the *stonewalling* obstruction of the past quarter century —Lord Cavadon> <he can go in and *stonewall* and say, "I don't know anything about what you are talking about" —J.W. Dean III> ~ *vt* : to refuse to comply or cooperate with <intention to *stonewall* further requests for . . . evidence —*Newsweek*>

stop* *vb* — **stop a stock** *of a stock-market specialist* : to agree to a later sale or purchase of a specified number of shares at the price current when the agreement is made

stop out* *vt* : to sell securities of (a shareowner) on a stop order

storage ring *n* : a device for storing a beam of high-energy particles collected from an accelerator until needed for collision with a second beam

STP \ˌe(ˌ)stēˈpē\ *n* [fr. *STP,* trademark for a motor fuel additive] : a psychedelic drug chemically related to mescaline and amphetamine — called also *DOM*

straight* *adj* : of, relating to, or characterized by heterosexuality <does occasionally feel the strain of living in two worlds: the *straight* world of his work, and the gay world of his friends and lovers —Robert Athanasiou, Phillip Shaver, & Carol Tavris> <division persists between gay and *straight* feminists —Myrna Lamb>

straight* *n* **1** : one who adheres to conventional attitudes and mores <the hippie who cadged a dime from a *straight* —Milton Mayer> **2** : a nonuser of illicit drugs <everybody coming here on wings from the whole world, *straights* and heads both —Hank Heifetz> **3** : one who is heterosexual <*straights* and gays>

straight–ahead \ˈstrād-əˈhed\ *adj* : being well within the limits of a particular musical style : unembellished <*straight-ahead* rock 'n' roll> <*straight-ahead,* searching jazz with no gimmicks —David Spitzer>

straight–arrow \ˌstrād-ˈarō, -arə(w)\ *adj* : rigidly proper and conventional <the *straight-arrow* guy and his girl, the latter a believer in early marriage and eternal obligation —*Time*>— **straight arrow** *n*

strand·ed \ˈstrandəd\ *adj* : having a strand or strands esp. of a specified kind or number — usu. used in combination <the double-*stranded* molecule of DNA> — **strand·ed·ness** \-nəs\ *n*

strangeness* *n* : a quantum characteristic of a strongly interacting elementary particle indicated by a number equal to its hypercharge minus its baryon number that indicates the possible transformations upon strong interaction with other elementary particles

strange particle *n* : a short-lived unstable elementary particle (as a kaon) that is created in high-energy particle collisions and has a strangeness quantum number different from zero

strat·i·fi·ca·tion·al grammar \ˈstrad-əfəˈkāshnəl-, -shənᵊl-\ *n* [*stratification* + *-al,* adj. suffix] : a grammar based on the theory that language consists of a series of hierarchically related strata linked together by representational rules

strat·i·fied charge engine \ˈstrad-əˌfīd-\ *n* : an internal-combustion engine in which the fuel charge is divided into two layers of differing concentration within the cylinder with a rich mixture in a small section close to the spark plug and a lean mixture in the remainder of the cylinder so that the engine runs on an overall leaner mixture

Stra·vin·ski·an *or* **Stra·vin·sky·an** \strəˈvin(t)skēən\ *adj* [Igor Fëdorovich *Stravinsky* †1971 Am. (Russ.-born) composer] : of, relating to, or suggestive of Igor Stravinsky or his music <mixture of pungent dissonance, *Stravinskian* rhythms and French chic —H.C. Schonberg>

strawberry jar *n* [fr. its slight resemblance to a strawberry] : a usu. large upright ceramic jar with pocketed openings in the sides into which small plants can be inserted for growing in soil contained in the jar

streak·ing \ˈstrēkiŋ\ *n* : the lightening (as by chemicals) of a few long strands of hair to produce a streaked effect — compare FROSTING

stream* *n, Brit* : one of several curricula of study to which students are assigned according to their needs or levels of ability : track

streaming* *n, Brit* : TRACKING

street·scape \ˈstrētˌskāp\ *n* [*street* + *-scape* (as in *landscape*)] **1** : a view of a street **2** : a work of art depicting a view of a street

street theater *n* : GUERRILLA THEATER

strep·to·ni·grin \ˌstreptəˈnīgrən\ *n* [NL *strepto-* (fr. *Streptomyces flocculus,* actinomycete from which it is produced) + L *nigr-, niger* black + E *-in* chemical compound; prob. fr. its dark color] : a toxic antibiotic $C_{25}H_{22}N_4O_8$ from an actinomycete (*Streptomyces flocculus*) that interferes with DNA metabolism

stretch receptor *n* : a sensory end organ in a muscle that is sensitive to stretch in the muscle, consists of small striated muscle fibers richly supplied with nerve fibers, and is enclosed in a connective tissue sheath : muscle spindle

strewn field *n* : an area in which tektites are found

stri·a·tion* \strī'āshən\ *n* : one of the alternate dark and light cross bands of a myofibril of striated muscle

stride piano *n* [fr. the repeated strides taken by the left hand] : a style of jazz piano playing in which the right hand plays the melody while the left hand alternates between a single note and a chord played an octave or more higher

strike* *n* : a perfectly thrown ball <fired a *strike* to first base>

striking price *n* : a price agreed upon as that at which an option contract (as a put or call) can be exercised

strip city *n* : an urban area forming a long narrow strip

stro·mat·o·lite \strō'mad·ᵊl,īt\ *n* [L *stromat-, stroma* bed covering + E connective *-o-* + *-lite* mineral, rock, fossil, deriv. of Gk *lithos* stone] : a laminated sedimentary fossil formed from layers of blue-green algae — **stro·mat·o·lit·ic** \-,mad·ᵊl'id·ik\ *adj*

strong interaction *also* **strong force** *n* : a fundamental interaction experienced by elementary particles (as hadrons) that is more powerful than any other known force and is responsible for the binding together of neutrons and protons in the atomic nucleus and for processes of particle creation in high-energy collisions

stro·phoid \'strō,fȯid\ *n* [F *strophoïde,* fr. Gk *strophos* twisted band (fr. *strephein* to twist) + *-oïde* something similar] : a plane curve that is generated by a point whose distance from the y-axis along a variable straight line which always passes through a fixed point is equal to the y-intercept and that has the equation $\rho = \alpha\,(\sec\theta \pm \tan\theta)$ in polar coordinates

structural gene *n* : a gene determining the amino acid sequence of a protein (as an enzyme) through a specific messenger RNA

strung out *adj* **1 :** addicted to a drug <thinking of all drug users as hard-core addicts *strung out* on heroin —B.R. Hershenson> **2 :** physically debilitated from or as if from long-term drug addiction <dreaming of himself as a footloose cowboy, although he was to spend much of his life (and end it) *strung out,* ill, and living with his mother —*New Yorker*>

student's t distribution *n, often cap S* [*Student,* pen name of W. S. Gossett †1937 Brit. statistician] : T DISTRIBUTION

student union *n* : a building on a college campus that is devoted to student activities and that usu. contains lounges, auditoriums, offices, and game rooms

stuff shot *n* : DUNK SHOT

sub·cel·lu·lar \¦səb¦selyələ(r)\ *adj* [*sub-* under (fr. L *sub*) + *cellular*] : of less than cellular scope or level of organization <*subcellular* particles>

sub·com·pact \'səb¦käm,pakt\ *n* : an automobile smaller than a compact

sub·duc·tion* \səb'dəkshən\ *n* : the action or process of the edge of one crustal plate descending below the edge of another — **sub·duct** \səb'dəkt\ *vb*

sub·em·ployed \¦səbəm¦plȯid\ *adj* : subjected to subemployment <a more relevant approach to understanding social conditions . . . would be to measure those who have been *subemployed* for any significant period of time —Michael Marien>

sub·em·ploy·ment \-'plȯimənt\ *n* : inadequate employment including unemployment, part-time employment, and full-time employment that does not provide a living wage

sub·field \'səb,fēld\ *n* **1 :** a subset of a mathematical field that is itself a field **2 :** a subdivision of a field (as of study) <each of the 12 *subfields* in physics that are discussed in the report —*Chem. & Engineering News*>

sub·group* \-,grüp\ *n* : a subset of a mathematical group that is itself a group

sub·mil·li·me·ter \¦səb¦milə,mēd·ə(r)\ *adj* : being less than a millimeter in a specified measurement <a *submillimeter* wave>

sub·mi·to·chon·dri·al \-,mīd·ə'kändrēəl\ *adj* : of, relating to, composed of, or being parts and esp. fragments of mitochondria <*submitochondrial* membranes> <*submitochondrial* particles>

sub·or·di·na·tor \sə'bȯrdᵊn,ād·ər, -'bȯ(ə)d-\ *n* : one that subordinates; *esp* : a subordinating conjunction

sub·pro·gram \'səb,prō,gram, -prōgrəm\ *n* : a semi-independent portion of a program (as for a computer)

sub·ring \-ˌriŋ\ *n* : a subset of a mathematical ring which is itself a ring

sub·sat·el·lite \ˈsəbˈsad·ᵊlˌīt\ *n* **1** : a political entity within the sphere of influence of another entity that is itself a satellite of a stronger power **2** : an object carried into orbit in and subsequently released from an artificial satellite

sub·se·quence \ˈsəbˈsēkwən(t)s, -ˌkwen-\ *n* : a mathematical sequence that is part of another sequence

sub·shell \ˈsəbˌshel\ *n* : any of the one or more orbitals making up an electron shell of an atom

sub·til·i·sin \ˌsəbˈtiləsən\ *n* [NL *subtilis,* specific epithet of *Bacillus subtilis,* species to which *Bacillus amyloliquefaciens* was once thought to belong + E *-in* chemical compound] : an extracellular protease produced by a soil bacillus (*Bacillus amyloliquefaciens*)

sub·to·pia \ˌsəbˈtōpēə\ *n* [*sub*urbs + *-topia* (as in *utopia*)] *chiefly Brit* : the suburbs of a city <those who can happily shoot a pheasant on a nursery farm in *subtopia* —Christopher Wordsworth> — **sub·to·pi·an** \-ēən\ *adj, chiefly Brit*

sub·vi·ral \ˈsəbˈvīrəl\ *adj* : relating to, being, or caused by a piece or a structural part (as a protein) of a virus <*subviral* infection>

suc·cor·ance* \ˈsəkərən(t)s\ *n* : a dependence on or an active seeking for nurturant care — **suc·cor·ant** \ˈsəkərənt\ *adj*

sudden infant death syndrome : death of an infant in apparently good health due to unknown causes that occurs usu. before one year of age — called also *cot death, crib death*

suicide pact *n* : an agreement between two or more individuals wherein they commit suicide together or one kills the other or others and then commits suicide

suicide squad *n* [fr. the fact that kickoffs and punts are more dangerous than other plays] : a special squad used on kickoffs and punts in football

sui·cid·ol·o·gy \ˌsüəˌsīˈdäləjē\ *n* [*suicide* + connective *-o-* + *-logy* science, theory, deriv. of Gk *logos* word] : the study of suicide and suicide prevention — **sui·cid·ol·o·gist** \-jəst\ *n*

sul·fo·nyl·urea \ˌsəlfəˌnilˈ(y)ürēə\ *n* [NL, fr. ISV *sulfonyl* + NL *urea*] : any of several hypoglycemic compounds related to the sulfonamides and used in the oral treatment of diabetes

sul·phide* \ˈsəlˌfīd\ *n* : a ceramic form and esp. a portrait bas-relief enclosed in clear glass where it glitters like silver

sum* *n* : UNION 1

sun·roof \ˈsənˌrüf, -ˌrůf\ *n* [fr. its letting in the sunlight] : an automobile roof having a panel that can be opened

sun·seek·er \ˈsənˌsēkə(r)\ *n* **1** : a person who travels to an area of warmth and sun esp. in winter <the cream of cruising comfort for the winter *sunseekers* —B.D. Walker> **2** : a photoelectric device on a spacecraft or artificial satellite that maintains a constant fix on the sun and forms a part of the navigational system of the vehicle

su·per·alloy \ˈsüpərˈalȯi, -rəˈlȯi\ *n* [*super-* over (fr. L *super*) + *alloy*] : any of various high-strength often complex alloys having resistance to high temperature

su·per·cluster \ˈsüpə(r)ˌkləstə(r)\ *n* : a large cluster of galaxies

su·per·continent \ˈsüpə(r)ˈkänt(ᵊ)nənt\ *n* : a hypothetical former large continent from which other continents broke off and drifted away — called also *protocontinent*

su·per·current \-ˈkərənt\ *n* : a current of electricity flowing in a superconductor

su·per·fec·ta \ˈsüpə(r)ˌfektə\ *n* [blend of *super-* and *perfecta*] : a variation of the perfecta in which a bettor must select the first four finishers of a race in the correct order of finish in order to win — compare TRIFECTA

su·per·group \ˈsüpə(r)ˌgrüp\ *n* : a rock group made up of former members of other rock groups <the long-awaited *supergroup,* star-studded, sexy, talented —David Sapp>

su·per·jet \-ˌjet\ *n* [*super*sonic + *jet*] : a supersonic jet airplane

su·per·mol·e·cule \-ˈmäləˌkyü(ə)l\ *n* : a large molecule (as of protein or rubber) built up from smaller chemical structures : macromolecule — **su·per·mo·lec·u·lar** \ˈsüpə(r)məˈlekyələ(r)\ *adj*

su·per·plas·ti·ci·ty \ˌsüpə(r)ˌplastˈisəd·ē\ *n* : the quality or state of having enhanced ductility as a result of microstructural change brought about by heat and mechanical treatment — used of an alloy — **su·per·plas·tic** \-ˈplastik\ *adj or n*

su·per·po·ten·cy \-ˈpōtᵊn(t)sē\ *n* : the quality or state of being superpotent

su·per·po·tent \-ˈpōtᵊnt\ *adj* : of greater than normal or acceptable potency <in regard to safety, assays are available which are intended to ensure that tablets are not *superpotent* —L.C. Lasagna>

supersonic transport *n* : a large transport airplane designed to operate at supersonic speed

su·per·star \ˈsüpərˌstär, ˈsüpəˌstȧ\ *n* : a star (as in sports or the movies) who is considered extremely talented, has great public appeal, and can usu. command a high salary — **su·per·star·dom** \ˌsüpərˈstärdəm, ˌsüpəˈstȧdəm\ *n*

support* *n* : SUPPORT LEVEL

support hose *n* : elastic stockings

support level *or* **support area** *n* : a price level on a declining market at which a security resists further decline due to increased attractiveness to traders and investors

sup·press* \səˈpres\ *vt* : to inhibit the genetic expression of <*suppress* a mutation>

sup·pres·sant \səˈpresᵊnt\ *n* : an agent (as a drug) that tends to suppress or reduce in intensity rather than eliminate something (as appetite)

su·pra·cel·lu·lar \ˌsüprəˈselyələ(r)\ *adj* [*supra-* over, transcending (fr. L *supra* above, beyond) + *cellular*] : of greater than cellular scope or level of organization

su·pre·mo \səˈprē(ˌ)mō, süˈp-\ *n, pl* **-mos** *often cap* [Sp & It, fr. *supremo,* adj., supreme, fr. L *supremus*] *Brit*: one who is highest in rank or authority <the Russians . . . have just appointed a new energy *supremo* —*London Times*>

surf·able \ˈsərfəbəl, ˈsə̄f-, ˈsəif-\ *adj* : suitable for surfing

sur·face–ef·fect ship \ˈsərfəsəˌfekt-, ˈsə̄f-, ˈsəif-\ *n* : a ground-effect machine that operates over water

surface feeder *n* : a duck (as a mallard or shoveler) that feeds by dabbling

surface structure *n* **1** : a formal representation of the phonetic form of a sentence **2** : the structure which such a representation describes — compare DEEP STRUCTURE

surface–to–air missile \ˌsərfəstəˈa(ə)r, ˌsə̄f-, ˌsəif-, -ˈe(ə)r\ *n* : a usu. guided missile launched from the ground against a target in the air — called also *SAM*

surf and turf : seafood (as lobster tails or shrimp) and a beefsteak (as filet mignon) served as a single course

surf·er's knot \ˈsərfə(r)z-, ˈsə̄f-, ˈsəif-\ *n* : a knobby lump just below a surfer's knee or on the upper surface of his foot caused by friction and pressure between surfboard and skin

sur·jec·tion \(ˌ)sərˈjekshən\ *n* [F, fr. *sur* over, on, onto + *-jection* (as in *projection* projection)] : a mathematical function that is an onto mapping

sur·jec·tive \-ˈjektiv\ *adj* [F, fem. of *surjectif,* fr. *sur* onto + *-jectif* (as in *projectif* projective)] : ONTO <a set of *subjective* functions>

su·shi \ˈsüˌshē, -(ˌ)shi\ *n* [Jap] : a dish consisting of a cake of rice with raw fish, vegetables, and a vinegar sauce

swing* *vi* **1** : to be lively and up-to-date <he digs the hip scene and *swings* —Stan Sauerhaft> **2** : to engage in sex freely <couples who *swing* are incapable of intimate relationships even with each other, and use wife-swapping as a safety valve —*Time*>

swing* *also* **swing pass** *n* : a play in football in which a backfield receiver runs to the outside to take a short pass

swing–by \ˈswiŋˌbī\ *n, pl* **swing–bys** : an interplanetary mission in which a space vehicle utilizes the gravitational field of a planet near which it passes for changing course

swing·er* \ˈswiŋə(r)\ *n* **1** : a lively and up-to-date person who indulges in what is considered fashionable <reputation as a *swinger* since coming to Washington, where . . . he is everybody's prize catch for a dinner party —Martin Mayer> **2** : one who engages freely in sex <one of the *swingers,* who, ironically, is at this moment too sexually exhausted to take advantage of the compliance of the woman he most wants —Henry Hewes>

swing·ing* \-iŋ\ *n* : the practice of engaging in sex freely; *specif* : the exchanging of sex partners

swing–wing \ˈswiŋˌwiŋ\ *adj* : having an airplane wing whose outer portion folds back along the fuselage to give the plane an arrowlike platform at high speeds

switched–on \(ˈ)swichtˈȯn, -ˈän\ *adj* : attuned to what is new and exciting <with-it in the *switched-on* world of psychedelic art —Elenore Lester>

symmetric group *n* : a permutation group that is composed of all of the permutations of *n* things

symmetric ma·trix \-ˈmā·triks\ *n* : a matrix that is its own transpose

symmetry* *n* : a rigid motion of a geometric figure that determines a one-to-one mapping onto itself

sym·pa·tho·lyt·ic \ˌsimpəthōˈlid·ik\ *n* : a sympatholytic agent

sym·pa·tho·mi·met·ic \ˈsimpə(ˌ)thōməˈmed·ik, -mīˈm-\ *n* : a sympathomimetic agent

syn·an·throp·ic \(ˌ)sinənˈthräpik, -anˈth-\ *adj* [*syn-* with (deriv. of Gk *syn*) + *anthropic*] : ecologically associated with man <*synanthropic* flies> — **syn·an·thro·py** \səˈnan(t)thrəpē\ *n*

syn·ap·to·ne·mal complex *or* **syn·ap·ti·ne·mal complex** \səˌnaptəˌnēməl-\ *n* [*synapt*ic + connective *-o-* or *-i-* + *-nema* one having, being, or resembling a thread (deriv. of Gk *nēma* thread) + *-al,* adj. suffix] : a complex tripartite protein structure that spans the region between synapsed chromosomes in meiotic prophase

syn·ap·to·some \səˈnaptəˌsōm\ *n* [*synapt*ic + connective *-o-* + *-some* body, deriv. of Gk *sōma*] : a structure that is recovered from homogenized nerve tissue and prob. represents pinched-off nerve endings <noradrenaline uptake by *synaptosomes* prepared from rat brain —*Current Contents*>

syn·chro·tron radiation \ˈsiŋk(r)əˌträn, ˈsin-\ *n* [from its having been first observed in a synchrotron] : electromagnetic radiation emitted by high-energy charged relativistic particles (as electrons) when they are accelerated by a magnetic field (as in a nebula)

syn·ec·tics \səˈnektiks\ *n pl but usu sing in constr* [perh. fr. Gk *synektik*tein to bring forth together (fr. *syn-* together, with + *ektiktein* to bring forth, fr. *ex-* out + *tiktein* to beget) + E *-s* (as in *dialectics*)] : a theory or system of problem-stating and problem-solving based on creative thinking that involves free use of metaphor and analogy in informal interchange within a carefully selected small group of individuals of diverse personality and areas of specialization — **syn·ec·tic** \-tik\ *adj* — **syn·ec·ti·cal·ly** \-tək(ə)lē\ *adv*

syn·er·gism* \ˈsinə(r)ˌjizəm\ *n* : interaction of discrete agencies (as of industrial firms or physical equipment) in combination such that the total effect is greater than the sum of the individual effects <neither of these vocalists has very high-class equipment and no *synergism* occurs when they team up —Noel Coppage>

syn·ge·ne·ic \ˈsinjəˈnēik\ *adj* [Gk *syngeneia* kinship (fr. *syn-* together, with + *genos* kind, kin) + E *-ic*] : sufficiently alike genetically to be antigenically similar <*syngeneic* grafts between members of an inbred strain> — compare ALLOGENEIC

syn·tac·tic foam \sənˈtaktik-\ *n* [*syntactic* fr. Gk *syntaktikos* putting together] : a plastic in which preformed cells (as tiny hollow glass spheres) have been incorporated, which can withstand great pressures (as at ocean depths), and which floats

syn·thase \ˈsinˌthās, -āz\ *n* [*synth*esis + *-ase* enzyme] : an enzyme that catalyzes the synthesis of a substance without involving the breaking of a high-energy bond in a nucleoside triphosphate (as ATP)

synthetic division *n* : a simplified method of dividing one polynomial by another of the first degree by writing down only the coefficients of the several powers of the variable and changing the sign of the constant term in the divisor so as to replace the usual subtractions by additions

systems analysis *n* : the act, process, or profession of studying an activity (as a procedure, a business, or a physiological function) typically by mathematical means in order to determine its desired or essential end and how this may most efficiently be attained

systems analyst *n* : a specialist in systems analysis

T

T* *abbr* **1** tera- **2** tesla

TA \(ˌ)tē'ā\ *n* : a teaching assistant <appointed several *TAs* to grade papers for the professors>

TA *abbr* transactional analysis

ta·bla \'täblə, 'təb-\ *n* [Hindi *tablā*, fr. Ar *ṭabla*] : a pair of small different-sized hand drums used esp. in Hindu music

ta·can \'taˌkan\ *n* [*tac*tical *a*ir *n*avigation] : a system of navigation employing ultra-high frequency signals to determine the distance and bearing of an aircraft from a transmitting station

tach \'tak\ *n* [short for *tachometer*] : a device for indicating speed of rotation : tachometer

tach·ism \'taˌshizəm\ *n, often cap* [F *tachisme*, fr. *tache* stain, spot, blob + *-isme* -ism, action, state] : ACTION PAINTING — **tach·ist** \'tashəst\ *adj or n, often cap*

tachy·on \'takēˌän\ *n* [*tachy-* rapid (fr. Gk *tachys*) + *-on* elementary particle] : a hypothetical particle that travels faster than light and behaves in a manner opposite to that of ordinary particles so that with an increase in velocity its energy decreases

tad* \'tad\ *n* : a very small or insignificant amount or degree : bit <could inject at least a *tad* more variety into their work —Richard Cromelin> <one perhaps a *tad* more liberal than the other but not essentially different —Steve Wise>

tag·me·mic grammar \(ˌ)tagˌmēmik-\ *n* [*tagmeme* + *-ic*, adj. suffix] : a grammar that describes language in terms of the relationship between grammatical function and the class of items which can perform that function

tag sale *n* [fr. the tag on each item indicating its price] : GARAGE SALE

ta·ka \'täkə\ *n, pl* **taka** *or* **takas** [Bengali *ṭākā*, fr. Skt *ṭaṅka* coin] **1** : the basic monetary unit of Bangladesh **2** : a coin or note representing one taka

take* *vb* — **take a position** *of a security dealer* : to hold in his own account stock bought in the course of trading — **take the mickey** *chiefly Brit* : to joke or kid <he was making out he was only *taking the mickey*, but I could see he meant it —Bill Naughton> — **take the mickey out of** *chiefly Brit* : to tease or make fun of <a machine-gun barrage of one-liners and jokes that *took the mickey out of* everyone there —Peter Bogdanovich>

take* *n* — **on the take** : paid for illegal favors <crooked county commissioners . . . *on the take* —Aaron Latham>

take–out \'tāk(ˌ)au̇t\ *adj* : designed for the sale of food that is not to be consumed on the premises <a *take-out* counter in a restaurant>

[1]**ta·la** \'tälə\ *n* [Skt *tāla* hand-clapping, musical beat, alter. of *tāḍa* beating, fr. *tāḍāyati* he beats] : one of the ancient traditional metrical patterns of Hindu music

[2]**tala** *n, pl* **tala** *or* **talas** [Samoan, fr. E *dollar*] **1** : the basic monetary unit of Western Samoa **2** : a coin or note representing one tala

talking head *n* : the televised image of the head of a person who is talking <bored by a set of *talking heads* discoursing more or less dispassionately —H.S. Ashmore>

talk show *n* : a radio or television program in which usu. well-known persons engage in discussions or are interviewed; *also* : PHONE-IN

tam·ba·la \(ˌ)täm'bälə\ *n, pl* **tambala** *or* **tambalas** [native name in Malawi, lit., cockerel] **1** : a monetary unit of Malawi equal to $^{1}/_{100}$ kwacha **2** : a coin representing one tambala

tank suit *n* : a one-piece bathing suit with shoulder straps

tank top *n* [fr. its resemblance to a tank suit] : a sleeveless collarless shirt with shoulder straps and no front opening

tape deck *n* **1 a** : a mechanism that moves a tape past a magnetic head (as of a tape recorder) **b** : a device that contains such a mechanism and provisions usu. for the recording as well as the playback of magnetic tapes and that usu. has to be connected to a separate audio system **2 :** TAPE PLAYER

tape player *n* **:** a self-contained device for the playback of recorded magnetic tapes

tar·get·able \'tärgəd·əbəl\ *adj* **:** capable of being aimed at a target <missiles with *targetable* warheads>

target language *n* **1 :** a foreign language that is the subject of study **2 :** a language into which a translation (as by machine) is made — compare SOURCE LANGUAGE

tar pit *n* **:** an area in which natural bitumens collect and are exposed at the earth's surface and which tends to trap animals and preserve their hard parts

tart up *vt* [*tart* prostitute] *chiefly Brit* **:** to add superficial adornment to <*tarted up* pubs and restaurants for the spenders —Arnold Ehrlich>

tax haven *n* **:** a country or territory in which taxes are low or nonexistent and which is thus attractive to foreign investors

taxi squad *n* [fr. the practice of a former owner of a professional team who employed such surplus players as drivers for a taxi fleet which he also owned] **:** a group of professional football players under contract who practice with a team but are ineligible to participate in official games

taxon *abbr* taxonomic; taxonomy

tax selling *n* **:** concerted selling of securities late in the year to establish gains and losses for income-tax purposes

tax shelter *n* **:** a factor (as special depreciation allowances) that reduces the taxes on current earnings either to a corporation or its stockholders

tax–shel·tered \ˌtak(s)ˌsheltə(r)d\ *adj* **1 :** characterized or produced by a tax shelter <a *tax-sheltered* investment> <*tax-sheltered* income> **2 :** of, relating to, or involving investments relieved by law from the payment of tax on income often for a particular period or under particular circumstances <*tax-sheltered* retirement plans>

Tay·lor's series *also* **Taylor series** \'tālə(r)-\ *n* [Brook *Taylor* †1731 Eng. mathematician] **:** a power series that gives the expansion of a function $f(x)$ in the neighborhood of a point a provided all derivatives exist and the series converges and that has the form

$$f(x) = f(a) + \frac{f^{[1]}(a)}{1!}(x-a) + \frac{f^{[2]}(a)}{2!}(x-a)^2 + \ldots + \frac{f^{[n]}(a)}{n!}(x-a)^n + \ldots$$

where $f^{[n]}(a)$ is the derivative of nth order of $f(x)$ evaluated at a

Tay–Sachs disease \ˌtāˈsaks-\ *n* [Waren *Tay* †1927 Eng. physician and Bernard P. *Sachs* †1944 Am. neurologist] **:** a fatal hereditary disorder of lipid metabolism characterized by the accumulation of sphingolipid esp. in nervous tissue due to an enzyme deficiency

T cell *n* [*t*hymus-derived *cell*] **:** a lymphocyte differentiated in the thymus, characterized by specific surface antigens, and specialized for cell-mediated immunity (as in the defense against viruses and cancer and the rejection of foreign tissues) — compare B CELL

t distribution *n* **:** a probability density function that is used esp. in testing hypotheses concerning means of normal distributions whose standard deviations are unknown and that is the distribution of a random variable

$$t = \frac{u\sqrt{n}}{v}$$

where u and v are themselves independent random variables and u has a normal distribution with mean 0 and a standard deviation of 1 and v^2 has a chi-square distribution with n degrees of freedom — called also *student's t distribution*

tea break *n, chiefly Brit* **:** a short rest period during the working day for the drinking of tea

tea ceremony *n* **:** a Japanese ceremony consisting of the serving and taking of tea in accordance with an elaborate ritual **:** chanoyu

teach–in \'tēˌchin\ *n* **:** an extended meeting usu. held on a college campus for lectures, debates, and discussions on important issues (as U.S. foreign policy)

teaching machine *n* : any of various mechanical devices for presenting a program of instructional material

team foul *n* : one of a designated number of personal fouls the players on a basketball team may commit during a given period of play before the opposing team begins receiving bonus free throws

team handball *n* : a game developed from soccer which is played between two teams of seven players each and in which the ball is thrown, caught, and dribbled with the hands

tear·gas \'ti(ə)r,gas, 'tiə,-\ *vt* : to use tear gas on < tired of being maced and clubbed and *teargassed* by the police —R.J. Glessing >

tech·ne·tron·ic \,teknə-;tränik\ *adj* [*techn*ological + elec*tronic*] : shaped or influenced by the changes wrought by advances in technology and communications < our modern *technetronic* society >

tech·nol·o·gize \tek'nälə,jīz\ *vt* **-gized; -giz·ing** : to affect or alter by technology < *technologized* American society >

tech·nop·o·lis \tek'näpələs\ *n* [*techno-* art, craft, technical, technological (fr. Gk *technē* art, craft) + *-polis* city, deriv. of Gk *polis*] : a society strongly influenced by and heavily dependent on technology < we must civilize *technopolis,* where barbarism and anonymity are well entrenched —M.W. Fishwick > — **tech·no·pol·i·tan** \(,)teknə'pälət°n, -tən\ *adj*

tech·no·struc·ture \,teknō;strəkchə(r)\ *n* : a large-scale corporation or system of corporate enterprises; *also* : a group of professionals who control a technostructure

teeny \'tēnē\ *n, pl* **teen·ies** : a teenager

teeny·bop·per \-,bäpə(r)\ *n* : a teenager and esp. a teenaged girl; *esp* : one who is enthusiastically devoted to pop music and to current fads < thousands of *teenyboppers* shriek ecstatically, tears streaming down their faces —D.J. Heckman >

TEFL \'tefəl\ *abbr* teaching English as a foreign language

tele·di·ag·no·sis \,telə,dīəg;nōsəs\ *n* [*tele-* distant (deriv. of Gk *tēle* far off) + *diagnosis*] : the diagnosis of physical or mental ailments based on data received from a patient by means of telemetry and closed-circuit television

tele·fac·sim·i·le \-fak;simə(,)lē\ *n* : a system for the transmission and reproduction of fixed graphic matter (as printing) by means of signals transmitted (as between libraries) over telephone wires

tele·lec·ture \'telə,lekchə(r)\ *n* **1** : a loudspeaker connected to a telephone line for amplifying voice communication **2** : a lecture delivered to an audience by telelecture

te·lem·e·try \tə'lemə,trē\ *n* **1** : the science or process of telemetering data **2** : data transmitted by telemetry **3** : BIOTELEMETRY

tele·pro·cess·ing \,telə;präs,esiŋ, -;prös-, -səsiŋ\ *n* : computer processing via remote terminals

tel·ex \'te,leks\ *n* [*tele*printer + *ex*change] : a communication service involving teletypewriters connected by wire through automatic exchanges — **telex** *vt*

telo·phase* \'telə,fāz, 'tēl-\ *n* : a stage in meiosis that is usu. the final stage in the first and second meiotic divisions but may be missing in the first and that is characterized by formation of the nuclear membrane and by changes in coiling and arrangement of the chromosomes

tem·peh \'tem,pā\ *n* [Indonesian *témpé*] : an Asiatic food prepared by fermenting soybeans with a rhizopus

tem·plate* \'templət\ *n* : a molecule (as of RNA) in a biological system that carries the genetic code for another macromolecule

temporal sum·ma·tion \-(,)sə'māshən\ *n* : sensory summation that involves the addition of single stimuli over a short period of time

ten·der·om·e·ter \,tend(ə)'räməd·ə(r)\ *n* [*tender* + connective *-o-* + *-meter* instrument for measuring, deriv. of Gk *metron* measure] : a device for determining the maturity and tenderness of samples of fruits and vegetables

-tene \,tēn\ *adj comb form* [*-tene,* n. comb. form, deriv. of Gk *tainia* ribbon, band] : having (such or so many) chromosomal filaments < poly*tene* > < pachy*tene* >

ten·sio·met·ric \ˌten(t)sēəˈme·trik\ *adj* [*tensio*n + *-metric* measuring, deriv. of Gk *metron* measure] : of, relating to, or involving the measurement of tension or tensile strength — **ten·si·om·e·try** \ˌten(t)sēˈämə·trē\ *n*

tent trailer *n* : a 2-wheeled automobile-drawn trailer having a canvas shelter that can be opened up above the body to provide camping facilities

teo·na·na·catl \ˌtāōˌnänəˈkätᵊl\ *n* [Nahuatl, fr. *teotl* god + *nanacatl* mushroom] : any of several New World mushrooms (*Psilocybe* and related genera of the family Agaricaceae) that are sources of hallucinogens

te·pa \ˈtēpə\ *n* [*t*ri- three (fr. L & Gk) + *e*thylene + *p*hosphorus + *a*mide] : a soluble crystalline compound $C_6H_{12}N_3OP$ that is related to ethylenimine and that is used esp. as a chemosterilant of insects, an alleviant in some kinds of cancer, and in finishing and flame-proofing textiles

tera- \ˈterə\ *comb form* [ISV, fr. Gk *teras* monster] : trillion <*tera*ton> <*tera*hertz>

te·rato·gen \təˈrad·əjən, ˈterəd·əjən, -ˌjen\ *n* [*terato-* monster (fr. Gk *teret-, teras*) + *-gen* producer, deriv. of Gk *genēs* born] : a teratogenic agent (as a drug or virus)

ter·i·ya·ki \ˌterēˈ(y)äkē\ *n* [Jap, fr. *teri* sunshine + *yaki* roast] : a dish of Japanese origin consisting of meat, chicken, or shellfish that is grilled or broiled after being marinated in a spicy soy sauce

terminal* *n* : a device (as a teletypewriter) through which a user can communicate with a computer

ter·ra \ˈterə\ *n, pl* **ter·rae** \-r(ˌ)ē, -rˌī\ [NL, fr. L, land] : any of the relatively light-grayish highland areas on the surface of the moon

Ter·ran \ˈterən\ *n* [*Terra,* the planet Earth (fr. L *terra* Earth) + E *-an,* n. suffix] : an inhabitant of the earth <the way *Terrans* may appear to inhabitants of outer space —Jane Manthorne>

TESL \ˈtesəl\ *abbr* teaching English as a second language

tes·la \ˈteslə\ *n* [ISV, Nikola *Tesla* †1943 Am. electrician and inventor] : a unit of magnetic flux density in the mks system equivalent to one weber per square meter

test ban *n* : a self-imposed ban on the atmospheric testing of nuclear weapons that is mutually agreed to by countries possessing such weapons

test–drive \ˈtes(t)ˌdrīv\ *vt* **-drove; -driv·en; -driv·ing** : to drive (a motor vehicle) before buying in order to evaluate performance

tet·ra·ben·a·zine \ˌte·trəˈbenəˌzēn\ *n* [*tetra-* four (deriv. of Gk *tetra-*) + *benzo*[*a*]-quinoli*zine,* fr. *benzo-* related to benzene or benzoic acid + *a* (an indicator of position) + *quinolin*e + a*zine*] : a serotonin antagonist $C_{19}H_{27}NO_3$ that is used esp. in the treatment of psychosis and anxiety

tet·ra·func·tion·al \ˌte·trəˈfəŋ(k)shnəl, -shənᵊl\ *adj* : of, relating to, or being a compound with four sites in the molecule that are highly reactive (as in polymerization)

tet·ra·hy·dro·can·nab·i·nol \ˌte·trəˌhīdrəkəˈnabəˌnȯl\ *n* [*tetrahydro-* combined with four hydrogen atoms + *cannabinol,* a phenol obtained from hemp] : a physiologically active liquid from hemp plant resin that is the chief intoxicant in marijuana — called also *THC*

tet·ra·hy·me·na \ˌte·trəˈhīmənə\ *n* [NL, fr. *tetra-* + Gk *hymēn* membrane] **1** *cap* : a genus of free-living ciliate protozoans much used for genetic and biochemical research **2** : a member of the genus *Tetrahymena* and esp. *T. pyriformis*

tet·ra·pyr·role *also* **tet·ra·pyr·rol** \ˌte·trəˈpiˌrōl, -rȯl, -əpəˈr-\ *n* : a chemical group consisting of four pyrrole rings joined either in a straight chain (as in phycobilins) or in a ring (as in chlorophyll)

Texas citrus mite *n* : a red spider (*Eutetrarychus banksi*) that causes leaf injury to citrus trees

TG* *abbr* **1** transformational-generative **2** transformational grammar

thal·as·se·mic \ˌthaləˈsēmik\ *adj* : of, relating to, or affected with thalassemia — **thalassemic** *n*

tha·lid·o·mide \thəˈlidəˌmīd, -əməd\ *n* [ph*thal*im*ide* + connective *-o-* + i*mide*] : a sedative and hypnotic drug $C_{13}H_{10}N_2O_4$ that has been the cause of malformation in infants born to mothers using it during pregnancy

THC \ˌtē(ˌ)āchˈsē\ *n* [*t*etra*h*ydro*c*annabinol] : TETRAHYDROCANNABINOL

theater of the absurd : theater that seeks to represent the absurdity of man's existence in a meaningless universe by bizarre or fantastic means

theme park *n* : an amusement park in which the structures and settings are based on a central theme

therapeutic index *n* : a measure of the relative desirability of a drug for the attaining of a particular medical end that is usu. expressed as the ratio of the largest dose producing no toxic symptoms to the smallest dose routinely producing cures

thermal pol·lu·tion \-pə'lüshən\ *n* : the discharge of heated liquid (as waste water from a factory) into natural waters at a temperature detrimental to existing ecosystems

ther·mo·form \'thərmə,fȯrm\ *vt* [*thermo-* heat (fr. Gk *thermē*) + *form*] : to give a final shape to (as a plastic) with the aid of heat and usu. pressure — **thermoform** *n* — **ther·mo·form·able** \¦thərmə¦fȯrməbəl\ *adj*

ther·mo·gram* \'thərmə,gram\ *n* **1** : a photographic record made by thermography **2** : a temperature-weight change graph obtained in thermogravimetry

ther·mo·graph* \-,graf\ *n* **1** : THERMOGRAM **2** : the apparatus used in thermography

ther·mo·gra·vim·e·try \¦thər(,)mōgrə¦vimə·trē\ *n* [ISV *thermo-* + *gravimetry;* prob. orig. formed in F] : the determination (as with a thermobalance) of weight changes in a substance at a high temperature or during a gradual increase in temperature — **ther·mo·grav·i·me·tric** \-,gravə̇¦me·trik\ *adj*

ther·mo·phys·i·cal \¦thərmō¦fizə̇kəl, -mə-\ *adj* : of, relating to, or concerned with the physical properties of materials as affected by elevated temperatures

ther·mo·sphere \'thərmə,sfi(ə)r\ *n* : the part of the earth's atmosphere that begins at about 50 miles above the earth's surface, extends to outer space, and is characterized by steadily increasing temperature with height — **ther·mo·spheric** \¦thərmə¦sfi(ə)rik, -¦sfer-\ *adj*

the·ta rhythm \'thād·ə-, 'thēd·ə-\ *n* : a relatively high amplitude brain wave pattern between approximately 4 and 9 hertz that is characteristic esp. of the hippocampus but occurs in many regions of the brain including the cortex

thia·ben·da·zole \,thīə'bendə,zōl\ *n* [*thia*zole + benzimi*dazole*] : a drug $C_{10}H_7N_3S$ used in the control of parasitic roundworms and in the treatment of fungus infections

thi·a·zide \'thīə,zīd, -əzə̇d\ *n* [*thi-* sulfur (deriv. of Gk *theion*) + di*azine* + diox*ide*] : any of several drugs used as oral diuretics esp. in the control of high blood pressure

thing* *n* : a personal choice of activity — often used with *do* <letting students do their own *thing* —*Newsweek*>

think tank *also* **think factory** *n* : an institute, corporation, or group organized for interdisciplinary research (as in military strategy or technological and social problems) <corporate wise men who ponder others' problems, for a stiff fee, in the seclusion of *think tanks* —Leonard Iaquinta> — **think tank·er** \-¦taŋkə(r)\ *n*

thin–lay·er chro·ma·tog·ra·phy \¦thin,lāər,krōmə'tägrəfē, -,le(ə)r-\ *n* : chromatography in which the absorbent medium is in a thin layer (as of silica gel, alumina, or cellulose) — **thin–layer chro·ma·to·graph·ic** \-krō,mad·ə'grafik, -,krōməd·ə-\ *adj*

thi·o·rid·a·zine \,thīə'ridə,n, n, -əzə̇n\ *n* [*thio-* sulfur (deriv. of Gk *theion*) + pipe*ridine* + phenothi*azine*] : a phenothiazine used in the hydrochloride $C_{21}H_{26}N_2S_2.HCl$ as a tranquilizer for relief of anxiety states and in the treatment of schizophrenia

third market *n* [fr. its distinction from the organized exchanges and the market in unlisted securities] : the over-the-counter market in listed securities

third–stream \¦thərd,strēm, ¦thə̄d-, ¦thəid-\ *adj* : of, relating to, or being music that incorporates elements of classical music and jazz

third world *n, often cap T&W* [trans. of F *tiers monde*] **1** : a group of nations esp. in Africa and Asia that are not aligned with either the Communist or the non-Communist blocs <the anti-American feeling that the fight against the Viet Cong has caused in much of the Afro-Asian *Third World* —*Newsweek*> **2** : an aggregate of minority groups within a larger predominant culture <Community High, for example, has 65 *Third World* students and 120 whites —*Time*> **3** : the aggregate of the underdeveloped nations of the world <the *Third World* consists, by definition, of poor rural

societies —J.K. Galbraith > — **third world·er** \-¦wər(ə)ldə(r), -¦wəl-, -¦wəil-\ *n, often cap T&W*

tho·rac·ic gland \thə'rasik-\ *n* : PROTHORACIC GLAND

threads *n pl* : clothes < specializing in *threads* to fit the fashion-conscious soul brother —*Newsweek* >

thrift shop *n* : a shop that sells secondhand articles and esp. clothes and is often run for charitable purposes

through·put* \'thrü,pu̇t\ *n* : output, production < the *throughput* of a computer >

throw·away \¦thrōə,wā\ *adj* **1** : that may be thrown away : disposable < *throwaway* containers > < this flashlight is sturdy and well made for a *throwaway* item —*Consumer Reports* > **2** : written or spoken (as in a play) in a low-key or unemphasized manner < *throwaway* lines > **3** : nonchalant, casual < all put together with such style, such *throwaway* chic —Peter Buckley >

thrust chamber *n* : a jet engine that consists of a combustion chamber in which solid or liquid fuel is ignited and that is used for the propulsion of a missile or vehicle (as an airplane)

thrus·tor *also* **thrust·er** \'thrəstə(r)\ *n* : an engine (as a jet engine) that develops thrust by expelling a jet of fluid or a stream of particles : reaction engine

thrust stage *n* : a theater stage surrounded on three sides by the audience; *also* : a forestage that is extended into the auditorium to increase the stage area

thumb piano *n* : any of various musical instruments of African origin (as the kalimba, mbira, or zanza) that consist essentially of a resonator and a set of tuned metal or wooden strips that are plucked with the thumbs or fingers

thy·la·koid \'thīlə,kȯid\ *n* [ISV *thylak-* (fr. Gk *thylakos* sack) + *-oid* one that resembles; prob. orig. formed in G] : a membranous lamella of protein and lipid in plant chloroplasts where the photochemical reactions of photosynthesis take place

thy·mec·to·mize \thī'mektə,mīz\ *vt* **-mized; -miz·ing** : to subject to thymectomy < studies in rats *thymectomized* at birth >

thy·mi·co·lym·phat·ic \¦thīmə(,)kōlim¦fad·ik\ *adj* [*thymic* + connective *-o-* + *lymphatic*] : of, relating to, or affecting both the thymus and the lymphatic system

thy·ris·tor \thī'ristə(r)\ *n* [*thyr*atron + trans*istor*] : any of several semiconductor devices that act as switches, rectifiers, or voltage regulators

thy·ro·cal·ci·to·nin \¦thīrō,kalsə¦tōnən\ *n* [*thyro*id + *calcitonin*] : a polypeptide hormone from the thyroid gland that tends to lower the level of calcium in the blood plasma

thy·roid–stim·u·lat·ing hor·mone \¦thī,rȯid¦stimyə,lād·iŋ'hȯr,mōn, -'hȯ(ə),mōn\ *n* : a hormone secreted by the anterior pituitary that regulates the formation and secretion of thyroid hormone

tick off* *vt* : to make angry or indignant < the cancellation really *ticked* me *off* >

ticky–tacky \'tikē¦takē\ *n* [coined by Malvina Reynolds *b*1900 Am. songwriter] : sleazy or shoddy material used esp. in the construction of look-alike tract houses < sprawling suburbs are filled with more than enough neon, plastic and *ticky-tacky* —J.P. Sterba > — **ticky–tacky** *adj*

tight end *n* : an offensive end in football who lines up within two yards of the tackle

time di·la·tion \-dī'lāshən\ *also* **time di·la·ta·tion** \-,dilə'tāshən, -,dīlə-\ *n* : a slowing of time on a system moving at a velocity approaching that of light relative to an observer as predicted by the theory of relativity

time reversal *n* : a formal operation in mathematical physics that reverses the order in which a sequence of events occurs

time reversal in·vari·ance \-(')in¦verēən(t)s, -¦var-\ *n* : a principle in physics: if a given sequence of events is physically possible the same sequence in the opposite order is also possible

time–shar·ing \'tīm,she(ə)riŋ, -,sha(ə)riŋ\ *n* : simultaneous use of a central computer by many users at remote locations — **time–shared** \-,she(ə)rd, -,sha(ə)rd, -,sheəd, -,shaəd\ *adj*

times sign *n* : the symbol × used to indicate multiplication

time–test·ed \\'tīm,testəd\\ *adj* : having effectiveness that has been proved over a long period of time <a *time-tested* formula>

time trial *n* : a competitive event (as in auto racing) in which individuals are successively timed over a set course or distance

ting ware \\'ting-\\ *also* **ting yao** \\-'yaủ\\ *n, often cap T* [*Ting* fr. *Ting Chou,* town southwest of Peking, China, where it was originally made; *Ting yao* fr. *Ting* + Chin (Pek) *yao*[2] pottery] : a Chinese porcelain ware known since Sung times that is typically expertly potted, often decorated with engraved underglaze designs, and characteristically glazed with a milk-white to creamy white or less often an iron-red glaze

tis·sue* *vt* **tis·sued; tis·su·ing** : to remove (as cleansing cream) with a tissue

tis·su·lar \\'tish(y)ələ(r)\\ *adj* [*tissue* + *-lar* (as in *cellular*)] : of or relating to organismic tissue <*tissular* lesions> <*tissular* grafts>

T lym·pho·cyte \\'tē'lim(p)fə,sīt\\ *n* [*t*hymus-derived *lymphocyte*] : T CELL

TM* *abbr* transcendental meditation

together *adj* **1** : appropriately prepared, organized, or balanced <a super-delicious, beautifully *together* album —Clayton Riley> **2** : composed in mind or manner : self-possessed <a warm, sensitive, reasonably *together* girl —*East Village Other*> — often used as a generalized term of approval <don't let the out-of-the-way location put you off, it's every bit as *together* as any place downtown —Jay Hoffman>

to·ka·mak \\'tōkə,mak, 'täk-\\ *n* [Russ] : a toroidal device for producing controlled nuclear fusion that involves the confining and heating of a gaseous plasma by means of an internal electric current and its attendant magnetic field

toke \\'tōk\\ *n* [origin unknown] *slang* : a puff on a marijuana cigarette <every well-bred person passes a joint to his nearest neighbor and waits for it to come back before taking a second *toke* —R.A. Sokolov> — **toke** *vb, slang*

to·ken·ism \\'tōkə,nizəm\\ *n* : the policy or practice of making only a token effort (as to desegregate or provide equal employment opportunities) <creeping *tokenism* but little more . . . the top woman in every bank is outranked by at least 100 men —Carol Greitzer> — **to·ken·is·tic** \\-istik\\ *adj*

Tom* \\'täm\\ *n* : an Uncle Tom <I don't see why he wants to talk that I'm a *Tom,* that I don't stand up for the black man —Joe Frazier> <it had always proven sufficient for him to label his opponent a *Tom* and read the *New York Times* editorials supporting the hapless fellow from a sound truck to back up the charge —R.M. Levine>

tom *vi* **tommed; tom·ming** *often cap* : UNCLE TOM <the history of the American Negro from a *tomming* laughing boy to a fierce enduring militant —Pete Hamill>

ton* *n* **1** *Brit* : a speed of 100 miles per hour — often used in the phrase *do the ton* or *do a ton* <the first cars were doing the *ton* barely ten years after Victoria's Diamond Jubilee —*London Times*> ; called also *ton-up* **2** *Brit* : a score of 100 runs in cricket : a century

tool *n* : a design (as on the binding of a book) made by tooling

toothpick* *n* : a small often elaborate container for a supply of toothpicks at table

to·po·cen·tric \\¦täpə¦sen·trik, ¦tōp-\\ *adj* [*topo-* place (deriv. of Gk *topos*) + *-centric* centered] : relating to, measured from, or as if observed from a particular point on the earth's surface : having or relating to such a point as origin <*topocentric* coordinates>

to·po·log·i·cal* \\,täpə'läjəkəl, ,tōp-\\ *adj* : being or involving properties unaltered under a homeomorphism <continuity and connectedness are *topological* properties>

topological group *n* : a mathematical group which is also a topological space, whose multiplicative operation is continuous such that given any neighborhood of a product there exist neighborhoods of the elements composing the product with the property that any pair of elements representing each of these neighborhoods form a product belonging to the given neighborhood, and whose operation of taking inverses is continuous such that for any neighborhood of the inverse of an element there exists a neighborhood of the element itself in which every element has its inverse in the other neighborhood

to·po·log·i·cal·ly equivalent \\,täpə¦läjək(ə)lē-, ,tōp-\\ *adj* : related by a homeomorphism <two *topologically equivalent* figures can be made to coincide if subjected to a suitable elastic motion>

topological space *n* : a set with a collection of subsets satisfying the conditions that both the empty set and the set itself belong to the collection, the union of any number of the subsets is also an element of the collection, and the intersection of a finite number of the subsets is an element of the collection

topological transformation *n* : a one-to-one mapping in topology between two figures that is continuous in both directions : homeomorphism

to·pos \'tō,pōs, 'tä,p-\ *n, pl* **to·poi** \-,pȯi \ [Gk, place, commonplace, topic] : a stock rhetorical theme or topic

torpedo* *n, pl* **-does** : HOAGIE

torque \'tȯ(ə)rk, 'tȯ(ə)k\ *vt* **torqued; torqu·ing** : to impart torque to : cause to twist (as about an axis) <after a day the spinning satellite is magnetically *torqued* into a new orientation so that another great circle can be scanned — W. D. Metz> — **torqu·er** \-ə(r)\ *n*

total* *vt* : to make a total wreck of (a car) <had *totaled* a couple of cars and had been involved in a few motorcycle accidents —Anthony Mancini>

total environment *n* : ENVIRONMENT

tot lot *n* : a small playground for young children

tough* *adj, slang* : excellent, splendid, great — used as a generalized term of approval <the barbecue . . . was well attended, and judged "real *tough*" . . . by boys as well as girls —Judy Van Vliet Cook>

touring car* *n* : a usu. 2-door sedan as distinguished from a sports car

tourist trap *n* : a place (as a shop, restaurant, or resort area) where tourists are exploited <advised us to get out of a lousy *tourist trap* like Paris —Alexander King>

tow–away zone \'tōə,wā-\ *n* : a no-parking zone from which parked vehicles may be towed away

town house* *n* : a single-family house of two or sometimes three stories connected to another house by a common sidewall

track·ing \'trakiŋ\ *n* : the policy or practice of assigning students to a curricular track < *tracking* generally tends to segregate students of different backgrounds —Jerome Karabel>

track record *n* : a record of accomplishments <a modern university president is expected to have practical vision, a good *track record* in administration, and national prominence —W.G. Bennis>

tract house *n* : one of many similarly designed houses built on a tract of land

trade–off \'trā,dȯf\ *n* **1** : a balancing of desirable considerations or goals all of which are not attainable at the same time <the education versus experience *trade-off* which governs personnel practices —H.S. White> **2** : a giving up of one thing in return for another : exchange <the shipper is willing to make a *trade-off,* paying more for freight service to pay less for handling and for carrying inventory —J.F. Spencer>

trail bike *n* : a small motorcycle designed for uses other than on highways and for easy transport (as on an automobile bumper)

train·ee·ship \trā'nē,ship\ *n* : the position or status of a trainee; *specif* : one involving a program of advanced training and study esp. in a medical science and usu. bearing a stipend and allowances (as for travel)

trans·ac·tion·al analysis \tran(t)'sakshnəl-, -shənᵊl-, -n'za-\ *n* : a system of psychotherapy involving analysis of individual episodes of social interaction for insight that will aid communication (as by the substitution of constructive mature verbal exchanges for destructive immature ones)

trans·am·i·nate \tran(t)'samə,nāt, -n'za-\ *vb* **-nat·ed; -nat·ing** [back-formation fr. *transamination*] *vi* : to induce or catalyze a transamination ~ *vt* : to induce or catalyze the transamination of

tran·scen·den·tal* \,tran(t)s,en'dentᵊl, -sən-\ *adj* : being, involving, or representing a function (as $\sin x$, $\log x$, e^x) that cannot be expressed by a finite number of algebraic operations involving the variable and constants < *transcendental* curves>

transcendental meditation *n* : a technique of meditation in which the mind is released through the use of a mantra and which is intended to foster calm, creativity, and spiritual well-being

transcribe* *vt* **-scribed; -scrib·ing** : to cause (as DNA) to undergo genetic transcription

tran·scrip·tion* \tran(t)s'kripshən\ *n* : the process of constructing a messenger RNA molecule using a DNA molecule as a template with resulting transfer of genetic information to the messenger RNA — compare TRANSLATION

trans·duce \tran(t)s'd(y)üs, -nz'-\ *vt* **-duced; -duc·ing** [L *transducere* to lead across, transfer, fr. *trans-* + *ducere* to lead] **1** : to convert (as energy or a message) into another form **2** : to bring about the transfer of (as a gene) from one microorganism to another by means of a viral agent

trans·earth \¦tran,zərth, -,zəth, -,zəith\ *adj* [*trans-* across (fr. L *trans*) + *earth*] : of or relating to the entry of a spacecraft into a trajectory between a celestial body (as the moon) and the earth and to the travel of the spacecraft in the direction of the earth < *transearth* injection > < *transearth* burn >

transfer RNA *n* : a relatively small RNA that transfers a particular amino acid to a growing polypeptide chain at the ribosomal site of protein synthesis during translation — compare MESSENGER RNA

transform* *vt* : to cause (a cell) to undergo genetic transformation

trans·form* \'tran(t)s,fórm, -,fó(ə)m\ *n* **1** : a mathematical element obtained from another by transformation **2** : a linguistic structure (as a sentence) produced by means of a transformation < "the duckling is killed by the farmer" is a *transform* of "the farmer kills the duckling" >

transformation* *n* **1** : genetic modification of a bacterium by incorporation of free DNA from another ruptured bacterial cell **2** : one of an ordered set of rules that specify how to convert the deep structures of a language into surface structures

trans·for·ma·tion·al \¦tranzfə(r)¦māshənᵊl, -n(t)sf-, -shnəl\ *adj* : of, relating to, or based on linguistic transformation < *transformational* theory > < *transformational* rules >

transformational grammar *n* : a grammar that generates the deep structures of a language and relates these to the surface structures by means of transformations

trans·for·ma·tion·al·ist \,tranzfə(r),māshənᵊləst, -n(t)sf-, -shnəl-\ *n* : an exponent of transformational grammar

trans·fu·sion·al \tranz'fyüzhənᵊl, -n(t)s'f-, -zhnəl\ *adj* : of, relating to, or caused by transfusion < *transfusional* shock > < *transfusional* reactions >

transistor* *or* **transistor radio** *n* : a transistorized radio < conversations always seemed to be carried on over a background of *transistors* or record machines —G. A. Plimpton >

transition* *n* : a genetic mutation in RNA or DNA that results from the substitution of one purine base for the other or of one pyrimidine base for the other

translate* *vt* **-lat·ed; -lat·ing** : to subject (as genetic information) to translation in protein synthesis

translation* *n* : the process of forming a protein molecule at a ribosomal site of protein synthesis from information contained in messenger RNA — compare TRANSCRIPTION

trans·lu·nar \(')tran(t)s¦lünə(r), -nz¦l-\ *adj* : of or relating to the entry of a spacecraft into a trajectory between a celestial body (as the earth) and the moon and to the travel of the spacecraft in the direction of the moon < *translunar* injection > < *translunar* burn >

trans·mem·brane \-¦mem,brān\ *adj* : taking place, existing, or arranged from one side to the other of a membrane < a *transmembrane* potential >

transmitter* *n* : NEUROTRANSMITTER

trans·mu·ta·tion* \,tran(t)smyü'tāshən, ,tranzm-\ *n* : the effect of controlled reduction firing on certain chiefly Oriental copper-containing and/or iron-containing ceramic glazes (**transmutation glazes**) that is typically a variegation of colors (as purple, blue, and red) and a thick often bubbly consistency

transport* *n* : a mechanism for moving tape and esp. magnetic tape past a sensing or recording head

trans·pose* \'tran(t)s,pōz, -nz,p-\ *n* : a matrix formed by interchanging the rows and columns of a given matrix

trans·ra·cial \(ˈ)tran(t)sˌrāshəl, -nzˌr-\ *adj* : involving two or more races < *transracial* adoption >

trans·sex·u·al \-ˌseksh(ə)wəl, -shəl\ *n* : a person with a psychological urge to belong to the opposite sex that may be carried as far as surgical modification of the sex organs to mimic the other sex — **transsexual** *adj* — **trans·sex·u·al·ism** \tranˈseksh(ə)wəˌlizəm, -shəˌlizəm\ *n*

trans·tho·rac·ic \ˌtran(t)sthəˌrasik, -nzth-\ *adj* : done or made by way of the thoracic cavity — **trans·tho·rac·i·cal·ly** \-ˌrasək(ə)lē\ *adv*

tran·yl·cy·pro·mine \ˌtranᵊlˈsīprəˌmēn, -əmən\ *n* [*tran*s- + phen*yl* + *cy*clic + *pro*pyla*mine*] : an antidepressant drug $C_9H_{11}N$ that is an inhibitor of monoamine oxidase

trash* *vt* **1** : to turn into trash: as **a** : to vandalize or wreck < *trash* a college ROTC building —Susan Brownmiller > < beer and food stands had been liberated then *trashed* —Larry Sloman > **b** : to smash or destroy < *trashing* store windows > < a career politician finally smelling the White House is not much different from a bull elk in the rut. He will stop at nothing, *trashing* anything that gets in his way —H.S. Thompson > **c** : to spoil or ruin < *trashing* the environment > < so-called developers have already *trashed* several other good streets in Montreal —J.W. Maclellan > < *trash* his own lumpish songs by bawling in a voice that is both ear-splitting and off-pitch —Stephen Holden > **d** : to run down : disparage < Uncle Tomming in the very act of seeming to *trash* Whitey —Brendan Gill > **2** : to throw into the trash : discard < a lot of silly ideas being floated which had best be *trashed* as quickly as possible —*Christian Science Monitor* > **3** : to throw trash on < it started with two varsity guys *trashing* my lawn —Pam Graham > **~** *vi* : to trash something esp. as a form of protest < those who stopped marching when the marching turned to *trashing* —Elinor Langer > — **trash·er** \ˈtrashə(r)\ *n*

travel trailer *n* : a trailer drawn esp. by a passenger automobile and equipped for use (as while traveling) as a dwelling

treat·abil·i·ty \ˌtrēd·əˈbiləd·ē\ *n* : the condition of being treatable < an interpretation of the law based on *treatability* of felonious behavior >

trendy \ˈtrendē, -di\ *adj* **trend·i·er; -est** : very fashionable : up-to-date < he's a *trendy* dresser —*Sunday Mirror (London)* > < such supposedly *trendy* topics as drug use among the young, pollution and nuclear holocaust —Elizabeth Janeway > < I hear *trendy* clergymen asking God to attend to our balance of payments —Malcolm Muggeridge > — **trend·i·ly** \-dəlē, -dᵊlē\ *adv* — **trend·i·ness** \-dēnəs, -dən-\ *n* — **trendy** *n*

trial* *n* : one of a number of repetitions of an experiment < what is the probability of getting *k* successes in *n trials* >

tri·am·cin·o·lone \ˌtrīamˈsinᵊlˌōn\ *n* [*tri-* three + *am*yl + *cin*ene, a terpene + prednis*olone*] : a corticoid drug $C_{21}H_{27}FO_6$ used esp. in treating psoriasis and allergic skin and respiratory disorders

triangle inequality *n* [fr. its application to the distances between three points in a coordinate system] : an inequality stating that the absolute value of a sum is less than or equal to the sum of the absolute value of the terms

tri·chlor·fon \(ˈ)trīˈklō(ə)rˌfän, -ˈklȯ(ə)r-\ *n* [*tri-* three + *chlor*ine + *-fon* (irreg. fr. *phosphonate*)] : a crystalline compound $C_4H_8Cl_3O_4P$ that is used as an insecticide and anthelmintic

trickle–down theory \ˌtrikəlˌdau̇n-\ *n* : an economic theory that financial benefits given to big business will in turn pass down to smaller businesses and consumers

tri·fec·ta \(ˈ)trīˌfektə\ *n* [*tri-* + per*fecta*] : a variation of the perfecta in which a bettor must select the first 3 finishers of a race in the correct order of finish in order to win — called also *triple;* compare SUPERFECTA

tri·fluo·per·a·zine \ˌtrīˌflüōˌperəˌzēn, -əzən\ *n* [*tri-* + *fluo*rine + pi*perazine*] : a phenothiazine tranquilizer $C_{21}H_{24}F_3N_3S$ used esp. in the treatment of psychotic conditions (as schizophrenia)

tri·flu·ra·lin \trīˈflu̇rələn\ *n* [*tri-* + *flu*o*r*ine + ani*line*] : an herbicide $C_{13}H_{16}F_3N_3O_4$ used in the control of weeds (as pigweed and annual grasses)

tri·func·tion·al \(ˈ)trīˌfəŋ(k)shnəl, -shənᵊl\ *adj* : of, relating to, or being a compound with three sites in the molecule that are highly reactive (as in polymerization)

tri·jet \ˌtrīˌjet\ *adj* : powered with three jet engines <a *trijet* airplane> — **tri·jet** \ˈtrīˌjet\ *n*

tri·ma·ran \ˌtrīməˌran\ *n* [*tri-* + *-maran* (as in *catamaran*)] : a fast pleasure sailboat with three hulls side by side

trip* *n* **1** : an intense visionary experience undergone by a person who has taken a psychedelic drug (as LSD); *broadly* : an exciting experience <orgasm . . . is the ultimate *trip* —D.R. Reuben> **2** : pursuit of an absorbing or obsessive interest : kick <he's on a nostalgia *trip*> **3** : way of life : SCENE <the whole super-star *trip* —Joe Eszterhas>

trip *vi* **tripped; trip·ping** : to get high on a drug : turn on — often used with *out* <the pot generation (roughly, those who use marijuana frequently and *trip* out occasionally) —Pauline Kael> — **trip·per** \ˈtripə(r)\ *n*

triple* *n* : TRIFECTA

triple jump *n* : a jump for distance in track-and-field athletics usu. from a running start and combining a hop, a stride, and a jump in succession : hop, step, and jump

triplet* *n* **1** : a group of three elementary particles (as positive, negative, and neutral pions) with different charge states but otherwise similar properties **2** *or* **triplet state** : any state of an elementary particle having one quantum unit of spin

trivial* *adj* : relating to or being the mathematically simplest case; *specif* : characterized by having all variables equal to zero <a *trivial* solution to an equation>

tRNA \ˌtēˌärˌenˌā\ *n* [*t*ransfer *RNA*] : TRANSFER RNA

trog·lo·bite \ˈträgləˌbīt\ *n* [alter. (influenced by *troglodyte*) of *troglobiont*] : an animal living in or restricted to caves; *esp* : one occurring in the lightless waters of caves : troglobiont — **trog·lo·bit·ic** \ˌträgləˈbid·ik\ *adj*

troi·ka* \ˈtrȯikə\ *n* **1** : an administrative or ruling body of three <replaced by a *troika* of three coequal secretaries-general —*Newsweek*> **2** : a group of three <astrology, yoga, and poetry are the *troika* of humanities that most interest him —A.J. Liebling>

tro·phic level \ˈtrōfik-\ *n* : one of the hierarchical strata of a food web characterized by organisms which are the same number of steps removed from the primary producers

tro·po·col·la·gen \ˌträpəˈkäləjən, ˌtrōp-\ *n* [*trop-* turn, change, tropism (fr. Gk *tropos* turn) + *collagen*] : a soluble precursor of collagen with elongated molecules that form the elementary building units of collagen fibers

trust fund* *n* : a governmental fund consisting of moneys accepted for a specified purpose (as civil service retirement) that is administered as a trust separately from other funds and is expended only in furthering the specified purpose

truth set *n* : a mathematical or logical set containing all the elements that make a given statement of relationships true when substituted in it <the equation x + 7 = 10 has as its *truth set* the single number 3>

tryp·sin·iza·tion \ˌtripsənəˈzāshən, trəpˌsin-, -ˌīˈz-\ *n* : the action or process of trypsinizing

T–time \ˈtēˌtīm\ *n* [prob. fr. *t* (abbr. for *time*)] : the time of initial firing of a rocket vehicle or missile

tube* *n* **1** : a television set <switched on the big . . . color *tube* over the bar —*Rolling Stone*>; *broadly* : television <hardly a moment next fall when gunplay can't be found somewhere on the *tube* —R.K. Doan> <no politician can lightly offend the men who govern the *tube* —Leonard Ross> **2** : CURL

tu·grik \ˈt(y)üˌgrik\ *n* [Mongolian *dughurik*, lit., round thing, wheel] **1** : the basic monetary unit of Outer Mongolia **2** : a coin or note representing one tugrik

tu·mori·gen·e·sis \ˌt(y)ümərəˈjenəsəs\ *n* [*tumor* + connective *-i-* + *genesis*] : the formation of tumors

tu·mor·i·gen·ic \ˌt(y)ümərəˈjenik\ *adj* : producing or tending to produce tumors; *also* : carcinogenic <*tumorigenic* cells> — **tu·mor·i·ge·nic·i·ty** \ˌt(y)ümərəjəˈnisəd·ē\ *n*

tune out *vt* : to become unresponsive to : ignore <the children *tuned out* their mother's commands> ~ *vi* : to dissociate oneself from what is happening <when things get a bit too much, she simply *tunes out* temporarily —Ann Nietzke>

tunnel* *n* : CURL

tun·nel di·ode \-ˈdī,ōd\ *n* : a semiconductor device that has two stable states when operated in conjunction with suitable circuit elements and a source of voltage, is capable of extremely rapid transformations between the two by means of the tunnel effect of electrons, and is used for amplifying, switching, and computer information storage and as an oscillator

tunnel vision* *n* : extreme narrowness of viewpoint : narrowmindedness <computer specialists develop a type of *tunnel vision* consisting of statistical-empirical-digital thinking —L.J. Peter>

-tu·ple \,təpəl, ,tüp-\ *n comb form* [quin*tuple*, sex*tuple*] : set of (so many) elements — often used of sets with ordered elements <the ordered 2-*tuple* (*a, b*)>

tur·bo·cop·ter \ˈtərbō,käptər, -bə,k-\ *n* [*turbo-* turbine + heli*copter*] : a helicopter in which motive power for the rotor is provided by one or more gas turbine engines

tur·bo·elec·tric \ˌtərbōəˌlektrik, -ēˌl-\ *adj* : involving or depending as a power source on electricity produced by turbine generators <ships with *turboelectric* drive>

tur·bo·fan \ˈtərbō,fan, -bə-\ *n* **1** : a fan that is directly connected to and driven by a turbine and is used to supply air for cooling, ventilation, or combustion **2** : a jet engine having a turbofan

tur·bo·pump \-,pəmp\ *n* : a pump that is driven by a turbine

tur·bo·shaft \-,shaft\ *n* : a gas turbine engine that is similar in operation to a turboprop engine but instead of being used to power a propeller is used through a transmission system for powering other devices (as helicopter rotors and pumps)

Tu·ring machine \ˈt(y)u̇riŋ-\ *n* [A. M. *Turing* †1954 Eng. mathematician] : a hypothetical computing machine that has an unlimited amount of information storage and is not subject to malfunctioning

turkey Tet·raz·zi·ni \-,te·trəˌzēnē, -ni\ *n* [Luisa *Tetrazzini* — more at CHICKEN TETRAZZINI] : an au gratin dish consisting of turkey meat, noodles, mushrooms, and almonds in a velouté sauce

turn·around* \ˈtərnə,rau̇nd, ˈtən-, ˈtəin-\ *n* **1** : the readying of a pad and the installation of the booster for the next spacecraft launching **2** *or* **turnaround time** : the time required to receive, process, and return something <reprography has reached a very high state of technical perfection, mainly owing to the user's requirement for rapid *turnaround time* —A.B. Veaner>

Turner's syndrome \ˈtərnər-, ˈtənə-, ˈtəinə-\ *n* [Henry Herbert *Turner* *b* 1892 Am. physician] : a genetically determined condition that is associated with the presence of one X chromosome and no Y chromosome and that is characterized by an outwardly female phenotype with incomplete and infertile gonads

turn off* *vi* : to lose interest : withdraw <the kids *turn off* or drift into another world —Edwin Sorensen> **~** *vt* : to cause to turn off <dropouts who are *turned off* by . . . political phoniness —Hendrik Hertzberg> — **turn–off** \ˈtər,nȯf, ˈtə,nȯf, ˈtəi,nȯf\ *n*

turn on* *vt* **1** : to cause to undergo an intense visionary experience esp. by taking a drug (as LSD or marijuana) **2** : to excite pleasurably : stimulate <the ballet . . . was *turning* the audience *on* like magic —Clive Barnes> **~** *vi* **1** : to undergo an intense visionary experience esp. as a result of taking a drug; *broadly* : to get high **2** : to become pleasurably excited <*turns on* instead with classical music or jazz —Julie M. Heldman> — **turn–on** \ˈtər,nȯn, ˈtə,n-, ˈtəi,n-, -än\ *n*

turn·over* \ˈtər,novər; ˈtə,nōvə, ˈtəi,n-\ *n* : the act or an instance of a team's losing possession of a ball through error or a minor violation of the rules (as in basketball or football)

TV dinner *n* [fr. its saving the television viewer from having to interrupt his viewing to prepare a meal] : a quick-frozen packaged dinner that requires only heating before it is served

twin double *n* : a system of betting (as on horse races) in which the bettor must select the winners of two consecutive pairs of races in order to win

two–tailed test \ˌtü,tā(ə)l(d)-\ *n* : a statistical test for which the critical region consists of all values of the test statistic greater than a given value plus the values less than another given value — called also *two-sided test, two-tail test;* compare ONE-TAILED TEST

ty·lo·sin \ˈtīləsə̇n\ *n* [origin unknown] : an antibacterial antibiotic $C_{45}H_{77}NO_{17}$ from an actinomycete (*Streptomyces fradiae*) used in veterinary medicine and as a feed additive

type I error \ˌtīpˈwən-\ *n* : rejection of the null hypothesis in statistical testing when it is true

type II error \ˌtīpˈtü-\ *n* : acceptance of the null hypothesis in statistical testing when it is false

U

U \ˈyü\ *adj* [*u*pper class] : characteristic of the upper classes < the deference that the *U* British accent creates —Gershon Legman >

ubi·qui·none \yüˈbikwə̇ˌnōn; ˌyübə̇kwə̇ˈn-, -ˈkwiˌn-\ *n* [blend of L *ubique* everywhere and E *quinone;* fr. its occurrence in nature] : a quinone that functions as an electron transfer agent between cytochromes in the Krebs cycle — called also *coenzyme Q*

ufol·o·gy \yüˈfäləjē\ *n* [*UFO* + *-logy* theory, science, deriv. of Gk *logos* word] : the study of unidentified flying objects — **ufol·o·gist** \-jə̇st\ *n*

ul·tra·fiche \ˈəltrəˌfēsh, *also* -ˌfish\ *n* [*ultra-* beyond, extremely (fr. L *ultra* beyond) + *fiche*] : a microfiche of printed matter that is very greatly reduced (as 100 to 1)

ul·tra·high \ˌəltrəˈhī\ *adj* : very high : exceedingly high < *ultrahigh* vacuum > < at *ultrahigh* temperatures >

ul·tra·mi·cro·fiche \ˌəltrəˈmīkrōˌfēsh, *also* -ˌfish\ *n* : ULTRAFICHE

ul·tra·mi·cro·tome \-ˈmīkrəˌtōm\ *n* : a microtome for cutting extremely thin sections for electron microscopy — **ul·tra·mi·crot·o·my** \-(ˌ)mīˈkräd·əmē, -mi\ *n*

ul·tra·min·ia·ture \-ˈminēəˌchu̇(ə)r, -ˈminə̇-, -ˈminyə-, -ə̇chə(r), -ˌchu̇ə, -ˌt(y)u̇(ə)r, -ˌt(y)u̇ə\ *adj* : very small : subminiature < *ultraminiature* cameras > — **ul·tra·min·ia·tur·iza·tion** \-ˌminēəˌchu̇rə̇ˈzāshən, -ˌminə̇ˌ-, -ˌminyə-, -ə̇chər-, -ˌt(y)u̇r-\ *n*

ul·tra·pure \ˌəltrəˈpyu̇(ə)r, -ˈpyu̇ə\ *adj* : of the utmost purity < an *ultrapure* reagent >

ul·tra·thin \-ˈthin\ *adj* : exceedingly thin < *ultrathin* sections for use in electron microscopy >

umbilical *n* [short for *umbilical cord*] **1** : a cable conveying power to a rocket or spacecraft before takeoff **2** : a tethering or supply line (as for an astronaut outside a spacecraft or an aquanaut underwater) < he is to be connected to the craft by a 30-foot *umbilical* —Neal Stanford >

una·ry* \ˈyünərē, -ri\ *adj* : having or consisting of a single element, item, or component : monadic

un·bun·dling \ənˈbənd(ᵊ)liŋ\ *n* : separate pricing of products and services < *unbundling* left . . . customers free to shop around for bargains in systems-engineering, programming and employee education —*Time* > — **un·bun·dle** \(ˌ)ənˈbəndᵊl\ *vb*

Un·cle Tom \ˌəŋkəlˈtäm\ *vi* **Un·cle Tommed; Un·cle Tom·ming** : to behave like an Uncle Tom < I didn't sell out or *Uncle Tom* when I got famous —Muhammad Ali >

Uncle Tom·ism \-ˈtäˌmizəm\ *n* : behavior or attitudes characteristic of an Uncle Tom < has taken the trouble . . . to disguise his *Uncle Tomism* in a profusion of African garb —N.J. Loftis > — **Uncle Tom·ish** \-ˈtämish\ *adj*

un·der·achieve \ˌəndərəˈchēv\ *vi* : to perform below an expected level of proficiency < the intellectually capable but *underachieving* youngster —*Children's House* > — **un·der·achieve·ment** \-mənt\ *n* — **un·der·achiev·er** \-ə(r)\ *n*

un·der·class \ˈəndə(r)ˌklas\ *n* [prob. trans. of Sw *underklass*] : the lowest stratum of society usu. composed of disadvantaged minority groups < the problems of the black *underclass* —Godfrey Hodgson > < copy editors and other *underclasses* of the publishing community —V.S. Navasky >

un·der·coat·ing* \ˈəndə(r)ˌkōd·iŋ\ *n* : a usu. asphalt-based waterproof coating applied to the undersurface of a vehicle

underground* *adj* : existing, produced, or published outside the establishment esp. by the avant-garde < *underground* movies > < the *underground* press >; *also* : of or relating to the avant-garde underground < the *underground* life-style, once intended to be a shocking fist in the face of the Establishment, is now predictable —John Lahr >

underground* *n* : a usu. avant-garde group or movement that functions outside the establishment

un·der·kill \ˈəndə(r)ˌkil\ *n* [*under* + *-kill* (as in *overkill*)] : lack of the force required to defeat an enemy < models in which human sacrifice is weighed impersonally in a calculation of *underkill* and overkill —Kingman Brewster, Jr. >

un·der·pop·u·la·tion \ˌ¦əndə(r)ˌpäpyəˈlāshən\ *n* : the state of being underpopulated

un·der·steer \ˈəndərˌsti(ə)r, -dəˌstiə\ *n* : the tendency of an automobile to turn less sharply than the driver intends; *also* : the action or an instance of understeer — **un·der·steer** \ˌ¦əndər¦sti(ə)r, -də¦stiə\ *vi*

un·der·whelm \ˌ¦əndə(r)¦(h)welm, -eu̇m\ *vt* [*under* + *-whelm* (as in *overwhelm*)] : to fail to impress or stimulate < then the movie opened, and the critics were *underwhelmed* —Lee Dembart >

un·dock* \ˌənˈdäk\ *vt* : to disconnect or uncouple < *undock* the lunar module from the command module >

un·flap·pa·ble \ˌənˈflapəbəl\ *adj* : marked by assurance and self-control : imperturbable < trying very hard to remain cool and *unflappable* —E.V. Cunningham > — **un·flap·pa·bil·i·ty** \-ˌflapəˈbilәd·ē\ *n* — **un·flap·pa·bly** \-ˈflapəblē\ *adv*

union* *n* **1** : the set of all elements belonging to one or more of a given collection of two or more sets — called also *join, sum* **2** : the mathematical or logical operation of converting separate sets to a union < does set multiplication distribute . . . over *union* —*School Mathematics Study Group: Introd. to Matrix Algebra* >

¹uni·sex \ˈyünәˌseks, -nēˌ-\ *n* [*uni-* one, single (deriv. of L *unus* one) + *sex*] : the quality or state of not being distinguishable (as by hair or clothing) as to sex < is *unisex* the ideal or will the New Woman be molded into a wholly new human pattern unleashing unprecedented torrents of feminine energy? —John Cogley >

²unisex *adj* **1** : not distinguishable as male or female < a *unisex* face > < how *unisex* the Chinese appeared to be —Jonathan Mirsky > **2** : suitable or designed for both males and females < *unisex* clothes > < a *unisex* boutique >

uni·sex·u·al \ˌ¦yünә¦seksh(ə)wəl, -shəl\ *adj* : UNISEX < the *unisexual* badly-needs-a-bath bunch was in deep trouble —Jerry Hopkins > — **uni·sex·u·al·i·ty** \-ˌseksh(ə)ˈwalәd·ē\ *n*

uni·tar·i·ly \ˌyünəˈterəlē\ *adv* : in a unitary manner

uni·tar·i·ty \ˌyünəˈterәd·ē\ *n* : the requirement in quantum mechanics that the S matrix be a unitary transformation between initial and final states of motion

uni·tary ma·trix \ˌ¦yünəˌterē¦mā·triks\ *n* : a matrix that has an inverse and a transpose whose corresponding elements are pairs of conjugate complex numbers

unitary transformation *n* : a linear transformation of a vector space that leaves scalar products unchanged

unit circle *n* : a circle whose radius is one unit of length long

uni·term \ˈyünəˌtərm, -ˌtə̄m, -ˌtəim\ *n* : a single term used as a descriptor in document indexing

unit pricing *n* : the pricing of products (as packaged foods) whereby the unit price esp. by the ounce or pound is indicated along with the total price

unit train *n* : a railway train that transports a single commodity directly from producer to consumer

universal set *n* : a set that contains all elements relevant to a particular discussion or problem : universe of discourse

un·linked \ˌ¦ən¦liŋkt\ *adj* [*un-* not + *linked*] : not belonging to the same genetic linkage group < *unlinked* genes >

un·per·son \ˈən¦pərs^{ə}n, -¦pəs-, -¦pəis-\ *n* : an individual who usu. for political or ideological reasons is removed completely from recognition, consideration, or memory <became an *unperson* when he was removed from the Lenin Mausoleum —Henry Tanner>

up·date \ˈəpˌdāt\ *n* **1** : the act or an instance of updating <this roseate-faced institution . . . has come through successive *updates* with its gentility intact —Creighton Whitmore> **2** : current information for updating something <navigational *update* for a spacecraft computer> **3** : an up-to-date version, account, or report <*updates* of a machine-readable catalog . . . can be produced easily by a simple sorting operation —Concetta N. Sacco>

up·field \ˈəp¦fē(ə)ld\ *adv or adj* : in or into the part of the field toward which the offensive team is headed <marched *upfield* on a 74-yard scoring drive>

[1]**up front** *adj* : uninhibitedly honest : candid <the most sensitive, open, *up front,* uninhibited . . . student in the class —L.J. Peter>

[2]**up front** *adv* : in advance <actors demanding $1 million *up front*>

up·man·ship \ˈəpmənˌship\ *n* [short for *one-upmanship*] : the art or practice of going a friend or competitor one better or keeping one jump ahead of him : one-upmanship <real-estate people believe that social *upmanship* has much to do with the suburban boom —Tris Coffin>

upper* *n* : a stimulant drug; *esp* : amphetamine — compare DOWNER 1

up·tick \ˈəpˌtik\ *n* **1** : a stock market transaction at a price above the last previous transaction in the same security — compare DOWNTICK **2** : an increase in business or prosperity : upbeat <building of new theaters is on the *uptick* —M.J. Edmands>

up·tight \ˌ¦əpˈtīt\ *adj* **1** : being in financial difficulties : broke <surtax was another blow to an industry already *uptight* —*Chem. & Engineering News*> **2 a** : showing signs of tension or uneasiness : apprehensive <I was a little *uptight* about it at first —Phyllis Craig> **b** : angry, indignant <I've been doing that voice in Negro theaters for years. Nobody ever got *uptight* —Flip Wilson> **3** : rigidly conventional <*uptight* and antiseptic white community —J.M. Culkin> — **uptight** *n* — **up·tight·ness** \-nəs\ *n*

up·time \ˈəpˌtīm\ *n* : the time during which a piece of equipment (as a computer) is functioning or is able to function <*uptime* as a percentage of scheduled machine time was better than 99% —*Datamation*>

up·val·ue \ˌ¦əp¦val(ˌ)yü, -¦valyə(w)\ *vt* : to assign a higher value to; *specif* : to officially revalue (a currency) upward — **up·val·u·a·tion** \-ˌvalyə¦wāshən\ *n*

upward mo·bil·i·ty \-mōˈbilə̇d·ē\ *n* : the capacity or facility for rising to a higher social or economic class of society <the lives of quiet desperation so many couples live in the rat race of *upward mobility* —Judith Crist> — **upwardly mobile** *adj*

ura·nia \yůˈrānēə, -nyə\ *n* [NL, fr. *uranium* + *-a* oxide] : URANIUM DIOXIDE

uranium di·ox·ide \-(ˈ)dī¦äkˌsīd\ *n* : a dioxide UO_2 of uranium obtained as a brown to black crystalline powder by heating uranium trioxide or tri-uranium oct-oxide in hydrogen or carbon monoxide and formerly used in gas mantles and in ceramic glazes

uranium tri·ox·ide \-(ˈ)trī¦äkˌsīd\ *n* : a brilliant orange compound UO_3 that is formed in the course of refining uranium and that has been used as a coloring agent for ceramic wares

uranium 238 *n* : an isotope of uranium of mass number 238 that absorbs fast neutrons to form a uranium isotope of mass number 239 which then decays through neptunium to form plutonium of mass number 239

ur·ban·ol·o·gist \ˌərbəˈnäləjə̇st, ˌəb-, ˌəib-\ *n* [fr. *urbanology* (fr. *urban* + connective *-o-* + *-logy* theory, science, deriv. of Gk *logos* word) + *-ist,* n. suffix] : one who specializes in the problems of cities <the slow death of an urban community — one whose case history is all too familiar to *urbanologists* —Seth King> — **ur·ban·ol·o·gy** \-jē\ *n*

urban renewal *n* : a construction program to replace or restore substandard buildings in an urban area

urban sprawl *n* : the spreading of urban developments (as houses and shopping centers) on undeveloped land near a city <the *urban sprawl* which is rapidly devouring the remaining green spaces of the populous eastern seaboard —L.W. Cassels>

ureo·tel·ic \yə¦rēə¦telik, ¦yůr-\ *adj* [*urea* +connective *-o-* + *tel-* end, complete (deriv. of Gk *telos* end) + *-ic,* adj. suffix; fr. the fact that urea is the end product] : excreting nitrogen mostly in the form of urea <mammals are *ureotelic* animals> — **ureo·te·lism** \-l,izəm, ,yůrē'ätᵊl,-\ *n*

uri·co·tel·ic \¦yůrəkō¦telik\ *adj* [*uric* (acid) + connective *-o-* + *tel-* + *-ic;* fr. the fact that uric acid is the end product] : excreting nitrogen mostly in the form of uric acid <birds are *uricotelic* animals>— **uri·co·te·lism** \-l,izəm, ,yůri'kätᵊl,-\ *n*

uro·ki·nase \¦yůrə¦kī,nās, -,nāz\ *n* [*urine* + connective *-o-* + *kinase*] : an enzyme that is similar to streptokinase, is found in human urine, and is used to dissolve blood clots (as in the heart)

ur·ti·car·io·gen·ic \,ərd·ə¦karēə¦jenik, -¦ker-\ *adj* [*urticaria* + connective *-o-* + *-genic* produced by, producing] : being an agent or substance that induces or predisposes to urticarial lesions (as wheals on the skin)

V

vac·ci·nee \¦vaksə¦nē\ *n* [*vaccinate* + *-ee* recipient of an action] : a vaccinated individual

val·in·o·my·cin \,valə(,)nō'mīsᵊn\ *n* [*valine,* a crystalline amino acid + connective *-o-* + *-mycin* substance obtained from a fungus, fr. *streptomycin*] : an antibiotic $C_{54}H_{90}N_6O_{18}$ produced by a streptomyces (*Streptomyces fulvissimus*)

val·ue–add·ed tax \¦val(,)yü¦adəd-, ¦valyə¦wadəd-\ *n* : an incremental excise that is levied on the value added at each stage of the processing of a raw material or the production and distribution of a commodity and that typically has the impact of a sales tax on the ultimate consumer

van·co·my·cin \,vaŋkə'mīsᵊn, ,van-\ *n* [*vanco-* (arbitrary prefix) + *-mycin*] : an antimicrobial agent from an actinomycete (*Streptomyces orientalis*) that is effective against spirochetes

vanilla *adj* [fr. the fact that vanilla ice cream is considered the standard flavor] : lacking distinction : bland <there's nothing fancy about this design. It's just plain *vanilla* —*Newsweek*> <convinced her that sunny outdoor California was a big *vanilla* void compared with the intellectual East —Judith Sims>

vanity plate *n* : an automobile registration plate bearing letters, numbers, or a combination of these chosen by the owner

va·rac·tor \və'raktər, (')va¦r-, (')ve¦r-\ *n* [*varying* + *reactor*] : a semiconductor device whose capacitance varies with the applied voltage

variable annuity *n* : an annuity contract which is backed primarily by a fund of common stocks and the payments on which fluctuate with the state of the economy

vas·cu·li·tis \,vaskyə'līd·əs\ *n, pl* **vas·cu·li·ti·des** \-'līd·ə,dēz \ [NL, fr. *vascul-* vascular (fr. L *vasculum* small vessel) + *-itis* disease, inflammation] : inflammation of a blood or lymph vessel

va·so·active \¦vā(,)zō¦aktiv, ¦vā(,)sō-, ¦va(,)zō-\ *adj* [*vaso-* vessel (fr. L *vas*) + *active*] : affecting the blood vessels esp. in respect to the degree of their relaxation or contraction — **va·so·ac·tiv·i·ty** \-(,)ak¦tivəd·ē\ *n*

VAT *abbr* value-added tax

VC* *abbr* Vietcong

vector* *n* : an element of a vector space

vector space *n* : a set representing a generalization of a system of vectors and consisting of elements which comprise a commutative group under addition, each of which is left unchanged under multiplication by the multiplicative identity of a field, and for which multiplication under the multiplicative operation of the field is commutative, closed, distributive such that both $c(A + B) = cA + cB$ and $(c + d)A = cA + dA$, and associative such that $(cd)A = c(dA)$ where A, B are elements of the set and c, d are elements of the field

ve·gan \ˈvejən, ˈvēgən\ *n* [by contraction fr. *vegetarian*] : an extreme vegetarian : one that consumes no animal food or dairy products

ve·gan·ism \ˈvejəˌnizəm, ˈvēgə-\ *n* : extreme vegetarianism

ventriculo- *comb form* [NL, fr. L *ventriculus* stomach, ventricle of the heart] **1** : ventricle < *ventriculo*tomy > **2** : ventricular and < *ventriculo*atrial >

ve·ris·mo \vāˈrēz(ˌ)mō, veˈr-, -ˈriz-\ *n* [It, fr. *vero* true, fr. L *verus*] : artistic use of contemporary everyday material in preference to the heroic or legendary esp. in grand opera : verism

ver·ni·er* \ˈvərnēər, ˈvənēə(r, ˈvəinēə(r\ *also* **vernier engine** *n* : any of two or more small supplementary rocket engines or gas nozzles mounted on a missile or rocket vehicle and designed to make fine adjustments in the speed or course or to control the attitude

vesico- *comb form* [NL, fr. L *vesico* bladder] : of or relating to the urinary bladder and < *vesico*ureteral >

vex·il·lol·o·gy \ˌveksəˈläləjē\ *n* [L *vexillum* flag + E connective *-o-* + *-logy* theory, science, deriv. of Gk *logos* word] : the study of flags — **vex·il·lo·log·i·cal** \ˌveksələ̇-läjəkəl, (ˌ)vekˌsiləˌlä-\ *adj* — **vex·il·lol·o·gist** \ˌveksəˈläləjəst\ *n*

vibe \ˈvīb\ *n* [short for *vibration*] : a characteristic aura, spirit, or atmosphere : vibration < there was a beautiful *vibe* about them —Yoko Ono > — usu. used in pl. < the good guy is someone who radiates good *vibes* . . . to others and is not psychotic about doing his own thing —Franklin Chu >

vi·bra·harp \ˈvībrəˌhärp, -ˌhäp\ *n* [fr. *Vibra-Harp*, a former trademark] : a vibraphone — **vi·bra·harp·ist** \-pəst\ *n*

vi·bron·ic \(ˈ)vīˌbränik\ *adj* [*vibr*ation + electr*onic*] : of or relating to transitions between molecular energy states when modified by vibrational energy

vic·tim·less \ˈviktəmləs\ *adj* : having no victim < *victimless* crimes such as drunkenness, drug use, gambling, consensual illicit sex —Jonathan Kwitny >

vic·tim·ol·o·gy \ˌviktəˈmäləjē\ *n* [*victim* + connective *-o-* + *-logy* theory, science, deriv. of Gk *logos* word] : the study of the ways in which the behavior of a victim of a crime may have led to or contributed to his victimization — **vic·tim·ol·o·gist** \-jəst\ *n*

Vic·to·ri·ana \(ˌ)vikˌtōrēˈänə, -tȯr-, -ˈanə\ *n* [NL, neut. pl. of *Victorianus* Victorian] : materials concerning or characteristic of the Victorian age < at home in his favorite armchair surrounded by assorted *Victoriana*, newspapers, and shaggy fur throws —Margaret R. Weiss >

vid·eo·cas·sette \ˌvidēˌōkəˌset\ *n* : a video tape recording mounted in a cassette

vid·eo·phone \ˈvidēəˌfōn, -ēōˌ-\ *n* : a telephone equipped for transmission of video as well as audio signals so that users can see each other

¹vid·eo·tape \-ˌtāp\ *n* **1** : a recording of a television production on magnetic tape **2** : the magnetic tape used in a videotape

²videotape *vt* : to make a videotape of < *videotaping* their classroom work in order to undertake the most exacting self-scrutinization —T.J. Cottle >

Vi·et·nam·iza·tion \vēˌetnəməˈzāshən, ˌvyet-, -ˌmīˈz-, *also* ˌvēət- *or* ˌvēt-\ *n* : the act or process of transferring to the responsibility of the Vietnamese; *specif* : the disengagement of the United States from the war in Vietnam — **Vi·et·nam·ize** \vēˈetnəˌmīz, ˈvyet-, *also* ˈvēət-, ˈvēt-\ *vb*

-ville \ˌvil, *esp South* vəl\ *n suffix* [*-ville*, suffix occurring in names of towns, fr. F, fr. OF, fr. *ville* farm, village] : place or category of a specified nature < squares *ville* > < dulls *ville* >

VIN *abbr* vehicle identification number

vin·blas·tine \vinˈblaˌstēn, -ˈblastən\ *n* [contr. of *vincaleukoblastine*] : an alkaloid $C_{46}H_{58}N_4O_9$ from Madagascar periwinkle used to relieve human neoplastic diseases

vin·ca·leu·ko·blas·tine \ˌviŋkəˌlükəˌblaˌstēn, -ˌblastən; -ˌlükə(ˌ)blaˈstēn\ *n* [NL *Vinca* periwinkle + E *leukoblast* + *-ine* chemical substance] : VINBLASTINE

vin·cris·tine \vinˈkriˌstēn, viŋˈk-, -ˈkristᵊn\ *n* [NL *Vinca* + L *crista* crest + E *-ine*] : an alkaloid $C_{46}H_{56}N_4O_{10}$ from Madagascar periwinkle used to relieve some human neoplastic diseases (as leukemias)

vi·ri·on \ˈvīrēˌän, ˈvir-\ *n* [ISV *viri-* (fr. NL *virus*) + *-on* particle, unit] : a complete virus particle that consists of an RNA or DNA core with a protein coat sometimes with external envelopes and that is the extracellular infective form of a virus

virtual memory *n* : external memory (as magnetic disks) for a computer that can be used as if it were an extension of the computer's internal memory

visual lit·er·a·cy \-ˈlid·ərəsē, -ˈli·trəsē, -si\ *n* : the ability to discriminate and interpret the visible actions, objects, and symbols encountered in one's environment

vital signs *n pl* : the pulse rate, respiratory rate, body temperature, and sometimes blood pressure of a person

vi·ta·min·iza·tion \ˌvīd·əmənəˈzāshən, *Brit also* ˌvit-\ *n* : the action or process of vitaminizing

vocabulary* *n, pl* **-lar·ies** : a list or collection of terms or codes available for use (as in an indexing system)

voice–over \ˈvȯiˌsōvə(r)\ *n* : the voice of an unseen narrator heard in a motion picture or television program or commercial <narrates in *voice-over,* explaining how to make both maple syrup and maple sugar —*Booklist*>; *also* : the voice of a visible character indicating his thoughts but without motion of his lips <it's cheating to have the Bard's soliloquies recited as *voice-overs* while the camera lingers on still faces —Liz Smith>

voiceprint \ˈvoisˌprint\ *n* : a spectrographically produced individually distinctive pattern of certain voice characteristics that is an effective agent of identification

VOLAR *abbr* volunteer army

volcanogenic \ˌvälkənəˈjenik, ˌvȯl-\ *adj* [*volcano* + *-genic* produced by, producing] : of volcanic origin <*volcanogenic* sediments>

-vol·tine \ˈvōlˌtēn, ˈvȯl-\ *adj comb form* [F, fr. It *volta* time, occasion, lit., turn fr. *voltare* to turn, fr. (assumed) VL *volvitare,* freq. of L *volvere* to roll] : having (so many) generations or broods in a season or year <multi*voltine*>

VP* *abbr* verb phrase

VSO *abbr* very superior old — used of brandy 12 to 17 years old

VSOP *abbr* very superior old pale — used of brandy 18 to 25 years old

V/STOL \ˈvēˌstōl, -ȯl\ *abbr* vertical short takeoff and landing

VTOL \ˈvēˌtōl, -ȯl\ *abbr* vertical takeoff and landing

VVSOP *abbr* very very superior old pale — used of brandy 25 to 40 years old

W

wafer* *n* : a thin slice of material (as silicon or gallium arsenide) used as a base for an electronic component or components (as an integrated circuit)

wafer* *vt* **1** : to prepare (as hay or alfalfa) in the form of small compressed cakes suggestive of crackers **2** : to divide (as a silicon rod) into wafers

waffle* *vi* **waf·fled; waf·fling** : to talk indecisively or evasively : equivocate <has *waffled* miserably in his economic and foreign affairs stances —*Christian Science Monitor*>

waffle *n* : empty or pretentious words <a lot of rather vague *waffle* about how nice he was —Dan Davin>

wa·hi·ne* \wäˈhēnē, -(ˌ)nā\ *n* [*wahine* a Polynesian woman, fr. Maori & Hawaiian, woman] : a girl surfer

wake surfing *n* : the sport of riding (as on a surfboard) the wake of a powerboat

walking catfish *n* : an Asiatic catfish (*Clarias batrachus*) that is able to move about on land and has been inadvertently introduced into Florida waters

walk–up* \ˌwȯˌkəp\ *adj* : designed to allow pedestrians to be served without entering a building <the *walk-up* window of a bank>

wall* *n* — **up against the wall** : in or into a tight or difficult situation <high costs . . . have finally driven a ghastly number of colleges and universities *up against the wall* —G. W. Bonham>

Wan·kel engine \ˌväŋkəl-, ˌwaŋ-\ *n* [Felix *Wankel* *b*1902 Ger. engineer, its inventor] : an internal-combustion rotary engine that has a rounded triangular rotor functioning as a piston and rotating in a space in the engine and that has only two major moving parts

war–game \ˈwȯ(ə)rˌgām, ˈwȯ(ə)ˌ-\ *vt* : to plan or conduct in the manner of a war game <*war-gamed* an invasion —*Newsweek*> ~ *vi* : to conduct a war game — **war–gam·er** \-ə(r)\ *n*

warning track *or* **warning path** *n* : a usu. dirt or cinder strip around the outside edge of a baseball outfield to warn a fielder running to make a catch that he is approaching a wall, a fence, or bleachers

WASP *or* **Wasp** \ˈwäsp, ˈwȯsp\ *n* [*w*hite *A*nglo-*S*axon *P*rotestant] : an American of northern European and esp. British stock and of Protestant background; *esp* : a member of the dominant and most privileged class of people in the U.S. <some are *WASPs* with names that sound like banks and colleges —Jesse Kornbluth> — **Wasp·dom** \-spdəm\ *n* — **Wasp·ish** \-spəsh\ *adj* — **Wasp·ish·ness** \-spəshnəs\ *n*

waste* *vt* **wast·ed; wast·ing** : to kill or severely injure <comes back and *wastes* one of the ushers with a kick that opens up one side of his face —Robert Greenfield> <demanding that he hurry and . . . *waste* the Vietnamese so that the attack could press forward —*Time*>

water bed *n* : a bed whose mattress is a plastic bag filled with water

wa·ter·flood \ˈwȯd·ə(r)ˌfləd, ˈwä-\ *vi* : to pump water into the ground around an oil well nearing depletion in order to force out additional oil

Wa·ter·ford glass \-fə(r)d-, -(ˌ)fȯ(ə)rd-, -(ˌ)fȯ(ə)d-\ *n* [*Waterford*, city in southern Ireland where it was originally made] : an 18th and 19th century hand-blown flint glass often with a bluish cast

wa·ter·fowl·er \ˈwȯd·ə(r)ˌfau̇lə(r), ˈwä-\ *n* : a hunter of waterfowl

wa·ter·fowl·ing \-liŋ\ *n* : the occupation or pastime of hunting waterfowl

water toothpick *or* **water pick** *n* : a tooth-cleaning device that cleans by directing a stream of water over and between teeth

Wat·son–Crick \ˌwätsənˌkrik, *also* ˌwȯt-\ *adj* : of or relating to the Watson-Crick model <*Watson-Crick* helix> <*Watson-Crick* structure>

Watson–Crick model *n* [J. D. *Watson* *b*1928 Am. biologist and F.H.C. *Crick* *b*1916 Eng. biologist] : a model of DNA structure in which the molecule is a cross-linked double-stranded helix, each strand is composed of alternating links of phosphate and deoxyribose, and the strands are cross-linked by pairs of purine and pyrimidine bases projecting inward from the deoxyribose sugars and joined by hydrogen bonds with adenine paired with thymine and with cytosine paired with guanine

wave function* *n* : a quantum-mechanical function whose absolute value squared represents the relative probability of finding a given elementary particle within a specified volume of space

way–out \ˈwāˌau̇t\ *adj* : FAR-OUT <perhaps a little closer to reality than some of the weird, *way-out* designs created by Detroit auto makers —Ed Janicki> — **way–out·ness** \(ˈ)wāˈau̇tnəs\ *n*

weak interaction *or* **weak force** *n* : a fundamental interaction experienced by elementary particles that is responsible for some particle decay processes, for nuclear beta decay, and for emission and absorption of neutrinos

we·del \ˈvādᵊl, ˈwe-\ *vi* [back-formation fr. *wedeln*] : to ski downhill by means of wedeln

we·deln \ˈvādᵊl(ə)n, ˈwe-\ *n, pl* **wedelns** *or* **wedeln** [G, fr. *wedeln* to fan, wag the tail, fr. *wedel* fan, tail, fr. OHG *wadal;* akin to ON *vēl* bird's tail] : a style of skiing in which the skier moves the rear of the skis from side to side making a series of short quick turns while following the fall line

weirdo \ˈwi(ə)r(ˌ)dō, ˈwiə(ˌ)dō\ *n, pl* **weirdos** : one that is unusually strange, eccentric, or queer <small-town bigots who hate pacifists, pot smokers and long-haired *weirdos* —Vincent Canby> <reported backstage that a real *weirdo* was waiting outside in the line wearing a bizarre outfit —George Malko>

well-formed \ˌwelˌfȯ(ə)rmd, -ˌfȯ(ə)md\ *adj* : produced by the correct application of a set of transformations : grammatical <grammar . . . specifies the infinite set of *well-formed* sentences —Jerry Fodor & Jerrold J. Katz> — **well-formed·ness** \ˌwelˈfȯ(ə)rm(ə̇)dnə̇s, -ˈfȯ(ə)m-\ *n*

well-or·dered \ˌwelˌȯrdərd, -ˌȯ(ə)dəd\ *adj* : partially ordered with every subset containing a first element and exactly one of the relationships "greater than", "equal to", or "less than" holding for any given pair of elements

well-or·der·ing \-ˈȯrd(ə)riŋ, -ˈȯ(ə)d-\ *n* : an instance of being well-ordered

wet* *adj* — **wet behind the ears** : immature, inexperienced <I was a little offended. I thought they shouldn't betray their extreme youthfulness. Maybe, I thought, they were a little *wet behind the ears* —Walter Cronkite>

wet look *n* : a glossy effect on fabrics that is produced by coating with urethane

WF \ˌdəbə(l)yüˈef, -b(ə)yəˈ(w)ef\ *n* [*w*ithdrawn *f*ailing] : a grade assigned by a teacher to a student who withdraws from a course with a failing grade

wheel·er-dealer \ˌhwēlə(r)ˌdēlə(r), ˌwē-\ *n* [irreg. fr. *wheel and deal*] : a shrewd operator esp. in business or politics <rich but rickety conglomerates thrown together overnight by some high stepping *wheeler-dealer* —Tom Wicker>

wheel·ie \ˈhwē(ə)lē, ˈwē-\ *n* : a maneuver in which a wheeled vehicle (as a motorcycle, bicycle, or dragster) is balanced momentarily on its rear wheel or wheels

wheels *n pl, slang* : a motor vehicle : automobile <no chick ever got hot pants for a guy who didn't have his own *wheels* —William Jeanes>

whip·sawed \ˈhwipˌsȯd, ˈwip-\ *adj* : subjected to a double market loss through trying inopportunely to recoup a loss by a subsequent short sale of the same security

whisker* *n* : a thin hairlike crystal (as of sapphire or a metal) of great strength used esp. to reinforce composite structural material

white amur \-(ˈ)äˌmu̇(ə)r, -əˈm-, -u̇ə\ *n* [*amur* fr. *Amur* river, NE Asia] : GRASS CARP

white room \ˈhwītˌrüm, ˈwīt-, -ˌru̇m\ *n* : CLEAN ROOM <an artist was also in the *white room* on top of the Pad 14 gantry as the astronaut was buttoned into his tiny Mercury spacecraft —R.N. Watts, Jr.>

whit·ey \ˈhwīd·ē, ˈwī-\ *n, often cap* : the white man : white society <Negro leaders who are seen as stooges for *Whitey* —*Times Lit. Supp.*> — usu. used disparagingly

whiz kid *n* [alter. (influenced by *whiz*) of *quiz kid*] : a person who is unusually intelligent, clever, or successful esp. at an early age <a 19-year-old *whiz kid* . . . could read at 2, turned out a historical novel at 14 and entered Oxford at 16. She speaks 11 languages and can read 22 —*People*>

Whorf·ian hypothesis \ˈhwōrfēən, ˈw-, -ȯr-\ *n* [Benjamin Lee *Whorf* †1941 Am. anthropologist] : a theory in linguistics: an individual's language determines his conception of the world

Wic·ca \ˈwikə\ *n* [OE *wicca* wizard; akin to OE *wicce* witch, *wiccian* to practice witchcraft] : the cult or religion of witchcraft — **Wic·can** \ˈwikən\ *adj or n*

wide receiver *n* : a football receiver who normally lines up several yards to the side of the offensive formation

wig·let \ˈwiglə̇t\ *n* : a small wig used esp. to enhance a hairstyle

Wild·ean \ˈwī(ə)ldēən\ *adj* [Oscar Fingal O'Flahertie Wills *Wilde* †1900 Eng. (Irish-born) writer] : of, relating to, or suggestive of Oscar Wilde or his writings <a *Wildean* wit and dandy —*Times Lit. Supp.*>

Wil·son's disease \ˈwilsənz-\ *n* [Samuel A. K. *Wilson* †1937 Eng. neurologist] : a hereditary disease that is determined by an autosomal recessive gene and is marked esp. by cirrhotic changes in the liver and severe mental disorder due to a ceruloplasmin deficiency and resulting inability to metabolize copper

wimp \'wimp\ *n* [perh. fr. Brit. slang *wimp* girl, woman, of unknown origin] : a weak or ineffectual person <the American people are such *wimps* that they will take just about anything we dish out —Barney Matthews> — **wimpy** \-pē, -pi\ *adj*

wind·blast \'win(d),blast\ *n* **1** : a gust of wind **2** : the destructive effect of air friction on a pilot ejected from a high-speed airplane

wind·chill \'win,chil\ *or* **windchill factor** *or* **windchill index** *n* : a still-air temperature with the same cooling effect on exposed human flesh as a given combination of temperature and wind speed

wind down *vt* : to cause a gradual lessening of usu. with the intention of bringing to an end : DE-ESCALATE <*winding down* the war> <anti-inflation action to *wind down* federal spending —*Amer. Libraries*> ~ *vi* **1** : to draw gradually toward an end <the dress strike appears to be *winding down* —Sandy Parker> **2** : relax, unwind <inside, amid the odor of sweat and cigaret smoke and beer and whisky, perhaps 20 auto workers are *winding down* after their work turn —Everett Groseclose>

window* *n* **1** : a range of wavelengths in the electromagnetic spectrum to which a planet's atmosphere is transparent **2** : an interval of time within which a rocket or spacecraft must be launched to accomplish a particular mission **3** : an area at the limits of the earth's sensible atmosphere through which a spacecraft must pass for successful reentry

wipe·out \'wī,paůt\ *n* **1** : the act or an instance of wiping out; *esp* : complete or utter destruction **2** : a fall from a surfboard caused usu. by losing control, colliding with another surfer, or being knocked off by a wave

wishbone* *n* : a variation of the T formation in which the halfbacks line up farther from the line of scrimmage than the fullback does

witch of Agne·si \-än'yāzē, -zi\ *or* **witch** *n* [Maria Gaetana *Agnesi* †1799 It. mathematician; prob. fr. its resemblance to the outline of a witch's hat] : a plane cubic curve that is symmetric about the y-axis and approaches the x-axis as an asymptote, that is constructed by drawing lines from the origin intersecting an upright circle tangent to the x-axis at the origin and taking the locus of points of intersection of pairs of lines parallel to the x-axis and y-axis each pair of which consists of a line parallel to the x-axis through the point where a line through the origin intersects the circle and a line parallel to the y-axis through the point where the same line through the origin intersects the line parallel to the x-axis through the point of intersection of the circle and the y-axis, and that has the equation $x^2y = 4a^2(2a-y)$

wok \'wäk\ *n* [Chin (Cant) *wôk*] : a bowl-shaped cooking utensil used esp. in the preparation of Chinese food

Wolf–Ra·yet star \,wůlfrī'ā-\ *n* [Charles *Wolf* †1918 & Georges *Rayet* †1906 Fr. astronomers] : any of a class of white stars which are found mainly in the Milky Way and Magellanic Clouds and whose spectra are characterized by very broad bright lines esp. of hydrogen, helium, carbon, and nitrogen that indicate very hot unstable stars

won \'wȯn, 'wän\ *n, pl* **won** [Korean *wån*] **1** : the basic monetary unit of Korea **2** : a coin or note representing one won

wooden rose *n* : a tuberous half-hardy trailing vine (*Ipomoea tuberosa*) grown in warm regions esp. for its hard showy yellow rose-shaped calyx and seed capsule

word* *n* : a combination of electrical or magnetic impulses conveying a quantum of information in communications and computer work

work·a·hol·ic \,wərkə'hȯlik, ,wək-, ,wəik-, *sometimes* -'häl-\ *n* [*work* +connective *-a-* + *-holic* (as in *alcoholic*)] : a compulsive worker <the office grind, a *workaholic* who had made a small name for himself by exposing Washington restaurants with dirty kitchens —Timothy Crouse>

work·a·hol·ism \'wərkə,hȯ,lizəm, 'wək-, 'wəik-, *sometimes* -,hä,l-\ *n* : an obsessive need to work <informs us that *workaholism* increased markedly "since lay-offs became widespread" —*East Village Other*>

work·fare \'wərk,fa(ə)r, 'wək-, 'wəik-, -,fe(ə)r, -,faə, -,feə\ *n* [*work* + wel*fare*] : a welfare program designed to encourage people to work

workload \-,lōd\ *n* : the amount of work performed or capable of being performed (as by a mechanical device) usu. within a specified period

work–to–rule \ˌwərktəˈrül, ˌwə̄k-, ˌwəik-\ *n, Brit* : the practice of working according to the strictest interpretation of the rules so as to slow down production and force employers to comply with demands <local hospitals have banned the admission of non-urgent cases because of the *work-to-rule* which has closed some operating theatres —*Evening Post (Nottingham)*> — **work–to–rule** *vi*

world line *n* : the aggregate of all positions in space-time of any individual particle that retains its identity

worry beads *n pl* [fr. the belief that the fingering releases nervous tension] : a string of beads to be fingered so as to keep one's hands occupied <the incessant click of *worry beads* falling through the hands of the older men having an evening glass of ouzo or coffee under strings of electric lights —John Weston>

WP \ˌdəbə(l)yüˈpē, -b(ə)yəˈ-\ *n* [*w*ithdrawn *p*assing] : a grade assigned by a teacher to a student who withdraws from a course with a passing grade

W particle *n* [*W*, abbr. for *weak*] : a hypothetical massive elementary particle held to be responsible for the weak interaction

wrap·around \ˈrapəˌraund\ *adj* : of or relating to a flexible printing surface wrapped around a plate cylinder

wrist wrestling *n* : a form of arm wrestling in which opponents interlock thumbs instead of gripping hands

wu–ts'ai \ˈwütˈsī\ *n* [Chin (Pek) *wu*³ *ts'ai*³ five colors] : a 5-colored overglaze enamel decoration used on Chinese porcelain since the Ming period

X

X \ˈeks\ *adj, of a motion picture* : of such a nature that admission is denied to persons under a specified age (as 17) — compare G, PG, R

Xan·a·du \ˈzanəˌd(y)ü\ *n* [*Xanadu,* locality in *Kubla Khan* (1798) poem by Samuel T. Coleridge †1834 Eng. poet] : a place of idyllic beauty <this is a *Xanadu* only about half an hour by electric train from the . . . hum of the parent city —William Sansom>

xe·nate \ˈzēˌnāt, ˈze-\ *n* [ISV *xenon* + *-ate* salt or ester of an acid] : a salt of xenic acid

xe·nic \ˈzēnik, ˈzen-\ *adj* [*xen-* guest, foreigner, strange (deriv. of Gk *xenos* stranger, guest, host) + *-ic,* adj. suffix] : of, relating to, or employing a culture medium containing one or more unidentified organisms <*xenic* cultivation of insect larvae> — **xe·ni·cal·ly** \-ək(ə)lē\ *adv*

xe·nic acid \ˌzēnik-, ˌze-\ *n* [*xenic* fr. ISV *xenon* + *-ic,* adj. suffix] : a weak acid known only in the form of its hydrate ($XeO_3.xH_2O$) and obtained by hydrolysis from xenon fluorides

xe·no·bi·ol·o·gy \ˌzenō(ˌ)bīˈäləjē, ˌzē-, -ji\ *n* [*xeno-* guest, stranger, strange (deriv. of Gk *xenos* stranger, guest, host) + *biology*] : EXOBIOLOGY

xe·no·ge·ne·ic \-jəˌnēik\ *adj* [*xeno-* + *-geneic,* alter. of *-genic* producing, produced by] : derived from, originating in, or being a member of another species <a *xenogeneic* antibody> <*xenogeneic* hosts>

xe·no·graft \ˈzenəˌgraft, ˈzē-\ *n* : a tissue graft carried out between members of different species

xe·non hexa·flu·o·ride \ˈzēˌnänˌheksəˈflu̇(ə)rˌīd, ˈzen-\ *n* : a highly reactive colorless crystalline compound XeF_6

xenon te·tra·flu·o·ride \-ˌte·trə-\ *n* : a colorless crystalline compound XeF_4 that sublimes readily in air and is formed by heating xenon with fluorine under pressure

xi* \ˈzī, ˈksī\ *or* **xi particle** *n* **:** an unstable elementary particle existing in negative and neutral charge states with masses respectively 2585 and 2572 times the mass of an electron

X-ray astronomy *n* **:** astronomy dealing with investigations of celestial bodies by means of the X rays they emit

X-ray dif·frac·tion \-dəˈfrakshən\ *n* **:** a scattering of X rays by the atoms of a crystal that produces an interference effect so that the diffraction pattern gives information on the structure of the crystal or the identity of a crystalline substance

X-ray star *n* **:** a luminous starlike celestial object emitting a major portion of its radiation in the form of X rays

xu \ˈsü\ *n, pl* **xu** [Vietnamese, fr. F *sou* sou] **1 :** a monetary unit of North Vietnam equal to $^{1}/_{100}$ dong **2 :** a coin representing one xu

Y

YAG \ˈyag\ *n* [*y*ttrium *a*luminum *g*arnet] **:** a synthetic yttrium aluminum garnet of marked hardness and high refractive index that is used esp. as a gemstone and in laser technology

Ya·ma·to-e \yäˈmätəˌwā\ *also* **Ya·ma·to** \-ˈmä(ˌ)tō\ *n* [Jap *yamato-e,* fr. *Yamato* Japan + *e* picture, painting] **:** a movement in Japanese art arising in medieval times and marked by the treatment of Japanese themes with Japanese taste and sentiment

yard sale *n* **:** GARAGE SALE

ya·yoi \(ˈ)yäˈyȯi\ *adj, often cap* [*Yayoi,* site in Tokyo, Japan, where remains of the period were discovered] **:** of, relating to, or being typical of a Japanese cultural period extending from about 200 B.C. to A.D. 200, being generally neolithic but including the beginning of work in metal, and characterized esp. by unglazed wheel-thrown pottery (**Yayoi ware**) usu. without ornamentation but often of florid shape

Yellow Pages *n pl* **:** the section of a telephone directory that lists business and professional firms and people alphabetically by category and includes classified advertising

yen·ta \ˈyen·tə\ *n* [Yiddish *yente* vulgar and sentimental woman, fr. the name *Yente*] **:** a talkative or gossipy person and esp. such a woman <a head floor nurse — a *yenta* whose own vocal equipment could drown out the brass section of the Hamburg Philharmonic —Robert Craft>

yé-yé \ˈyā(ˌ)yā\ *adj* [F, fr. E *Yeah-yeah,* exclamation often interpolated in rock 'n' roll performances] **:** of, relating to, or featuring rock 'n' roll as it developed in France <op-art boutiques crowding the elegant Parisian boulevards, . . . *yé-yé* discotheques in quaint old houses —*Newsweek*>

yield to maturity : the total rate of return to an owner holding a bond to maturity expressed as a percentage of cost

YIG \ˈyig\ *n* [*y*ttrium *i*ron *g*arnet] **:** a synthetic yttrium iron garnet having ferrimagnetic properties that is used esp. as a filter for selecting or tuning microwaves

Yi-hsing ware \ˈyēˈshiŋˌ-\ *also* **Yi-hsing** *or* **Y-hsing yao** \ˌyēˌshiŋˈyau̇\ *n* [*Yi-hsing* fr. *Yi-hsing* (*Ihing*), town in southern Kiangsu province, China; *Yi-hsing yao* fr. *Yi-hsing* + Chin (Pek) *yao*^{2} pottery] **:** reddish yellow pottery made at Ihing in Kiangsu, China, and introduced into Europe by the Portuguese **:** boccaro

yo-yo* \ˈyō(ˌ)yō\ *n, pl* **yo-yos :** a stupid or foolish person <you don't want to look like a *yo-yo* in front of a hundred guys —B.R. Brown>

yo-yo *vi* **yo-yoed; yo-yo·ing :** to move from one position to another repeatedly <I'll be *yo-yoing* back and forth from the Coast —Telly Savalas> **:** as **a :** to vacillate <the Supreme Court has *yo-yoed* on the issue of the right to travel —F.P. Graham> **b :** to fluctuate <bond prices will *yo-yo* —W.S. Pinkerton, Jr.>

Z

zaf·tig *also* **zof·tig** \ˈzäftig, ˈzȯf-\ *adj* [Yiddish *zaftik* juicy, succulent, fr. G *saftig,* fr. *saft* juice, sap, fr. OHG *saf*] *of a woman* : having a full rounded figure : pleasingly plump <nice-looking, sort of *zaftig,* Jewish girl. A little thick in the thighs and ankles, but definitely one of your look-back ladies —Albert Goldman>

zai·bat·su \(ˈ)zīˈbät(ˌ)sü\ *n pl* [Jap, fr. *zai* money, wealth + *batsu* clique, clan] : the powerful financial and industrial conglomerates of Japan <the *zaibatsu* . . . countered military influence to a substantial extent before 1937 —Vera M. Dean>

zaire \ˈzī(ə)r, zäˈi(ə)r\ *n* [F *zaïre,* fr. *Zaïre* (formerly Congo), country in west central Africa, fr. *Zaïre,* former name of Congo river] **1** : the basic monetary unit of Zaire **2** : a note representing one zaire

Zair·ian *or* **Zair·ean** \ˈzī(ə)rēən, zīˈi(ə)r-\ *n* : a native or inhabitant of Zaire — **Zairian** *or* **Zairean** *adj*

1zap \ˈzap\ *interj* [imit.] **1** — used to express the sound made by or as if by a gun <*zap!* You're sterile> **2** — used to indicate a sudden or instantaneous occurrence <you hold the wires in place and *zap* — it's done —Gary Scott>

2zap *vb* **zapped; zap·ping** *vt* **1 a** : to destroy or kill by or as if by shooting <cartoon heros were *zapping* cartoon villains and monsters —Edith Efron> <*zapped* the crocodile with a bullet right through the eye —*Time*> **b** : to hit suddenly and forcefully <can *zap* him with long or short alarm sounds —*Esquire*> <the vibes given off by a contented pair . . . *zap* prospective interlopers like poison darts —Miranda Hostler> **2** : to propel suddenly or speedily <film can instantly *zap* us anywhere in time —Jacob Brackman> **~** *vi* : to go speedily : zoom, zip <*zap* off on a jet to someplace like Miami —H.S. Thompson>

ze·atin \ˈzēətən, -tᵊn\ *n* [NL *Zea,* generic name of maize + E *-tin* (as in *kinetin*)] : a cytokinin first isolated from maize endosperm

zebra crossing *n, Brit* : a crosswalk marked by a series of broad white stripes

zel·ko·va* \ˈzelkəvə, zelˈkōvə\ *n* : a plant of the genus *Zelkova; esp* : a tall widely spreading Japanese tree (*Z. serrata*) resembling the American elm and replacing the latter as an ornamental and shade tree because of its resistance to Dutch elm disease

ze·ner di·ode \ˌzānə(r)ˌdī(ˌ)ōd\ *n, often cap Z* [Clarence Melvin *Zener b*1905 Am. physicist] : a silicon semiconductor device used esp. as a voltage regulator

zero vector *n* : a vector which is of zero length and all of whose components are zero

zilch \ˈzilch, ˈziu̇ch\ *n* [origin unknown] : nothing, zero <right now the credibility of the Administration is *zilch* —R.J. Dole> <overnight, my desirability as a commercial voice dropped from sky high to *zilch* —Orson Bean>

zing·er \ˈziŋə(r)\ *n* : a pointed witty remark or retort <the critics got in their *zingers* —Caryl Rivers>

zingy \ˈziŋē, -ŋi\ *adj* **zing·i·er; -est** **1** : enjoyably exciting <a *zingy* musical> **2** : strikingly attractive or appealing <wore a *zingy* new outfit>

zinj·an·thro·pine \zinˈjan(t)thrəˌpīn\ *n* [*zinjanthropine* adj., fr. *zinjanthropus* + *-ine,* adj. suffix] : any of several closely related primitive extinct African hominids including zinjanthropus — **zinjanthropine** *adj*

zip code \ˈzip-\ *n, often cap Z&I&P* [*ZIP* fr. *z*one *i*mprovement *p*lan] : a 5-digit code that identifies each postal delivery area in the U.S.

zip–code \ˈzipˌkōd\ *vt* : to furnish with a zip code

zir·ca·loy \ˌzərkəˈlȯi\ *n* [*zirc*onium + *al*l*oy*] : any of several zirconium alloys notable for corrosion resistance and stability over a wide range of radiation and temperature exposures

zone* *n* : a designated area (as a row on a punch card or a channel on magnetic tape) in which bits signifying information other than digits are recorded (as in Hollerith code or EBCDIC)

zone melting *n* : a technique for the purification of a crystalline material and esp. a metal in which a molten region travels through the material to be refined, picks up impurities at its advancing edge, and then allows the purified part to recrystallize at its opposite edge

zone refine *vt* : to produce or refine by zone melting

zonked \ˈzäŋkt, ˈzȯŋkt\ *also* **zonked–out** \ˌzäŋkˌdau̇t, ˌzȯŋk-\ *adj* [origin unknown] : being under the influence of alcohol or a drug (as LSD) : high <crazies wander the streets *zonked* on acid —W.P. Rock>

zo·ri \ˈzōrē, ˈzȯrē\ *n, pl* **zori** [Jap, *zōri,* lit., straw sandals, fr. *sō-* grass, vegetation + *-ri* footwear] : a flat thonged sandal usu. made of straw, cloth, leather, or rubber

Zorn's lemma \ˈzȯ(ə)rnz-, ˈtsȯ-\ *n* [Max August *Zorn* *b*1906 Ger. mathematician] : a lemma in set theory: if a set is partially ordered and if each subset for which every pair of elements is related by exactly one of the relationships "less than", "equal to", or "greater than" has an upper bound in the set, the set contains at least one element for which there is no greater element in the set

ZPG *abbr* zero population growth

zup·pa in·gle·se \ˌtsüpə·iŋˈglā(ˌ)zā, ˌzü-, -inˈg-, -(ˌ)sā, -ˈglāsē, -zē\ *n, often cap I* [It, lit., English soup] : a dessert consisting of sponge cake and custard or pudding that is flavored with rum, covered with cream, and garnished with fruit